THE LIFE & LETTERS OF
PETER ILICH TCHAIKOVSKY

THE LIFE & LETTERS OF PETER ILICH TCHAIKOVSKY

BY MODESTE TCHAIKOVSKY
EDITED FROM THE RUSSIAN
WITH AN INTRODUCTION BY
ROSA NEWMARCH: ILLUSTRATED

University Press of the Pacific
Honolulu, Hawaii

The Life and Letters of Peter Ilich Tchaikovsky

by
Modeste Tchaikovsky

ISBN: 1-4102-1612-8

Reprinted from the 1904 edition

University Press of the Pacific
Honolulu, Hawaii
http://www.universitypressofthepacific.com

TO

SERGEÏ IVANOVICH TANEIEV

AND TO ALL

WHO STILL CHERISH THE MEMORY OF

PETER ILICH TCHAIKOVSKY

I DEDICATE THIS WORK

INTRODUCTION

IN offering to English and American readers this
abridged edition of *The Life and Letters of Peter
Ilich Tchaikovsky*, my introduction must of necessity
take the form of some justification of my curtailments and excisions.

The motives which led to this undertaking, and the
reasons for my mode of procedure, may be stated in a few
words.

In 1900 I published a volume dealing with Tchaikovsky,[1]
which was, I believe, the first attempt to embody in book
form all the literature—scattered through the byways of
Russian journalism—concerning the composer of the
Pathetic Symphony.

In the course of a year or two—the book having sold
out in England and America—a proposal was made to me
to prepare a new edition. Meanwhile, however, the
authorised *Life and Letters*, compiled and edited by the
composer's brother, Modeste Ilich Tchaikovsky, was being
issued in twenty-five parts by P. I. Jurgenson, of Moscow.[2]

---

[1] *Tchaikovsky, his Life and Works*: with extracts from his writings and
the diary of his tour abroad in 1888. Grant Richards, London, 1900.

[2] *Zijn Piotra Ilicha Tchaikovskavo*. P. Jurgenson, Moscow. Three
volumes.

This original Russian edition was followed almost immediately by a German translation, published in Leipzig by the same firm.[1]

In November, 1901, the late P. I. Jurgenson approached me on the subject of a translation, but his negotiations with an American firm eventually fell through. He then requested me to find, if possible, an English publisher willing to take up the book. Both in England and America the public interest in Tchaikovsky seemed to be steadily increasing. Frequent calls for copies of my small book—by this time out of print—testified that this was actually the case.

An alternative course now lay before me : to revise my own book, with the help of the material furnished by the authorised *Life and Letters*, or to take in hand an English translation of the latter. The first would have been the less arduous and exacting task ; on the other hand, there was no doubt in my mind as to the greater value and importance of Modeste Tchaikovsky's work.

The simplest—and in many ways most satisfactory—course seemed at first to be the translation of the Russian edition in its entirety. Closer examination, however, revealed the fact that out of the 3,000 letters included in this book a large proportion were addressed to persons quite unknown to the English and American publics ; while at the same time it contained a mass of minute and almost *local* particulars which could have very little significance for readers unversed in every detail of Russian musical life.

---

[1] *Das Leben Peter Iljitsch Tschaikowsky's*, translated by Paul Juon. P. Jurgenson, Leipzig. Two volumes.

Another practical question confronted me.   What publisher would venture upon launching this biographical three-decker, with its freight of 3,000 letters, amounting to nearly 2,000 pages of closely printed matter? Such colossal biographies, however valuable as sources of information to the specialist, are quite beyond all possibility of purchase or perusal by the general public. That the author himself realised this, seems evident from the fact that the German edition was lightened of about a third of the original contents.

Following the lines of these authorised abridgments, while using my own judgment as to the retention of some portions of the Russian text omitted in the German edition, I have condensed the work still further.

It may be true, as Carlyle has said, that mankind takes "an unspeakable delight in biography"; but it is equally certain that these "headlong days" which have witnessed the extinction of the three-volume novel are absolutely unfavourable to the success of the three-volume biography.

While admiring the patient and pious industry which has raised so colossal a monument to Tchaikovsky's memory, I cannot but feel that it would be unreasonable to expect of any nation but his own a hero-worship so devout that it could assimilate a *Tchaikovskiad* of such prodigious dimensions.

The present volume is the result of a careful selection of material. The leading idea which I have kept in view throughout the fulfilment of my task has been to preserve as far as possible the *autobiographical* character of the book. Wherever feasible, I have preferred to let Tchaikovsky himself tell the story of his life. For this reason the proportion of letters to the additional biographical matter is even greater in my version than in the German edition. When two or three letters of only moderate interest have followed in immediate succession, I have frequently condensed their contents into a single paragraph, keeping as closely as possible to the phraseology of the composer himself.

In one respect the present edition shows a clear improvement upon the German. In the latter the dates have been given throughout in the Old Style, thereby frequently causing confusion in the minds of Western readers. In the English version—with a few unimportant exceptions — the dates are given according to both calendars.

The most romantic episode of Tchaikovsky's life—his friendship extending over thirteen years with a woman to whom he never addressed a direct personal greeting—is told in a series of intimate letters. In these I have spared all but the most necessary abridgements.

The account of his tour in America, which takes the form of a diary kept for the benefit of his near relatives, cannot fail to amuse and interest all those who remember the favourable impression created by his appearance at the inauguration of the Carnegie Hall, New York, in May, 1891.

The illustrations are the same as those published in the Russian and German publications, with two notable additions: the photograph of Tchaikovsky and Siloti, and the fine portrait by Kouznietsov.

My thanks are due to Mr. Grant Richards for permission to republish the facsimile from the score of the Overture "*1812*"; also to Mr. W. W. Manning and Mr. Adolf Brodsky for the kind loan of autographs.

In conclusion, let me say that in planning and carrying out this work it is not so much the needs of the specialist I have kept most constantly in view, as those of that large section of the musical public whose interest in Tchaikovsky has been awakened by the sincerely emotional and human elements of his music.

ROSA NEWMARCH

CONTENTS

PAGE

PART   I.   CHAPTERS I.-   V.   1840–1861   .   .   I

PART   II.   CHAPTERS I.- VII.   1861–1866   .   .   30

PART III.   CHAPTERS I.–XIII.   1866–1877   .   .   64

PART IV.   CHAPTERS I.–VIII.   1877–1878   .   . 204

PARV   V.   CHAPTERS I.- XX.   1878–1885   .   . 318

PART VI.   CHAPTERS I.–XIII.   1885–1888   .   . 468

PART VII.   CHAPTERS I.- XIX.   1888–1893   .   . 539

APPENDICES—A, B, C 726

ILLUSTRATIONS

ALPHABETICAL INDEX OF NAMES   .   .   . 773

ALPHABETICAL INDEX OF MUSICAL WORKS   .   . 779

"To regret the past, to hope in the future, and never to be satisfied with the present—this is my life."—P. TCHAIKOVSKY (*Extract from a letter*)

THE LIFE & LETTERS
OF PETER ILICH
TCHAIKOVSKY

PART I

I

ONE of the most characteristic traits of Peter Ilich Tchaikovsky was his ironical attitude towards his family's traditions of noble descent. He never lost an opportunity of making fun of their armorial bearings, which he regarded as "imaginary," and clung obstinately to the plebeian origin of the Tchaikovskys. This was not merely the outcome of his democratic convictions, but had its origin, partly in the pride which lay at the very root of his nature, and partly in his excessive conscientiousness. He would not consider himself a scion of the aristocracy, because his nearest ancestors could not boast of one *boyar*, nor one owner of patrimonial estates. His father was the sole serf-owner in the family, and *he* possessed a cook with a numerous progeny—ten souls in all.

But if he was unconcerned as to family descent, he was far from indifferent as to nationality. The aristocratic pretensions of his relatives aroused his mockery, but the mere suggestion of their Polish origin stirred him

B

to instant wrath.   Love of Russia and all things Russian
was so deeply rooted in him that, while he cared nothing
for questions of pedigree, he rejoiced to discover among
his earliest ancestors on his father's side one orthodox
Russian from the district of Kremenschug.

Tracing back Tchaikovsky's pedigree, we do not find
a single name connected with music.   There is not one
instance of a professional musician, and only three can be
considered amateurs—his mother's brother, Michael Assier;
her sister Catharine, in her day a well-known amateur in
Petersburg society; and the composer's mother herself,
who sang the fashionable ballads of her youth with feeling
and expression.   All the rest of the family—Assiers and
Tchaikovskys alike—not only lacked musical talent, but
were indifferent to the art.   Thus it is almost impossible
to ascertain from whom Peter Ilich inherited his genius,
if indeed there can be any question of heredity.   His one
certain inheritance seems to have been an abnormally
neurotic tendency, which probably came to him through
his grandfather Assier, who suffered from epilepsy.   If
it is true, as a modern scientist asserts, that "genius" is
merely an abnormal physical condition, then it is possible
that Tchaikovsky may have inherited his musical gift, at
the same time as his "nerves," from the Assier family.

Little is known of the early life of the composer's father,
Ilia Petrovich Tchaikovsky.   In old age he rarely spoke
of his youth, and did not care to be questioned about it.
Not that he had any painful memories to conceal, but
it was his habit to avoid all reference to himself, and only
to speak of his past when he had some amusing anecdote
to relate, or when he was induced by others to recall some
glad, or sorrowful, event of bygone days.

Ilia Petrovich Tchaikovsky was educated at the School
of Mining Engineers, which he left in 1817 at the age
of twenty-two, having been awarded the distinction of

a silver medal. In the same year he was appointed to an inspectorship in the Mining and Geological Department. His career cannot have been brilliant, since it took him twenty years to rise to the rank corresponding to a lieutenant-colonel. But the fact that at thirty he was already a member of the Scientific Committee of the Institute of Mining Engineers, and lectured on mining law and statistics, proves him to have been a capable and industrious member of his profession.

In private life, all who knew him agreed as to his sympathetic, jovial, and straightforward character. Benevolence —or more correctly speaking, a universal affection—was one of his chief characteristics. In youth, manhood, and old age he loved his neighbour, and his faith in him remained unshaken. His trustfulness knew no limits; and even the loss of his entire fortune, due to misplaced confidence, did not avail to make him suspicious of his fellow-men. To the end of his days, everyone he met was "an excellent, honourable, good fellow." Disillusionment cut him to the quick, but had no power to obscure his rosy views of human nature. It would be difficult to find a man who possessed so many devoted friends.

Although a capable specialist, as regards general culture and intelligence Ilia Petrovich had only a mediocre equipment. He had no great taste for art and science. Music and the drama interested him most. In his youth he played the flute a little, but gave it up early in life.

On September 11th (23rd), 1827, Ilia Petrovich married Maria Carlovna Keiser, by whom he had one daughter. Shortly afterwards he was left a widower and, in October, 1833, married, for a second time, Alexandra Andreievna Assier.

Almost as little is known of the childhood and youth of the composer's mother as of his father. As early as 1816 she was left motherless, and was brought up in a Female Orphanage, where she completed her education in

1829. The instruction in this school appears to have been excellent. Alexandra Andreievna had a thorough knowledge of French and German. In addition, she played the piano a little and sang nicely. A satisfactory education for a girl who had neither means nor position.

Those who knew the composer's mother describe her as tall and distinguished-looking ; not precisely handsome, but with wonderfully expressive eyes. All agreed that there was something particularly attractive in her appearance. Peter Ilich recollected his mother as a tall woman, inclined to be stout, with wonderful eyes and beautiful hands, although by no means small. " Such hands do not exist nowadays, and never will again," he used to say in after life.

Alexandra Andreievna, unlike her husband, was rather reserved and chary of endearments. Her kindness, as compared to his universal amiability, seemed somewhat austere, and showed itself more frequently in act than in speech. The first child of this marriage was a daughter who died in infancy.

In 1837 Ilia Tchaikovsky was appointed inspector of the mines at Kamsko-Votinsk, in the Government of Viatka, where he settled with his wife. On May 9th (21st), 1838, a son was born to them—Nicholas Ilich ; while on April 28th (May 10th), 1840, a second son came into the world—Peter Ilich—the subject of this biography.

The position of manager in the case of such important mines as those of Votinsk closely resembled that of a wealthy landowner living on his estate. In some respects it was even more advantageous, because he had every luxury in life provided for him : a fine house, a staff of servants, and almost unlimited control over a number of human beings. Ilia Tchaikovsky even had at command a small army of a hundred Cossacks, and a little court, consisting of such employés in the mines as had any claim to social position. The fine salary, thanks to the wise economy of his wife, sufficed not only for every comfort, but even admitted of something being put by for less prosperous times.

The allowance provided for social purposes sufficed for widespread hospitality, and, owing to the affability of the host, and the characteristic charm of his wife, the Tchaikovskys' house was the favourite resort of all the neighbouring society. This circle had nothing in common with the uncultured provincial society of those days. It was composed chiefly of young men from St. Petersburg, holding various Government appointments in the district, and of one highly intellectual English family. The proximity of Asia and the remoteness from civilised centres were scarcely perceptible.

About the period of Peter Ilich's earliest recollections, two new members were added to the Tchaikovsky family —a girl, Alexandra, born December 28th, 1842 (January 9th, 1843), and a son, Hyppolite, born April 10th (22nd), 1844. The care of the younger children now so exclusively occupied the mother's attention that she was obliged to engage a governess for her eldest son, Nicholas, and a niece, Lydia, who lived with the family. While on a visit to St. Petersburg she became acquainted with Fanny Dürbach, and brought her back to Votinsk in November, 1844.

In view of the lasting influence which her personality exercised upon Peter Ilich, some account of this lady should be given here.

Fanny Dürbach had been specially trained as a teacher, and had already had some experience in her work. She knew French and German thoroughly, and was a strict Protestant. She is still living at Montbeillard, near Belfort, where she continues to give lessons. The poverty in which she lived impressed me still more on my visit to her in 1894, because I knew that two years earlier my brother Peter Ilich had implored her to accept a regular allowance, which she absolutely refused. "I am content with what I have," she told him; "as far as I can be, after the heavy blows fate has dealt me, I am happy." The expression of her face, wonderfully young for a woman of seventy-two, and the light in her large black eyes, bespoke such true peace of mind and purity of heart that I felt sure neither her physical ailments, nor the lack of luxury in her surroundings, had power to darken the light of her declining days.

Although Fanny Dürbach's connection with the Tchai-kovsky family lasted only four years, her memory lives with them to-day, while all her successors have long been forgotten. She, too, had retained a vivid recollection of "the happiest time in her life," and her account of her arrival at Votinsk gives an animated picture of the patriarchal life of the Tchaikovsky family.

"I travelled from Petersburg with Madame Tchai-kovsky and her son Nicholas. The journey took three weeks, during which time we became so friendly that we were quite intimate on our arrival. All the same, I felt very shy. Had it only depended upon Madame Tchai-kovsky and her boy, all had been well; but there was still the prospect of meeting strangers and facing new conditions of life. The nearer we drew to the journey's end, the more restless and anxious I became. On our arrival, a single moment sufficed to dispel all my fears. A number of people came out to meet us, and in the general greet-ing and embracing it was difficult to distinguish relatives from servants. All fraternised in the sincerity of their joy. The head of the family kissed me without ceremony, as though I had been his daughter. It seemed less like a first arrival than a return home. The next morning I began my work without any misgivings for the future."

II

Peter Ilich was four and a half years old when Fanny came to be governess to Nicholas and his cousin Lydia, and on the first day his mother had to yield to his tearful entreaties to share the lessons of the elder children. Henceforward he always learnt with them, and resented being excused any task on the grounds of his youth. He was wonderfully quick in overtaking his fellow-pupils, and at six could read French and German fluently. He learnt Russian with a tutor.

From the beginning, Fanny was especially attracted by her youngest pupil ; not only because he was more gifted and conscientious than the others, nor because he was more docile than Nicholas, but because in all the child's ways there was something original and uncommon, which exercised an indefinable charm on everyone who came in contact with him.

In looks he did not compare favourably with Nicholas, and was never so clean and tidy. His clothes were always in disorder. Either he had stained them in his absent-mindedness, or buttons were missing, or his hair was only half-brushed, so that by the side of his spruce and impeccable brother he did not show to advantage at first sight. But when the charm of his mind, and still more of his heart, had time to work, it was impossible not to prefer him to the other children. This sympathetic charm, this gift of winning all hearts, Tchaikovsky retained to the last day of his life.

To my inquiry in what way the boy's charm showed itself most, our old governess replied:—

"In no one particular thing, but rather in all his ways and actions. At lessons no child was more industrious or quicker to understand; in playtime none was so full of fun. When we read together none listened so attentively as he did, and when on holidays I gathered my pupils around me in the twilight and let them tell tales in turn, no one could improvise so well as Peter Ilich. I shall never forget these precious hours of my life. In daily intercourse we all loved him, because we felt he loved us in return. His sensibility was extreme, therefore I had to be very careful how I treated him. A trifle wounded him deeply. He was brittle as porcelain. With him there could be no question of punishment; the least criticism or reproof, that would pass lightly over other children, would upset him alarmingly."

The weak and unhappy always found in him a staunch protector. Once he heard with indignation that someone was intending to drown a cat. When he discovered the monster who was planning this crime, he pleaded so eloquently that pussy's life was saved.

Another proof of his compassion for the suffering was his extraordinary sympathy for Louis XVII. Even as a grown man his interest in the unhappy prince survived. In 1868 he bought a picture representing him in the Temple, and had it framed. This picture, and the portrait of Anton Rubinstein, remained for a long while the only adornments of his walls.

The boy was also influenced by that enthusiastic patriotism—not without a touch of Chauvinism—which characterised the reign of Nicholas I. From this early period dates that exclusive affection for everything Russian which lasted his whole lifetime. Sometimes his love for his country was shown in a very droll way. Fanny used to relate the following story :—

" Once, during the recreation hour, he was turning over the pages of his atlas. Coming to the map of Europe, he smothered Russia with kisses and spat on all the rest of the world. When I told him he ought to be ashamed of such behaviour, that it was wicked to hate his fellow-men who said the same 'Our Father' as himself, only because they were not Russians, and reminded him that he was spitting upon his own Fanny, who was a Frenchwoman, he replied at once : 'There is no need to scold me ; didn't you see me cover France with my hand first?'"

Continuing her reminiscences, Fanny said :—

" As our leisure hours were few, I insisted on devoting them to physical exercise; but often I met with some opposition from Pierre, who would go straight from his lessons to the piano. Otherwise he was obedient, and generally enjoyed romping with his sisters. Left to himself, he preferred to play the piano, or to read and write poetry."

In the autumn of 1846 his half-sister Zinaïda left the Catharine Institute, in St. Petersburg, and, her education being finished, returned to live at home. With the arrival of this pretty and lively school-girl the house became even merrier and brighter than before. To the boy's imagination, the new-comer seemed a visitant from a fairy world.

In February, 1848, Ilia Tchaikovsky retired with the rank of major-general. He was anxious to get an appointment as manager of private mines, and with this object in view left Votinsk, with all his family, for a long visit to Moscow. As it was intended on their arrival to send Lydia and the elder boys to school, Fanny now took leave of her friends for good. Not until forty-four years had elapsed did she renew her acquaintance with the family in the person of Peter Ilich.

Besides Fanny's reminiscences, which form so valuable an addition to the biography of Tchaikovsky, she also preserved the books in which her favourite pupil set down his thoughts in leisure hours ; more often than not in the form of verse. The old lady could not be persuaded to let these relics leave her keeping, but she willingly made extracts from them.

These manuscript books naturally contain nothing of real artistic or literary value, but they are not the less interesting on that account. They show the origin and give the explanation of Tchaikovsky's artistic tendency, and are not merely interesting from a biographical point of view, but as documents in which we may study the evolution of genius. These childish verses prove a precocious desire for expression, before the right medium had been discovered. Here the future musician is knocking at the wrong door.

There are two copy-books and a few loose pages. The handwriting, although not beautiful, is well formed and firm. The pages show traces of carelessness. They would have been very differently written, had they been intended for other eyes than his own. We find here a miscellany of verses, extracts, rough copies of letters, attempts to draw houses, odd words and phrases, all jotted down without any connection.

The first book opens with a translation from a French reading-primer, *L'éducation maternelle*. It bears the date 1847, with a French signature, and is followed by several poems, of which two are in Russian and the rest in French. They may be divided into three groups: the poems relating to God; those which have a patriotic tendency; and those which display his sympathy for the weak and suffering and his love of animals.

The first poem, dated 1847, is called:

L'ENFANT PARLE À SON ANGE GARDIEN

Tez ailes dorées ont volé chez moi (?)
Ta *voi* m'a *parler*
O ! que j'etais heureuse
Quant tu *venait* chez moi
Tes ailes *son blanc* et *pur* aussi
Viens encore une *foix*
Pour parler de Dieu puissant !

Later on come some notes headed : " La force, l'activité."
" Il avait dans sa vie la force et l'activité ! "

When we recollect the ebullient activity of Peter Ilich's
musical career, and his unflagging energy, we cannot help
giving to these fortuitous entries, if not a predictive significance, at least that of a conscious homage to the qualities
he most admired.

His patriotic ardour found vent in four poems, dated
1847, of which the following is a specimen :

Terre ! *apresent* tu *est* loin de moi
Je ne te *voi* plus, o patrie cherie !
Je t'embrasse. O ! pays *adorée*
Toi, oh Russie *aimé*
Vien ! vien ! aupre de moi
Toi, place où je suis né
Je te salut ! oh, terre cherie
Longtemps quand je suis né
Je n'avais ni memoire, ni raison
Ni de dons pour parler
Oh, je ne savais pas que ma Patrie est Russie !

He also attempted an historical essay in verse on Joan
of Arc, whom he had learnt to know from Masson's *Les
Enfants célèbres*. It is entitled :

THE HEROINE OF FRANCE

On t'aime, on ne t'oublie pas
Heroıne si belle !
Tu as sauvé la France
Fılle d'un berger !
Mais qui fait ces actions si belles !

Barbare anglais vous ont tuée,
Toute la France vous admire
Tes cheveux blonds jusqu'à tes genoux
Ils sont très beau
Tu étais si célèbre
Que l'ange Michel t'apparut.
Les célèbres on pense à eux
Les mechants on les oublie !

After 1848 there are no more poetical effusions, perhaps because Fanny was no longer there to preserve such documents; but more probably because the boy had just begun to discover in music a new medium for the expression of his sentiments.

At Votinsk there were no musicians, with the exception of a few indifferent amateur pianists. The mother sang a little, but only played the piano for her children to dance to ; at least, from the time of her marriage, we never hear of a more serious *répertoire*. No other member of the household could do even as much. Unfortunately Fanny was not at all musical, so that the place of music master to the future composer fell to the lot of an inanimate object—an orchestrion which his father brought home with him after a visit to St. Petersburg.

This orchestrion was a superior one, with a varied programme. Peter Ilich himself considered that he owed his first musical impressions to this instrument, which he was never tired of hearing. A composition by Mozart had a particular fascination for him, and his passionate worship of this master dates from this period of childhood, when Zerlina's " Aria," or any melody from *Don Juan*, played by the orchestrion, awoke in him " a beatific rapture." Thanks to this instrument, he first became acquainted with the music of Bellini and Donizetti, so that even the love of Italian opera, which he cherished all his life, may be said to have originated in the same way.

Very early in life he displayed a remarkable ear and quick musical perception. No sooner had he acquired some rudimentary knowledge from his mother, than he could repeat upon the piano all he heard on the orchestrion. He found such delight in playing that it was frequently necessary to drag him by force from the instrument. Afterwards, as the next best substitute, he

would take to drumming tunes upon the window-panes.
One day, while thus engaged, he was so entirely carried
away by this dumb show that he broke the glass and
cut his hand severely. This accident led his parents to
reflect upon the child's incurable tendency and consider
the question of his musical education. They decided to
engage as pianoforte teacher a young lady called Marie
Markovna Palchikov. This was about a year after Fanny's
arrival. Where this teacher came from, and how far she
understood her business, we cannot say. We only know
she came on purpose to teach Peter Ilich, who kept a
pleasant recollection of her. But she cannot entirely have
satisfied the requirements of the future composer, because
already in 1848 he could read at sight as easily as she
did. Nor can her knowledge of musical literature have
been extensive, for her pupil could not remember a single
item in her repertory.

We know from Fanny's own testimony that the boy
spent every spare moment at the piano, and that she did
her utmost to prevent it. A musician's life did not offer
to her mind a radiant prospect. She took more pleasure
in her pupil's literary efforts, and called him in fun "the
juvenile Poushkin." She also observed that music had a
great effect upon his nervous system. After his music
lesson, or after having improvised for any length of time,
he was invariably overwrought and excited. One evening
the Tchaikovskys gave a musical party at which the
children were allowed to be present. At first Peter Ilich
was very happy, but before the end of the evening he
grew so tired that he went to bed before the others.
When Fanny visited his room she found him wide awake,
sitting up in bed with bright, feverish eyes, and crying to
himself. Asked what was the matter, he replied, although
there was no music going on at the time: "Oh, this music,
this music! Save me from it! It is here, here," pointing
to his head, "and will not give me any peace."

Occasionally a Polish officer visited Votinsk. He was an excellent amateur and played Chopin's "Mazurkas" particularly well. His coming was a red-letter day for Peter Ilich. Once he learnt two mazurkas all by himself, and played them so charmingly that the officer kissed him when he had done. "I never saw Pierre so radiantly happy as that day," says Fanny.

This is all I have been able to glean with regard to Peter Ilich's musical development at this period of his life.

III

The Tchaikovsky family arrived in Moscow early in October, 1848. Here they were predestined to misfortune and disappointment. The father had confided to one of his friends at Votinsk that he had received the offer of a fine appointment. On arriving in Moscow, he discovered that the treacherous friend had betrayed his confidence and made use of the information to secure the tempting berth for himself. Added to this, an epidemic of cholera had just broken out in the town, and the children's maid nearly fell a victim to the disease. The uncertainty of their position, the absence of their father—who, on hearing of the trick which had been played him, hastened to Petersburg—the grim spectre of the cholera, all combined to make their sojourn in Moscow anything but a happy one. These things cut deep into the sensitive disposition of Peter Ilich. Just at this moment he stood in the greatest need of loving and careful supervision, and yet at no time did he suffer more from neglect, for his mother was too preoccupied, and too anxious about the future of the family, to spare time and consideration for the moods of its individual members. The children were left to her stepdaughter, herself still half a child, and devoid of all experience.

Zinaïda was the only one who did not make a pet of Peter,
and it seems more than probable that the young poet
found her anything but a just and patient teacher. Under
these circumstances his recollections of the happy past
became more and more idealised, and his retrospective
yearnings more intense.

Early in November the family removed to Petersburg
and took up their abode on the Vassily Ostrov, near the
Exchange.

Here their first impressions were more favourable than
in Moscow. The modern capital was the mother's native
place, and almost like home to the father. Both had many
friends and relatives residing there. No unexpected disagreeables awaited them in St. Petersburg, and they settled
down once again to a peaceful home life.

But now the real trials of life began for Peter Ilich.
Immediately after their arrival, he and his brother Nicholas
were sent to a boarding-school. From Fanny's tender
care they passed straight into the hands of an unsympathetic teacher, and found themselves among a host of
boys, who received the new-comers with the customary
greeting of whacks and thumps. The work, too, was very
hard. They left home at eight in the morning and did
not return till five in the afternoon. The home preparation
was so severe that sometimes the boys sat over their books
till midnight. Besides all this, Peter had regular music
lessons with the pianist Philipov. Judging from the rapid
progress he made in a short time, this teacher must have
been thoroughly competent. Such hard work was very
fatiguing, especially as the boys were drinking in new
æsthetic impressions at the same time. The Tchaikovskys
frequently took the children to the opera and theatre.

If the singing and playing of mediocre amateurs had
excited the future composer to such an extent that their
music haunted him for hours ; if a mechanical organ could
completely enchant him—how infinitely more intense must

have been the first impression made by a full orchestra!
What an agitation, and at the same time what an unhealthy
stimulus to his over-sensibility!

This nervous tension began to be apparent, not only in
his pallor and emaciation, but in frequent ailments that kept
him from school. There was also a moral reaction, and
the boy became capricious, irritable, and unlike his former
self.

In December both brothers had measles; but while
in Nicholas the ailment ran its usual course, Peter's
nervous irritability was much increased by the illness, and
the doctors believed he was suffering from some spinal
trouble. All work was forbidden, and the invalid rested
until June, 1849. After a time, quiet and freedom from
lessons improved the boy's physical health, but his moral
character did not entirely regain its former cheerful
serenity. The wound was healed, but the scar remained.

Early in 1849 Ilia Tchaikovsky was appointed manager
of works on the Yakovliev property at Alapaiev and
Nijny-Neviansk.

Having left his eldest son at a boarding-school, to be
prepared for the School of Mining Engineers, he quitted
Petersburg with the rest of his family, and settled in the
little town of Alapaiev.

The position was not so brilliant as the one he had held
under the Government, but the house was roomy and comfortable, and the Tchaikovskys soon made themselves at
home and endeavoured to revive the patriarchal style in
which they had lived at Votinsk.

The change from St. Petersburg, while it proved beneficial to Peter's health, did not cure his indolence, ca-
priciousness, and irritability. On the contrary, they
seemed to increase, because his present surroundings
suggested comparisons with his ideal life at Votinsk,
which were unfavourable to Alapaiev. He was lonely,

for he missed Nicholas; although at the same time he was jealous of the continual congratulations over each letter which came from Petersburg, announcing his brother's progress and success. The family were delighted, and compared him with Peter, whose studies did not progress rapidly under such an indifferent teacher as Zinaïda. "Pierre is not himself," wrote his mother at this time. "He has grown idle, learns nothing, and often makes me cry with vexation."

Even Peter himself confesses his indolence in a letter dated July 7th (19th) :—

"MA CHÈRE M-ELLE FANNY,—Je vous prie beaucoup de me pardonner que je ne vous ai ecrit si longtemps. Mais comme vous savez que je ne ment pas, c'est *ma paresse* qui en est cause, mais ce n'est pas *l'oublie*, parceque je Vous aime toujours comme je vous aimez avant. Nicholas apprend très bien."[1]

Receiving no reply to this, he wrote again at the end of June. At last an answer came, in which, apparently, Fanny scolded her old pupil, for one of his cousins wrote at this time: "When your letter came, Aunty read it aloud, and Peterkin cried bitterly. He loves you so."

A real improvement in the boy's character dated from the arrival of a new governess, Nastasia Petrov. His mother was soon able to report to Fanny that "Pierre is behaving better and learns willingly with his new teacher."

On May 1st (13th), 1850, twin boys were added to the Tchaikovsky family—Anatol and Modeste. Peter Ilich informed Fanny of the event in the following letter :—

"[ALAPAIEV, *May 2nd* (*14th*), 1850.]

"CHÈRE ET BONNE MELLE FANNY,—C'est avec une grande joie que j'ai appris la nouvelle que vous avez un

---

[1] MY DEAR MISS FANNY,—I beg you to forgive me for not having written all this time. But as you know I do not tell lies, it is *my laziness* that is the cause, not *forgetfulness*, because I love you the same as before. Nicholas works very well, etc.

C

élève *siban* et si diligent. Je veux aussi Vous apprendre, ma chère Fanny, une nouvelle qui peutêtre Vous rejouira un peu ; c'est la naissance de mes frères qui sont jumeaux (la nuit du premier Mai). Je les ai déjà vus plusieurs fois, mais chaque fois que je les vois je crois que ce sont des Anges qui ont descendu sur la terre."[1]

Meanwhile he had made great progress in music. No doubt he had profited greatly by Philipov's instruction, as well as by the other musical impressions he had received in Petersburg. Now, he not only played the pieces he was learning, but would often improvise, "just for myself alone when I feel sad," as he says in one of his letters. His musical idiom was growing richer, and music had become to him what poetry had been at Votinsk. Henceforth we hear no more about verses. He had found the right medium of expression for all that was in his soul. About this time he began to compose, although his attempts were merely improvisations. Musical sounds, according to his own account, followed him everywhere, whatever he was doing. His parents did nothing, however, to further his musical education, partly because they were afraid of a return of his nervous disorder, and partly because they had no intention of making their son a professional musician. No one at Alapaiev took any interest in his musical talent, and he kept his thoughts to himself ; either from pride, or because as yet he had no great confidence in his own gifts. The fact that his character was changing may also have had something to do with his reserve. He felt he possessed something that none of his associates could share, and, inwardly conscious of his power, he was mortified that it should pass unobserved, and that no one should be interested in his artistic aspirations.

---

[1] DEAR, GOOD MISS FANNY,—It is with great joy I hear the news of your having so good and industrious a pupil. I want also to give you some news, my dear Fanny, which may please you a little ; it is of the birth of my twin brothers (on the night of May 1st). I have already seen them several times, but each time I think they are angels descended to earth.

When he went to St. Petersburg for the second time, he was no longer a child. His natural qualities were unchanged, but experience had somewhat hardened him. He was better fitted for the battle of life, but his susceptibilities and his enthusiasms were a trifle blunted.

His young life had already a past, for he had learnt to suffer. Nor did the future appear any more in a rainbow glory, since he realised that it would bring renunciation as well as joy. But he carried a treasure in his heart, a light hidden from all eyes but his own, which was to bring him comfort and courage in the hour of trial.

IV

Early in August, 1850, Madame Tchaikovsky went to Petersburg, accompanied by her daughter, her stepdaughter, and Peter Ilich.

The parents had originally intended to place both their sons at the School of Mining Engineers. Their reason for altering this plan and sending Peter to the School of Jurisprudence has not transpired. Probably it was highly recommended to them by an old friend of Ilia Tchaikovsky's, M. A. Vakar, who had already the charge of Nicholas. This gentleman's brother, Plato Vakar, who was to play an important part in the life of Peter Ilich, was a lawyer, a fine man with a brilliant career in prospect. It is not at all improbable that the Tchaikovskys resolved to send their son to the school of which he was such an admirable example.

Peter Ilich was too young to pass straight into the School of Jurisprudence. It was necessary that for two years he should attend the preparatory classes. At first, all his Sundays and half-holidays were spent with his mother, who

also visited him on every opportunity; so that in the beginning he did not feel the transition from home to school life
so severely. But his mother could not remain in Petersburg
after the middle of October, and then came one of the
most terrible memories of Peter's life—the day of her
departure.

When the actual moment of parting came, he completely
lost his self-control and, clinging wildly to his mother, refused to let her go. Neither kisses, nor words of comfort,
nor the promise to return soon, were of any avail. He saw
nothing, heard nothing, but hung upon her as though he
was part and parcel of the beloved presence. It became
necessary to carry off the poor child by force, and hold him
fast until his mother had driven away. Even then he broke
loose, and with a cry of despair, ran after the carriage, and
clung to one of the wheels, as though he would bring the
vehicle to a standstill.

To his life's end Tchaikovsky could never recall this
hour without a shiver of horror. This first great trouble
of his life was only partly obliterated by a still greater
grief—the death of his mother. Although in after life he
passed through many sad experiences, and knew disappointment and renunciation, he could never forget the sense of
resentment and despair which possessed him as the carriage
containing his beloved mother passed out of sight. The
shadow of this parting darkened the first year of his school
life. Home-sickness and yearning effaced all other impressions, and destroyed all his earlier tendencies, desires,
and thoughts. For two whole years it is evident from
his letters that he lived only in the hope of seeing his
parents again. He knew no other preoccupations or distractions.

Hardly had the boy's mother left St. Petersburg, when
an epidemic of scarlet fever broke out in the school. The
Vakars hastened to take Peter into their own house, but

unhappily the boy, although he escaped illness himself, carried the infection with him. The eldest son, the pride of the home, developed the complaint and died of it. Not a word of reproach was breathed to Peter Ilich, the unhappy cause of the disaster; but the boy could not rid himself of the sense that the parents must regard him with secret bitterness. It is not surprising that just at this time life seemed to him cold and cheerless, and that he longed more than ever for his own people.

The Vakars left Petersburg in April, 1851, and a new home was found for the two brothers in the family of M. Weiss. This change does not appear to have had much effect on Peter Ilich. The tone of his letters remains as homesick as before. But in the following May, Plato Vakar and his wife took the boys into their own house, where they remained until their parents returned to settle in St. Petersburg. In these surroundings Peter's spirits brightened perceptibly.

In September his father came alone and spent three weeks with his boys. His departure was not so tragic an event as had been the mother's a year earlier. Peter was now older, and had learnt to do without his parents. Henceforth his letters are calmer; his entreaties to his mother to come occur less frequently, and are sometimes put in a playful manner.

In May, 1852, the Tchaikovsky family returned to St. Petersburg. His modest savings and the pension he drew from the Government enabled Ilia Tchaikovsky to retire from work and live reunited with his children.

This period of the composer's life offers few interesting events. The monotony of his schooldays was only broken by his Sunday *exeat* which was spent at home.

In 1854 his half-sister, Zinaïda, was married; and in the course of the same year a tragic event took place, which cast a gloom over the family for long days to come. Two years later, in 1856, Peter Ilich refers to this loss in a letter to Fanny :—

"First I must give you some very sad news. A terrible grief befell us more than two years since. Four months after Zinaïda's marriage my mother was taken ill with cholera. Thanks to the care of her doctor, she rallied, but not for long. Three days later she was taken from us without even time to bid us good-bye."

This occurred in July, 1854, and the troubles of the bereaved family did not end here. On the day of his wife's funeral Ilia Tchaikovsky was also seized with cholera ; but although for several days he was in great danger, his life was eventually spared to his family. In his bereaved condition he now found it impossible to keep house. Consequently the younger children were sent to various schools and institutions, while he himself made a home in the household of his brother, Peter Petrovich Tchaikovsky, who was then residing in Petersburg.

The period between 1852 and 1854 had a twofold influence upon Tchaikovsky's character. The tears he had shed, the suffering he had experienced during the two years spent away from home, had reformed his nature, and brought back, in all his old candour and charm, the boy we knew at Votinsk. The irritability, idleness, insincerity, and dissatisfaction with his surroundings had now given place to his old frankness of character, which had formerly fascinated all who came in contact with him.

On the other hand, the former freedom in which his mind and soul developed was now greatly restricted by his way of life, which, although wholesome in some respects, was a direct hindrance to his artistic development. His musical progress, which had made such strides between 1848 and 1849, now came to a standstill that lasted ten years.

Of the thirty-nine letters written during his first two

years of school-life, only two have any reference to music.
Once he speaks of having played a polka for his comrades,
and adds that he had been practising a piece learnt three
years previously, Another time he writes to his parents
that some day he will relate them the story of *Der
Freischütz*, and recalls having heard *A Life for the Tsar*
on his first visit to Petersburg.

It would, however, be incorrect to conclude from this
that he lived without musical impressions. He had strong
predilections, and, as he himself says, Weber's inspired
creation, together with *A Life for the Tsar* and certain
airs from *Don Giovanni*—learnt by means of the orchestrion
at Votinsk—occupied the highest niches in the temple of
his gods. But he had no one to share his musical enthusiasms. At that period there was not a single amateur
among his acquaintances. Everyone with whom he came
in contact regarded music merely as a pastime, without
serious significance in life. Meeting with little sympathy
from his relatives or teachers, and even less from his
schoolmates, he kept his secret aspirations to himself. He
showed a certain reticence in all that concerned his music.
When asked to play, he did so unwillingly, and hurried to
get the performance over. But when he sat down to the
piano, believing himself to be alone, he seemed quite absorbed in his improvisations.

The only person with whom he could discuss his musical
taste was his aunt, Mme. E. A. Alexeiev. Her knowledge
of instrumental music was limited, but she could advance
her nephew's acquaintance with vocal—especially operatic
—music. Thanks to her, he learnt to know the whole of
Don Giovanni, and was never tired of reading the pianoforte
score.

"The music of *Don Juan*," he wrote in 1878, "was the
first to make a deep impression upon me. It awoke a
spiritual ecstasy which was afterwards to bear fruit. By its
help I penetrated into that world of artistic beauty where

only great genius abides. It is due to Mozart that I devoted my life to music. He gave the first impulse to my efforts, and made me love it above all else in the world."

But although Tchaikovsky shrank from sharing his deeper musical emotions with anyone, he was quite willing to take part with those who regarded music as a mere recreation. He sang bravura airs with a facility of vocalisation any *prima donna* might have envied. Once he learnt, with his aunt, the exceedingly florid duet in *Semiramide*, and sang the soprano part admirably. He was very proud of his wonderful natural shake.

About this time one of his most characteristic peculiarities first showed itself: his docility and compliance to the opinions of others on all questions save those concerned with music. Here he would brook no interference. In spite of any attempts to influence his judgment in this respect, he adhered to his own views and followed only his own inward promptings. In all other matters he was malleable as wax.

V

Tchaikovsky's school life had little or no effect upon his subsequent career. The period between 1852–1859 reveals to us not so much the evolution of an artist, as that of an amiable, but mediocre, official, of whom scarcely a trace was to be found some five years later.

The biographical material of this period is necessarily very scanty, being limited to the somewhat hazy reminiscences of his relatives and school friends. Naturally enough it did not occur to anyone to take notes of the comings and goings of a very ordinary young man.

Among the masters and pupils at the School of Jurisprudence no one seems to have exercised any lasting influence, moral or intellectual, upon Tchaikovsky.

He was studious and capable. Many of his studies interested him, but neither he, nor any of his schoolmates, could recall one particular subject in which he had won distinction. On the other hand, mathematics alone seem to have offered any serious difficulty to him.

The scholars of the School of Jurisprudence were drawn chiefly from the upper middle classes, consequently Tchaikovsky found himself from the first among his social equals. His final year was not especially brilliant, but, besides the composer himself, it included the poet Apukhtin and the famous lawyer Gerard.

According to the latter's account, the scholars of that year aimed high. All took a keen interest in literature. Even the lower forms possessed a school magazine, to which Apukhtin, Maslov, Aertel, Gerard, and Tchaikovsky were contributors. A " History of the Literature of our Form," very smartly written, emanated—so Maslov says— from Tchaikovsky's pen.

Among the composer's schoolfellows Vladimir Stepano- vich Adamov takes the first place. Although they spent but a few months in the same class, the mutual attraction was so strong that they remained intimate friends until death severed the connection. Adamov was a typical scholar of the hard-working kind, yet at the same time he had æsthetic aspirations and tastes. He was a passionate lover of nature and very fond of music, although he never became more than an indifferent amateur singer. The friends often went together to the Italian Opera. Adamov left the school with a gold medal and rose rapidly to a high place in the Ministry of Justice. His premature death in 1877 was a severe blow to Tchaikovsky, for Adamov was one of the few intimate friends to whom he cared to confide his artistic aspirations.

Apukhtin, who came to school in 1853, at thirteen, was a

youthful prodigy.   His poetical gifts were already the admiration not only of his comrades, but of the outer world.
He possessed the same personal charm as Tchaikovsky,
but was far more sophisticated and self-conscious.   The
universal admiration to which he was accustomed, the
interest of such writers as Tourgeniev and Fet, tended to
encourage his vanity.   The path to fame lay clearly before
him.

Apukhtin's tendencies were decidedly sceptical.   He was
the exact opposite of Tchaikovsky.   Their temperaments
were radically different.   But both loved poetry, and
shared that delicate " flair " for all that is choice—that
mysterious " something " which draws artists together, no
matter when or where they chance to meet.   The contrast
in all other respects only served to open new horizons to
both and draw the bonds of friendship closer.

As a friend and schoolmate, Tchaikovsky displayed the
same qualities which distinguished him as a child at
Votinsk.   Now, as subsequently in the Ministry of Justice,
at the Conservatoires of Petersburg and Moscow, throughout Europe and across the Atlantic, we watch him drawing
all hearts towards himself, while the circle of his friendships
was constantly widening.

By the time he passed out of the preparatory classes,
his ideal faith in the order of things was shaken.   He
no longer worked with a kind of religious fervour for
work's sake.   Henceforward he did just what was necessary
to avoid punishment and to enable him to qualify for an
official post, without any real interest in the work.   As to
music, neither he, nor any of his circle, had any confidence
in an artistic career.   He scarcely realised in what direction
he was drifting ; yet with the change from youth to manhood came also the desire to taste the pleasures and
excitements of life.   The future appeared to him as an
endless festival, and as nothing had come, so far, to mar
his happiness, he gave himself up to this delightful illusion.

With an impulsive temperament, he took life easily: a good-natured, careless young man, unencumbered by serious aspirations or intentions.

In 1855, in consequence of the mother's death, the family life of the Tchaikovskys underwent great changes.

Ilia Tchaikovsky was a good father, but he did not understand the education of the younger children. Realising this fact—and partly because he found his loneliness unbearable—he now resolved to share the home of his brother, Peter Petrovich Tchaikovsky.

Peter Petrovich was a white-haired man of seventy, every inch a soldier, who had seen many campaigns, and bore many honourable scars. He was exceedingly religious, and up to the time of his marriage had led a life devoted to prayer, fasting, and warfare. He might have belonged to some mediæval order of knighthood. Stern towards himself, he demanded blind obedience from his wife and children; when he found that they did not respond to his influence, he shut himself apart in grim disapproval and wrote endless tracts on mystical subjects.

Madame Peter Tchaikovsky, although a little in awe of her husband, permitted her children to enjoy all the amusements natural to their age—balls, concerts, and other worldly dissipations. The young people of both families led a merry, careless existence until the spring of 1858, when Ilia Tchaikovsky, thanks to his over-confidence in humanity, suddenly lost his entire fortune and was obliged in his declining days to seek a new appointment. Fortunately this was forthcoming and, as the Director of the Technological Institute, he found himself once more in comfortable circumstances. A married sister-in-law Elizabeth Schobert, and her family, now joined the Tchaikovsky household, established in the official residence that went with the new appointment.

On May 13th (25th), 1859, Peter Ilich left the School of Jurisprudence and entered the Ministry of Justice as a first-class clerk. This event, which would have meant so much to any other young man, signified little to Tchaikovsky. He did not take his new work seriously, although he had no presentiment of his future destiny. How little his official occupations really interested him is evident from the fact that a few months after he had changed his vocation he could not remember the nature of his work in the Ministry of Justice. He only recollected one of his colleagues, because of "something rather unusual that seemed to flash from his eyes." Twenty-five years later Tchaikovsky met this man again in the person of the celebrated landscape painter Volkov.

One "traditional" anecdote, and the brief history of Peter Ilich as an official is complete. He had been entrusted with a signed document from the chief of his department, but on his way to deliver it he stopped to talk with someone, and in his absence of mind never noticed that, while talking, he kept tearing off scraps of the paper and chewing them—a trick he always had with theatre tickets or programmes. There was nothing for it but to re-copy the document and, however unpleasant, to face his chief for a fresh signature.

Tchaikovsky delighted in nature and the freedom of the country. In winter the theatre was his chief amusement, especially the French play, the ballet, and the Italian opera. He was particularly fascinated by ballets of the fantastic or fairy order, and gradually came to value more and more the art of dancing.

The acting of Adelaide Ristori made a profound impression upon Tchaikovsky. His greatest admiration, however, was for the singer Lagroua. She was not a beautiful woman, but, in the part of Norma, she displayed such tragic pathos, such plastic art, that she was worthy to be compared with the greatest actresses.

In 1860 Tchaikovsky's youngest sister and constant companion, Alexandra Ilinichna, was married to Leo Vassilievich Davidov, and went to live in the Government of Kiev. During the following year several other members of the family went out into the world, so that the cheerful family life came to an end, and a shade of melancholy crept over the remainder of the household.

At this period Tchaikovsky's attitude to his father and his aunts was slightly egotistical and contemptuous. This was only a passing phase. He was not actually wanting in affection for his own people, but was simply bored in their society. At this age he could not endure a quiet life at home.

Under such auspices dawned the year 1861, destined to inaugurate a new epoch in the life of Tchaikovsky.

PART II

I

AT this time there were two music masters at the School of Jurisprudence. Karel, who taught the piano, until he was succeeded by Bekker, and Lomakin, the professor of singing.

It is not known whether Tchaikovsky ever took lessons with Karel. With Bekker he did learn for a time, but the lessons made no impression upon his memory.

The singing lessons he received from Lomakin amounted to little more than choral practices. Lomakin was a very competent man, who brought the school choir to a pitch of perfection; but he had not time to train individual voices, consequently he exercised no direct influence on Tchaikovsky, although he observed his beautiful soprano voice and his great talent for music.

Besides these masters, Tchaikovsky took piano lessons at home from Rudolf Kündinger.

Kündinger had come to Russia at eighteen, and delighted the public of St. Petersburg by his brilliant virtuosity. Having attracted many pupils, he settled in Petersburg. In 1855 the elder Tchaikovsky engaged him to teach his son. Kündinger afterwards regretted that he kept no record of these lessons. The boy struck him as talented, but nothing made him suspect the germ of a great composer. One thing which impressed Kündinger was his remarkable power of improvisation. Another was his fine feeling for harmony. Kündinger would often show his pupil his own compositions, and accept his suggestions as regards harmony, finding them invariably to the point, although at that time Tchaikovsky knew nothing of the theory of music.

His father consulted Kündinger as to the wisdom of allowing his son to devote himself entirely to music. The teacher's advice was directly to the contrary. "I had to take into consideration the wretched status of a professional musician in Russia at that time," said Kündinger afterwards; "besides I had no real faith in Peter Ilich's gift for music."

If such specialists as Lomakin and Kündinger saw nothing phenomenal in Tchaikovsky, it is hardly surprising that others should have failed to do so. His school friends valued his musical talents, but were far from suspecting him to be a future celebrity. His relations, especially his sisters and cousins, thought his improvisation of dance music a pleasant accomplishment, but otherwise regarded his music as "useless trifling." His father, alone, took the matter at all seriously. He engaged a good teacher, and encouraged his son to study steadily. In a word, he did all that a man could do, who knew absolutely nothing of music and musicians.

Tchaikovsky had only one morning and two evenings in the week in which he was free to devote himself to music. Consequently he had no opportunity of grounding himself in the art. When and how could he become acquainted with the symphonic masterpieces of the great German composers? Symphony concerts were then rare in St. Petersburg. The future composer had no alternative but to study these works in pianoforte arrangements. But such music was expensive and beyond his slender means. This explains why his musical knowledge was so limited at that time. We cannot say how many of the works of Beethoven, Mozart, and Schubert he knew prior to 1861; it is certain that his knowledge was not half so extensive as that of any good amateur of the present day. For instance, he knew nothing of Schumann, nor the number and keys of Beethoven's symphonies. He frequented the Italian Opera, which was his sole opportunity of hearing a good orchestra, chorus, and first-rate soloists. Russian opera was then at a low ebb, and he only went to hear his favourite work, *A Life for the Tsar*. All the other operas he heard were sung by Italians. To these artists he owed not only his passion for *Don Juan* and *Freischütz*, but also his acquaintance with Meyerbeer, Rossini, Donizetti, and Verdi, for whom he had a genuine enthusiasm.

During the fifties the celebrated singing master Piccioli was living in Petersburg. He was a Neapolitan by birth, who had come to the Russian capital some ten years earlier and settled there. His wife was a friend of Alexandra Schobert, and in this way he became acquainted with the Tchaikovskys. Although nearly fifty, he was very intimate with Peter, who was but seventeen. But as to Piccioli's real age, no one knew the truth, for he kept it dark. He certainly dyed his hair and painted his face, and cruel tongues did not hesitate to assert that he would never see seventy again, and that he kept at the back of his head a small apparatus for smoothing out his wrinkles. I remember how, as children, my brother Anatol and I took great pains to discover this apparatus, and how we finally decided it must be concealed somewhere under his collar. As regards music, Piccioli gave utterance to such violently fanatical views and convictions, and knew so well how to defend them with persuasive eloquence, that he could have won over even a less pliant nature than that of Tchaikovsky. He acknowledged only Rossini, Bellini, Donizetti, and Verdi. He scorned and hated with equal thoroughness the symphonies of Beethoven, the works of Bach, *A Life for the Tsar*, and all the rest. Outside the creations of the great Italian melodists he admitted no music whatever. In spite of his eloquence, the Italian

could not win over Tchaikovsky heart and soul to his way
of thinking, because the latter was not given to partiality,
and also because his own musical tastes were already
firmly implanted, and could not be so easily modified.
He carried within him an Olympia of his own, to the
deities of which he did homage with all his soul.   Nevertheless, the friendship between himself and Piccioli remained unbroken, and to this he owed, in a great measure,
his thorough acquaintance with the music of the Italian
operatic school.

Since 1850 Tchaikovsky's talent as a composer had only
found expression in improvisations for the piano. Although
he had composed a good many valses, polkas, and "Rêveries
de Salon," which were probably no worse than similar
pieces invented by his "composer" friends, he could not
bring himself to put his thoughts on paper—perhaps from
excessive modesty, perhaps from pride.   Once only did he
write out a song, composed to words by the poet Fet: "My
genius, my angel, my friend," a mere empty amateur
effusion.   Yet, as time passed, his musical consciousness,
his realisation of his true vocation, undoubtedly increased.
Later in life he said, that even at school, the thought
of becoming a composer haunted him incessantly, but,
feeling that no one in his circle had any faith in his talents,
he seldom mentioned the subject.   Occasionally he made
a prophetic utterance.   Once, about the close of 1862,
soon after he had joined the classes at the Conservatoire,
he was talking to his brother Nicholas.   Nicholas, who
was one of those who did not approve of his brother's wish
to study music, held forth on the subject, assuring him he
had not the genius of a Glinka, and that the wretched lot
of a mediocre musician was not an enviable one.   At first
Peter Ilich made no reply, but as they were parting he said:
"Perhaps I shall not turn out a Glinka, but one thing
I can assure you—you will be proud some day to own me
as a brother."   The look in his eyes, and the tone in which

D

he spoke these words, were never forgotten by Nicholas Tchaikovsky.

The slowness and unproductiveness of Tchaikovsky's musical development in the fifties was closely connected with his frivolous mode of life. His nature—in reality lovable and accessible to all—and his fertile genius seemed both hushed in a profound slumber; but at the moment of his awakening, his musical gifts as well as all his other good qualities simultaneously reappeared. With the superficial amateur vanished also the mere society man; with the strenuous, zealous inquirer returned also the tender, grateful son, the kind and thoughtful brother.

The change took place quite unobserved. It is difficult to give the exact moment of its commencement, for it was not preceded by any important events. Undoubtedly, it may be observed as early as 1861, when Peter Ilich began once more to think of an artistic career and entered into closer relationship with his family, striving to find at home that satisfaction for his higher spiritual needs, which he had failed to discover in his previous way of living. He had grown weary of an easy-going life, and the desire to start afresh made itself increasingly felt. He began to be afraid lest he might be overwhelmed in this slough of a petty, useless, and vicious existence. In the midst of this feverish pursuit of pleasure there came over him— so he said—moments of agonising despair. Whether satiety came to him from some unknown event in his life, or whether it gradually crept into his soul, no one can tell, for he passed through these heavy hours alone. Those around him only observed the change when it had already taken place, and the dawn of a new life had gladdened his spiritual vision.

In a letter to his newly-married sister Alexandra, written in March, 1861, he speaks of an incident which may be regarded as the first step towards his musical career. His father, on his own initiative, had actually proposed that he should devote himself entirely to music.

"At supper they were talking of my musical talent," writes Peter Ilich, "and father declared it was not yet too late for me to become an artist. If it were only true! But the matter stands thus: that my talent, supposing I really have any, would hardly develop now. They have made me an official, although a poor one; I try as hard as I can to improve and to fulfil my duties more conscientiously, and at the same time I am to be studying thorough-bass!"

Another incident, as ordinary as the one just related, marks the change in Tchaikovsky's relations with his family, and throws a clearer light upon this revolution in his spiritual life.

After the marriage of our sister Alexandra, the twins, Anatol and myself, then about ten years old, were often very lonely. From three o'clock in the afternoon—when we returned from school—until bedtime, we were left to our own resources. One long and wearisome evening, as we sat on the drawing-room window-sill kicking our heels, Peter came in and found us. From our earliest infancy he inspired us, not so much with love as with respect and adoration. A word from him was like a sacred treasure. He, on the contrary, took no notice of us; we had no existence for him.

The mere fact that he was in the house, and that we could see him, sufficed to distract our dullness and cheer us up; but great indeed was our astonishment when, instead of passing us by unobserved as usual, he stopped to say: "Are you dull, boys? Would you like to spend the evening with me?" To this day I cannot forget that memorable evening; memorable indeed for us, since it was the beginning of a new existence.

The wisest and most experienced of teachers, the dearest and tenderest of mothers, could not have replaced Peter

Ilich in our life from that hour; for he was all this, and our friend and comrade besides. All we thought and felt we could tell him without any fear lest it would fail to interest him. His influence upon us was unbounded. We, on our side, became the first care and aim of his life. We three formed, as it were, a family within the family. A year later Peter wrote to his sister :—

"My attachment to these little folk grows from day to day. I am very proud of this feeling, perhaps the best which my heart has known. When I am unhappy I have only to think of them, and my life seems better worth living. I try as far as possible to give them a mother's love and care. . . ."

II

In spite of the important conversation at the supper-table, in spite of the spiritual regeneration of Peter Ilich and the change in his relations towards his family, his life remained externally the same. He kept his official berth, and continued to go into society, frequenting dances and theatres. Of all the pleasures he pursued, of all the desires he cherished, only one remained unfulfilled—a tour abroad.

But now even this wish was to be satisfied.

An old friend of his father's had to go abroad on business. As he was no linguist, it was necessary to take a companion who would act as interpreter, and he proposed that Peter Ilich should accompany him in this capacity. Accordingly in June, 1861, the former writes to his sister:—

"As you probably have heard already, I am to go abroad. You can imagine my delight. . . This journey seems to me at times an alluring, unrealisable dream. I shall not believe in it until I am actually on the steamer. I—in Paris! In Switzerland! It seems ridiculous to think of it !"

In July Tchaikovsky started with his friend, but not by steamer.

Their first halting-place was Berlin. In those days every Russian considered it his duty to run down this city. To this duty—or rather custom—Peter Ilich contributed his due. After he had visited Kroll's, and a dancing saloon, and seen Offenbach's *Orphée aux Enfers*, he writes with youthful *naïveté*: "Now we know our Berlin thoroughly, and have had enough of it!"

After Berlin came Hamburg, which Tchaikovsky found "a considerable improvement." Brussels and Antwerp did not please him at all. At Ostend they stayed three days. "It is beautiful here," he wrote. "I love the sea, especially when it foams and roars, and these last days it has been furious."

Next they went on to London. "Our visit would be very pleasant were it not for the anxiety about your health," he wrote to his father. "Your letters are awaiting me in Paris, and my heart yearns for them, but we must remain here a few days longer. London is very interesting, but makes a gloomy impression. The sun is seldom visible, and it rains all the time." Here Tchaikovsky heard Patti for the first time, and although later in life she fascinated him, now he could see "nothing particular" in her.

As might be expected, Paris pleased him best of all the towns he visited. Life in the French capital he found delightful. The six weeks which he spent in Paris were the culmination of his pleasure trip. But in the midst of his enjoyment he experienced a complete disenchantment with his travelling companion. After a series of painful misunderstandings they separated, and Peter Ilich returned to Russia alone about the end of September.

Intellectually and artistically, Tchaikovsky profited little by this journey. Indeed, it is astonishing how little sensitive he seems to have been at that time to all such impressions. In the three months he was abroad he only acquired one positive piece of information—where one could derive the greatest pleasure. And yet his journey was not altogether wasted. In the first place, it brought home to him the strength of his attachment to his own people. He missed the twins most of all. " Take care, father, that Toly and Modi[1] are not idle." "Are Toly and Modi working well?" "Don't forget to tell the examiner that Toly and Modi are prepared for the upper division," so runs the gist of his letters.

Secondly, on this journey he learnt to realise the in-evitable end of an idle and pleasure-seeking life, and to recognise that it led to nothing, and that existence held other and nobler aims than the pursuit of enjoyment. The various distractions of Parisian life brought about a wholesome reaction, and on the threshold of a new career he could look quietly on the termination of his former life, conscious only of an ardent desire to step from the shadow into God's daylight.

Soon after his return he wrote the following letter to his sister :—

" *October 23rd (November 4th)*, 1861.

" What shall I tell you about my journey? It is better to say nothing. If ever I started upon a colossal piece of folly, it was this same trip abroad. You remember my companion? Well, under the mask of *bonhomie*, which made me believe him to be a worthy man, was concealed the most commonplace nature. You can imagine if it was pleasant to spend three months with such a fellow-traveller. Added to which I ran through more money than I could afford and got nothing for it. Do you see what a fool I have been? But do not scold me. I have behaved like a child—nothing more. . . . You know I have a weakness : as soon as I have any money I squander it in pleasure. It is vulgar, wanting in good sense—I know it —but it seems in my nature. Where will it all lead? What can I hope from the future? It is terrible to think of. I know there will come a time when I shall no longer

---

[1] Diminutives of Anatol and Modeste.

be able to fight against the difficulties of life. Until then I will do all I can to enjoy it. For the last fortnight all has gone badly with me; my official work has been very bad. Money vanishes like smoke. In love—no luck. But a better time will come soon.

"P.S.—I have begun to study thorough-bass, and am making good progress. Who knows, perhaps in three years' time you will be hearing my opera and singing my arias."

III

The most remarkable feature in the process of Tchaikovsky's transformation from a smart Government official and society dandy into a musical student lies in the fact that, with all its apparent suddenness and irrevocableness, there was nothing hasty or emotional about the proceeding. Not once, by word or deed, can we discern that he cherished any idea of future renown. He scaled no rugged heights, he put forth no great powers; but every move in his new career was carefully considered, steadily resolved upon, and, in spite of a certain degree of caution, firmly established. His peace of mind and confidence were so great that they seemed part of his environment, and all hindrances and difficulties vanished of their own accord and left the way open to him.

The psychological aspect of this transformation, the pathetic side of the conflict which he sustained for over two years, must always remain unrevealed; not because his correspondence at this time was scanty, but because Peter Ilich maintained a jealous guard over the secrets of his inner and spiritual life in which no stranger was permitted to intermeddle. He chose to go through the dark hours alone, and remained outwardly the same serene and cheerful young man as before. But if this reincarnation was quite ordinary in its process, it was the more radical and decisive.

Tchaikovsky's situation is very clearly shown in four letters written to his sister about this period, each letter corresponding with one of the four phases of his evolution. These letters throw a clear light upon the chief psychological moments of these two eventful years of his life.

The first, dated October 23rd (November 4th), 1861, has been already quoted. Tchaikovsky just mentions in the postscript that he has begun his musical studies as a matter of no importance whatever—and that in itself is very enlightening. At that moment his harmony lessons with Zaremba were only a detail in the life of a man of the world, as were the Italian conversation lessons he was taking at the same time. His chief interest was still his official career, and most of his leisure was still given up to social enjoyment. The second letter shows matters from a somewhat different point of view. Although only written a few weeks later, it puts his musical studies in a new light. On December 4th (16th), 1861, Tchaikovsky writes:—

"I am getting on well. I hope soon to get a rise, and be appointed 'clerk for special duty.' I shall get an additional twenty roubles to my salary and less work. God grant it may come to pass! . . . I think I have already told you that I have begun to study the theory of music with success. You will agree that, with my rather exceptional talents (I hope you will not mistake this for bragging), it seems foolish not to try my chances in this direction. I only dread my own easy-going nature. In the end my indolence will conquer: but if not, I promise you that I shall do something. Luckily it is not yet too late."

Between the second and third letters eight months elapsed. During this period Peter Ilich had to refute his self-condemnation as regards indolence, and to prove that it actually "was not yet too late" to accomplish something.

I recollect having made two discoveries at this time which filled me with astonishment. The first was that the two ideas "brother Peter" and "work" were not necessarily opposed; the second, that besides pleasant and interesting music, there existed another kind, exceedingly unpleasant and wearisome, which appeared nevertheless to be the more important of the two. I still remember with what persistency Peter Ilich would sit at the piano for hours together playing the most "abominable" and "incomprehensible" preludes and fugues. . . . My astonishment knew no bounds when he informed me he was writing exercises. It passed my understanding that so charming a pastime as music should have anything in common with the mathematical problems we loathed. Outwardly Peter Ilich's life underwent one remarkable change. Of all his friends and acquaintances he now only kept up with Apukhtin and Adamov.

Besides his work for Zaremba's classes, Tchaikovsky devoted many hours to the study of the classical composers. Yet, in spite of all this, his official work still remained the chief aim of his existence. During the summer of 1862 he was more attentive to his official duties than before, because in the autumn a desirable vacancy was expected to occur, to which he had every claim, so that it was important to prove to his chief, by extra zeal and diligence, that he was worthy of the post. His labour was wasted; the place was not bestowed upon him. His indignation at being "passed over" knew no bounds, and there is little doubt that this incident had a great deal to do with his resolution to devote himself entirely to music. The last ties which bound him to the bureaucratic world snapped under the strain of this act of "injustice."

Meanwhile several changes had taken place in the family life of the Tchaikovskys. Their aunt Madame Schobert had left them. Nicholas had received an appointment in the provinces. Hyppolite was in the navy and had been sent on a long voyage. The family was now reduced to four members—the father, Peter Ilich, and the twins. The latter, deprived of their aunt's care, found in their brother more than ever both a tutor and a guardian.

Tchaikovsky's third letter to his sister, dated September 10th (22nd), 1862, brings us to a still more advanced phase of his transformation. His official work has now taken quite a subordinate position, while music is regarded as his speciality and life-work, not only by himself, but by all his relatives.

"I have entered the newly-opened Conservatoire," he says, "and the course begins in a few days. As you know, I have worked hard at the theory of music during the past year, and have come to the conclusion that sooner or later I shall give up my present occupation for music. Do not imagine I dream of being a great artist. . . . I only feel I must do the work for which I have a vocation. Whether I become a celebrated composer, or only a struggling teacher—'tis all the same. In any case my conscience will be clear, and I shall no longer have any right to grumble at my lot. Of course, I shall not resign my present position until I am sure that I am no longer a clerk, but a musician."

He had relinquished social gaiety. "I always have my midday meal at home," he wrote at this time, "and in the evening I often go to the theatre with father, or play cards with him." Soon he had not even leisure for such distractions. His musical studies were not restricted to two classes in the week, but began to absorb almost all his time. Besides which he began to make new friends at the Conservatoire—mostly professional musicians—with whom he spent the rest of his leisure.

Among these, Laroche plays so important a part in Tchaikovsky's artistic and intimate life that it is necessary to say something of his personality before proceeding further.

Hermann Laroche, the well-known musical writer and critic, was born in St. Petersburg, May 13th (25th), 1845. His father, a Hanoverian by birth, was established in that city as a French teacher. His mother was a highly educated woman, and was careful to make her son an accomplished linguist. His musical talent was displayed at an early age. At ten he had already composed a march and an overture. He began his systematic musical education in 1860, at Moscow, under the guidance of Dubuque. At first he wished to be a virtuoso, but his teachers persuaded him to relinquish the idea, because his hands were not suited to the piano, and they laid more stress on his talent for composing.

When he entered the Conservatoire in the autumn of 1862, Laroche surpassed all his fellow-students in musical knowledge, and was also a highly educated and well-read young man.

Tchaikovsky and Laroche met for the first time in October, 1862, at the class of the professor of pianoforte, Gerke. Hermann Laroche was then seventeen years of age. The important results of this friendship in Tchaikovsky's after-life will be seen as this book proceeds; at the outset its importance was threefold. In the first place, he found in this fellow-student, who was far better versed in musical literature than himself, an unofficial guide and mentor; secondly, Laroche was the first critic of Tchaikovsky's school compositions—the first and also the most influential, for, from the beginning, Peter Ilich placed the greatest confidence in his judgment; and thirdly, Laroche supplanted all former intimacies in Tchaikovsky's life, and became his dearest companion and friend. The variety of his interests, the keenness of his critical judgments, his unfailing liveliness and wit, made the hours of leisure which Tchaikovsky now spent with him both pleasant and profitable; while Laroche's inexperience of the practical side of life, and his helplessness in his relations with others, amused Tchaikovsky and gave him an opportunity of helping and advising his friend in return.

Early in 1863 Tchaikovsky resigned his place in the

Ministry of Justice, and resolved to give himself up entirely to music. His material prospects were not bright. His father could give him board and lodging; the rest he must earn for himself. But his will was firm, for by this time his self-confidence and love of his art had taken firm root.

The fourth and last letter to his sister, which sets forth the reasons which induced him to give up his official appointment, reveals altogether a new man.

"*April* 15*th* (27*th*), 1863.

"DEAR SASHA,—From your letter which reached father to-day, I perceive that you take a lively interest in my situation and regard with some mistrust the step I have decided to take. I will now explain to you more fully what my hopes and intentions really are. My musical talent—you cannot deny it—is my only one. This being so, it stands to reason that I ought not to leave this God-sent gift uncultivated and undeveloped. For this reason I began to study music seriously. So far my official duties did not clash with this work, and I could remain in the Ministry of Justice. Now, however, my studies grow more severe and take up more time, so I find myself compelled to give up one or the other. . . . In a word, after long consideration, I have resolved to sacrifice the salary and resign my post. But it does not follow that I intend to get into debt, or ask for money from father, whose circumstances are not very flourishing just now. Certainly I am not gaining any material advantage. But first I hope to obtain a small post in the Conservatoire next season (as assistant professor); secondly, I have a few private lessons in view; and thirdly—what is most important of all—I have entirely renounced all amusements and luxuries, so that my expenditure has very much decreased. Now you will want to know what will become of me when I have finished my course. One thing I know for certain. I shall be a good musician and shall be able to earn my daily bread. The professors are satisfied with me, and say that with the necessary zeal I shall do well. I do not tell you all this in a boastful spirit (it is not my nature), only in order to speak openly to you without any false modesty. I cherish a dream; to come to you for a whole year after my studies are finished to compose a great work in your quiet surroundings. After that—out into the world."

In the autumn of 1863, after a visit to Apukhtin, Tchaikovsky returned to Petersburg, externally and inwardly a changed man. His hair had grown long, and he wore a somewhat shabby, but once fashionable coat, a relic of his "foppish days"; so that in the new Tchaikovsky the former Peter Ilich was hardly recognisable. His circumstances at this time were not brilliant. His father had taken a very modest lodging in Petersburg, and could give his son nothing but bare board and lodging. To supply his further needs, Peter Ilich took some private teaching which Anton Rubinstein found for him. These lessons brought in about fifty roubles a month (£5).

The sacrifice of all the pleasures of life did not in the least embitter or disturb him. On the contrary, he made light of his poverty, and at no time of his life was he so cheerful and serene as now. In a small room, which only held a bed and a writing-table, he started bravely on his new, laborious existence, and there he spent many a night in arduous work.

IV

Laroche gives the following account of the years Tchaikovsky spent at the Conservatoire of St. Petersburg :—

" At the Conservatoire, founded by Anton Rubinstein in 1861, under the patronage of the Grand-Duchess Helen, the curriculum consisted of the following subjects: Choral Singing (Lomakin and Dütsch), Solo Singing (Frau Nissen-Soloman), Pianoforte (Leschetitzky and Beggrov), Violin (Wieniawsky), Violoncello (Schuberth), and Composition (Zaremba). Of all these subjects Tchaikovsky studied the last only.

" Nicholas Ivanovich Zaremba was then forty years of age. A Pole by birth, he had studied law at the University of St. Petersburg, and had been a clerk in one of the Government offices. . . Music —especially composition— he had studied in Berlin under the celebrated theorist Marx, whom he almost worshipped. As a composer, Zaremba is not known to me. Never once, either in class or during his private lessons, did he say so much as a word about his own compositions. Only on one occasion he invited Peter Ilich to his house and, when they were alone together, showed him the manuscript of a string quartet of his own. The following day Peter Ilich told me the work was 'very nice, in the style of Haydn.'

" Zaremba had many of the qualities of an ideal teacher. Although, if I am not mistaken, teaching was somewhat new to him, he appeared fully equipped, with a course mapped out to the smallest details, firm in his æsthetic views, and inventive in illustrating his subject. . . . As became an out-and-out follower of Marx, Zaremba was a progressive liberal as regards music, believed in Beethoven (particularly in his latest period), detested the bondage of the schools, and was more disposed to leave his pupils to themselves than to restrict and hamper them with excessive severity. He taught on Marx's method, with one deviation: he followed up his harmony course by one on strict counterpoint, using a text book of Heinrich Bellermann's. I do not think, however, that he taught this on his own initiative, but possibly at Rubinstein's expressed wish.

" I have spoken of Zaremba as progressive. He was actually an enthusiastic admirer of Beethoven's later period; but he stopped short at Beethoven, or rather at Mendelssohn. The later development of German music, which started from Schumann, was unknown to him. He knew nothing of Berlioz and ignored Glinka. With regard to the latter he showed very plainly his alienation from Russian soil. Tchaikovsky, who was more disposed towards empiricism, and by nature antagonistic to all abstractions, did not admire Zaremba's showy eloquence, nor yet that structure of superficial logic, from the shelter of which he thundered forth his violent and arbitrary views. The misunderstanding between pupil and teacher was aggravated by the fact that Zaremba most frequently cited the authority of Beethoven, while, following the example of his master, Marx, he secretly — and sometimes openly — despised Mozart. Tchaikovsky, on the contrary, had more respect than enthusiasm for Beethoven, and never aimed at following in his footsteps. His judgment was always somewhat sceptical; his need of independence remarkable. During all the years I knew him, he never once submitted blindly to any influence, nor swore by anyone in *verba magistri.* His personal feelings sometimes coloured his views. Zaremba, however, exercised no such fascination for him. Neither in Tchaikovsky the composer, nor in Tchaikovsky the professor, do we find any subsequent traces of Zaremba's teaching. This is the more remarkable, because the composer went to him as a beginner to be grounded in the rudiments of musical theory, so that he had every opportunity of making a deep and lasting impression. I must, however, relate one occurrence which partially contradicts my statement that Zaremba had no influence whatever upon his pupil. When in 1862, or the following year, I expressed my admiration for the energy and industry with which Tchaikovsky was working, he replied that when he first attended Zaremba's classes he had not been so zealous, but had worked in 'a very superficial way, like a true amateur,' until on one occasion Zaremba had drawn him aside and impressed upon him the necessity of being more earnest and industrious, because he possessed a fine talent. Deeply touched, Peter Ilich resolved to conquer his indolence, and from that moment worked with untiring zeal and energy.

"From 1861–2 Tchaikovsky learnt harmony, and from 1862–3 studied strict counterpoint and the church modes under Zaremba, with whom, in September, 1863, he began also to study form ; while about the same time he passed into Rubinstein's class for instrumentation.

"The great personality of the Director of the Conservatoire inspired us students with unbounded affection, mingled with not a little awe. In reality no teacher was more considerate and kindly, but his forbidding appearance, his hot temper and roughness, added to the glamour of his European fame, impressed us profoundly.

"Besides the direction of the Conservatoire, he taught the piano, and his class was the desired goal of every young pianist in the school, for although the other professors (Gerke, Dreyschock, and Leschetitzky) had excellent reputations, they were overshadowed by Rubinstein's fame and by his wonderful playing. In his class, which then consisted of three male students and a host of women, Rubinstein would often set the most comical tasks. On one occasion, for instance, he made his pupils play Czerny's "Daily Studies" in every key, keeping precisely the same fingering throughout. His pupils were very proud of the ordeals they were made to undergo, and their narrations aroused the envy of all the other classes. As a teacher of theory Anton Rubinstein was just the opposite of Zaremba. While the latter was remarkably eloquent, the former was taciturn to the last degree. Rubinstein spoke a number of languages, but none quite correctly. In Russian he often expressed himself fluently and appropriately, but his grammar was sometimes faulty, which was very noticeable in his exposition of a theoretical problem, demanding logical sequence. Yet it was remarkable that this deficiency in no way spoilt his lectures. With Zaremba, all was systematic, each word had its own place. With Rubinstein, reigned a fascinating disorder. I believe that ten minutes before the lesson he did not know what he was going to talk about, and left all to the inspiration of the moment. Although the literary form of his lectures suffered in consequence, and defied all criticism, they impressed us deeply, and we attended them with great interest. Rubinstein's extraordinary practical knowledge, his breadth of view, his experience as a composer—almost incredible for a man of thirty—invested his words with an authority of which we could not fail to be sensible. Even the paradoxes he indulged in, which sometimes irritated and sometimes amused us, bore the stamp of genius and thought. As I have said, Rubinstein had no system whatever. If he observed in the course of a lesson that he was not in touch with his pupils, he was not discouraged, and always discovered some new way—as also in his pianoforte class—by which to impart some of his original ideas. On one occasion he set Tchaikovsky the task of orchestrating

Beethoven's D minor sonata in four different ways. Peter
Ilich elaborated one of these arrangements, introducing the
English horn and all manner of unusual accessories, for
which the master reprimanded him severely. I must add
that Rubinstein was sincerely attached to Tchaikovsky,
although he never valued his genius at its true worth. It
is not difficult to understand this, because Tchaikovsky's
artistic growth was perfectly normal and equal, and quite
devoid of any startling developments. His work, which
was generally of level excellence, lacked that brilliancy
which rejoices the astonished teacher.

" Rubinstein, on the contrary, cast a magic spell over
Tchaikovsky. The pupil, who kept his complete independence of judgment, and even made fun of his master's lack
of logic and grammar in his lectures, contemplated, not
without bitterness, his mass of colourless and insipid compositions. But neither the peculiarities of the teacher, nor
the ever-increasing weakness of his works, could under-
mine Tchaikovsky's regard for him as a man. This sentiment remained with him to the last, although his relations
with Anton were never so intimate as with his brother,
Nicholas Rubinstein. At this period of our lives Tchaikovsky's personal respect for his master was of the greatest
service to him. It made his work easier and gave impulse
to his powers. Rubinstein observed his pupil's zeal, and
made increasing demands upon his capacity for work. But
the harder the tasks set him, the more energetic Tchaikovsky became. Sometimes he spent the whole night upon
some score he wished to lay before his insatiable teacher
on the following day. This extraordinary industry does
not appear to have injured his health.

"The silent protest Tchaikovsky raised against Zaremba's
methods affected in a lesser degree his relations with
Rubinstein. The latter had grown up in the period
of Schubert, Mendelssohn and Schumann, and recognised
only their orchestra, that is, the orchestra of Beethoven,
with the addition of three trombones—natural horns and
trumpets being replaced by chromatic ones. We young
folk, however, were enthusiasts for the most modern
of orchestras. Tchaikovsky was familiar with this style
of orchestration from the operas of Meyerbeer and Glinka.

E

He also heard it at the rehearsals of the Musical Society (to which, as students, we had free access), where Rubinstein conducted works by Meyerbeer, Berlioz, Liszt and Wagner. Finally, in 1862, Wagner himself visited Petersburg, and made us acquainted in a series of concerts, not only with the most famous excerpts from his earlier operas, but also with portions of the *Nibelungen Ring*. It was not so much Wagner's music as his instrumentation which impressed Tchaikovsky. It is remarkable that, with all his love for Mozart, he never once attempted, even as a *tour de force*, to write for the classical orchestra. His medium of expression was the full modern orchestra, which came after Meyerbeer. He did not easily acquire the mastery of this orchestra, but his preference for it was already established. Rubinstein understood it admirably, and explained its resources scientifically to his pupils, in the hope that having once learnt its secrets, they would lay it aside for ever. In this respect he experienced a bitter disappointment in Tchaikovsky.

" In spring the students were generally set an important task to be completed during the summer holidays. In the summer of 1864 Tchaikovsky was expected to write a long overture on the subject of Ostrovsky's [1] drama, *The Storm*. This work he scored for the most 'heretical' orchestra : tuba, English horn, harp, tremolo for violins *divisi*, etc. When the work was finished he sent it to me by post, with the request that I would take it to Rubinstein (I cannot remember why he could not attend in person). I carried out his wish, and Rubinstein told me to return in a few days to hear his opinion. Never in the course of my life have I had to listen to such a homily on my own sins as I then endured vicariously (it was Sunday morning too !). With unconscious humour, Rubinstein asked : ' How dared you bring me such a specimen of your own composition,' and proceeded to pour such vials of wrath upon my head that apparently he had nothing left for the real culprit, for when Peter Ilich himself appeared a few days later, the Director received him amiably, and only made a few remarks upon the overture. . . .

[1] The greatest Russian dramatist. His most celebrated plays are : *The Storm, The Forest, The Poor Bride, Snow White, The Wolf and the Sheep.*

"One of Rubinstein's most urgent desires was the organisation of a school orchestra. In the early days of the Conservatoire, however, there was no immediate hope of realising this wish. Apart from the numerous violinists, attracted by the name of Wieniawsky, there were few, during the first year, who could play any other orchestral instrument even tolerably well. Rubinstein, who at that time had no great income, spent at least 1,500 roubles in the gratuitous tuition of those instruments he needed for his orchestra. There was an immediate response among those who were enterprising. Tchaikovsky expressed a wish to learn the flute. He studied for two years, and became a satisfactory second flute in this orchestra. On one occasion he took part in a flute quartet of Kuhlau's at a musical evening in honour of Madame Clara Schumann's visit to Petersburg. Afterwards, finding no special use for this accomplishment, he gave it up entirely.

"Of even less importance were the organ lessons he took for a time from the famous Heinrich Stiehl. The majestic tone of this instrument, heard in the mystic twilight of the empty Lutheran church in Petersburg, made a profound impression upon Tchaikovsky's poetic temperament. But the impression was fleeting; his imagination was attracted in other directions, and he grew more and more remote from the works of Bach. He never composed a single piece for this instrument."

V

"In the biography of an artist," continues Laroche, "side by side with his individual evolution, the close observation of all external influences with which he comes in contact plays an important part. In Tchaikovsky's case, I place among these influences, the musical repertory which was familiar to him, and such compositions as he specially studied or cared for. During the whole of his time at the Conservatoire, especially during the first two years, I was constantly with him, and am therefore a fair judge of the works which more or less left their impress upon his mind. I can enumerate almost all the compositions we played together during his first year : Beethoven's *Ninth Symphony*, Schumann's *Third Symphony*, his *Paradise and the Peri*, and *Lohengrin*. Tchaikovsky grumbled when I made him play long vocal works with endless recitatives, which became very wearisome on the piano, but the beauty of the more connected parts soon re-awakened his enthusiasm. Wagner gave him the least pleasure. He simply made light of *Lohengrin*, and only became reconciled to the whole opera much later in life.

"One day he remarked fearlessly : 'I am sure of this —Serov has more talent for composition than Wagner.' Schumann's *Third Symphony* and Rubinstein's '*Ocean*' *Symphony* made the greatest impression upon him. Later on, under the bâton of the composer, our enthusiasm for the latter continually increased. Many readers will be surprised to hear that one of Tchaikovsky's earliest crazes was for Henri Litolff—but only for the two overtures, *Robespierre* and *Les Girondistes*. I can say without exaggeration that, after hearing these two overtures and Meyerbeer's *Struensee*, Tchaikovsky was always an impassioned lover of programme music. In his early overtures, including *Romeo and Juliet*, the influence of Litolff is easily perceptible, while he approached Liszt—who did far more to inspire the young generation—with hesitation and mistrust. During his student years, *Orpheus* was the only one of Liszt's symphonic poems which attracted him. The *Faust Symphony* he only valued long afterwards. It is but fair to state that Liszt's symphonic poems, which enslaved a whole generation of Russian composers, only exercised an insignificant and ephemeral influence upon Tchaikovsky.

"It is important to observe that, at this early period, he showed many curious and morbid musical antipathies which he entirely outgrew. These dislikes were not for particular composers, but for certain styles of composition, or, more strictly speaking, for their quality of sound. For instance, he did not like the combination of piano and orchestra, nor the timbre of a string quartet or quintet, and least of all the effect of the piano with one or more stringed instruments. Although, for the sake of experience, he had studied the general repertory of chamber music and pianoforte concertos, and now and then was charmed by a work of this nature, he afterwards took the first opportunity of condemning its 'detestable' quality of tone. Not once, but hundreds of times, he has vowed in my presence never to compose a pianoforte concerto, nor a violin and piano sonata, nor any work of this class. As regards the violin and pianoforte sonata, he has kept his word. Not less strange was his determination, at this time, never to write any small pieces for piano, or songs. He spoke of the latter with the greatest dislike. But this hatred must have been quite Platonic, for the next minute he was growing enthusiastic with me over the songs of Glinka, Schumann, or Schubert.

"At this period in his life it was a kind of mania to declare himself quite incapable in certain branches of his art. For instance, he often declared he was absolutely unable to conduct. The art of conducting goes frequently with that of accompanying, and he was an excellent accompanist. This fact alone should have sufficed to prove the groundlessness of his assertions. At the Conservatoire the advanced students in the composition class were expected to conduct the school orchestra in turn. Tchaikovsky stood first on the list. I cannot remember whether he distinguished himself on this occasion, but I know that nothing particularly dreadful happened, and that he made no evident fiasco. Nevertheless he made this first experience the confirmation of his opinion. He declared that having to stand at the raised desk in front of the orchestra produced such nervous sensations that all the time he felt his head must fall off his shoulders; in order to prevent this catastrophe, he kept his left hand under his chin and only conducted with his right. This fixed idea lasted for years.

"In 1868 Tchaikovsky was invited to conduct the dances from his opera *The Voyevode* at a charity concert given in Moscow. I still see him before me, the bâton in his right hand, while his left firmly supported his fair beard!

"Tchaikovsky s ardent admiration for Glinka, especially for the opera *A Life for the Tsar*, included also this composer's incidental music to the tragedy *Prince Kholmsky*. As regards *Russlan and Lioudmilla*, his views varied at first. Early in the sixties he knew only a few numbers from Glinka's second opera, which pleased him unreservedly. He was equally delighted with the music and libretto of Serov's opera *Judith*, which he heard in 1863. It is remarkable that while a few masterpieces, such as *Don Juan*, *A Life for the Tsar*, and Schubert's *Symphony in C*, took their places once and for ever in his appreciation, his judgment of other musical works was subject to considerable fluctuation. One year he was carried away by Beethoven's *Eighth Symphony*, the next he pronounced it 'very nice, but nothing more.' For years he declared the music to *Faust* by Pugni (a well-known composer of ballets) was infinitely superior to Gounod's opera, and afterwards he described the French composer's work as 'a masterpiece.' Therefore it is all the more remarkable that he remained faithful to Serov's opera *Judith* to the end of his days.

"His attitude to Serov's literary work was exceedingly sceptical. We both attended the popular lectures given by this critic in 1864, and were amused at his desperate efforts to overthrow the authority of the Conservatoire, to abase Glinka and to exalt Verstovsky.[1] Serov's attack upon Rubinstein would in itself have lowered him in the eyes of so devoted an adherent as Tchaikovsky, but he disliked him still more for such expressions as 'the spiritual contents of music,' 'the organic unity of the music drama,' and similar phrases, under which Serov concealed his vacillation and extraordinary lack of principle.

"Tchaikovsky's personal relations with the composer of *Judith* are only known to me in part. They met, if I am not mistaken, in the autumn of 1864, and I was the means of their becoming acquainted. One of our fellow-students named Slavinsky, who visited Serov, invited

[1] Alexis Nicholaevich Verstovsky, the composer of a popular opera, *Askold's Grave*.

me to go with him to one of his 'composer's Tuesdays.'
About a year later I introduced Tchaikovsky to Serov. I
recollect how on that particular evening Dostoievsky talked
a great deal—and very foolishly—about music, as literary
men do, who know nothing whatever about it. Serov's
personality did not please Tchaikovsky, and I do not think
he ever went again, although he received a pressing invitation to do so.

"Besides N. A. Hubert and myself, I cannot recall a
single student at the Conservatoire with whom Tchaikovsky kept up a lasting intimacy. He was pleasant to all,
and addressed a few in the familiar second person singular.
Among these passing friends I may mention Gustav Kross,
afterwards the first to play Tchaikovsky's pianoforte concerto in public; Richard Metzdorf, who settled in Germany
as a composer and Capellmeister; Karl van Ark, who
became a professor at the Petersburg Conservatoire;
Slavinsky and Joseph Lödscher. Of these fellow-students,
the name of Nicholas Hubert occurs most frequently in
subsequent pages. In spite of his foreign name, Hubert
was really of Russian descent. From his childhood he
lived only in and for music, and very early in life had
to earn his living by teaching. The number of lessons he
gave, combined with his weak and uncertain health, prevented him from working very hard at the Conservatoire,
but he impressed us as talented and clever. He was fond
of assembling his friends round the tea-table in his large,
but scantily-furnished room, when the evening would be
spent in music and discussion. Tchaikovsky, Lödscher
and myself were the most regular guests at these evenings.
The real intimacy, however, between Tchaikovsky and
Hubert did not actually begin until many years later—
about the middle of the eighties."

With this chapter Laroche's reminiscences of Tchaikovsky come to an end.

VI

In the autumn of 1863 the mother of Leo Davidov, who had married Tchaikovsky's sister, came to settle in St. Petersburg.

Alexandra Ivanovna, widow of the famous Decembrist, Vassily Davidov, was a vigorous, kindly clever old lady, who had seen and suffered much in her day. Of her very numerous family, four daughters and her youngest son had accompanied her to Petersburg. Two of these daughters, Elizabeth and Vera, became very friendly with Tchaikovsky, thanks to their common love of music.

Peter Ilich never felt more at home than at the Davidovs. Apart from the pleasure of acting as a guide to Vera in musical matters—introducing her to the works of Schumann, Berlioz, and Glinka, whose charm he had only just discovered for himself—he thoroughly enjoyed talking to her mother and sister.

Tchaikovsky was always deeply interested in his country's past, especially in the period of Catherine II. and Alexander I. Alexandra Davidov was, so to speak, a living chapter of history from the last years of Alexander's reign, and had known personally many famous men of the time, among them the poet Poushkin, who often visited the Davidovs at Kamenka. Consequently Tchaikovsky delighted in hearing her recall the joys and sorrows of those far-off days.

Her daughter Elizabeth, an elderly spinster, also excited his interest. She had been entrusted by her mother, when the latter had voluntarily followed her husband into exile, to the care of Countess Tchernischov-Kruglikov, and grew up in a house frequented by all the notabilities of the early years of Nicholas I.'s reign.

She knew Gogol and Poushkin, and had made many journeys to Europe and Siberia. Besides which she was deeply interested in art and literature, and had a decided talent for drawing.

Among the few acquaintances who continued to show a friendly attitude to Tchaikovsky, in spite of his becoming a musician, was Prince Alexis Galitsin. He helped the struggling student and teacher by recommending him to private pupils, and invited him to spend the summer on his estate, Trostinetz, in the Government of Kharkov.

Life at the Prince's country-seat seemed to Tchaikovsky like a fairy tale. One event will suffice to show the attention with which he was treated by his host. On his name-day, June 29th (July 11th), the Prince gave an entertainment in his honour. After early service there was a breakfast, and in the evening, after dark, a walk through the forest, the paths being illuminated by torches, which made a grand effect. In the heart of the woods a tent had been raised, in which a banquet was prepared; while, on the open green around it, all kinds of national amusements were organised in honour of the musician.

During this visit, Tchaikovsky composed and orchestrated his first independent musical work, the overture to his favourite Russian play, *The Storm*, by Ostrovsky. He had already hankered to write an opera on this play, consequently when Rubinstein set him to compose an overture by way of a holiday task, he naturally selected the subject which had interested him for so long. On page 30 of his instrumentation sketch-book for 1863–4 he made a pencil note of the programme of this overture :—

" Introduction ; adagio (Catharine's childhood and life before marriage) ; allegro (the threatening of the storm) ; her longing for a truer love and happiness ; allegro appassionato (her spiritual conflict). Sudden change to evening on the banks of the Volga : the same conflict, but with traces of feverish joy. The coming of the storm (repetition of the theme which follows the adagio and the further development of it). The Storm: the climax of her desperate conflict—Death."

The next important composition, which was not lost, like so many of Tchaikovsky's early works, was the " Dances of the Serving Girls," afterwards employed as a ballet in his opera, *The Voyevode*. It is impossible to fix the precise date at which these dances were composed, but early in 1865 they were already finished and orchestrated.

VII

In 1865 Tchaikovsky's father married—for the third time —a widow, Elizabeth Alexandrov. This event made no difference to the life of Peter Ilich, for he was attached to his stepmother, whom he had known for several years, and to whom he often went for advice in moments of doubt and difficulty. The summer of this year was spent with his sister at Kamenka.

Kamenka, of which we hear so much in the life of Peter Ilich, is a rural spot on the banks of the Tiasmin, in the Government of Kiev, and forms part of the great estate which Tchaikovsky's brother-in-law had inherited from the exiled Decembrist Vassily Davidov. The place has historical associations, having been the centre of the revolutionary movement which disturbed the last years of Alexander I. Here, too, the poet Poushkin came as a visitor, and his famous poem, " The Prisoner in the Caucasus," is said to have been written at Kamenka. The property actually belonged to an elder brother, Nicholas Davidov, who practically resigned it to the management of Tchaikovsky's brother-in-law, preferring the pleasures of his library and garden to the responsibilities of a great landowner.

Kamenka did not boast great natural charms, nevertheless Tchaikovsky enjoyed his visit there, and soon forgot the luxuries of Trostinetz.

Nicholas Davidov, although a kindly and sympathetic nature, held decided opinions of his own, which were not altogether in keeping with the liberalism then in vogue. This strong-minded man, who thought things out for himself, impressed Tchaikovsky, and changed his political outlook. Throughout life the composer took no very strong political views; his tendencies leaned now one way, now another; but from the time of his acquaintance with Nicholas Davidov his views were more disposed towards conservativism. It was, however, the happy household at Kamenka that exercised the greatest influence upon Tchaikovsky. Henceforth his sister's family became his favourite refuge, whither, in days to come, he went to rest from the cares and excitements of life, and where, twelve years later, he made a temporary home.

Perhaps these pleasant impressions were also strengthened by the consciousness of work well accomplished. Anton Rubinstein had set him a second task—the translation of Gevaert's treatise on *Instrumentation*. This he carried out admirably, besides the composition of the overture.

At Kamenka he had one disappointing experience. He had heard so much of the beauty of the Little Russian folk-songs, and hoped to amass material for his future compositions. This was not to be. The songs he heard seemed to him artificial and retouched, and by no means equal in beauty or originality to the folk melodies of Great Russia. He only wrote down one song while at Kamenka—a tune sung daily by the women who worked in the garden. He first used this melody in a string quartet, which he began to compose in the autumn, but afterwards changed it into the *Scherzo à la russe* for pianoforte, Op. 1. No. 1. Towards the end of August, Tchaikovsky returned to Petersburg with his brothers.

" Petersburg welcomed us with a deluge of rain," he wrote to his sister on his return. But in many other respects also the town made an unfavourable impression upon Tchaikovsky. In the first place, the question of a lodging gave him considerable trouble. The room which he had engaged for eight roubles a month was small and uncomfortable. The longer he stayed, the more he disliked it. He tried various quarters without finding the quiet which was the first essential, and, in November, finally took possession of a room lent him by his friend, Apukhtin, who was going away for a time.

Another unpleasant experience took the form of an obstinate affection of the eyes, which hindered him from working regularly. Lastly, he began to feel some anxiety as to his future livelihood when his course at the Conservatoire should have come to an end. To continue in his present course of existence seemed to him terrible. The small income, which hitherto only had to serve him for his lesser needs, had now to cover board and lodging— in fact, his entire expenses.

We may guess how hard was his struggle with poverty, when we find him once more assailed by doubts as to his wisdom in having chosen the musical profession, and even contemplating the idea of returning to the service of the State. Some of his friends echoed his momentary cry of weakness. One seriously proposed that he should accept the fairly good pay of an inspector of meat. To the great advantage of all consumers, and to the glory of Russian music, the proposal came to nothing.

Simultaneously with Tchaikovsky's hardest struggle for existence, came also the first hopes of artistic success. These triumphs were very modest as compared to those which lay in store for him; but at that period of his life the praise of his masters, the applause of his fellow-students, and the first public performance of his works, sufficed to fill him with happiness and self-confidence. The performance of his " Dances of the Serving Maids," at one of the summer concerts at Pavlovsk, conducted by the " Valse King," Johann Strauss, greatly cheered the young composer.

His satisfaction was still further increased when Nicholas Rubinstein, following the example of his illustrious brother, resolved to open a Conservatoire in Moscow, and engaged Tchaikovsky as Professor of Harmony.

Nicholas Rubinstein had first approached Serov, who was not unwilling to accept the post. But the extraordinary success of his opera *Rogneda* in St. Petersburg, and the failure of *Judith* in Moscow, caused him to change his mind and wish to remain in that capital where he was best appreciated. This took place in 1865. Nicholas Rubinstein, seeing no other way out of the difficulty, decided to offer the professorship to one of the students of the Petersburg Conservatoire, and his brother put forward the claims of Tchaikovsky. Although the honour was great, the emolument was not attractive, for it amounted only to fifty roubles (£5) a month; that is to say, to something less than the modest income he had hitherto managed to earn in Petersburg. Nevertheless, in November, he decided to accept the post.

The remaining successes of this period relate to his compositions.

In spite of his eyes being affected, and his constant change of quarters, the time had not been barren. He had composed a string quartet in B♭ major,[1] and an overture in F major.[2] The quartet was played at one of the pupils' concerts at the Conservatoire, October 30th (November 11th), 1865, and a fortnight later the overture was performed by the school orchestra, under the bâton of the composer.

[1] Of this quartet only the first movement remains intact. The others must have been destroyed by the composer at a later date.

[2] Tchaikovsky afterwards arranged this overture for full orchestra, in which form it was given several times in Moscow and Petersburg.

In November of this year, Tchaikovsky set to work upon a cantata for chorus and orchestra, a setting of Schiller's *Ode to Joy*.[1]

This task had been set him by Anton Rubinstein, and was intended for performance at the prize distribution, which took place at the end of the school year. On December 31st, 1865 (January 12th, 1866), the cantata was performed by the pupils of the Conservatoire in the presence of the Directors of the Russian Musical Society, the Board of Examiners, the Director of the Court Chapel, Bachmetiev, and the Capellmeisters of the Imperial Opera, Kajinsky, Liadov and Ricci.

The composer himself was not present, as he wished to avoid the *vivâ voce* examination, which ought to have preceded the performance of the cantata. Anton Rubinstein was exceedingly displeased, and threatened to withhold Tchaikovsky's diploma until he submitted to this public test. Matters were not carried so far. Apparently the young composer had given sufficient proof of his knowledge in the cantata itself, and he received not only his diploma, but a silver medal in addition.

In spite of this official success, the cantata did not win the approval of the musical authorities.

Evidently Rubinstein was not satisfied with it, since he put off Tchaikovsky's request that the cantata might be performed by the Russian Musical Society, by saying that he could only agree on condition that "great alterations" were made in the score, for in its original form it was not good enough to place beside the works of other Russian composers — Sokalsky, Christianovich, Rimsky-Korsakov, and Balakirev. Serov's opinion of this composition was not more favourable.

In the opposite camp to Serov—among that young Russian school which flocked round Dargomijsky, and

---

[1] The manuscript of this cantata is in the archives of the St. Petersburg Conservatoire.

included Balakirev, Rimsky-Korsakov, and Cæsar Cui, the cantata met with even less approval. Three months after its performance Cui, then critic of the St. Petersburg *Viedomosti*, wound up his notice of the work as follows :—

"In a word, I will only say that composers of the calibre of Reinthaler and Volkmann will probably rejoice over Mr. Tchaikovsky's cantata, and exclaim, 'Our number is increased.'"

Such were the judgments passed upon his first work by the musical lights and the Press.

Laroche, however, was of a different opinion. He sent the following letter to Tchaikovsky in Moscow :—

"PETERSBURG (MIDNIGHT),

"*January* 11*th* (23*rd*), 1866.

". . . I will tell you frankly that I consider yours is the greatest musical talent to which Russia can look in the future. Stronger and more original than Balakirev, loftier and more creative than Serov, far more refined than Rimsky-Korsakov. *In you I see the greatest—or rather the sole—hope of our musical future. Your own original creations will probably not make their appearance for another five years. But these ripe and classic works will surpass everything we have heard since Glinka.* To sum up: I do not honour you so much for what you *have* done, as for what the force and vitality of your genius *will* one day accomplish. The proofs you have given so far are but solemn pledges to outdo all your contemporaries."

PART III

I

TCHAIKOVSKY'S first impressions of Moscow practically resolve themselves into his association with a few Muscovites, with whom he was destined to be linked to the end of his days. His subsequent life is so inseparably connected with the narrow circle of his friends in the old capital, that the reader needs to be introduced to some of them individually, before I pass on to my brother's career as a teacher and composer.

At the head of these musical friends stands Nicholas Rubinstein, of whom it is no exaggeration to say that he was the greatest influence throughout Tchaikovsky's after career. No one, artist or friend, did so much for the advancement of his fame, gave him greater support and appreciation, or helped him more to conquer his first nervousness and timidity, than the Director of the Moscow Conservatoire. Nicholas Rubinstein is intimately associated with every event in Tchaikovsky's private and public life. Everywhere we shall come upon traces of his helpful influence. It is not too much to assert that, during the first years of Tchaikovsky's life there, all Moscow was personified in Nicholas Rubinstein.

Laroche, in his *Reminiscences*, gives the following sketch of the director :—

"Nicholas Rubinstein was born June 2nd (14th), 1835. Like his celebrated brother, he showed a remarkable and precocious talent for music. It is said he learnt quicker, and was considered to have more genius than Anton. But while the latter devoted himself entirely to music and studied in Berlin, Nicholas elected for a university education. . . . As a student at the Moscow University, and even later—until the establishment of the Russian Musical Society—he earned his living by teaching the pianoforte. He had a number of pupils, and, as he himself told me, earned at one time as much as 7,000 roubles (over £700) a year. On his marriage he was compelled to give up playing in public, on account of the objections raised by his wife's relations. His domestic life was not happy, and the differences of opinion between himself and his wife's family led to a rupture two years later. His unusual powers were first recognised when he succeeded in founding the Moscow Conservatoire. Besides being a most gifted pianist, he had great talent as a conductor, and organiser of many schemes. He could represent all branches of musical society in his own person. Although he spent all his nights at the 'English Club,' playing cards for high stakes, he managed to take part in every social event, and was acquainted with all circles of Moscow society, commercial, official, artistic, scientific, and aristocratic."

"As regards art," says Kashkin, "Nicholas Rubinstein was purely an idealist; he admitted no compromise, and was entirely above personal likes or dislikes. He was always ready to help a fellow-artist, especially a Russian, and, without stopping to consider his means, simply gave whatever he had by him at the moment.

"Externally he differed greatly from his brother Anton. Nicholas Rubinstein was short and stoutly built; fair-complexioned, with curly hair. He had a dreamy expression, a languor of speech, and an air of aristocratic weariness, which was contradicted by the indefatigable energy of his temperament. Probably this languor proceeded from the fact that he scarcely ever slept.

"He was Tchaikovsky's senior by five years only; but in these early days of their intercourse the difference between their ages seemed much greater. This was partly accounted for by the fact that Tchaikovsky came to

F

Moscow in a somewhat subordinate position, whereas the name of Rubinstein was one of the most popular in the town; but the difference in character was also very great. Rubinstein belonged to the class of dominating and ruling personalities; his was a forceful character which impressed all who came in contact with him. Tchaikovsky, on the contrary, was yielding and submissive in matters of daily existence, although inwardly he protested against all attempts to influence and coerce him, and generally preserved his freedom of opinion, at least as regards music. This self-assertion did not, however, come naturally to him, and for that reason he loved solitude. He avoided his fellow-men, because he did not know how to hold his own among them; while at the same time he disliked submitting to the will of others, but this was not his attitude in 1866. At this time he was grateful for Nicholas Rubinstein's almost paternal care, and bowed to his decision, even in the matter of dress.

"Their friendly relations were sometimes strained, but never broken, although Peter Ilich was occasionally irritated by Rubinstein's masterful guidance, and was scolded in return for not being sufficiently docile."

"Rubinstein's right hand," says Laroche, "was Constantine Albrecht, the Inspector of the Conservatoire. He was about five years older than Tchaikovsky, and had held the post of 'cellist at the Opera House since the age of fifteen. Albrecht was a very capable and, in many respects, a very interesting man, although he was not popular with the public. Tchaikovsky was strongly attracted to him, and soon after his arrival in Moscow arranged to take his meals daily at his house. Albrecht's views, or rather convictions, were extraordinarily paradoxical.

"In politics he took the Conservative side, but as regards music he was probably the most advanced radical in Moscow. Wagner, Liszt, Beethoven in his last period, and certain things of Schumann, were all he would acknowledge. I must add, by way of an eccentricity, his admiration for Dargomijsky's *Roussalka*. He was an admirable choral conductor, and did good work in this branch of his art, for many of the pupils trained by him turned out excellent teachers. Besides music, Albrecht took great interest in natural science and mathematics. In summer he was an enthusiastic hunter of beetles and butterflies. But for the subjects in which a musician should be interested—history, poetry, *belles-lettres* he showed the most complete indifference. I doubt if he had ever read a novel. . . ."

Tchaikovsky had a very high opinion of Albrecht as a composer, and often regretted that so much talent should be wasted. But it was his kindliness of heart, and above all his innate sense of humour, which appealed most to Peter Ilich.

Very different, and far more important, were Tchaikovsky's relations with P. I. Jurgenson, the first—and always the chief—publisher of his works.

Peter Ivanovich Jurgenson was born at Reval in 1836, and his childhood was spent in very poor and depressing circumstances. At nineteen he entered a music warehouse in Petersburg, where he soon won his employer's confidence, and rose to be manager to the firm of Schildbach, in Moscow. Two years later, in 1861, he made a daring venture and set up business on his own account. In Nicholas Rubinstein he found a powerful friend and ally, who supported his enterprise for twenty years with unfailing energy. By 1866 Jurgenson had passed through his worst experiences, and began to play a prominent part in the musical life of Moscow. Courageous and enterprising, he was one of the most active adherents of Nicholas Rubinstein, that "Peter the Great" of musical Moscow, to whom he rendered valuable assistance in founding the Conservatoire. Jurgenson was the first Russian publisher to bring out the works of the classical school in cheap editions, and also the compositions of young native composers, including those of Tchaikovsky.

Although he came from the Baltic provinces, Jurgenson was an ardent Russian patriot, and soon won the affection of Peter Ilich, who was always a welcome guest in his house.

At the present moment the firm of Jurgenson is almost the sole possessor of Tchaikovsky's compositions. Among the 200,000 engraving-plates which are preserved in their fireproof safes more than 70,000 belong to the works of this composer.

The fourth of Tchaikovsky's intimate friends, Nicholas Kashkin, received him on his arrival with the cordiality of an old comrade, for he already knew him from Laroche's enthusiastic description.

" . . . Nicholas Dmitrievich Kashkin was the son of a well-known and respected bookseller in the town of Voronejh," says Laroche in his reminiscences. From childhood he displayed great aptitude for the piano, and by dint of self-teaching, made such progress that he could execute difficult music, and was highly thought of in his native place. Yet he was conscious that he lacked proper training, and at twenty-two went to study with Dubuque, in Moscow.

Although Kashkin had no influence on Tchaikovsky's development, their relations were very friendly. When the latter came to Moscow, Kashkin was already married and a professor at the Conservatoire. He and his young wife took a great liking to the lonely composer, and the intimacy ripened very quickly. All the teachers at the Conservatoire, including Nicholas Rubinstein, valued Kashkin's advice. All his friends regarded him as a critic *par excellence*. Many years later he gave up teaching at the Conservatoire, and became a professional critic. But even in this difficult calling, which so often leads to misunderstanding and bitter enmities, he managed to keep all his old friends, and even to make new ones.

If I add to the names of N. Rubinstein, Albrecht, Jurgenson, and Kashkin, two fellow-students already mentioned — Laroche and Hubert — the list of Tchaikovsky's intimate friends is complete. This little circle was destined to give unfailing support to the growing reputation of the composer, and to remain in the closest personal relations with him to the end of his life. Amid these friends he found encouragement and sympathy at the time when he stood most in need of them.

II

Tchaikovsky left St. Petersburg early in January, 1866. At this time his letters show his depth of tenderness for his own people, his first feelings of loneliness in the strange city, his indifference to his surroundings, and finally his gradual attachment to Moscow, which ended in being " the dearest town in the world."

To Anatol and Modeste Tchaikovsky.

" 3.30 *p.m., January 6th* (18*th*).

" MY DEAR BROTHERS,—My journey, although sad, is safely over. I thought about you the whole way, and it grieved me to think that lately I had overshadowed you with my own depression, although I fought hard against it. Do not, however, doubt my affection, even if I do not always show it outwardly. I am staying at the Hotel Kokorev. I have already seen Rubinstein and been intro- duced to two directors of the Musical Society. Rubinstein was so pressing in his invitation to me to live with him that I could not refuse, and shall go there to-morrow. . . . I hug you both. Do not cease to love me. Give my remembrances to everyone. Write! I will write again soon. I have just written to Dad. You must also do so."

To the same.

" MOSCOW, *January* 10*th* (22*nd*).

" DEAR BROTHERS,—I am now living with Nicholas Rubinstein. He is a very kind and sympathetic man.

He has none of his brother's unapproachable manner, but in other respects he is not to be compared with Anton—as an artist. I have a little room next to his bedroom, and, truth to tell, I am afraid the scratching of my pen must disturb him after he goes to bed, for our rooms are only divided by a thin partition. I am very busy (upon the orchestration of the C minor overture composed during the summer). I sit at home nearly all day, and Rubinstein, who leads rather an excitable life, cannot sufficiently marvel at my industry. I have been to both theatres. The opera was very bad, so for once I did not get as much artistic enjoyment from it as from the play. . . . I have hardly made any new acquaintances except Kashkin, a friend of Laroche's and a first-rate musician, whom I have got to know very well indeed.

"Sometimes I feel rather melancholy, but as a rule I am possessed by an insatiable craving for work, which is my greatest consolation. . . . I have promised Rubinstein my overture shall be performed here before I send it to Petersburg. Yesterday at bedtime I thought a great deal about you both. I pictured to myself all the horrors of the first night after the holidays, and fancied how Modi would hide his nose under the bed-clothes and cry bitterly. How I wish I could have comforted him! It is not a meaningless phrase, Modi, when I tell you to grind and grind and grind, and to make friends with your respectable companions, but not with that crazy fellow X. . . . I am afraid you will be left behind in your class and be one of those who get into the master's black books. I have no fears for Toly, so I send him no advice. Toly, my dear, conquer your indolence as a correspondent and write to me. Hearty kisses!"

The overture in C minor, referred to in this letter, was submitted to Nicholas Rubinstein a few days later. His opinion, however, was unfavourable, and he declared the work unsuitable for performance by the Musical Society. Tchaikovsky then sent the work to Petersburg, in order that Laroche might ask Anton Rubinstein to perform it there. "I have left your overture with Rubinstein," Laroche wrote in reply, "and repeated your request *verbatim*. He replied by a low, ironical bow. But this is just his way." The overture was not approved by Anton Rubinstein, nor did it meet with a happier fate when Laroche tried to persuade Liadov to give it a place at one of the opera concerts. Long afterwards Tchaikovsky himself shared this adverse opinion of the work, and wrote upon the cover of the manuscript, " Awful rubbish."

To his sister, Alexandra Davidov.

"*January* 15*th* (27*th*).

". . . I have nothing particular to tell you about my life and work. I am to teach the theory of music, and yesterday I held the preliminary examination. Many pretty girls presented themselves. . . . I like Moscow very well, but I doubt if I shall ever get accustomed to it; I have been too long rooted in Petersburg."

To A. and M. Tchaikovsky.

"*January* 15*th* (27*th*).

"MY DEAR BROTHERS,—Do not waste your money on stamps. It would be better to write only once a week, a long letter in the form of a diary. . . .

"I get on very well with everyone, especially with Rubinstein, Kashkin, Albrecht, and Osberg.[1] I have also made friends with a family of the name Tchaikovsky.[2] I have eaten a great deal at their house, but I did not take part in the dancing, although I was attired in Rubinstein's dress-coat. The latter looks after me like a nurse, and insists upon doing so. To-day he forced me to accept half a dozen new shirts (you need not mention this to the Davidovs or anyone else), and to-morrow he will carry me off to his tailor to order me a frock-coat. He is a wonderfully kind man, but I cannot understand how he has won

---

[1] Professor of singing at the Conservatoire.
[2] All traces of this family appear to be lost, but it is evident they were not relatives of the composer.

his great reputation as a musician. He is rather ordinary in this respect, not to be compared to his brother.[1]

"In mentioning my friends here, I must not omit Rubinstein's servant Alexander. He is a worthy old man, and possesses a splendid white cat which is now sitting on my lap, while I stroke it gently. My pleasantest pastime is to think of the summer. Lately I have felt drawn to Sasha, Leo, and their children, and have now decided to spend the summer with you at their house."

To A. and M. Tchaikovsky.

"*Sunday, January 30th* (*February* 11th).

". . . I laugh heartily over Dickens's *Pickwick Papers*, with no one to share my mirth; but sometimes this thought incites me to even wilder hilarity. I recommend you to read this book; when one wants to read fiction it is best to begin with such an author as Dickens. He has much in common with Gogol; the same inimitable and innate humour and the same masterly power of depicting an entire character in a few strokes. But he has not Gogol's depth. . . .

"The idea of an opera begins to occupy my attention. All the libretti Rubinstein has given me are utterly bad. I have found a subject, and intend to write words myself. It will simply be the adaptation of a tragedy. The poet Plestcheiev is living here, and has promised to help me."

To his sister, Alexandra Davidov.

"*February* 7th (19th).

"I am gradually becoming accustomed to Moscow, although sometimes I feel very lonely. My classes are very successful, to my great astonishment; my nervousness is vanishing completely, and I am gradually assuming the airs of a professor. My home-sickness is also wearing off, but still Moscow is a strange place, and it will be long before I can contemplate without horror the thought of remaining here for years—perhaps for ever. . . ."

---

[1] Later on Tchaikovsky completely altered his opinion.

To Modeste Tchaikovsky.

(*The middle of February.*)

"MY DEAR FRIEND MODI,—I have been very busy lately, and therefore have not written for a long while. Rubinstein has entrusted me with some important work which has to be finished by the third week in Lent. . . .

"Life glides on quietly and monotonously, so that I have hardly anything to tell you. I often visit the Tarnovskys, whose niece is the loveliest girl I ever saw in my life. I am very much taken with her, which causes Rubinstein to be a perfect nuisance. The moment we arrive at the house the others begin to tease us and leave us together. At home she is called 'Mufka,' and just now I am wondering whether I dare use this name for her too. I only need to know her a little better. Rubinstein has also been in love with her, but his sentiments have now grown cooler.

"My nerves are in good condition; I am very calm and even cheerful. I often console myself with thoughts of Easter, spring, and the summer holidays."

The work to which Tchaikovsky refers at the beginning of this letter was the instrumentation of his overture in F major, which had been originally scored for the small orchestra of the Petersburg Conservatoire. In later years the composer must have destroyed the fuller arrangement of the work, although at this time he seems to have been satisfied with the result.

To A. and M. Tchaikovsky.

"*March 6th* (18*th*).

". . . My overture was performed on Friday, and had a good success. I was unanimously recalled, and—to be grandiloquent—received with applause that made the welkin ring. More flattering still was the ovation I met with at the supper which Rubinstein gave after the concert . . . After supper he proposed my health amid renewed applause. I go into these details because it is my first public success, and consequently very gratifying."

At the end of March Tchaikovsky, eager as a schoolboy at the beginning of his holidays, left Moscow for Petersburg, where he stayed until April 4th (16th).

To A. and M. Tchaikovsky.

"Moscow, *April 7th* (19*th*).

"Brothers! Forgive me for not having written before. The journey was safely accomplished. The news of the attempt upon the Emperor's life reached us at the station where we stopped for tea, but only in a very vague form.[1] We pictured to ourselves that he was actually dead, and one lady wept bitterly, while another began to extol all the virtues of the new sovereign. Only at Moscow I learnt the true account. The rejoicings here were beyond belief; yesterday at the Opera, where I went to hear *A Life for the Tsar*, when the Poles appeared on the stage the entire public began to shout, 'Down with the Poles!' In the last scene of the fourth act, in which the Poles put Sousanin to death, the singer who was taking this part resisted with such realistic violence that he knocked down several of the 'Polish' chorus-singers. When the rest of the 'Poles' saw that this outrage to art and to the truth delighted the public, they promptly fell down of their own accord, and the triumphant Sousanin walked away, shaking his fists at them, amid the vociferous applause of the Muscovites. At the end of the opera the Emperor's portrait was brought on the stage, and an indescribable tumult followed."

To Alexandra Davidov.

"*April 8th* (20*th*).

"I am going to act as advocate for two mortals who are just crazy about Kamenka. You write that Toly and Modi might be left in Petersburg, but I am determined not to tell them your point of view. They would utterly lose heart—especially Toly. One of my chief reasons for caring to spend the summer at Kamenka is to be with them, and your house is the only place where we can be together for a time. If you only knew how these little

---

[1] Karakovich's attempt upon Alexander II., April 4th (16th), 1866.

fellows cling to me (and I return their love a hundredfold), you would not find it in your heart to separate us. Arrange, my dear, for this visit to come off. Very likely I shall be able to take part of the expense off your hands."

Before the summer holidays came, Tchaikovsky's health was in an unsatisfactory condition. He complains in his letters of insomnia, nervousness, and the throbbing sensations in his head, to which he often refers as "my apoplectic symptoms." At the end of April his depression became very apparent, and he wrote to his brother Anatol :—

"My nerves are altogether shaken. The causes are: (1) the symphony, which does not sound satisfactory; (2) Rubinstein and Tarnovsky have discovered that I am easily startled, and amuse themselves by giving me all manner of shocks all day long; (3) I cannot shake off the conviction that I shall not live long, and shall leave my symphony unfinished. I long for the summer and for Kamenka as for the Promised Land, and hope to find rest and peace, and to forget all my troubles there. Yesterday I determined to touch no more wine, spirits, or strong tea.

"I hate mankind in the mass, and I should be delighted to retire into some wilderness with very few inhabitants. I have already secured my ticket in the *diligence* for May 10th (22nd)."

The visit to Kamenka, to which he had looked forward through the winter and spring, did not actually come to pass. In consequence of the state of the high-roads, the diligence was unable to run beyond Dovsk; the remainder of the journey had to be undertaken, at the traveller's own risk and expense, in a private post-chaise. Tchaikovsky's funds did not permit of this extra strain, and the visit to his sister was abandoned. With the assistance of his father, Anatol was sent to Kamenka, while Peter Ilich, with Modeste, went for a time to his sister's mother-in-law at Miatlev, near Petersburg.

In spite of the beauty of scenery and his pleasure in being with his excellent friends, Elizabeth and Vera Davidov, in spite of being near his father and the poetical impression derived from a trip to Lake Ladoga, Tchaikovsky did not altogether enjoy his holiday at Miatlev. The cause of this was his G minor symphony, afterwards known as *Winter Day Dreams*. Not one of his compositions gave him so much trouble as this symphony.

He began this work in Moscow during the spring, and it was the cause of his nervous disorders and numerous sleepless nights. These difficulties were partly caused by his want of experience in composition, and partly by his habit of working by night as well as by day. At the end of June he had a terrible nervous breakdown, and the doctor who was called in to see him declared he had narrowly escaped madness, and that his condition was very serious. The most alarming symptoms of the illness were his hallucinations and a constant feeling of dread. That he suffered intensely is evident from the fact that he never again attempted to work through the night.

In consequence of his illness, Tchaikovsky was unable to finish the symphony during the summer. Nevertheless, before his return to Moscow he resolved to submit it to his former masters, Anton Rubinstein and Zaremba, hoping they might offer to let it be heard at the Musical Society.

Once more he was doomed to disappointment. His symphony was severely criticised, rejected, and pronounced unworthy of performance. It was the first completely independent work which he had composed after leaving the Petersburg Conservatoire. The only other work upon which he was engaged at this time was the orchestration of his F major and C minor overtures, which still remain unpublished.

III

1866–1867

At the end of August Tchaikovsky returned to Moscow without any trace of the hostile feeling with which he had gone there in the previous January. In this change of attitude his artistic sensibility unquestionably played a part. After the severe judgment of the authorities in Petersburg upon his symphony, he could not fail to contrast this reception unfavourably with the acknowledgments of the Moscow musical world. He had learnt, too, the value of his colleagues, N. Rubinstein, Albrecht and Kashkin, and looked forward to meeting them again. Finally, he had the pleasant prospect of an increased salary, commencing from September. He must have rejoiced to feel his extreme poverty had touched its limits, and an income of over £120 a year seemed almost wealth to him. "I have money enough and to spare," he wrote to his brothers in November.

The ties which bound him to Petersburg were slackening. His attachment to his father remained unchanged, but he was growing accustomed to his separation; moreover, the twins stood less in need of his tender solicitude, since they were once more living at home with their father.

And yet he still hankered after the recognition of St. Petersburg; Moscow was still "a strange city"; a provincial town, the appreciation of which was hardly worth the conquest.

In 1866 the Conservatoire outgrew its quarters in Rubinstein's house, and it became necessary to locate it in a larger building. Rubinstein now moved into quarters nearer the new Conservatoire, and Tchaikovsky continued to live with him.

The opening of the buildings took place on September 1st (13th), and was attended by most of the leaders of Moscow society. The consecration service was followed by a banquet at which many toasts were given, and even Tchaikovsky himself drank to the health of Rubinstein, after making a cordial and eloquent speech in his honour. Kashkin, the only witness of the event now living, writes :—

"The banquet was followed by music, and Tchaikovsky, who was determined that the first music to be heard in the hall of the Conservatoire should be Glinka's, opened the impromptu concert by playing the overture to *Russlan and Lioudmilla* from memory."

The influx of new colleagues which followed the enlargement of the Conservatoire made very little difference to Tchaikovsky's intimate circle. He admired Laub's incomparable playing without entering into closer relations with him. He had more in common with Kossmann, an excellent musician and a man of culture. His acquaintance with the violinist Wieniawsky was of short duration, since at the end of six months the latter resigned his post as teacher, and they never met again. He often spent the evening with Dubuque, a most hospitable man, and a famous pianist, who was considered the finest interpreter of Field's Nocturnes and other works which were accounted modern in those days. To these acquaintances we may add Anton Door, the well-known pianist, now residing in Vienna.

Among such of Tchaikovsky's friends as did not belong to the musical profession, the generous art patron Prince Vladimir Odoevsky takes the first place. Peter Ilich was grateful for the interest which this enlightened man took in him and his work. In 1878 he says in one of his letters :—

"He was the personification of kindness, and combined the most all-embracing knowledge, including the art of music. . . . Four days before his death he came to the concert to hear my orchestral fantasia, *Fatum*. How jovial he was when during the interval he came to give me his opinion! The cymbals which he unearthed and presented to me are still kept at the Conservatoire. He did not like the instruments himself, but thought I had a talent for introducing them at the right moment. So the charming old fellow searched all Moscow until he discovered a pair of good 'piatti,' and sent them to me with a precious letter."

In the literary and dramatic world Tchaikovsky had two good friends—the dramatist Ostrovsky and Sadovsky. He won the sympathy of these distinguished men entirely by his own personality, since neither of them cared greatly for music.

During the season 1866-7 the composer made another friendship which was of great importance to his future career. Vladimir Petrovich Begichev, Intendant of the Imperial Opera, Moscow, enjoyed a considerable reputation—first as an elderly Adonis, secondly as the hero of many romantic episodes in the past, and thirdly as the husband of his wife, a lady once renowned for her singing and for her somewhat sensational past. By her first husband Madame Begichev had two sons—Constantine and Vladimir Shilovsky. These young men were strongly attracted to art and literature, and played a considerable part in Tchaikovsky's subsequent career.

Soon after his arrival in Moscow Tchaikovsky began to compose an overture on the Danish National Hymn, which N. Rubinstein had requested him to have ready for the approaching marriage of the Tsarevitch with the Princess Dagmar, to be played in the presence of the royal pair during their visit to Moscow.

As with all his commissioned works, Tchaikovsky had completed this overture before the appointed day, although he had to compose under the most unfavourable conditions. Rubinstein's house was beset all day long by

professors from the Conservatoire and other visitors, who
did not hesitate to intrude into Tchaikovsky's room, so
that he found no peace at home, and had to take refuge
in a neighbouring inn, "The Great Britain," which was
very little frequented during the daytime. When finished,
he dedicated the overture to the Tsarevitch, and received
in return a pair of jewelled sleeve-links, which he immediately sold to Dubuque. Tchaikovsky, who generally
judged his early works very severely, kept a favourable
recollection of this overture, and wrote to Jurgenson, in
1892 :—

"My Danish Overture may become a popular concert
work, for, as far as I can remember, it is effective and,
from a musical standpoint, far superior to '1812.'"

After making some alterations in his symphony—undertaken at the desire of Anton Rubinstein and Zaremba—
Tchaikovsky, setting aside N. Rubinstein, desired to
hear the judgments of his old teachers, so greatly was he
still under the influence of Petersburg opinion. He only
permitted the least important movement to be heard at
a Moscow Symphony Concert in December—the scherzo,
which had very little success. In Petersburg the work
was once more refused, but afterwards the two middle
movements (adagio and scherzo) were performed in
February, 1867. The reception was not encouraging, only
one anonymous critic speaking warmly in praise of the
music.

In Tchaikovsky's nature, side by side with his gentle
and benevolent attitude towards his fellow-men, there
existed an extraordinary memory for any injury; not
in the ordinary sense of a desire for revenge, but in the
more literal meaning of unforgetfulness. He hardly ever
forgot a slight to his artistic pride. If it was offered by
one whom he had hitherto loved, he grew suddenly cold to
him—and for ever. Not only for months or years, but for

decades, he would bear such a wound unhealed in his heart, and it took a great deal to make him forget an inconsiderate word, or an unfriendly action. It was no doubt the result of having been spoilt as a child. From his earliest infancy he had been kept from all unpleasantness, or even indifference, so that what would have appeared a pin-prick to many seemed to him a mortal blow.

Not only the episode of the symphony—which afterwards won a fair measure of success in St. Petersburg—but many other events contributed to estrange Tchaikovsky from the city of his first affections. Gradually the circle of his friends there decreased, and the most intimate of them all, Laroche, was appointed Professor at the Moscow Conservatoire in December, 1867. Besides which that little school of gifted "young Russians," under the leadership of Balakirev, and the protection of Dargomijsky, which included Moussorgsky, Cui, Borodin and Rimsky-Korsakov, were gaining more and more acknowledgment and weight in Petersburg. This circle, supported by the pens of Cui and Stassov, who held extremely modern views and were opposed to the Conservatoire and Anton Rubinstein, made a very unsympathetic impression upon Tchaikovsky.

The hostility with which he regarded this group of composers had its origin in his distrustful attitude towards society generally. He met all strangers with dislike, but at the first friendly advance, or kind word, he forgave them, and even thought them sympathetic.

So it was with his intercourse with the members of the New School in St. Petersburg. Until 1868 none of them were known to him personally, but all the same he was hostile to them. This was sufficient to awaken in him the notion that they were all disposed to be his enemies, and when in 1867 Anton Rubinstein resigned the conductorship of the Symphony Concerts, and it passed into the hands of this school, he decided that Petersburg was now a hostile

G

camp, whereas in reality they were simply neutral, or indifferent, to him.

Meanwhile, by closer acquaintance with Nicholas Rubinstein, Tchaikovsky had begun to recognise his worth as an
executant, a conductor, and an indefatigable worker;
while the presence of such musicians as Laub and Kossmann, and such intimate friends as Kashkin, Albrecht and
Laroche, reconciled him to Moscow as a musical centre
where it was worth while to be appreciated.

The earliest of Tchaikovsky's letters in 1867 is dated
May 2nd (14th); therefore it is difficult to fix the precise
date at which he began to compose his opera, *The
Voyevode.* In any case he received the first part of the
libretto from Ostrovsky in March or April. I remember
that in the summer the first act was not even finished. At
the very outset he was delayed in his work because he
lost the manuscript, and Ostrovsky had to rewrite it from
memory.

To Anatol Tchaikovsky.

"*May 2nd (14th),* 1867.

"All last week I was out of humour; first, because
of the bad weather; secondly, from shortness of money;
and thirdly, from despair of ever again finding the libretto.
. . . Recently I made the acquaintance of Professor
Bougaiev at his house. He is an extraordinarily learned
man. He talked until late into the night about astronomy
and its latest discoveries. Good God! How ignorant we
are when we leave school! I shudder when I chance to
come across a really well-read and enlightened man! . . ."

In the summer of 1867 Tchaikovsky decided to visit
Finland with one of the twins, his funds not being sufficient
to allow of his taking both of them. With his usual
naïveté as regards money matters, he set off with Anatol,
taking about £10 in his pocket, which he believed would
suffice for the trip. At the end of a few days in Viborg,
finding themselves nearly penniless, they took the first

boat back to Petersburg.   There a great disappointment
awaited them.   Their father, from whom they hoped to
obtain some assistance, had already left for a summer
holiday in the Ural Mountains.   The brothers then spent
their last remaining shillings in reaching Hapsal by
steamer, where they were certain of finding their faithful
friends the Davidovs.   They travelled as "between deck"
passengers and suffered terribly from the cold.   But
notwithstanding these misadventures, out of which they
derived more amusement than discomfort, Peter Ilich
enjoyed the summer holidays.   His spirits were excellent,
and he worked hard at *The Voyevode*, while his leisure
was spent in the society of his dear friends.   The evenings
were devoted to reading, and they were particularly
interested in the dramatic works of Alfred de Musset.
This kind of life entirely satisfied Tchaikovsky's simple
and steadfast nature, and his happy frame of mind is
reflected in the *Chant sans paroles*, which he composed
at this time and dedicated—with two additional pieces for
piano—to Vera Vassilievna Davidov, under the title of
Souvenir de Hapsal.

On August 15th (27th), Tchaikovsky left Hapsal for
Moscow, spending a week in Petersburg on his way.

IV

1867–1868

"Perhaps you may have observed"—writes Tchaikovsky
to his sister—"that I long intensely for a quiet, peaceful life,
such as one lives in the country.   Vera Davidov may have
told you how we often spoke in fun of our future farm,
where we intended to end our days.   As regards myself it
is no joke.   I am really attracted to this idea because,
although I am far from being old, I am already very tired

of life. Do not laugh; if you always lived with me you would see it for yourself. The people around me often wonder at my taciturnity and my apparent ill-temper, while actually I do not lead an unhappy existence. What more can a man want whose prospects are good, who is liked, and whose artistic work meets with appreciation? And yet, in spite of these favourable circumstances, I shrink from every social engagement, do not care to make acquaintances, love solitude and silence. All this is explained by my weariness of life. In those moments when I am not merely too lazy to talk, but too indolent even to think, I dream of a calm, heavenly, serene existence, and only realise this life in your immediate neighbourhood. Be sure of this: you will have to devote some of your maternal devotion to your tired old brother. Perhaps you may think such a frame of mind naturally leads a man to the consideration of matrimony. No, my dear future companion! My weariness has made me *too indolent* to form new ties, *too indolent* to found a family, *too indolent* to take upon myself the responsibility of wife and children. In short, marriage is to me inconceivable. How I shall come to be united with your family I know not as yet; whether I shall become the owner of a plot of ground in your neighbourhood, or simply your boarder, only the future can decide. One thing is clear: my future happiness is impossible apart from you."

Tchaikovsky never gives the true reason for his yearning after solitude and a life of "heavenly quiet and serenity," but it certainly did not proceed from "misanthropy," "indolence," or weariness of life.

He was no misanthropist, for, as everyone who knew him must agree, it would be difficult to find any man who gave out more sympathy than he did. Laroche says:—

"The number of people who made a good impression on him, who pleased him, and of whom he spoke in their absence as 'good' and 'sympathetic,' sometimes astounded me. The power of seeing the best side of people and of things was a gift inherited from his father, and it was precisely this love of his fellow-creatures which made him so beloved in return. He was no misanthropist, rather a philanthropist in the true sense of the word. Neither is there greater justice in his self-accusation of 'indolence.' Those who have followed him through his school-life, his official career, and his student days at the Conservatoire, will be of my opinion. But a glance at the number of his works, which reaches seventy-six, including ten operas and three ballets; at his letters (I possess, in all, four thousand); at his literary work (sixty-one articles); at his translations and arrangements, and his ten years' teaching, will suffice to convince the most sceptical that his nature knew no moods of *dolce far niente.*"

As regards his "weariness of life," he himself disposes of it in the same letter, when he speaks of yearning for a calm and happy existence. Those who are really world-weary have no longing for any kind of existence. Neither misanthropy, indolence, nor weariness were his permanent moods. His indefinite craving for an easier life was caused by his creative impulse, which, waxing ever stronger and stronger, awoke the desire for more leisure to devote to it. This longing for freedom reached a climax in 1877, and brought about a complete change in his life.

For the time being it was useless to think of solitude or freedom. All he could hope for was the comparative liberty of his summer vacation. Town life was a necessity to him from the material and moral point of view, and although he complained of its being oppressive, I believe that had he been compelled by fate to reside in the country —as he did some years later—he would, at this earlier period of his career, have had much more cause for complaint.

To Anatol Tchaikovsky.

"August 31st, 1867 (September 12th).

" . . . At present I have nothing to do, and loaf about the town all day. . . . Ostrovsky still keeps me on the trot. I read in the Petersburg papers that he had com-

pleted my libretto, but it is not so. I had some difficulty
in dragging the first half of the lost act out of him. I am
wandering about with the intention of buying a large
writing-table to make my room more comfortable, so that
I can work at my opera at home. I am determined to
finish it during the winter. Last night we celebrated
Dubuque's birthday, and I came back rather the worse for
liquor.

"I have spent two evenings running at the 'English
Club.' What a delightful club! It would be jolly to belong to it, but it costs too much. . . ."

To Anatol Tchaikovsky.

(*About the end of October.*)

"I am getting along all right. On Saturday our first
concert takes place, to which I look forward, for, generally
speaking, the people here prefer carnal to spiritual enter-
tainments, and eat and drink an incredible amount. The
concert will supply me with a little musical food, of which
I am badly in need, for I live like a bear in his cave, upon
my own substance, that is to say, upon my compositions,
which are always running in my head. Try as I may, it is
impossible to lead a quiet life in Moscow, where one must
over-eat and drink. This is the fifth day in succession
that I have come home late with an overloaded stomach.
But you must not imagine I am idle: from breakfast till
the midday meal I work without a break."

To Modeste Tchaikovsky.

"*November 25th (December 7th).*

"Our mutual friend Klimenko is in Moscow, and visits
us almost daily.

"The Opera is progressing fairly well. The whole
of the third act is finished, and the dances from it—which
I orchestrated at Hapsal—will be given at the next
concert."

Ivan Alexandrovich Klimenko, whose name will often

occur in the course of this book, had previously made Laroche's acquaintance at one of Serov's "Tuesday evenings." An architect by profession, Kashkin describes him as a very gifted amateur. He was devotedly attached to Tchaikovsky, and one of the first to prophesy his significance for Russian music.

At the second symphony concert, which took place early in December, "The Dances of the Serving Maids," from *The Voyevode*, were given. They had an undeniable success, and were twice repeated in Moscow during the season.

On December 12th (24th) Tchaikovsky wrote to his brother Anatol as follows :—

"You ask if I am coming to Petersburg. Wisdom compels me to say no. In the first place I have not money for the journey, and secondly, Berlioz is coming here at Christmas, and will give two concerts—one popular, and another in the place of our fourth symphony evening. I shall put off my visit until the Carnival or Lent. . . ."

Berlioz went to Moscow about the end of December, 1867, direct from St. Petersburg, where he had been invited by the directors of the Musical Society—chiefly at the instigation of Dargomijsky and Balakirev — to conduct a series of six concerts.

This was not his first visit to Russia. As early as 1847 he had been welcomed in Petersburg, Moscow and Riga, by the instrumentality of Glinka, who regarded him as "the greatest of contemporary musicians." He then met with an enthusiastic reception from the leaders of the Russian musical world, Prince Odoevsky and Count Vielgorsky, and not only made a large sum, but was equally fêted by the public. It is interesting to note that not only Berlioz himself, but his Russian admirers seem to have deluded themselves into the belief that he was "understood" and "appreciated" in Russia. Prince

Odoevsky, who published an article extolling Berlioz's genius the very day before his first concert in Petersburg, exclaims in one of his letters to Glinka :—

"Where are you, friend? Why are you not with us? Why are you not sharing our joy and pleasure? Berlioz has been 'understood' in St. Petersburg!! Here, in spite of the scourge of Italian cavatina, which has well-nigh ruined Slavonic taste, we showed that we could still appreciate the most complicated contrapuntal music in the world. There must be a secret sympathy between his music and our intimate Russian sentiment. How else can this public enthusiasm be explained?"

I am of opinion that it is more easily explicable by the fact that Berlioz was a gifted conductor, and that the public had been prepossessed in his favour by the laudatory articles of Prince Odoevsky himself. Judging from the neglect of this famous composer in the present day (*Faust* is the only one of his works which is still popular), this is surely the right point of view.

Twenty years later, in 1867, the enthusiastic welcome he received here was chiefly due to his attraction as a conductor, and to the enthusiasm of that small group of Russian musicians to whom he owed his invitation to our country.

Tchaikovsky, whose views were entirely opposed to those of this circle, held "his own opinions" in this, as in other matters. Although he fully appreciated the important place which Berlioz filled in modern music, and recognised him as a great reformer of the orchestra, he felt no enthusiasm for his music. On the other hand, he had the warmest admiration for the man, in whom he saw "the personification of disinterested industry, of ardent love for art, of a noble and energetic combatant against ignorance, stupidity, vulgarity, and routine. . . ." He also regarded him as "an old and broken man, persecuted alike by fate and his fellow-creatures," whom he cordially

desired to console and cheer—if only for the moment—
by the expression of an ungrudging sympathy.

On February 3rd (15th) Tchaikovsky's G minor symphony was given at the Musical Society, when its success surpassed all expectations. "The adagio pleased best," Tchaikovsky wrote to his brothers. The composer was vociferously recalled, and, according to Countess Kapnist, appeared upon the platform in rather untidy clothes, hat in hand, and bowed awkwardly.

On February 19th (March 2nd) a charity concert was given in the Opera House in aid of the Famine Fund. This was an event in Tchaikovsky's life, for he made his first public appearance as a conductor, the "Dances" from *The Voyevode*, being played under his bâton. On this occasion, too, he first became acquainted with the work of Rimsky-Korsakov, whose "Serbian Fantasia" was included in the programme.

Tchaikovsky's opinion of himself as a conductor we have learnt already from Laroche. Kashkin gives the following account of this concert :—

"When I went behind the scenes to see how the *débutant* was feeling, he told me that to his great surprise he was not in the least nervous. Before it came to his turn I returned to my place. When Tchaikovsky actually appeared on the platform, I noticed that he was quite distracted ; he came on timidly, as though he would have been glad to hide, or run away, and, on mounting to the conductor's desk, looked like a man who finds himself in some desperate situation. Apparently his composition was blotted out from his mind ; he did not see the score before him, and gave all the leads at the wrong moment, or to the wrong instruments. Fortunately the band knew the music so well that they paid no attention whatever to Tchaikovsky's beat, but laughing in their sleeves, got through the dances very creditably in spite of him. Afterwards Peter Ilich told me that in his terror he had a feeling that his head would fall off his shoulders unless he held it tightly in position."

That he had no faith in his powers of conducting is evident from the fact that ten years elapsed before he ventured to take up the bâton again.

In a notice of the concert, which appeared in *The Entr'acte*, Tchaikovsky was spoken of as a " mature " musician, whose work was remarkable for " loftiness of aim and masterly thematic treatment " ; while Rimsky-Korsakov's " Serbian Fantasia " was dismissed as " colourless and inanimate."

Had such a judgment been pronounced a few months earlier, at a time when Tchaikovsky knew nothing of the composer, and regarded the entire Petersburg School as his enemies, who knows whether he would not have felt a certain satisfaction—a kind of " Schadenfreude "—at its appearance ? Now, however, circumstances were altered. Not only had he become well acquainted with the "Serbian Fantasia " at rehearsal, and learnt to regard both the work and its composer with respect, but during the last two or three months he had been more closely associated with the leader of the New School, Mily Balakirev, and had become convinced that, far from being his enemies, the Petersburg set were all interested in his career.

The result of this pleasing discovery was a burning desire to show his sympathy for a gifted colleague, and he wrote an article in direct contradiction to the criticism of the *Entr'acte*. This was the beginning of his literary activity. The article aroused considerable attention in Moscow, and was warmly approved. Nor did it escape observation in St. Petersburg. Consequently, when Tchaikovsky visited his father at Easter, he was received in a very friendly spirit by " The Invincible Band."[1]

The rallying-point of " The Band " was Dargomijsky's house. The composer, although confined to his bed by a mortal illness, was working with fire and inspiration at his

---

[1] Under this sobriquet were grouped the followers of the New Russian School : Dargomijsky, Cui, Balakirev, Rimsky-Korsakov, and others.

opera, *The Stone Guest*. His young friends regarded this work as the foundation-stone of the great temple of " The Music of the Future," and frequently assembled at the " Master's " to note the progress of the new creation and show him their own works. Even Tchaikovsky, who had already met Dargomijsky at Begichev's in Moscow, found himself more than once among the guests, and made many new acquaintances on these occasions.

At Balakirev's, too, he met many musicians who held the views of the New Russian School. Although Tchaikovsky entered into friendly relations with the members of " The Invincibles," he could not accept their tenets, and with great tact and skill remained entirely independent of them. While he made friends individually with Balakirev, Rimsky-Korsakov, Cui and Vladimir Stassov, he still regarded their union with some hostility.

He laughed at their ultra-progressive tendencies and regarded with contempt the naive and crude efforts of some members of " The Band " (especially Moussorgsky). But while making fun of these " unheard-of works of genius," which " throw all others into the shade," and indignant at their daring attacks upon his idol Mozart, Tchaikovsky was also impressed by the force and vitality displayed in some of their compositions, as well as by their freshness of inspiration and honourable intentions, so that far from being repulsed, he learnt to feel a certain degree of sympathy and a very great respect for this school.

This dual relationship reacted in two different ways. Tchaikovsky never hesitated to express quite openly his antipathy to the tendencies of these innovators, while he refused to recognise the dilettante extravagances of Moussorgsky as masterpieces, and always made it evident that it would be distasteful to him to win the praise of Stassov and Cui, and with it the title of " genius," by seeking originality at the expense of artistic beauty. At the same time he acted as the propagandist of " The

Band " in Moscow, was their intermediary with the Moscow section of the Musical Society, and busied himself with the performance or publication of their works. When in 1869 the Grand Duchess Helena Paulovna desired to carry out a change in the management of the symphony concerts, and Balakirev retired from the conductorship, Tchaikovsky appeared for the second time as the champion of " The Band," and protested against the proceedings of the Grand Duchess in an energetic article, in which he displayed also his sympathy with the leader of the New Russian School. During the period when he was engaged in musical criticism, he lost no opportunity of giving public expression to his respect and enthusiasm for the works of Balakirev and Rimsky-Korsakov.

But the most obvious sign of his sympathy with " The Band " is the fact that he dedicated three of his best works to individual members—*Fatum* and *Romeo and Juliet* to Balakirev and *The Tempest* to Vladimir Stassov. Here undoubtedly we may see the indirect influence which the New School exercised upon Tchaikovsky. He would not amalgamate with them ; nor would he adopt their principles. But to win their sympathy, without actually having recourse to a compromise ; to accept their advice (*Romeo and Juliet* was suggested by Balakirev and *The Tempest* by Stassov) ; to triumph over the tasks they set him and to show his solidarity with " The Band," only in so far as they both aimed at being earnest in matters of art—all this seemed to him not only interesting, but worthy of his vocation.

" The Invincible Band " repaid Tchaikovsky in his own coin. They criticised some of his works as pedantic, " behind the times," and *routinier*, but at the outset of his career they took the greatest interest in him, respected him as a worthy rival, strove to win him over to their views, and continued to consider him " among the elect," even after the failure of their efforts at conversion.

The relations between Tchaikovsky and "The Band" may be compared to those existing between two friendly neighbouring states, each leading its independent existence, meeting on common grounds, but keeping their individual interests strictly apart.

During the summer of this year Tchaikovsky went abroad with his favourite pupil Vladimir Shilovsky, accompanied by the lad's guardian, V. Begichev, and a friend named De Lazary. In spite of a lingering wish to spend his holidays with his own people in some quiet spot, the opportunity seemed too good to be lost. His travelling companions were congenial, and his duties of the lightest—merely to give music lessons to young Shilovsky.

From Paris he wrote to his sister on July 20th (August 1st), 1868 :—

"Originally we intended to visit the most beautiful places in Europe, but Shilovsky's illness, and the need of consulting a certain great doctor with all possible speed, brought us here, and has kept us against our will. . . . The theatres are splendid, not externally, but as regards the staging of pieces and the skill with which effects are produced by the simplest means. They know how to mount and act a play here in such a way that, without any remarkable display of histrionic talent, it is more effective than it would be with us, since it would probably lack rehearsal and *ensemble.*

"As regards music, too, in the operas I have heard I remarked no singer with an exceptional voice, and yet what a splendid performance! How carefully everything is studied and thought out! What earnest attention is given to every detail, no matter how insignificant, which goes to make up the general effect! We have no conception of such performances. . . . The noise and bustle of Paris is far less suited to a composer than the quiet of such a lake as the Thuner See, not to mention the stinking, but beloved, Tiasmin,[1] which is happy in flowing by the house

---

[1] The river at Kamenka.

that holds some of my nearest and dearest. How have they passed this summer?"

Tchaikovsky returned to his duties at Moscow about the end of August.

V

1868–1869

Externally, Tchaikovsky's life had remained unchanged during this period. His lessons at the Conservatoire slightly increased, and his salary consequently rose to over 1,400 roubles (£140). Under these circumstances he began to think of finding separate quarters, since his life with Nicholas Rubinstein was unfavourable to his creative work. The latter, however, would not consent to this, and Tchaikovsky himself had doubts as to whether his income would suffice for a separate establishment.

To Modeste Tchaikovsky.

"*September 3rd (15th).*

"I have been working like a slave to-day. The day before yesterday I received an unexpected summons to attend at the theatre. To my great surprise I found two choral rehearsals of my opera (*The Voyevode*) had already been given, and the first solo rehearsal was about to take place. I have undertaken the pianoforte accompaniment myself. I doubt the possibility of getting up such a difficult work in a month, and already I shiver with apprehension at all the hurry-skurry and confusion which lie before me. The rehearsals will take place almost daily. The singers are all pleased with the opera. . . ."

To Anatol Tchaikovsky.

"*September 25th (October 7th).*

". . . When I saw that it was impossible to study my opera in so short a time, I informed the directors that so

long as the Italian company remained in Moscow and
absorbed the time of both chorus and orchestra, I would
not send in the score of my work.   I wrote to Gedeonov
to this effect.   In consequence, the performance is postponed until the Italians leave Moscow.   I have a little
more leisure now.   Besides, Menshikova already knows
the greater part of her rôle by heart.   I lunched with her
to-day, and she sang me several numbers from the opera,
by no means badly.   Time, on the whole, goes quickly
and pleasantly.

"I have some good news to give you about my future
work.   A few days ago I was lunching with Ostrovsky,
and he proposed, entirely of his own accord, to write a
libretto for me.   The subject has been in his mind for the
last twenty years, but he has never spoken of it to anyone
before; now his choice has fallen upon me.

"The scene is laid in Babylon and Greece, in the time
of Alexander of Macedon, who is introduced as one of
the characters.   We have representatives of two great
races of antiquity: the Hebrews and the Greeks.   The
hero is a young Hebrew, in love with one of his own race,
who, actuated by ambitious motives, betrays him for the
sake of Alexander.   In the end the young Hebrew becomes a prophet.   You have no idea what a fine plot it
is!   Just now I am writing a symphonic sketch, *Fatum*.[1]
The Italian opera is creating a furore.   Artôt is a splendid
creature.   She and I are good friends."

"Early in 1868," says Laroche, "an Italian opera company visited Moscow for a few weeks, at the head of which
was the impresario Merelli.   Their performances at the
Opera drew crowded houses.   The company consisted of
fifth-rate singers, who had neither voices nor talent; the
one exception was a woman of thirty, not good-looking,
but with a passionate and expressive face, who had just
reached the climax of her art, and soon afterwards began
to go off, both in voice and appearance.

"Désirée Artôt, a daughter of the celebrated horn-player
Artôt, and a niece of the still more renowned violinist,

---

[1] In my volume upon Tchaikovsky I have called this work *Destiny*.—R. N.

had been trained by Pauline Viardot-Garcia. Her voice was powerful, and adapted to express intense dramatic pathos, but unfortunately it had no reserve force, and began to deteriorate comparatively early, so that six or seven years after the time of which I am speaking it had completely lost its charm. Besides its dramatic quality, her voice was suitable for florid vocalisation, and her lower notes were so good that she could take many mezzo-soprano parts; consequently her repertory was almost un-limited. . . . It is not too much to say that in the whole world of music, in the entire range of lyrical emotion, there was not a single idea, or a single form, of which this admirable artist could not give a poetical interpretation. The timbre of her voice was more like the oboe than the flute, and was penetrated by such indescribable beauty, warmth, and passion, that everyone who heard it was fascinated and carried away. I have said that Désirée Artôt was not good-looking. At the same time, without recourse to artificial aids, her charm was so great that she won all hearts and turned all heads, as though she had been the loveliest of women. The delicate texture and pallor of her skin, the plastic grace of her movements, the beauty of her neck and arms, were not her only weapons; under the irregularity of her features lay some wonderful charm of attraction, and of all the many 'Gretchens' I have seen in my day, Artôt was by far the most ideal, the most fascinating.

"This was chiefly due to her talent as an actress. I have never seen anyone so perfectly at home on the stage as she was. From the first entrance, to the last cry of triumph or despair, the illusion was perfect. Not a single movement betrayed intention or pre-consideration. She was equally herself in a tragic, comic, or comedy part."

To Anatol Tchaikovsky.

"*October* 21*st* (*November* 2*nd*).

"I am very busy writing choruses and recitatives to Auber's *Domino Noir*, which is to be given for Artôt's benefit. Merelli will pay me for the work. I have be-come very friendly with Artôt, and am glad to know something of her remarkable character. I have never met a kinder, a better, or a cleverer woman.

"Anton Rubinstein has been here. He played divinely, and created an indescribable sensation. He has not altered, and is as nice as ever.

"My orchestral fantasia *Fatum* is finished."

To Modeste Tchaikovsky.

(*November.*)

"Oh, Moding, I long to pour my impressions into your artistic soul. If only you knew what a singer and actress Artôt is!! I have never experienced such powerful artistic impressions as just recently. How delighted you would be with the grace of her movements and poses!"

To Modeste Tchaikovsky.

(*December.*)

". . . I have not written to you for a long while, but many things now make it impossible for me to write letters, for all my leisure is given to one—of whom you have already heard—whom I love dearly.

"My musical situation is as follows: Two of my pianoforte pieces are to be published in a day or two. I have arranged twenty-five Russian folksongs for four hands, which will be published immediately, and I have orchestrated my fantasia *Fatum* for the fifth concert of the Musical Society.

"Recently a concert was given here for the benefit of poor students, in which 'the one being' sang for the last time before her departure, and Nicholas Rubinstein played my pianoforte piece dedicated to Artôt."

To his father.

"*December* 26th (*January* 7th, 1869).

"MY DEAR, KIND DAD!—To my great annoyance, circumstances have prevented my going to Petersburg. This journey would have cost me at least a hundred roubles, and just now I do not possess them. Consequently I must

H

send my New Year's wishes by letter. I wish you happiness and all good things. As rumours of my engagement will doubtless have reached you, and you may feel hurt at my silence upon the subject, I will tell you the whole story. I made the acquaintance of Artôt in the spring, but only visited her once, when I went to a supper given after her benefit performance. After she returned here in autumn I did not call on her for a whole month. Then we met by chance at a musical evening. She expressed surprise that I had not called, and I promised to do so, a promise I should never have kept (because of my shyness with new friends) if Anton Rubinstein, in passing through Moscow, had not dragged me there. Afterwards I received constant invitations, and got into the way of going to her house daily. Soon we began to experience a mutual glow of tenderness, and an understanding followed immediately. Naturally the question of marriage arose at once, and, if nothing hinders it, our wedding is to take place in the summer. But the worst is that there are several obstacles. First, there is her mother, who always lives with her, and has considerable influence upon her daughter. She is not in favour of the match, because she considers me too young, and probably fears lest I should expect her daughter to live permanently in Russia. Secondly, my friends, especially N. Rubinstein, are trying might and main to prevent my marriage. They declare that, married to a famous singer, I should play the pitiable part of 'husband of my wife'; that I should live at her expense and accompany her all over Europe; finally, that I should lose all opportunities of working, and that when my first love had cooled, I should know nothing but disenchantment and depression. The risk of such a catastrophe might perhaps be avoided, if she would consent to leave the stage and live entirely in Russia. But she declares that in spite of all her love for me, she cannot make up her mind to give up the profession which brings her in so much money, and to which she has grown accustomed. At present she is on her way to Moscow. Meanwhile we have agreed that I am to visit her in summer at her country house (near Paris), when our fate will be decided.

" If she will not consent to give up the stage, I, on my

part, hesitate to sacrifice my future; for it is clear that I shall lose all opportunity of making my own way, if I blindly follow in her train. You see, Dad, my situation is a very difficult one. On the one hand, I love her heart and soul, and feel I cannot live any longer without her; on the other hand, calm reason bids me to consider more closely all the misfortunes with which my friends threaten me. I shall wait, my dear, for your views on the subject.

"I am quite well, and my life goes on as usual—only I am unhappy now she is not here."

Tchaikovsky received the following letter in reply:—

"*December* 29*th*, 1868 (*January* 10*th*, 1869).

"MY DEAR PETER,—You ask my advice upon the most momentous event in your life. . . . You are both artists, both make capital out of your talents; but while she has made both money and fame, you have hardly begun to make your way, and God knows whether you will ever attain to what she has acquired. Your friends know your gifts, and fear they may suffer by your marriage—I think otherwise. You, who gave up your official appointment for the sake of your talent, are not likely to forsake your art, even if you are not altogether happy at first, as is the fate of nearly all musicians. You are proud, and therefore you find it unpleasant not to be earning sufficient to keep a wife and be independent of her purse. Yes, dear fellow, I understand you well enough. It is bitter and unpleasant. But if you are both working and earning together there can be no question of reproach; go your way, let her go hers, and help each other side by side. It would not be wise for either of you to give up your chosen vocations until you have saved enough to say: 'This is *ours*, we have earned it in common.'

"Let us analyse these words: 'In marrying a famous singer you will be playing the pitiable part of attendant upon her journeys; you will live on her money and lose your own chances of work.' If your love is not a fleeting, but solid sentiment, as it ought to be in people of your age; if your vows are sincere and unalterable, then all these misgivings are nonsense. Married happiness is based upon mutual respect, and you would no more permit your wife to be a kind of servant, than she would ask you to be her lackey. The travelling is not a matter of any importance, so long as it does not prevent your composing— it will even give you opportunities of getting your operas or symphonies performed in various places. A devoted friend will help to inspire you. When all is set down in black and white, with such a companion as your chosen one, your talent is more likely to progress than to deteriorate. (2) Even if your first passion for her does cool somewhat, will 'nothing remain but disenchantment and depression'? But why should love grow cold? I lived twenty-one years with your mother, and during all that time I loved her just the same, with the ardour of a young man, and respected and worshipped her as a saint. . . . There is only one question I would ask you; have you proved each other? Do you love each other truly, and for all time? I know your character, my dear son, and I have confidence in you, but I have not as yet the happiness of knowing the dear woman of your choice. I only know her lovely heart and soul through you. It would be no bad thing if you proved each other, not by jealousy —God forbid—but by time. . . .

"Describe her character to me in full, my dear. Does she translate that tender word 'Désirée'? A mother's wish counts for nothing in love affairs, but give it your consideration."

Tchaikovsky to his brother Anatol.

(*January.*)

"Just now I am very much excited. *The Voyevode* is about to be performed. Everyone is taking the greatest pains, so I can hope for a good performance. Menshikova will do very well; she sings the 'Nightingale' song in the second act beautifully. The tenor is not amiss, but the bass is bad. If the work goes well I shall try to arrange for you both to come here in the Carnival Week, so that you may hear it.

"I have already begun upon a second opera, but I must not tell you about the subject, because I want to keep it a secret that I have anything in hand. How astonished they will be to find in summer that half the opera is already put together! (I hope in summer I shall have some chance of working). . . .

"With regard to the love affair I had early in the winter, I may tell you that it is very doubtful whether I shall enter Hymen's bonds or not. Things are beginning to go rather awry. I will tell you more about it later on. I have not time now."

During this month (January) Désirée Artôt, without a word of explanation to her first lover, was married to the baritone singer Padilla at Warsaw.

The news reached Tchaikovsky at a moment when his whole mind, time, and interests were absorbed by the production of his first opera, and, judging from the tone of his letters, it was owing to these circumstances that it affected him less painfully than might have been expected.

In any case, after the first hours of bitterness, Tchaikovsky bore no grudge against the faithless lady. She remained for him the most perfect artist he had ever known. As a woman she was always dear to his memory. A year later he had to meet her again, and wrote of the prospect as follows :—

"I shall have very shortly to meet Artôt. She is coming here, and I cannot avoid a meeting, because immediately after her arrival we begin the rehearsals for *Le Domino Noir* (for which I have written recitatives and choruses), which I shall be compelled to attend. This woman has caused me to experience many bitter hours, and yet I am drawn to her by such an inexplicable sympathy that I begin to look forward to her coming with feverish impatience."

They met as friends. All intimate relations were at an end.

"When, in 1869, Artôt reappeared at the Moscow Opera," says Kashkin, "I sat in the stalls next to Tchaikovsky, who was greatly moved. When the singer came on, he held his opera glasses to his eyes and never lowered them during the entire performance ; but he must have seen very little, for tear after tear rolled down his cheeks."

Twenty years later they met once more. Youthful love and mutual sympathy had then given place to a steady friendship, which lasted the rest of their lives.

On January 30th (February 11th), 1869, *The Voyevode* was given for the first time for the singer Menshikova's benefit.

The opera was very well received. The composer was recalled fifteen times and presented with a laurel wreath. The performance, however, was not without mishaps. Rapport, who took the lover's part, had been kept awake all night by an abscess on his finger, and was nearly fainting. " If Menshikova had not supported him in her arms, the curtain must have been rung down," wrote Tchaikovsky to his brothers.

Kashkin says the chorus on a folksong, which occurred early in the opera, pleased at once, and the " Nightingale " song became a favourite. The tenor solo, "Glow, O Dawn-light," based upon the pentatonic scale, and the duet between Olona and Maria, " The moon sails calmly," and the last quartet all met with great success.

But the stormy ovation at the first performance, the enthusiasm of the composer's friends, and the appreciation of one or two specialists, could not create a lasting success. The opera was only heard five times, and then disappeared from the repertory for ever.

The first words of disapprobation and harsh criticism came from an unexpected quarter—from Laroche. It was not only his " faint praise " of this work, but the contemptuous attitude which Laroche now assumed towards Tchaikovsky's talent as a whole, which wounded the composer so deeply that he broke off all connection with his old friend.

Soon after the production of *The Voyevode* Tchaikovsky's

symphonic fantasia *Fatum* (or *Destiny*) was given for the first time at the eighth concert of the Musical Society. By way of programme for this work, which he dedicated to Balakirev, Tchaikovsky chose the following lines from Batioushkov :—

> " Thou knowest what the white-haired Melchisedek
> Said when he left this life : Man is born a slave,
> A slave he dies. Will even Death reveal to him
> Why thus he laboured in this vale of tears,
> Why thus he suffered, wept, endured—then vanished ?"

To the choice of this motto attaches a history in which a certain Sergius Rachinsky played a part. This gentleman, Professor of Botany at the Moscow University, was one of Tchaikovsky's earliest and most enthusiastic admirers. Rachinsky was a lover of music and literature, but held the most unusual views upon these, as upon all other subjects. For instance, he saw nothing in Ostrovsky, then at the height of his fame, but discerned in Tchaikovsky, who was hardly known to the world, the making of a "great" composer.

When, in 1871, the musician dedicated to Rachinsky his first quartet, the latter exclaimed with enthusiasm: "C'est un brevet d'immortalité que j'ai reçu."

Originally *Fatum* had no definite programme.

"When the books for the concert were about to be printed," relates Rachinsky, "Rubinstein, who was always very careful about such details, considered the bare title *Fatum* insufficient, and suggested that an appropriate verse should be added. It chanced that I, who had not heard a note of the new work, had dropped in upon Rubinstein, and the verses of Batioushkov flashed across my mind. Rubinstein asked me to write them down at once, and added them to the programme-book with the composer's consent."

The quotation, therefore, has not the significance of a

programme, but was merely an epigraph added to the score.

The composer declared that *Fatum* had a "distinct success" with the public, and added that he "considered it the best work he had written so far," and "others are of my opinion." From this we may gather that, with the exception of Laroche, Tchaikovsky's musical friends were pleased with this composition.

Fatum was given almost simultaneously by the Petersburg section of the Musical Society, under Balakirev's direction. But here the fantasia fell flat, and pleased neither the public nor the musicians.

Nevertheless, Cui did not handle the young composer so severely as on the occasion of his Diploma Cantata. He found fault with a good deal in *Fatum*, but described the music as being on the whole "agreeable, but not inspired," the instrumentation "somewhat rough," and the harmonies "bold and new, if not invariably beautiful."

Balakirev—to whom the work was dedicated—did not admire it, and his feelings were shared by the rest of the "Invincible Band." He wrote to Tchaikovsky as follows :—

"Your *Fatum* has been played, and I venture to hope the performance was not bad—at least everyone seemed satisfied with it. There was not much applause, which I ascribe to the hideous crash at the end. The work itself does not please me ; it is not sufficiently thought out, and shows signs of having been written hastily. In many places the joins and tacking-threads are too perceptible. Laroche says it is because you do not study the classics sufficiently. I put it down to another cause : you are too little acquainted with modern music. You will never learn freedom of form from the classical composers. You will find nothing new there. They can only give you what you knew already, when you sat on the students' benches and listened respectfully to Zaremba's learned discourses upon 'The Connection between Rondo-form and Man's First Fall.'

"At the same concert *Les Préludes* of Liszt was performed. Observe the wonderful form of this work; how one thing follows another quite naturally. This is no mere motley, haphazard affair. Or take Glinka's *Night in Madrid;* in what a masterly fashion the various sections of this overture are fused together! It is just this organic coherence and connection that are lacking in *Fatum*. I have chosen Glinka as an example because I believe you have studied him a great deal, and I could see all through *Fatum* you were under the influence of one of his choruses.

"The verse you chose as an epigraph is altogether beneath criticism. It is a frightful specimen of manufactured rhyme. If you are really so attracted to Byronism, why not have chosen a suitable quotation from Lermontov? With the object of making the verse run smoother I left out the first two lines (Melchisedek seemed really too absurd!), but apparently I perpetrated a blunder. Our entire circle dropped upon me and assured me that the whole of the introduction to *Fatum* was intended to express the awful utterance of Melchisedek himself. Perhaps they are right. If so, you must forgive my excellent intention. . . . I write to you quite frankly, and feel sure you will not on this account abandon your intention of dedicating *Fatum* to me. This dedication is very precious, as indicating your regard for me, and on my part I reciprocate your feeling."

Tchaikovsky did not resent Balakirev's opinion, although it may have wounded him. That he was grateful for the friendly tone of the letter, in which Balakirev's confidence in his talent was clearly perceptible, is evident from the fact that three months later he appeared in the press as the champion of the leader of the "Invincible Band." Moreover, after a short time, he shared Balakirev's opinion of his work, and destroyed the score of *Fatum*.

Early in the season Tchaikovsky began to look out for material for a new opera. The chief requisite he asked was that the scene should not be laid in Russia. The discussion with Ostrovsky of a plot from the period of

Alexander the Great, mentioned in his letter of September 25th, had come to nothing. Without applying to another librettist, he began to search for a ready-made text. Great was his joy to discover a book among the works of Count Sollogoub, based upon his favourite poem, Joukovsky's " Undine."

Without reflection, or closer inspection of the libretto, he began to compose with fervour, even in the midst of the rehearsals for *The Voyevode;* that is in January, 1869. By February he had already written most of the first act. The two following acts he wrote in April, and began the orchestration in the course of the same month. He hoped to complete the first act in May, and the remainder during the summer, and to send the whole score to the Direction of the Petersburg Opera by November, when Gedeonov had given him a formal promise to produce it.

This feverish work, the many excitements of the winter season, his anxiety about the elder of the twins, who had to pass his final examination at the School of Jurisprudence, and all the trouble and correspondence involved in trying to find him an opening in Moscow, told upon Tchaikovsky's nerves. His health was so far impaired that he gradually lost strength, until he became quite exhausted, and the doctor ordered him to the seaside, or to an inland watering-place, enjoining absolute repose.

The summer was spent with his sister at Kamenka, where the whole family was gathered together, with the exception of Nicholas. In June they celebrated the wedding of his brother, Hyppolite, to Sophia Nikonov, and Tchaikovsky, having recovered his spirits, took a leading part in all the festivities.

The score of *Undine* was finished by the end of July, and the composer returned to Moscow earlier than usual— about the beginning of August.

VI

1869–1870

To Anatol Tchaikovsky.

"*August* 11*th* (23*rd*), 1869.

". . . We have taken new quarters; my room is upstairs, and there is a place for you too. I made every possible pretext for living alone, but I could not manage it. However, now I shall pay my own expenses and keep my own servant. . . . Begichev has taken my opera to Petersburg. Whether it is produced or not, I have finished with it and can turn to something else. Balakirev is staying here. We often meet, and I always come to the conclusion that—in spite of his worthiness—his society weighs upon me like a stone. I particularly dislike the narrowness of his views, and the persistence with which he upholds them. At the same time his short visit has been of benefit to me in many respects."

To Anatol Tchaikovsky.

"*August* 18*th* (30*th*).

" I have no news to give. Balakirev leaves to-day. Although he has sometimes bored me, I must in justice say that he is a good, honourable man, and immeasurably above the average as an artist. We have just taken a touching farewell of each other. . . .

" I gave an evening party not long since. Balakirev, Borodin, Kashkin, Klimenko, Arnold and Plestcheiev were among the guests.

" I met Laroche in The Hermitage and said ' Good-day,' but I have no intention of making it up with him."

Towards the end of September, 1869, Tchaikovsky set to work upon his overture to *Romeo and Juliet,* to which he had been incited by Balakirev's suggestions. Indeed, the latter played so important a part in the genesis of this work that it is necessary to speak of it in detail.

Balakirev not only suggested the subject, but took such

a lively interest in the work that he kept up a continuous current of good advice and solicitations. In October he wrote :—

"It strikes me that your inactivity proceeds from your lack of concentration, in spite of your 'snug workshop.' I do not know your method of composing, mine is as follows : when I wrote my *King Lear*, having first read the play, I felt inspired to compose an overture (which Stassov had already suggested to me). At first I had no actual material, I only warmed to the project. An Introduction, 'maestoso,' followed by something mystical (Kent's Prediction). The Introduction dies away and gives place to a stormy allegro. This is Lear himself, the discrowned, but still mighty, lion. By way of episodes the characteristic themes of Regan and Goneril, and then—a second subject —Cordelia, calm and tender. The middle section (storm, Lear and the Fool on the heath) and repetition of the allegro : Regan and Goneril finally crush their father, and the overture dies away softly (Lear over Cordelia's corpse), then the prediction of Kent is heard once more, and finally the peaceful and solemn note of death. You must understand that, so far, I had no definite musical ideas. These came later and took their place within my framework. I believe you will feel the same, if once you are inspired by the project. Then arm yourself with goloshes and a walking-stick and go for a constitutional on the Boulevards, starting with the Nikitsky ; let yourself be saturated with your plan, and I am convinced by the time you reach the Sretensky Boulevard some theme or episode will have come to you. Just at this moment, thinking of your overture, an idea has come to me involuntarily, and I seem to see that it should open with a fierce 'allegro with the clash of swords.' Something like this :

" I should begin in this style. If I were going to write
the overture I should become enthusiastic over this germ,
and I should brood over it, or rather turn it over in my
mind until something vital came of it.

" If these lines have a good effect upon you I shall
be very pleased. I have a certain right to hope for this,
because your letters do me good. Your last, for instance,
made me so unusually light-hearted that I rushed out into
the Nevsky Prospect; I did not walk, I danced along, and
composed part of my *Tamara* as I went."

When Balakirev heard that Tchaikovsky was actually
at work, he wrote in November :—

" I am delighted to hear that the child of your fancy
has quickened. God grant it comes to a happy birth.
I am very curious to know what you have put into the
overture. Do send me what you have done so far, and
I promise not to make any remarks—good or bad—until
the thing is finished."

After Tchaikovsky had acceded to Balakirev's request,
and sent him the chief subjects of his overture, he received
the following answer, which caused him to make some
modifications in the work :—

" . . . As your overture is all but finished, and will soon
be played, I will tell you what I think of it quite frankly
(I do not use this word in Zaremba's sense). The first
subject does not please me at all. Perhaps it improves in
the working out—I cannot say—but in the crude state in
which it lies before me it has neither strength nor beauty,
and does not sufficiently suggest the character of Father
Lawrence. Here something like one of Liszt's chorales—
in the old Catholic Church style—would be very appropriate (*The Night Procession, Hunnenschlacht,* and *St.
Elizabeth*); your motive is of quite a different order, in the
style of a quartet by Haydn, that genius of " burgher "
music which induces a fierce thirst for beer. There is
nothing of old-world Catholicism about it; it recalls rather

the type of Gogol's *Comrade Kunz*, who wanted to cut off his nose to save the money he spent on snuff. But possibly in its development your motive may turn out quite differently, in which case I will eat my own words.

" As to the B minor theme, it seems to me less a theme than a lovely introduction to one, and after the agitated movement in C major, something very forcible and energetic should follow. I take it for granted that it will really be so, and that you were too lazy to write out the context.

" The first theme in D flat major is very pretty, although rather colourless. The second, in the same key, is simply fascinating. I often play it, and would like to hug you for it. It has the sweetness of love, its tenderness, its longing, in a word, so much that must appeal to the heart of that immoral German, Albrecht. I have only one thing to say against this theme: it does not sufficiently express a mystic, inward, spiritual love, but rather a fantastic passionate glow which has hardly any nuance of Italian sentiment. Romeo and Juliet were not Persian lovers, but Europeans. I do not know if you will understand what I am driving at—I always feel the lack of appropriate words when I speak of music, and I am obliged to have recourse to comparison in order to explain myself. One subject in which spiritual love is well expressed— according to my ideas — is the second theme in Schumann's overture, *The Bride of Messina*. The subject has its weak side too ; it is morbid and somewhat sentimental at the end, but the fundamental emotion is sincere.

" I am impatient to receive the entire score, so that I may get a just impression of your clever overture, which is—so far—your best work ; the fact that you have dedicated it to me affords me the greatest pleasure. It is the first of your compositions which contains so many beautiful things that one does not hesitate to pronounce it good as a whole. It cannot be compared with that old Melchisedek, who was so drunk with sorrow that he must needs dance his disgusting *trepak* in the Arbatsky Square. Send me the score soon ; I am longing to see it."

But even in a somewhat modified form, Balakirev was

not quite satisfied with the overture. On January 22nd (February 3rd), 1871, he wrote as follows :—

" I am very pleased with the introduction, but the end is not at all to my taste. It is impossible to write of it in detail. It would be better if you came here, so that I could tell you what I think of it. In the middle section you have done something new and good ; the alternating chords above the pedal-point, rather *à la Russlan*. The close becomes very commonplace, and the whole of the section after the end of the second subject (D major) seems to have been dragged from your brain by main force. The actual ending is not bad, but why those accentuated chords in the very last bars? This seems to contradict the meaning of the play, and is inartistic. Nadejda Nicholaevna[1] has scratched out these chords with her own fair hands, and wants to make the pianoforte arrangement end pianissimo. I do not know whether you will consent to this alteration."

When this arbitrary treatment of the composer's intention had been carried through, the indefatigable critic wrote once more :—

" It is a pity that you, or rather Rubinstein, should have hurried the publication of the overture. Although the new introduction is a decided improvement, yet I had still a great desire to see some other alterations made in the work, and hoped it might remain longer in your hands for the sake of your future compositions. However, I hope Jurgenson will not refuse to print a revised and improved version of the overture at some future time.

To Anatol Tchaikovsky.

" *October 7th* (19*th*).

" The Conservatoire begins already to be repugnant to me, and the lessons I am obliged to give fatigue me as

---

[1] Madame Rimsky-Korsakov, *née* Pourgold. In his final arrangement Tchaikovsky omitted these chords himself.

they did last year. Just now I am not working at all. *Romeo and Juliet* is finished. Yesterday I received a commission from Bessel. He asked me to arrange Rubinstein's overture to *Ivan the Terrible*. I have had a letter from Balakirev scolding me because I am doing nothing. I hear nothing definite about my opera: they say it will be performed, but the date is uncertain. I often go to the opera. The sisters Marchisio are good, especially in *Semiramide.* Yet when I hear them I am more and more convinced that Artôt is the greatest artist in the world."

To Modeste Tchaikovsky.

"*November* 18*th* (30*th*).

"Yesterday I received very sad news from Petersburg. My opera is to wait until next season, because there is not sufficient time to study the two operas which stand before mine in the repertory: Moniuszko's *Halka* and Dütsch's *Croat.* I am not likely therefore to come to Petersburg. From the pecuniary point of view the postponement of my opera is undesirable. Morally, too, it is bad for me; that is to say, I shall be incapable of any work for two or three weeks to come."

To Modeste Tchaikovsky.

"*January* 13*th* (25*th*), 1870.

"Balakirev and Rimsky-Korsakov have been here. We saw each other every day. Balakirev begins to respect me more and more. Korsakov has dedicated a charming song to me. My overture pleased them both, and I like it myself. Besides the overture, I have recently composed a chorus from the opera *Mandragora*, the text of which, by Rachinsky, is already known to you. I intended to write music to this libretto, but my friends dissuaded me, because they considered the opera gave too little scope for stage effects. Now Rachinsky is writing another book for me, called *Raymond Lully*."

Kashkin was one of the friends who dissuaded Tchaikovsky from composing *Mandragora*. The latter played him a 'Chorus of Insects' from the unfinished work, which pleased him very much. But he thought the subject more suitable for a ballet than an opera. A fierce argument took place which lasted a long time. Finally, with tears in his eyes, Tchaikovsky came round to Kashkin's view, and relinquished his intention of writing this opera. It made him very unhappy and more chary in future of confiding his plans to his friends.

Laroche gives the following account of this unpublished chorus :—

"'The Elves' Chorus' is intended for boys' voices in unison, with accompaniment for mixed chorus and orchestra. The atmosphere of a calm moonlight night (described in the text) and the fantastic character of the scene are admirably reproduced. In this chorus we find not only that silky texture, that softness, distinction, and delicacy which Tchaikovsky shows in all his best work, but far more marked indications of maturity than in any of his earlier compositions. The orchestration is very rich, and on the whole original, although the influence of Berlioz is sometimes noticeable."

To his sister, A. Davidov.

"*February 5th* (*17th*)."

"One thing troubles me: there is no one in Moscow with whom I can enter into really intimate, familiar, and homely relations. I often think how happy I should be if you, or someone like you, lived here. I have a great longing for the sound of children's voices, and for a share in all the trifling interests of a home—in a word, for family life.

"I intend to begin a third opera; this time on a subject borrowed from Lajetnikov's tragedy, *The Oprichnik*. My *Undine* is to be produced at the beginning of next season, if they do not fail me. Although the spring is still far off and the frosts are hardly over yet, I have already begun to think of the summer, and to long for the early spring sunshine, which always has such a good effect upon me."

I

To Modeste Tchaikovsky.

"*March 3rd* (15*th*), 1870.

". . . The day after to-morrow my overture *Romeo and Juliet* will be performed. There has been a rehearsal already: the work does not seem detestable. But the Lord only knows! . . .

"In the third week of Lent excerpts from my opera *Undine* will be played at Merten's[1] concert. I am very curious to hear them. Sietov writes that there is every reason to believe the opera will be given early next season."

Merten's concert took place on March 16th (28th). Kashkin says it gave further proof how hardly Tchaikovsky conquered the public sympathy.

"In the orchestration of the aria from *Undine*," he says, "the pianoforte plays an important and really beautiful part. Nicholas Rubinstein undertook to play it; yet, in spite of the wonderful rendering of the piece, it had very little success. After the adagio from the *First Symphony*— also included in the programme—even a slight hissing was heard. The Italian craze was still predominant at the Opera House, so that it was very difficult for a Russian work to find recognition."

Romeo and Juliet, given at the Musical Society's Concert on March 4th (16th), had no success.

On the previous day the decision in the case of "Schebalsky *v.* Rubinstein" had been made public, and the Director of the Conservatoire had been ordered to pay 25 roubles, damages for the summary and wrongful dismissal of this female student. Rubinstein refused to pay, and gave notice of appeal, but the master's admirers immediately collected the small sum, in order to spare him

---

[1] Conductor at the Opera House.

the few hours' detention which his refusal involved. This event gave rise to a noisy demonstration when he appeared in public. Kashkin says :—

"From the moment Nicholas Rubinstein came on the platform, until the end of the concert, he was made the subject of an extraordinary ovation. No one thought of the concert or the music, and I felt indignant that the first performance of *Romeo and Juliet* should have taken place under such conditions."

So it came about that the long-desired evening, which he hoped would bring him a great success, brought only another disillusionment for Tchaikovsky. The composer's melancholy became a shade darker. " I just idle away the time cruelly," he writes, " and my opera, *The Oprichnik*, has come to a standstill at the first chorus."

To Modeste Tchaikovsky.

" *March* 25*th* (*April* 6*th*).

" I congratulate you on leaving school. Looking back over the years that have passed since I left the School of Jurisprudence, I observe with some satisfaction that the time has not been lost. I wish the same for you. . . ."

To Anatol Tchaikovsky.

"*April* 23*rd* (*May* 5*th*).

" Rioumin [1] wants to convert me at any price. He has given me a number of religious books, and I have promised to read them all. In any case, I now walk in ways of godliness. In Passion week I fasted with Rubinstein.

" About the middle of May I shall probably go abroad. I am partly pleased at the prospect and partly sorry, because I shall not see you."

---

[1] Constantine Ivanovich Rioumin, the guardian of Vladimir Shilovsky.

To I. A. Klimenko.

"*May 1st* (13*th*), 1870.

". . . First I must tell you that I am sitting at the open window (at four a.m.) and breathing the lovely air of a spring morning. It is remarkable that in my present amiable mood I am suddenly seized with a desire to talk to you—to you of all people, you ungrateful creature! I want to tell you that life is still good, and that it is worth living on a May morning; and so, at four o'clock in the morning, I am pouring out my heart to you, while you, O empoisoned and lifeless being, will only laugh at me. Well, laugh away; all the same, I assert that life is beautiful in spite of everything! This 'everything' includes the following items: 1. Illness; I am getting much too stout, and my nerves are all to pieces. 2. The Conservatoire oppresses me to extinction; I am more and more convinced that I am absolutely unfitted to teach the theory of music. 3. My pecuniary situation is very bad. 4. I am very doubtful if *Undine* will be performed. I have heard that they are likely to throw me over. In a word, there are many thorns, but the roses are there too. . . .

" As regards ambition, I must tell you that I have certainly not been flattered of late. My songs were praised by Laroche, although Cui has 'slated' them, and Balakirev thinks them so bad that he persuaded Khvostova—who wanted to sing the one I had dedicated to her—not to ruin with its presence a programme graced by the names of Moussorgsky & Co.

" My overture, *Romeo and Juliet*, had hardly any success here, and has remained quite unnoticed. I thought a great deal about you that night. After the concert we supped, a large party, at Gourin's (a famous restaurant). No one said a single word about the overture during the evening. And yet I yearned so for appreciation and kindness! Yes, I thought a great deal about you, and of your encouraging sympathy. I do not know whether the slow progress of my opera, *The Oprichnik* is due to the fact that no one takes any interest in what I write; I am very doubtful if I shall get it finished for at least two years."

Tchaikovsky spent only a few days in St. Petersburg before going abroad. There he heard the final verdict upon his opera *Undine*. The conference of the Capell-meisters of the Imperial Opera, with Constantine Liadov at their head, did not consider the work worthy of production. How the composer took this decision, what he felt and thought of it, we can only guess from our knowledge of his susceptible artistic *amour propre*. At the time, he never referred to the matter, either in letters or in conversation. Eight years afterwards he wrote as follows :—

"The Direction put aside my *Undine* in 1870. At the time I felt much embittered, and it seemed to me an injustice ; but in the end I was not pleased with the work myself, and I burnt the score about three years ago."

Tchaikovsky travelled from St. Petersburg to Paris without a break, being anxious to reach his friend Shilovsky with all possible speed. He half feared to find him already on his death-bed. The young man was extremely weak, but able to travel to Soden at the end of three days. The atmosphere of ill-health in which Tchaikovsky found himself—Soden is a resort for consumptive patients—was very depressing, but he determined to endure it for his friend's sake.

"The care of Volodya,"[1] he wrote, "is a matter of conscience with me, for his life hangs by a thread . . . his affection for me, and his delight on my arrival, touched me so deeply that I am glad to take upon myself the rôle of an Argus, and be the saviour of his life."

But by coming abroad he sacrificed all opportunity of seeing the twins and his sister Alexandra during the summer vacation.

[1] Short for Vladimir.

To Modeste Tchaikovsky.

"SODEN, *June 24th (July 6th).*

"We lead a monotonous existence, and are dreadfully bored, but for this very reason my health is first-rate. The saline baths do me a great deal of good, and, apart from them, the way of living is excellent. I am very lazy, and have not the least desire to work. A few days ago a great festival took place at Mannheim, on the occasion of the hundredth anniversary of Beethoven's birth. This festival, to which we went, lasted three days. The programme was very interesting, and the performance superb. The orchestra consisted of various bands from the different Rhenish towns. The chorus numbered 400. I have never heard such a fine and powerful choir in my life. The well-known composer, Lachner, conducted. Among other things I heard for the first time the difficult *Missa Solennis.* It is one of the most inspired musical creations.

"I have been to Wiesbaden to see Nicholas Rubinstein. I found him in the act of losing his last rouble at roulette, which did not prevent our spending a very pleasant day together. He is quite convinced he will break the bank before he leaves Wiesbaden. I long to be with you all."

The outbreak of the Franco-Prussian war drove all the visitors at Soden into the neutral territory of Switzerland. It was little less than a stampede, and Tchaikovsky describes their experiences in a letter to his brother Modeste, dated July 12th (24th), 1870:—

"INTERLAKEN.

"We have been here three days, and shall probably remain a whole month. . . . The crush in the railway carriages was indescribable, and it was very difficult to get anything to eat and drink. Thank God, however, here we are in Switzerland, where everything goes on in its normal course. Dear Modi, I cannot tell you what I feel in the presence of these sublime beauties of Nature, which no one can imagine without beholding them. My astonishment, my admiration, pass all bounds. I rush about like one possessed, and never feel tired. Volodi, who takes no delight in Nature, and is only interested in the Swiss cheeses, laughs heartily at me. What will it be like a few days hence, when I shall scramble through the passes and over glaciers by myself! I return to Russia at the end of August."

Tchaikovsky spent six weeks in Switzerland, and then went on to Munich, where he stayed two days with his old friend Prince Galitsin. From thence he returned to St. Petersburg by Vienna, which delighted him more than any other town in the world. From Petersburg he went direct to Moscow in order to take up his work at the Conservatoire.

During the whole of his trip abroad Tchaikovsky, according to his own account, did no serious work beyond revising his overture *Romeo and Juliet*. Thanks to the exertions of N. Rubinstein and Professor Klindworth, the overture, in its new form, was published in Berlin the following season, and soon found its way into the programmes of many musical societies in Germany.

"Karl Klindworth came from London to Moscow in 1868," says Laroche. "He was then thirty-eight, and at the zenith of his physical and artistic powers. He was tall and strongly built, with fair hair and bright blue eyes. His appearance accorded with our ideas of the Vikings of old ; he was, in fact, of Norwegian descent. He cordially detested London, where he had lived many years, although he spoke English fluently. London was at that time quite unprepared for the Wagnerian propaganda, and, apart from this, life had neither meaning nor charm for Klindworth. As a pupil of Bülow and Liszt, he had been devoted to the Wagnerian cult from his youth. He was invited by Nicholas Rubinstein to come to Moscow as teacher of the pianoforte ; but he was not popular, either as a pianist, or in society. . . . It would seem as though there could be no common meeting-ground between this Wagnerian fanatic and Tchaikovsky. If one desired to be logical, it would further appear that, as a composer, Tchaikovsky would not only fail to interest Klindworth, but must seem to him quite in the wrong, since Wagner has written that concert and chamber music have long since had their day.   But luckily men are devoid of the sense of logical sequence, and Klindworth proved a man of far more heart than one would have thought at first sight. Tchaikovsky charmed him from the first, not merely as a man, but as a composer.   Klindworth was one of the first to spread Tchaikovsky's works abroad.   It was owing to him that they became known in London and New York; and it was through him also that Liszt made acquaintance with some of them.   In Klindworth, Tchaikovsky found a faithful but despotic friend.   Speaking picturesquely, Peter Ilich trembled before him like an aspen-leaf, did not dare openly to give his real opinions upon the composer of the *Nibelungen Ring*, and I believe he embellished as far as possible the views expressed in his articles from Bayreuth in order not to irritate Klindworth."

While I am mentioning the important event of Tchaikovsky's earliest introduction to Western Europe, I must recall the prophetic words of a young critic, then at the outset of his career.   Five years before the appearance of the overture *Romeo and Juliet*, in 1866, Laroche had written to his friend :—

"Your creative work will not really begin for another five years; but these mature and classic works will surpass all that we have produced since Glinka's time."

Being no musical critic, it is not for me to say whether, in truth, in all Russian musical literature nothing so remarkable as *Romeo and Juliet* had appeared since Glinka. I can only repeat what has been said by many musical authorities—that my brother's higher significance in the world of art dates from this work.   His individuality is here displayed for the first time in its fulness, and all that he had hitherto produced seems—as in Laroche's prophecy —to have been really preparatory work.

VII

1870–1871

During this period Tchaikovsky's spirits were, generally speaking, fairly bright. Only occasionally they were damped by anxiety about the twins, of whom the younger had left the School of Jurisprudence and obtained a post in Simbirsk.[1] His lack of experience led him into many blunders and mistakes, which gave trouble to his elder brother Peter. His affection and over-anxiety caused the latter to exaggerate the importance of these small errors of judgment, and he concerned himself greatly about the future of his precious charge.

To I. A. Klimenko.

" October 26th (November 7th), 1870.

" . . . Anton Rubinstein is staying here. He opened the season, playing the Schumann Concerto at the first concert (not very well), and also Mendelssohn's Variations and some Schumann Studies (splendidly). At the Quartet evening he played in his own Trio, which I do not much like. At an orchestral rehearsal, held specially for him, he conducted his new *Don Quixote* Fantasia. Very interesting; first-rate in places. Besides this he has composed a violin concerto and a number of smaller pieces. Extraordinary fertility! Nicholas Rubinstein lost all his money at roulette during the summer. At the present moment he is working, as usual, with unflagging energy.

" I have written three new pieces,[2] and a song,[3] as well as going on with my opera and revising *Romeo and Juliet.*"

---

[1] Modeste.
[2] Op. 9. Three pieces for piano—" Rêverie," " Polka de Salon," " Mazurka."
[3] " So schnell vergessen."

To Anatol Tchaikovsky.

(About the beginning of November.)

" . . . My time is very much occupied. I have foolishly undertaken to write music for a ballet *Cinderella*, at a very small fee. The ballet has to be performed in December, and I have only just begun it ; but I cannot get out of the work, for the contract is already signed. *Romeo and Juliet* will be published in Berlin and performed in several German towns. . . ."

To his sister, A. I. Davidov.

" *December 20th*, 1870 (*January 1st*, 1871).

" DEAREST,—Your letter touched me deeply, and at the same time made me feel ashamed. I wonder that you could doubt, even for an instant, the constancy of my affection for you ! My silence proceeds partly from idleness, and partly from the fact that I need great peace of mind to write satisfactorily, and I hardly ever attain it. Either I am at the Conservatoire, or I am seizing a free hour for composition in feverish haste, or someone wants me to go out, or I have visitors at home, or I am so tired out I can only fall asleep. . . . I have already told you what an important part you play in my life—although you do not live near me. In dark hours my thoughts fly to you. 'If things go very badly with me, I shall go to Sasha,' I say to myself; or, 'I think I will do this, I am sure Sasha would advise it'; or, 'Shall I write to her? What would she think of this . . .?' What a joy to think that if I could get away from these surroundings into another atmosphere I should sun myself in your kindly heart ! Next summer I will not fail to come to you. I shall not go abroad."

To his father.

" *February 14th* (*26th*).

" MY VERY DEAR FATHER,—You say it would not be a bad thing if I wrote to you at least once a month.

" No, not once a month, but at least once a week I

ought to send you news of all I am doing, and I wonder you have not given me a good scolding before this! But I will never again leave you so long without a letter. The news of the death of uncle Peter Petrovich[1] came to me several days ago. God give him everlasting peace, for his honest and pure soul deserved it! I hope, dear, you are bearing this trouble bravely. Remember that poor uncle, with his indifferent health and his many old wounds, had enjoyed a fairly long life."

This letter closes Tchaikovsky's correspondence for the year 1870–1. It is very probable that some of his letters may have been lost, but undoubtedly after February, 1871, he corresponded less frequently than before.

Being very short of funds, he decided to act upon Rubinstein's advice to give a concert. To add to the interest of the programme he thought it well to include some new and important work of his own. He could not expect to fill the room, and an expensive orchestral concert was therefore out of the question. This led to the composition of the first String Quartet (D major). Tchaikovsky was engaged upon this work during the whole of February.

The concert took place on March 16th (28th) in the small hall of the Nobles' Assembly Rooms. Thanks to the services of the Musical Society's quartet, with F. Laub as leader, Nicholas Rubinstein at the piano, and Madame Lavrovsky — then at the height of her popularity — as vocalist, Tchaikovsky had a good, although not a crowded, house.

In his reminiscences Kashkin says that among those who attended this concert was the celebrated novelist, I. S. Tourgeniev, who was staying in Moscow at the time, and was interested in the young composer, about whom he had heard abroad. This attention on the part of the great writer did not pass unnoticed, and was decidedly advan-

---

[1] The uncle whose establishment the Tchaikovskys shared in 1855.

tageous for the musician. Tourgeniev expressed great appreciation of Tchaikovsky's works, although he arrived too late to hear the chief item on the programme, the Quartet in D major.

At the end of May Tchaikovsky went to Konotop, where his eldest brother Nicholas Ilich was residing, and from thence to visit Anatol in Kiev. Afterwards the two brothers travelled to Kamenka, where they spent most of the summer. Tchaikovsky, however, devoted part of his holidays to his intimate friends Kondratiev and Shilovsky.

Kondratiev's property (the village of Nizy, in the Government of Kharkov) was beautifully situated on the prettiest river of Little Russia, the Psiol, and united all the natural charms of South Russia with the light green colouring of the northern landscape so dear to Tchaikovsky. Here in the hottest weather, instead of the oppressive and parched surroundings of Kamenka, he looked upon luxuriant pastures, enclosed and shaded by ancient oaks. But what delighted him most was the river Psiol with its refreshing crystal waters.

The place pleased Tchaikovsky, but his friend's style of living was not to his taste. It was too much like town life, with its guests and festivities, and he preferred Shilovsky's home at Ussovo, which was not so beautifully situated, but possessed the greater charms of simplicity, solitude, and quiet. Here he spent the last days of his vacation very happily, and for many years to come Ussovo was his ideal of a summer residence, for which he longed as soon as the trees and fields began to show the first signs of green.

VIII

1871–1872

As I have already remarked, it was not Tchaikovsky's nature to force the circumstances of life to his own will. He could wait long and patiently—and hope still longer. As in his early youth he had kept his yearning for music hidden in his heart, until the strength of his desire was such that nothing could shake his firm hold upon his chosen vocation, so now, from the beginning of his musical career, he was possessed by an intense longing to break away from all ties which withheld him from the chief aim of his existence—to compose.

Just as a few years earlier he continued his work in the Ministry of Justice in spite of its monotony, and kept up his social ties as though he were waiting until a complete disgust for his empty and aimless life should bring about a revulsion, so it was with him now. Although his duties at the Conservatoire were repugnant to him, and he often complained of the drawbacks of town life, which interfered with his creative work, he went on in his usual course, as though afraid that his need of excitement and pleasure was not quite satisfied, and might break out anew.

The time for the realisation of his dream of complete freedom was not yet come. Moscow was still necessary to his everyday life, and was not altogether unpleasant to him. He was still dependent on his surroundings. To break with them involved many considerations. Above all, he must have emancipated himself, although in a friendly way, from the influence of Nicholas Rubinstein. This was the first step to take in the direction of liberty. With all his affection and gratitude, with all his respect for Rubinstein as a man and an artist, he suffered a good deal under the despotism of this truest and kindest of friends. From morning till night he had to conform to his will in all the trifling details of daily existence, and this was the more unbearable because their ideas with regard to hours and occupations differed in most respects.

Tchaikovsky had already made two attempts to leave Rubinstein and take rooms of his own. But only now was he able to carry out his wish. Nicholas Rubinstein absolutely stood in need of companionship, and Tchaikovsky was fortunate in finding someone, in the person of N. A. Hubert, ready and willing to take his place.

So it chanced that Tchaikovsky reached his thirty-second year before he began to lead an entirely independent existence. His delight at finding himself the sole master of his little flat of three rooms was indescribable. He took the greatest pains to make his new home as comfortable as possible with the small means at his disposal. His decorations were not sumptuous: a portrait of Anton Rubinstein, given to him by the painter Madame Bonné in 1865; a picture of Louis XVII. in the house of the shoemaker Simon, given to him by Begichev in Paris; a large sofa and a few cheap chairs, comprised the composer's entire worldly goods.

He now engaged a servant, named Michael Sofronov. Tchaikovsky never lost sight of this man, although he was afterwards replaced by his brother Alexis, who played rather an important part in his master's life.

At this time the composer's income was slightly increased. His salary at the Conservatoire rose to 1,500 roubles a year (£150), while from the sale of his works, and from the Russian Musical Society,[1] he received about 500 roubles more.

Besides these 2,000 roubles, Tchaikovsky had another

[1] At the instigation of Nicholas Rubinstein, the Musical Society paid the composers about 200 to 300 roubles for new works performed at their Symphony Concerts.

small source of income, namely, his earnings as a musical critic. His employment in this capacity came about thus. In 1871, Laroche, who wrote for the *Moscow Viedomosti*, was offered a post at the St. Petersburg Conservatoire, and passed on his journalistic work to N. A. Hubert, who, partly from ill-health and partly from indolence, neglected the duties he had undertaken. Fearing that Katkov, who edited the paper, might appoint some amateur as critic, and so undo the progress in musical matters which had been made during the past years, Tchaikovsky and Kashkin came to Hubert's aid and "devilled" for him as long as he remained on the staff. Tchaikovsky continued to write for the *Viedomosti* until the winter of 1876.

To Anatol Tchaikovsky.

"*December 2nd* (14*th*).

"I must tell you that at Shilovsky's urgent desire I am going abroad for a month. I shall start in about ten days' time, but no one—except Rubinstein—is to know anything about it; everyone is to think I have gone to see our sister."

To Anatol Tchaikovsky.

"NICE, *January 1st* (13*th*), 1872.

"I have been a week at Nice. It is most curious to come straight from the depths of a Russian winter to a climate where one can walk out without an overcoat, where orange trees, roses, and syringas are in full bloom, and the trees are in leaf. Nice is lovely. But the gay life is killing. . . . However, I have many pleasant hours; those, for instance, in the early morning, when I sit alone by the sea in the glowing—but not scorching—sunshine. But even these moments are not without a shade of melancholy. What comes of it all? I am old, and can enjoy nothing more. I live on my memories and my hopes. But what is there to hope for?

"Yet without hope in the future life is impossible. So I dream of coming to Kiev at Easter, and of spending part of the summer with you at Kamenka."

By the end of January Tchaikovsky was back in Moscow.

In 1871 a great Polytechnic Exhibition was organised in this town in celebration of the two hundredth anniversary of the birth of Peter the Great. The direction of the musical section was confided to Nicholas Rubinstein, but when he resigned, because his scheme was too costly to be sanctioned by the committee, the celebrated 'cellist, K. Davidov, was invited to take his place. He accepted, and named Laroche and Balakirev as his coadjutors. Balakirev was not immediately disposed to undertake these duties, saying that he would first like to hear the opinion of Nicholas Rubinstein as to the part which the Petersburg musicians were to take in the matter. After two months of uncertainty, the committee decided to dispense with his reply, and invited Rimsky-Korsakov to take his place. At the same time Asantchevsky (then Director of the Petersburg Conservatoire), Wurm, and Leschetitzky were added to the musical committee.

This originally Muscovite committee, which ended in being made up of Petersburgers, decided among other projects to commission from Tchaikovsky a Festival Cantata, the text of which was to be specially written for the occasion by the poet Polonsky.

By the end of December, or the beginning of January, the libretto was finished. When Tchaikovsky undertook to do any work within a fixed limit of time, he always tried to complete it before the date of contract expired. On this occasion he was well beforehand with the work, and sent in the cantata to the committee by the 1st of April. As he had only received the words towards the end of January, after his return from Nice, he could not have had more than two months in which to complete this lengthy and complicated score.

In April he was at work again upon *The Oprichnik*, and must have finished it early in May.

This, however, is a matter of conjecture, as between

January 31st (February 12th) and May 4th (16th), there does not exist a single one of his letters.

On May 4th (16th), 1872, the score of *The Oprichnik* was sent to Napravnik in Petersburg.

The Festival Cantata was performed on May 31st (June 12th) at the opening of the Polytechnic Exhibition, and shortly afterwards Tchaikovsky left Moscow for Kamenka, where he spent the whole of June. Here he began his Second Symphony in C minor. Early in July he went to Kiev, and from thence to Kondratiev at Nizy, accompanied by his brother Modeste. A part of this journey had to be accomplished by diligence. On the return journey the two brothers were to travel together as far as Voroshba, where Peter Ilich branched off for Shilovsky's house at Ussovo, and Modeste went on to Kiev. Between Sumy and Voroshba was a post-house, at which the horses were generally changed.

We were in the best of spirits—it is Modeste who recounts the adventure—and partook of a luxurious lunch, with wine and liqueurs. These stimulants had a considerable effect upon our empty stomachs, so that when we were informed of the fact that there were no fresh post-horses at our disposal, we lost our tempers and gave the overseer a good talking to. Peter Ilich quite lost his head, and could not avoid using the customary phrase: " Are you aware to whom you are talking? " The post-master was not in the least impressed by this worn-out phraseology, and Peter Ilich, beside himself with wrath, demanded the report-book. It was brought, and thinking that the unknown name of Tchaikovsky would carry no weight, Peter Ilich signed his complaint: " Prince Volkonsky, Page-in-Waiting." The result was brilliant. In less than a quarter of an hour the horses were harnessed, and the head-ostler had been severely reprimanded for not having told the post-master that a pair had unexpectedly returned from a journey.

K

Arrived at Voroshba, Peter Ilich hurried to the ticket-office and discovered with horror that he had left his pocket-book, containing all his money and papers, at the post-station. What was to be done? He could not catch the train, and must therefore wait till the next day. This was tiresome; but far worse was the thought that the post-master had only to look inside the pocket-book to see Peter Ilich's real name on his passport and visiting-cards. While we sat there, feeling crushed, and debating what was to be done, my train came in. I was forced to steam off to Kiev, after bestowing the greater part of my available cash—some five or six roubles—upon the unhappy pseudo-Prince.

Poor Peter Ilich spent a terrible night at the inn. Mice and rats—of which he had a mortal terror—left him no peace. He waged war all night with these pests, which ran over his bed and made a hideous noise. The next morning came the news that the post-master would not entrust the pocket-book to the driver of the post-waggon; Peter Ilich must go back for it himself. This was a worse ordeal than even the rats and the sleepless night. . . . As soon as he arrived he saw at once that the post-master had never opened the pocket-book, for his manner was as respectful and apologetic as before. Peter Ilich was so pleased with this man's strict sense of honour that before leaving he inquired his name. Great was his astonishment when the post-master replied, "*Tchaikovsky*"! At first he thought he was the victim of a joke, but afterwards he heard from his friend Kondratiev that the man's name was actually the same as his own.

Tchaikovsky spent the rest of the summer at Ussovo, where he completed the symphony commenced at Kamenka.

IX

1872–1873

Immediately after his return to Moscow, Tchaikovsky moved into new quarters, which were far more comfortable than his first habitation.

We have already seen the motives which first induced him to take up journalism. Now he felt it not only a matter of honour and duty towards the interests of the Conservatoire to continue this work, but found it also a welcome means of adding to his income, seeing that he lived entirely upon his own resources. His literary efforts had been very successful during the past year, and had attracted the attention of all who were interested in music. Nevertheless his journalistic work, like his lessons at the Conservatoire, was burdensome. He told himself "it must be done," and did it with the capability that was characteristic of him, but without a gleam of enthusiasm or liking for the work. His writing was interesting and showed considerable literary style ; the general character of his articles bespoke the cultivated and serious musician, who is disinterested and just, and has a complete insight into his art —but nothing more. We cannot describe him as a preacher of profound convictions, who has power to carry home his ideas ; or as a critic capable of describing a work, or a composer, in a few delicate or striking words. Reading his articles, we seem to be conversing with a clever and gifted man, who knows how to express himself clearly ; we sympathise with him, earnestly wish him success in his campaign against ignorance and charlatanism, and share his desire for the victory of wholesome art over the public taste for "the Italians," "American valses," and the rest. In these respects we may say that Tchaikovsky's labours were not lost.

To Modeste Tchaikovsky.

"Moscow, *November 2nd* (14*th*).

"Modi, my conscience pricks me. This is the punishment for not having written to you for so long. What can I do when the symphony, which is nearing completion, occupies me so entirely that I can think of nothing else? This *work of genius* (as Kondratiev calls it) will be performed as soon as I can get the parts copied. It seems to me to be my best work, at least as regards correctness of form, a quality for which I have not so far distinguished myself. . . . My quartet has created a sensation in Petersburg."

To I. A. Klimenko.

"Moscow, *November 15th* (27*th*).

". . . Since last year nothing particular has happened in our lives here. We go to the Conservatoire as formerly, and occasionally meet for a general 'boose,' and are just as much bored as last year. Boredom consumes us all, and the reason is that we are growing old. Yes, it is useless to conceal that every moment brings us nearer to the grave. . . .

"As regards myself, I must honestly confess that I have but one interest in life : my success as a composer. But it is impossible to say that I am much spoilt in this respect. For instance, two composers, Famitzin and myself, send in our works at the same time. Famitzin is universally regarded as devoid of talent, while I, on the contrary, am said to be highly gifted. Nevertheless, *Sardanapalus* is to be given almost immediately, whereas so far nothing has been settled as to the fate of *The Oprichnik*. This looks as though it were going to fall 'into the water'[1] like *Undine*. For an Undine to fall into the water is not so disastrous; it is her element. But imagine a drowning Oprichnik, how he would battle with the waves! He would certainly perish. But if I went to his rescue I should be drowned too ; therefore I have taken my oath never to dip pen in ink again if my *Oprichnik* is refused."

[1] Russian equivalent for "falling through."

To Ilia Petrovich Tchaikovsky.

"November 22nd (December 4th).

" MY DEAR, GOOD FATHER,—. . . As regards marriage,
I must confess that I have often thought of finding myself
a suitable wife, but I am afraid I might afterwards regret
doing so. I earn almost enough (3,000 roubles a year), but
I know so little about the management of money that I am
always in debt and dilemma. So long as a man is alone,
this does not much signify. But how would it be if I had
to keep a wife and family?

" My health is good : only one thing troubles me a little
—my eyesight, which is tried by my work. It is so much
weaker than formerly that I have been obliged to get
a pair of eyeglasses, which I am told are very becoming
to me. My nerves are poor, but this cannot be helped,
and is not of much consequence. Whose nerves are not
disordered in our generation—especially among artists?"

To Modeste Tchaikovsky.

"December 10th (22nd).

"You say that Anatol has told you about my depression.
It is not a question of depression, only now and then
a kind of misanthropical feeling comes over me which has
often happened before. It comes partly from my nerves,
which sometimes get out of gear for no particular reason,
and partly from the rather uncertain fate of my compositions. The symphony, on which I build great hopes,
will not be performed apparently before the middle of
January, at the earliest.

" Christine Nilsson is having a great triumph here. I
have seen her twice, and I must own she has made great
progress as an actress since I heard her for the first time
in Paris. As regards singing, Nilsson stands alone. When
she opens her mouth one does not hear anything remarkable at first; then suddenly she takes a high C, or holds
a sustained note pianissimo, and the whole house thunders
its applause. But with all her good qualities she does not
please me nearly so well as Artôt. If the latter would
only return to Moscow I should jump for joy."

During the Christmas holidays Tchaikovsky was called unexpectedly to St. Petersburg to hear the verdict of the committee upon his opera, *The Oprichnik*. The committee consisted of the various Capellmeisters of the Imperial Theatre and Opera : Napravnik (Russian opera), Bevignani (Italian opera), Rybassov (Russian plays), Silvain Mangen (French plays), Ed. Betz (German plays), and Babkov (ballet). With the exception of Napravnik, Tchaikovsky had no great opinion of these men, and considered them much inferior to himself as judges of music. It seemed to him particularly derogatory to have to appear before this Areopagus in person. He did his best to avoid this formality, but in vain.

The meeting which he dreaded so much passed off quite satisfactorily. *The Oprichnik* was unanimously accepted.

During this visit to St. Petersburg Tchaikovsky was frequently in the society of his friends of the " Invincible Band "; and it was evidently under their influence that he took a Little Russian folksong as the subject of the Finale of the Second Symphony. " At an evening at the Rimsky-Korsakovs the whole party nearly tore me to pieces," he wrote, " and Madame Korsakov implored me to arrange the Finale for four hands." On this same occasion Tchaikovsky begged Vladimir Stassov to suggest a subject for a symphonic fantasia. A week had hardly passed before Stassov wrote the following letter :—

" ST. PETERSBURG,

" *December* 30*th*, 1872 (*January* 11*th*, 1873).

" DEAR PETER ILICH,—An hour after we had parted at the Rimsky-Korsakovs'—that is to say, the moment I was alone and could collect my thoughts—I hit upon the right subject for you. I have not written the last three days because I had not absolutely made up my mind. Now listen, please, to my suggestion. I have not only thought of one suitable subject—I have three. I began by looking at Shakespeare, because you said you would prefer a

Shakesperean theme.   Here I came at once upon the poetical *Tempest*, so well adapted for musical illustration, upon
which Berlioz has already drawn for his fine choruses in
Lelio.   To my mind you might write a splendid overture on this subject.   Every element of it is so full of
poetry, so grateful.   First the Ocean, the Desert Island,
the striking and rugged figure of the enchanter Prospero,
and, in contrast, the incarnation of womanly grace—
Miranda, like an Eve who has not as yet looked upon any
man (save Prospero), and who is charmed and fascinated
by the first glimpse of the handsome youth Ferdinand,
thrown ashore during the tempest.   They fall in love with
each other; and here I think you have the material for
a wonderfully poetical picture.   In the first half of the
overture Miranda awakens gradually from her childish
innocence to a maidenly love; in the second half, both
she and Ferdinand have passed through 'the fires of passion'—it is a fine subject.   Around these leading characters
others might be grouped (in the middle section of the
work): the monstrous Caliban, the sprite Ariel, with his
elfin chorus.   The close of the overture should describe
how Prospero renounces his spells, blesses the lovers, and
returns to his country."

Besides *The Tempest* Stassov suggested two alternative
subjects—Scott's *Ivanhoe* and Gogol's *Tarass Boulba*.
Tchaikovsky, however, decided upon the Shakespearean
subject, and after informing Stassov of his decision,
received the following letter :—

"St. Petersburg,

"*January* 21st (*February 2nd*), 1873.

" I now hasten to go into further details, and rejoice in
the prospect of your work, which should prove a worthy
pendant to your *Romeo and Juliet*.   You ask whether it is
necessary to introduce the tempest itself.   Most certainly.
Undoubtedly, most undoubtedly.   Without it the overture
would cease to be an overture ; without it the entire programme would fall through.

" I have carefully weighed every incident, with all their
pros and cons, and it would be a pity to upset the whole

business. I think the sea should be depicted twice—at the opening and close of the work. In the introduction I picture it to myself as calm, until Prospero works his spell and the storm begins. But I think this storm should be different from all others, in that it breaks out *at once* in all its fury, and does not, as generally happens, work itself up to a climax by degrees. I suggest this original treatment because this particular tempest is brought about by enchantment and not, as in most operas, oratorios, and symphonies, by natural agencies. When the storm has abated, when its roaring, screeching, booming and raging have subsided, the Enchanted Island appears in all its beauty and, still more lovely, the maiden Miranda, who flits like a sunbeam over the island. Her conversation with Prospero, and immediately afterwards with Ferdinand, who fascinates her, and with whom she falls in love. The love theme (crescendo) must resemble the expanding and blooming of a flower; Shakespeare has thus depicted her at the close of the first act, and I think this would be something well suited to your muse. Then I would suggest the appearance of Caliban, the half-animal slave; and then Ariel, whose motto you may find in Shakespeare's lyric (at the end of the first act), 'Come unto these yellow sands.' After Ariel, Ferdinand and Miranda should reappear; this time in a phase of glowing passion. Then the imposing figure of Prospero, who relinquishes his magic arts and takes farewell of his past; and finally the sea, calm and peaceful, which washes the shores of the desert island, while the happy inhabitants are borne away in a ship to distant Italy.

"As I have planned all this in the order described, it seems to me impossible to leave out the sea in the opening and close of the work, and to call the overture " Miranda." In your first overture you have unfortunately omitted all reference to Juliet's nurse, that inspired Shakespearean creation, and also the picture of dawn, on which the love-scene is built up. Your overture is beautiful, but it might have been still more so. And now, please note that I want your new work to be wider, deeper, more mature. That it will have beauty and passion, I think I am safe in predicting. So I wish you all luck and—*vogue la galère!*"

To V. Stassov.

"*January 27th (February 8th),* 1873.

"HONOURED VLADIMIR VASSILIEVICH,—I scarcely know how to thank you for your excellent, and at the same time most attractive, programme. Whether I shall be successful I cannot say, but in any case I intend to carry out every detail of your plan. I must warn you, however, that my overture will not see the light for some time to come: at least, I have no intention of hurrying over it. A number of tiresome, prosaic occupations, among them the pianoforte arrangement of my opera, will, in the immediate future, take up the quiet time I should need for so delicate a work. The subject of *The Tempest* is so poetical, its programme demands such perfection and beauty of workmanship, that I am resolved to suppress my impatience and await a more favourable moment for its commencement.

" My symphony was performed yesterday, and met with great success; so great in fact that N. Rubinstein is repeating it at the tenth concert 'by general request.' To confess the truth, I am not altogether satisfied with the first two movements, but the finale on *The Crane*[1] theme has turned out admirably. I will speak to Rubinstein about sending the score; I must find out the date of the tenth concert. I should like to make a few improvements in the orchestration, and I must consider how long this will take, and whether it will be better to send the score to Nadejda Nicholaevna,[2] or to wait until after the concert.

"Laroche paid me the compliment of coming to Moscow on purpose to hear my symphony. He left to-day."

The Second Symphony appeared in the programme of the Musical Society's concert of January 6th (18th), 1873, and was very well received. Laroche spoke very appreciatively of the new work.

---

[1] A Little Russian folksong.
[2] Madame Rimsky-Korsakov, who was going to make the pianoforte arrangement of the symphony for four hands.

The symphony was repeated at the tenth concert, when the composer was recalled after each movement and presented with a laurel-wreath and a silver goblet.

To his father, I. P. Tchaikovsky.

"*February 5th (17th).*

"Time flies, for I am very busy. I am working at the pianoforte arrangement of my opera (*The Oprichnik*), writing musical articles, and contributing a biography of Beethoven to *The Grajdanin*.[1] I spend all my evenings at home, and lead the life of a peaceable and well-disposed citizen of Moscow. At last a very cold winter has set in. To-day the frost is so intense that the noses of the Muscovites risk becoming swollen and frost-bitten. But as I keep indoors, I am very snug and warm in my rooms."

To the same.

"*April 7th (19th).*

"For nearly a whole month have I been sitting diligently at work. I am writing music to Ostrovsky's fairy tale, *Sniegourotchka* ('Little Snow White'), and consequently my correspondence has been somewhat neglected. In addition to this, I cut my hand so severely the day before yesterday that it was two hours before the doctor could stop the bleeding and apply a bandage. Consequently I can only write with difficulty, so do not be surprised, my angel, at my writing so seldom."

To the same.

"*May 24th (June 5th).*

"I have been feverishly busy lately with the preparations for the first performance of *Sniegourotchka*, the pianoforte arrangement of my symphony, the examinations at the Conservatoire, the reception of the Grand Duke Constantine Nicholaevich, etc. The latter was enthusiastic over my symphony, and paid me many compliments."

[1] Only the opening chapters of this work appeared.

I have already said that life was precious to Tchaikovsky. This was noticeable in many ways, among others his passion for keeping a diary. Every day had its great value for him, and the thought that he must bid eternal farewell to it, and lose all trace of its experiences, depressed him exceedingly. It was a consolation to save something from the limbo of forgetfulness, so that in time to come he might recall to mind the events through which he had lived. In old age he believed it would be a great pleasure to reconstruct the joys of the past from these short sketches and fragmentary jottings which no one else would be able to understand. He preferred the system of brief and imperfect notes, because in reading through the diaries of his childhood and youth, in which he had gone more fully into his thoughts and emotions, he had felt somewhat ashamed. The sentiments and ideas which he found so interesting, and which once seemed to him so great and important, now appeared empty, unmeaning and ridiculous, and he resolved in future only to commit facts to paper, without any commentary.[1] Disillusioned by their contents, he destroyed all his early diaries. About the close of the seventies Tchaikovsky started a new diary, which he kept for about ten years. He never showed it to anyone, and I had to give him my word of honour to burn it after his death. After all, he did so himself, and only spared what might be seen by strangers.

His first attempt at a diary dates from 1873. He began it in expectation of many impressions during his tour abroad, the very day he left Nizy.

---

[1] Many of the entries in Tchaikovsky's diaries are so devoid of characteristic interest that I have thought fit to curtail the number of quotations in this volume, selecting only those which had some reference to his work or his views of life.—R. N.

*Extracts from the diary kept during the summer
of* 1873.

"KIEV, *June* 11*th* (23*rd*), 1873.

"Yesterday, on the road from Voroshba to Kiev, music came singing and echoing through my head after a long interval of silence. A theme in embryo, in B major, took possession of my mind and almost led me on to attempt a symphony. Suddenly the thought came over me to cast aside Stassov's not too successful *Tempest* and devote the summer to composing a symphony which should throw all my previous works into the shade. Here is the embryo :—

" On the road to . . .

"What is more wearisome than a railway journey and tiresome companions? An Italian, an indescribable fool, has tacked himself on to me, and I hardly know how to get rid of him. He does not even know where he is going, nor where to change his money. I changed mine at a Jew's in Cracow. What a bore it all is! Sometimes I think of Sasha and Modi, and my heart is fit to break. At Volochisk great agitation, and my nerves upset. With the exception of the Italian, my fellow-travellers are bearable. I scarcely slept all night. The old man is a retired officer with the old, original whiskers. At the present moment the Italian is boring a lady. Lord, what an ass! I must get rid of him by some kind of dodge."

"*June* 29*th* (*July* 11*th*).

"I had four long hours to wait in Myslovitz; at last I am on the road to Breslau. The Italian is enchanted to think I shall travel with him to Liggia. He bores me to extinction. Oh, what an idiot! At Myslovitz I had an indifferent meal, and afterwards went for a walk through the pretty town. I can imagine my Italian's face, and what he will say, when I suddenly vanish at Breslau! He will be left sitting there! My money goes like water!"

"Jean Prosco, Constantinople,
"Breslau.

"After all I had not the heart to deceive my Italian. I told him beforehand I intended to stop in Breslau. He almost dissolved into tears, and gave me his name, which I have put down above."

"3 *a.m.*

"How I love solitude sometimes! I must confess I am only staying here in order to put off my arrival in Dresden and the society of the Jurgensons. To sit like this— alone, to be silent, and to think! : . ."

"*Not far from Dresden.*

"Theme for the first allegro, introduction from the same, but in 4/4 time."

"DRESDEN, *July* 2*nd* (14*th*).

"I arrived here yesterday at six o'clock. As soon as I had secured a room I hurried to the theatre. *Die Jüdin* (*The Jewess*) was being played—very fine. My nerves are terrible. Without waiting for the end, I went to find the Jurgensons at the hotel. Supper. Took tea with the Jurgensons. To-day I took a bath. Sauntered about the town with Jurgenson. Midday dinner at the table d'hôte. Very shortly we start for Saxon Switzerland. My frame of mind is not unbearable."

"DRESDEN.

"The weather has broken up, and we have decided to turn back from our trip. We made the descent from the Bastei by another road between colossal rocks. We halted at a restaurant in the midst of the most sublime scenery. Breakfasted on the banks of the Elbe (*omelette aux confitures*) and returned to Dresden by boat. Our rooms were no longer to be had, and they have given me a wretched one."

Throughout the whole of his tour through Switzerland we find similar brief entries, recording very little beyond the state of the weather, the names of the hotels at which they stayed, and the quality of the meals provided.

At Cadenabbia (Como) the diary comes to an end with the following entry:—

"The journey (from Milan) was not long, and it was very pleasant on the steamer. We are staying at the lovely Hotel Bellevue."

After Tchaikovsky's return to Russia, early in August, he went straight to his favourite summer resort Ussovo. The fortnight which he spent there in complete solitude seemed to Tchaikovsky, in after days, one of the happiest periods in his existence. Life abroad, under similar circumstances, he found painful and unbearable, whereas in his own country the presence even of a servant sufficed to spoil his solitude, and the sense of increased energy and strength, which always came to him in the lonely life of the country, was unknown in the bustle and stress of the city. In a letter written in 1878 he recalls this visit to Ussovo in the following words :—

To N. F. M. (von Meck).

"*April 22nd (March 4th),* 1878.

" I know no greater happiness than to spend a few days quite alone in the country. I have only experienced this delight once in my life. This was in 1873. I came straight from Paris—it was early in August—to stay with a bachelor friend in the country, in the Government of Tambov. My friend, however, was obliged to go to Moscow for a few days, so I was left all alone in that lovely oasis amid the steppes of South Russia. I was in a highly strung, emotional mood ; wandered for whole days together in the forest, spent the evenings on the low-lying steppe, and at night, sitting at my open window, I listened to the solemn stillness, which was only broken at rare intervals by some vague, indefinable sound. During this fortnight, without the least effort—just as though I were under the influence of some supernatural force—I sketched out the whole of *The Tempest* overture. What an unpleasant and tiresome awakening from my dreams I experienced on my friend's return ! All the delights of direct intercourse with the sublimities and indescribable beauties of nature vanished in a trice ! My corner of Paradise was transformed into the prosaic house of a well-to-do country gentleman. After two or three days of boredom I went back to Moscow."

Tchaikovsky went to Ussovo about the 5th or 6th of August, and by the 7th (19th) had already set to work upon *The Tempest.* By August 17th (29th) this symphonic poem was completely sketched out in all its details, so that the composer could go straight on with the orchestration on his return to Moscow. The Countess Vassilieva-Shilovsky made me a present of this manuscript, upon which are inscribed the dates I have just mentioned. At the present time the manuscript is in the Imperial Public Library, St. Petersburg.

X

1873–1874

As soon as Tchaikovsky returned to Moscow, on September 1st, he set to work upon the orchestration of *The Tempest.*

In the second half of the month he moved into new quarters in the Nikitskaya (House Vishnevsky).

Nothing particularly eventful had happened since last year, either in his career as professor or musical critic. His daily life ran in the same grooves as before, with this difference only : the things which once seemed to him new and interesting now appeared more and more wearisome and unprofitable, and his moods of depression became more frequent, more intense, and of longer duration.

To V. Bessel. "*September,* 1873.

"Be so kind as to do something for *The Oprichnik.* Yesterday they told me at the Opera House that the Direction had quite decided to produce it in Moscow during the spring. Although, with the exception of Kadmina, I have no strong forces to reckon upon here, yet I think we had better not raise any objections. Let them do it if they like. The *repétiteur* has assured me that no expense shall be spared in mounting the opera brilliantly. The rehearsals will be carried on throughout the season. As regards *The Oprichnik*, I think it would be best to dedicate it to the Grand Duke Constantine Nicholaevich."

To the same.

" *October* 10th (22nd)."

"DEAR FRIEND,—I have written to Gedeonov and told him that you are my representative as regards everything pertaining to the production of *The Oprichnik*. As to the pianoforte arrangement, you must wait patiently for a little while. When you meet Stassov, please tell him I have quite finished *The Tempest*, according to his programme, but I shall not send him the work until I have heard it performed in Moscow."

To the same.

" *October* 18th (30th)."

"DEAR FRIEND,—Although I expected your bad news, I cannot conceal the fact that I am very much annoyed by it. It seems to be a foregone conclusion that I shall never hear a good performance of one of my operas. It is useless for you to hope that *The Oprichnik* will be mounted next year. It will never be given at all, for the simple reason that I am not personally known to any of the 'great people' of the world in general, or to those of the Petersburg Opera in particular. Is it not ridiculous that Moussorgsky's *Boris Godounov*, although refused by the Committee, should have been chosen by Kondratiev[1] for his benefit? Madame Platonova, too, interests herself in this work, while no one wants to hear anything about mine, which has been accepted by the authorities. It goes without saying that I will not consent to have the opera performed in Moscow unless it is produced in Petersburg too. My conscience pricks me that the work will involve

---

[1] G. Kondratiev, baritone singer, and afterwards manager of the Marvinsky Theatre.

L

you in some expense, but I hope I may have some opportunity of compensating you.

"As to the dedication to the Grand Duke, would it not look strange to dedicate it to him now that the fate of the work is so uncertain? An unperformed opera seems to me like a book in manuscript. Would it not be better to wait? I am impatiently expecting the corrections of the symphony."

To the same.

"*October* 30*th* (*November* 11*th*).

"DEAR FRIEND,—Hubert has given me the good news that luck has turned for the opera. I am so glad! Keep it a complete secret that I want to be in Petersburg for the first symphony concert, in order to hear my symphony. . . . Let me know the date and secure me a ticket for the gallery. But not a word, for Heaven's sake, or my little joke will be turned into something quite unpleasant."

To Modeste Tchaikovsky.

"*November* 28*th* (*December* 10*th*).

". . . My pecuniary situation will shortly be improved. *The Tempest* is to be performed next week, when I shall receive the customary 300 roubles from the Musical Society. This sum will put me in good heart again. I am very curious to hear my new work, from which I hope so much. It is a pity you cannot hear it too, for I think a great deal of your wise opinion.

"This year, for the first time, I have begun to realise that I am rather lonely here, in spite of many friends. There is no one to whom I can open my heart—like Kondratiev, for instance."

At the third concert of the Moscow Musical Society *The Tempest* was given with great success, and repeated during the same season at an extra concert.

From E. Napravnik to Peter Ilich Tchaikovsky.

"*December* 16th (28th).

"Although we shall probably not begin the rehearsals of your opera before the second week in Lent, may I ask you to lighten the work somewhat for the soloists and chorus by making a few cuts, *i.e.* all those repetitions in words and music which are not essential to the development of the drama? I assure you the work will only gain by it. Besides this, I advise you to alter the orchestration, which is too heavy, and over-brilliant in places; it overwhelms the singers and puts them completely in the shade. I hope you will take my remarks in good part, as coming from one who for eleven years has been exclusively occupied with operatic art."

To E. Napravnik.

"*December* 18th (30th).

"HONOURED SIR,—Your remarks have not hurt my feelings: on the contrary, I am much obliged to you. Above all I am glad that your letter has given me the opportunity of making your acquaintance, and talking things over personally with you. I will do everything you think necessary as regards the distribution of the parts, the shortening of the scenes, and the changes in the orchestration. In order to discuss things in detail, I will go to Petersburg next Sunday and call upon you. . . . Pray do not mention my coming to anyone, as my visit will be short, and I do not want to see anyone but yourself."

To A. Tchaikovsky.

"*January* 26th (*February* 7th), 1874.

"The difficulties with the Censor are happily settled; in fact, I am at peace as regards the opera, and convinced that Napravnik will take the greatest pains with it. I have written a new quartet, and it is to be played at a *soirée* given by Nicholas Rubinstein."

The new quartet mentioned in this letter was begun about the end of December, or beginning of January. In his reminiscences, Kashkin gives the following account of its first performance at N. Rubinstein's :—

"Early in 1874 the Second Quartet (F major) was played at a musical evening at Nicholas Rubinstein's. I believe the host himself was not present, but his brother Anton was there. The executants were Laub, Grijimal, and Gerber. All the time the music was going on Rubinstein listened with a lowering, discontented expression, and, at the end, declared with his customary brutal frankness that it was not at all in the style of chamber music ; that he himself could not understand the work, etc. The rest of the audience, as well as the players, were charmed with it."

On March 10th (22nd) the Quartet was played at one of the Musical Society's chamber concerts, and according to *The Musical Leaflet*, had a well-deserved success.

On February 25th (March 9th), the Second Symphony was performed for the first time in Petersburg, under Napravnik's direction. It was greatly applauded, especially the finale ; but, in the absence of the composer, its success was not so remarkable, nor so brilliant, as it had been a year earlier in Moscow. The symphony won the approval of the "Invincible Band," with the exception of Cæsar Cui, who expressed himself in the St. Petersburg *Viedomosti* as follows :—

"The Introduction and first Allegro are very weak ; the poverty of Tchaikovsky's invention displays itself every moment. The March in the second movement is rough and commonplace. The Scherzo is neither good nor bad ; the trio is so innocent that it would be almost too infantile for a 'Sniegourotchka.' The best movement is the Finale, and even then the opening is as pompously trivial as the introduction to a *pas de deux*, and the end is beneath all criticism."

Towards the end of March, Tchaikovsky went to St. Petersburg to attend the rehearsals of *The Oprichnik*, and took up his abode with his father.   During his first interviews with Napravnik his pride suffered many blows to which he was not accustomed.   Somewhat spoilt by Nicholas Rubinstein's flattering attitude towards every note of his recent orchestral works, he was rather hurt by the number of cuts Napravnik considered it necessary to make in the score of his opera.   Afterwards he approved of them all, but at the moment he felt affronted.

From the very first rehearsal Tchaikovsky was dissatisfied with his work.   On March 25th he wrote to Albrecht :—

"Kindly inform all my friends that the first performance takes place on Friday in Easter week, and let me know in good time whether they intend to come and hear it, so that I may secure tickets for them.   Frankly speaking, I would rather none of you came.   *There is nothing really fine in the work.*"

To his pupil, Serge Taneiev, he writes in the same strain :—

"Serioja,[1] if you really seriously intend to come here on purpose to hear my opera, I implore you to abandon the idea, for there is *nothing good in it*, and it would be a pity if you travelled to Petersburg on that account."

The more the opera was studied, the gloomier grew Tchaikovsky's mood.   One day, unsuspicious of the true reason of his depression, I ventured to criticise *The Oprichnik* rather severely, and made fun of the scene in which Andrew appears in Jemchoujny's garden, merely to "draw" him for some money.   My brother lost his temper and flew out at me fiercely.   I was almost reduced to tears, for at the time I could not guess the real reason for his anger.

---

[1] Diminutive of Serge.

It was not until long after that I realised my criticism had wounded his artistic feelings in the most sensitive spot.

Against Tchaikovsky's wish, almost the entire teaching staff of the Moscow Conservatoire, with N. Rubinstein at their head, appeared in Petersburg for the first night of *The Oprichnik*, April 12th (24th), 1874.

Although none of the singers were remarkable, yet no individual artist marred the *ensemble*. The chorus and orchestra were the best part of it. The performance ran smoothly. The scenery and costumes were rather old, for the authorities did not care to risk the expense of a very luxurious setting for a new work by a composer whose name was not as yet a guarantee for a brilliant success.

On the face of it, the work seemed to have a great success. After the second act the composer was unanimously called before the curtain. The public seemed to be in that enthusiastic mood which is the true criterion of the success of a work.

In a box on the second tier sat the composer's old father with his family. He beamed with happiness. But when I asked him which he thought best for Peter, this artistic success or the Empress Anne's Order, which he might have gained as an official, he replied : " The decoration would certainly have been better." This answer shows that in his heart of hearts he still regretted that his son had ceased to be an official. Not that this feeling sprang from petty ambition, or from any other prosaic or egotistical reason, but because he believed that the life of the ordinary man is safer and happier than that of the artist.

After the performance the directors of the Moscow and Petersburg sections of the Russian Musical Society gave a supper in honour of Tchaikovsky at the Restaurant Borcille.

In the course of the evening, Asantchevsky, then principal of the St. Petersburg Conservatoire, delivered an address, in which he informed the composer in flattering terms that the directors of the Petersburg section of the Musical Society had decided to award him the sum of 300 roubles, being a portion of the Kondratiev Bequest for the benefit of Russian composers.

The Press notices of *The Oprichnik* were as contradictory as they were numerous. The opinions of Cæsar Cui and Laroche represented as usual the two opposite poles of criticism. The former declared that while

"the text might have been the work of a schoolboy, the music is equally immature and undeveloped. Poor in conception, and feeble throughout, it is such as might have been expected from a beginner, but not from a composer who has already covered so many sheets of paper. Tchaikovsky's creative talents, which are occasionally apparent in his symphonic works, are completely lacking in *The Oprichnik*. The choruses are rather better than the rest, but this is only because of the folksong element which forms their thematic material. . . . Not only will *The Oprichnik* not bear comparison with other operas of the Russian school, such as *Boris Godounov*,[1] for instance, but it is even inferior to examples of Italian opera."

In these words Cui apparently believed he had given the death-blow to the composer of *The Oprichnik*.

Laroche's view (in *The Musical Leaflet*) is quite opposed to that of Cæsar Cui. He says :—

"While our modern composers of opera contend with each other in their negation of music, Tchaikovsky's opera does not bear the stamp of this doubtful progress, but shows the work of a gifted temperament. The wealth of musical beauties in *The Oprichnik* is so great that this opera takes a significant place not only among Tchaikovsky's own works, but among all the examples of Russian dramatic music. When to this rare melodic gift we add a fine harmonic style, the wonderful, free, and often daring

[1] By Moussorgsky.

progression of the parts, the genuinely Russian art of inventing chromatic harmonies for diatonic melodies, the frequent employment of pedal-points (which the composer uses almost too freely), the skilful manner in which he unites the various scenes into an organic whole, and finally the sonorous and brilliant orchestration, we have a score which displays many of the best features of modern operatic music, while at the same time it is free from most of the worst faults of contemporary composition."

The most harsh and pitiless of critics, however, was the composer himself, who wrote a fortnight after the first performance as follows :—

" *The Oprichnik* torments me. This opera is so bad that I always ran away from the rehearsals (especially of Acts iii. and iv.) to avoid hearing another note. . . . It has neither action, style, nor inspiration. I am sure it will not survive half a dozen performances, which is mortally vexatious."

This prediction was not fulfilled, for by March 1st (13th), 1881, *The Oprichnik* was given fourteen times. This does not amount to a great deal; but when we remember that not a single new opera of the Russian school—*Boris Godounov*,[1] *The Stone Guest*, *William Ratcliff*, *Angelo*— had exceeded sixteen performances, and many had only reached eight, we must admit that *The Oprichnik* had more than the average success.

The third day after the performance of his opera Tchaikovsky started for Italy. Besides wishing to rest after the excitement of the last few days, he went as correspondent for the *Russky Viedomosti* to attend the first performance in Italy of Glinka's *A Life for the Tsar*. The opera was translated into Italian by Madame Santagano-Gortshakov and, thanks to her initiative, was brought out at the Teatro dal Verme in Milan.

---

[1] *Boris Godounov*, Moussorgsky; *The Stone Guest*, Dargomijsky; *Ratcliff* and *Angelo*, Cæsar Cui.

To M. Tchaikovsky.

"VENICE, *April* 17*th* (29*th*), 1874.

"All day long I have been walking up and down the Piazza San Marco. . . . My soul was very downcast. Why? For many reasons, one of which is that I am ashamed of myself. Instead of going abroad and spending money, I ought really to have paid your debts and Anatol's—and yet I am hurrying off to enjoy the beautiful South. The thought of my wrong-doing and selfishness has so tormented me that only now, in putting my feelings on paper, does my conscience begin to feel somewhat lighter. So forgive me, dear Modi, for loving myself better than you and the rest of mankind.

"Perhaps you will think I am posing as a benefactor. Not in the least. I know my egotism is limitless, or I should not have gone off on my trip while you had to remain at home. . . . Now I will tell you about Venice. It is a place in which—had I to remain for long—I should hang myself on the fifth day from sheer despair. The entire life of the place centres in the Piazza San Marco. To venture further in any direction is to find yourself in a labyrinth of stinking corridors which end in some *cul-de-sac*, so that you have no idea where you are, or where to go, unless you are in a gondola. A trip through the Canale Grande is well worth making, for one passes marble palaces, each one more beautiful and more dilapidated than the last. In fact, you might suppose yourself to be gazing upon the ruined scenery in the first act of *Lucrezia.* But the Doge's Palace is beauty and elegance itself; and then the romantic atmosphere of the Council of Ten, the Inquisition, the torture chambers, and other fascinating things. I have thoroughly 'done' this palace within and without, and dutifully visited two others, and also three churches, in which were many pictures by Titian and Tintoretto, statues by Canova, and other treasures. Venice, however—I repeat it—is very gloomy, and like a dead city. There are no horses here, and I have not even come across a dog.

"I have just received a telegram from Milan. *A Life for the Tsar* will not be performed before May 12th (new style), so I have decided to leave to-morrow for Rome, and afterwards go on to Naples, where I shall expect to find a letter from you."

To Anatol Tchaikovsky.

"ROME, *April 20th (May 2nd)*, 1874.

"DEAR TOLY,—. . . Solitude is a very good thing, and I like it—in moderation. To-day is the eighth day since I left Russia, and during the whole of this time I have not exchanged a friendly word with anyone. Except the hotel servants and railway officials, no human being has heard a word from my lips. I saunter through the city all the morning and have certainly seen most glorious things: the Colosseum, the Capitol, the Vatican, the Pantheon, and, finally—the loftiest triumph of human genius—St. Peter's. Since the midday meal I have been to the Corso, but here I was overcome by such 'spleen' that I am striving to shake it off by writing letters and drinking tea. . . . Except for certain historical and artistic sights, Rome itself, with its narrow streets, is not interesting, and I cannot understand spending one's whole life here, as many Russians do. I have sufficient funds to travel all over Italy. As regards money, from the moment I left Russia I have not ceased to reproach myself for my unfeeling egotism. If you only knew how my conscience has pricked me! But I had made up my mind to travel through Italy. It is too foolish; if I had wanted distraction I might just as well have gone to Kiev or the Crimea—it would have been cheap and as good. Dear Toly, I embrace you heartily. What would I give to see you suddenly appear on the scene!"

To Modeste Tchaikovsky.

"FLORENCE, *April 27th (May 9th)*, 1874.

"You are thinking: 'Lucky fellow, first he writes from Venice and then from Florence.' Yet all the while, Modi, you cannot imagine anyone who suffers more than I do. At Naples it came to such a pass that every day I shed tears from sheer home-sickness and longing for my dear folk. . . . But the chief ground of all my misery is *The Oprichnik*. Finally, the same terrible weather has followed me here. The Italians cannot remember a similar spring. At Naples, where I spent six days, I saw nothing, because in bad weather the town is impassable. The last two days it was impossible to go out. I fled post-haste, and shall go straight to Sasha[1] without stopping at Milan. I have very good grounds for avoiding Milan, for I hear from a certain Stchurovsky that the performance of *A Life for the Tsar* will be bungled. . . . In Florence I only had time to go through the principal streets, which pleased me very much. I hate Rome, and Naples too; the devil take them both! There is only one town in the world for me—Moscow, and perhaps I might add Paris."

Without waiting for the performance of *A Life for the Tsar* at Milan, which did not take place until May 8th (20th), Tchaikovsky returned to Moscow early in this month.

For a short time his dissatisfaction with *The Oprichnik* filled him with such doubt of his powers that his spirits flagged. But his energy quickly recovered itself. No sooner had he returned to Moscow, than he was possessed by an intense desire to prove to himself and others that he was equal to better things than *The Oprichnik*. The score of this work seemed like a sin, for which he must make reparation at all costs. There was but one way of atonement—to compose a new opera which should have no resemblance to *The Oprichnik*, and should wipe out the memory of that unhappy work.

In the course of this season, the Russian Musical Society organised a prize competition for the best setting of the opera, *Vakoula the Smith*.

While Serov was still engaged upon his opera, *The Power of the Evil One*, he was suddenly seized with a desire to compose a Russian comic opera, and chose a fantastic poem by Gogol. When he informed his patroness, the Grand Duchess Helena Pavlovna, of his project, she declared herself

---

[1] His sister, Madame Davidov.

willing to have a libretto prepared by the poet Polonsky at
her own cost. Serov died before he had time to begin the
opera, and the Grand Duchess resolved to honour his
memory by offering two prizes for the best setting of the
libretto he had been unable to use. In January, 1873, the
Grand Duchess Helena died, and the directors of the Imperial Musical Society proceeded to carry out her wishes
with regard to the libretto of *Vakoula the Smith*.

The latest date at which the competitors might send in
their scores to the jury was fixed for August 1st (13th)
1875. The successful opera was afterwards to be performed at the Imperial Opera House in Petersburg.

At first Tchaikovsky hesitated to take part in the competition, lest he should be unsuccessful. But having read
Polonsky's libretto, he was fascinated. The originality
and captivating local colour, as well as the really poetical
lyrics with which the book is interspersed, commended
it to Tchaikovsky's imagination, so that he could no longer
resist the impulse to set it to music. At the same time he
feared the competition, not so much because he desired
the prize, as because, in the event of failure, he could not
hope to see his version of the libretto produced at the
Imperial Opera. This was his actual motive in trying to
discover, before finally deciding the matter, whether Anton
Rubinstein, Balakirev, or Rimsky-Korsakov were intending
to compete. As soon as he had ascertained that these
rivals were not going to meet him in the field, he threw
himself into the task with ardour.

At the beginning of the summer vacation Tchaikovsky
went to stay with Kondratiev at Nizy, and set to work
without loss of time. He was under the misapprehension
that the score had to be ready by August 1st of that year
(1874), besides which he felt a burning desire to wipe out
the memory of *The Oprichnik* as soon as possible. By
the middle of July, when he left Nizy for Ussovo, he had
all but finished the sketch of the opera, and was ready to

begin the orchestration. At Ussovo he redoubled his efforts, and the work was actually completed by the end of August. The entire opera had occupied him barely three months. He wrote no other dramatic work under such a long and unbroken spell of inspiration. To the end of his days Tchaikovsky had a great weakness for this particular opera. In 1885 he made some not very important changes in the score. It has been twice re-named; once as *Cherevichek* ("The Little Shoes"), and later as *Les Caprices d'Oxane*, under which title it now appears in foreign editions.

During this season Tchaikovsky's reputation greatly increased. The success of his Second Symphony, and the performance of *The Oprichnik*, made his name as well known in Petersburg as it had now become in Moscow.

In his account of the first performance of *A Life for the Tsar*, at Milan, Hans von Bülow, referring to Tchaikovsky, says:—[1]

"At the present moment we know but one other who, like Glinka, strives and aspires, and whose works—although they have not yet attained to full maturity—give the complete assurance that such maturity will not fail to come. I refer to the young professor of composition at the Moscow Conservatoire—Tchaikovsky. A beautiful string quartet by him has won its way in many German towns. Many of his works deserve equal recognition—his pianoforte compositions, two symphonies, and an uncommonly interesting overture to *Romeo and Juliet*, which commends itself by its originality and luxuriant flow of melody. Thanks to his many-sidedness, this composer will not run the danger of being neglected abroad, as was the case with Glinka."

[1] *Allgemeine Zeitung*, No. 148 (1874), "Musikalisches aus Italien."

XI

1874–1875

It was not until his return to Moscow that Tchaikovsky found out his mistake as to the date of the competition. This discovery annoyed him exceedingly. Like all composers, he burned with impatience to hear his work performed as soon as possible. In his case such impatience was all the greater, because he was not accustomed to delay; hitherto Nicholas Rubinstein had brought out his works almost before the ink was dry on the paper. Besides which Tchaikovsky had never before been so pleased with any offspring of his genius as with this new opera. The desire to see *Vakoula* mounted, and thus to wipe out the bad impression left by *The Oprichnik*, became almost a fixed idea, and led him to a course of action which in calmer moments would have seemed to him reprehensible.

Tchaikovsky never had the art of keeping a secret, especially when it was a question of the rehabilitation of his artistic reputation, such as it seemed to him at present, for he believed it to have been damaged by " the detestable *Oprichnik*." Consequently he never took the least trouble to conceal the fact that he was taking part in this competition. For a man of his age he showed an inconceivable degree of *naïveté*, and went so far as to try to induce the directors of the Opera in Petersburg to have *Vakoula* performed before the result of the competition was decided. From the letter which I give below, it is easy to see how little he thought at the moment of the injustice he was inflicting upon the other competitors, and how imperfectly he realised the importance of silence in such an affair as a competition, in which anonymity is the first condition of impartial judgment.

To E. Napravnik.

"*October* 19*th* (31*st*), 1874.

"I have learnt to-day that you and the Grand Duke are much displeased at my efforts to get my opera performed independently of the decision of the jury. I very much regret that my strictly private communication to you and Kondratiev should have been brought before the notice of the Grand Duke, who may now think I am unwilling to submit to the terms of the competition. The matter can be very simply explained. I had erroneously supposed that August 1st (13th), 1874, was the last day upon which the compositions could be sent in to the jury, and I hurried over the completion of my work. Only on my return to Moscow did I discover my mistake, and that I must wait more than a year for the decision of the judges. In my impatience to have my work performed (which is far more to me than any money) I inquired, in reply to a letter of Kondratiev's—whether it might not be possible to get my work brought out independently of the prize competition. I asked him to talk it over with you and give me a reply. Now I see that I have made a stupid mistake, because I have no rights over the libretto of the opera. You need only have told Kondratiev to write and say I was a fool, instead of imputing to me some ulterior motive which I have never had. I beg you to put aside all such suspicions, and to reassure the Grand Duke, who is very much annoyed, so Rubinstein tells me.

"Let me express my thanks for having included *The Tempest* in your repertory. I must take this opportunity of setting right a little mistake in the instrumentation. I noticed in the introduction, where all the strings are divided into three, and each part has its own rhythm, that the first violins sounded too loud—first, because they are more powerful than the others, and secondly, because they are playing higher notes. As it is desirable that no distinct rhythm should be heard in these particular passages, please be so kind as to make the first violins play *ppp* and the others simply *p*."

To Modeste Tchaikovsky.

"*October 29th (November 10th).*

"Just imagine, Modi, that up to the present moment I am still slaving at the pianoforte arrangement of my opera. . . . I have no time for answering all my letters. Many thanks for both yours; I am delighted to find that you write with the elegance of a Sévigné. Joking apart, you have a literary vein, and I should be very glad if it proved strong enough to make an author of you. Then, at last, I might obtain a good libretto, for it seems a hopeless business; one seeks and seeks, and finds nothing suitable. Berg, the poet, (editor of the *Grajdanin*, the *Niva*, and other Russian publications), suggested to me a subject from the period of the Hussites and Taborites. I inquired if he had any decided plan. Not in the least; he liked the idea of their singing hymns!!! I would give anything just now to get a good historical libretto—not Russian.

" . . . I sit at home a good deal, but unfortunately I do not get much time for reading. I work or play. I have studied *Boris Godounov* and *The Demon* thoroughly. As to Moussorgsky's music, it may go to the devil for all I care: it is the commonest, lowest parody of music. In *The Demon* I have found some beautiful things, but a good deal of padding, too. On Sunday the Russian Quartet, that has brought out my quartet in D, is playing here.

"I am glad my second quartet finds favour with you and Mademoiselle Maloziomov.[1] It is my best work; not one of them has come to me so easily and fluently as this. I completed it as it were at one sitting. I am surprised the public do not care for it, for I have always thought, among this class of works, it had the best chance of success."

I cannot understand how my brother can have inferred from my letter that the quartet had no success. It must

[1] A fellow-student of Tchaikovsky's, *dame de compagnie* of Anton Rubinstein's class and the intimate friend of the master. Afterwards teacher of pianoforte at the St. Petersburg Conservatoire.

have pleased, since it was repeated at least once during the season. Cui spoke of it as a "beautiful, talented, fluent work, which showed originality and invention." Laroche considered it "more serious and important than the first quartet"; and Famitzin thought it showed "marked progress. The first movement displayed as much style as Beethoven's A minor quartet."

On November 1st (13th) Napravnik conducted the first performance of *The Tempest* in St. Petersburg.

From V. V. Stassov to Tchaikovsky.

"*November* 13th (25th), 10 a.m.

"I have just come from the rehearsal for Saturday's concert. Your *Tempest* was played for the first time. Rimsky-Korsakov and I sat alone in the empty hall and overflowed with delight.

"Your *Tempest* is fascinating! Unlike any other work! The tempest itself is not remarkable, or new; Prospero, too, is nothing out of the way, and at the close you have made a very commonplace cadenza, such as one might find in the finale of an Italian opera—these are three blemishes. But all the rest is a marvel of marvels! Caliban, Ariel, the love-scene—all belong to the highest creations of art. In both love-scenes, what passion, what languor, what beauty! I know nothing to compare with it. The wild, uncouth Caliban, the wonderful flights of Ariel—these are creations of the first order.

"In this scene the orchestration is enchanting.

"Rimsky and I send you our homage and heartiest congratulations upon the completion of such a fine piece of workmanship. The day after to-morrow (Friday) we shall attend the rehearsal again. We could not keep away. . . ."

The Tempest not only pleased Stassov and "The Band," but won recognition even in the hostile camp. Laroche alone was dissatisfied. He considered that in his programme music Tchaikovsky approached Litolff as regards form and instrumentation, and Schumann and Glinka as regards

M

harmony. *The Tempest* would not bear criticism as an organic whole. " Beautiful, very beautiful, are the details," he continues, " but even these are not all on a level; for instance, the tempest itself is not nearly so impressive as in Berlioz's fantasia on the same subject. Tchaikovsky's storm is chiefly remarkable for noisy orchestration, which is, indeed, of so deafening a character that the specialist becomes curious to discover by what technical means the composer has succeeded in concocting such a pandemonium."

To Anatol Tchaikovsky.

" *November* 21*st* (*December* 3*rd*).

" Toly, your general silence makes me uneasy. I begin to think something serious has happened, or one of you is ill. I am particularly puzzled about Modeste. I am aware that my *Tempest* was performed a few days ago. Why does no one write a word about it? After my quartet, Modeste wrote at considerable length, and also Mademoiselle Maloziomov. Now—not a soul, except Stassov. Most strange!

" I am now completely absorbed in the composition of a pianoforte concerto. I am very anxious Rubinstein should play it at his concert. The work progresses very slowly, and does not turn out well. However, I stick to my intentions, and hammer pianoforte passages out of my brain : the result is nervous irritability. For this reason I should like to take a trip to Kiev for the sake of the rest, although this city has lost nine-tenths of its charms for me now Toly does not live there. For this reason, too, I hate *The Oprichnik* with all my heart.[1] . . .

" To-morrow the overture to my 'unfinished opera' will be given here."

The " unfinished opera" is none other than *Vakoula the Smith*. The overture had no success, but Tchaikovsky received the customary fee of 300 roubles from the Musical Society.

---

[1] Tchaikovsky had to visit Kiev for the first performance of *The Oprichnik* in that city.

To Modeste Tchaikovsky.

" *November* 26*th* (*December* 8*th*).

". . . You do not write a word (about *The Tempest*), and Maloziomova is silent too. Laroche's criticism has enraged me. With what *schadenfreude* he points out that I imitate Litolff, Schumann, Berlioz, Glinka, and God knows whom besides. As though I could do nothing but compile! I am not hurt that he does not like *The Tempest*. I expected as much, and I am quite contented that he should merely praise the details of the work. It is the general tone of his remarks that annoys me; the insinuation that I have borrowed everything from other composers and have nothing of my own. . . ."

The hyper-sensitiveness which Tchaikovsky shows in this letter is a symptom of that morbid condition of mind, of which more will be said as the book advances.

On December 9th Tchaikovsky attended the first performance of *The Oprichnik* at Kiev, and wrote an account of the event for the *Russky Viedomosti*. The opera had a great success, and remained in the repertory of the Kiev Opera House throughout the entire season.

To Modeste Tchaikovsky.

"*January* 6*th* (18*th*) 1875.

"I am very pleased with your newspaper article. You complain that writing comes to you with difficulty, and that you have to search for every phrase. But do you really suppose anything can be accomplished without trouble and discipline? I often sit for hours pen in hand, and have no idea how to begin my articles. I think I shall never hammer anything out; and afterwards people praise the fluency and ease of the writing! Remember what pains Zaremba's exercises cost me. Do you forget how in the summer of '66 I worked my nerves to pieces over my First Symphony? And even now I often gnaw my nails to the quick, smoke any number of cigarettes, and pace up and down my room for long, before I can evolve a particular motive or theme. At other times writing comes easily, thoughts seem to flow and chase each other as they go. All depends upon one's mood and condition of mind. But even when we are not disposed for it we must force ourselves to work. Otherwise nothing can be accomplished.

"You write of being out of spirits. Believe me, I am the same."

To Anatol Tchaikovsky.

"*January 9th (21st).*

"I cannot endure holidays. On ordinary days I work at fixed hours, and everything goes on like a machine. On holidays the pen falls from my hand of its own accord—I want to be with those who are dear to me, to pour out my heart to them; and then I am overcome by a sense of loneliness, of desolation. . . . It is not merely that there is no one here I can really call my friend (like Laroche or Kondratiev), but also during these holidays I cannot shake off the effects of a cruel blow to my self-esteem—which comes from none others than Nicholas Rubinstein and Hubert. When you consider that these two are my best friends, and in all Moscow no one should feel more interest in my compositions than they, you will understand how I have suffered. A remarkable fact! Messrs. Cui, Stassov, and Co. have shown, on many occasions, that they take far more interest in me than my so-called friends! Cui wrote me a very nice letter a few days ago. From Korsakov, too, I have received a letter which touched me deeply. . . . Yes, I feel very desolate here, and if it were not for my work, I should become altogether depressed. In my character lurk such timidity of other people, so much shyness and distrust—in short, so many characteristics which make me more and more misanthropical. Imagine, nowadays, I am often drawn towards the monastic life, or something similar. Do not fancy I am physically out of health. I am quite well, sleep well, eat even better; I am only in rather a sentimental frame of mind—nothing more."

Tchaikovsky has told so well the tale of Rubinstein's injury to his self-esteem in one of his subsequent letters to Frau von Meck, that I think it advisable to publish the entire letter in this particular chapter of the book.

To N. F. von Meck.

"SAN REMO, *January* 21*st* (*February* 2*nd*), 1878.

". . . In December, 1874, I had written a pianoforte concerto. As I am not a pianist, it was necessary to consult some virtuoso as to what might be ineffective, impracticable, and ungrateful in my technique. I needed a severe, but at the same time friendly, critic to point out in my work these external blemishes only. Without going into details, I must mention the fact that some inward voice warned me against the choice of Nicholas Rubinstein as a judge of the technical side of my composition. However, as he was not only the best pianist in Moscow, but also a first-rate all-round musician, and, knowing that he would be deeply offended if he heard I had taken my concerto to anyone else, I decided to ask him to hear the work and give me his opinion upon the solo parts. It was on Christmas Eve, 1874. We were invited to Albrecht's house, and, before we went, Nicholas Rubinstein proposed I should meet him in one of the class-rooms at the Conservatoire to go through the concerto. I arrived with my manuscript, and Rubinstein and Hubert soon appeared. The latter is a very worthy, clever man, but without the least self-assertion. Moreover, he is exceedingly garrulous, and needs a string of words to say 'yes' or 'no.' He is incapable of giving his opinion in any decisive form, and generally lets himself be pulled over to the strongest side. I must add, however, that this is not from cowardice, but merely from lack of character.

" I played the first movement. Never a word, never a single remark. Do you know the awkward and ridiculous sensation of putting before a friend a meal which you have cooked yourself, which he eats—and holds his tongue? Oh, for a single word, for friendly abuse, for *anything* to break the silence ! For God's sake say *something !* But Rubinstein never opened his lips. He was preparing his thunderbolt, and Hubert was waiting to see which way the wind would blow. I did not require a judgment of my work from the artistic side; simply from the technical point of view. Rubinstein's silence was eloquent. 'My dear friend,' he seemed to be saying to himself, 'how can I speak of the details, when the work itself goes entirely against the grain?" I gathered patience, and played the concerto straight through to the end. Still silence.

"'Well?' I asked, and rose from the piano. Then a torrent broke from Rubinstein's lips. Gentle at first, gathering volume as it proceeded, and finally bursting into the fury of a Jupiter-Tonans. My concerto was worthless, absolutely unplayable; the passages so broken, so disconnected, so unskilfully written, that they could not even be improved; the work itself was bad, trivial, common; here and there I had stolen from other people; only one or two pages were worth anything; all the rest had better be destroyed, or entirely rewritten. 'For instance, *that?*' 'And what meaning is there in *this?*' Here the passages were caricatured on the piano. 'And look there! Is it possible that anyone could?' etc., etc., etc. But the chief thing I cannot reproduce: the *tone* in which all this was said. An independent witness of this scene must have concluded I was a talentless maniac, a scribbler with no notion of composing, who had ventured to lay his rubbish before a famous man. Hubert was quite overcome by my silence, and was surprised, no doubt, that a man who had already written so many works, and was professor of composition at the Conservatoire, could listen calmly and without contradiction to such a jobation, such as one would hardly venture to address to a student before having gone through his work very carefully. Then he began to comment upon Rubinstein's criticism, and to agree with it, although he made some attempt to soften the harshness of his judgment. I was not only astounded, but deeply mortified, by the whole scene. I require friendly counsel and criticism; I shall always be glad of it, but there was no trace of friendliness in the whole proceedings. It was a censure delivered in such a form that it cut me to the quick. I left the room without a word and went upstairs. I could not have spoken for anger and agitation. Presently

Rubinstein came to me and, seeing how upset I was, called me into another room.   There he repeated that my concerto was impossible, pointed out many places where it needed to be completely revised, and said if I would suit the concerto to his requirements, he would bring it out at his concert. 'I shall not alter a single note,' I replied, 'I shall publish the work precisely as it stands.'   This intention I actually carried out."

Not only did Tchaikovsky publish the concerto in its original form, but he scratched out Rubinstein's name from the dedication and replaced it by that of Hans von Bülow.   Personally, Bülow was unknown to him, but he had heard from Klindworth that the famous pianist took a lively interest in his compositions, and had helped to make them known in Germany.

Bülow was flattered by the dedication, and, in a long and grateful letter, praised the concerto very highly—in direct opposition to Rubinstein—saying, that of all Tchaikovsky's works with which he was acquainted this was "the most perfect."

" The ideas," he wrote, " are so lofty, strong, and original. The details, which although profuse, in no way obscure the work as a whole, are so interesting.   The form is so perfect, mature, and full of style—in the sense that the intention and craftsmanship are everywhere concealed.   I should grow weary if I attempted to enumerate all the qualities of your work—qualities which compel me to congratulate, not only the composer, but all those who will enjoy the work in future, either actively or passively (*réceptivement*)."

I have already mentioned that Tchaikovsky, in spite of a nature fundamentally noble and generous, was not altogether free from rancour.   The episode of the pianoforte concerto proves this.   It was long before he could forgive Rubinstein's cruel criticism, and this influenced their friendly relations.   It is evident from the style of his letter to Nadejda von Meck, from the lively narration of every episode and detail of the affair, that the wound still smarted as severely as when it had been inflicted three years earlier.

In 1878 Nicholas Rubinstein entirely healed the breach, and removed all grounds of ill-feeling when, with true nobility and simplicity, recognising the injustice he had done to the concerto in the first instance, he studied and played it, abroad and in Russia, with all the genius and artistic insight of which he was capable.

To Anatol Tchaikovsky.

"*March 9th (21st).*

" The jester Fate has willed that for the last ten years I should live apart from all who are dear to me. . . . If you have any powers of observation, you will have noticed that my friendship with Rubinstein and the other gentlemen of the Conservatoire is simply based on the circumstance of our being colleagues, and that none of them give me the tenderness and affection of which I constantly stand in need. Perhaps I am to blame for this ; I am very slow in forming new ties. However this may be, I suffer much for lack of someone I care for during these periods of hypochondria. All this winter I have been depressed to the verge of despair, and often wished myself dead. Now the spring is here the melancholy has vanished, but I know it will return in greater intensity with each winter to come, and so I have made up mind to live away from Moscow all next year. Where I shall go I cannot say, but I must have entire change of scene and surroundings. . . . Probably you will have read of Laub's death in the papers."

To Modeste Tchaikovsky.

"*March 12th (24th).*

" I see that Kondratiev has been giving you an over-coloured account of my hypochondriacal state. I have suffered all the winter, but my physical health is not in the least impaired. . . . Probably I wrote to Kondratiev in a fit of depression, and should find my account very much exaggerated if I were to read the letter now. You seem inclined to reproach me for being more frank with Kondratiev than with you. That is because I love you and Anatol ten times more than I love him ; not that he does not like me, but only in so far as I do not interfere with his comfort, which is the most precious thing in the world to him. If I had confided my state to you, or Anatol, you would have taken my troubles too much to heart; whereas Kondratiev would certainly not let them cause him any anxiety. As to what you say about my antipathy towards you, I pass it by as a joke. Upon what do you found your supposition ? It makes me angry to see that you are not free from any of my own faults—that much is certainly true. I wish I could find any of my idiosyncrasies missing in you—but I cannot. You are too like me : when I am vexed with you, I am vexed with myself, for you are my mirror, in which I see reflected the true image of all my own weaknesses. From this you can conclude that if you are antipathetic to me, this antipathy proceeds fundamentally from myself. Ergo—you are a fool, which no one ever doubted. Anatol wrote me a letter very like yours. Both letters were like a healing ointment to my suffering spirit. . . . The death of Laub has been a terrible grief to me. . . ."

Following upon these letters, it becomes necessary to give some account of the mental and moral disorder which attacked Tchaikovsky during the course of this season, and gradually took firmer hold upon him, until in 1877 it reached a terrible crisis which nearly proved fatal to his existence.

The desire for liberty, the longing to cast off all the fetters which were a hindrance to his creative work, now began to assume the character of an undeclared, but chronic, disease, which only showed itself now and again in complaints against destiny, in poetical dreams of "a calm, quiet home," of "a peaceful and happy existence." Such aspirations came and went, according to the impressions and interests which filled his mind and imagination. If we read the letters of this period carefully, we cannot fail to observe how every fluctuation in his circumstances influenced his spiritual condition. We see it when he separated from Rubinstein and started a home of his own. His independence, his new friendships, once more reconciled him to existence, and his affection for Moscow—or at least for the life it afforded—then reached its climax. For a little while his longings for something better were stifled. But as early as 1872 his dissatisfaction and desire to escape from his surroundings make themselves felt; although only infrequently and lightly expressed.

In November 1873, we find him speaking frankly of his disenchantment with his Moscow friends, and complaining of his isolation and the lack of anyone who understood him. So far, these were only recurrent symptoms of a chronic malady.

We see that in the spring of 1874, when he was away from Moscow and from the friends of whom he had complained, he wished for their society again, wrote to them in affectionate terms, and, during the whole of his visit to Petersburg, as later on to Italy, he was always looking forward to his return to "dear Moscow, where alone I can be happy."

By 1875 the chronic malady had made considerable progress. It did not return at intervals as heretofore, but had become a constant trouble. According to his own account, he was depressed all the winter, sometimes to the verge of despair. He felt he had reached a turning-point in his existence, similar to that in the sixties. But then the desired goal had been his musical career, whereas now, it was "to live as he pleased."

Tchaikovsky now resembled those invalids who do not recognise the true cause of their sufferings, and therefore have recourse to the wrong treatment. He believed the reason for his state lay in the absence of intimate friends, and that his one chance of a cure was to be found among "those who were dear to him" and "who alone could save him from the torments of solitude" from which he suffered. I lay stress upon this error of Tchaikovsky's, because, becoming more and more of a fixed idea, it finally led the composer to take an insane step which almost proved his undoing.

One symptom of Tchaikovsky's condition was the morbid sensibility of his artistic temperament. Even before the episode of the B♭ minor concerto, he chanced one day to play part of *Vakoula the Smith* before some of his friends.

"He was too nervous to do justice to the work," says Kashkin, "and rendered the music in a pointless and spiritless fashion, which produced an unfavourable impression upon his little audience. Tchaikovsky, observing the cool attitude of his hearers, played the opera hurriedly through to the end and left the piano, annoyed by our lack of appreciation."

At any other time such criticism would have been a momentary annoyance, soon forgotten. But just then, following upon his keen disappointment in *The Oprichnik* and the exaggerated hopes he had set upon *Vakoula*, he was much mortified at this reception of his "favourite child." Not only was he annoyed, but he considered himself affronted by what seemed to him an unjust criticism. Hence the bitterness with which, at that period, he spoke of his Moscow friends. They, however, kept the same warmth of feeling for him, as was amply proved during the crisis of 1877.

With the coming of spring Tchaikovsky's depression passed away, and he spent the Easter holidays very happily in the society of the twins, who came to visit him in Moscow.

On May 4th (16th) *The Oprichnik* was performed for the first time in Moscow. But all the composer's thoughts were now concentrated on his "favourite child, *Vakoula the*

Smith." "You cannot imagine," he wrote to his brother Anatol, "how much I reckon upon this work. I think I might go mad if it failed to bring me luck. I do not want the prize—I despise it, although money is no bad thing—but I want my opera to be performed."

Shortly before leaving Moscow for the summer, he was commissioned by the Imperial Opera to write a musical ballet entitled *The Swan Lake.* He did not immediately set to work upon this music, but went to Ussovo at the end of May, where he began his Third Symphony in D major. Late in June he visited his friend Kondratiev at Nizy, where he was exclusively occupied with the orchestration of this symphony until July 14th (26th), when he went to stay with his sister Madame Davidov at Verbovka. By August 1st the symphony was finished, and Tchaikovsky took up the ballet music, for which he was to receive a fee of 800 roubles (about £80). The first two acts were ready in a fortnight.

Verbovka, the Davidovs' estate, was in the neighbourhood of Kamenka, and Tchaikovsky was so fond of this spot that it became his favourite holiday resort, and cast the charms of Ussovo entirely in the shade. The summer of 1875 was spent not only in the society of his sister and her family, but also in that of his father and his brother Anatol.

XII

1875–1876

To N. A. Rimsky-Korsakov.

"Moscow, *September 10th (22nd),* 1875.

"MOST HONOURED NICHOLAI ANDREIEVICH,—Thanks for your kind letter. You must know how I admire and bow down before your artistic modesty and your great strength of character! These innumerable counterpoints, these sixty fugues, and all the other musical intricacies which you have accomplished—all these things, from a man who had already produced a *Sadko* eight years previously—are the exploits of a hero. I want to proclaim them to all the world. I am astounded, and do not know how to express all my respect for your artistic temperament. How small, poor, self-satisfied and naïve I feel in comparison with you! I am a mere *artisan* in composition, but you will be an *artist*, in the fullest sense of the word. I hope you will not take these remarks as flattery. I am really convinced that with your immense gifts—and the ideal conscientiousness with which you approach your work—you will produce music that must far surpass all which so far has been composed in Russia.

"I await your ten fugues with keen impatience. As it will be almost impossible for me to go to Petersburg for some time to come, I beg you to rejoice my heart by sending them as soon as possible. I will study them thoroughly and give you my opinion in detail. . . . The Opera Direction has commissioned me to write music for the ballet *The Swan Lake*. I accepted the work, partly because I want the money, but also because I have long had a wish to try my hand at this kind of music.

"I should very much like to know how the decision upon the merits of the (opera) scores will go. I hope you may be a member of the committee. The fear of being rejected—that is to say, not only losing the prize, but with it all possibility of seeing my *Vakoula* performed—worries me very much.

"Opinions here as regards *Angelo*[1] are most contradictory. Two years ago I heard Cui play the first act, which produced an unsympathetic impression upon me, especially in comparison with *Ratcliff*, of which I am extremely fond."

Contrary to custom, Petersburg, not Moscow, enjoyed the first hearing of Tchaikovsky's latest work. At the first Symphony Concert of the Musical Society, on De-

---

[1] An opera by Cæsar Cui.

cember 1st, Professor Kross played the Pianoforte Concerto. Both composer and player were recalled, but at the same time the work was only a partial success with the public. The Press, with one exception, was unfavourably disposed towards it. Famitzin spoke of the Concerto as "brilliant and grateful, but difficult for virtuosi." All the other critics, including Laroche, were dissatisfied. The latter praised the Introduction for its "clearness, triumphal solemnity, and splendour," and thought the other movements did not display the melodic charm to be expected from the composer of *The Oprichnik* and *Romeo and Juliet*. "The Concerto," he continued, "was ungrateful for pianists, and would have no future."

At the first Symphony Concert in Moscow, November 7th (19th), Tchaikovsky's Third Symphony was produced for the first time with marked success.

To N. A. Rimsky-Korsakov.

"MOSCOW, *November* 12*th* (24*th*), 1875.

"MOST HONOURED NICHOLAI ANDREIEVICH,—To-day for the first time I have a free moment in which to talk to you. Business first.

"1. It goes without saying that Rubinstein will be much obliged if you will send him *Antar*.[1] We shall await the score impatiently, and also the quartet, which interests me very much. . . .

"2. Jurgenson will be glad if you will let him have the quartet. Have I explained your conditions correctly? I told him you expected a fee of fifty roubles, and the pianoforte arrangement was to be made at his expense. I know a young lady here who arranged my second quartet very well. So if your wife will not undertake to do it herself, we might apply to her. . . .

"I went direct from the station to the rehearsal of my symphony. It seems to me the work does not contain any very happy ideas, but, as regards form, it is a step in

---

[1] Rimsky-Korsakov's Second Symphony, or "Eastern Suite," Op 9.

advance. I am best pleased with the first movement, and also with the two Scherzi, the second of which is very difficult, consequently not nearly so well played as it might have been if we could have had more rehearsals. Our rehearsals never last more than two hours; we have three, it is true, but what can be done in two hours? On the whole, however, I was satisfied with the performance. . . .

" . . . A few days ago I had a letter from Bülow, enclosing a number of American press notices of my Pianoforte Concerto. The Americans think the first movement suffers from 'the lack of a central idea around which to assemble such a host of musical fantasies, which make up the breezy and ethereal whole.' The same critic discovered in the finale 'syncopation on the trills, spasmodic interruptions of the subject, and thundering octave passages'! Think what appetites these Americans have: after every performance Bülow was obliged to repeat *the entire finale!* Such a thing could never happen here."

The first performance of the Concerto in Moscow took place on November 21st (December 3rd), 1875, when it was played by the young pianist Serge Taneiev, the favourite pupil of N. Rubinstein and Tchaikovsky. Taneiev had made his first appearance in public in January of the same year. On this occasion he played the ungrateful Concerto of Brahms, and won not only the sympathy of the public, but the admiration of connoisseurs. Tchaikovsky's account of Taneiev's *début* is not quite free from affectionate partiality, but it is so characteristic that it deserves quotation :—

"The interest of the Seventh Symphony concert was enhanced by the first appearance of the young pianist Serge Taneiev, who brilliantly fulfilled all the hopes of his teachers on this occasion. Besides purity and strength of touch, grace, and ease of execution, Taneiev astonished everyone by his maturity of intellect, his self-control, and the calm objective style of his interpretation. While possessing all the qualities of his master, Taneiev cannot be regarded as a mere copyist. He has his own artistic individuality, which has won him a place among virtuosi from the very outset of his career. . . ."

Tchaikovsky was delighted with Taneiev's rendering of his own Concerto, and wrote :—

" The chief feature of his playing lies in his power to grasp the composer's intention in all its most delicate and minute details, and to realise them precisely as the author heard them himself."

In November, 1875, Camille Saint-Saëns came to conduct and play some of his works in Moscow. The short, lively man, with his Jewish type of features, attracted Tchaikovsky and fascinated him not only by his wit and original ideas, but also by his masterly knowledge of his art. Tchaikovsky used to say that Saint-Saens knew how to combine the grace and charm of the French school with the depth and earnestness of the great German masters. Tchaikovsky became very friendly with him, and hoped this friendship would prove very useful in the future. It had no results, however. Long afterwards they met again as comparative strangers, and always remained so.

During Saint-Saëns' short visit to Moscow a very amusing episode took place. One day the friends discovered they had a great many likes and dislikes in common, not merely in the world of music, but in other respects. In their youth both had been enthusiastic admirers of the ballet, and had often tried to imitate the art of the dancers. This suggested the idea of dancing together, and they brought out a little ballet, *Pygmalion and Galatea*, on the stage of the Conservatoire. Saint-Saëns, aged forty, played the part of Galatea most conscientiously, while Tchaikovsky, aged thirty-five, appeared as Pygmalion. N. Rubinstein formed the orchestra. Unfortunately, besides the three performers, no spectators witnessed this singular entertainment.

The fate of *Vakoula the Smith* was Tchaikovsky's chief preoccupation at this time. The jury consisted of A. Kireiev, Asantchevsky, N. Rubinstein, Th. Tolstoi, Rimsky-Korsakov, Napravnik, Laroche, and K. Davidov.

Tchaikovsky's score, so Laroche relates, was of course copied out in a strange autograph, "but the motto, which was identical with the writing in the parcel, was in Tchaikovsky's own hand. 'Ars longa, vita brevis' ran the motto, and the characteristic features of the writing were well known to us all, so that from the beginning there was not the least room for doubt that Tchaikovsky was the composer of the score. But even if he had not had the *naïveté* to write this inscription with his own hand, the style of the work would have proclaimed his authorship. As the Grand Duke remarked laughingly, during the sitting of the jury: '*Secret de la comédie.*'"

The result of the prize competition was very much talked of in Petersburg. Long before the decision of the jury was publicly announced, everyone knew that their approval of *Vakoula* was unanimous.

In October Rimsky-Korsakov wrote to Tchaikovsky as follows :—

"I do not doubt for a moment that your opera will carry off the prize. To my mind, the operas sent in bear witness to a very poor state of things as regards music here. . . . Except your work, I do not consider there is one fit to receive the prize, or to be performed in public."

Towards the end of October the individual views of the jury were collected in a general decision, and Tchaikovsky received a letter from the Grand Duke Constantine Nicholaevich, in his own handwriting, congratulating him as the prize-winner of the competition.

During October Modeste Tchaikovsky retired from the Government service in order to become private tutor to a deaf and dumb boy, Nicholas Konradi. The child's

N

parents decided to send young Tchaikovsky to Lyons for a year, to study a special system of education for deaf mutes.

The composer and his brother left Russia together towards the end of December. "Even the various difficulties and unpleasant occurrences of this trip could not damp our cheerful spirits," says Modeste Tchaikovsky. My delight in the journey, and the interest I felt in everything I saw "abroad," infected my brother. He enjoyed my pleasure, laughed at the innocence of his inexperienced travelling companion, and threw himself energetically into the part of guide to an impressionable tourist.

From Berlin we travelled to Geneva, where we spent ten days with my sister and her family (the Davidovs). Afterwards we went on to Paris. Here my brother experienced one of the strongest musical impressions of his life.

On March 3rd (15th), 1873, Bizet's opera *Carmen* was given for the first time. Vladimir Shilovsky, who was in Paris at the time, attended this performance. Captivated by the work, he sent the pianoforte score to his teacher in Moscow. My brother was never so completely carried away by any modern composition as by *Carmen*. Bizet's death, three months after the production of the work, only served to strengthen his almost unwholesome passion for this opera.

During our visit to Paris *Carmen* was being played at the Opera Comique. We went to hear it, and I never saw Peter Ilich so excited over any performance. This was not merely due to the music and the piquant orchestration of the score, which he now heard for the first time, but also to the admirable acting of Galli-Marié, who sang the title-rôle. She reproduced the type of Carmen with wonderful realism, and at the same time managed to combine with the display of unbridled passion an element of mystical fatalism which held us spell-bound.

Two days later we parted. My brother returned to Russia, while I remained in France.

On January 25th (February 6th) the Third Symphony was performed in Petersburg under Napravnik's bâton. Cui criticised it in the following words :—

"The public remained cool during the performance of the work, and applauded very moderately after each movement. At the end, however, the composer was enthusiastically recalled. This symphony must be taken seriously. The first three movements are the best; the only charm of the fourth being its sonority, for the musical contents are poor. The fifth movement, a polonaise, is the weakest. On the whole the new symphony shows talent, but we have a right to expect more from Tchaikovsky."

Laroche said :—

"The importance and power of the music, the beauty and variety of form, the nobility of style, originality and rare perfection of technique, all contribute to make this symphony one of the most remarkable musical works produced during the last ten years. Were it to be played in any musical centre in Germany, it would raise the name of the Russian musician to a level with those of the most famous symphonic composers of the day."

To Modeste Tchaikovsky.

"Moscow, *February* 10*th* (*22nd*).

"I am working might and main to finish a quartet[1] which—you may remember—I started upon in Paris. Press opinions upon my symphony—Laroche not excepted —are rather cold. They all consider I have nothing new to say, and am beginning to repeat myself. Can this really be the case? After finishing the quartet I will rest for a time, and only complete my ballet. I shall not embark upon anything new until I have decided upon an opera. I waver between two subjects, *Ephraim* and *Francesca*. I think the latter will carry the day."

[1] No. 3, Op. 30.

Ephraim was a libretto written by Constantine Shilovsky upon a love-tale of the court of Pharaoh, at the period of the Hebrew captivity.

Francesca da Rimini was a ready-made libretto by Zvantsiev, which had been suggested to Tchaikovsky by Laroche. It was based upon the fifth canto of Dante's *Inferno*.

Neither of these books satisfied the composer. After seeing *Carmen* he only cared for a similar subject: a libretto dealing with real men and women who stood in closer touch with modern life ; a drama which was at once simple and realistic.

The new Quartet No. 3 was played for the first time at a concert given by the violinist Grijimal, March 18th. Later on it was repeated at a chamber music evening of the Musical Society. On both occasions its success was decisive.

In May Tchaikovsky was out of health and was ordered by the doctors to take a course of waters at Vichy. He reached Lyons on June 27th (July 9th), where he met Modeste, and made the acquaintance of his brother's pupil, to whom he became much attached.

His first impressions of Vichy were far from favourable, but the local physician persuaded him to remain at least long enough for a "demi-cure," from which he derived great benefit. He then rejoined Modeste and young Konradi for a short time, and went to Bayreuth at the end of July, where a lodging had been secured for him by Karl Klindworth.

To M. Tchaikovsky.

"BAYREUTH, *August 2nd* (14*th*).

". . . I arrived here on July 31st (August 12th), the day before the performance. Klindworth met me. I found a number of well-known people here, and plunged straightway into the vortex of the festival, in which I whirl all day long like one possessed. I have also made the acquaintance of Liszt, who received me most amiably. I called on Wagner, who no longer sees anyone. Yesterday the performance of the *Rheingold* took place. From the scenic point of view it interested me greatly, and I was also much impressed by the truly marvellous staging of the work. Musically, it is inconceivable nonsense, in which here and there occur beautiful, and even captivating, moments. Among the people here who are known to you are Rubinstein—with whom I am living—Laroche and Cui.

"Bayreuth is a tiny little town in which, at the present moment, several thousand people are congregated. . . . I am not at all bored, although I cannot say I enjoy my visit here, so that all my thoughts and efforts are directed to getting away to Russia, *viâ* Vienna, as soon as possible. I hope to accomplish this by Thursday."

In the articles Tchaikovsky sent to the *Russky Viedomosti*, he describes his visit to Bayreuth in detail :—

"I reached Bayreuth on August 12th (new style), the day before the first performance of the first part of the Trilogy. The town was in a state of great excitement. Crowds of people, natives and strangers, gathered together literally from the ends of the earth, were rushing to the railway-station to see the arrival of the Emperor. I witnessed the spectacle from the window of a neighbouring house. First some brilliant uniforms passed by, then the musicians of the Wagner Theatre, in procession, with Hans Richter, the conductor, at their head ; next followed the interesting figure of the 'Abbé' Liszt, with the fine, characteristic head I have so often admired in pictures ; and, lastly, in a sumptuous carriage, the serene old man, Richard Wagner, with his aquiline nose and the delicately ironical smile which gives such a characteristic expression to the face of the creator of this cosmopolitan and artistic festival. A rousing 'Hurrah' resounded from thousands of throats as the Emperor's train entered the station. The old Emperor stepped into the carriage awaiting him, and drove to the palace. Wagner, who followed immediately in his wake, was greeted by the crowds with as much enthusiasm as the Emperor. What pride, what overflowing emotions must have filled at this moment the heart of that little man who, by his energetic will and great talent, has defied all obstacles to the final realisation of his artistic ideals and audacious views!

" I made a little excursion through the streets of the town. They swarmed with people of all nationalities, who looked very much preoccupied, and as if in search of something. The reason of this anxious search I discovered only too soon, as I myself had to share it. All these rest-less people, wandering through the town, were seeking to satisfy the pangs of hunger, which even the fulness of artistic enjoyment could not entirely assuage. The little town offers, it is true, sufficient shelter to strangers, but it is not able to feed all its guests. So it happened that, even on the very day of my arrival, I learnt what 'the struggle for existence' can mean. There are very few hotels in Bayreuth, and the greater part of the visitors find accom-modation in private houses. The tables d'hôte prepared in the inns are not sufficient to satisfy all the hungry people; one can only obtain a piece of bread, or a glass of beer, with immense difficulty, by dire struggle, or cunning strata-gem, or iron endurance. Even when a modest place at a table has been stormed, it is necessary to wait an eternity before the long-desired meal is served. Anarchy reigns at these meals; everyone is calling and shrieking, and the exhausted waiters pay no heed to the rightful claims of an individual. Only by the merest chance does one get a taste of any of the dishes. In the neighbourhood of the theatre is a restaurant which advertises a good dinner at two o'clock. But to get inside it and lay hold of anything in that throng of hungry creatures is a feat worthy of a hero.

" I have dwelt upon this matter at some length with the design of calling the attention of my readers to this promi-nent feature of the Bayreuth Melomania. As a matter of fact, throughout the whole duration of the festival, food forms the chief interest of the public; the artistic repre-sentations take a secondary place. Cutlets, baked potatoes, omelettes, are discussed much more eagerly than Wagner's music.

" I have already mentioned that the representatives of all

civilised nations were assembled in Bayreuth. In fact, even on the day of my arrival, I perceived in the crowd many leaders of the musical world in Europe and America. But the greatest of them, the most famous, were conspicuous by their absence. Verdi, Gounod, Thomas, Brahms, Anton Rubinstein, Raff, Joachim, Bülow had not come to Bayreuth. Among the noted Russian musicians present were: Nicholas Rubinstein, Cui, Laroche, Famitsin, Klindworth (who, as is well known, has made the pianoforte arrangement of the Wagner Trilogy), Frau Walzeck, the most famous professor of singing in Moscow, and others.

" The performance of the *Rheingold* took place on August 1st (13th), at 7 p.m. It lasted without a break two hours and a half. The other three parts, *Walküre*, *Siegfried*, and *Götterdämmerung*, will be given with an hour's interval, and will last from 4 p.m. to 10 p.m. In consequence of the indisposition of the singer Betz, *Siegfried* was postponed from Tuesday to Wednesday, so that the first cycle lasted fully five days. At three o'clock we take our way to the theatre, which stands on a little hill rather distant from the town. That is the most trying part of the day, even for those who have managed to fortify themselves with a good meal. The road lies uphill, with absolutely no shade, so that one is exposed to the scorching rays of the sun. While waiting for the performance to begin, the motley troop encamps on the grass near the theatre. Some sit over a glass of beer in the restaurant. Here acquaintances are made and renewed. From all sides one hears complaints of hunger and thirst, mingled with comments on present or past performances. At four o'clock, to the minute, the fanfare sounds, and the crowd streams into the theatre. Five minutes later all the seats are occupied. The fanfare sounds again, the buzz of conversation is stilled, the lights turned down, and darkness reigns in the auditorium. From depths—invisible to the audience—in which the orchestra is sunk float the strains of the beautiful overture; the curtain parts to either side, and the performance begins. Each act lasts an hour and a half; then comes an interval, but a very disagreeable one, for the sun is still far from setting, and it is difficult to find any place in the shade. The second interval, on the contrary, is the most beautiful part of the day. The sun is already near the horizon; in the air one feels the coolness of evening, the wooded hills around and the charming little town in the distance are lovely. Towards ten o'clock the performance comes to an end. . . ."

To M. Tchaikovsky.

"VIENNA, *August 8th (20th)*, 1876.

"Bayreuth has left me with disagreeable recollections, although my artistic ambition was flattered more than once. It appears I am by no means as unknown in Western Europe as I believed. The disagreeable recollections are raised by the uninterrupted bustle in which I was obliged to take part. It finally came to an end on Thursday. After the last notes of the *Gotterdämmerung*, I felt as though I had been let out of prison. The *Nibelungen* may be actually a magnificent work, but it is certain that there never was anything so endlessly and wearisomely spun out.

"From Bayreuth I went first to Nuremberg, where I spent a whole day and wrote the notice for the *Russky Viedomosti*. Nuremberg is charming! I arrived in Vienna to-day and leave to-morrow for Verbovka."

Laroche contributes the following account of Tchaikovsky's visit to the Bayreuth festival :—

"The effort of listening and gazing during the immensely long acts of the Wagner Trilogy (especially of *Rheingold* and the first part of *Gotterdammerung*, which both last without interval for two hours), the sitting in a close, dark amphitheatre in tropical heat, the sincere endeavour to understand the language and style of the book of the words—which is so clumsy and difficult in its composition that even to Germans themselves it is almost inaccessible —all produced in Tchaikovsky a feeling of great depression, from which he only recovered when it came to an end and he found himself at a comfortable supper with a glass of beer. . . ."

Such was the impression produced upon Tchaikovsky by the *Nibelungen.* He himself recorded the following observations upon Wagner's colossal work :—

" I brought away the impression that the Trilogy contains many passages of extraordinary beauty, especially symphonic beauty, which is remarkable, as Wagner has certainly no intention of writing an opera in the style of a symphony. I feel a respectful admiration for the immense talents of the composer and his wealth of technique, such as has never been heard before. And yet I have grave doubts as to the truth of Wagner's principles of opera. I will, however, continue the study of this music—the most complicated which has hitherto been composed.

" Yet if the ' Ring ' bores one in places, if much in it is at first incomprehensible and vague, if Wagner's harmonies are at times open to objection, as being too complicated and artificial, and his theories are false, even if the results of his immense work should eventually fall into oblivion, and the Bayreuth Theatre drop into an eternal slumber, yet the *Nibelungen Ring* is an event of the greatest importance to the world, an epoch-making work of art."

Morally and physically exhausted, pondering uninterruptedly on his own future, and imbued with the firm conviction that " things could not go on as they were," Tchaikovsky returned from foreign countries, travelling through Vienna to Verbovka.

There a hearty welcome from his relations awaited him, and all the idyllic enjoyments of the country. The happy family life of the Davidovs was the best thing to calm and comfort Tchaikovsky, but, at the same time, it strengthened a certain intention in which his morbid imagination discerned the one means of " salvation," but which actually became the starting-point of still greater troubles and worries. On August 19th (31st) he wrote to me from Verbovka :—

" I have now to pass through a critical moment in my life. By-and-by I will write to you about it more fully ;

meanwhile I must just tell you that I *have decided to get married.* This is irrevocable. . . ."

XIII

1876–1877

To Modeste Tchaikovsky.

" Moscow, *September* 10*th* (*22nd*), 1876.

" . . . Nearly two months have passed since we parted from each other, but they seem to me centuries. During this time I have thought much about you, and also about myself and my future. My reflections have resulted in the firm determination to marry some one or other."

To Modeste Tchaikovsky.

" Moscow, *September* 17*th* (*29th*).

" Time passes uneventfully. In this colourless existence, however, lies a certain charm. I can hardly express in words how sweet is this feeling of quiet. What comfort—I might almost say happiness—it is to return to my pleasant rooms and sit down with a book in my hand! At this moment I hate, probably not less than you do, that beautiful, unknown being who will force me to change my way of living. Do not be afraid, I shall not hurry in this matter; you may be sure I will approach it with great caution, and only after much deliberation."

To A. Tchaikovsky.

" *September* 20*th* (*October* 2*nd*).

" Toly, I long for you again. I am worried with the thought that while you were staying in Moscow I did not treat you kindly enough. If such a thought should come to you too, know (you know it already) that my lack of tenderness by no means implies a lack of love and attachment. I was only vexed with myself, and vexed assuredly, because I deceived you when I said I had arrived at an

important turning-point in my existence. That is not
true ; I have not arrived at it, but I think of it and wait
for *something* to spur me on to action.   In the meantime,
however, the quiet evening hours in my dear little home,
the rest and solitude—I must confess to this—have great
charms for me.   I shudder when I think I must give it all
up.   And yet it will come to pass. . . ."

To Rimsky-Korsakov.

" Moscow, *September 29th (October 11th),* 1876.

" DEAR FRIEND,—As soon as I had read your letter
I went to Jurgenson and asked him about the quartet.   I
must tell you something which clearly explains Jurgenson's
delay.   When you sent the parts of your quartet to
Rubinstein last year, it was played through by our Quartet
Society, Jurgenson being present.   Now your quartet by
no means pleased these gentlemen, and they expressed
some surprise that Jurgenson should dream of publishing
a work which appeared destined to fall into oblivion.   This
may have cooled the ardour of our publisher.   In the
approaching series of Chamber Concerts the quartet will
probably be performed, and I fancy the members of the
Society will retract their opinion when they get to know
your work better.   I am convinced of this, because I know
how your quartet improves on acquaintance.   The first
movement is simply delicious, and ideal as to form.   It
might serve as a pattern of purity of style.   The andante is
a little dry, but just on that account very characteristic—
as reminiscent of the days of powder and patches.   The
scherzo is very lively, piquant, and must sound well.   As
to the finale, I freely confess that it in no wise pleases me,
although I acknowledge that it may do so when I hear it,
and then I may find the obtrusive rhythm of the chief theme
less frightfully unbearable.   I consider you are at present
in a transition period ; in a state of fermentation ; and no
one knows what you are capable of doing.   With your
talents and your *character* you may achieve immense
results.   As I have said, the first movement is a pattern of
virginal purity of style.   It has something of Mozart's
beauty and unaffectedness.

"You ask whether I have really written a third quartet. Yes, it is so. I produced it last winter, after my return from abroad. It contains an "Andante funèbre," which has had so great a success that the quartet was played three times in public in the course of a fortnight."

To A. Davidov.

"*October 6th (18th).*

". . . Do not worry yourself about my marriage, my angel. The event is not yet imminent, and will certainly not come off before next year. In the course of next month I shall begin to look around and prepare myself a little for matrimony, which for various reasons I consider necessary."

To Modeste Tchaikovsky.

"*October 14th (26th).*

"I have only just finished the composition of a new work, the symphonic fantasia, *Francesca da Rimini*. I have worked at it *con amore*, and believe my love has been successful. With regard to the *Whirlwind*, perhaps it might correspond better to Doré's picture; it has not turned out quite what I wanted. However, an accurate estimate of the work is impossible, so long as it is neither orchestrated nor played."

To E. Napravnik.

"*October 18th (30th).*

"I have just read in a Petersburg paper that you intend to give the dances from my opera *Vakoula* at one of the forthcoming symphony concerts. Would it be possible to perform my new symphonic poem, *Francesca da Rimini*, instead? I am actually working at the orchestration of this work, and could have the score ready in two or three weeks. It would never have occurred to me to trouble you with my new work, had I not seen that my name was already included in your programmes. As you have been so kind as to grant me a little room at your concerts, I hope you will agree to my present proposal. I must frankly confess that I am somewhat troubled about the fate of my opera.   So far, I have not even heard whether the choral rehearsals have begun.   Perhaps you will be so kind as to send me word about the performance of *Vakoula.*"

To A. Davidov.

"*November 8th (20th).*"

" Probably you were not quite well, my little dove,[1] when you wrote to me, for a note of real melancholy pervaded your letter.   I recognised in it a nature closely akin to my own.   I know the feeling only too well.   In my life, too, there are days, hours, weeks, aye, and months, in which everything looks black, when I am tormented by the thought that I am forsaken, that no one cares for me. Indeed, my life is of little worth to anyone.   Were I to vanish from the face of the earth to-day, it would be no great loss to Russian music, and would certainly cause no one great unhappiness.   In short, I live a selfish bachelor's life.   I work for myself alone, and care only for myself. This is certainly very comfortable, although dull, narrow, and lifeless.   But that *you*, who are indispensable to so many whose happiness you make, that *you* can give way to depression, is more than I can believe.   How can you doubt for a moment the love and esteem of those who surround you ?   How could it be possible not to love you ? No, there is no one in the world more dearly loved than you are.   As for me, it would be absurd to speak of my love for you.   If I care for anyone, it is for you, for your family, for my brothers and our old Dad.   I love you all, not because you are my relations, but because you are the best people in the world. . . ."

At the end of October Tchaikovsky came to Petersburg to be present at the first performance of his *Vakoula the Smith.*   This time the composer had not been disenchanted by his work ; on the contrary, every rehearsal gave him more and more pleasure, and the hope of success increased.   The appreciation shown him by the singers

---

[1] There is no real English equivalent for the term "*goloubouska.*"

engaged in the work; the enthusiastic verdict of the connoisseurs who had become acquainted with the pianoforte
arrangement, and of those who were able to attend the
rehearsals; finally, the lavish expenditure with which the
Direction was mounting the piece—everything encouraged
Tchaikovsky to feel assured of great success.

Since the first production of *The Oprichnik* the popularity of Tchaikovsky's name had considerably increased.
Not only musicians, and those who attended the symphony
concerts, but also the public—in the widest sense of the
word—expected something quite out of the common.
Long before November 24th (December 6th), the day
fixed for the first performance of *Vakoula*, the tickets were
already sold out.

The production had been very carefully prepared; the
principals endeavoured to do their best. The overture
was well received, as also the first scene. Then the
enthusiasm of the audience cooled, and the succeeding
numbers—with the exception of the " Gopak "[1]—obtained
but scant applause. The opera failed to please; people
had come to be amused, expecting something brilliant,
humorous, and lively, in the style of *The Barber of Seville*,
or *Domino Noir*, consequently they were disappointed.
Nevertheless, the composer was recalled several times,
although not without some opposition on the part of a
small, but energetic, party.

Tchaikovsky himself, in a letter to Taneiev, writes as
follows :—

" *Vakoula* was a brilliant failure. The first two acts left
the audience cold. During the scene between the Golova
and the Dyak there was some laughter, but no applause.
After the third and fourth acts I had several calls, but also
a few hisses from a section of the public. The second
performance was somewhat better, but one cannot say that
the opera pleased, or is likely to live through six performances.

[1] A characteristic Russian dance.

" It is worth notice that at the dress rehearsal even Cui prophesied a brilliant success for the work. This made the blow all the harder and more bitter to bear. I must freely confess that I am much discouraged. I have nothing to complain of with regard to the mounting of the work. Everything, to the smallest details, had been well studied and prepared . . . in short, I alone am in fault. The opera is too full of unnecessary incidents and details, too heavily orchestrated, and not sufficiently vocal. Now I understand your cool attitude when I played it over to you at Rubinstein's. The style of *Vakoula* is not good opera style—it lacks movement and breadth."

The opinions of the Press on the new work were very similar. No one " praised it to the skies," but no one damned it. All expressed more or less esteem for the composer, but none were quite contented with his work.

To S. I. Taneiev.

" Moscow, *December 2nd* (14*th*), 1876.

". . . I have just heard that my *Romeo* was hissed in Vienna. Do not say anything about it, or Pasdeloup may take fright; I hear he thinks of doing it.

" Yes, indeed, dear friend, there are trying times in life! " *Francesca* has long been finished, and will now be copied out."

Hans Richter, who conducted the Vienna performance of *Romeo*, declared that the comparative failure of the work did not amount to a fiasco. Certainly at the concert itself a few hisses were heard, and Hanslick wrote an abusive criticism of it in the *Neue Freie Presse*, but at the same time much interest, even enthusiasm, was shown for the new Russian work.

Hardly had Tchaikovsky swallowed the bitter Viennese pill, than he received equally disagreeable news from Taneiev in Paris.

Taneiev to Tchaikovsky.

"PARIS, *November 28th (December 10th)*, 1876.

"I have just come from Pasdeloup's concert, where your *Romeo* overture was shamefully bungled. The tempi were all too fast, so that one could scarcely distinguish the three

notes 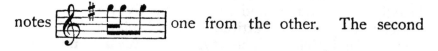 one from the other. The second

subject was played by the wind as if they had only to support the harmony, and did not realise they had the subject.

"The following was especially bad :—

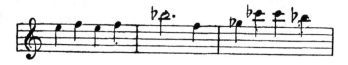

not a single crescendo, not a single diminuendo. At the repetition of the accessory theme in D major

the bassoons played their fifth in the bass so energetically that they drowned the other parts. There were no absolutely false notes, but the piece produced a poor effect. Pasdeloup obviously understood nothing about it, and does not know how such a piece should be played. No wonder the Overture did not please the public and was but coolly received. It was as painful to me as if I had been taking part in the concert myself. Pasdeloup alone, however, was to blame, not the public. The Overture is by no means incomprehensible ; it only needs to be well interpreted.

"I played your concerto to Saint-Saëns ; everyone was much pleased with it. All musicians here are greatly interested in your compositions."

To S. Taneiev.

"MOSCOW, *December 5th* (*17th*), 1876.

"DEAR SERGIUS,—I have just received your letter. Good luck and bad always come together; it is proverbial, and I am not surprised to hear of the non-success of my *Francesca*, as just now all my compositions are failures. But your letter suggested an idea to me. Last year Saint-Saëns advised me to give a concert of my own compositions in Paris. He said such a concert would be best given with Colonne's orchestra at the Châtelet, and would not cost very much."

S. Taneiev to Tchaikovsky.

"PARIS, *December 16th* (*28th*), 1876.

"Saint-Saëns advises you more strongly than ever to give a concert, in order to produce your *Romeo and Juliet*. . . . '*Cela l'a posé, cette overture*,' was his remark. You must give your concert in the Salle Herz, with Colonne's orchestra. All expenses, including two rehearsals, will come to 1,500 francs. Two rehearsals will not be sufficient; we should need at least three. Even then, 2,000 francs would be the maximum expenditure. The orchestra are paid five francs for each rehearsal, and ten for the concert. The most favourable time would be February or March."

To S. Taneiev.

"MOSCOW, *January 29th* (*February 10th*), 1877.

"DEAR SERGIUS,—My concert will not come off. In spite of gigantic efforts on my part, I cannot raise the necessary funds.

"I am in despair.

"I can write no more to-day. Forgive me for the trouble I have given you over my unlucky plans. Thank you for your letter."

In spite of the bitterness left by the comparative failure of *Vakoula*, and the many other blows which his artistic ambitions had to suffer, Tchaikovsky, after his return to

o

Moscow, did not lose his self-confidence, nor let his energy flag for a moment. On the contrary, although grieved at the fate of his " favourite offspring, *Vakoula,*" and at his unlucky *début* as a composer in Vienna and Paris, although suffering from a form of dyspepsia, he was not only interested in the propaganda of his works abroad, but composed his *Variations on a Rococo Theme* for violoncello, and corresponded with Stassov about an operatic libretto. The choice of the subject—*Othello*—emanated from Tchaikovsky himself. When Stassov tried to persuade him that this subject was not suitable to his temperament, he refused to listen to arguments, and would only consider this particular play. About the middle of September Stassov sent him the rough sketch which he began to study zealously. But it went no further. On January 30th Stassov wrote to him : " Do as you will, but I have not finished *Othello* yet. Hang me if you please—but it is not my fault." Tchaikovsky himself had also begun to feel less eager, for he remarks in a letter to Stassov that he is not to trouble about a new subject.

At this time the composer was in such good health, and so active-minded, that he gave up his original intention of spending Christmas at Kamenka, and stayed on in Moscow.

In December Tchaikovsky wrote to his sister, A. Davidov :—

" A short time ago Count Leo Tolstoi was here. He called upon me, and I am proud to have awakened his interest. On my part, I am full of enthusiasm for his ideal personality."

For a long time past—since the first appearance of Tolstoi's works—Tchaikovsky had been one of his most ardent admirers, and this admiration had gradually become a veritable cult for the name of Tolstoi. It was characteristic of the composer that everything he cared for, but did not actually know face to face, assumed abnormal proportions in his imagination. The author of *Peace and War* seemed to him, in his own words, "not so much an ordinary mortal as a demi-god." At that time the personality and private life—even the portrait—of Tolstoi were almost unknown to the great public, and this was a further reason why Tchaikovsky pictured him as a sage and a magician. And lo, this Olympian being, this unfathomable man, descended from his cloud-capped heights and held out his hand to Tchaikovsky.

Ten years later we find in Tchaikovsky's "diary" the following record of this meeting :—

"When first I met Tolstoi I was possessed by terror and felt uneasy in his presence. It seemed that this great searcher of human hearts must be able to read at a glance the inmost secrets of my own. I was convinced that not the smallest evil or weakness could escape his eye ; therefore it would avail nothing to show him only my best side. If he be generous (and that is a matter of course), I reflected, he will probe the diseased area as kindly and delicately as a surgeon who knows the tender spots and avoids irritating them. If he is not so compassionate, he will lay his finger on the wound without more ado. In either case the prospect alarmed me. In reality nothing of the sort took place. The great analyst of human nature proved in his intercourse with his fellow-men to be a simple, sincere, whole-hearted being, who made no display of that omniscience I so dreaded. Evidently he did not regard me as a subject for dissection, but simply wanted to chat about music, in which at that time he was greatly interested. Among other things, he seemed to enjoy depreciating Beethoven, and even directly denying his genius. This is an unworthy trait in a great man. The desire to lower a genius to the level of one's own *misunderstanding* of him is generally a characteristic of narrow-minded people."

Tolstoi not only wished to talk about music in general, but also to express his interest in Tchaikovsky's own compositions. The latter was so much flattered that he asked

Nicholas Rubinstein to arrange a musical evening at the Conservatoire in honour of the great writer. On this occasion the programme included the Andante from Tchaikovsky's string quartet in D major, during the performance of which Tolstoi burst into tears.

"Never in the whole course of my life," wrote the composer in his diary, "did I feel so flattered, never so proud of my creative power, as when Leo Tolstoi, sitting by my side, listened to my Andante while the tears streamed down his face."

Shortly after this memorable evening Tolstoi left Moscow, and wrote the following letter to Tchaikovsky from his country estate Yasnaya Polyana :—

"DEAR PETER ILICH,—I am sending you the songs, having looked them through once more. In your hands they will become wonderful gems; but, for God's sake, treat them in the Mozarto-Haydn style, and not after the Beethoven-Schumann-Berlioz school, which strives only for the sensational. How much more I had to tell you! But there was no time, because I was simply enjoying myself. My visit to Moscow will always remain a most pleasant memory. I have never received a more precious reward for all my literary labours than on that last evening. How charming is (Nicholas) Rubinstein! Thank him for me once more. Aye, and all the other priests of the highest of all arts, who made so pure and profound an impression upon me! I can never forget all that was done for my benefit in that round hall. To which of them shall I send my works? That is to say, who does not possess them?

"I have not looked at your things yet. As soon as I have done so, I shall write you my opinion—whether you want it or not—because I admire your talent. Good-bye, with a friendly hand-shake.

"Yours,

"L. TOLSTOI."

To this Tchaikovsky replied :—

"MOSCOW, *December 24th*, 1876 (*January 5th*, 1877).

"HONOURED COUNT,—Accept my sincere thanks for the songs. I must tell you frankly that they have been taken down by an unskilful hand and, in consequence, nearly all their original beauty is lost. The chief mistake is that they have been forced artificially into a regular rhythm. Only the Russian choral-dances have a regularly accentuated measure; the legends (Bylini) have nothing in common with the dances. Besides, most of these songs have been written down in the lively key of D major, and this is quite out of keeping with the tonality of the genuine Russian folksongs, which are always in some indefinite key, such as can only be compared with the old Church modes. Therefore the songs you have sent are unsuitable for systematic treatment. I could not use them for an album of folksongs, because for this purpose the tunes must be taken down exactly as the people sing them. This is a difficult task, demanding the most delicate musical perception, as well as a great knowledge of musical history. With the exception of Balakirev—and to a certain extent Prokounin—I do not know anyone who really understands this work. But your songs can be used as symphonic material—and excellent material too— of which I shall certainly avail myself at some future time. I am glad you keep a pleasant recollection of your evening at the Conservatoire. Our quartet played as they have never done before. From which you must infer that one pair of ears, if they belong to such a great artist as yourself, has more incentive power with musicians than a hundred ordinary pairs. You are one of those authors of whom it may be said that their personality is as much beloved as their works. It was evident that, well as they generally play, our artists exerted themselves to the utmost for one they honoured so greatly. What I feel I must express: I cannot tell you how proud and happy it made me that my music could so touch you and carry you away.

"Except Fitzenhagen, who cannot read Russian, your books are known to all the other members of the quartet.

But I am sure they would be grateful if you gave them each one volume of your works. For myself, I am going to ask you to give me *The Cossacks;* if not immediately, then later on, when next you come to Moscow—an event to which I look forward with impatience. If you send your portrait to Rubinstein, do not forget me."

With this letter personal intercourse between Tchaikovsky and Count Tolstoi came to an end. It is remarkable that this was not against the composer's wishes, even if he did nothing actually to cause the rupture. The attentive reader will not fail to have gathered from the last words quoted from his diary that his acquaintance with Tolstoi had been something of a disappointment. It vexed him that "the lord of his intellect" should care to talk of "commonplace subjects unworthy of a great man." It hurt him to see all the little faults and failings of this divinity brought out by closer proximity. He feared to lose faith in him, and consequently to spoil his enjoyment of his works. This delight was at one time somewhat disturbed by his hyper-sensitiveness. In a letter to his brother, Tchaikovsky criticises *Anna Karenina,* which had then just begun to make its appearance in the *Russky Vestnik.*

"After your departure," he writes, "I read *Anna Karenina* once more. Are you not ashamed to extol this revolting and commonplace stuff, which aspires to be psychologically profound? The devil take your psychological truth when it leaves nothing but an endless waste behind it."

Afterwards, having read the whole novel, Tchaikovsky repented his judgment, and acknowledged it to be one of Tolstoi's finest creations.

In the presence of Tolstoi, Tchaikovsky felt ill at ease, in spite of the writer's kind and simple attitude towards his fellow-men. From a fear of wounding or displeasing him in any way, and also in consequence of his efforts not to betray his admiration and delight, the musician never quite knew how to behave to Tolstoi, and was always conscious of being somewhat unnatural—of playing a part. This consciousness was intolerable to Tchaikovsky, consequently he avoided future intercourse with the great man.

Greatly as Tchaikovsky admired Tolstoi the writer, he was never in sympathy with Tolstoi the philosopher. In his diary for 1886, writing of *What I Believe*, he says :—

"When we read the autobiographies or memoirs of great men, we frequently find that their thoughts and impressions—and more especially their artistic sentiments—are such as we ourselves have experienced and can therefore fully understand. There is only one who is incomprehensible, who stands alone and aloof in his greatness—Leo Tolstoi. Yet often I feel angry with him : I almost hate him. Why, I ask myself, should this man, who more than all his predecessors has power to depict the human soul with such wonderful harmony, who can fathom our poor intellect and follow the most secret and tortuous windings of our moral nature—why must he needs appear as a preacher, and set up to be our teacher and guardian? Hitherto he has succeeded in making a profound impression by the recital of simple, everyday events. We might read between the lines his noble love of mankind, his compassion for our helplessness, our mortality and pettiness. How often have I wept over his words without knowing why! . . . Perhaps because for a moment I was brought into contact —through his medium—with the Ideal, with absolute happiness, and with humanity. Now he appears as a commentator of texts, who claims a monopoly in the solution of all questions of faith and ethics. But through all his recent writings blows a chilling wind. We feel a tremor of fear at the consciousness that he, too, is a mere man ; a creature as much puffed up as ourselves about 'The End and Aim of Life,' 'The Destiny of Man,' 'God,' and 'Religion' ; and as madly presumptuous, as ineffectual as some ephemera born on a summer's day to perish at eventide. Once Tolstoi was a Demigod. Now he is only a Priest. . . . Tolstoi says that formerly, knowing nothing, he was mad enough to aspire to teach men out of his ignorance. He regrets this. Yet here he is beginning to teach us again. Then we must conclude he is no longer ignorant. Whence this self-confidence? Is it not foolish presumption? The true sage knows only that he knows nothing."

It is said that in nature peace often precedes a violent storm. This is twice observable in the life of Tchaikovsky. Let us look back to the period of his Government service, to the strenuous industry and zeal he displayed in his official duties in 1862—just before he took up the musical profession. Never was he more contented with his lot, or calmer in mind, than a few months before he entered the Conservatoire. It was the same at the present juncture. Shortly before that rash act, which cut him off for ever from Moscow, which changed all his habits and social relations, and was destined to be the beginning of a new life; just at the moment, in fact, when we might look for some dissatisfaction with fate as a reason for this desperate resolve, Tchaikovsky was by no means out of spirits. On the contrary, in January and February 1877, he gave the impression of a man whose mind was at rest, who had no desires, and displayed more purpose and cheerfulness than before. This mood is very evident in a playful letter dated January 2nd (14th), 1877 :—

To Modeste Tchaikovsky.

"HONOURED MR. MODESTE ILICH,—I do not know if you still remember me. I am your brother and a professor at the Moscow Conservatoire. I have also composed a few things : operas, symphonies, overtures, etc. Once upon a time you honoured me by your personal acquaintance. Last year we were abroad together and spent a time which I shall never forget. You used frequently to write me long and interesting letters.   Now all this seems like a beautiful dream. . . .

"Just before the holidays, my dear brotherkin, I made the acquaintance of Count Tolstoi.   This pleased me very much.   I have also received a kind and precious letter from his Grace.   When he heard the 'Andante' from my first quartet he shed tears of emotion.   I am very proud of this, my dear brotherkin, and you really should not forget me, my dear brotherkin, because I have now become a great swell.   Farewell, my brotherkin.

"Your brother,

"PETER."

On February 20th (March 4th) the first performance of Tchaikovsky's ballet, *The Swan Lake*, took place.   The composer was not to be blamed for the very moderate success of this work.   The scenery and costumes were poor, while the orchestra was conducted by a semi-amateur, who had never before been confronted with so complicated a score.

To his sister, A. Davidov.

"February 22nd (March 6th).

"I have lately found courage to appear as a conductor. I was very unskilful and nervous, but still I managed to conduct, with considerable success, my 'Russo-Serbian March' in the Opera House.   Henceforward I shall take every opportunity of conducting, for if my plan of a concert tour abroad comes off, I shall have to be my own conductor."

On February 25th (March 9th) the symphonic fantasia *Francesca da Rimini* was performed for the first time at the tenth symphony concert in Moscow.   It had a splendid reception, and was twice repeated during the month of March.   In his notice of the concert Kashkin praises not only the music itself, but its inspired interpretation by Nicholas Rubinstein.

In the course of this season Tchaikovsky began his Fourth Symphony. Probably the real reason why he lost his interest in the libretto of *Othello* is to be found in his entire devotion to this work.

In March and April he began to suffer again from mental depression. This is evident from many of his letters written at this time.

To I. A. Klimenko.

"*May 8th (20th).*

"I am very much changed—especially mentally—since we last met. There is no trace of gaiety and love of fun left in me. Life is terribly empty, wearisome and trivial. I am seriously considering matrimony as a lasting tie. The one thing that remains unaltered is my love of composing. If things were only different, if I were not condemned to run against obstacles at every step—my work at the Conservatoire, for instance, which restricts me more each year—I might accomplish something of value. But alas, I am chained to the Conservatoire!"

In the early spring of 1877 Modeste Tchaikovsky sent his brother a libretto based upon Nodier's novel, *Ines de Las-Sierras*. The musician was not attracted by it; he had already another plan in view. In May he wrote to his brother :—

"Recently I was at Madame Lavrovsky's.[1] The conversation fell upon opera libretti. X. talked a lot of rubbish, and made the most appalling suggestions. Madame Lavrovsky said nothing and only laughed. Suddenly, however, she remarked : 'What about *Eugene Oniegin ?*' The idea struck me as curious, and I made no reply. Afterwards, while dining alone at a restaurant, her words came back to me, and, on consideration, the idea did not seem at all ridiculous. I soon made up my mind, and set off at once in search of Poushkin's works. I had some trouble in finding them. I was enchanted when I read the

[1] E. A Lavrovsky, a famous singer and a teacher at the Conservatoire.

work.   I spent a sleepless night; the result—a sketch of a
delicious opera based upon Poushkin's text.   The next day
I went to Shilovsky, who is now working post-haste at my
sketch.

"You have no notion how crazy I am upon this subject.
How delightful to avoid the commonplace Pharaohs,
Ethiopian princesses, poisoned cups, and all the rest of
these dolls' tales! *Eugene Oniegin* is full of poetry.   I
am not blind to its defects.   I know well enough the work
gives little scope for treatment, and will be deficient in
stage effects; but the wealth of poetry, the human quality
and simplicity of the subject, joined to Poushkin's inspired
verses, will compensate for what it lacks in other respects."

To N. F. von Meck.

"*May 27th (June 8th*).

". . . The plan of my symphony is complete.   I shall
begin upon the orchestration at the end of the summer."

To Modeste Tchaikovsky.

"GLIEBOVO, *June 6th* (18*th*).

"At first I was annoyed by your criticism of Oniegin,
but it did not last long.   Let it lack scenic effect, let it
be wanting in action!   I am in love with the image of
Tatiana, I am under the spell of Poushkin's verse, and
I am drawn to compose the music as it were by some
irresistible attraction.   I am lost in the composition of the
opera."

PART IV

I

1877–1878

SOME time during the seventies, a violinist named Joseph Kotek entered Tchaikovsky's theory class at the Conservatoire.

He was a pleasant-looking young man, good-hearted, enthusiastic, and a gifted virtuoso. His sympathetic personality and talented work attracted Tchaikovsky's notice, and Kotek became a special favourite with him. Thus a friendship developed between master and pupil which was not merely confined to the class-room of the Conservatoire.

Kotek was poor, and, on leaving the Conservatoire, was obliged to earn his living by teaching, before he began to tour abroad.

At that time there lived in Moscow the widow of a well-known railway engineer, Nadejda Filaretovna von Meck. This lady asked Nicholas Rubinstein to recommend her a young violinist who could play with her at her house.

Rubinstein recommended Kotek. No young musician could have desired a better post. Nadejda von Meck, with her somewhat numerous family, lived part of the year in Moscow and the rest abroad, or upon her beautiful estate in the south-west of Russia. Kotek, therefore, besides a good salary, enjoyed a chance of seeing something of the world, and had also leisure to perfect himself on his instrument.

Kotek soon discovered that Nadejda von Meck shared his own admiration for Tchaikovsky's genius. An amateur of music in general, she was particularly interested in Tchaikovsky's works, a predilection which was destined to have considerable influence upon the composer's future career. Nadejda von Meck was not only interested in the composer, but also in the man. She endeavoured to learn something of his private life and character, and cross-questioned everyone who had come in contact with him. Consequently her acquaintance with Kotek was doubly agreeable, because he could tell her a great deal about the composer who had given her such keen artistic enjoyment.

From Kotek she learnt to know Tchaikovsky in his daily life, and her affection for him continually increased. Naturally she found out about his pecuniary needs and his longing for freedom, and in this way she formed a wish to take some active part in his private life, and to make it her first duty to allay his material anxieties.

Through Kotek she commissioned the composer, at a high fee, to arrange several of his own works for violin and piano. Gradually, through the medium of the young violinist, constant intercourse was established between the patroness and the composer. On his side Tchaikovsky, who liked whatever was original and unconventional, took the liveliest interest in all Kotek detailed to him about "the eccentricities" of Nadejda von Meck. Flattered and touched by the knowledge that he was a household name in the family of this generous admirer, Tchaikovsky sent her messages of grateful thanks by Kotek. Nadejda von Meck, elated that her favourite composer did not disdain to execute her commissions, returned similar expressions of gratitude and sympathy.

This was the commencement of the unusual relations between Tchaikovsky and Nadejda von Meck.

This friendship was of great importance in Tchaikovsky's life, for it completely changed its material conditions and consequently influenced his creative activity; moreover, it was so poetical, so out of the common, so different from anything that takes place in everyday society, that, in order to understand it, we must make closer acquaintance with the character of this new friend and benefactress.

Nadejda Filaretovna von Meck was born January 29th (February 10th), 1831, in the village of Znamensk (in the Government of Smolensk).[1] Although her parents were not rich, yet she enjoyed the advantage of an excellent home education. Her father was an enthusiastic music-lover, and his taste descended to his daughter. She would listen to him playing the violin for hours together; but as he grew older the parts were reversed, and Nadejda and her sister would play pianoforte duets to their father. In this way she acquired an extensive knowledge of musical literature.

No information is forthcoming as regards her general education. But from her voluminous correspondence with Tchaikovsky, his brother Modeste derives the impression that she was a proud and energetic woman, of strong convictions, with the mental balance and business capacity of a man, and well able to struggle with adversity; a woman, moreover, who despised all that was petty, commonplace, and conventional, but irreproachable in all her aspirations and in her sense of duty; absolutely free from sentimentality in her relations with others, yet capable of deep feeling, and of being completely carried away by what was lofty and beautiful.

In 1848 Nadejda Filaretovna married K. von Meck, an engineer employed upon the Moscow-Warsaw line, and with her marriage began a hard time in her life. As a

[1] Her parents' name was Frolovsky.

devoted wife and mother, Frau von Meck had a great deal
to endure, from which, however, she emerged triumphant
in the end.

" I have not always been rich," she says in one of
her letters to Tchaikovsky ; " the greater part of my life
I was poor, very poor indeed.   My husband was an
engineer in the Government service, with a salary of
1500 roubles a year (£150), which was all we had to live
upon, with five children and my husband's family on our
hands.   Not a brilliant prospect, as you see !   I was nurse,
governess, and sewing-maid to my children, and valet to
my husband ; the housekeeping was entirely in my hands;
naturally there was plenty of work, but I did not mind
that.   It was another matter which made life unbearable.
Do you know, Peter Ilich, what it is to be in the Government service ?   Do you know how, in that case, a man
must forget he is a reasoning being, possessed of will-
power and honourable instincts, and must become a
puppet, an automaton ?   It was my husband's position
which I found so intolerable that finally I implored him to
send in his resignation.   To his remark that if he did so
we should starve, I replied that we could work, and that
we should not die of hunger.   When at last he yielded to
my desire, we were reduced to living upon twenty kopecks
a day (5d.) for everything.   It was hard, but I never
regretted for a moment what had been done."

Thanks to this energetic step, taken at the entreaty of
his wife, Von Meck became engaged in private railway
enterprises, and gradually amassed a fortune and put by
some millions of roubles.

In 1876 Nadejda was left a widow.   Of eleven children,
only seven lived with her.   The others were grown up, and
had gone out into the world.   She managed her complicated affairs herself, with the assistance of her brother
and her eldest son.   But her chief occupation was the
education of her younger children.

After her husband's death, Nadejda von Meck gave up

going into society ; she paid no more visits, and remained, in the literal sense of the word, "invisible" to all but the members of her domestic circle.[1]

Nadejda von Meck was a great lover of nature, and travelled constantly. She also read much, and was passionately fond of music, especially of Tchaikovsky's works.

The peculiar characteristic of the close and touching friendship between Nadejda von Meck and Tchaikovsky was the fact that they never saw each other except in a crowd—an accidental glimpse at a concert or theatre. When they accidentally came face to face they passed as total strangers. To the end of their days they never exchanged a word, scarcely even a casual greeting. Their whole intercourse was confined to a brisk correspondence. Their letters, which have been preserved intact, and serve as the chief material for this part of my book, are so interesting, and throw such a clear light on the unique relations between this man and woman, that the publication of the entire correspondence on both sides would be of profound interest.

But the time has not yet come for such an undertaking. I may only use this valuable material (says Modeste Tchaikovsky) in so far as it forwards the chief aim of this book—to tell the story of Tchaikovsky's life. I may only write of Nadejda von Meck as my brother's "best friend" and benefactress, without intruding upon her intimate life which she has described in her frank, veracious, and lengthy letters.

Shortly after she had sent Tchaikovsky a commission, through Kotek, for a violin and pianoforte arrangement, he received his first letter from Nadejda von Meck.

---

[1] She carried her seclusion to such lengths that Tchaikovsky's sister and brother-in-law, Alexandra and Lèo Davidov, never saw Nadejda von Meck, although their daughter married one of her sons. Their friendly intercourse was carried on entirely by correspondence. Nicholas Rubinstein was almost the only visitor from the outside world whom she cared to receive.

N. F. von Meck to Tchaikovsky.

"*December* 18*th* (30*th*), 1876.

"HONOURED SIR,—Allow me to express my sincere thanks for the prompt execution of my commission. I deem it superfluous to tell you of the enthusiasm I feel for your music, because you are doubtless accustomed to receive homage of a very different kind to any which could be offered you by so insignificant a person, musically speaking, as myself. It might, therefore, seem ridiculous to you ; and my admiration is something so precious that I do not care to have it laughed at. Therefore I will only say one thing, which I beg you to accept as the literal truth—that your music makes life easier and pleasanter to live."

From Tchaikovsky to N. F. von Meck.

"*December* 19*th* (31*st*), 1876.

"HONOURED MADAM,—I thank you most cordially for the kind and flattering things you have written to me. On my part, I can assure you that, amid all his failures and difficulties, it is a great comfort to a musician to know that there exists a handful of people—of whom you are one— who are genuine and passionate lovers of music."

Two months later he received another commission, and a longer letter, which paved the way to intimate friendship and lasting influence.

N. F. von Meck to Tchaikovsky.

"Moscow, *February* 15*th* (27*th*), 1877.

"DEAR SIR—PETER ILICH,—I do not know how to express my thanks for your kind indulgence for my impatience. Were it not for the real sympathy I feel for you, I should be afraid you might want to get rid of me ; but I value your kindness too greatly for this to happen.

"I should like to tell you a great deal about my fantastic feelings towards you, but I am afraid of taking up your leisure, of which you have so little to spare. I will only say

P

that this feeling—abstract as it may be—is one of the best and loftiest emotions ever yet experienced by any human being. Therefore you may call me eccentric, or mad, if you please; but you must not laugh at me. All this would be ridiculous, if it were not so sincere and serious. "Your devoted and admiring

"N. F. VON MECK."

From Tchaikovsky to N. F. von Meck.

"*February* 16*th* (28*th*), 1877.

"DEAR MADAM—NADEJDA FILARETOVNA,—Accept my hearty thanks for the too lavish fee with which you have repaid such a light task. I am sorry you did not tell me all that was in your heart. I can assure you it would have been very pleasant and interesting, for I, too, warmly reciprocate your sympathy. This is no empty phrase. Perhaps I know you better than you imagine.

"If some day you will take the trouble to write me all you want to say, I shall be most grateful. In any case I thank you from my heart for your expressions of appreciation, which I value very highly."

N. F. Meck to Tchaikovsky.

"MOSCOW, *March* 7*th* (19*th*), 1877.

"DEAR SIR—PETER ILICH,—Your kind answer to my letter proved a greater joy than I have experienced for a long while, but—you know human nature: the more we have of a good thing, the more we want. Although I promised not to be a nuisance, I already doubt my own powers of refraining, because I am going to ask you a favour which may seem to you very strange; but anyone who lives the life of an anchorite—as I do—must naturally end by regarding all that relates to society and the conventionalities of life as empty and meaningless terms. I do not know how you look upon these matters, but—judging from our short acquaintance—I do not think you will be disposed to criticise me severely; if I am wrong, however, I want you to say so frankly, without circumlocution, and to refuse my request, which is this: give me one of your photographs. I have already two, but I should like one from you personally; I want to read in your face the inspiration, the emotions, under the influence of which you write the music which carries us away to that world of ideal feelings, aspirations and desires which cannot be satisfied in life. How much joy, but how much pain is there in this music! Nor would we consent to give up this suffering, for in it we find our highest capacities; our happiness, our hopes, which life denies us. *The Tempest* was the first work of yours I ever heard. I cannot tell you the impression it made upon me! For several days I was half out of my mind. I must tell you that I cannot separate the man from the musician, and, as the high priest of so lofty an art, I expect to find in him, more than in ordinary men, the qualities I most reverence. Therefore after my first impression of *The Tempest* I was seized with the desire to know something of the man who created it. I began to make inquiries about you, took every opportunity of hearing what was said of you, stored up every remark, every fragment of criticism, and I must confess that just those things for which others blamed you were charms in my eyes—everyone to his taste! Only a few days ago—in casual conversation—I heard one of your opinions, which delighted me, and was so entirely in accordance with my own that I felt suddenly drawn to you by more intimate and friendly ties. It is not intercourse that draws people together, so much as affinities of opinion, sentiment, and sympathy, so that one person may be closely united to another, although in some respects they remain strangers.

"I am so much interested to know all about you that I could say at almost any hour where you are, and—up to a certain point—what you are doing. All I have observed myself, all I have heard of you from others—the good and the bad—delights me so much that I offer you my sincerest sympathy and interest. I am glad that in you the musician and the man are so completely and harmoniously blended.

" There was a time when I earnestly desired your personal acquaintance; but now I feel the more you fascinate me, the more I shrink from knowing you. It seems to me

I could not then talk to you as I do now, although if we met unexpectedly I could not behave to you as to a stranger.

"At present I prefer to think of you from a distance, to hear you speak and to be at one with you in your music. I am really unhappy never to have had the opportunity of hearing *Francesca da Rimini*; I am impatient for the appearance of the pianoforte arrangement.

"Forgive me all my effusions; they cannot be of any use to you; yet you will not regret that you have been able to infuse a little life—especially by such ideal ways and means—into one who, like myself, is so nearly at the end of her days as to be practically already dead.

"Now one more 'last request,' Peter Ilich. There is one particular number in your *Oprichnik* about which I am wildly enthusiastic. If it is possible, please arrange this for me as a funeral march for four hands (pianoforte). I am sending you the opera in which I have marked the passages I should like you to arrange. If my request is tiresome, do not hesitate to refuse; I shall be regretful, but not offended. If you agree to it, take your own time, because it will be an indulgence I have no right to expect. Will you allow me to have your arrangements published, and if so, should I apply to Jurgenson or Bessel?

"Furthermore, allow me in future to drop all formalities of 'Dear Sir,' etc., in my letters to you; they are not in my style, and I shall be glad if you will write to me without any of this conventional politeness. You will not refuse me this favour?

"Yours, with devotion and respect,
"N. F.

"P.S.—Do not forget to answer my first request."

Tchaikovsky to N. F. von Meck.

"Moscow, *March* 16*th* (28*th*), 1877.

"You are quite right, Nadejda Filaretovna, in thinking that I am able to understand your inward mind and temperament. I venture to believe that you have not made a mistake in considering me a kindred spirit. Just as you have taken the trouble to study public opinion about me, I, too, have lost no opportunity of learning something about you and your manner of life. I have frequently been interested in you as a fellow-creature in whose temperament I recognised many features in common with my own. The fact that we both suffer from the same malady would alone suffice to draw us together. This malady is misanthropy; but a peculiar form of misanthropy, which certainly does not spring from hatred or contempt for mankind. People who suffer from this complaint do not fear the evil which others may bring them, so much as the disillusionment, that craving for the ideal, which follows upon every intimacy. There was a time when I was so possessed by this fear of my fellow-creatures that I stood on the verge of madness. The circumstances of my life were such that I could not possibly escape and hide myself. I had to fight it out with myself, and God alone knows what the conflict cost me!

" I have emerged from the strife victorious, in so far that life has ceased to be unbearable. I was saved by work— work which was at the same time my delight. Thanks to one or two successes which have fallen to my share, I have taken courage, and my depression, which used often to drive me to hallucinations and insanity, has almost lost its power over me.

" From all I have just said, you will understand I am not at all surprised that, although you love my music, you do not care to know the composer. You are afraid lest you should miss in my personality all with which your ideal imagination has endowed me. You are right. I feel that on closer acquaintance you would not find that harmony between me and my music of which you have dreamt.

" Accept my thanks for all your expressions of appreciation for my music. If you only realised how good and comforting it is to a musician to know one soul feels so deeply and so intensely all that he experienced himself while planning and finishing his work! I am indeed grateful for your kind and cordial sympathy. I will not say what is customary under the circumstances: that I am unworthy of your praise. Whether I write well or ill, I write from an irresistible inward impulse. I speak in music because I have something to say. My work is 'sincere,' and it is a great consolation to find you value this sincerity.

"I do not know if the march will please you . . . . if not, do not hesitate to say so. Perhaps, later on, I might be more successful.

"I send you a cabinet photograph ; not a very good one, however. I will be photographed again soon (it is an excruciating torture to me), and then I shall be very pleased to send you another portrait."

From N. F. von Meck.

"*March* 18*th* (30*th*), 1877.

"Your march is so wonderful, Peter Ilich, that it throws me—as I hoped—into a state of blissful madness ; a condition in which one loses consciousness of all that is bitter and offensive in life. . . . Listening to such music, I seem to soar above all earthly thoughts, my temples throb, my heart beats wildly, a mist swims before my eyes and my ears drink in the enchantment of the music. I feel that all is well with me, and I do not want to be reawakened. Ah, God, how great is the man who has power to give others such moments of bliss !"

About the end of April, at a moment when Tchaikovsky found himself in great pecuniary straits, he received another commission from his benefactress. This time Frau von Meck asked for an original work for violin and pianoforte, and proposed a very extravagant fee in return.

Tchaikovsky replied as follows :—

"*May* 1*st* (13*th*), 1877.

"HONOURED NADEJDA FILARETOVNA,—In spite of obstinate denials on the part of a friend who is well known to both of us,[1] I have good reason to suppose that your letter, which I received early this morning, is due to a well-intentioned ruse on his part. Even your earlier commissions awoke in me a suspicion that you had more than one reason for suggesting them : on the one hand, you

[1] J. Kotek.

really wished to possess arrangements of some of my works; on the other—knowing my material difficulties—you desired to help me through them. The very high fees you sent me for my easy tasks forced me to this conclusion. This time I am convinced that the second reason is almost wholly answerable for your latest commission. Between the lines of your letter I read your delicacy of feeling and your kindness, and was touched by your way of approaching me. At the same time, in the depths of my heart, I felt such an intense *unwillingness* to comply with your request that I cannot answer you in the affirmative. I could not bear any insincerity or falsehood to creep into our mutual relations. This would undoubtedly have been the case had I disregarded my inward promptings, manufactured a composition for you without pleasure or inspiration, and received from you an unsuitable fee in return. Would not the thought have passed through your mind that I was ready to undertake any kind of musical work provided the fee was high enough? Would you not have had some grounds for supposing that, had you been poor, I should not have complied with your requests? Finally, our intercourse is marred by one painful circumstance—in almost all our letters the question of money crops up. Of course it is not a degradation for an artist to accept money for his trouble; but, besides labour, a work such as you now wish me to undertake demands a certain degree of what is called inspiration, and at the present moment this is not at my disposal. I should be guilty of artistic dishonesty were I to abuse my technical skill and give you false coin in exchange for true—only with a view to improving my pecuniary situation.

"At the present moment I am absorbed in the symphony[1] I began during the winter. I should like to dedicate it to you, because I believe you would find in it an echo of your most intimate thoughts and emotions. Just now any other work would be a burden—work, I mean, that would demand a certain mood and change of thought. Added to this, I am in a very nervous, worried and irritable state, highly unfavourable to composition, and even my symphony suffers in consequence."

[1] No. 4 in F minor.

Tchaikovsky's refusal did not offend Frau von Meck; on the contrary, she was deeply grateful for his honourable and straightforward explanation. The incident only served to strengthen the friendship between them, and the result of their closer and more outspoken intercourse was a remittance of 3,000 roubles to pay his debts. Having made herself his sole creditor, she now became his benefactress and patroness, and from this time forward took charge of his material welfare. But not only in this way did she warm and brighten the course of Tchaikovsky's life; of greater value was the deep sympathy in which her generosity had its root, a sympathy which shows in every line of her letters.

" I am looking after you for my own sake," she wrote. " My most precious beliefs and sympathies are in your keeping; your very existence gives me so much enjoyment, for life is the better for your letters and your music; finally, I want to keep you for the service of the art I adore, so that it may have no better or worthier acolyte than yourself. So, you see, my thought for your welfare is purely egotistical and, so long as I can satisfy this wish, I am happy and grateful to you for accepting my help."

II

To Anatol Tchaikovsky.

" GLIEBOVO, *June 23rd (July 5th),* 1877.

" DEAR ANATOL,—You are right in supposing that I am hiding something from you, but you have made a false guess as to what this 'something' really is. Here is the whole matter. At the end of May an event took place which I kept from you and from all my family and friends, so that you should none of you worry yourselves with unnecessary anxieties as to whether I had done wisely or not. I wanted to get the business over and confess it afterwards. I am going to be married. I became engaged at the end of May, and meant to have the wedding early in July, without saying a word to anyone. Your letter shook my resolve. I could not avoid meeting you, and I felt I could not play a comedy of lies as to my reason for not being able to go to Kamenka. Besides I came to the conclusion that it was not right to get married without Dad's blessing. So I decided to make a clean breast of it. The enclosed letter is for Dad. Do not worry about me. I have thought it over, and I am taking this important step in life with a quiet mind. You will realise that I am quite calm when I tell you—with the prospect of marriage before me—I have been able to write two-thirds of my opera.[1] My bride is no longer very young, but quite suitable in every respect, and possessed of one great attraction : she is in love with me. She is poor, and her name is Antonina Ivanovna Milioukov. I now invite you to my wedding. You and Kotek will be the sole witnesses of the ceremony. Ask father not to say a word about it to anyone. I will write to Sasha and to the rest of my brothers myself."

To his father, I. P. Tchaïkovsky.

"GLIEBOVO, *June 23rd (July 5th)*, 1877.

"DEAR FATHER,—Your son Peter intends to marry. But as he must not be united without your blessing upon his new life, he writes to ask for it. My bride is poor, but a good, honourable woman, who is deeply attached to me. Dear Dad, you know a man does not rush thoughtlessly into marriage at my age, so do not be anxious. I am sure my future wife will do all she can to make my life peaceful and happy. . . . Take care of yourself, dear, and write to me at once. I kiss your hands."

To N. F. von Meck.

"Moscow, *July 3rd (15th)*, 1877.

"First of all I must tell you that at the end of May I became engaged, to my own surprise. This is how it

---

[1] *Eugene Oniegin.*

came about. One day I received a letter from a girl whom I had already seen and met. I learnt from this letter that for a long time past she had honoured me with her love. The letter was so warm and sincere that I decided to answer it, which I had always carefully avoided doing in other cases of the kind. Without going into the details of this correspondence, I will merely say that I ended by accepting her invitation to visit her. Why did I do this? Now it seems as though some hidden force drew me to this girl. When we met I told her again that I could only offer gratitude and sympathy in exchange for her love. But afterwards I began to reflect upon the folly of my proceedings. If I did not care for her, if I did not want to encourage her affections, why did I go to see her, and where will all this end? From the letters which followed, I came to the conclusion that, having gone so far, I should make her really unhappy and drive her to some tragic end were I to bring about a sudden rupture. I found myself confronted by a painful dilemma : either I must keep my freedom at the expense of this woman's ruin (this is no empty word, for she loved me intensely), or I must marry. I could but choose the latter course. Therefore I went one evening to my future wife and told her frankly that I could not love her, but that I would be a devoted and grateful friend ; I described to her in detail my character, my irritability, my nervous temperament, my misanthropy—finally, my pecuniary situation. Then I asked her if she would care to be my wife. Her answer was, of course, in the affirmative. The agonies I have endured since that evening defy description. It is very natural. To live thirty - seven years with an innate antipathy to matrimony, and then suddenly, by force of circumstances, to find oneself engaged to a woman with whom one is not in the least in love—is very painful. To give myself time to consider and grow used to the idea, I decided not to upset my original plans, but to spend a month in the country just the same. I did so, and the quiet, rural life among congenial friends, surrounded by beautiful scenery, has had a very beneficial effect. I consoled myself with the thought that we cannot escape our fate, and there was something fatalistic in my meeting with this girl.   Besides, I know from experience that the terrible, agitating *unknown* often proves beneficial and *vice versâ*.   How often we are disappointed in the happiness which we have expected and striven to attain!   Let come what come may!

"Now a few words as to my future wife.   Her name is Antonina Ivanovna Milioukov, and she is twenty-eight. She is rather good-looking, and of spotless reputation.   She keeps herself, and lives alone—from a feeling of independence—although she has a very affectionate mother.   She is quite poor and of moderate education, but apparently very good and capable of a loyal attachment.

"During the month of July I finished a large part of the opera, and might have accomplished more but for my agitated frame of mind.   I have never regretted my choice of subject for an instant.   I cannot understand how it is that you who love music cannot appreciate Poushkin, who, by the power of his genius, often oversteps the limitations of poetry and enters the illimitable sphere of music.   This is no mere phrase.   Apart from the substance and form of his verses, they have another quality, something in their sequence of sound which penetrates to our inmost soul. This 'something' is music.

"Wish that I may not lose courage in the new life which lies before me.   God knows I am filled with the best of intentions towards the future companion of my life, and if we are both unhappy I shall not be to blame.   My conscience is clear.   If I am marrying without love, it is because circumstances have left me no alternative.   I gave way thoughtlessly to her first expressions of love; I ought never to have replied to them.   But having once encouraged her affection by answering her letter and visiting her, I was bound to act as I have done.   But, as I say, my conscience is clear: I have neither lied to her, nor deceived her. I told her what she could expect from me, and what she must not count upon receiving."

Tchaikovsky sent a similar intimation to his sister at Kamenka, and to his brother Modeste.   As he had anticipated, his father was the only person who really rejoiced at the news.   He replied as follows :—

From I. P. Tchaikovsky.

"PAVLOVSK, *June 27th (July 9th),* 1877.

"MY DEAR SON PETER,—Toly gave me your letter in which you ask for my blessing upon your marriage. This news delighted me so that I was ready to jump for joy. God be praised! The Lord's blessing be upon you! I have no doubt that your chosen bride is equally worthy of the same good wishes which your father—an old man of eighty-three—and all your family bestow upon you; and not your family only, but all who have come in contact with you.

" Is it not so, dear Antonina Ivanovna? After yesterday you must give me leave to call you my God-sent daughter, and to bid you love your chosen husband, for he is indeed worthy of it. And you, dear bridegroom, let me know the day and hour of your wedding, and I will come myself (if you agree to it) to give you my blessing. . . ."

Of all Tchaikovsky's family, Anatol was the only one able to go to Mocsow, and he arrived too late to prevent his brother from taking the rash and foolish step he had decided upon.

The marriage took place on July 6th (18th).

I shall not attempt to follow step by step the whole sad story of my brother's marriage. First of all, I do not possess the necessary sense of impartiality; secondly, I have no evidence for the other side of the case, nor any hope of procuring it in the future; and thirdly, I do not wish to hurt the legitimate sensitiveness of several people still living, I can only say that from the first hour of his married life Tchaikovsky had to pay the penalty of his rash and ill-considered act and was profoundly miserable.

On the evening of the wedding-day the newly married couple left for St. Petersburg and returned to Moscow at the end of a week. They then paid a short visit to the bride's mother, who lived in the country, after which it was settled that Tchaikovsky should go alone to Kamenka, while his wife prepared the new home in Moscow.

On July 26th (August 7th) he wrote to N. F. von Meck: " I leave in an hour's time. A few days longer, and I swear I should have gone mad."

To N. F. von Meck.

"KAMENKA, *August 2nd* (14*th*), 1877.

" If I were to say that I had returned to my normal condition, it would not be true. But this is impossible. Only time can cure me, and I have no doubt that gradually I shall become reconciled. I am quiet here, and begin to look the future in the face without fear. One thing annoys me; I am absolutely incapable of taking up my work. Yet it would be the finest remedy for my morbid state of mind. I must hope that the hunger for work will return ere long."

To N. F. von Meck.

"*August* 11*th* (23*rd*), 1877.

" I am much better. . . . I feel *sure* I shall now triumph over my difficult and critical situation. I must struggle against *my feeling of estrangement* from my wife and try to keep all her good qualities in view. For undoubtedly she has good qualities.

" I have so far improved that I have taken in hand the orchestration of *your* symphony. One of my brothers, whose judgment I value, is very pleased with such parts of it as I have played to him. I hope *you* will be equally pleased. That is the chief thing."

To N. F. von Meck.

"KAMENKA, *August* 12*th* (24*th*), 1877.

" You are right, Nadejda Filaretovna, there are times in life when one must fortify oneself to endure and create for oneself some kind of joy, however shadowy. Here is a case in point: either live with people and know that you are condemned to every kind of misery, or escape somewhere and isolate yourself from every possibility of intercourse, which, for the most part, only leads to pain and grief. My dream has always been to work as long as I had power to do so, and when I felt convinced that I could do no more, to hide myself somewhere, far away from the strife, and look on at the agitations of the human ant-hill. This dream of being at rest in some remote corner has been the great consolation and goal of my life. Now, by my own act, I have deprived myself of all hope of ever reaching this harbour of refuge. . . . My new tie forces me into the arena of life—there is no escape from it. As you say, there is nothing to be done, but to set to and create some artificial happiness. . . .

" Our symphony progresses. The first movement will give me a great deal of trouble as regards orchestration. It is very long and complicated ; at the same time I consider it the best movement. The three remaining movements are very simple, and it will be pleasant and easy to orchestrate them. The Scherzo will have quite a new orchestral effect, from which I expect great things. At first only the string orchestra is heard, always pizzicato. In the trio the wood-wind plays by itself, and at the end of the Scherzo all three groups of instruments join in a short phrase. I think this effect will be interesting."

To N. F. von Meck.

" KAMENKA, *August* 30*th* (*September* 11*th*), 1877.

" The weather grows more and more autumnal. The fields are bare, and it is time I took my departure. My wife writes that our rooms are now ready. . . ."

To N. F. von Meck.

" Moscow, *September* 12*th* (24*th*), 1877.

" I have not yet been to the Conservatoire. My classes only begin to-day. The arrangements of our home leave nothing to be desired. My wife has done all she possibly could to please me. It is really a comfortable and pretty home. All is clean, new and artistic.

" The orchestration of the first movement of our symphony is quite finished. Now I shall give myself a few days to grow used to my new life. In any case the symphony will not be ready before the end of the winter."

To Anatol Tchaikovsky.

"Moscow, *September* 12*th* (24*th*), 1877.

". . . My wife came to meet me. Poor woman, she has gone through some miserable experiences in getting our home ready; while awaiting my arrival she has had to change her cook twice. She had to take one into the police court. Twice she was robbed, and for the last few days she has been obliged to remain at home all day, not daring to leave the place in the care of the cook. But our home pleases me; it is pretty, comfortable, and not altogether wanting in luxury."

Shortly after writing this letter Tchaikovsky's health broke down. According to a telegram which he sent to Petersburg, he left Moscow suddenly on September 24th (October 6th) in a condition bordering upon insanity.

Anatol says that his brother was scarcely recognisable when he met him on the platform of the Nicholas Station in Petersburg; his face had entirely changed in the course of a month. From the station he was taken to the nearest hotel, where, after a violent nervous crisis, he became unconscious, in which state he remained for forty-eight hours. When this crisis was over, the doctors ordered a complete change of life and scene as the sole chance of recovery. Anatol went immediately to Moscow, hastily arranged his brother's affairs, left his wife to the care of her family, for the time being, and then took the invalid away as soon as possible.

Not once in the whole course of his life—neither at the time nor subsequently—did Tchaikovsky, in speech or writing, lay the blame for this unhappy incident upon his wife. Following his example, therefore, I cannot complete this chapter without exonerating her from every shadow of responsibility for all that happened.

Tchaikovsky himself declared that "she always behaved honourably and with sincerity," never consciously deceived him and was "unwittingly and involuntarily" the cause of all her husband's misery.

As to Tchaikovsky's treatment of his wife, the sternest judge must admit that it was frank and honourable and that he did not attempt to mislead her. Both of them believed, under the influence of an abnormal and fatal exaltation, that, after self-revelation, they understood each other and were honestly convinced they would get on together. It was not until they entered into closer relationship that they discovered, to their horror, they were far from having told each other all; that a gulf of misunderstanding lay between them which could never be bridged over, that they had been wandering as it were in a dream, and had unintentionally deceived each other.

Under the circumstances separation was the only solution of the difficulty, the sole method of regaining their peace of mind and of saving Tchaikovsky's life.

On October 3rd (15th) the composer reached Berlin, accompanied by his brother Anatol. The dangerous crisis in his illness was over and a slow convalescence began.

III

Tchaikovsky selected Clarens as his first resting-place, and settled down at the Villa Richelieu on the shore of the Lake of Geneva.

He had only money enough to last five or six weeks; but at the end of that time he had no inclination—nor was he in a condition—to return to his work in Moscow. His constitution was so shaken and impaired by his nervous illness that at least a year's rest was necessary for his complete restoration.

There was some hope of getting a little money in the

winter, if the Principal of the Petersburg Conservatoire, Karl Davidov, appointed him delegate for the forthcoming exhibition in Paris. But the chance was very uncertain, and even if he were nominated, the office was not very well suited to Tchaikovsky, because it demanded not only great energy, but constant social intercourse, whereas the condition of his health needed complete repose.

All the same, Tchaikovsky would have been glad of the appointment as affording the one means of remaining longer abroad.

This anxiety as to his future counteracted in some degree the benefit derived from the quiet and solitude of Clarens. To escape from his difficulties Tchaikovsky was obliged to have recourse to the kindness of Nicholas Rubinstein and Nadejda von Meck.

Rubinstein interested himself in the matter of the delegation, and wrote as follows :—

" It has been decided to send you all the money which is left over from the expenses of your classes in monthly instalments. Try to calm yourself; take care of your health, and fear nothing. You are far too highly valued as a musician to be compromised by secondary considerations."

Tchaikovsky replied, expressing his gratitude and reporting the progress of his opera.

"The first act of *Eugene Oniegin* will soon be in your hands," he writes. "I shall be very happy if it pleases you. I composed it with great enthusiasm. A performance at the Conservatoire is just my ideal. The opera is intended for a modest setting and a small theatre."

From Nicholas Rubinstein to Tchaikovsky.

" FRIEND PETER,—I am very glad you are getting better and gradually returning to work. I am full of curiosity about *Eugene Oniegin*. Be so kind as to assign the parts. Even

Q

if they have to be changed afterwards, it is important to know your views. Can I also count on the Symphony?

" I have seen Frau von Meck. We talked a great deal about you. I think she will send you another commission, or money direct."

Rubinstein was not mistaken. Even before she received Tchaikovsky's letter asking for assistance, Nadejda von Meck had decided to take upon herself the responsibility of his maintenance, and asked him to accept an annual allowance of 6,000 roubles (£600). In reply to his request, which was accompanied by many apologies, she wrote as follows :—

". . . . Are we really such strangers? Do you not realise how much I care for you, how I wish you all good? In my opinion it is not the tie of sex or kindred which gives these rights, but the sense of mental and spiritual communion. You know how many happy moments you have given me, how grateful I am, how indispensable you are to me, and how necessary it is that you should remain just as you were created ; consequently what I do is not done for your sake, but for my own. Why should you spoil my pleasure in taking care of you, and make me feel that I am not very much to you after all? You hurt me. If I wanted something from you, of course you would give it me—is it not so? Very well, then we cry quits. Do not interfere with my management of your domestic economy, Peter Ilich.

" I do not know what you think, but for my part I would rather we kept our friendship and correspondence to ourselves. Therefore in talking to Nicholas Rubinstein I spoke of you as a complete stranger ; I inquired, as though quite in the dark, your reasons for leaving Moscow, where you had gone, how long you were going to remain away, and so on. He was anxious, I thought, to make me take a warmer interest in you, but I kept to the part of a disinterested admirer of your talents."

Thus, thanks to his new friend, Tchaikovsky became an independent man as regards his material welfare, and a new life opened out before him, such as hitherto he had only imagined as an unrealisable dream.   He had attained that freedom of existence which was indispensable to his creative activity.   Now, at last, he was at liberty to employ his time as he pleased, and to arrange his manner of living to suit his own tastes and requirements.

IV

In consequence of this entire change of circumstances, Tchaikovsky abandoned his original idea of spending the whole winter in Clarens.   In thanking his benefactress for her generous help, he says :—

"I shall only remain here until—thanks to you—I receive the wherewithal to go to Italy, which calls me with all its force.   It is very quiet and very beautiful here, but somewhat depressing.

"You say liberty is unattainable, and that there is no method of procuring it.   Perhaps it is impossible to be completely free ; but even this comparative freedom is the greatest joy to me.   At least I can work.   Work was impossible in the vicinity of one who was so much to me externally, while remaining a stranger to my inner life.   I have been through a terrible ordeal, and it is marvellous that my soul still lives, though deeply wounded."

To N. F. von Meck.

"CLARENS, *October* 25*th* (*November* 6*th*), 1877.

"Your letter is so warm and friendly that it would suffice of itself to reawaken in me the desire for life, and to help me to endure all its miseries.   I thank you for everything, my invaluable friend.   I do not suppose that I shall ever have an opportunity of proving that I am ready to make any sacrifice for you in return ; I think you will never be compelled by circumstances to demand any supreme service from my friendship ; therefore I can only please and serve you by means of my music. Nadejda Filaretovna, every note which comes from my pen in future is dedicated to you! To you I owe this reawakened love of work, and I will never forget for a moment that you have made it possible to carry on my career. Much, much still remains for me to do! Without false modesty, I may tell you that all I have done so far seems to me poor and imperfect compared with what I *can*, *must*, and *will* do in the future.

"I like my present quarters very well. Apart from the glorious view of the lake and mountains of Savoy, with the Dent du Midi, which I get from my windows, I am pleased with the villa itself. . . . But I must confess I am continually haunted by the thought of a long visit to Italy, so that I have decided to start for Rome with my brother about a fortnight hence. Afterwards we shall go on to Naples or Sorrento. After a few days amid the mountains, have you never had the yearning, from which I think no northerner ever escapes, for wide horizons and the unbounded expanse of the plains? . . . Gradually I am going back to my work, and I can now definitely say that *our* Symphony will be finished by December at the latest, so you will be able to hear it this season. May this music, which is so closely bound up with the thought of you, speak to you and tell you that I love you with all my heart and soul, O my best and incomparable friend!"

To N. F. von Meck.

"CLARENS, *October* 30*th* (*November* 11*th*), 1877.

" . . . Whenever I think calmly over all I have been through, I come to the conclusion that there is a Providence who has specially cared for me. Not only have I been saved from ruin—which seemed at one time inevitable—but things are now well with me, and I see ahead the dawn-light of happiness and success. As regards religion, I must confess I have a dual temperament, and to this day I have found no satisfactory solution of the problem. On the one hand, my reason obstinately refuses to accept the dogmatic teaching either of the orthodox Russian, or of any other Christian Church. For instance, however much I may think about it, I can see no sense in the doctrine of retribution and reward. How is it possible to draw a hard-and-fast line between the sheep and the goats? What is to be rewarded and what is to be punished? Equally impossible to me is the belief in immortality. Here I am quite in accord with the pantheistic view of immortality and the future life.

"On the other hand, my whole upbringing, customs of childhood, and the poetical image of Christ and all that belongs to His teaching, are so deeply implanted in me, that involuntarily I find myself calling upon Him in my grief and thanking Him in my happiness."

To N. F. von Meck.

"FLORENCE, *November 6th* (18*th*), 1877.

"I am ashamed, not without reason, to have to write you a melancholy letter. At first I thought I would not write at all, but the desire to talk with you a little got the upper hand. It is impossible to be insincere with you, even when I have the best of reasons for concealing my thoughts.

"We came here quite unexpectedly. I was so unwell in Milan that I decided to remain a day here, which our tickets permit us to do. My indisposition is not of such great importance. The real trouble is my depression—a wearing, maddening depression, which never leaves me for a moment. In Clarens, where I was living an absolutely quiet life, I was often overcome by melancholy. Not being able to account for these attacks of depression, I attributed them to the mountains. What childishness! I persuaded myself that I need only cross the frontiers of Italy, and a life of perfect happiness would begin! Nonsense! Here I feel a hundred times worse. The weather is glorious, the days are as warm as in July, there is something to see, something to distract me, and yet I am tormented by an overwhelming, gigantic depression. How to account for it I do not know. If I had not asked all my correspondents to address their letters to me in Rome, I think I should not travel any further. I must get as far as that, it is clear, but I am not fit just now for a tourist's life. . . . I have not come here for sight-seeing, but to cure myself by work. At the present moment it seems to me impossible to work in Italy, especially in Rome. I regret *terribly* the peace and quiet of Clarens, where I had made a successful effort to return to my work, and I am seriously wondering whether it might not be better to return there. . . . What will become of me when my brother goes? I cannot think of that moment without a shudder. But I neither wish, nor am I able, to return to Russia. You see how I keep turning in this *cercle vicieux*. . . ."

To N. F. von Meck.

" ROME, *November 7th (19th),* 1877.

" . . . We arrived in Rome quite early this morning. This time I entered the famous city with a troubled heart. How true it is that we do not draw our happiness from our surroundings, but from our inward being! This has been sufficiently proved by my present tour in Italy.

" . . . I am still quite a sick man. I cannot bear the least noise as yet. Yesterday in Florence, and to-day in Rome, every vehicle that rolled by threw me into an insane rage ; every sound, every cry exasperated my nerves. The crowds of people flowing through the narrow streets annoy me so that every stranger I meet seems to me an enemy. Now, for the first time, I begin to realise the folly of my journey to Rome. My brother and I have just been to St. Peter's : all I have gained by it is overwhelming physical fatigue. Of the noisy streets, the bad air, the dirt, I will say nothing. I know my morbid condition makes me see only the bad side of Rome in all its hatefulness, while the beauties of the city seem veiled to my eyes ; but this is a poor consolation. Yesterday I discussed with my brother what we should do next, and came to this conclusion. It is evident that I cannot continue my tour. If I feel ill in Florence and Rome, it will be just as bad in Naples. A fortnight hence my brother must leave me ; in order somewhat to prolong our time together, I have decided to accompany him as far as Vienna. I have also come to the conclusion that I ought not to be left alone. Therefore I have sent for my servant, who is leading an idle life in Moscow. I shall await his coming in Vienna, and then return to Clarens, where I think of staying.

"To-morrow, or the next day, we shall go to Venice for a few days before starting for Vienna. Venice is quiet, and I can work there ; and it is very important I should do so. . . ."

To Nicholas Rubinstein.

"ROME, *November 8th (20th)*, 1877.

"I am agitated by uncertainty as to whether the first act [1] will please you or not. Pray do not give it up on your first impressions : they are often so deceptive. I wrote that music with such love and delight ! The following numbers were specially dear to me : (1) the first duet behind the scenes, which afterwards becomes the quartet ; (2) Lensky's Arioso ; (3) the scene in Tatiana's room ; (4) the chorus of maidens. If you can tell me it pleases you and Albrecht (I value his opinion so highly), it will make me very happy. As soon as I have finished the first scene of the second act and sent it to you, I will attack the Symphony with all zeal, and so I implore you to keep a place for it at the Symphony Concerts.

"I thank you, dear friend, with all my heart for the many things you have done for me, and for your kind letter, in which I recognise with joy your loyal friendship. But, for God's sake, do not summon me back to Moscow before next September. I know I shall find nothing there but terrible mental suffering."

To N. F. von Meck.

"VENICE, *November 11th (23rd)*, 1877.

"DEAR NADEJDA FILARETOVNA,—The last day in Rome compensated for all my troubles, but it was also rather fatiguing. In the morning I had to go in search of the Symphony (No. 4), which had been sent from Clarens. I inquired at the post office, at the station, at various other offices. Everywhere they received me politely, looked for

---

[1] Of *Eugene Oniegin.*

the parcel, and failed to find it. Imagine my anxiety. If the Symphony had been lost, I should never have had the energy to rewrite it from memory. At last I requested that it should be diligently sought for, and—behold the parcel was discovered! It was a great comfort.

"Afterwards I visited the Capitol with my brother. I found much that was interesting here and which touched me directly—for instance, the statue of the Dying Gladiator. I cannot say the same of the Venus of the Capitol, which still leaves me quite cold, as on my first visit. At two o'clock we went to the Palace of the Cæsars, and looked into the Villa Borghese as we passed, to see the collection of pictures. Here, too, I was capable of taking in some artistic impressions. One picture particularly attracted my attention—the Death of a Saint (Jerome, if I am not mistaken), by Domenicchino. But I must tell you frankly that I am no enthusiastic amateur of pictures, and I lack any profound insight into the subtleties of painting or sculpture. I soon get tired in the galleries. Among a number of pictures there are seldom more than two or three which remain firmly fixed in my mind's eye; but these I study in every detail, and endeavour to enter into their spirit, while I run through the others with a superficial glance. . . . Besides the picture by Domenicchino, some of Raphael's pleased me very much, especially the portraits of Cæsar Borgia and Sixtus V.[1]

"The grandest, the most overpowering, of all the sights I saw was the Palace of the Cæsars. What gigantic proportions, what wealth of beauty! At every step we are reminded of the past ; we endeavour to reconstruct it and the further we explore it, the more vivid are the gorgeous pictures which crowd the imagination. The weather was lovely. Every moment we came upon some fresh glimpse of the city, which is as dirty as Moscow, but far more picturesquely situated, and possessing infinitely greater

[1] The condition of Tchaikovsky's health is probably accountable for many errors in this letter. In 1877 the pictures of which he speaks were not in the *Villa*, but in the *Palazzo* Borghese. Domenicchino's picture was in the Vatican. The portraits of Cæsar Borgia and Sixtus V. were not by Raphael. The latter was not made Pope until sixty-five years after the death of the celebrated painter.

historical interest.   Quite close by are the Colosseum and the ruined Palace of Constantine.[1]   It is all so grand, so beautiful, so rare!   I am very glad to have left Rome under this ineffaceable impression.   I wanted to write to you in the evening, but after packing I was too tired to move a finger.

"At six o'clock this morning we arrived in Venice. Although I had not been able to close my eyes all night, and although it was still quite dark and cold when we got here, I was charmed with the characteristic beauty of the place.   We are staying at the Grand Hôtel.   In front of our windows is S. Maria della Salute, a graceful, pretty building on the Canale Grande."

To N. F. Von Meck.

"VENICE, *November* 16th (28th), 1877.

" . . . I have received a very comforting letter from my sister, and am busy with the orchestration of the first scene of the second act of my *Oniegin*.

"Venice is a fascinating city.   Every day I discover some fresh beauty.   Yesterday we went to the Church of the Frati, in which, among other art treasures, is the tomb of Canova.   It is a marvel of beauty!   But what delights me most is the absolute quiet and absence of all street noises.   To sit at the open window in the moonlight and gaze upon S. Maria della Salute, or over to the Lagoons on the left, is simply glorious!   It is very pleasant also to sit in the Piazza di San Marco (near the Café) in the afternoon and watch the stream of people go by. The little corridor-like streets please me, too, especially in the evening when the windows are lit up.   In short, Venice has bewitched me.   To-day I have been considering whether it would not be better to stay here than at Clarens —Clarens is quiet, cheap, and nice, but often dull; here nature is less beautiful, but there is more life and movement, and this is not of the kind that bewilders and confuses me. . . . To-morrow I will look for a furnished apartment.   If I succeed in finding one—I shall be just as undecided as before."

[1] The Basilica.

To N. F. von Meck.

"VENICE, *November* 18*th* (30*th*), 1877.

". . . The few days spent here have done me a great deal of good. First, I have been able to work a little, so that my brother will take the second scene of the opera —not quite finished—back to Moscow with him. Secondly, I feel much better, although I was not very well yesterday. It is only a slight chill, however. Thirdly, I am quite in love with my beautiful Venice, and have decided to come back here after parting from my brother in Vienna. Do not laugh, for Heaven's sake, at my uncertainty and vacillation. This time my decision is irrevocable. I have gone so far as to take a very nice apartment in the Riva dei Chiavoni.

"To-morrow I go to Vienna. On my return I will begin to work at the Symphony—*our* Symphony.

"Do you know what enrages me in Venice?—The vendors of the evening papers. If I go for a walk across the Piazza di San Marco I hear on every side, '*Il Tempo! La Gazzetta di Venezia! Vittoria dei Turchi!*' This '*Vittoria dei Turchi*' is shouted every evening. Why do they never cry one of our actual victories? Why do they try to attract customers by fictitious Turkish successes? Can it be that peaceful, beautiful Venice, who once lost her strength in fighting these same Turks, is as full of hatred for Russia as all the rest of Western Europe?

"Beside myself with indignation, I asked one of them, '*Ma dovè la vittoria?*' It turned out that a Turkish victory was really a reconnaissance, in which the Russians had had about one hundred casualties. 'Is that a victory?' I asked him angrily. I could not understand his reply, but he cried no more 'victories.' One must acknowledge the amiability, politeness, and obligingness of the Italians. These qualities of theirs strike one very forcibly when one comes direct from Switzerland, where the people are gloomy, unfriendly, and disinclined for a joke. To-day, when I met the same vendor of papers, he greeted me civilly, and instead of calling out, 'Grande vittoria dei Turchi'—with which words the others were recommending their wares—he began to cry, 'Gran combattimento a

Plevna, vittoria dei Russi!' I knew he lied, but it pleased me all the same, since it expressed the innate courtesy of a poor man.

"When will it end, this terrible war, in which such unimportant results have to be won at such vast sacrifices? And yet it must be fought out to the end, until the enemy is utterly vanquished. This war cannot and must not be settled by compromises and side issues. One or the other must give in. But how disgraceful it seems to speak of such a life-and-death struggle while sitting in a bright, comfortable, well-lit room, knowing neither hunger nor thirst, and well protected from bad weather and all other physical deprivations and discomforts! From moral and spiritual troubles we are none of us safe. As to my own, I know one remedy and alleviation—my work. But our strength is not always equal to our work. Oh, my God, if I could only find strength and gladness of heart for new works! Just now I can only go on patching up the old ones."

To N. F. von Meck.

"VIENNA, *November* 20th (*December* 2nd), 1877.

". . . Yesterday evening found us in Vienna. The journey across the Semmering left a fascinating impression. The weather was fine. On the journey I read and re-read your letter, my dear friend.

". . . Now it is evident that theoretically you have separated yourself from the Church and from dogmatic belief. I perceive that after years of thought you have framed for yourself a kind of religio-philosophic catechism. But it strikes me you are mistaken in supposing that parallel with the bulwarks of the old, strong faith which you have overthrown, you have raised new ones, so sure and reliable that you can afford to do away entirely with the old lines of defence. Herein lies precisely the sceptic's tragedy: once he has broken the ties which bind him to traditional belief, he passes from one set of philosophical speculations to another, always imagining he will discover that inexhaustible source of strength, so needful for the battle of life, with which the believer is fully equipped. You may say what you please, but a faith—not that which proceeds from mere deficiency of reasoning power and is simply a matter of routine—but a faith founded on reason and able to reconcile all misconceptions and contradictions arising from intellectual criticism—such a belief is the supreme happiness. A man who has both intellect and faith (and there are many such) is clad, as it were, in a panoply of armour which can resist all the blows of fate. You say you have fallen away from the accepted forms of religion and have made a creed for yourself. But religion is an element of reconciliation. Have you this sense of being reconciled? I think not. For if you had, you would never have written that letter from Como. Do you remember? That yearning, that discontent, that aspiration towards some vague ideal, that isolation from humanity, the confession that only in music—the most ideal of all the arts—could you find any solution of these agitating questions, all proved to me that your self-made religion did not give that absolute peace of mind which is peculiar to those who have found in their faith a ready-made answer to all those doubts which torment a reflective and sensitive nature. And, do you know—it seems to me you only care so much for my music because I am as full of the ideal longing as yourself. Our sufferings are the same. Your doubts are as strong as mine. We are both adrift in that limitless sea of scepticism, seeking a haven and finding none.

"Are not these the reasons why my music touches you so closely? I also think you are mistaken in calling yourself a realist. If we define 'realism' as contempt for all that is false and insincere—in life as in art—you are undoubtedly a 'realist.' But when we consider that a true realist would never dream of seeking consolation in music, as you do, it is evident you are far more of an idealist. You are only a realist in the sense that you do not care to waste time over sentimental, trivial, and aimless dreams, like so many women. You do not care for phrases and empty words, but that does not mean you are a realist. Impossible! Realism argues a certain limited outlook, a thirst for truth which is too quickly and easily satisfied. A realist does not actually feel eager to comprehend the essential problems of existence; he even denies the need of seeking truth, and does not believe in those who are searching for reconcilement and religion, philosophy, or art. Art—especially music—counts for nothing with the realist, because it is the answer to a question which his narrow intellect is incapable of posing. For these reasons I think you are wrong in declaring you have enrolled under the banner of realism. You say music only produces in you a pleasant, purely physical, sensation. Against this I distinctly protest. You are deceiving yourself. Do you really only care for music in the same way that I enjoy a bottle of wine or a pickled gherkin? Nay, you love music as it should be loved : that is to say, you give yourself up to it with all your soul and let it exercise its magic spell all unconsciously upon your spirit.

"Perhaps it may seem strange that I should doubt your self-knowledge. But, to my mind, you are, first of all, a very good woman, and have been so from your birth up. You honour what is good because the aspiration towards the right, as well as the hatred of lies and evil, is innate in you. You are clever, and consequently sceptical. An intelligent man cannot help being a sceptic; at least he must at some period of his life experience the most agonising scepticism. When your innate scepticism led you to the negation of tradition and dogma you naturally began to seek some way of escape from your doubts. You found it *partly* in the pantheistic point of view, and *partly* in music; but you discovered no perfect reconcilement with faith. Hating all evil and falsehood, you enclose yourself in your narrow family circle in order to shut out the consciousness of human wickedness. You have done much good, because, like your innate love of nature and art, this doing good is an invincible craving of your soul. You help others, not in order to purchase that eternal happiness which you neither quite believe in nor quite deny, but because you are so made that you cannot help doing good."

To N. F. Von Meck.

"VIENNA, *November* 23*rd* (*December* 5*th*), 1877.

"The continuation of my letter :—
"My feeling about the Church is quite different to yours.

For me it still possesses much poetical charm. I very often attend the services. I consider the liturgy of St. John Chrysostom one of the greatest productions of art. If we follow the service very carefully, and enter into the meaning of every ceremony, it is impossible not to be profoundly moved by the liturgy of our own Orthodox Church. I also love vespers. To stand on a Saturday evening in the twilight in some little old country church, filled with the smoke of incense ; to lose oneself in the eternal questions, *whence*, *why*, and *whither ;* to be startled from one's trance by a burst from the choir ; to be carried away by the poetry of this music ; to be thrilled with quiet rapture when the Golden Gates of the Iconostasis are flung open and the words ring out, 'Praise the name of the Lord!' —all this is infinitely precious to me! One of my deepest joys!

"Thus, from one point of view, I am firmly united to our Church. From other standpoints I have—like yourself —long since lost faith in dogma. The doctrine of retribution, for instance, seems to me monstrous in its injustice and unreason. Like you, I am convinced that if there is a future life at all, it is only conceivable in the sense of the indestructibility of matter, in the pantheistic view of the eternity of nature, of which I am only a microscopic atom. I cannot believe in a personal, individual immortality.

" How shall we picture to ourselves eternal life after death? As endless bliss? But such endless joy is inconceivable apart from its opposite—eternal pain. I entirely refuse to believe in the latter. Finally, I am not sure that life beyond death is desirable, for it would lose its charm but for its alternations of joy and sorrow, its struggle between good and evil, darkness and light. How can we contemplate immortality as a state of eternal bliss? According to our earthly conceptions, even bliss itself becomes wearisome if it is never broken or interrupted. So I have come to the conclusion, as the result of much thinking, that there is no future life. But conviction is one thing, and feeling and instinct another. This denial of immortality brings me face to face with the terrible thought that I shall never, never, again set eyes upon some of my dear dead. In spite of the strength of my *convictions*, I shall never reconcile myself to the thought that my dear mother, whom I loved so much, actually *is not;* that I shall never have any chance of telling her how, after twenty-three years of separation, she is as dear to me as ever.

" You see, my dear friend, I am made up of contradictions, and I have reached a very mature age without resting upon anything positive, without having calmed my restless spirit either by religion or philosophy. Undoubtedly I should have gone mad but for *music.* Music is indeed the most beautiful of all Heaven's gifts to humanity wandering in the darkness. Alone it calms, enlightens, and stills our souls. It is not the straw to which the drowning man clings ; but a true friend, refuge, and comforter, for whose sake life is worth living. Perhaps there will be no music in heaven. Well, let us give our mortal life to it as long as it lasts."

To N. F. von Meck.

" VIENNA, *November 26th (December 8th),* 1877.

" I am still in Vienna. Yesterday I heard that my servant would leave Moscow on Saturday. Although I have given him the most minute instructions what to do on the journey, I have no idea how he will cross the frontier, not knowing a single word of any foreign language. I fancy there will be many tragic-comic episodes. Sometimes I think it is not very wise to have a Russian servant. And yet—I do not know what I should have done, since I cannot endure complete solitude. Besides which I know it will be a comfort to my brother to feel I am not quite alone. I have seen Wagner's *Walküre.* The performance was excellent. The orchestra surpassed itself; the best singers did all within their powers—and yet it was wearisome. What a Don Quixote is Wagner ! He expends his whole force in pursuing the impossible, and all the time, if he would but follow the natural bent of his extraordinary gift, he might evoke a whole world of musical beauties. In my opinion Wagner is a symphonist by nature. He is gifted with genius which has wrecked itself upon his tendencies ; his inspiration is paralysed by theories which he has invented on his own account, and which, *nolens volens,* he wants to bring into practice. In his efforts to attain *reality, truth*, and *rationalism* he lets *music* slip quite out of sight, so that in his four latest operas it is, more often than not, conspicuous by its absence. I cannot call that music which consists of kaleidoscopic, shifting phrases, which succeed each other without a break and never come to a close, that is to say, never give the ear the least chance to rest upon musical form. Not a single broad, rounded melody, nor yet one moment of repose for the singer! The latter must always pursue the orchestra, and be careful never to lose his note, which has no more importance in the score than some note for the fourth horn. But there is no doubt Wagner is a wonderful symphonist. I will just prove to you by one example how far the symphonic prevails over the operatic style in his operas. You have probably heard his celebrated *Walkürenritt?* What a great and marvellous picture! How we actually seem to see these fierce heroines flying on their magic steeds amid thunder and lightning! In the concert-room this piece makes an extraordinary impression. On the stage, in view of the cardboard rocks, the canvas clouds, and the soldiers who run about very awkwardly in the background—in a word, seen in this very inadequate theatrical heaven, which makes a poor pretence of realising the illimitable realms above, the music loses all its powers of expression. Here the stage does not enhance the effect, but acts rather like a wet blanket. Finally I cannot understand, and never shall, why the *Nibelungen* should be considered a literary masterpiece. As a national saga—perhaps, but as a libretto—distinctly not!

"Wotan, Brünnhilda, Fricka, and the rest are all so impossible, so little human, that it is very difficult to feel any sympathy with their destinies. And how little life! For three whole hours Wotan lectures Brünnhilda upon her disobedience. How wearisome! And with it all, there are many fine and beautiful episodes of a purely symphonic description.

"Yesterday Kotek[1] and I looked through a new symphony by Brahms (No. 1 in C minor), a composer whom the Germans exalt to the skies. He has no charms for me.

---

[1] Kotek, who was then studying with Joachim in Berlin, joined Tchaikovsky for a few days in Vienna.

I find him cold and obscure, full of pretensions, but without any real depths. Altogether it seems to me Germany is deteriorating as regards music. I believe the French are now coming to the front. Lately I have heard Délibes' very clever music—in its own style—to the ballet *Sylvia*. I became acquainted with this music in the pianoforte arrangement some time ago, but the splendid performance of it by the Vienna orchestra quite fascinated me, especially the first part. *The Swan Lake* is poor stuff compared to *Sylvia*. Nothing during the last few years has charmed me so greatly as this ballet of Délibes and *Carmen*."

To N. F. von Meck.

"Vienna, *November 27th (December 9th),* 1877.

"Kotek and my brother have gone to the Philharmonic concert, at which my favourite Third Symphony of Schumann is being played. I preferred to remain at home alone. I was afraid I might meet some of the local musicians with whom I am acquainted. If only I came across one, by to-morrow I should have to call on at least ten musical 'lions,' make their acquaintance, and express my gratitude for their favours. (Last year, without any initiative on my part, my overture *Romeo and Juliet* was performed here and unanimously hissed.) No doubt I should do much towards making my works known abroad if I went the round of the influential people, paying visits and compliments. But, Lord, how I hate that kind of thing! If you could only hear the offensively patronising tone in which they speak of Russian music! One reads in their faces: 'Although you are a Russian, my condescension is such that I honour you with my attention." God be with them! Last year I met Liszt. He was sickeningly polite, but all the while there was a smile on his lips which expressed the above words pretty plainly. At the present moment, as you will understand, I am less than ever in the mood to be civil to these gentlemen."

R

To N. F. von Meck.

"Vienna, *November 29th* (*December 10th*), 1877.

"My brother only left at a quarter to eleven. I will not go into my feelings; you know what they are. My servant arrived yesterday at five o'clock. I was quite wrong in supposing he would encounter any serious difficulties on account of his ignorance of the language; and equally wrong as to his first impressions of foreign lands. He is, like all Russian peasants, as plucky as he is quick-witted, and knows how to get out of the most difficult situations; consequently he crossed the frontier as easily as though he had been in the habit of making the journey frequently. As to his impressions, he thinks the houses in Vienna far inferior to those in Moscow, and Moscow altogether incomparably more beautiful. The news of the capture of Plevna has made the separation from my brother more bearable. When the waiter brought my early coffee yesterday, with the announcement, 'Plevna has fallen,' I nearly embraced him! It seems from the papers as though Austria was not best pleased, and was rather aggrieved at the capitulation of the flower of the Turkish army."

To N. F. von Meck.

"Venice, *December 3rd* (*15th*), 1877.

". . . There is one thing in your letter with which I cannot agree in the least—your view of music. I particularly dislike the way in which you compare music with a form of intoxication. I think this is quite wrong. A man has recourse to wine in order to stupefy himself and produce an illusion of well-being and happiness. But this dream costs him very dear! The reaction is generally terrible. But in any case wine can only bring a momentary oblivion of all our troubles—no more. Has music a similar effect? Music is no illusion, but rather a revelation. Its triumphant power lies in the fact that it reveals to us beauties we find in no other sphere; and the apprehension of them is not transitory, but a perpetual reconcilement to life. Music enlightens and delights us. It is extremely difficult to analyse and define the process of musical enjoyment, but it has nothing in common with intoxication. It is certainly not a physiological phenomenon. Of course the nerves—therefore to some extent our physical organs—take part in our musical impressions and, in this sense, music gives physical delight: but you must own it is exceedingly difficult to draw a hard-and-fast line between the physical and psychical functions; for instance, thought is a physiological process in so far as it pertains to the functions of the brain. But when all is said and done, this is only a matter of words. If we both look upon the enjoyment of music from opposite points of view, at least one thing is certain: our love of it is equally strong, and that is sufficient for me. I am glad you apply the word *divine* to the art to which I have dedicated my life.

"In your philosophy I altogether approve your views of good and evil. These views are perhaps rather fatalistic, but full of Christian charity towards your weak and sinful fellow-creatures. You are quite right in saying that it is foolish to expect wisdom and virtue from a person not endowed with these qualities. Here again I hit upon the obvious difference between your personality and mine; I have always compelled myself to regard the evil in man's nature as the inevitable negation of good. Taking this point of view (which originates, if I am not mistaken, with Spinoza), I ought never to feel anger or hatred. Actually, however, no moment passes in which I am not prepared to lose my temper, to hate and despise my fellow-creatures, just as though I was not aware that each person acts according to the decree of fate. I know that you are a stranger to the least feeling of spite or contempt. You elude the blows aimed at you by others, and never retaliate. In short, you carry your philosophy into your workaday life. I am different; I think one thing and do another.

"I will just give you an instance. I have a friend called Kondratiev; he is a very nice, pleasant fellow, with only one fault—egotism. But he can cloak this failing under such charming, gentlemanly disguises that it is impossible to be angry with him for long. In September, when I was passing through the climax of my suffering in Moscow, and was looking about in a paroxysm

of depression for someone to come to my aid, Kondratiev
—who was then living on his property in the Government
of Kharkov—chanced to write to me one of his usual
kindly letters, assuring me of his friendship. I did not
want to reveal my state to my brothers at that time, for fear
of making them unhappy. My cup of misery was overflowing. I wrote to Kondratiev, telling him of my terrible
and hopeless condition. The meaning of my letter, expressed between the lines, was : 'I am going under, save
me! Rescue me, but be quick about it!' I felt sure that
he, a well-to-do and independent man, who was—as he
himself declared—ready to make any sacrifice for friendship's sake, would immediately come to my assistance.
Afterwards you know what happened. Not until I was in
Clarens did I receive the answer to my letter, which had
reached Moscow a week after my flight from thence. In
this reply Kondratiev said he was sorry for my plight, and
concluded with the following words : 'Pray, dear friend,
pray. God will show you how to overcome your sad condition.' A cheap and simple way of getting out of the
difficulty! To-night I have been reading the third volume
of Thackeray's splendid novel *Pendennis*. 'The Major' is
a living type, who frequently reminds me of Kondratiev.
One episode recalled my friend so vividly that I sprang
out of bed, then and there, and wrote him in terms of
mockery which disclosed all my *temper*. When I read your
letter I felt ashamed. I wrote to him again, and asked
pardon for my unreasonable anger. See what a good
influence you have on me, dear friend! You are my
Providence and my comforter!"

To N. F. von Meck.

"VENICE, *December 9th (21st)*, 1877.

"I am working diligently at the orchestration of *our*
Symphony, and am quite absorbed in the task.

"None of my earlier works for orchestra have given me
such trouble as this; but on none have I expended such
love and devotion. I experienced a pleasant surprise
when I began to work at it again. At first I was only
actuated by a desire to bring the unfinished Symphony to

an end, no matter what it cost me.   Gradually, however, I fell more and more under the spell of the work, and now I can hardly tear myself away from it.

"Dear Nadejda Filaretovna, I may be making a mistake, but it seems to me this Symphony is not a mediocre work, but the best I have done so far.   How glad I am that it is *ours*, and that, hearing it, you will know how much I thought of you with every bar.   Would it ever have been finished but for you?   When I was still in Moscow and believed my end to be imminent, I made the following note upon the first sketch, which I had quite forgotten until I came upon it just now: 'In case of my death I desire this book to be given to N. F. von Meck.' I wanted you to keep the manuscript of my last composition.   Now I am not only well, but have to thank you for placing me in such a position that I can devote myself entirely to my work, and I believe a composition is taking form under my pen which will not be destined to oblivion. I may be wrong, however; all artists are alike in their enthusiasm for their latest work.   In any case, I am in good heart now, thanks to the interest of the Symphony. I am even indifferent to the various petty annoyances inflicted upon me by the hotel-keeper.   It is a wretched hotel; but I do not want to leave until the question of my brother's coming is decided."

To N. F. von Meck.

"VENICE, *December* 12th (24th), 1877.

"To-day I have received the pleasant news that Modeste and his nice pupil are coming to join me.   The boy's father (Konradi) has only consented to this arrangement on condition that I will go to some place where the climate is suitable for his son.   He suggests San Remo, where there are plenty of comfortable hotels and pensions. . . . I have had a letter from my brother Anatol, which was very comforting.   They are just as fond of me as ever at Kamenka; I am quite at rest on this score.   I had a fancy that they only pitied me, and this hurt me very deeply!   Lately I have begun to receive letters from them. . . . but my brother has reassured me that all the folk at Kamenka—a group of beings who are very, very dear to me—have forgiven me, and understand I acted blindly, and that my fault was involuntary."

To N. F. von Meck.

"MILAN, *December* 16th (28th), 1877.

"I only arrived here at four o'clock, and after a short walk in the charming town went to the theatre in the evening. Unfortunately, not to La Scala, which was closed to-night, but to Dal Verme, where four years ago *A Life for the Tsar* was produced. This evening *Ruy Blas*, by Marcetti, was given. This opera has made a stir in Italy for some years, so I hoped to hear something interesting. It proved, however, to be a dull, commonplace imitation of Verdi, but lacking the strength and sincere warmth which characterise the coarse, but powerful, works of this composer. The performance was worse than mediocre. Sometimes it awoke sad thoughts in my mind. A young queen comes upon the stage, with whom everyone is in love. The singer who took this part seemed very conscientious and did her utmost. How far she was, however, from resembling a beautiful, queenly woman who has the gift of charming every man she sets eyes upon! And the hero, Ruy Blas! He did not sing so badly, but instead of a handsome young hero, one saw—a lackey. Not the smallest illusion! Then I thought of my own opera. Where shall I find a Tatiana such as Poushkin dreamed of, and such as I have striven to realise in music? Where is the artist who can approach the ideal Oniegin, that cold-hearted dandy, impregnated to the marrow of his bones with the fashionable notion of 'good tone'? Where is there a Lensky, that youth of eighteen, with the flowing locks and the gushing and would-be-original manners of a poetaster *à la* Schiller? How commonplace Poushkin's charming characters will appear on the stage, with all its routine, its drivelling traditions, its veterans— male and female—who undertake without a blush to play the parts of girl-heroines and beardless youths! Moral: it is much pleasanter to write purely instrumental music which involves fewer disappointments. What agony I have had to go through during the performance of my operas, more especially *Vakoula!* What I pictured to myself had so little resemblance to what I actually saw on the stage of the Maryinsky Theatre! What an Oxane, what a Vakoula! You saw them?

"After the opera to-night there was a very frivolous ballet with transformation scenes, a harlequin, and all manner of astonishing things; but the music was dreadfully commonplace. At the same time it amused while the opera performance irritated me. Yet *Ruy Blas* is an excellent operatic subject.

"From Venice I carried away a charming little song. I had two pleasant musical experiences while in Italy. The first was in Florence. I cannot remember whether I told you about it before. One evening Anatol and I suddenly heard someone singing in the street, and saw a crowd in which we joined. The singer was a boy about ten or eleven, who accompanied himself on a guitar. He sang in a wonderfully rich, full voice, with such warmth and finish as one rarely hears, even among accomplished artists. The intensely tragic words of the song had a strange charm coming from these childish lips. The singer, like all Italians, showed an extraordinary feeling for rhythm. This characteristic of the Italians interests me very much, because it is directly contrary to our folksongs as sung by the people."

To N. F. von Meck.

"SAN REMO, *December 20th,* 1877 (*January 1st,* 1878).

"I have found an abode in the Pension "Joli"; four poorly furnished rooms which form a little separate flat at a comparatively low rent.

"The situation of San Remo is truly enchanting. The little town lies on a hill, and is closely packed together. The lower town consists almost exclusively of hotels, which are all overcrowded. San Remo has become the fashion since our Empress stayed here. To-day, without exaggeration, we are having summer weather. The sun was almost unbearable, even without an overcoat. Everywhere one sees olive trees, palms, oranges, lemons, heliotrope, jasmine—in short, it is gloriously beautiful. And yet—shall I tell you or not? When I walk by the sea I am seized with a desire to go home and pour out all my yearning and agitations in a letter to you, or to Toly. Why? Why should a simple Russian landscape, a walk through our homely villages and woods, a tramp over the fields and steppes at sunset, inspire me with such an intense love of nature that I throw myself down on the earth and give myself up to the enchantment with which all these humble things can fill me? Why? I only observe the fact without attempting to explain it.

"I am very glad, however, that I continued my walk, for had I listened to my inner promptings, you would have had to endure another of my jeremiads. I know I shall feel quite differently to-morrow, especially when I begin the finale of my Symphony; but to-day? I am unequal to describing exactly what I feel, or what I want. To return to Russia—no. It would be terrible to go back; for I know I shall return a different man.

" And here?—There is no more lovely spot on earth than San Remo, and yet I assure you that neither the palms, nor the oranges, nor the beautiful blue sea, nor the mountains, make the impression upon me which they might be expected to do. Consolation, peace, well-being I can only draw from within. The success of the Symphony, the consciousness that I am writing something good, will reconcile me to-morrow to all the friction and worry of previous days. The arrival of my brother will be a great joy. I have a curious feeling towards nature—at least towards such a luxuriant nature as surrounds me here. It dazzles me, gets on my nerves, makes me angry. I feel at such moments as though I were going out of my mind. But enough of all this . . . really I am like the old woman whose fate Poushkin describes in his fable of 'The Fisherman and the little Fish.' The greater reason I have to be happy, the more discontented I become. Since I left Russia a few dear souls have shown me such proofs of affection as would suffice to make the happiness of a hundred men. I see that as compared to millions of people who are really unhappy, I should regard myself as a spoilt child of fortune, and yet I am not happy, not

happy, not happy. There are moments of happiness.
There is also that preoccupation with my work which often
possesses me so entirely that I forget everything not
directly connected with my art. But happiness does not
exist for me. However, here is my jeremiad after all; it
seems to have been inevitable! And it is ridiculous,
besides, being in some sort indelicate. But since once for
all you are my best friend, dear Nadejda Filaretovna, must
I not tell you all, *all* that goes on in my queer, morbid
soul? Forgive me this. To-morrow I shall regret it; to-
day it has been a relief to grumble to you a little. Do not
attach too much importance to it. Do you know what I
sometimes feel on such days as this? It comes over me
suddenly that no one really loves me, or can love me,
because I am a pitiable, contemptible being. And I have
not strength to put away such thoughts . . . but there—
I am beginning my lamentations over again.

"I quite forgot to tell you, I spent a day in Genoa. In
its way it is a fine place. Do you know Santa Maria di
Carignano, from the tower of which one gets such a
wonderful view over the whole town? Extraordinarily
picturesque!"

Shortly after Tchaikovsky left Russia for this tour
abroad, he was asked to represent his country as musical
delegate at the Paris Exhibition. The part was not suited
to his nervous and retiring nature, but, as the prospect
seemed remote, he had not given a definite refusal, and by
December had almost entirely forgotten the proposal.
Then, to his extreme annoyance, he received a communication from the Minister of Finance, nominating him to the
post with a fee of 1,000 francs per month. Tchaikovsky
was thrown into the greatest consternation at this news, as
we may gather from the letters he wrote at this time.

"How shall I escape from this dilemma?" he says to
Nadejda von Meck. "I cannot prevent my brother's
coming here, because I have no idea where he is just
now. . . . Neither is there time for me to take counsel

with my friends. Who knows, perhaps it might be good for me to come out of my cell and plunge, against my will, into the stream of Paris life? But if only you knew what it would cost me! It goes without saying that I have not been able to do a stroke of work to-day. O God, when shall I eventually find peace?"

To Anatol Tchaikovsky.

"SAN REMO, *December 23rd*, 1877 (*January 4th*), 1878.

". . . . The day before yesterday I tried to imagine what you would say if you were here. I believe you would advise me to go to Paris.

"But if you saw my miserable face to-day, and could watch me striding up and down my room like a madman, you would certainly say—Stay where you are! Now that I have decided to refuse the post I shall be tormented with the thought that you, Nadejda von Meck, and the others, will be vexed with me. . . . There is one thing I have hidden from you; since the day you left I have taken several glasses of brandy at night, and during the day I drink a good deal. I cannot do without it.

"I never feel calm except when I have taken a little too much. I have accustomed myself so much to this secret tippling that I feel a kind of joy at the sight of the bottle I keep near me. I can only write my letters after a nip. This is a proof that I am still out of health.

"In Paris I should have to be drinking from morning till night to be equal to all the excitement. My hope is in Modeste. A quiet life in a pleasant spot and plenty of work—that is what I need. In a word, for God's sake do not be angry with me that I cannot go to Paris."

To N. F. von Meck.

"SAN REMO, *December, 24th*, 1877 (*January 5th*, 1878).

"I have just received your letter, and must answer it fully. The young Petersburg composers are very gifted, but they are all impregnated with the most horrible presumptuousness and a purely amateur conviction of their superiority to all other musicians in the

universe. The one exception, in later days, has been
Rimsky-Korsakov. He was also an 'auto-dictator' like
the rest, but recently he has undergone a complete change.
By nature he is very earnest, honourable, and conscientious. As a very young man he dropped into a set
which first solemnly assured him he was a genius, and
then proceeded to convince him that he had no need
to study, that academies were destructive to all inspiration
and dried up creative activity. At first he believed all
this. His earliest compositions bear the stamp of striking
ability and a lack of theoretical training. The circle to
which he belonged was a mutual admiration society.
Each member was striving to imitate the work of another,
after proclaiming it as something very wonderful. Consequently the whole set suffered from one-sidedness, lack
of individuality and mannerisms. Rimsky-Korsakov is the
only one among them who discovered, five years ago, that
the doctrines preached by this circle had no sound basis,
that their mockery of the schools and the classical masters,
their denial of authority and of the masterpieces, was
nothing but ignorance. I possess a letter dating from that
time which moved me very deeply. Rimsky-Korsakov
was overcome by despair when he realised how many unprofitable years he had wasted, and that he was following
a road which led nowhere. He began to study with such
zeal that the theory of the schools soon became to
him an indispensable atmosphere. During one summer
he achieved innumerable exercises in counterpoint and
sixty-four fugues, ten of which he sent me for inspection.
From contempt for the schools, Rimsky-Korsakov suddenly
went over to the cult of musical technique. Shortly
after this appeared his symphony and also his quartet.
Both works are full of obscurities and—as you will justly
observe—bear the stamp of dry pedantry. At present
he appears to be passing through a crisis, and it is hard
to predict how it will end. Either he will turn out a great
master, or be lost in contrapuntal intricacies.

"C. Cui is a gifted amateur. His music is not original, but
graceful and elegant; it is too coquettish—'made up'—so
to speak. At first it pleases, but soon satiates us. That
is because Cui's speciality is not music, but fortification,

upon which he has to give a number of lectures in the
various military schools in St. Petersburg. He himself
once told me he could only compose by picking out his
melodies and harmonies as he sat at the piano. When he
hit upon some pretty idea, he worked it up in every detail,
and this process was very lengthy, so that his opera
Ratcliff, for instance, took him ten years to complete.
But, as I have said, we cannot deny that he has talent of
a kind—and at least taste and instinct.

"Borodin—aged fifty—Professor of Chemistry at the
Academy of Medicine, also possesses talent, a very great
talent, which however has come to nothing for the want of
teaching, and because blind fate has led him into the
science laboratories instead of a vital musical existence.
He has not as much taste as Cui, and his technique is so
poor that he cannot write a bar without assistance.

"With regard to Moussorgsky, as you very justly remark,
he is 'used up.' His gifts are perhaps the most remarkable of all, but his nature is narrow and he has no aspirations towards self-perfection. He has been too easily led
away by the absurd theories of his set and the belief in
his own genius. Besides which his nature is not of the
finest quality, and he likes what is coarse, unpolished, and
ugly. He is the exact opposite of the distinguished and
elegant Cui.

"Moussorgsky plays with his lack of polish—and even
seems proud of his want of skill, writing just as it comes
to him, believing blindly in the infallibility of his genius.
As a matter of fact his very original talent flashes forth
now and again.

"Balakirev is the greatest personality of the entire
circle. But he relapsed into silence before he had accomplished much. He possesses a wonderful talent which
various fatal hindrances have helped to extinguish. After
having proclaimed his agnosticism rather widely, he
suddenly became 'pious.' Now he spends all his time in
church, fasts, kisses the relics—and does very little else.
In spite of his great gifts, he has done a great deal of
harm. For instance, he it was who ruined Korsakov's
early career by assuring him he had no need to study.
He is the inventor of all the theories of this remarkable

circle which unites so many undeveloped, falsely developed, or prematurely decayed, talents.

"These are my frank opinions upon these gentlemen. What a sad phenomenon! So many talents from which—with the exception of Rimsky-Korsakov—we can scarcely dare to hope for anything serious. But this is always our case in Russia : vast forces which are impeded by the fatal shadow of a Plevna from taking the open field and fighting as they should. But all the same, these forces exist. Thus Moussorgsky, with all his ugliness, speaks a new idiom. Beautiful it may not be, but it is new. We may reasonably hope that Russia will one day produce a whole school of strong men who will open up new paths in art. Our roughness is, at any rate, better than the poor, would-be-serious pose of a Brahms. The Germans are hopelessly played out. With us there is always the hope that the moral Plevna will fall, and our strength will make itself felt. So far, however, very little has been accomplished. The French have made great progress. True, Berlioz has only just begun to be appreciated, ten years after his death ; but they have many new talents and opponents of routine. In France the struggle against routine is a very hard matter, for the French are terribly conservative in art. They were the last nation to recognise Beethoven. Even as late as the forties they considered him a *madman* or an *eccentric*. The first of French critics, Fétis, bewailed the fact that Beethoven had committed so many sins against the laws of harmony, and obligingly *corrected* these mistakes twenty-five years later.

"Among modern French composers Bizet and Délibes are my favourites. I do not know the overture *Patrie*, about which you wrote to me, but I am very familiar with Bizet's opera *Carmen*. The music is not profound, but it is so fascinating in its simplicity, so full of vitality, so sincere, that I know every note of it from beginning to end. I have already told you what I think of Délibes. In their efforts towards progress the French are not so rash as our younger men ; they do not, like Borodin and Moussorgsky, go beyond the bounds of possibility."

V

To N. F. von Meck.

"SAN REMO, *January* 1st (13th), 1878.

" Returning to San Remo, I found a mass of letters and your telegram. This time I actually heard from you the first intelligence of Radetzky's victory.[1] Thank you for the good news and all your wishes. Whatever may chance, the year before me can bring nothing worse than the last. At any rate the present leaves nothing to be desired, except for my unhappy disposition, which always exaggerates the evil and does not sufficiently rejoice in the good. Among my letters was one from Anatol, who writes a great deal about my wife and the whole unhappy affair. All goes well, but directly I begin to think over the details of a past which is still too recent, my misery returns. I have also received a letter from the committee of the Russian section of the Paris Exhibition, which has made me regret my refusal. My conscience still pricks me. Is it not foolish and egotistical on my part to decline the office of delegate? I write this to you, because I am now in the habit of telling you *everything*. . . ."

To N. G. Rubinstein.

"SAN REMO, *January* 1st (13th), 1878.

" . . . From Albrecht's telegram, which I found here on my return from Milan, I gather that you are vexed with me for having declined to act as delegate. Dear friend, you know me well ; could I really have helped the cause of Russian music in Paris? You know how little gift I have for organising. Added to which there is my misanthropical shyness, which is becoming a kind of incurable malady. What would have been the result? I should only worry myself to death with both the French and the Russian rabble, and nothing would be carried out. As regards myself, or any personal profit it might bring me,

---

[1] The Shipka Pass.

it will be sufficient to say that, without exaggeration, I would rather be condemned to penal servitude than act as delegate in Paris. Were I in a different frame of mind, I might agree that the visit could be of use to me; but not at present. I am ill, mentally and physically; just now I could not live in any situation in which I had to be busy, agitated, and conspicuously before the world. . . . Now as regards the symphony (No. 4) I despatched it to you from Milan on Thursday. Possibly it may not please you at first sight, therefore I beg you not to be too hasty in your judgment, but only to write me your opinion after you have heard it performed. I hope you will see your way to bringing it out at one of the later concerts. It seems to me to be my best work. Of my two recent productions—the opera and the symphony—I give decided preference to the latter. . . . You are the one conductor in all the world on whom I can rely. The first movement contains one or two awkward and recurrent changes of time to which I call your special attention. The third movement is to be played *pizzicato*; the quicker the better, but I do not quite know how fast it is possible to play *pizzicato*."

To S. I. Taneiev.

"SAN REMO, *January 2nd* (14*th*), 1878.

". . . Very probably you are quite right in saying that my opera is not effective for the stage. I must tell you, however, I do not care a rap for such effectiveness. It has long been an established fact that I have no dramatic vein, and now I do not trouble about it. If it is really not fit for the stage, then it had better not be performed! I composed this opera because I was moved to express in music all that seems to cry out for such expression in *Eugene Oniegin*. I did my best, working with indescribable pleasure and enthusiasm, and thought very little of the treatment, the effectiveness, and all the rest. I spit upon 'effects'! Besides, what are effects? For instance, if *Aïda* is effective, I can assure you I would not compose an opera on a similar subject for all the wealth of the world; for I want to handle human beings, not puppets. I would gladly compose an opera which was completely lacking in startling effects, but which offered characters resembling my own, whose feelings and experiences I shared and understood. The feelings of an Egyptian Princess, a Pharaoh, or some mad Nubian, I cannot enter into, or comprehend. Some instinct, however, tells me that these people must have felt, acted, spoken, and expressed themselves quite differently from ourselves. Therefore my music, which—entirely against my will—is impregnated with Schumannism, Wagnerism, Chopinism, Glinkaism, Berliozism, and all the other 'isms' of our time, would be as out of keeping with the characters of *Aïda* as the elegant speeches of Racine's heroes—couched in the second person plural—are unsuited to the real Orestes or the real Andromache. Such music would be a *falsehood*, and all falsehoods are abhorrent to me. Besides, I am reaping the fruits of my insufficient harvest of book-learning. Had I a wider acquaintance with the literatures of other countries, I should no doubt have discovered a subject which was both suitable for the stage and in harmony with my taste. Unfortunately I am not able to find such things for myself, nor do I know anyone who could call my attention to such a subject as Bizet's *Carmen*, for example, one of the most perfect operas of our day. You will ask what I actually require. I will tell you. Above all I want no kings, no tumultuous populace, no gods, no pompous marches—in short, none of those things which are the attributes of 'grand opera.' I am looking for an intimate yet thrilling drama, based upon such a conflict of circumstance as I myself have experienced or witnessed, which is capable of touching me to the quick. I have nothing to say against the fantastic element, because it does not restrict one, but rather offers unlimited freedom. I feel I am not expressing myself very clearly. In a word, Aïda is so remote, her love for Radames touches me so little—since I cannot picture it in my mind's eye—that my music would lack the vital warmth which is essential to good work. Not long since I saw *L'Africaine* in Genoa. This unhappy African, what she endures! Slavery, imprisonment, death under a poisoned tree, in her last moment the sight of her rival's triumph—and yet I never once pitied her! But what

effects there were : a ship, a battle, all manner of dodges!
When all is said and done, what is the use of these effects?
. . . With regard to your remark that Tatiana does not
fall in love with Oniegin at first sight, allow me to say—
you are mistaken. She falls in love at once. She does
not learn to know him first, and then to care for him.
Love comes suddenly to her. Even before Oniegin comes
on the scene she is in love with the hero of her vague
romance. The instant she sets eyes on Oniegin she in-
vests him with all the qualities of her ideal, and the love
she has hitherto bestowed upon the creation of her fancy
is now transferred to a human being.

"The opera *Oniegin* will never have a success; I feel
already assured of that. I shall never find singers capable,
even partially, of fulfilling my requirements. The routine
which prevails in our theatres, the senseless performances,
the system of retaining invalided artists and giving no
chance to younger ones: all this stands in the way of my
opera being put on the stage. I would much prefer to
confide it to the theatre of the Conservatoire. Here, at
any rate, we escape the commonplace routine of the opera,
and those fatal invalids of both sexes. Besides which, the
performances at the Conservatoire are private, *en petit
comité.* This is more suitable to my modest work, which
I shall not describe as an opera, if it is published. I should
like to call it 'lyrical scenes,' or something of that kind.
This opera has no future! I was quite aware of this when
I wrote it; nevertheless, I completed it and shall give it to
the world if Jurgenson is willing to publish it. I shall
make no effort to have it performed at the Maryinsky
Theatre ; on the contrary, I should oppose the idea as far
as possible. It is the outcome of an invincible inward
impulse. I assure you one should only compose opera
under such conditions. It is only necessary to think of
stage effects to a certain extent. If my enthusiasm for
Eugene Oniegin is evidence of my limitations, my stupidity
and ignorance of the requirements of the stage, I am very
sorry ; but I can at least affirm that the music *proceeds in
the most literal sense from my inmost being.* It is not
manufactured and forced. But enough of *Oniegin.*

"Now a word as to my latest work, the Fourth Sym-

S

phony, which must have reached Moscow by now. What will you think of it? I value your opinion highly, and fear your criticism. I know you are absolutely sincere, that is why I think so much of your judgment. I cherish one dream, one intense desire, which I hardly dare disclose, lest it should seem selfish. You must write and play, and play and write, for your own self, and you ought not to waste time on *arrangements*. There are but two men in Moscow —nay, in the whole world—to whom I would entrust the arrangement of my symphony for four hands. One of these is Klindworth, and the other a certain person who lives in the *Oboukhov pereoulok*. The latter would be all the dearer to me, if I were not afraid of asking too much. Do not hesitate to refuse my request. Yet if you feel able to say 'yes,' I shall jump for joy, although my corpulence would be rather an impediment to such behaviour."

To K. K. Albrecht.

"SAN REMO, *January 8th* (*20th*), 1878.

" To-day I received your letter. Had it come a fortnight ago I should no doubt have reflected whether in refusing the office of delegate I had done something foolish or wrong. Now, however, the matter is decided, and on mature consideration I am convinced I was wise not to undertake a business so antipathetic to my temperament. . . . Let us thoroughly consider the question In what way could I have been useful as a delegate: First, to the cause of Russian music, and secondly, to myself?

" 1. *As regards Russian music*. . . . What could I have done, under the circumstances, to interest the Parisians in our music? How could I (unless funds were forthcoming) arrange concerts and evenings for chamber music? What a poor figure I should have cut beside the other delegates, who were well supplied with money! But even had funds been forthcoming, what could I have done? Can I conduct anything? I might have beaten time to my own compositions, but I could not fill up the programmes with my works. I must, on the contrary, have put them aside in order to bring forward the compositions of Glinka, Dargomijsky, Serov, Rimsky-Korsakov, Cui, and Borodin.

And for all this I should have had to prepare myself, unless I risked bringing disgrace upon Russian music. That I should have disgraced it is certain. Then all Russia would have blamed me afterwards, and with justification. I do not deny the fact that a man of temperament, skill, and talent for organisation could do much. But you know that apart from my speciality I am a useless sort of being. So, you see, I should have been of *no service to Russian music,* even if the Government had allowed me sufficient money to carry out any plans.

"2. *As concerns myself.* . . . I must say that the idea of making the acquaintance of the Parisian musical lights seemed to me the most terrible part of the business. To make myself amiable and pay court to all the ragtag and bobtail is not in my line. Pride shows itself in many different ways. In my case it takes the form of avoiding all contact with people who do not know or appreciate my worth. For instance, it would be unbearable to have to stand humbly before Saint-Saëns and to be honoured by his gracious condescension, when in my heart of hearts I feel myself *as far above him as the Alps.* In Paris my self-respect (which is very great in spite of my apparent modesty) would suffer hourly from having to mix with all kinds of celebrities who would look down upon me. To bring my works to their notice, to convince them that I am of some consequence—this is impossible to me. . . . Now let us leave the question of my own reputation and speak of my health. Physically I feel very well, at any rate better than could be expected ; but mentally I am still far from sound. In a word, I am on the verge of insanity. I can only live in an atmosphere of complete quiet, quite away from all the turmoil of great cities. In order that you may realise how changed I am, let me tell you that now I spit—yes, spit upon the thought of all success or notoriety abroad. I beg and pray one thing only : to be let alone. I would gladly be dropped in some remote desert, if I could thus avoid contact with my fellow-men. . . . I cannot live without work, and when I can no longer compose I shall occupy myself with other musical matters. But I will not lift a finger to push my works in the world, because I do not care about it one way or the other. Anyone can play or sing my works if they please ; if no one pleases—it is all the same to me, for, as I tell you, I *spit, spit, spit* upon the whole business ! ! !   Once again, I repeat: were I rich I should live in complete seclusion from the world and only occasionally visit Moscow, to which I am deeply attached. . . . I am grieved, my dear Karl, that you are vexed with me.   But listen : I have learnt from bitter experience that we cannot do violence to our nature without being punished for it.   My whole self, every nerve, every fibre in me, protests against undertaking this post of delegate, and I subscribe to this protest.

"Karl, I recommend to you most highly my latest work. I mean my symphony. Feel kindly towards it, for I cannot be at rest without your praise. You do not guess how I value your opinion. Give Kashkin my best thanks for his letter and show him this one by way of reply, as it will serve for him too. Your warm words about *Eugene Oniegin* are 1,000,000,000,000 times more to me than the condescension of any Frenchmen. I embrace you both, and also Rubinstein. But as to fame, I *spit, spit,* yes, *spit* upon it."

To. N. F. von Meck.

"SAN REMO, *January* 14*th* (26*th*), 1876.

" Two nights running we have had a gale from the north-west. It howled and whistled until I had the shivers. Last night it rattled and shook my window so that I could not sleep and began to think over my life. I do not know whence it came, but suddenly a very pleasant thought passed through my mind. I thought that I had never yet shown my gratitude to you in its fullest extent, my best and dearest friend. I saw clearly that all you are doing for me, with such untiring goodness and sympathy, is so beyond measure generous that I am not really worthy of it. I recollected the crisis when I found myself on the verge of an abyss, and believed that all was over, that nothing remained but to vanish from the face of the earth, and how, at the same time, an inward voice reminded me of you and predicted that you would hold out your hand to me. The inner voice proved true. You and my brothers have given me back my life. Not only am I still living, but I can work ;

without work life has no meaning for me.   I know you do
not want me to be pouring out assurances of my gratitude
every moment; but let me say once for all that I owe you
everything, everything; that you have not only given me
the means to come through a very difficult crisis without
anxiety, but have brought the new elements of light and
gladness into my life.   I am now speaking of your friendship, my dear, kind Nadejda Filaretovna, and I assure you
since I have found in you so eternally good a friend, I can
never be quite unhappy again.   Perhaps the time will
come when I shall no longer require the material assistance you have bestowed upon me with such admirable
delicacy of feeling, such fabulous generosity; but I shall
never be able to do without the moral aid and comfort I
have derived from you.   With my undecided character,
which is innate in me, and with my faculty for getting out
of heart, I am happy in the consciousness of having so
good a friend at hand, who is always ready to help me and
point out the right course of action.   I know you will not
only be the upholder of my good and wise achievements,
but also a judge of my faults; a compassionate judge,
however, who has my welfare at heart.   All this I said to
myself as I lay awake last night, and determined to write
it to you to-day.   In doing so I am merely satisfying my
great desire to open my heart to you.

"Such a strange coincidence happened this morning! A
letter from N. Rubinstein[1] was put into my hands.   He
has returned from his journey, and lost no time in replying to my letter, in which I excused myself for shirking
the duties of delegate.   His letter breathes savage wrath.
This would not matter so much, but that the whole tone of
the communication is so dry, so lacking in cordial feeling,
so exaggerated! He says my illness is a mere fraud, that I
am only *putting it on*, that I prefer the *dolce far niente*
aspect of life, that I am drifting away from my work, and
that he deeply regrets having shown me so much sympathy,
because it has only encouraged my indolence! !! etc., etc."

This lack of sympathy and complete misunderstanding
of his motives provoked a sharp reply on Tchaikovsky's

---

[1] Unfortunately this letter has been lost.

part. But in calmer moments he saw clearly all the artistic benefit he had derived from N. Rubinstein's friendship, and never ceased to feel grateful for it.

To Nicholas Rubinstein.

"SAN REMO, *January* 14*th* (26*th*), 1878.

". . . . I received your letter to-day. It would have annoyed me very much, had I not told myself you were keeping in view my ultimate recovery. To my regret, however, you seem to see what is good for me precisely where I—and several others—see what is inimical to my health ; in the very thing which appears to me an unprofitable and aimless exertion. . . . All you have written to me, and also your manner of saying it, only proves *how little you know me*, as I have frequently observed on former occasions. Possibly you may be right, and I am only *putting it on ;* but that is precisely the nature of my illness. . . . From your letter I can only gather the impression that in you I possess a great benefactor, and that I have proved an ungrateful and unworthy recipient of your favours. It is useless to try this tone ! I know how much I am indebted to you ; but, in the first place, your reproaches cool my gratitude, and, secondly, it annoys me when you pose as a benefactor in a matter in which you have proved yourself quite the reverse.

". . . But, enough of this. Let us rather speak of those things in which you have really been my benefactor. Not possessing any gifts as a conductor, I should certainly have failed to make a name, had not so admirable an interpreter of my works been always at hand. Without you I should have been condemned to perpetual maltreatment. You are the one man who has rightly understood my works. Your extraordinary artistic instinct enables you to take a difficult work—without any previous study—and carry it through with only two rehearsals. I must beg you once again to bring this power to bear upon my opera and symphony. As regards the former—much as I desire it—I shall not be hurt if you find it impossible to perform it this season. The symphony, on the other hand, must be given soon, for in many ways it would seriously inconvenience me if the performance were postponed. . . . I have often told you that in spite of my loathing for the duties of a professor, and the thought of being tied for life to the Conservatoire, custom has now made it impossible for me to live anywhere but in Moscow and in your society."

To N. F. von Meck.

"SAN REMO, *January* 15*th* (27*th*), 1878.

"We have just returned from a beautiful excursion to Colla. . . . To-day was exquisite; a real spring day. We hired a donkey for Kolya,[1] so that he might take part in the outing. It was not a very steep climb, and all the way the olive trees shut out the views of the sea and town, but all the same it was beautiful. Once I walked ahead of the others and sat under a tree, when suddenly there came over me that feeling of intense delight which I so often experienced during my country rambles in Russia, and for which I have longed in vain since I have been here. I was alone in the solemn stillness of the woods. Such moments are wonderful, indescribable, not to be compared with any other experience. The indispensable condition is—solitude. I always like walking alone in the country. The companionship of anyone as dear to me as my brother has its charms, but it is quite a different thing. In a word, I was happy. First of all I felt a great desire to write to you, and on the way home yet another pleasure awaited me. Do you love flowers? I am passionately fond of them, especially the wild flowers of the field and forest. To my mind the queen of flowers is the lily-of-the-valley; I love it to distraction. Modeste, who is equally fond of flowers, is all for the violet, so that we often fall out on the subject. I declare that violets smell of pomade, and he retorts that my lilies look like nightcaps. In any case I recognise in the violet a dangerous rival to the lily-of-the-valley, and am very fond of it. There are plenty of violets to be bought in the streets here, but as I had failed to find a single flower, even after the most diligent search, I began to regard this as the special privilege of the children of the soil. To-day, on my way home, I had the luck to come

---

[1] Nicholas Konradi, pupil of Modeste Tchaikovsky.

upon a place where they grew in profusion. This is the second subject of my letter. I send you a few sweet blossoms gathered by my own hand. May they remind you of the South, the sun, and the sea!"

To N. F. von Meck.

"SAN REMO, *January 25th (February 6th)*, 1878.

"I am feeling splendidly well. My physical health is first-rate; my head clear and strong. I observe myself with delight, and have come to the conclusion that I am now completely recovered. Do you know, my dear friend, people have not been altogether wrong in reporting that I had gone out of my mind? When I look back on all I did, and all the follies I committed, I am unwillingly forced to the conclusion that my brain was temporarily affected, and has only now returned to its normal state. Much in my recent condition now takes on the semblance of a strange dream; something remote, a weird nightmare in which a man bearing my name, my likeness, and my consciousness acted as one acts in dreams: in a meaningless, disconnected, paradoxical way. That was not my sane self, in full possession of logical and reasonable will-powers. Everything I did then bore the character of an unhealthy conflict between will and intelligence, which is nothing less than insanity. Amid these nightmares which darkened my world during this strange and terrible — but fortunately brief—period, I clung for salvation to the one or two beings who were dearest to me, who seemed sent to draw me out of the abyss. To you, and to my two dear brothers, *to all three of you*, I owe, not only my life, but my mental and physical recovery."

To P. I. Jurgenson.

"SAN REMO, *January 26th (February 7th)*, 1878.

"Your letter reached me to-day, dear Peter Ivanovich. You are very kind. I am deeply touched by your liberality. All the same, I will not accept any money for the opera unless it should be performed in some important theatre, and, even then, nothing approaching to the large sum you propose. The fee for the symphony I wish to pass on to Taneiev. For the translations I cannot take anything from you, because I think them very poor. As regards a fee for the violin and 'cello pieces, we will speak of it later.

"Dearest friend, I am only too thankful that you are not parsimonious to me and are so willing to publish my works. But this is nothing new. I have always appreciated your large-hearted liberality. *Merci, merci, merci!*"

To Nicholas Rubinstein.

"San Remo, *January 30th (February 11th),* 1878.

"Dear Friend,—I have read your letter with great pleasure. . . . If I expressed myself too sharply, please forget it. Now let us drop the subject entirely.

"I think you have acted wisely in postponing my opera until next year. I agree with you that it is better to have it studied without undue haste and to perform the work in its entirety. You may rest assured that I shall not give the work to the Petersburg Conservatoire. So far, I have not been asked to do so; if I were invited, I should refuse. I hope this letter may reach you about the moment of the first rehearsal of my (Fourth) Symphony. I am very anxious about the Scherzo. I think I told you that the quicker it can go, the better. Now I begin to think it should not be taken *too* fast. However, I entrust myself entirely to your intelligence, and believe you will find out the right *tempo* better than I can.

"I have read your letter a second time. You ask if I care to have your advice. Of course I do. You know I am always ready to accept the advice of a judicious friend and that I have frequently sought yours, not only in matters concerning music, but in my daily life. It was not the advice you gave me in your letter which hurt me, but the harsh, dry tone (at least so it seemed to me) of your communication, the reproach to my indolence, and the insinuation that I only refused to go to Paris because N. von Meck was allowing me enough to live upon; in short, you entirely misunderstood the true motives of my conduct.

"I have become terribly misanthropical, and dread the thought of having to change my present mode of life, in which I hardly come in contact with anyone. At the same time I am weary of ˌit, and would gladly relinquish all the natural beauties and the climate of this place to be once more in my beloved Moscow."

To N. F. von Meck.

"SAN REMO, *February* 1*st* (13*th*), 1878.

" MY DEAR FRIEND,—Yesterday I forgot to thank you for the Schopenhauer.[1]

"Has not the thought occurred to you that now I am quite recovered I ought to return to Russia to take up my duties at the Conservatoire and my old ways of life ? The thought constantly passes through my mind, and perhaps it might be good for me in every way if I decided to act upon it. And yet, with all my longing for Russia, and my attachment to Moscow, I should find it terribly hard suddenly to give up this life of freedom and the convalescence I am now enjoying, and return to my teaching and my various complications—in a word, to my old life. I shudder at the very thought. Give me your frank opinion. Answer me this question, entirely oblivious of the fact that you are making me an allowance. The fact that I profited by your wealth to travel abroad for my health's sake does not weigh upon me seriously. I know the sentiment which prompted your offer of pecuniary assistance, and I have long since grown to regard the situation as quite normal. My relations with you are outside the scope of everyday friendship. From you I can accept assistance without any sense of embarrassment. This is not the difficulty.

" Since Rubinstein told me I was drifting into indolence and feigning ill-health (that was his expression) I have been somewhat troubled by the thought that perhaps it was actually my duty to hasten back to Moscow. Help me to decide this question, kind friend, without showing me excessive indulgence.

" On the other hand, if they have been able to do without me for six months, surely now—when there remain but three months before the vacation—I shall not be greatly missed . . . To sum up the foregoing arguments : although

---

[1] *The World as Will and Idea.*

I may now be equal to resuming my duties, it would be very hard upon me to be forced to do so, because I am most anxious to give myself a longer convalescence in order to return in September altogether a new man, having forgotten—as far as forgetfulness is possible—the unhappy events of six months ago. My request to you involves a strange contradiction. I ask you to tell me the truth and, without allowing yourself to be influenced by any side issues, to exact the fulfilment of my duty ; while at the same time you will read between the lines : for God's sake do not insist on my returning to Moscow now, for it will make me profoundly miserable.

" I remember writing to you in a very depressed frame of mind from Florence, for I was out of spirits at the time. Florence itself was in no way to blame for my mood. Now I am feeling quite well again, I have conceived a great wish to return there, chiefly because Modeste has never been in Italy and I know how he would enjoy all the art treasures in that city. He has far greater feeling for the plastic arts than I have, and possibly his enthusiasm may be communicated to me. So I have decided to await the coming of spring in Florence and then go to Switzerland *via* Mont Cenis. Early in April I shall return to Russia, probably to Kamenka, where I shall stay until September.

" I will not attempt to conceal from you, most invaluable of friends, that the consciousness of having achieved two works on a large scale, in both of which, it seems to me, I have made a distinct advance, is a great source of consolation. The rehearsals for the symphony will commence soon. Would you find it possible—if you are quite well by then—to attend one of them? One gains so much by hearing a new and lengthy work twice. I am so anxious you should like this symphony! It is impossible to get a true idea of it at one hearing. The second time it grows clearer. Much that escapes us at first then attracts our attention ; the details fall into place ; the leading ideas assume their proper proportions as compared with the subordinate matter. It would be such an excellent thing if you could manage this.

" I am in a rose-coloured mood. Glad the opera is finished, glad spring is at hand, glad I am well and free, glad to feel safe from unpleasant meetings, but happiest of all to possess in your friendship, and in my brothers' affection, such sure props in life, and to be conscious that I may eventually perfect my art. I trust this feeling is no self-deception, but a just appreciation of my powers. I thank you for all, for all."

VI

To N. F. von Meck.

"FLORENCE, *February 9th (21st),* 1878.

"We arrived in Florence to-day. A charming and attractive town. I came here with the pleasantest feelings, and thought how different the place appeared to me two months ago. What a change has taken place in my mental state! What a sad and sorry creature I was then—and now, how well I am! What glad days lie before me! Once again I am able to delight in life, in the full, luxuriant life of Italy.

"This evening we wandered through the streets. How beautiful! A mild evening; the life and bustle of the thoroughfares; the brilliant illumination of the shop-windows! What fun it is to mix with the crowd, unknown and unrecognised! Italy is beginning to cast over me her magic spell. I feel so free here, so cheerful, amid the turmoil and hum of life.

"But in spite of the enjoyments of life in Italy, in spite of the good effect it has upon me—I am, and shall ever be, faithful to my Russia. Do you know, I have never yet come across anyone so much in love with Mother Russia —especially Great Russia—as myself? The verses by Lermontov which you sent me only depict one side of our native land: that indefinable charm which lies in our modest, plain, poor, but wide and open landscape. I go further. I am passionately devoted to the Russian people, to the language, to the Russian spirit, to the fine Russian type of countenance and to Russian customs. Lermontov says frankly: 'the sacred traditions of our past' do not move his soul. I love these traditions. I believe my

ILIA PETROVICH TCHAIKOVSKY, THE COMPOSER'S FATHER, IN 1860

THE HOUSE IN WHICH TCHAIKOVSKY WAS BORN, AT VOTINSK

THE TCHAIKOVSKY FAMILY IN 1848

PETER ILICH TCHAIKOVSKY. ALEXANDRA ANDREIEVNA (THE MOTHER). ZINAIDA ILYINICHA.
NICHOLAS ILICH. HYPPOLITE ILICH. ILIA PETROVICH (THE FATHER).
7. ALEXANDRA ILYINICHA. (CENTRE)

From an old Daguerrotype)

ALEXANDRA ANDREIEVNA TCHAIKOVSKY, THE COMPOSER'S MOTHER, IN 1848

TCHAIKOVSKY IN 1859

THE COMPOSER'S FATHER WITH HIS TWIN SONS MODESTE AND ANATOL, 1855

TCHAIKOVSKY IN 1859

TCHAIKOVSKY IN 1863

TCHAIKOVSKY IN 1868

TCHAIKOVSKY IN 1873

TCHAIKOVSKY IN 1874

TCHAIKOVSKY IN 1877

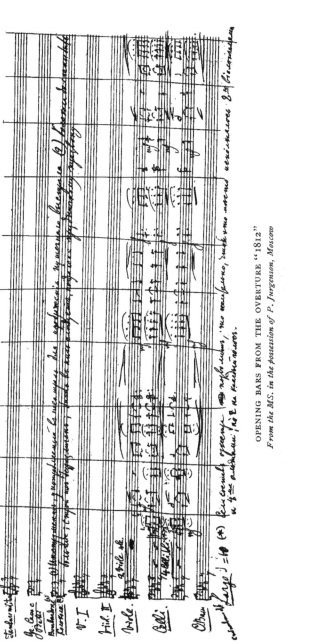

OPENING BARS FROM THE OVERTURE "1812"

From the MS. in the possession of P. Jurgenson, Moscow

FRAGMENT FROM A LETTER IN WHICH TCHAIKOVSKY SKETCHES A THEME
FOR "THE ENCHANTRESS"

TCHAIKOVSKY IN 1888

(From a photograph by Reitlinger, Paris)

ALEXANDER SILOTI   PETER ILICH TCHAIKOVSKY

TCHAIKOVSKY'S HOUSE AT FROLOVSKOE

THE HOUSE IN WHICH TCHAIKOVSKY LIVED AT KLIN

(HIS LAST HOME)

TCHAIKOVSKY'S BEDROOM AT KLIN

SITTING-ROOM AT KLIN

TCHAIKOVSKY IN 1893
(From a photograph taken in London)

sympathy for the Orthodox faith, the tenets of which have long been undermined in me by destructive criticism, has its source in my innate affection for its national element. I could not say what particular virtue or quality it is which endears Russia and the Russians to me.   No doubt such qualities exist.   A lover, however, does not love for such reasons, but because he cannot help himself.

" This is why I feel so angry with those among us who are ready to perish of hunger in a garret in Paris, and who seem to enjoy running down everything Russian ; who can spend their whole lives abroad without regret, on the grounds that there are fewer comforts to be had in Russia. I hate these people ; they trample in the mud all that to me is inexpressibly precious and sacred.

" But to return to Italy.   It would be a heavy punishment to be condemned to spend my life in this beautiful land ; but a temporary sojourn here is another matter. Everything in Italy exercises a charm for one who is travelling for health and relaxation. . . . This conviction has so gained ground with me that I am beginning to wonder if, instead of going to Switzerland, it might not be better to visit Naples.   Naples continually beckons and calls to me !   I have not yet definitely decided.   It will be wiser to think it over.   Of course I shall let you know the result of my reflections in good time.

" I think you must have been amused by the letter in which I told you I was going to give you a brief outline of Schopenhauer's philosophy.   It is evident that you are thoroughly acquainted with the subject, while I have hardly yet reached the essential question : the moral aspect of the matter.   It strikes me you make a very just evaluation of his curious theories.   His final deductions contain something hurtful to human dignity, something dry and egotistical, which is not warmed by any love towards mankind. However, as I have said, I have not yet got to the root of the matter.   In the exposition of his views upon the meaning of intelligence and will, and their interrelationship, there is much truth and ingenuity.   Like yourself, I marvel how a man who has never attempted to carry out in his own life his theories of austere asceticism should preach to others the complete renunciation of all the joys of life.   In

any case the book interests me immensely, and I hope to
discuss it further with you after a more thorough study of
its contents.   Meanwhile, just one observation : how can a
man who takes so low a view of human intelligence, and
accords it so subordinate a position, display at the same
time such self-assurance, such a haughty belief in the infallibility of his own reason, heaping contempt upon the
views of others, and regarding himself as the sole arbiter
of truth?   What a contradiction!   To declare at each step
that the reasoning faculty in man is something fortuitous,
a function of the brain (therefore merely a physiological
function), and as weak and imperfect as all human things—
and at the same time to set such value upon his own process of reasoning!   A philosopher like Schopenhauer, who
goes so far as to deny to mankind anything beyond an
instinctive desire to perpetuate his species, ought, first of
all, to be prepared to acknowledge the complete uselessness
of all systems of philosophy.   A man who is convinced
that non-existence is the best thing of all should endeavour
to act up to his conviction ; should suppress himself, anni-
hilate himself, and leave those in peace who desire to live.
So far, I cannot quite make out whether he really believes
himself to be doing mankind a great service by his philosophy.   What use is it to prove to us that there can be nothing
more lamentable than existence?   If the blind instinct of
perpetuation is so strong in us, if no power suffices to
weaken our love of individual life, why should he poison
this life with his pessimism?   What end does this serve?
It might seem as though he were advocating suicide ; but
on the contrary, he forbids self-destruction.   These are
questions which arise in my mind, and to which perhaps I
may find answers when I have finished the book.

"You ask me, my friend, if I have known love other
than platonic.   Yes and no.   If the question had been
differently put, if you had asked me whether I had ever
found complete happiness in love, I should have replied no,
and again, no.   Besides, I think the answer to this question
is to be heard in my music.   If, however, you ask me
whether I have felt the whole power and inexpressible
stress of love, I must reply yes, yes, yes ; for often and
often have I striven to render in music all the anguish and

the bliss of love. Whether I have been successful I do not know, or rather I leave others to judge. I do not in the least agree with you that music cannot interpret the universal nature of love. On the contrary, I think only music is capable of doing so. You say words are necessary. O no! This is just where words are not needed, and where they have no power; a more eloquent language comes in, which is music. Look at the poetical forms to which poets have recourse in order to sing of love; they simply usurp the spheres which belong inseparably to music. Words clothed in poetical forms cease to be mere words; they become partly music. The best proof that love-poetry is really more music than words lies in the fact that such poetry—if you read it carefully from the point of view of words rather than of music—contains very little meaning. (I refer you to the poet Fet, whom I greatly admire.) And yet it has a meaning, and a very profound one, although it is more musical than literary.

"I am delighted that you value instrumental music so highly. Your observation that words often spoil music and degrade it from its highest level is perfectly true. I have often felt this very keenly, and perhaps therein lies the reason why I am more successful with instrumental than with vocal music."

On February 10th (22nd), Tchaikovsky's Fourth Symphony was performed for the first time at one of the symphony concerts of the Russian Musical Society. It did not produce, either upon the public or the Press, that impression which the composer had confidently awaited. Most of the papers passed it over in silence, and the remainder only record an indifferent success, both for the work and its performance.

To N. F. von Meck.

"FLORENCE, *February 12th (24th)*, 1878.

"Early yesterday came your telegram, dear friend. It gave me inexpressible pleasure. I was more than anxious to know how you liked the Symphony. Probably you would have given me some friendly sign of your sympathy, even if you had not cared much about it. From the warm tone of your telegram, however, I see that you are satisfied, on the whole, with the work which was written for you. In my heart of hearts I feel sure it is the best thing I have done so far. It seems rather strange that not one of my friends in Moscow has thought it worth while to give me any news of the Symphony, although I sent off the score nearly six weeks ago. At the same time as your telegram I received one signed by Rubinstein and all the others. But it only stated the fact that the work had been very well performed. Not a word as to its merits; perhaps that is intended to be understood. Thank you for your news of the success of 'my favourite child,' and the cordial words of your telegram. My thoughts were in the concert-room. I calculated the moment when the opening phrase would be heard, and endeavoured, by following every detail, to realise the effect of my music upon the public. The first movement (the most complicated, but also the best) is probably far too long, and would not be completely understood at the first hearing. The other movements are simple. . . .

"I have not finished Schopenhauer yet, and am saving up my opinions upon it for some future letter. I have been twice with my brother to the Uffizi and Palazzo Pitti. Thanks to Modeste, I took in a good many artistic impressions. He was lost in ecstasy before the masterpieces of Raphael and Leonardo da Vinci. We also visited an exhibition of modern pictures, and discovered a few fine works. If I am not mistaken, the spirit of realism has entered into modern Italian painting. All the pictures I have seen here by painters of the present day are more remarkable for the truthful presentment of details than for profound or poetic thought. The figures are very lifelike, even when the conception is crude. For instance, a page drawing aside a curtain; both page and curtain are so real that one actually expects to see some movement. An old Pompeiian woman, leaning back in an ancient chair and indulging in a burst of Homeric laughter, makes one want to laugh too. All this has no pretensions to profound thought, but the drawing and colouring are astonishingly truthful.

" As regards music, Italy is in a bad way. Such a town as Florence, for instance, has no opera house. There are theatres, but nothing is given in them because there is no impresario."

To N. F. von Meck.

" FLORENCE, *February* 16*th* (28*th*), 1878.

". . . Of all that I have seen here the chapel of the Medici in San Lorenzo has made the most profound impression upon me. It is grandiose and beautiful. Here, for the first time, I realised the greatness of Michael Angelo in its fullest significance. I think he has a spiritual affinity with Beethoven. The same breadth and power, the same daring courage, which sometimes almost oversteps the limits of the beautiful, the same dark and troubled moods. Probably this idea is not original. Taine gives a very ingenious comparison between Raphael and Mozart. But whether anyone has ever drawn a parallel between Michael Angelo and Beethoven I cannot say.

" I have finished Schopenhauer. I do not know what impression this philosophy might have made upon me had I come to know it in some other place, under different surroundings. Here it seems to me only a brilliant paradox. I think Schopenhauer's inconsequence lies in his ultimate conclusions. When he has proved that non-existence is better than existence, we say to ourselves: granted, but what are we to do? It is in his reply to this question that he shows his weakness. Logically, his theories lead direct to suicide. But Schopenhauer evidently shrinks from this dangerous method of shifting the burden of life, and not daring to recommend self-destruction as a universal method of carrying his philosophy into practice, he falls into a curious sophistry and endeavours to prove that the man who commits suicide merely lays stress on his love of life. This is neither logical nor ingenious. As regards ' Nirvana,' this is a species of insanity not worth discussion. But, in any case, I have read Schopenhauer with the greatest interest, and found in him much that is extraordinarily clever. His definition of love is original, although a few details are somewhat distorted

T

and wrested from the truth. You are quite right in saying that we must regard with suspicion the views of a philosopher who bids us renounce all joy in life and stamp out every lust of the flesh, while he himself, without any qualms of conscience, enjoyed the pleasures of existence to the day of his death, and had a very good notion of managing his affairs for the best."

To N. F. von Meck.

"FLORENCE, *February* 17*th* (*March* 1*st*), 1878.

"What joy your letter brought me to-day, dearest Nadejda Filaretovna! I am inexpressibly delighted that the symphony pleases you: that, hearing it, you felt just as I did while writing it, and that my music found its way to your heart.

"You ask if in composing this symphony I had a special programme in view. To such questions regarding my symphonic works I generally answer: nothing of the kind. In reality it is very difficult to answer this question. How interpret those vague feelings which pass through one during the composition of an instrumental work, without reference to any definite subject? It is a purely lyrical process. A kind of musical shriving of the soul, in which there is an encrustation of material which flows forth again in notes, just as the lyrical poet pours himself out in verse. The difference consists in the fact that music possesses far richer means of expression, and is a more subtle medium in which to translate the thousand shifting moments in the mood of a soul. Generally speaking, the germ of a future composition comes suddenly and unexpectedly. If the soil is ready—that is to say, if the disposition for work is there—it takes root with extraordinary force and rapidity, shoots up through the earth, puts forth branches, leaves, and, finally, blossoms. I cannot define the creative process in any other way than by this simile. The great difficulty is that the germ must appear at a favourable moment, the rest goes of itself. It would be vain to try to put into words that immeasurable sense of bliss which comes over me directly a new idea awakens in me and begins to assume

a definite form.   I forget everything and behave like a
madman.   Everything within me starts pulsing and quiver-
ing; hardly have I begun the sketch ere one thought
follows another.   In the midst of this magic process it
frequently happens that some external interruption wakes
me from my somnambulistic state: a ring at the bell, the
entrance of my servant, the striking of the clock, reminding
me that it is time to leave off.   Dreadful, indeed, are such
interruptions.   Sometimes they break the thread of inspiration for a considerable time, so that I have to seek it again
—often in vain.   In such cases cool headwork and technical
knowledge have to come to my aid.   Even in the works of
the greatest master we find such moments, when the
organic sequence fails and a skilful join has to be made, so
that the parts appear as a completely welded whole.
But it cannot be avoided.   If that condition of mind and
soul, which we call *inspiration*, lasted long without intermission, no artist could survive it.   The strings would
break and the instrument be shattered into fragments.   It
is already a great thing if the main ideas and general
outline of a work come without any racking of brains, as
the result of that supernatural and inexplicable force we
call inspiration.

"However, I have wandered from the point without
answering your question.   *Our* symphony has a programme.
That is to say, it is possible to express its contents in
words, and I will tell you—and you alone—the meaning of
the entire work and of its separate movements.   Naturally I can only do so as regards its general features.

"The Introduction is the germ, the leading idea of the
whole work.

"This is Fate, that inevitable force which checks our
aspirations towards happiness ere they reach the goal,
which watches jealously lest our peace and bliss should be
complete and cloudless—a force which, like the sword of

Damocles, hangs perpetually over our heads and is always embittering the soul. This force is inescapable and invincible. There is no other course but to submit and inwardly lament.

"The sense of hopeless despair grows stronger and more poignant. Is it not better to turn from reality and lose ourselves in dreams?

O joy! A sweet and tender dream enfolds me. A bright and serene presence leads me on.

How fair! How remotely now is heard the first theme of the Allegro! Deeper and deeper the soul is sunk in dreams. All that was dark and joyless is forgotten.
  " Here is happiness!
  " It is but a dream, Fate awakens us roughly.

So all life is but a continual alternation between grim truth and fleeting dreams of happiness. There is no haven. The waves drive us hither and thither, until the sea engulfs us. This is, approximately, the programme of the first movement.

"The second movement expresses another phase of suffering. Now it is the melancholy which steals over us when at evening we sit indoors alone, weary of work, while the book we have picked up for relaxation slips unheeded from our fingers. A long procession of old memories goes by. How sad to think how much is already *past and gone!* And yet these recollections of youth are sweet. We regret the past, although we have neither courage nor desire to start a new life. We are rather weary of existence. We would fain rest awhile and look back, recalling many things. There were moments when young blood pulsed warm through our veins and life gave all we asked. There were also moments of sorrow, irreparable loss. All this has receded so far into the past. How sad, yet sweet to lose ourselves therein!

"In the third movement no definite feelings find expression. Here we have only capricious arabesques, intangible forms, which come into a man's head when he has been drinking wine and his nerves are rather excited. His mood is neither joyful nor sad. He thinks of nothing in particular. His fancy is free to follow its own flight, and it designs the strangest patterns. Suddenly memory calls up the picture of a tipsy peasant and a street song. From afar come the sounds of a military band. These are the kind of confused images which pass through our brains as we fall asleep. They have no connection with actuality, but are simply wild, strange, and bizarre.

"The fourth movement. If you can find no reasons for happiness in yourself, look at others. Go to the people. See how they can enjoy life and give themselves up entirely to festivity. A rustic holiday is depicted. Hardly have we had time to forget ourselves in the spectacle of other people's pleasure, when indefatigable Fate reminds us once more of its presence. Others pay no heed to us. They do not spare us a glance, nor stop to observe that we are lonely and sad. How merry, how glad they all are! All their feelings are so inconsequent, so simple. And will you still say that all the world is immersed in sorrow? Happiness does exist, simple and unspoilt. Be glad in others' gladness. This makes life possible.

"I can tell you no more, dear friend, about the symphony.

Naturally my description is not very clear or satisfactory. But there lies the peculiarity of instrumental music; we cannot analyse it. 'Where words leave off, music begins,' as Heine has said.

"It is growing late. I will not tell you anything about Florence in this letter. Only one thing—that I shall always keep a happy memory of this place.

"P.S.—Just as I was putting my letter into the envelope I began to read it again, and to feel misgivings as to the confused and incomplete programme which I am sending you. For the first time in my life I have attempted to put my musical thoughts and forms into words and phrases. I have not been very successful. I was horribly out of spirits all the time I was composing this symphony last winter, and this is a true echo of my feelings at the time. But only an echo. How is it possible to reproduce it in clear and definite language? I do not know. I have already forgotten a good deal. Only the general impression of my passionate and sorrowful experiences has remained. I am very, very anxious to know what my friends in Moscow say of my work.

"Last night I went to the People's Theatre, and was very much amused. Italian humour is coarse, and lacks grace and delicacy, but it carries everything before it."

To N. F. von Meck.

"FLORENCE, *February 20th (March 4th)*, 1878.

"To-day is the last day but one of the Carnival. . . . My window is open. I am drinking in with delight the cool night air after a hot spring day. How strange, how odd, but yet how sweet, to think of my dear and distant country! There it is still winter! Probably you are sitting near the stove in your study. Fur-clad figures go to and fro in your house. The silence is unbroken by any sound of wheels, since all conveyances are turned into sleighs. How far we are apart! You amid winter snows, and I in a land where spring is green, and my window stands open at 11 p.m.! And yet I look back with affection to our seasons. I love our long, hard winters. How beautiful it is! How magical is the suddenness of our spring, when it bursts upon us with its first message! I delight in the trickle of melting snow in the streets, and the sense of something life-giving and exhilarating that pervades the atmosphere! With what delight we welcome the first blade of grass, the first sprouting seed, the arrival of the lark and all our summer guests! Here, spring comes by gradual stages, so that we cannot actually fix the time of its awakening.

"Do you remember I once wrote to you from Florence about a boy with a lovely and touching voice? A few days ago I met some street-singers, and inquired about him. They knew him, and promised to bring him to me on the Lung' Arno at nine o'clock. Punctual to the moment I appeared at the place of meeting. The man who had promised was there with the boy. A curious crowd stood around them. As the numbers increased, I beckoned him aside and led the way into a side street. I had my doubts as to whether it was the same boy. 'As soon as I begin to sing,' he said, 'you will be convinced that I am the same. Give me a silver piece of fifty centimes first.' These words were spoken in a glorious voice, which seemed to come from his inmost soul. What I felt when he began to sing is beyond all words!

"I wept, I trembled, I was consumed with pure delight. He sang once more, 'Perchè tradirmi, perchè lasciarmi!' I do not remember any simple folksong ever having made such an impression upon me. This time the lad sang me a charming new melody, which I intend to make him sing again, so that I may write it down for my own use on some future occasion. I pitied this child. He seems to be exploited by his father and other relatives. Just now, during the Carnival, he is made to sing from morning till night, and will continue to do so until his voice vanishes for good and all. . . . If he belonged to a respectable family he might have some chance of becoming a great artist. One must live for a time with Italians in order to understand their supremacy in vocal art. Even as I write, I can hear in the distance a wonderful tenor singing some song with all his might. But even when the quality of the voice is not beautiful, every Italian can boast that he is a singer by nature. They all have a true *émission* (production), and sing from their chests, not from their throats and noses as we do."

To N. F. von Meck.

"CLARENS, *March 3rd* (15*th*), 1878.

"I have been very much occupied with music the last few days, as the weather has made going out impossible. To-day I played nearly all day with Kotek. Do you know the *Symphonie Espagnole,* by the French composer, Lalo? The piece has been recently brought out by that very modern violinist, Sarasate. It is for solo violin and orchestra, and consists of five independent movements, based upon Spanish folksongs. The work has given me great enjoyment. It is so fresh and light, and contains piquant rhythms and melodies which are beautifully harmonised. It resembles many other works of the modern French school with which I am acquainted. Like Leo Délibes and Bizet, Lalo is careful to avoid all that is *routinier,* seeks new forms without trying to be profound, and is more concerned with musical beauty than with tradition, as are the Germans. The young generation of French composers is really very promising."

To N. F. von Meck.

"CLARENS, *March 5th* (17*th*), 1878.

"It is delightful to talk to you about my own methods of composition. So far I have never had any opportunity of confiding to anyone these hidden utterances of my inner life; partly because very few would be interested, and partly because, of these few, scarcely one would know how to respond to me properly. To you, and you alone, I gladly describe all the details of the creative process, because in you I have found one who has a fine feeling and can understand my music.

"Do not believe those who try to persuade you that composition is only a cold exercise of the intellect. The only music capable of moving and touching us is that which flows from the depths of a composer's soul when he is stirred by inspiration. There is no doubt that even the greatest musical geniuses have sometimes worked without inspiration. This guest does not always respond to the first invitation. We must *always* work, and a self-respecting artist must not fold his hands on the pretext that he is not in the mood. If we wait for the mood, without endeavouring to meet it half-way, we easily become indolent and apathetic. We must be patient, and believe that inspiration will come to those who can master their *disinclination.* A few days ago I told you I was working every day without any real inspiration. Had I given way to my disinclination, undoubtedly I should have drifted into a long period of idleness. But my patience and faith did not fail me, and to-day I felt that inexplicable glow of inspiration of which I told you; thanks to which I know beforehand that whatever I write to-day will have power to make an impression, and to touch the hearts of those who hear it. I hope you will not think I am indulging in self-laudation, if I tell you that I very seldom suffer from this disinclination to work. I believe the reason for this is that I am naturally patient. I have learnt to master myself, and I am glad I have not followed in the steps of some of my Russian colleagues, who have no self-confidence and are so impatient that at the least difficulty they are ready to throw up the sponge. This is why, in spite of great gifts, they accomplish so little, and that in an amateur way.

You ask me how I manage my instrumentation. I never compose in the *abstract ;* that is to say, the musical thought never appears otherwise than in a suitable external form. In this way I invent the musical idea and the instrumentation simultaneously. Thus I thought out the scherzo of our symphony—at the moment of its composition—exactly as you heard it. It is inconceivable except as *pizzicato.* Were it played with the bow, it would lose all its charm and be a mere body without a soul.

As regards the Russian element in my works, I may tell you that not infrequently I begin a composition with the intention of introducing some folk-melody into it. Sometimes it comes of its own accord, unintentionally (as in the finale of our symphony). As to this national element in my work, its affinity with the folksongs in some of my melodies and harmonies proceeds from my having spent my childhood in the country, and having, from my earliest years, been impregnated with the characteristic beauty of our Russian folk-music. I am passionately fond of the national element in all its varied expressions. In a word, I am Russian in the fullest sense of the word."

To N. F. von Meck.

"CLARENS, *March 7th* (*19th*), 1872.

"The wintry weather still continues. To-day it has never ceased snowing. However, I am not at all bored, and time passes very quickly while I am at work. The sonata and concerto interest me greatly. For the first time in my life I have begun to work at a new piece before finishing the one on hand. Hitherto I have invariably followed the rule not to take up a new composition until the old was completed. This time I could not resist the pleasure of sketching out the concerto, and allowed myself to be so carried away that the sonata has been set aside ; but I return to it at intervals.

"I have read the two volumes of *Russian Antiquities* with delight. As they were already cut, I conclude you have read them yourself.

"Do you not think, dear friend, that Serov's letters are extremely interesting ? At least I find them so, because I well remember the period to which the correspondence belongs. I made Serov's acquaintance just at the moment when *Judith*[1] was first performed, and I attended many of the rehearsals. The work roused my enthusiasm at the time, and Serov seemed to me a genius. Afterwards I was bitterly disappointed in him, not only as a man, but as a composer. His personality was never very sympathetic to me. His petty vanity and self-adoration, which often showed themselves in the most naïve way, were repugnant and incomprehensible in so gifted and clever a man. For he was remarkably clever in spite of his small-minded egotism.

"All the same, he was an interesting personality. At the age of forty-three he had not composed *anything at all ;*

---

[1] Serov's first opera.

he had made some attempts, but was either inflated by his self-admiration, or else he entirely lost heart. Finally, after twenty-five years of irresolution, he set to work upon *Judith*, and astonished the world, which expected from him a dull and pretentious work, in the style of Grand Opera. It was supposed that a man who had reached maturity without having produced a single composition could not be greatly gifted. But the world was wrong. The novice of forty-three presented the public of St. Petersburg with an opera which, in every respect, must be described as *beautiful*, and shows no indications whatever of being the composer's *first work*. I do not know whether you have heard *Judith*, dear friend ; the opera has many good points. It is written with unusual warmth, and sometimes rises to great emotional heights. It had considerable success with the public, and was extraordinarily well received by musical circles, especially by the younger generation. Serov, who had hitherto been unknown, and led a very humble life, in which he had been obliged to fight poverty, became suddenly the hero of the hour, the idol of a certain set, in fact, a celebrity. This unexpected success turned his head, and he began to regard himself as a genius. The childishness with which he sings his own praises in his letters is quite remarkable. Never before was there such originality of style, or such beauty of melody. And Serov actually had proved himself a gifted composer, but not a genius of the first order. His second opera, *Rogneda*, is already a falling off from the first. Here he is evidently striving for effect, frequently degenerates into the commonplace, and attempts to impress the gallery by coarse and startling effects. This is all the more remarkable because, as a true Wagnerian, he inveighed in speech and in writing against Meyerbeer's vulgar and flashy style. *The Power of the Evil One* is still weaker. Serov is, in reality, a very peculiar and interesting musical phenomenon. If we consider his voluminous critical articles, we shall observe that his practice does not agree with his principles ; he composes his music on methods diametrically opposed to those which he advocates in his writings. I have held forth at length upon Serov, because I am still under the influence of his letters. which I read yesterday, and all day to-day I can think of nothing else. I recall the arrogance with which he behaved to me, and how I longed for his recognition. Now I know that this very clever and highly cultured man possessed one weakness: he could not appreciate anyone but himself. He disparaged the success of others; detested those who had become famous in his own art, and frequently gave way to impulses of small-minded egotism. On the other hand, one forgave him all, on account of what he suffered before success raised him from poverty, and because he bore his troubles in a strong, manly spirit for love of his art. Having regard to his birth, education, and connections, he might have had a brilliant career, but his love for music won the day. How painful it was to me to learn from his letters that he met with neither support nor encouragement at home but, on the contrary, with derision, mistrust, and hostility!

"I do not know how to thank you, my dear, for the collection of poems you have sent me. I am particularly delighted with those of A. Tolstoi, of whom I am very fond, and—apart from my intention to use some of his words for songs—it will be a great pleasure to read a few of his longer poems again. I am specially interested in his *Don Juan*, which I read long ago."

To N. F. von Meck.

"CLARENS, *March* 14*th* (26*th*), 1878.

"I have just been reading the newspapers, and am thoroughly depressed. Undoubtedly a war is imminent. It is terrible. It seems to me that now I am no longer absorbed in my personal troubles, I feel far more keenly all the wounds inflicted upon our Fatherland, although I have no doubt that in the end Russia—indeed, the whole Slavonic world—will triumph, if only because we have truth and honour on our side. I am glad I shall be in Russia during the war. How many unpleasant moments have I endured abroad, seeing the satisfaction (*Schadenfreude*) which greeted the news of every small misfortune that befell us, and the ill-feeling which was provoked by any victory on our part! Let us hope our cup of bitterness may pass from us. There are good men to be found among us in every walk of life—with one exception. I am now speaking of my own special line. Whether the (Moscow) Conservatoire was somewhat too forcibly planted upon Muscovite soil by the despotic hand of N. Rubinstein, or whether the Russian intellect is not made to grasp the theory of music, it is certain that there is nothing more difficult than to find a good teacher of harmony. I have come to this conclusion because—in spite of the low valuation I set upon my teaching capacities, in spite, too, of my loathing for a professor's work—I am indispensable to the Conservatoire. If I resigned my post, it would be hardly possible to find anyone to take my place. This is the reason why I hold it to be my duty to remain there until I feel sure the institution would not suffer from my departure. I am telling you all this, my dear, because I have been constantly wondering of late whether it might not be possible to slip this heavy load from my shoulders.

" How unpleasant teaching will be after these months of freedom ! I can give you no adequate idea how derogatory this kind of work can be to a man who has not the smallest vocation for it. Among the male students I have to deal with a considerable number of raw youths who intend, however, to make music their profession : violinists, horn-players, teachers, and so on. Although it is very hard to have to explain to such lads, for twelve consecutive years, that a triad consists of a third and fifth, I feel at least that I am instilling into them some indispensable knowledge. Here, at any rate, I am of some use. But the ladies' classes ! O Lord ! Out of the sixty or seventy girls who attend my harmony lessons there are, at the utmost, five who will really turn out musicians. All the rest come to the Conservatoire simply for occupation, or from motives which have nothing to do with music. It cannot be said that these young ladies are less intelligent, or industrious, than the men. Rather the reverse ; the women are more conscientious and make greater efforts. They take in a new rule far quicker—but only up to a certain point. Directly this rule ceases to be applied mechanically, and it becomes a question of initiative, all these young women, although inspired with the best intentions in the world, come hopelessly to grief. I often lose my patience and my head, forget all that is going on, and go into a frantic rage, as much with myself as with them. I think a more patient teacher might produce better results. What makes one despair is the thought that it is all to no purpose : a mere farce! Out of the crowd of girls I have taught in the Conservatoire only a very small number came to the classes with a serious aim in view. For how few of them is it worth while to torment and exhaust myself, to wear myself to thread-paper! For how few is my teaching of any real importance! There are many other unpleasant aspects of my work.

"And yet I am *bound* to continue it. I am delighted at what you tell me about my pupils' sympathy. I always feel they must hate me for my irritability, which sometimes overstepped the bounds of reason; as well as for my scolding and eternal discontent. I was very glad to be convinced of the contrary."

To P. I. Jurgenson.

"CLARENS, *March* 15th (27th), 1878.

". . . The violin concerto is rapidly nearing completion. I hit upon the idea quite accidentally, began to work at it, was completely carried away, and now the sketch is all but finished. Altogether a considerable number of new compositions are hanging over your head : seven little pieces, two songs, and a pianoforte sonata which I have begun. By the end of the summer I shall have to engage a railway truck to convey them all to you. I can hear your energetic expletive : 'The devil take you!'"

To N. F. von Meck.

"CLARENS, *March* 16th (28th), 1878.

"Yesterday I received your letter with the news of Rubinstein's concert. I am so glad you were pleased with my concerto. I was convinced from the first that Nicholas Grigorievich would play it splendidly. The work was originally intended for him, and took into consideration

his immense virtuosity.   It is good to see from your letter
how attentively you follow every new musical event.
Hardly has a new concerto by Max Bruch appeared
than you know all about it.   I do not know it yet; nor
the concerto by Goldmark which you mention.   I only
know one of his orchestral works, the overture to *Sakun-
tala*, and a quartet.   Both compositions are clever and
sympathetic.   Goldmark is one of the few German composers who possess some originality and freshness of
invention.

"Why do you not care for Mozart?   In this respect our
opinions differ, dear friend.   I not only like Mozart, I
idolise him.   To me the most beautiful opera ever written
is *Don Juan*.   You, who possess such a fine musical taste,
must surely love this pure and ideal artist.   It is true
Mozart used up his forces too generously, and often wrote
without inspiration, because he was compelled by want.
But read his biography by Otto Jahn, and you will see
that he could not help it.   Even Bach and Beethoven
have left a considerable number of inferior works which
are not worthy to be spoken of in the same breath as
their masterpieces.   Fate compelled them occasionally
to degrade their art to the level of a handicraft.   But
think of Mozart's operas, of two or three of his symphonies, his Requiem, the six quartets dedicated to Haydn,
and the D minor string quintet.   Do you feel no charm
in these works?   True, Mozart reaches neither the depths
nor heights of Beethoven.   And since in life, too, he
remained to the end of his days a careless child, his
music has not that subjectively tragic quality which is so
powerfully expressed in that of Beethoven.   But this did
not prevent him from creating an objectively tragic type,
the most superb and wonderful human presentment ever
depicted in music.   I mean Donna Anna, in *Don Juan*.
Ah, how difficult it is to make anyone else see and feel
in music what we see and feel ourselves!   I am quite incapable of describing to you what I felt on hearing *Don
Juan*, especially in the scene where the noble figure of the
beautiful, proud, revengeful woman appears on the stage.
Nothing in any opera ever impressed me so profoundly.
And afterwards, when Donna Anna recognises in Don

Juan the man who has wounded her pride and killed her father, and her wrath breaks out like a rushing torrent in that wonderful recitative, or in that later aria, in which every note in the orchestra seems to speak of her wrath and pride and actually to quiver with horror—I could cry out and weep under the overwhelming stress of the emotional impression.   And her lament over her father's corpse, the duet with Don Ottavio, in which she vows vengeance, her arioso in the great sextet in the churchyard —these are inimitable, colossal operatic scenes !

" I am so much in love with the music of *Don Juan* that even as I write to you I could shed tears of agitation and emotion.   In his chamber music, Mozart charms me by his purity and distinction of style and his exquisite handling of the parts.   Here, too, are things which can bring tears to our eyes.   I will only mention the adagio of the D minor string quintet.   No one else has ever known as well how to interpret so exquisitely in music the sense of resigned and inconsolable sorrow.   Every time Laub played the adagio I had to hide in the farthest corner of the concert-room, so that others might not see how deeply this music affected me. . . .

" I could go on to eternity holding forth to you upon this sunny genius, for whom I cherish a cult.   Although I am very tolerant to other people's musical views, I must confess, my dear, that I should like very much to convert you to Mozart.   I know that would be difficult.   I have met one or two others, besides yourself, who have a fine feeling for music, yet nevertheless failed to appreciate Mozart.   I should have tried in vain to make them discover the beauties of his music.   Our musical sympathies are often affected by purely external circumstances.   The music of *Don Juan* was the first which stirred me profoundly.   It roused in me a divine enthusiasm which was not without after-results.   Through its medium I was transplanted to that region of artistic beauty where only genius dwells. Previously I had only known the Italian opera.   It is thanks to Mozart that I have devoted my life to music. All these things have probably played a part in my exclusive love for him—and perhaps it is foolish of me to expect those who are dear to me to feel towards Mozart as I do. But if I could do anything to change your opinion—it would make me very happy. If ever you tell me that you have been touched by the adagio of the D minor quintet I shall rejoice."

To N. F. von Meck.

"CLARENS, *March* 19*th* (31*st*), 1878.

" . . . You need not be troubled about my fame abroad, my dear. If I am destined ever to acquire such fame, it will come of its own accord, although in all probability not while I am alive to see it. When you come to think that during my many trips abroad I have never called on influential people, or sent them my compositions, that I have never pushed my reputation in other countries, we must be satisfied with any little success which my works may win. Do you know, all my pianoforte compositions are reprinted in Leipzig, and my songs also, with translations of the words? My principal works (with the exception of the operas) can be procured without difficulty in most of the large towns of France, Germany, and England. I myself bought my Third Symphony, arranged for four hands, and my Third Quartet, in Vienna. I have even come across some transcriptions hitherto unknown to me: the Barcarole for piano (Op. 37*a*) arranged for violin and piano, the andante from the First Quartet for flute. Brandus, in Paris, keeps all my works in stock. There are many reasons why my symphonic works are so seldom heard of abroad. In the first place I am a Russian, and consequently looked upon with prejudice by every Western European. Secondly—also because I am a Russian—there is something exotic in my music which makes it inaccessible to foreigners. My overture to *Romeo and Juliet* has been played in every capital, but always without success. In Vienna and Paris it was hissed. A short time ago it met with no better reception in Dresden. In some other towns (London and Hamburg) it was more fortunate, but, all the same, my music has not been included in the standard repertory of Germany and other countries. Among musical circles abroad my name is not unknown. A few men have been specially interested in me, and

U

taken some pains to include my works in their concert programmes; but have generally met with insurmountable obstacles. For instance, Hans Richter, the Bayreuth conductor. In spite of all protests, he put my overture into the programme of one of the eight Philharmonic concerts which he conducts in Vienna. Disregarding its failure, he wished this season to do my Third Symphony; but after one rehearsal the directors of the Philharmonic pronounced the work 'too Russian,' and it was unanimously rejected. There is no doubt that I could do a great deal to spread my works abroad if I went the round of all the European capitals, calling upon the 'big wigs,' and displaying my wares to them. But I would rather abandon every joy in life. Good Lord! what one must undergo, what wounds to one's self-respect one must be prepared to receive before one can catch the attention of these gentlemen! I will give you an instance. Supposing I wanted to become known in Vienna: Brahms is the musical lion of Vienna. Consequently, I should have to pay my respects to him. Brahms, the celebrity—and I, the unknown composer. I may tell you, however, without false modesty, that I place myself a good deal higher than Brahms. What could I say to him? If I were an honourable and sincere man I should have to say something of this kind: 'Herr Brahms, I regard you as an uninspired and pretentious composer, without any creative genius whatever. I do not rate you very highly, and look down upon you with disdain. But you could be of some use to me, so I have come to call upon you.' But if I were a dishonest man, then I should say exactly the opposite. I cannot adopt either course.

"I need not go into further details. You alone—with the exception of my brothers—can fully enter into my feelings. My friends in Moscow cannot reconcile themselves to my having declined to act as delegate in Paris. They cannot believe that my association with such distinguished names as Liszt (who represents Hungary) and Verdi would not do much to promote my reputation. My dear friend, I have the reputation of being modest. But I will confess to you that my modesty is nothing less than a secret, but immense, *amour propre*. Among all living musicians there is not one before whom I would willingly lower my crest. At the same time, Nature, who endowed me with such pride, denied me the capacity for showing off my wares. *Je ne sais pas me faire valoir.* I do not know how to meet fame half-way on my own initiative, and prefer to wait until it comes to me unsought. I have long since resigned myself to the belief that I shall not live to see the general recognition of my talents.

"You speak of Anton Rubinstein. How can I compare myself to him? He is at present the greatest pianist in the world. He combines the personalities of a remarkable virtuoso and a gifted composer, so that the latter is borne as it were upon the shoulders of the former. In my life-time I shall never attain to a tenth part of what he has accomplished. Now we are on the subject of Rubinstein, let me tell you this: as my teacher, he knew my musical temperament better than anyone else, so that he might have done much to further my reputation abroad. Un-fortunately, this 'great light' has always treated me with a loftiness bordering on contempt. No one has inflicted such cruel wounds upon my self-esteem as Rubinstein. Externally, he has always been amiable and friendly. But beneath this friendly manner he showed plainly that he did not think me worth a brass farthing! The one 'big wig' who has always been most kindly disposed towards me is Bülow. Unluckily, he has been forced almost to abandon his musical career on account of ill-health, and cannot therefore do much more on my behalf. Thanks to him, I am well known in England and America. I have a number of Press notices relating to myself which appeared in these countries, and were sent to me by Bülow.

"You need not worry yourself, my dear. If fame is destined for me, it will come with slow but sure steps. History convinces us that the success which is long delayed is often more lasting than when it comes easily and at a bound. Many a name which resounded through its own generation is now engulfed in the ocean of oblivion. An artist should not be troubled by the indifference of his contemporaries. He should go on working and say all he has been predestined to say. He should know that posterity alone can deliver a true and just verdict. I will tell you something more. Perhaps I accept my modest share with so little complaint because my faith in the judgment of the future is immovable. I have a foretaste during my lifetime of the fame which will be meted out to me when the history of Russian music comes to be written. For the present I am satisfied with what I have already acquired. I have no right to complain. I have met people on my way through life whose warm sympathy for my music more than compensates me for the indifference, misunderstanding, and ill-will of others."

VII

From S. I. Taneiev to Tchaikovsky.

"*March* 18th (30th), 1878.

". . . The first movement of your Fourth Symphony is disproportionately long in comparison with the others; it seems to me a symphonic poem, to which the three other movements are added fortuitously. The fanfare for trumpets in the introduction, which is repeated in other places, the frequent change of *tempo* in the tributary themes—all this makes me think that a programme is being treated here. Otherwise this movement pleases me.
But the rhythm ♪♪♪ appears too often and becomes wearisome.

"The Andante is charming (the middle does not particularly please me). The Scherzo is exquisite, and goes splendidly. The Trio I cannot bear: it sounds like a ballet movement.

"Nicholas Grigorievich (Rubinstein) likes the Finale best, but I do not altogether agree with him. The variations on a folksong do not strike me as very important or interesting.

"In my opinion the Symphony has one defect, to which I shall never be reconciled: in every movement there are phrases which sound like ballet music: the middle section of the Andante, the Trio of the Scherzo, and a kind of march in the Finale. Hearing the Symphony, my inner eye sees involuntarily 'our *prima ballerina,'* which puts me out of humour and spoils my pleasure in the many beauties of the work.

"This is my candid opinion. Perhaps I have expressed it somewhat freely, but do not be hurt. It is not surprising that the Symphony does not entirely please me. Had you not sent *Eugene Oniegin* at the same time, perhaps it might have satisfied me. It is your own fault. Why have you composed such an opera, which has no parallel in the world? *Oniegin* has given me such pleasure that I cannot find words to express it. A splendid opera! And yet you say you want to give up composing. You have never done so well. Rejoice that you have attained such perfection, and profit by it."

Tchaikovsky to Taneiev.

"CLARENS, *March 27th (April 8th),* 1878.

"DEAR SERGE,—I have read your letter with the greatest pleasure and interest. . . . You need not be afraid that your criticism of my Fourth Symphony is too severe. You have simply given me your frank opinion, for which I am grateful. I want these kind of opinions, not choruses of praise. At the same time many things in your letter astonished me. I have no idea what you consider 'ballet music,' or why you should object to it. Do you regard every melody in a lively dance-rhythm as 'ballet music'? In that case how can you reconcile yourself to the majority of Beethoven's symphonies, for in them you will find similar melodies on every page? Or do you mean to say that the Trio of my Scherzo is in the style of Minkus, Gerber, or Pugni? It does not, to my mind, deserve such criticism. I never can understand why 'ballet music' should be used as a contemptuous epiphet. The music of a ballet is not invariably bad, there are good works of this class—Délibes' *Sylvia,* for instance. And when the music is good, what difference does it make whether the Sobiesichanskaya[1] dances to it or not? I can only say that certain portions of my Symphony do not please you because *they recall the ballet,* not because they are intrinsically bad. You may be right, but I do not see why

---

[1] *Prima ballerina* of the Moscow Opera.

dance tunes should not be employed episodically in a symphony, even with the avowed intention of giving a touch of coarse, everyday humour. Again I appeal to Beethoven, who frequently had recourse to similar effects. I must add that I have racked my brains in vain to recall in what part of the Allegro you can possibly have discovered ' ballet music.' It remains an enigma. With all that you say as to my Symphony having a programme, I am quite in agreement. But I do not see why this should be a mistake. I am far more afraid of the contrary ; I do not wish any symphonic work to emanate from me which has nothing to express, and consists merely of harmonies and a purposeless design of rhythms and modulations. Of course, my Symphony is programme music, but it would be impossible to give the programme in words; it would appear ludicrous and only raise a smile. Ought not this to be the case with a symphony which is the most lyrical of all musical forms ? Ought it not to express all those things for which words cannot be found, which nevertheless arise in the heart and clamour for expression? Besides, I must tell you that in my simplicity I imagined the plan of my Symphony to be so obvious that everyone would understand its meaning, or at least its leading ideas, without any definite programme. Pray do not imagine I want to swagger before you with profound emotions and lofty ideas. Throughout the work I have made no effort to express any new thought. In reality my work is a reflection of Beethoven's Fifth Symphony ; I have not copied his musical contents, only borrowed the central idea. What kind of a programme has this Fifth Symphony, do you think ? Not only has it a programme, but it is so clear that there cannot be the smallest difference of opinion as to what it means. Much the same lies at the root of my Symphony, and if you have failed to grasp it, it simply proves that I am no Beethoven—on which point I have no doubt whatever. Let me add that there is not a single bar in this Fourth Symphony of mine which I have not truly felt, and which is not an echo of my most intimate spiritual life. The only exception occurs perhaps in the middle section of the first movement, in which there are some forced passages, some things which are laboured and artificial. I know you will laugh as you read these lines. You are a sceptic and a mocking-bird. In spite of your great love of music you do not seem to believe that a man can compose from his inner impulses. Wait awhile, you too will join the ranks! Some day, perhaps very soon, you will compose, not because others ask you to do so, but because it is your own desire. Only then will the seed which can bring forth a splendid harvest fall upon the rich soil of your gifted nature. I speak the truth, if somewhat grandiloquently. Meanwhile your fields are waiting for the sower. I will write more about this in my next. There were beautiful details in your score, it only lacks . . . but I will not forestall matters. In my next letter I will talk exclusively of yourself.

"There have been great changes in my life since I wrote that I had lost all hope of composing any more. The devil of authorship has awoke in me again in the most unexpected way.

"Please, dear Serge, do not see any shadow of annoyance in my defence of the Symphony; of course I should like you to be pleased with everything I write, but I am quite satisfied with the interest you always show me. You cannot think how delighted I am with your approval of *Oniegin*. I value your opinion very highly, and the more frankly you express it, the more I feel its worth. And so I cordially thank you, and beg you not to be afraid of over-severity. I want just those stinging criticisms from you. So long as you give me the truth, what does it matter whether it is favourable or not?"

To N. F. von Meck.

"*April 1st* (13*th*), 1878.

". . . It is very early. I slept badly, and after an unsuccessful attempt to doze off again, I got up and came to sit near the window, where I am now writing to you. What a wonderful morning! The sky is absolutely clear. A few little harmless clouds are floating over the mountains on either side the lake. From the garden comes the twitter of innumerable birds. The Dent du Midi is clear of mist, and glitters in the sunlight which catches its snow-clad peaks. The lake is smooth as a mirror. How beautiful it all is! Does it not seem hard that the fine weather should have come just as I am on the point of departure?

" As regards Mozart, let me add these words. You say my worship for him is quite contrary to my musical nature. But perhaps it is just because—being a child of my day— I feel broken and spiritually out of joint, that I find con-solation and rest in the music of Mozart, wherein he gives expression to that joy of life which was part of his sane and wholesome temperament, not yet undermined by re-flection. It seems to me that an artist's creative power is something quite apart from his sympathy with this or that great master. For instance, a man may admire Beethoven, and yet by temperament be more akin to Mendelssohn. Could there be a more glaring instance of inconsistency, for instance, than Berlioz the composer and champion of ultra-romanticism in music, and Berlioz the critic and adorer of Gluck? Perhaps this is just an example of the attraction which makes extremes meet, and causes a big, strong man to fall in love with a tiny, delicate woman, and *vice versâ*. Do you know that Chopin did not care for Beethoven, and could hardly bear to hear some of his works? I was told this by a man who knew him per-sonally. At any rate, I will conclude by saying that dissimilarity of temperament between two artists is no hindrance to their mutual sympathy."

To N. F. von Meck.

"VIENNA, *April 8th* (*20th*), 1878.

". . . My next letter will reach you from Russia.

" I was surprised to find the spring so much further advanced in Vienna than at Clarens. The trees there had scarcely begun to show green, while here there is a look of summer already. Vienna is so bright and sunny to-day, it would certainly have made a pleasant impression upon me had I not read the morning papers, which are full of poisonous, malicious, and abominable slanders about Russia. The *Neue Freie Presse* takes pains to inform its readers that the action of the girl who fired at Trepov has created a revolution in Russia, that the Emperor is in peril, and must flee from the country, etc., etc.

"Now, on the point of taking leave of foreign lands and turning my face homewards, a sound, sane man, full of renewed strength and energy—let me thank you once again, my dear and invaluable friend, for all I owe you, which I can never, never forget."

To N. F. von Meck.

"KAMENKA, *April 12th (24th).*

"At last we have arrived. The journey was long and tedious and my expectations were disappointed. I had always thought my home-coming would fill me with such sweet and profound sentiments. Nothing of the kind! A tipsy policeman who would hardly let us pass because he could not grasp that the number of passengers on my passport corresponded to the figure on his own; an officer of customs who demanded duty to the amount of fourteen gold roubles upon a dress I had bought for my sister for seventy francs; a conversation with a very importunate gentleman, bent on convincing me that the policy of England was the most humane in the world; the crowd of dirty Jews with their accompanying odours; the numbers of young conscripts who travelled in our train, and the farewell scenes with their wives and mothers at every station—all these things spoilt my pleasure in returning to my beloved native land. At Shmerinka we had to wait a few hours; unfortunately, as it was night, I could not see Brailov,[1] although I knew in which direction to look for it. . . . As my sister's house is rather crowded, she has taken a nice, quiet room near at hand for me. I have also a garden, well stocked with flowers, which will soon begin to exhale their lovely perfumes. My little home is very cosy and comfortable. There is even a piano in the tiny parlour next to my bedroom. I shall be able to work undisturbed.

". . . How glad I am, dear Nadejda Filaretovna, that you take such a just and sensible view of the agitating events which have been taking place in Petersburg and

---

[1] The country property of Nadejda von Meck.

Moscow! I did not expect you to think differently, although I feared lest your pity for Sassoulich personally —in any case a very diluted and involuntary sympathy— might possibly have influenced your opinion. It is *one thing*, however, to feel sorry for her, and to detest the arrogant and brutal conduct of the arbitrary Prefect of Petersburg, and quite *another thing* to approve of that display of unpatriotic sentiment by which her acquittal has been signalised, and with the Moscow riots. It seems to me that both these events are most disquieting at the present moment, and I am exceedingly glad that the Russian lower classes have shown the crazy leaders of our younger generation how little their orders are in accord with sound sense and the spirit of the nation. I am glad to feel once again that, in spite of a few differences as to details, we are in agreement on most important matters."

A few days after receiving this letter, N. F. von Meck invited Tchaikovsky to spend some weeks in the restful solitude of her estate at Brailov. "Of course she herself will not be there," he wrote to his brother on April 27th (May 9th). "I am delighted to accept her invitation." Meanwhile his days at Kamenka were fully occupied, as may be seen from the following extract from a letter to Nadejda von Meck, dated April 30th, 1878 :—

"I am working very hard. The sonata is already finished, as are also twelve pieces—of moderate difficulty —for pianoforte. Of course all this is only sketched out. To-morrow I shall begin a collection of miniature pieces for children. I thought long ago it would not be a bad thing to do all in my power to enrich the children's musical literature, which is rather scanty. I want to write a whole series of perfectly easy pieces, and to find titles for them which would interest children, as Schumann has done. I have planned songs and violin pieces for later on, and then, if the favourable mood lasts long enough, I want to do something in the way of Church music. A vast and almost untrodden field of activity lies open to composers here. I appreciate certain merits in Bortniansky, Berezovsky, and others ; but how little their music is in keeping with the Byzantine architecture, the ikons, and the whole spirit of the Orthodox liturgy! Perhaps you are aware that the Imperial Chapels have the monopoly of Church music, and that it is forbidden to print, or to sing in church, any sacred compositions which are not included in the published collections of these Chapels. Moreover, they guard this monopoly very jealously, and will not permit new settings of any portions of the liturgy under any circumstances whatever. My publisher, Jurgenson, has discovered a way of evading this curious prohibition, and if I write anything of this kind, he will publish it abroad. It is not improbable that I shall decide to set the entire liturgy of St. John Chrysostom. I shall arrange all this by July. I intend to rest absolutely during the whole of that month, and to start upon some important work in August. I should like to write an opera. Turning over books in my sister's library, I came upon Joukovsky's *Undine*, and re-read the tale which I loved as a child. In 1869 I wrote an opera on this subject, and submitted it to the Opera Direction. It was rejected. Although at the time I thought this very unjust, yet afterwards I became disillusioned with my own work, and was very glad it had not had the chance of being damned. Now I am again attracted to the subject."

To N. F. von Meck.

"KIEV, *May* 14*th* (26*th*), 1878.

"My telegram to-day, sent from Kiev, must have astonished you, dear friend. I left quite suddenly, as my sister had to come here sooner than she expected. . . . I could not wait at Kamenka for your letter containing directions for my journey to Brailov; but, in any case, I shall leave here on Tuesday, and arrive at Shmerinka at 7 a.m. on Wednesday."

To Modeste Tchaikovsky.

"BRAILOV, *May* 17*th* (29*th*), 1878.

"Seated in the carriage, after you left me, of course I dissolved in tears. The recollection of our meeting in

Milan came back to me.   How jolly it was!   The journey to Genoa and afterwards!   How beautiful it all seemed to me—and it was nearly six months ago!   Here followed a fresh burst of tears.

"One of my fellow-travellers, who seemed to know this neighbourhood, told us that Brailov belonged to the banker Meck, had cost three million roubles, and brought the owner a yearly income of 700,000 roubles, and other non-sense.   I was very much excited on the journey.   In the waiting-room at Shmerinka I was greeted by the same waiter—you remember him—who served our supper; I told him to inquire whether any horses had been sent from Brailov.   Two minutes later Marcel appeared.   He is not a Frenchman, but a native.   He was very attentive and amiable.   His coat and hat were infinitely superior to mine, so that I felt quite embarrassed as I took my seat in the luxuriously appointed carriage, while he mounted the box beside the coachman.   The house is really a palace.   At Marcel's invitation I entered the dining-room, where a huge silver samovar steamed on the table, together with a coffee-pot upon a spirit-lamp, cups of rare china, eggs, butter, etc.   I observed that Marcel had received his instructions; he did not attempt to converse, nor to stand behind my chair, but just served what was necessary and went away.   He inquired how I desired to arrange my day.   I *ordered* my midday meal at one o'clock, tea at nine, and a cold supper.   After coffee I explored the house, which contains a series of separate suites of rooms.   A large wing, built in stone for the accommodation of guests, is arranged like a kind of hotel; a long corridor with rooms on each side, which are always kept exactly as though they were inhabited.   The first floor, which I occupy, is furnished with the utmost comfort.   There are many bookcases containing very interesting illustrated publications.   In the music-room, a grand piano, a very fine harmonium, and plenty of music.   In Nadejda Filaret-ovna's study there are a few pictures.   At one o'clock I had dinner, a very exquisite, but rather slight, repast. The *Zakouska* (*hors d'œuvre*) excellent, the wine ditto. After dinner I looked through the music and strolled in the garden.   At four o'clock I ordered the carriage and took a drive. The neighbourhood of Brailov is not very pretty. There is no view from the windows. The garden is extensive and well stocked, especially with lilacs and roses, but it is not picturesque, nor sufficiently shady. On the whole I like the house best. . . ."

To N. F. von Meck.

"BRAILOV, *May* 18*th* (30*th*), 1878.

" How lovely, how free, it is in your country home! The sun has set, and over the wide fields in front of the main entrance the heat is already giving way to the cool evening breeze. The lilacs scent the air, and the cockchafers break the stillness with their bass note. The nightingale is singing in the distance. How glorious it is !"

To N. F. von Meck.

"BRAILOV, *May* 21*st* (*June* 2*nd*), 1878.

"My life at Brailov flows tranquilly on. In the early morning after coffee I stroll in the garden, and then slip out through the little wooden door in the wall near the stable, and, jumping the ditch, find myself in the old, forsaken garden of the monastery, where the monks used to wander of old, but which is now tenanted by all kinds of birds. Not infrequently the oriole and the nightingale are seen there. This garden is apparently deserted, for the paths are so overgrown and the greenery so fresh that one could fancy oneself in the heart of the forest. First I wander through it, then sit down in a shady place for an hour or so. Such moments of solitude amid the flowers and green branches are incomparable ; then I can watch every form of organic life which manifests itself silently, without a sound, yet speaks more forcibly of the illimitable and the eternal than the rumbling of bridges and all the turmoil of the streets. In one of your letters you say I shall not find a Gorge de Chaudière at Brailov. I do not want it ! Such places satisfy one's curiosity rather than one's heart and imagination ; one sees more English tourists than birds and flowers ; they bring more fatigue than enjoyment.

"After my walk I work at the violin pieces, one of which

is quite finished.   If I am not mistaken, it will please you, although the accompaniment is rather difficult in places, and this, I fear, will make you angry.

"Punctually at 1 p.m. Marcel summons me to the dining-room, where, in the middle of the elegantly appointed table, two big bouquets are arranged, which give me fresh cause for delight.   Then follows a real Balthazar's feast.   Each time I feel a little ashamed to sit down alone to such a liberal and sumptuous table.

"After dinner I walk in the garden, read, or write letters until 4.30, when I go for a drive.

"Yesterday the rain prevented me from taking my usual constitutional in the meadows facing the house.   At sunset I like a more open space, and these meadows enclosed by trees, lilac bushes, and the stream, offer a charming evening walk.

"Then I generally spend half an hour at your splendid harmonium.   I like to observe all its curious acoustic properties, which are called aliquot tones.   No doubt you have observed that when you play chords on the organ, besides the sound which comes from the notes struck, another sound is heard in the bass, which sometimes harmonises with the chord and sometimes results in a harsh discord.   Occasionally the most curious combinations are produced.   This is what I discovered yesterday.

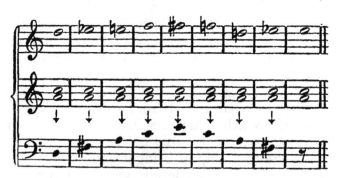

Try this acoustic experiment by drawing out register No. 1, that is to say Flute and Cor Anglais.   D and F sharp, A and C are perfectly in tune, but the E sounds rather sharp.

" At 9 p.m. the second Balthazar's feast takes place. Then I play and make myself acquainted with your musical library. Yesterday I played through a serenade for strings by Volkmann with great pleasure. A sympathetic composer. He has many simple and natural charms.

" Do you know that Volkmann is quite an old man and lives in the greatest poverty at Pesth ? Once the musicians in Moscow got up a small fund for him, amounting to 300 roubles, in gratitude for which he dedicated his Second Symphony to the Moscow Musical Society. I never could discover why he was so poor.

" At 11 p.m. I go to my room and undress. Marcel, the good-natured soldier-porter, and Alexis go to bed. I am left alone to read, dream, or recall the past ; to think of those near and dear to me ; to open the window and gaze out on the stars ; to listen to the sounds of night ; and finally—to go to bed.

" A wonderful life ! Like a vision, a dream ! Kind and beloved Nadejda Filaretovna, how grateful I am to you for everything ! Sometimes my sense of gratitude is so keen I feel I must proclaim it aloud."

To N. F. von Meck.

" BRAILOV, *May 23rd (June 4th),* 1878.

" As I walked through the woods yesterday I found a quantity of mushrooms. Mushrooming is my greatest delight in summer. The moment in which one first sees a plump, white mushroom is simply fascinating ! Passionate card-lovers may experience the same feeling when they see the ace of trumps in their hand. All night long I dreamed of large, fat, pink mushrooms. When I awoke I reflected that these *mushroomy dreams* were very childish. And, in truth, one would become a child again if one lived long all alone with Nature. One would become far more receptive to the simple, artless joys which she offers us.

" Do you know what I am preoccupied with at present? When I was sitting alone one evening at Kiev, while my sister and Modeste had gone to the theatre to see Rossi in

Romeo and Juliet, I read the play through once more. Immediately I was possessed with the idea of composing an opera on the subject. The existing operas of Bellini and Gounod do not frighten me. In both of them Shakespeare is mutilated and distorted until he is hardly recognisable. Do you not think that this great work of the arch-genius is well adapted to inspire a musician? I have already talked it over with Modeste; but he shrank from the magnitude of the task. Nothing venture, nothing have. I shall think over the plan of this opera and throw all my energies into the work for which I am reserving them."

To Modeste Tchaikovsky.

"BRAILOV, *May 25th (June 6th),* 1878.

"Modi, ever since I re-read *Romeo and Juliet, Undine, Berthalde, Gulbrand,* and the rest seem to me a pack of childish nonsense. Of course, I shall compose an opera on *Romeo and Juliet.* All your objections will vanish before the vast enthusiasm which possesses me. It shall be my finest work. It seems absurd that I have only just found out that fate has to some extent ordained me for this task. Nothing could be better suited to my musical temperament. No kings, no marches—in a word, none of the usual accessories of Grand Opera. Nothing but love, love, love. And then how delightful are the minor characters: Friar Lawrence, Tybalt, Mercutio! You need not be afraid of monotony. The first love duet will be very different from the second. In the first, brightness and serenity; in the second, a tragic element. From children, happily and carelessly in love, Romeo and Juliet have become passionate and suffering beings, placed in a tragic and inextricable dilemma. How I long to get to work on it!"

To Modeste Tchaikovsky.

"BRAILOV, *May 27th (June 8th),* 1878.

"Yesterday I played the whole of *Eugene Oniegin,* from beginning to end. The author was the sole listener. I am half ashamed of what I am going to confide to you in

secret: the listener was moved to tears, and paid the composer a thousand compliments. If only the audiences of
the future will feel towards this music as the composer
himself does!"

To N. F. von Meck.

"BRAILOV, *May 29th* (*June 10th*), 1878.

"I am spending my last days here. I need hardly tell
you why I cannot accept your hospitality any longer,
although I might remain until June 10th (22nd). I have
spent many unforgettable days here; I have experienced
the purest and most tranquil enjoyment. I have drunk in
the beauties and sympathetic surroundings of Brailov, so
that my visit will remain one of the most beautiful memories of my life. I thank you. Nevertheless it is time I
went away."

To N. F. von Meck.

"BRAILOV, *May 30th* (*June 11th*), 1878.

"I have given my pieces (which are dedicated to Brailov)
to Marcel, so that he may deliver them to you. The first
is the best, I think, but also the most difficult; it is called
Meditation. The second is a very quick Scherzo, and the
third a '*Chant sans Paroles.*' It was very hard to part with
them to Marcel. Just recently I had started copying
them! Then the lilacs were still in full bloom, the grass
uncut, and the roses had hardly begun to bud!"

VIII

To N. F. Meck.

"VILLAGE OF NIZI, *June 6th* (*18th*) 1878.

"Forgive me, my friend, for not having written to you
from Petersburg. In the first place, I was afraid my letter
might not reach you in time, and secondly, you cannot
imagine what a *hell* my three days' sojourn in Moscow
proved to be. They seemed more like three centuries. I
experienced the same joy when I found myself in the train

once more that I might have felt on being released from a narrow prison cell. I have come here in answer to the invitation of a hospitable old friend, Kondratiev, whom I formerly used to visit almost every summer. Here I composed *Vakoula* and many other works."

To N. F. von Meck.

"KAMENKA, *June 24th* (*July 6th*), 1878.

"You want to know my methods of composing? Do you know, dear friend, that it is very difficult to give a satisfactory answer to your question, because the circumstances under which a new work comes into the world vary considerably in each case.

"First, I must divide my works into two categories, for this is important in trying to explain my methods.

"(1) Works which I compose on my own initiative—that is to say, from an invincible inward impulse.

"(2) Works which are inspired by external circumstances: the wish of a friend, or a publisher, and *commissioned* works.

"Here I should add experience has taught me that the intrinsic value of a work has nothing to do with its place in one or the other of these categories. It frequently happens that a composition which owes its existence to external influences proves very successful; while one that proceeds entirely from my own initiative may, for various indirect reasons, turn out far less well. These indirect circumstances, upon which depends the mood in which a work is written, are of the very greatest importance. During the actual time of creative activity complete quiet is absolutely necessary to the artist. In this sense every work of art, even a musical composition, is *objective*. Those who imagine that a creative artist can—through the medium of his art—express his feelings at the moment when he is *moved*, make the greatest mistake. Emotions —sad or joyful—can only be expressed *retrospectively*, so to speak. Without any special reason for rejoicing, I may be moved by the most cheerful creative mood, and, *vice versâ*, a work composed under the happiest surroundings may be touched with dark and gloomy colours.

" In a word, an artist lives a double life: an everyday human life, and an artistic life, and the two do not always go hand in hand.

" In any case, it is absolutely necessary for a composer to shake off all the cares of daily existence, at least for a time, and give himself up entirely to his art-life.

" Works belonging to the first category do not require the least effort of will. It is only necessary to obey our inward promptings, and if our material life does not crush our artistic life under its weight of depressing circumstances, the work progresses with inconceivable rapidity. Everything else is forgotten, the soul throbs with an incomprehensible and indescribable excitement, so that, almost before we can follow this swift flight of inspiration, time passes literally unreckoned and unobserved.

" There is something *somnambulistic* about this condition. *On ne s'entend pas vivre.* It is impossible to describe such moments. Everything that flows from one's pen, or merely passes through one's brain (for such moments often come at a time when writing is an impossibility) under these circumstances is *invariably good*, and if no external obstacle comes to hinder the creative glow, the result will be an artist's best and most perfect work. Unfortunately such external hindrances are inevitable. A duty has to be performed, dinner is announced, a letter arrives, and so on. This is the reason why there exist so few compositions which are of equal quality throughout. Hence *the joins, patches, inequalities and discrepancies.*

" For the works in my second category it is necessary to *get into the mood.* To do so we are often obliged to fight with indolence and disinclination. Besides this, there are many other fortuitous circumstances. Sometimes the victory is easily gained. At other times inspiration eludes us, and cannot be recaptured. I consider it, however, the *duty* of an artist not to be conquered by circumstances. He must not wait. Inspiration is a guest who does not care to visit those who are indolent. The reproaches heaped upon the Russian nation because of its deficiency in original works of art are not without foundation, for the Russians are lazy. A Russian is always glad to procrastinate : he is gifted by nature, but at the same time nature has withheld from him the power of will. A man must learn to conquer himself, lest he should degenerate into *dilettantism*, from which even so colossal a talent as Glinka's was not free. This man, endowed with an extraordinary and special creative talent, achieved astonishingly little, although he attained a fairly ripe age. Read his *Memoirs*. You will see that he worked like a *dilettante*—on and off, when he was in the mood. However proud we may be of Glinka, we must acknowledge that he did not entirely fulfil his task, if we take into consideration the magnitude of his gifts. Both his operas, in spite of their astonishing and original beauty, suffer from glaring inequalities of style. Side by side with touches of genius and passages of imperishable beauty we find childish and weak numbers. What might not Glinka have accomplished had he lived amid different surroundings, had he worked like an artist who, fully alive to his power and his duty, develops his gifts to the ultimate limit of perfection, rather than as an amateur who makes music his pastime!

" I have explained that I compose either from an inward impulse, winged by a lofty and undefinable inspiration, or I simply *work*, invoking all my powers, which sometimes answer and sometimes remain deaf to my invocation. In the latter case the work created will always remain the mere product of labour, without any glow of genuine musical feeling.

" I hope you will not think I am boasting, if I say that my appeal to inspiration is very rarely in vain. In other words, that power which I have already described as a capricious guest has long since become fast friends with me, so that we are inseparable, and it only deserts me when my material existence is beset by untoward circumstances and its presence is of no avail. Under normal conditions I may say there is no hour of the day in which I cannot compose. Sometimes I observe with curiosity that uninterrupted activity, which—independent of the subject of any conversation I may be carrying on—continues its course in that department of my brain which is devoted to music. Sometimes it takes a preparatory form—that is, the consideration of all details that concern the elaboration of some projected work; another time it may be an entirely new and independent musical idea, and I make an effort to hold it fast in my memory. Whence does it come? It is an inscrutable mystery.

"Now I will try to describe my actual procedure in composition. But not until *after dinner*. *Au revoir*. If you only knew how *difficult*, yet at the same time how *pleasant* it is to talk to you about all this!

" *Two o'clock*.

"I usually write my sketches on the first piece of paper to hand. I jot them down in the most abbreviated form. A melody never stands alone, but invariably with the harmonies which belong to it. These two elements of music, together with the rhythm, must never be separated; every melodic idea brings its own inevitable harmony and its suitable rhythm. If the harmony is very intricate, I set down in the sketch a few details as to the working out of the parts; when the harmony is quite simple, I only put in the bass, or a figured bass, and sometimes not even this. If the sketch is intended for an orchestral work, the ideas appear ready-coloured by some special instrumental combination. The original plan of instrumentation often undergoes some modifications.

"The text must *never* be written after the music, for if music is written to given words only, these words invoke a suitable musical expression. It is quite possible to fit words to a short melody, but in treating a serious work such adaptation is not permissible. It is equally impossible to compose a symphonic work and afterwards to attach to it a programme, since every episode of the chosen programme should evoke its corresponding musical presentment. This stage of composition—the sketch—is remarkably pleasant and interesting. It brings an indescribable delight, accompanied, however, by a kind of unrest and nervous agitation. Sleep is disturbed and meals forgotten. Nevertheless, the development of the project proceeds tranquilly. The instrumentation of a work which is completely thought out and matured is a most enjoyable task.

"The same does not apply to the bare sketch of a work

for pianoforte or voice, or little pieces in general, which are sometimes very tiresome. Just now I am occupied with this kind of work. You ask: do I confine myself to established forms? Yes, and no. Some compositions imply the use of traditional forms; but only as regards their general features—the sequence of the various movements. The details permit of considerable freedom of treatment, if the development of the ideas require it. For example, the first movement of *our* Symphony is written in a very informal style. The second subject, which ought, properly speaking, to be in the major, is in a somewhat remote minor key. In the recapitulation of the principal part the second subject is entirely left out, etc. In the finale, too, there are many deviations from traditional form. In vocal music, in which everything depends on the text, and in fantasias (like *The Tempest* and *Francesca*) the form is quite free. You ask me about melodies built upon the notes of the harmony. I can assure you, and prove it by many examples, that it is quite possible, by means of rhythm and the transposition of these notes, to evolve millions of new and beautiful melodic combinations. But this only applies to homophonic music. With polyphonic music such a method of building up a melody would interfere with the independence of the parts. In the music of Beethoven, Weber, Mendelssohn, Schumann, and especially Wagner, we frequently find melodies which consist of the notes of the common chord; a gifted musician will always be able to invent a new and interesting fanfare. Do you remember the beautiful Sword-motive in the Nibelungen?

"I am very fond of a melody by Verdi (a very gifted man):

"How glorious and how fresh the chief theme of the first movement of Rubinstein's *Ocean* symphony:

"If I racked my brains a little, I should find countless examples to support my assertion. Talent is the sole secret. It knows no limitations: it creates the most beautiful music out of nothing. Could there be anything more trivial than the following melody?

Beethoven, Seventh Symphony:

or Glinka, *Jota aragonesa:*

"And yet what splendid musical structures Beethoven and Glinka have raised on these themes!"

To N. F. von Meck.

"KAMENKA, *June 25th (July 7th),* 1878.

"Yesterday, when I wrote to you about my methods of composing, I did not sufficiently enter into that phase of work which relates to the working out of the sketch. This phase is of primary importance. What has been set down in a moment of ardour must now be critically examined, improved, extended, or condensed, as the form requires. Sometimes one must do oneself violence, must sternly and pitilessly take part against oneself, before one can mercilessly erase things thought out with love and enthusiasm. I cannot complain of poverty of imagination, or lack of inventive power; but, on the other hand, I have always suffered from my want of skill in the management of form. Only after strenuous labour have I at last succeeded in making the form of my compositions correspond, more or less, with their contents. Formerly I was careless and did not give sufficient attention to the critical overhauling of my sketches. Consequently my *seams* showed, and there was no organic union between my individual episodes. This was a very serious defect, and I only improved gradually as time went on; but the form of my works will never be *exemplary*, because, although I can modify, I cannot radically alter the essential qualities of my musical temperament. But I am far from believing that my gifts have yet reached their ultimate development. I can affirm with joy that I make continual progress on the way of self-development, and am passionately desirous of attaining the highest degree of perfection of which my talents are capable. Therefore I expressed myself badly when I told you yesterday that I transcribed my works direct from the first sketches. The process is something more than copying; it is actually a critical examination, leading to corrections, occasional additions, and frequent curtailments.

"In your letter you express a wish to see my sketches. Will you accept the original sketch for my opera *Eugene Oniegin*? As the pianoforte score will be published in the autumn, it might interest you to compare the autograph sketches with the completed work. If so, I will send you the manuscript as soon as I return to Moscow. I suggest *Oniegin* because none of my works has been written with such fluency; therefore the manuscript is easy to read, as it contains few corrections."

To N. F. von Meck.

"VERBOVKA, *July 4th* (16*th*), 1878.

". . . My work progresses slowly. The sonata is finished, however, and to-day I have begun to write out some songs, composed partly abroad and partly at Kamenka, in April. I have heard from Jurgenson that four great Russian concerts, conducted by N. Rubinstein, are to take place in Paris. My Pianoforte Concerto, *The Tempest*, *Francesca*, and two movements from *our* Symphony are to be given. I will let you have further particulars, in case you care to time your visit to Paris so that it coincides with the concerts. Among those engaged to take part in them is Lavrovsky."

To N. F. von Meck.

"*July 25th* (*August 6th*), 1878.

"I write to you, dear friend, with a light heart, happy in the consciousness of having finished a work (the Liturgy). . . . People who go to work in feverish haste (like myself) are really the laziest folk. They get through their work as fast as possible in order to enjoy idleness. Now I can indulge to the full my secret delight in doing nothing."

To P. I. Jurgenson.

"VERBOVKA, *July 29th* (*August 10th*), 1878.

"DEAR FRIEND,—My manuscripts will have been taken to you. You will find plenty of material for your engravers. I send you five pieces, and besides these I shall shortly despatch three pieces for violin.

"I should like to receive the following fees :—[1]

	£	s.	d.
"1. Sonata (50 roubles) . . .	5	o	o
2. Twelve pieces (at 25 roubles each) .	30	o	o
3. The Children's Album (240 roubles)	24	o	o
4. Six songs (at 25 roubles) . .	15	o	o
5. Violin pieces (at 25 roubles each) .	7	10	o
6. The Liturgy	10	o	o
	91	10	o

[1] The rouble is here and elsewhere roughly calculated at 2*s*.

" In a round sum 900 roubles ; but having regard to the fact that I have written such a quantity at once, I will let you have the lot for 800 roubles."

To N. F. von Meck.

"*August 4th* (16*th*), 1878.

" With my usual habit of worrying and upsetting myself about things, I am now troubled because I did not get to Brailov in time—immediately after your departure.   I am afraid this may have caused some inconvenience to your servants.   But what could I do?   I wish someone could explain to me the origin of that curious exhaustion which comes upon me almost every evening, about which I have already written to you.   I cannot say it is altogether dis- agreeable, because it usually ends in a heavy, almost lethargic sleep, and such repose is bliss.   Nevertheless the attacks are tiresome and unpleasant, because of the vague anxiety, the undefinable yearning, which take an incon- ceivably strong hold upon my spirit, and end in a positive longing for Nirvana—*la soif du néant.*   Probably the cause of this psychological phenomenon is of quite a prosaic nature ; I think it is not so much a mental ailment as a result of bad digestion, a sequel of my catarrh of the stomach.   Unluckily we cannot get over the fact that the material influences the spiritual !   Too often, alas ! a pickled gherkin too much has played the most important part in the highest functions of the human intellect.   Forgive me, dear friend, for boring you with these continual com- plaints about my health, which are out of place, for in reality I am a perfectly sound man, and the little ailments about which I grumble are not serious.   I only want repose, and I shall certainly find it in Brailov.   Good Lord ! how I long for the dear house and the dear neighbourhood ! "

To N. F. von Meck.

"BRAILOV, *August* 14*th* (26*th*), 1878.

" I have brought a great many interesting books with me, among them *Histoire de ma vie,* by George Sand. The book is rather carelessly written—without logical sequence, like a clever gossip relating his own reminiscences, but with many digressions. But it has much sincerity, a complete absence of pose, and remarkably clever portraiture of the people among whom she moved in her youth. Your library, too, contains many books I cannot put down when I have once opened them. Among these is a superb edition of de Musset, one of my favourite authors. To-day, looking through this volume, I became so absorbed in *Andrea del Sarto* that—seated upon the floor—I was compelled to read the whole work to the end. I am passionately fond of all de Musset's dramatic works. How often have I thought of using one of his comedies or plays as an opera libretto! Unfortunately they are all too French, and not to be thought of in a translation ; for instance, *Le Chandelier*, or *On ne badine pas avec l'amour*. Some, less *local* in character, are lacking in dramatic movement, such as *Lorenzaccio*, or *Andrea del Sarto*. Others, again, contain too much philosophising, like *Les caprices de Marianne*.

"I cannot understand why French composers have hitherto neglected this rich source of inspiration."

To N. F. von Meck.

"BRAILOV, *August* 16*th* (28*th*), 1878.

"I return once more to Alfred de Musset. You must read his *Proverbes Dramatiques* from end to end. I recommend you especially *Les caprices de Marianne, On ne badine pas avec l'amour*, and *Le Chandelier*. Do not these things cry aloud for music? What thought! what wit! How profoundly felt and fascinating in their elegance! Yet in reading his works we feel that all is written with a light hand, not for the sake of the ideas ; that is, we never feel that these ideas have been forcibly obtruded upon the artistic material, thereby paralysing the free development of the characters and situations. Then I delight in his truly Shakespearean anachronisms : for instance, when an imaginary King of Bavaria discusses the art of Grisi with some fantastic Duke of Mantua. Like Shakespeare, de Musset does not keep to the *verities of place*, yet all the same we find among his characters, as among those of Shakespeare, many of those universal human presentments who, independent of time and locality, belong to the eternal truth. Only with de Musset the frame is narrower and the flight less lofty. Nevertheless, no other dramatic writer approaches Shakespeare so closely. *Les Caprices de Marianne* has made a peculiarly strong impression upon me, and I have thought of nothing else all day long but the possibility of turning it into an opera. I feel the necessity of considering a libretto. My enthusiasm for *Undine* has cooled. I am still captivated by *Romeo and Juliet*, but—first it is very difficult, and secondly, I am rather frightened of Gounod, who has already written a mediocre opera on this subject."

To N. F. Von Meck.

"VERBOVKA *August 25th (September 6th)*, 1878.

". . . I have already told you that at Brailov I jotted down the sketch of a scherzo for orchestra. Afterwards the idea came to me of composing a series of orchestral pieces out of which I could put together a Suite, in the style of Lachner. Arrived at Verbovka, I felt I could not restrain my impulse, and hastened to work out on paper my sketches for this Suite. I worked at it with such delight and enthusiasm that I literally lost count of time. At the present moment three movements are finished, the fourth is sketched out, and the fifth sits waiting in my head. . . . The Suite will consist of five movements : (1) Introduction and Fugue, (2) Scherzo, (3) Andante, (4) Intermezzo (*Echo du bal*), (5) Rondo. While engaged upon this work my thoughts were perpetually with you ; every moment I asked myself if such and such passages would please, or such and such melodies touch you ? Therefore my new work can only be dedicated to *my best friend.*

"To-morrow I travel straight to Petersburg to see my father and Anatol again, and shall remain there two or three days. Then I go to Moscow. I look to the future with a little apprehension, a little sadness, and a trifle of disgust."

To Modeste Tchaikovsky.

"KIEV, *August* 29*th* (*September* 10*th*), 1878.

"In to-day's paper (the *Novoe Vremya*) I found an article containing a mean, base and vulgar attack upon the Moscow Conservatoire. Very little is said about me personally; it simply states that I occupy myself exclusively with music and take no part in the intrigues.

"Going along in the train, with this paper in my hand, I resolved to resign my professorship. I should have done so immediately, and not returned to Moscow at all, if my rooms had not been already engaged, and if I had not been definitely expected at the Conservatoire. I have made up my mind to wait until December, then I will go to Kamenka for the holidays and write from there that I am indisposed. Of course I shall give private information of my intentions to Rubinstein, so that he may have time to engage another professor. So *vive la liberté*, and especially Nadejda Filaretovna! There is no doubt whatever that she will approve of my decision—consequently I shall be able to lead a glorious, wandering life, sometimes in Kamenka, sometimes in Verbovka, sometimes in Petersburg or abroad. . . .

"For God's sake go on with your novel! Work is the sole cure for *les misères de la vie humaine.* Besides, it gives you independence.

"You will say you have *no time* for writing because you are occupied all day with Kolya. All the same, I repeat: Write, write, write! I might offer myself as an example. I used to have six hours' exhausting teaching at the Conservatoire, besides living with Rubinstein—whose ways hindered me exceedingly—in a house next door to the Conservatoire, whence was borne the sound of unceasing scales and exercises which made it difficult to compose. Your occupations with Kolya may be somewhat heavier than my theory classes, but still I say, Write! Meanwhile I embrace you, dear Modi! What does anything matter when people love as I love you and you love me (forgive my self-assurance)!"

PART V

I

1878–1879

WHEN in 1877 Tchaikovsky declined to act as delegate for the Paris Exhibition, the office was accepted by Nicholas Rubinstein, who, in September, 1878, gave four important concerts at the Trocadéro, the programmes of which were drawn exclusively from the works of Russian composers.

Tchaikovsky was represented by the following works: the Pianoforte Concerto (B♭ minor), *The Tempest, Chant sans Paroles* (played by Nicholas Rubinstein), and "Serenade and Valse" for violin (played by Bartzevich). The success of these compositions, especially of the Concerto, thanks to Rubinstein's artistic interpretation, was so great that, judging by the opinions of Tchaikovsky's friends and opponents, the chief interest of all four concerts centred in them. Eye-witnesses declare they never saw such enthusiasm in any concert-room as was displayed on the first evening after the performance of the B♭ minor Concerto. The work was repeated with equal success at the fourth concert.

The Paris Press accorded the warmest greeting to Tchaikovsky, whose name was as yet almost unknown to them, the most appreciative criticisms being expended upon the Concerto. *The Tempest* came in for its share of applause, while the violin pieces were not so well received.

The importance of Tchaikovsky's success was, however, greatly overrated, both by himself and all his friends, including N. Rubinstein. They none of them realised that Paris forgets as lightly as it warms to enthusiasm. Scarcely six months elapsed before *The Tempest*, which had delighted the Parisian public at the Trocadéro, was received with suspicion and curiosity, as the unknown work of an unknown composer of queer Russian music.

About the same time, Bilse brought forward *Francesca da Rimini* in Berlin. Here, where Russian music had such propagandists as Hans von Bülow and Klindworth, Tchaikovsky was not altogether unknown; but although some of his works, like the Andante from the first quartet, were almost popular, yet the composer had been regarded with a certain disdain, and almost ignored by the majority of the German critics. This time it was different. On the same evening as *Francesca*, Bilse also conducted Brahms's Second Symphony, which, being a novelty, drew all the musical lights of Berlin to the concert. It was only thanks to these circumstances that *Francesca* was not entirely passed over by the critics. The Press split into two camps: one stood up for Brahms and attacked Tchaikovsky, the other took the opposite view. The hostile party was the stronger. Richard Würst called the work "a musical monstrosity."[1] "We know," he continued, "a few songs, pianoforte pieces, and a Cossack fantasia (?) by this composer; these compositions bear the stamp of an original talent, but are not pleasing on the whole. In the Symphonic Fantasia (*Francesca*) this unpleasantness is so obvious as to make us forget the originality of the composer. The first and last allegros, which depict the whirlwinds of hell, have neither subjects

---

[1] See the *Berliner Fremdenblatt*, September 17th, 1878.

nor ideas, but only a mass of sounds, and these ear-splitting effects seem to us, from an artistic point of view, too much even for hell itself. The middle section, which describes the unhappy fate of Francesca, Paolo, and myself, shows—in spite of its endless length—at least some trace of catching melody." Another critic, O. Lumprecht (*National Zeitung*, September 17th, 1878), applies to *Francesca* such terms as "madness," "musical contortions," etc.

Among the friendly party *Francesca* was favourably compared to the Brahms Symphony, especially by Moszkowski. Among private opinions should be mentioned that of Hans von Bülow, who wrote to Tchaikovsky shortly after the performance that he was far more charmed with *Francesca* than with *Romeo and Juliet*. Kotek says that Joachim was pleased with the work in spite of his prepossession in favour of his friend Brahms, while Max Bruch when asked his opinion of *Francesca* replied: "I am far too stupid to criticise such music." In spite of the overruling of unfavourable criticism, and its mediocre success with the public, Bilse had the courage to repeat *Francesca da Rimini* in the course of the same season.

Early in September Tchaikovsky returned to Moscow to take up his duties at the Conservatoire. His quarters were already prepared for him. Nevertheless, before returning to the town he had once loved and believed to be a necessary part of his happiness, he had already resolved "to leave it again at the earliest opportunity."

This curious discrepancy between his actions and his intentions, this external submission to, and inward protest against, the compelling circumstances of life, so characteristic of Tchaikovsky, has already become familiar to us. He was incapable of clearing a direct way for himself to some definite goal; he could only desire intensely and await with patience the course of events, until the obstacles gave way of themselves and the path was open to him at last.

After the mental collapse he had suffered, and during the pause in his creative activity in November and December, 1877, he thought of the return to his old life in Moscow with fear and trembling, while still regarding it as an inevitable necessity. The great distance which lay between himself and Moscow softened all its sharpness of outline, and veiled all the unpleasant side of life in that city. From far-away Italy and Switzerland he no longer looked back upon everyday Moscow, but saw rather the white City of the Tsars, with its flashing golden cupolas, which was so dear to his patriotic soul. He no longer saw the Conservatoire, with its tiresome classes and petty commonplace interests, but a little group of true friends for whom he yearned. All this drowned the resolve which already existed in his inmost heart, never to return to his old way of life. He attributed this dislike of his former existence to his ill-health, and cherished the hope that the ideal conditions of his life abroad would restore his nerves and soothe his irritability; he was convinced that he would completely recover, and take up his professorship once more with a stout heart.

But it proved otherwise. From the month of January, when he was able to arrange his life as he pleased, when, with improved health, the desire to compose awoke once more—from the moment, in fact, in which his real recovery began—life in Moscow seemed to him to be more dreadful and impossible; his connection with the Conservatoire, and with the social life of the capital, more and more unbearable; while the free, untrammelled existence in which nothing hindered his creative activity grew more attractive in his eyes. Never had Tchaikovsky been so lastingly happy as during the period dating from 1878. Never had "the calm, peaceful existence in solitude" appeared so alluring, nor his imagination so quick and so

Y

varied. Consequently everything which disturbed his existence at that happy time seemed hostile and unfavourable to its continuance.

Only the weak bond of his promise to return to the Conservatoire remained to be broken.

At the moment in which Tchaikovsky left the train in which he arrived and set foot on Moscow soil, he was possessed with " the idea " of leaving again as soon as possible. This thought gradually grew into a fixed idea, under the influence of which everything that had once been dear to him—his faithful friends included—stirred in him an exaggerated feeling of resentment and, by way of reaction, caused everything which reminded him of his freedom to appear in a rosy light. In his first letters from Moscow he scarcely speaks on any other topic but the irksomeness of life there, and the delight with which he looks back to every detail of his visits to Italy, Switzerland and Brailov.

There was nothing to be done, however, until Rubinstein's return from the Paris Exhibition, which would not be before the end of September.

" I had been anxiously awaiting his coming," wrote Tchaikovsky to Nadejda von Meck, " because I wanted to tell him, as soon as possible, of my intention to retire from the Conservatoire. He was received with great rejoicings, and a dinner in his honour was given at ' The Hermitage,' [1] at which I was present. In his reply to the first toast to his health, Rubinstein said he had been greatly gratified by the success of my works at his concerts, that the Conservatoire had reason to be proud of its connection with so famous a man, etc. The speech ended in an ovation to me. I need hardly tell you how painful this speech and ovation were.

" The next day I informed him of my future plans. I expected Nicholas Rubinstein to burst forth with indignation, and try to convince me that it was better for me

---

[1] A famous restaurant in Moscow.

to stay where I was. On the contrary, he listened to me laughingly, as one might to a tiresome child, and expressed his regret. He merely remarked that the Conservatoire would lose a great deal of its prestige with the withdrawal of my name, which was as good as saying that the pupils would not really suffer much by my resignation. Probably he is right, for I am a poor and inexperienced teacher—yet I anticipated greater opposition to my resignation."

It was decided that Tchaikovsky should stay on for a month or two at the Conservatoire, in order to give his successor Taneiev time to prepare for his classes; but when it was announced that Hubert, not Taneiev, was to succeed him, he "hastened the course of events" and informed Rubinstein that he should leave Moscow early in October.

From Moscow Tchaikovsky went to St. Petersburg, which was equally unsuited to his condition of mind. The invitations to dinners, suppers, and evening parties, fatigued him and wore him out. The bad impression which Petersburg left upon him on this occasion was increased by the disappointment he experienced as regards his favourite opera, *Vakoula the Smith*, which was just being given at the Maryinsky Theatre.

To N. F. von Meck.

"PETERSBURG, *October* 30*th* (*November* 11*th*), 1878.

"*Vakoula the Smith* went quite smoothly and well, just as it did at the first performance; but it was very stereotyped and colourless. All the while I felt angry with one man : that was *myself*. Good Lord! what heaps of unpardonable mistakes there are in this opera which I alone could have made! I have done my best to neutralise the effect of all those situations which were calculated to please. If only I had held the purely musical inspiration in check, and kept the scenic and decorative effects more in view! The entire opera suffers from a plethora of details and the tiresome use of chromatic harmonies. *C'est un menu sur-*

chargé de mets épicés.   It contains too many delicacies and not enough simple, wholesome fare.   The recent production of the opera has been a lesson to me for the future.   I think *Eugene Oniegin* is a step in advance."

II

At the beginning of November Tchaikovsky went to Kamenka, and here for the first time he began to breathe freely after two anxious and depressing months.

"I feel very well here," he wrote in November.   To "feel well" was the equivalent with him of "being equal to hard work."   As a matter of fact he composed more at Kamenka in a fortnight than during the two months he had spent in Moscow and Petersburg.   On November 13th (25th) he wrote to his brother Modeste :—

"Inspiration has come to me, so the sketch of the Suite is almost finished.   But I am anxious because I left the manuscript of the first three movements in Petersburg, and it may get lost.   I wrote the last two movements here. This short and—if I am not mistaken—excellent Suite is in five movements: (1) Introduction and Fugue, (2) Scherzo, (3) Andante, (4) March Miniature, (5) Giant's Dance."

To A. Tchaikovsky.

"FLORENCE, *November 21st (December 3rd)*, 1878.

". . . I came here yesterday, direct from Vienna, without visiting Venice.   I was met by Pakhulsky (Kotek's successor with N. F. von Meck), who took me to my quarters, which were warm and bright, and all ready for their admiring tenant.

"The apartment Nadejda Filaretovna has taken for me consists of a suite of five rooms: drawing-room, dining-room, bedroom, dressing-room, and a room for Alexis.

"In the drawing-room there is a splendid grand piano, on the writing-table every kind of stationery, and two

big bouquets. The furniture is luxurious.   I am delighted
that the house stands outside the town, and that I have
such a beautiful view from my windows!

"On the journey here I was troubled with the thought
that Nadejda Filaretovna would be living so close to me ;
that we might meet.   I even had a momentary suspicion
that she might invite me.   But a letter from her, which I
found upon my writing-table yesterday, completely set my
mind at rest. She will be leaving in three weeks, and
during that time probably we shall not see each other once."

To N. F. von Meck.

"FLORENCE, *November 20th (December 2nd)*, 1878.

". . . If you knew what a blessing this quiet, regular,
and solitary life is, especially in such sympathetic surroundings!   I shall begin the instrumentation of the
Suite with ardour, because I am strongly attracted to a
new subject for an opera: Schiller's *Maid of Orleans.*
. . . This idea came to me at Kamenka, while turning over
the pages of Joukovsky. The subject offers much musical
material. Verdi's opera, *Giovanna d'Arco,* is not taken
from Schiller in the first place, and secondly it is extremely
poor.   But I am glad I bought it. It will be very useful
to compare the libretto with the French."

"*November 22nd (December 4th)*, 1878.

" I have never thanked you, my good fairy, for the fine
instrument.   I often reproach myself for not being sufficiently grateful.   On the other hand I am afraid of weary-
ing you with my reiterated assurance of gratitude."

To P. I. Jurgenson.

"FLORENCE, *November 24th (December 6th)*, 1878.

" In the evening I often pace my verandah and enjoy the
utter stillness.   That strikes you as peculiar: how can
anyone enjoy the absence of all sound, you will ask?   If
you were a musician, perhaps you, too, would have the gift
of hearing, when all is still in the dead silence of night, the
deep bass note which seems to come from the earth in its
flight through space.   But this is nonsense! "

To N. F. von Meck.

"FLORENCE, *November 26th (December 8th)*, 1878.

"Please send me the Lalo Concerto again. I only looked through the first movement attentively, and found it rather insipid. After what you have written I should like to run through the work again.

"I read Italian pretty well, but speak it badly. Once upon a time I studied it and could speak fluently. That was in the days of my admiration for Ristori.

"I place Massenet lower than Bizet, Délibes, or even Saint-Saëns, but he, too, has—like all our French contemporaries—that element of freshness which is lacking in the Germans.

8 p.m.

"Modeste's telegram was a pleasant surprise. I had no idea the Symphony (No. 4) was going to be played yet. His news of its success is entirely trustworthy. First, because Modeste knows that I am not pleased when people send me exaggerated reports of such events; and secondly because the Scherzo was encored—an undoubted proof of success. After this news I am entirely lost in our Symphony. All day long I keep humming it, and trying to recall how, where, and under what impression this or that part of it was composed. I go back to two years ago, and return to the present with joy! What a change! What has not happened during these years! When I began to work at the Symphony I hardly knew you at all. I remember very well, however, that I dedicated my work to you. Some instinct told me that no one had such a fine insight into my music as yourself, that our natures had much in common, and that you would understand the contents of this Symphony better than any other human being. I love this child of my fancy very dearly. It is one of the things which will never disappoint me."

The success of the Fourth Symphony, at a concert of the Russian Musical Society in St. Petersburg, on November 25th (December 7th), was most brilliant, and the Press was almost unanimous in its acknowledgment of the fact.

To N. F. von Meck.

" FLORENCE, *November 27th (December 9th),* 1878.

" Permit me, dear friend, to give you my opinion of Lalo's Concerto, which I have played through several times, and begin to know pretty thoroughly. Lalo is very talented, there is no doubt about it, but he is either a very young man—because all his deficiencies may be referred to a certain immaturity of style—or he will not go far, since, in a man of ripe age, these deficiencies point to an organic, incurable fault. I do not consider the Concerto as good as the 'Spanish Symphony.' All that was wild, lawless, and rhapsodical in the latter—which I attributed to the oriental and Moorish character of the Spanish melodies—is to be found also in the Concerto, which, however, is not at all Spanish. Let us analyse the first movement. It does not consist of two themes, as is usually the case, but of several —of five, in fact.

" This is too much. A musical work must be digestible, and should not consist of too many ingredients. Then, of these themes, only the fifth can be considered successful. The rest are colourless, or, like the second, made up of scraps, which have no organic unity and lack definite outline. Thirdly, every one of these themes, except the fifth, shows a monotonous method, which occurs only too often in the 'Spanish Symphony': the alternation of rhythms of 3 and 2. If a man cannot keep his inspiration within the limits of balanced form, then he should strive, at least, to vary the rhythms of his themes; in this Concerto the rhythmical treatment is monotonous. I will say nothing about the laboured way in which the various episodes follow one another; it would take us too far afield. Then as to harmony. The Concerto is full of queer, wild harmonies. In a modest violin Concerto such spicy condiments are out of place; but apart from that, I must say they have a kind of crude character, because they are not the outcome of the essential musical idea, but are forced upon it, like a schoolboy's bravado put on for his teacher's benefit. Other passages—also in the schoolboy style—are really rather slovenly, so to speak. For instance, this 'smudge' *à la* Moussorgsky, which occurs twice over:

" If we play this horrible combination in quavers we get the following :—

" This is repulsive, and quite unnecessary, because it is based upon nothing, and at first I took it for a misprint.

Do not imagine, my friend, that it is the pedantic harmony master who speaks thus. I myself am very partial to dissonant combinations, when they have a motive, and are rightly used. But there are limits which must not be overstepped. Now, to enter into technical details, let me say that no breach of the laws of harmony, no matter whether it is harsh or not, really sounds well unless it has been made under the influence of the melodic origin. In other words, a dissonance should only be resolved harmonically, or melodically. If neither of these courses is adopted, we merely get abominations *à la* Moussorgsky. In the example cited above I might possibly be reconciled to the painful dissonance if, in the next bar, each part followed the melodic plan. But this is not the case with Lalo. With him abomination follows abomination. Now that I have done scolding, I will say something good. The various movements, although disconnected, show warmth and many beautiful details of harmony. On the whole the music has a piquant character peculiarly French, although not nearly so elegant as Bizet's work."

To N. F. von Meck.

" FLORENCE, *November* 28*th* (*December* 10*th*), 1878.

" Yesterday's performance at Pergola left a sad impression upon me. What a deterioration Italian music has suffered! What commonplace, yet pretentious stuff! What an incredibly poor performance as regards orchestra and chorus! The staging, too, was wretched. Such scenery in the town where Raphael and Michael Angelo once lived!"

To N. F. von Meck.

" FLORENCE, *December* 5*th* (17*th*), 1878.

" A great number of my works I regard as weak. Several of these (the minority) have been published. Of those unpublished, many no longer exist, such as the operas *Undine* and *The Voyevode* (which were never performed), the symphonic fantasia *Fatum*, a Festival overture on the Danish National Hymn, and a cantata; but you are welcome to those I have kept, in order to complete your collection. They are very poor, although they contain some episodes and details I should be sorry to see disappear for ever.

"Laroche does not call me the enemy of programme music, but thinks I have no gift for this kind of work; therefore he describes me as an anti-programme composer. He takes every opportunity of expressing his regret that I so frequently compose programme music. What is programme music? Since for you and me a mere pattern of sounds has long since ceased to be music at all, all music is programme music from our point of view. In the limited sense of the word, however, it means symphonic, or, more generally, instrumental music which illustrates a definite subject, and bears the title of this subject. Beethoven partly invented programme music in the 'Eroica' symphony, but the idea is still more evident in the 'Pastoral.' The true founder of programme music, however, was Berlioz, every one of whose works not only bears a definite title, but appears with a detailed explanation. Laroche is entirely opposed to a programme. He thinks the composer should leave the hearer to interpret the meaning of the work as he pleases; that the programme limits his freedom; that music is incapable of expressing the concrete phenomena of the physical and mental world. Nevertheless, he ranks Berlioz very highly, declares him to be an altogether rare genius and his music exemplary; but, all the same, he considers his programmes superfluous. If you care to hear my opinion on the subject, I will give it in a few words. I think the inspiration of a symphonic work can be of two kinds: subjective or objective. In the first instance it expresses the personal emotion of joy or sorrow, as when the lyric poet lets his soul flow out in verse. Here a programme is not only unnecessary, but impossible. It is very different when the composer's inspiration is stirred by the perusal of some poem, or by the sight of a fine landscape, and he endeavours to express his impressions in musical forms. In this case a programme is indispensable, and it is a pity Beethoven did not affix one to the sonata you mention. To my mind, both kinds of music have their *raison d'être*, and I cannot understand those who will only admit one of these styles. Of course, every subject is not equally suitable for a symphony, any more than for an opera ; but, all the same, programme music can and must exist. Who would insist in literature upon ignoring the epic and admitting only the lyric element?"

III

Shortly after writing the above letter Tchaikovsky left Florence for Paris. He did not remain there any length of time, but went to Clarens on December 28th in order to work at *The Maid of Orleans* in the quiet atmosphere of the Villa Richelieu.

To N. F. von Meck.

"CLARENS, *December* 31st (*January* 12th), 1878.

" To-day I began to work, and wrote out the first chorus of the first act. The composition of this work is rendered more difficult because I have no ready-made libretto, and have not yet come to any definite plan as to the general outline. Meanwhile, only the text for the first act is complete. This I have written myself, keeping as far as possible to Joukovsky's version, although I have drawn upon other sources : Barbier, for instance, whose tragedy has many good points. I find the versification very difficult."

To N. F. von Meck.

"CLARENS, *January* 8th (20th), 1879.

"I am very well pleased with my musical work. As regards the literary side of it, I believe it will cost me some days of my life. I cannot describe how it exhausts me. How many penholders I gnaw to pieces before a few lines grow perfect! How often I jump up in sheer despair because I cannot find a rhyme, or the metre goes wrong, or because I have absolutely no notion what this or that character would say at a particular moment! As regards rhyme, I think it would be a blessing if someone would publish a rhyming dictionary. If I am not mis-taken, there is one in German, and perhaps in Russian too, but I am not sure of it."

To P. I. Jurgenson.

"CLARENS, *January 14th (26th)*, 1879.

"There exist, as you are aware, three remarkable per-sonages, whom you know intimately : the feeble poetaster N. N.,[1] who has written a few verses for your editions of Russian songs; B. L.,[2] formerly musical critic of the *Russky Viedomosti*, and the composer and ex-professor, Mr. Tchaikovsky.

"An hour or two ago Mr. Tchaikovsky invited the two other gentlemen—who live with him—to follow him to the piano, and played them the second act of his new opera *The Maid of Orleans*. Mr. Tchaikovsky, who is on very intimate terms with Messrs. N. N. and B. L., conquered his timidity without much difficulty, and played his new work with great skill and inspiration. You should have seen the enthusiasm of these two gentlemen! Anyone might have supposed they had some share in the composi-tion of the opera, to see how they strutted about the room and admired the music. Finally, the composer, who had long tried to preserve his modesty intact, was infected by their enthusiasm, and all three rushed on to the balcony, as though possessed, to cool their disordered nerves and control their wild desire to hear the rest of the opera as soon as possible. In vain Messrs. N. N. and B. L. en-deavoured to persuade Mr. Tchaikovsky that operas could not be tossed out like pancakes, the latter began to despair over the weakness of human nature and the impossibility of transferring to paper in a single night all that had long been seething in his brain. Finally, the good folks induced the insane composer to calm him-self, and he sat down to write to a certain publisher in Moscow. . . ."

---

[1] The initials under which Tchaikovsky translated the German words of Rubinstein's songs.

Tchaikovsky's signature to his articles in the *Russky Viedomosti*.

To N. F. von Meck.

"*January 20th (February 1st)*, 1879.

" Of the music you sent me, I have only played, as yet, through the pieces by Grieg and two acts of Goldmark's opera, *The Queen of Sheba*. I do not know if I ever told you that I bought *Le Roi de Lahore* in Paris. Thus I possess two operas of the most modern French school. Let me tell you, dear friend, that I have no hesitation in giving the preference to *Le Roi de Lahore*. I know you do not care very much for Massenet, and hitherto I, too, have not felt drawn to him. His opera, however, has captivated me by its rare beauty of form, its simplicity and freshness of ideas and style, as well by its wealth of melody and distinction of harmony. Goldmark's opera does not greatly please me—just enough to interest me in playing it through. Yet it is the work of a good German master. But all the German composers of the present day write laboriously, with pretensions to depth of thought, and strive to atone for their extraordinary poverty of invention by exaggerated colouring. For instance, the duet in the second act. How unvocal! How little freedom it gives to the singer! What insipid melodies! Massenet's love duet, on the contrary, is far simpler, but a thousand times fresher, more beautiful, more melodious. . . .

" Learn to know this opera, dear friend, and give me your opinion upon it.

" My work progresses. I am composing the first scene of Act III."

To Modeste Tchaikovsky.

" CLARENS, *January 24th (February 5th)*, 1879.

" Do not be surprised if my letter is somewhat incoherent. I am very tired after my day's work. To-day I wrote the love duet in the second act, and it is very complicated, so that at the present moment my brain works with difficulty. I jumped from the first scene of the third act to the fourth, because it is not so easy, and I wanted to get the most difficult scene—between Lionel and Joan —off my mind. On the whole I am pleased with myself, but feel rather exhausted. In Paris, I will rest by returning to my Suite and leaving the two remaining scenes of the opera until my return to Russia.

"I have added a new joy to life. In Geneva I bought the pianoforte arrangements of several Mozart and Beethoven quartets, and I play one every evening. You have no idea how I enjoy this, and how it refreshes me! I would give anything for my *Maid of Orleans* to turn out as good as *Le Roi de Lahore*."

To N. F. von Meck.

"*January 25th* (*February 6th*), 1879.

"I will gladly follow your advice and write to Jurgenson to send a copy of *Eugene Oniegin* to Bülow. Generally speaking, I never send my works on my own initiative to musical celebrities, but Bülow is an exception, because he is really interested in Russian music and in me personally. He is the sole German musician who admits the possibility of the Russians rivalling the Germans as composers. Speaking of the German view of our compatriots, I do not think I ever told you about the fiasco of my *Francesca* in Berlin this winter. Bilse gave it twice. The second performance was a daring act on his part, since after the first hearing the entire Press was unanimous in damning my unfortunate fantasia. . . ."

IV

To P. I. Jurgenson.

"PARIS, *February 6th* (18*th*), 1879.

"Do you imagine I am going to dish you up my impressions of Paris? 'You are mistaken, friend,' as Kashkin is always saying. I only arrived early this morning. My departure from Clarens was highly dramatic. The landlady wept; the landlord shook me warmly by the hand; the maid (a very nice creature) also wept, so that I, too, was reduced to tears. I assure you I have never been so comfortable anywhere abroad as there. If circumstances permit, and no untoward changes occur in my life, I intend henceforth to spend a considerable part of each winter in Clarens. . . ."

To N. F. von Meck.

"*February* 10th (22nd), 1879.

" At the present moment I am engaged upon the great *ensemble* in the third act (septet and chorus), which presents many technical difficulties. The first part of the septet is finished, and very successful, if I am not mistaken. The brilliance and bustle of Paris have their advantages. The variety of circumstances and impressions distract my thoughts from the musical work. Perhaps this is the reason why the number which I expected to find most fatiguing has proved comparatively easy. For the books and music I am very grateful to you. . . ."

To P. I. Jurgenson.

" Paris, *February* 13th (25th), 1879.

" Here I live the life of an anchorite, and only emerge twice a day to satisfy the cravings of my stomach and take a little exercise.

" Last Sunday, however, I had a real musical treat. Colonne conducted one of my favourite works—Berlioz's *Faust.* The performance was excellent. It was so long since I had heard any good music that I was steeped in bliss, all the more because I was alone, with no acquaintances sitting by my side. What a work!! Poor Berlioz! As long as he was alive no one wanted to hear about him. Now the newspapers call him ' the mighty Hector. . . .' O God, how happy I am now! Did I ever dream that I should enjoy life so much?. . ."

To N. F. von Meck.

" Paris, *February* 19th (*March* 3rd), 1879.

" My whole life long I have been a martyr to my enforced relations with society. By nature I am a savage. Every new acquaintance, every fresh contact with strangers, has been the source of acute moral suffering. It is difficult to say what is the nature of this suffering. Perhaps it springs from a shyness which has become a mania, perhaps from absolute indifference to the society of my fellows, or perhaps the difficulty of saying, without effort, things about oneself that one does not really think (for social intercourse involves this)—in short, I do not really know what it is. So long as I was not in a position to avoid such intercourse, I went into society, pretended to enjoy myself, played a certain part (since it is absolutely indispensable to social existence), and suffered horribly all the time. I could wax eloquent on the subject. . . . To cut a long story short, however, I will merely tell you that two years ago Count Leo Tolstoi, the writer, expressed a wish to make my acquaintance. He takes a great interest in music. Of course, I made a feeble attempt to escape from him, but without success. He came to the Conservatoire and told Rubinstein he had not left the town because he wanted to meet me. Tolstoi is very sympathetic towards my musical gifts. It was impossible to avoid his acquaintance, which was obviously flattering and agreeable. We met, and I, assuming the part of a man who is immensely gratified, said I was very happy—most grateful— a whole series of indispensable but insincere phrases. ' I want to know you better,' he said ; ' I should like to talk to you about music.' Then and there, after we had shaken hands, he began to give me his musical views. He considers Beethoven lacks inspiration. We started with this. Thus this writer of genius, this searcher of human hearts, began by asserting, in a tone of complete assurance, what was most offensive to the stupidity of the musician. What is to be done under such circumstances? Discuss? Yes, I discussed. But could such a discussion be regarded as serious? Properly speaking, I ought to have felt honoured by his notice. Probably another would have been. I merely felt uncomfortable, and continued to enact the comedy—pretending to be grateful and in earnest. Afterwards he called upon me several times, and although after this meeting I came to the conclusion that Tolstoi, if somewhat paradoxical, was straightforward, good, and in his way had even a fine taste for music, yet, at the same time, I had no more to gain from his acquaintance than from that of any other man.

"The society of another fellow-creature is only pleasant when a long-standing intimacy, or common interests, make it possible to dispense with all effort. Unless this is the case, society is a burden which I was never intended by nature to endure.

"This is the reason, dear friend, why I have not called upon Tourgeniev. There are numbers of people I might visit here. Saint-Saëns, for instance, on whom I promised to call whenever I was in Paris. Anyone else in my place would make the acquaintance of the local musicians. It is a pity I cannot, for I lose a good deal by my misanthropy. Oh, if you only knew how I have struggled against this weakness, how hard I have contended with my strange temperament in this respect!

"Now I am at rest. I am finally convinced that at my age it is useless to continue my education. I assure you I have been very happy since I drew into my shell, and since music and books became my faithful and inseparable companions. As to intercourse with famous people, I know from experience that their works, musical or literary, are far more interesting than their personalities."

To Modeste Tchaikovsky.

"PARIS, *February 22nd (March 6th),* 1879.

"DEAR MODI,—Yesterday was a very important day for me. Quite unexpectedly I finished the opera. When you have written the last word of a novel you will understand what a joy it is to feel such a weight off your mind. To squeeze music out of one's brain every day for ten weeks is indeed an exhausting process. Now I can breathe freely!

"Yesterday evening I walked about Paris feeling quite another man. I even *sauntered,* and perhaps that is why my old love for the place is reawakened. Perhaps, too, the fact that Colonne intends to give my *Tempest* at the next Sunday concert has something to do with it. Now I see my name on all the hoardings and posters I feel quite at home. I will confess that although I am pleased, yet I am also rather anxious. I know beforehand that it will not be well played, and will be hissed by the public—the invariable

z

fate of all my compositions abroad. Therefore it would be better if the performance took place after I have left Paris. It cannot be helped, however. I shall have to endure some misery on Sunday, but not much, because I am only here as a bird of passage, and I know that the time is coming when I need not endure any more.

"In any case, yesterday and to-day I have strutted through the streets of Paris like a cock, and comforted myself with the feeling that I need not work. You would never have recognised your brother in a new overcoat, silk hat, and elegant gloves. . . ."

To N. F. von Meck.

"PARIS, *February* 24th (*March* 8th), 1879.

"Yesterday I saw *L'Assomoir*. It is interesting to sit through this piece, for it is highly entertaining to see washer-women getting up linen in the second scene, all the characters dead drunk in the sixth, and in the eighth, the death of a confirmed toper in an attack of *delirium tremens*. The play deals a double blow at that feeling for beauty which exists in us all. First, it is adapted from a novel written by a talented, but cynical, man who chooses to wallow in human filth, moral and physical. Secondly, to make it more effective and pander to the taste of the Boulevard public, a melodramatic element has been brought into the play which is not in keeping with the rest of it. In this way *L'Assomoir* loses on the stage its chief merit—the wonderfully realistic presentment of everyday life.

"But what do you think of Monsieur Zola, the high priest of the realistic cult, the austere critic who recognises no literary art but his own, when he allows perfectly unreal and improbable episodes and characters to be tacked on to his play—all for the sake of a royalty?"

To Modeste Tchaikovsky.

"PARIS, *February* 26th (*March* 10th), 1879.

"Yesterday was a very exciting day. In the morning at the Châtelet Concert the performance of my *Tempest* took place. The agonies I endured are the best proof that a country life is the most tolerable for me. What used to be a pleasure—the hearing of one of my own works—has now become a source of misery. The evening before I began to suffer from colic and nausea. My agitation continued to grow *crescendo* until the opening chords, and while the work was proceeding I felt I should die of the pain in my heart. It was not the fear of failure with the public, but because lately the first hearing of all my works has brought me the sharpest disappointment. Mendelssohn's *Reformation* symphony preceded *The Tempest*, and all the time I was admiring this fine masterpiece. I have not attained to the rank of a master. I still write like a gifted young man from whom much is to be expected. What surprised me chiefly was the fact that my orchestration sounded so poor. Of course, my reason told me I was exaggerating my own defects, but this was no great consolation. *The Tempest* was not badly played. The orchestra took pains, but showed no warmth of enthusiasm. One member of the band (a 'cellist) kept staring, smiling, and nodding his head, as much as to say : 'Excuse our playing such an extraordinary work ; it is not our fault ; we are ordered to play it, and we obey.' After the last bars had died away, there followed some feeble applause, mingled with two or three audible hisses, at which the whole room broke out into exclamations of 'O ! O !' which were intended as a kindly protest against the hisses. Then came silence. The whole business passed over me without leaving any special bitterness. I was only vexed to feel that *The Tempest*, which I have hitherto regarded as one of my most brilliant works, is in reality so unimportant. I left the room and, as the weather was very fine, took a two hours' stroll. On returning home I wrote a card to Colonne, telling him that I could only remain another day in Paris, and could not therefore call to thank him personally.

" I must soon leave Paris. I am reconciled to the failure of *The Tempest*. I speak of it as a failure *to myself*, but I console myself with the thought that after the opera and the Suite I shall at last compose a fine symphonic work. And so, in all probability, I shall strive for mastery until my last breath, without ever attaining it. Something is lacking in me—I can feel it—but there is nothing to be done."

The *Gazette Musicale* published Tchaikovsky's letter to Colonne, which ran as follows :—

"Sir,—As luck would have it, I came to Paris for one day only, the very one upon which you presented my *Tempest* to the public. I was at the Châtelet. I heard it, and hasten to thank you for the kind and flattering attention bestowed on my music, and for your fine interpretation of my difficult and ungrateful work. I also send my hearty thanks to the members of your splendid orchestra for the trouble they took to interpret every detail of the score in the most artistic way.

"As to the feeble applause and somewhat energetic hisses with which the public greeted my unlucky *Tempest*, they affected me deeply, but did not surprise me—I expected them. If a certain degree of prejudice against our Muscovite barbarity had something to do with this, the intrinsic defects of the work itself are also to blame. The form is diffuse and lacking in proportion. In any case the performance which, as I have said, was excellent, has nothing to do with the failure of the work.

"I should certainly have gone round to shake hands with you and express my gratitude in person, had not the state of my health prevented my doing so. I am only passing through Paris. I am obliged therefore, dear sir, to have recourse to my pen, in order to convey to you my thanks. Rest assured that my gratitude will not be effaced from my heart.

                     "Your devoted

                           "P. T."

In publishing this letter, the *Gazette Musicale* preceded it by a few lines in praise of "this rare witness to the noble and sincere modesty of a composer."

To N. F. von Meck.

"Paris, *February* 27th (*March* 11th), 1879.

"For the first time in my life I have read Rousseau's *Confessions*. I do not know if I ought to recommend the book to you, supposing you have never read it, for side by side with passages of genius, it contains much cynical information which makes it almost unfit for a woman to read. Nevertheless I cannot help admiring the astonishing strength and beauty of style, as well as the true and profound analysis of the human soul. Apart from this, I find an indescribable delight in recognising features in my own character which I have never met with before in any literary work, and which are here described with extraordinary subtlety. For instance, he explains why, being a clever man, he never succeeds in giving any impression of his cleverness when in society. He speaks of his misanthropical tendencies, and of the unbearable necessity of keeping up forced conversations, when, in order to keep the ball rolling, one is obliged to pour forth empty words which in no way express the result of intellectual work, or spiritual impulse. How subtle and true are his remarks upon the scourge of social life."

At the beginning of March Tchaikovsky returned to St. Petersburg. As invariably happened when his solitude was interrupted and a break in his work occurred, he now passed through a period of depression and discontent with his surroundings, which were actually in no way to blame for his frame of mind.

To N. F. von Meck.

"*March* 13*th* (25*th*), 1879.

". . . On Friday I go to Moscow with my brothers to attend the first performance of *Eugene Oniegin*, after which I shall return to Petersburg, where I remain until Easter."

To N. F. von Meck.

"PETERSBURG, *March* 19*th* (31*st*), 1879.

" I have just returned from Moscow. Instead of leaving on Friday, I went on Wednesday, because Jurgenson telegraphed that my presence was required at the last rehearsal. I arrived just before the costume rehearsal took place. The stage was fully lighted, but the hall itself was quite dark, which gave me the opportunity of concealing myself in a corner and listening to the opera undisturbed. On the whole the performance was very satisfactory. The orchestra and chorus got through their business splendidly. The soloists, on the other hand, left much to be desired. . . .

"These hours, spent in a dark corner of the theatre, were the only pleasant ones during my visit to Moscow. Between the acts I saw all my former colleagues once more. I observed with delight that the music of *Oniegin* seemed to win their favour. Nicholas Rubinstein, who is so parsimonious in praise, told me that he had 'fallen in love' with it. After the first act Taneiev wanted to express his sympathy, instead of which he burst into tears. I cannot really tell you how this touched me. . . . On Saturday (the day of the performance) my brothers and a few other Petersburgers, among them Anton Rubinstein, arrived early.

"Throughout the day I was greatly excited, especially as I had yielded to Nicholas Rubinstein's entreaty and declared my willingness to come before the curtain in case I should be called for.

"During the performance my excitement reached its zenith. Before it began, Nicholas Rubinstein invited me behind the scenes, where, to my horror, I found myself confronted by the whole Conservatoire. At the head of the professors stood Nicholas Grigorievich himself, who handed me a wreath, amid the hearty applause of the bystanders. Of course I had to say a few words in answer to Rubinstein's speech. God knows what it cost me! Between the acts I was recalled several times. I have never seen such an enthusiastic audience. I draw this conclusion from the fact that it was invariably myself—not the performers—who received a recall.

"After the performance there was a supper at 'The Hermitage,' at which even Anton Rubinstein was present. I have absolutely no idea whether my *Oniegin* pleased him or not. He never said a word to me on the subject. It was 4 a.m. before I returned home with a splitting headache, and spent a wretched night. I recovered during the return journey to Petersburg, and to-day I feel quite

refreshed.   I shall try not to go out during the next fortnight, but to give myself up in earnest to the instrumentation of my Suite."

To Tchaikovsky's account of the first performance, I can
only add my personal impression that the actual success of
the opera was poor, and the ovation given to my brother
was rather in consideration of former services than in
honour of the music itself, which had only a moderate
success.

This cool reception of a work, afterwards to become one
of Tchaikovsky's most popular operas, can be accounted for
in the first place by its indifferent interpretation.   It had
been carefully prepared, but was entrusted to inexperienced
students of the Conservatoire, instead of mature artists;
consequently the work was not represented in its best
light.   The comparatively recent period of the tale, and
the audacity of the librettist in representing upon the stage
the almost canonised personality of Tatiana, and, what
was still worse, the additions made to Poushkin's incomparable poem—all contributed to set public taste against
the opera.   Besides which, both libretto and music lacked
those dramatic incidents which generally evoke the public
enthusiasm.

Respecting Anton Rubinstein's judgment of *Eugene
Oniegin*, the widow of the great pianist said that her husband was not at all pleased with the opera at the first
hearing.   On his return to Petersburg he criticised the
work from beginning to end, and declared it to be utterly
wanting in the "grand opera style."   Some years later he
altered his opinion, and when his wife reminded him of the
first failure of the work, replied: "What do you know
about it?   No one who has been brought up upon gipsy
songs and Italian opera has any right to criticise such
a composition."

With the exception of Laroche, most of the critics praised
Eugene Oniegin, although without much enthusiasm.

V

Early in April Tchaikovsky left Petersburg for Kamenka.

To N. F. von Meck.

"KAMENKA, *April* 14*th* (*26th*), 1879.

"My opera reposes for the time being in my portfolio. I am working at the Suite. To-day I finished the score, and to-morrow I shall start upon the arrangement for four hands. . . .

"I have another fortnight's work to bestow upon the Suite. At Brailov I shall be able to give myself up entirely to my increasing love of nature. There is no other spot in the world which can offer me so much in this respect. To live in your house, to feel myself free and alone, to be able to visit the forests every day and wander all day among the flowers, to listen to the nightingale at night, to read your books, play upon your instruments and think of you—these are joys I cannot find elsewhere."

To P. Jurgenson.

"KAMENKA, *April* 22*nd* (*May* 4*th*), 1879.

"I am beginning to be proud of my works, now that I see what an extraordinary effect some of them make. Everyone here is crazy over the Andante, and when I played it with my brother as a pianoforte duet, one girl fainted away (this is a fact ! !). To make the fair sex faint is the highest triumph to which any composer can attain."

To N. F. von Meck.

"BRAILOV, *May* 5*th* (17*th*), 1879.

"Yesterday I began to study the score of *Lohengrin*. I know you are no great admirer of Wagner, and I, too, am far from being a desperate Wagnerite. I am not very sympathetic to Wagnerism as a principle. Wagner's personality arouses my antipathy, yet I must do justice to his great musical gift.   This reaches its climax in *Lohengrin*, which will always remain the crown of all his works. After *Lohengrin*, began the deterioration of his talent, which was ruined by his diabolical vanity.   He lost all sense of proportion, and began to overstep all limits, so that everything he composed after *Lohengrin* became incomprehensible, impossible music which has no future. What chiefly interests me in *Lohengrin* at present is the orchestration.   In view of the work which lies before me, I want to study this score very closely, and decide whether to adopt some of his methods of instrumentation.   His mastery is extraordinary, but, for reasons which would necessitate technical explanations, I have not borrowed anything from him.   Wagner's orchestration is too symphonic, too overloaded and heavy for vocal music.   The older I grow, the more convinced I am that symphony and opera are in every respect at the opposite poles of music. Therefore the study of *Lohengrin* will not lead me to change my style, although it has been interesting and of negative value."

To N. F. von Meck.

"Brailov, *May 7th* (19*th*), 1879.

"Yesterday I was talking to Marcel about the completion of the Catholic chapel, started long ago, but interrupted by order of the Government.   Now the necessary permission has been obtained, and the priest has funds for the work; but another difficulty exists which you alone can overcome.   One of your offices just touches the wall of the church, and could easily be transported to another spot.   Last year I went into the chapel in which the service is held, and I must honestly say that I was sorry to see this obvious proof of Catholic persecution . . . it is not large enough to hold a tenth part of the congregation. I am an energetic champion of religious freedom.   Marcel tells me the priest did not like to trouble you with his requests, therefore I am animated with a desire to come to his assistance.   I take the liberty of telling you that the Catholics of Brailov are hoping for your kind permission to have your building removed.   If this should prove to be impossible, at least forgive me, dear friend, for my untimely interference on their behalf."

To N. F. von Meck.

"BRAILOV, *May 9th* (*21st*), 1879.

"I have just been in the church attached to the monastery. There were many people, both in the church and in the courtyard of the building. I heard the blind 'lyre singer.' He calls himself 'lyre singer' on account of the instrument with which he accompanies himself, which, however, has nothing in common with the lyre of antiquity. It is curious that in Little Russia every blind beggar sings exactly the same tune with the same refrain. I have used part of this refrain in my Pianoforte Concerto.

"At the present moment I am writing on the balcony. Before me is the bunch of lilies of the valley from Simakov. I am never tired of looking at these enchanting creations of nature."

To N. F. von Meck.

"KAMENKA, *May 29th* (*June 10th*), 1879.

"To-day I finished the first act of my opera (*The Maid of Orleans*). It has grown into a somewhat bulky score. What a delight to look through a newly finished score! To a musician a score means something more than a collection of all kinds of notes and pauses. It is a complete picture, in which the central figures stand out clearly from the accessories and the background.

"To me every orchestral score is not merely a foretaste of oral delight, but also a joy to look upon. For this reason I am painfully particular about my scores, and cannot bear corrections, erasures, or blots."[1]

---

[1] In later years Tchaikovsky was less particular, and his scores became less neat.

To N. F. von Meck.

"KAMENKA, *June* 13*th* (25*th*), 1879.

"Early this morning I had a telegram from Jurgenson, to say he had won his case against Bachmetiev, the Director of the Imperial Chapel. I think I told you that early last year my Liturgy (of St. John Chrysostom) was confiscated from Jurgenson's by order of Bachmetiev. . . . Only those works which have been recognised by the Chapel can be publicly sold or performed. This is the reason why, until now, no Russian musicians have written Church music. After the confiscation of my composition, Jurgenson brought an action for damages against Bachmetiev, and has won his case. . . . This does not matter so much for my Liturgy, as for the principle involved.

"Twenty-five years ago to-day my mother died. It was the first profound sorrow of my life. Her death had a great influence on the fate of myself and our entire family. She was carried off by cholera, quite unexpectedly, in the prime of life. Every moment of that terrible day is still as clear in my remembrances as though it had happened yesterday."

On June 20th Tchaikovsky wrote to N. F. von Meck that he had received three very agreeable letters from abroad. In one Colonne expressed his respect in the kindliest manner, and assured Tchaikovsky that, in spite of the cold reception of *The Tempest*, his name should figure again in the programmes of the Châtelet. A second communication came from the 'cellist Fitzenhagen (professor at the Moscow Conservatoire), telling him of the impression he had created with the "Variations on a Rococo theme" at the Wiesbaden Festival. Liszt remarked on this occasion, "At last here is music again." The third letter —from Hans von Bülow—announced the great success of Tchaikovsky's first Pianoforte Concerto at the same festival. Von Bülow had already played it with even greater success in London.

Almost on the same day Tchaikovsky also heard the good news that his Liturgy had been performed in the University Church at Kiev.

VI

On August 7th Tchaikovsky finished the third act of *The Maid of Orleans* and, suffering from physical and nervous exhaustion, left Kamenka for Simaki,[1] as Nadejda von Meck was occupying her house at Brailov.

To N. F. von Meck.

" I am enchanted. I could not imagine more beautiful surroundings. The garden in which I have just been walking with Pakhulsky has surpassed all my expectations. The house is a splendid retreat! If you only realised how much I am in need just now of all the comforts which I get as your guest in this delightful spot!

" I intend to finish the orchestration of the last act of my opera while I am here, and shall begin work to-morrow. I shall get this heavy burden off my shoulders, and then I can draw breath and enjoy the incomparable sensation of having completed a long work."

To Modeste Tchaikovsky.

" SIMAKI, *August 9th (21st)*, 1879.

" I hasten to send you my first impressions of this place. A very, very old house, a shady garden with ancient oaks and lime trees; it is very secluded, but therein lies its charm. At the end of the garden flows a stream. From the verandah there is a fine view over the village and the forests. The absolute quiet and comfort of the place exactly suit my taste and requirements. I have at my disposal an old manservant called Leon, a cook whom I

---

[1] A smaller country house belonging to Nadejda von Meck in the vicinity of Brailov.

never see, and a coachman with a phaeton and four horses.
I could gladly dispense with the last, since it necessitates
my driving occasionally, while in reality I prefer to walk.
The proximity of Nadejda Filaretovna troubles me somewhat, although it is really folly. I know my seclusion will
not be disturbed. I am so accustomed to regard her as a
kind of remote and invisible genius that the consciousness
of her mortal presence in my neighbourhood is rather dis-
concerting. Yesterday I met Pakhulsky, who spent part
of the evening with me. But I told him plainly that I
wanted to be left quite alone for a few days."

To N. F. von Meck.

"*August* 11*th* (23*rd*), 1879.

"Pakhulsky told me that next time he came he was
to bring Milochka [1] with him. I am very fond of Milochka; it is a pleasure to look at the photograph of her
charming face. I am sure she is a dear, sweet, sympathetic
child. I love children, and could only say 'yes' to such a
proposal. But what I could not say to Pakhulsky I can
say to you.

"Forgive me, dear friend, and make fun of my mania if
you like—but I am not going to invite Milochka here, for
this reason: my relations towards you—as they exist at
present—are my chief happiness, and of the greatest importance to my well-being. I do not want them altered
by a hair's breadth. The whole charm and poetry of our
friendship lies in your being so near and so dear to me,
while at the same time I do not know you at all in the
ordinary sense of the word. This condition of things must
extend to your nearest belongings. I will love Milochka
as I have hitherto loved you. If she appeared before me
—*le charme serait rompu !*

"Every member of your family is dear to me—particularly Milochka—yet for God's sake let everything remain
as it has been. What could I say if she asked me why I
never went to see her mother? I should have to open our
acquaintance with a *lie.* This would be a grief to me,

---

[1] Frau von Meck's youngest daughter.

even though it were a trifling falsehood. Pardon my frankness, dear and noble friend. . . .

"If you have Beethoven's Sonatas, be so kind as to send them to me."

To Anatol Tchaikovsky.

"SIMAKI, *August* 18*th* (30*th*), 1879.

"Time slips away unobserved. Yesterday something very painful happened. About four o'clock in the afternoon I was walking in the woods, feeling sure I should not meet Nadejda Filaretovna, because it was her dinner-hour. It chanced, however, that I went out a little earlier, and she was dining somewhat later, so we ran against each other quite by chance. It was an awkward predicament. Although we were only face to face for a moment, I felt horribly confused. However, I raised my hat politely. She seemed to lose her head entirely and did not know what to do. She was in one carriage with Milochka, and the whole family followed in two others. I wandered into the forest in search of mushrooms, and when I returned to the little table where tea was prepared for me, I found my letters and newspapers awaiting me. It appears she sent a man on horseback to look for me, so that I might get my post at tea-time."

To N. F. von Meck.

"SIMAKI, *August* 27*th* (*September* 8*th*), 1879.

"Now I can almost say *finished!* I have worked at *The Maid of Orleans* from the end of November (Florence) to the end of August (Simaki), just nine months. It is remarkable that I began and finished this opera as the guest of my dear friend."

To N. F. von Meck.

"*August* 31*st* (*September* 12*th*), 1879.

"Do you not like such grey days as to-day? I love them. The beginning of autumn can only be compared to spring as regards beauty. It seems to me September, with its tender, melancholy colouring, has a special power to fill me with calm and happy feelings. Around Simaki there are many delightful spots which I like best to frequent at sunset, or on sunless days like to-day. For instance, if you turn to the right, past the kitchen garden, and take the lower path (parallel to the village) by the fen where the reeds grow. I am very fond of that spot. But by day the sun spoils the picturesque view of the village.

" At evening, too, or on a cloudy day, it is delightful to sit on some high-lying spot, and look over the old willows, or poplars, across to the village, with its modest church (what a charm is given to every rural landscape by these churches), and far away to the distant forests. I often spend an hour in this way. . . ."

To Modeste Tchaikovsky.

"August 31st (September 12th), 1879.

" I have just received a telegram from Anatol : ' Have just been dismissed in consequence of an unpleasantness in my department. Most anxious to speak to you.' I am starting for Petersburg at once. A great fear of the future possesses me. In spite of the many delightful moments spent here, I have had a continual foreboding of something unlucky, and always about Toly."

VII

1879–1880

To P. I. Jurgenson.

(Early in September.)

" You will be very much astonished to hear of my being in Petersburg. I was summoned by a telegram from my brother Anatol, announcing that in consequence of some unpleasantness he had to resign his position in the Government service. . . . I think the matter can be so arranged that he can keep his place. . . .

" I do not know how long I shall stay here. It depends upon the progress of my brother's affairs. O detested Petersburg !"

To N. F. von Meck.

"PETERSBURG, *September 13th (25th)*, 1879.

"I received your letter yesterday, dear friend. How I envied you when I read your account of the lovely autumn weather you were enjoying! The weather is not bad here, but what is the use of it to me?

"I often go to the opera, but I do not enjoy it much. The impossibility of escaping from innumerable acquaintances bores me dreadfully. No matter where I hide myself, there are always idle people who poison my pleasure in the music by their kind attentions. They will worry me with the usual commonplace questions: 'How are you?' 'What are you composing now?' etc. But the invitations are the most intolerable. It requires so much courage to refuse them.

"In one of your letters you asked me to tell you the whole method of procedure in order to get an opera accepted for performance. One has to send the score and pianoforte arrangement, with a written request for its performance, to the Direction of the Imperial Opera House. Then, in order to be successful, one must set in motion the whole machinery of solicitation and entreaty. This is just what I do not understand. My first two operas were performed, thanks to the assistance of the Grand Duke Constantine Nicholaevich who likes my music. How things will go this time I cannot say. I shall impress upon Jurgenson to do all that is necessary. Two days ago I was talking to Napravnik (one of the worthiest members of the musical world), who takes a lively interest in the fate of my opera. He told me it could not be performed this season, but advised me to send in the score as soon as possible."

To Anatol Tchaikovsky.

"Moscow, *September 20th (October 2nd)*, 1879.

"Forgive me for not having written before to-day. Yesterday it was impossible. . . . Rubinstein and Jurgenson soon put in an appearance, and compelled me to leave the tea, upon which I had just started, and go out to

breakfast with them. O Moscow! Scarcely has one
set foot in it before one must needs begin to drink! At
five o'clock I was invited to dinner at the Jurgensons',
where we began again. I cannot tell you how strange
and repugnant to me is this Moscow atmosphere of
swilling."

To N. F. von Meck.

"GRANKINO, *September* 25*th* (*October* 7*th*), 1879.

" I left Moscow on the 22nd. No sooner did the train
begin to move, and I saw the outskirts of the town, than
the black curtain, which had hung before my eyes during
the whole of my time in the two capitals, suddenly vanished.
I was once more free and happy.

" Here I found both your letters. I cannot tell you how
glad I was to read your dear words. It was a surprise to
hear our symphony was at last published, for the distracted
Jurgenson forgot to mention this. . . .

" I owe you everything: my life, the possibility of going
forward to distant goals, freedom, and that complete happiness which formerly I believed to be unattainable.

" I read your letters with such a sense of eternal gratitude and affection that I cannot put it into words. . . ."

To N. F. von Meck.

"KAMENKA, *October* 5*th* (17*th*), 1879.

" At the present moment—I do not know why—I am
going through an intense Italian craze. I feel so delighted,
so happy, at the mere thought that before long I, too, shall
be in Italy. Naples, Pompeii, Vesuvius . . . enchanting,
lovely!

" I found the proofs of the Suite here. In three days I
corrected and sent them back, so that I can now take a
holiday—read, walk, play, dream—to my heart's desire.
For how long? I do not know. At any rate, I will not
undertake any work during my first days in Naples. Do
you not think that in the land of *lazzarone* one must be
lazy too?"

To Anatol Tchaikovsky.

"KAMENKA, *October 7th* (19*th*), 1879.

"No news. I feel very well, only a little misanthropical now and then. To-day there are visitors. When there are none I feel quite at ease. We all sit and sew. I have hemmed and marked a pocket-handkerchief."[1]

To N. F. von Meck.

"KAMENKA, *October 9th* (21*st*), 1879.

"How can I thank you for the trouble you have taken about our symphony? I am delighted Colonne will play it. At the same time there is no doubt it will have no success whatever with the public. Perhaps it might rouse a spark of sympathy in the hearts of ten or twelve people —and that would be a great step in advance. . . . Only one thing troubles me. Does Colonne really want to be paid for doing the work? It would gratify me to know that his readiness to perform the symphony was not based upon pecuniary considerations."

To N. F. von Meck.

"KAMENKA, *October 12th* (24*th*), 1879.

"The last few days I have felt a secret dissatisfaction with myself, which has degenerated into boredom. I realised that I wanted work and began to occupy myself. The boredom immediately vanished and I felt relieved. I have begun a pianoforte concerto and intend to work at it without haste and over-fatigue.

"Have you read V. Soloviev's philosophical articles? They are admirably written ; very popular in form, so that they do not overstep the intelligence of the ordinary reader, yet very clever. I do not know to what conclusions the writer will eventually come. In the last number he proves very effectively the untenableness of positivism, which denies metaphysics, yet cannot get along without philosophy. Soloviev speaks in a very striking way of the

---

[1] This form of occupation, like sport, only amused Tchaikovsky for a very short time.

delusion of the materialists who, because they deny meta-physics, believe they are only dealing with what actually exists, that is, with the material; whereas the material has no objective existence, and is only a phenomenon, the result of the activity of our sense and intellect. I express his ideas very indifferently, but I advise you to read this book for yourself.

"Yesterday I heard from Anatol about the performance of *Vakoula the Smith*, which took place the previous week. The theatre was full, but the public cool, just as on former occasions. Anatol attributes this to the indifferent perfor-mance. But I can see with startling clearness that this attitude of reserve is the outcome of my own stupid mis-takes. I am glad to know that *The Maid of Orleans* is free from the faults of my earlier pseudo-opera style, in which I wearied my listeners with a superfluity of details, and made my harmony too complicated, so that there was no moderation in my orchestral effects. Besides which, I gave the audience no repose. I set too many heavy dishes before them. Opera style should be broad, simple, and decorative. *Vakoula* is not in true opera style, but is far more like symphonic or chamber music. It is only sur-prising that it has not proved a complete failure. It is possible that it may find favour with the public in course of time. I place it in the front rank of my works, although I see all its defects. It was a labour of love, an enjoyment, like *Oniegin*, the Fourth Symphony, and the Second Quartet."

To N. F. von Meck.

"KAMENKA, *October* 15*th* (27*th*), 1879.

"Only a month—and I shall be at Naples! I look for-ward to this as a child to his birthday, and the presents it will bring. Meanwhile things are going well with me. My latest musical creation begins to grow and display more characteristic features. I work with greater pleasure and try to curb my habitual haste, which has often been injurious to my work."

On October 21st Nicholas Rubinstein played Tchaikov-sky's Pianoforte Sonata at a concert of the Musical Society in Moscow. The success was so great that the famous pianist repeated it at his own concert in the course of the same season.

On November 11th the composer's First Suite had a decided success, judging by the newspapers. The short number which Tchaikovsky once thought of cutting out of the work was encored.

To Anatol Tchaikovsky.

"BERLIN, *November 11th (23rd)*, 1879.

"MY DEAR ANATOL,—I have had an ideal journey. I arrived in Berlin early this morning. After breakfast I went to see Kotek. The good man seemed wild with delight at seeing me again, and even I was glad. But at the end of two hours of musical tittle-tattle I was tired, and thankful he had to attend a rehearsal. Strange! The longer I live, the less I care for the society of my fellow-creatures. There is no doubt that I am fond of Kotek, but his chatter wearies me more than the severest physical exertion."

To N. F. von Meck.

"PARIS, *November 18th (30th)*, 1879.

"I know the Variations by Rimsky-Korsakov & Co.[1] very well. The work is original in its way and shows some remarkable talent for harmony in its authors. At the same time I do not care for it. It is too heavy and spun-out for a joke, and the everlasting repetition of the theme is—clumsy. As a work of art it is a mere nonentity. It is not surprising that a few clever men should have amused themselves by inventing all kinds of variations upon a commonplace theme; the surprising thing is their having published them. Only amateurs can suppose that every piquant harmony is worthy to be given to the public. Liszt, the old Jesuit, speaks in terms of exaggerated praise of every work which is submitted to his inspection. He is

---

[1] "Paraphrases," twenty-four variations and fourteen pieces for piano on a popular theme, by Borodin, Cui, Liadov, and Rimsky-Korsakov.

at heart a good man, one of the very few great artists who have never known envy (Wagner and in some measure Anton Rubinstein owe their success to him; he also did much for Berlioz); but he is too much of a Jesuit to be frank and sincere."

To P. Jurgenson.

"PARIS, *November* 19*th* (*December* 1*st*), 1879.

"DEAR FRIEND,—What happiness to get right away from one's own country! Not until I had passed the frontiers, did I breathe freely and feel at ease. On the journey I came across Joseph Wieniawsky, who was in the same corridor train. I immediately told him I was not alone, but travelling with a lady, upon which he winked at me slyly, as much as to say, 'Of course, we know, shocking dog!'

"At present I want to work slowly at my Concerto; later I mean to look through my old works, especially the Second Symphony, which I intend to revise thoroughly."

To N. F. von Meck.

"PARIS, *November* 21*st* (*December* 3*rd*), 1879.

"To-day, being a Saint's Day, Alexis went to church, and told me the Grand Duke Nicholas Nicholaevich, with all his suite in full uniform, had attended the service. I could not account for this until I took up the *Gaulois* at breakfast, and read of an attempt made in Moscow on the Tsar's life. . . . The Emperor escaped unharmed.

"I do not believe, dear friend, that we are in immediate danger of a war with Prussia. Such a war, although inevitable, is improbable during the lives of the present emperors. How can it be possible to think of war, when such horrors are taking place in our midst? . . . I think the Tsar would do well to assemble representatives throughout all Russia, and take counsel with them how to prevent the recurrence of such terrible actions on the part of mad revolutionaries. So long as all of us—the Russian citizens —are not called to take part in the government of the country, there is no hope of a better future."

To N. F. von Meck.

"PARIS, *November* 26*th* (*December* 8*th*), 1879.

"I am not altogether at one with you as regards Cui. I do not recognise in him any great creative power, although his music has a certain elegance, agreeable harmonies, and shows good taste, in which he is distinguished from the other members of 'the band,' especially Moussorgsky. By nature Cui is more drawn towards light and piquantly rhythmic French music; but the demands of 'the band' which he has joined compel him to do violence to his natural gifts and to follow those paths of would-be original harmony which do not suit him. Cui is now forty-four years of age and has only composed two operas and two or three dozen songs. He was engaged for ten years upon his opera *Ratcliff*. It is evident that the work was composed piecemeal, hence the lack of any unity of style."

To N. F. von Meck.

"PARIS, *November* 27*th* (*December* 9*th*), 1879.

"Now I will answer your question. My *Voyevode* is undoubtedly a very poor opera. I do not speak of the music only, but of all that goes to the making of a good opera. The subject is lacking in dramatic interest and movement, and the work was written hastily and carelessly. I wrote music to the words without troubling to consider the difference between operatic and symphonic style. In composing an opera the stage should be the musician's first thought, he must not abuse the confidence of the theatre-goer who comes *to see* as well as *to hear*. Finally, the style of music written for the stage should be the same as the decorative style in painting, clear, simple, and highly coloured. A picture by Meissonier would lose half its charm if exhibited on the stage; and subtle, delicately harmonised music would be equally inappropriate, since the public demands sharply defined melodies on a background of subdued harmony. In my *Voyevode* I have been chiefly concerned with filigree work, and have forgotten the requirements of the stage.

"The stage often paralyses a composer's inspiration, that

is why symphonic and chamber music are so far superior to opera. A symphony or sonata imposes no limitations, but in opera, the first necessity is to speak the musical language of the great public. . . . The final defect of *The Voyevode* lies in the heaviness of its orchestration, which overpowers the soloists. These are all the faults of inexperience; we must leave a whole series of failures behind us before we can attain to perfection. This is the reason why I am not ashamed of my first opera. It has taught me useful lessons. And you see, dear friend, how strenuously I have endeavoured to correct my errors. Even *Undine* (the opera I burnt), *The Oprichnik*, and *Vakoula* are not what they should be. I find this branch of art very difficult! I think *The Maid of Orleans* at last fulfils every requirement, but perhaps I deceive myself. If it is so, if it turns out that I have failed to grasp the true opera style, even in this work, then I shall be convinced of the justice of the opinion that I am by nature only a symphonic composer and should not attempt dramatic music. In that case, I shall abandon all attempts at opera."

To N. F. von Meck.

"PARIS, *December* 1879.

"I have read the proclamation you mention. It is impossible to conceive anything more astounding and cynical. How will such revolutionary proceedings forward the reforms with which, sooner or later, the Tsar will crown his reign? That which the Socialists are doing in the name of Russia is foolish and insolent. But equally false is their pretence of readiness to shake hands with all parties and to leave the Emperor in peace as soon as he summons a Parliament. This is not what they really aim at, for they mean to go further—to a socialist-republic, or to anarchy. But no one will swallow this bait. Even were a constitution granted to Russia in the remote future, the first act of the *Zemstvo* should be extermination of this band of murderers who hope to become the leaders of the country."

To N. F. von Meck.

"PARIS, *December 3rd* (15*th*), 1879.

"The sketch of my Concerto is finished and I am very pleased with it, especially with the Andante. Now I shall take in hand the revision of my Second Symphony, of which only the last movement can be left intact. I published this work through Bessel in 1872, as a return for the trouble he took over the performance of *The Oprichnik*. . . . For seven years he has led me a dance over the engraving of the score—always putting me off with the assurance that it would soon be ready. I was sometimes furious with him, but his lack of conscience has proved itself a blessing in disguise! . . . If I succeed in working steadily in Rome, I shall make a good work out of my immature, mediocre symphony."

VIII

After spending a few days in Turin, Tchaikovsky reached Rome on December 8th (20th), 1879. From thence he wrote, on the 12th (24th), to Frau von Meck :—

"Yesterday we made a pilgrimage to S. Pietro in Montorio. Probably you know the place, therefore I need not describe the beauty of the view from the terrace below the church. To-day I visited San Giovanni in Laterano and carried away some profound artistic impressions. I also went to Scala Santa. High Mass was being celebrated in the church. The choir sang a Mass *a capella* and also with the organ. Quite modern music, utterly unsuitable in church, but beautifully sung. What voices there are in Italy! The tenor gave a solo, in the style of a wretched operatic aria, in such a magnificent voice that I was quite carried away. But the Mass itself lacks that solemn, poetical atmosphere with which our liturgy is surrounded."

To N. F. von Meck.

"ROME, *December* 13*th* (25*th*), 1879.

"It is Christmas here to-day. We went to Mass at St. Peter's. What a colossal edifice—this cathedral!"

To N. F. von Meck.

"ROME, *December* 15*th* (27*th*), 1879.

"Yesterday we went up Monte Testaccio, with its lovely view of Rome and the Campagna. From there we visited S. Paolo Fuori le Mura, a basilica of huge proportions and vast wealth. To-day I am going for the first time to 'do' the Forum thoroughly. This has a three-fold interest for me because I am just reading Ampère's *Histoire romaine à Rome*, in which all that has taken place in this building is minutely described.

"I have a very good piano now. I got a few volumes of Bach's works from Ricordi, and play a number of them, alone, or four-handed, with my brother Modeste. But work will not come back to me. Rome and Roman life are too characteristic, too exciting and full of variety, to permit of my sticking to my writing-table. However, I hope the power of work will gradually return. Yesterday I heard a charming popular song, of which I shall certainly make use some future day."

To P. I. Jurgenson.

"ROME, *December* 19*th* (31*st*), 1879.

"DEAR FRIEND,—. . . Nicholas Rubinstein's opinion that my Suite is so difficult that it is impossible, has surprised and annoyed me very much. Either Rubinstein is mistaken, or I must give up composing; one or the other. Why, it is my chief anxiety to write more easily and simply as time goes on, and the more I try—the worse I succeed! It is dreadful!

"I asked Taneiev to write and tell me what actually constituted these terrible difficulties. I feel a little hurt that none of my friends telegraphed to me after the performance. I am forgotten. The one interest which

binds me to life is centred in my compositions. Every
first performance marks an epoch for me. Can no one
realise that it would have been a joy to receive a few
words of appreciation, by which I should have known that
my new work had been performed and had given pleasure
to my friends?

"I do not understand what you say about the 'Marche
Miniature.' We never cut it out. The March was to be
kept, but as it was not suitable as No. 5 it was to be
published at the end of the Suite. . . . For God's sake
answer my letters quicker. Your communication has
upset my nerves and I feel as ill as a dog."

To N. F. von Meck.

ROME, *December 22nd (January 3rd,* 1880), 1879.

" To-day I went to the Capitol with Modeste. We spent
an hour and a half in the Hall of the Emperors. The busts
are highly characteristic! What a revolting, sensual,
animal face Nero has! How sympathetic is Marcus Aure-
lius! How fine the old Agrippina! How repulsive Cara-
calla! Some of these countenances in no way bear out
one's idea of the originals. For instance, Julius Cæsar
altogether lacks power and greatness; he looks like a
Russian Councillor of State. And Trajan? Who could
guess from his narrow forehead, prominent chin, and commonplace expression, that the original of the portrait was
a great man? . . ."

A few days later, Tchaikovsky recounted to Nadejda
von Meck his impressions of the treasures of the Vatican :—

" The frescoes of Michel Angelo now appear less incomprehensible to me, although I do not share Modeste's
enthusiasm for them. His athletic, muscular figures, and
the gloomy vastness of his pictures, are gradually becoming more intelligible. His art now interests and overcomes
me, but it does not delight me, or touch my heart. Raphael
is still my favourite—the Mozart of painters. Guercino's
pictures please me very much, some of his Madonnas are so

angelically beautiful, they fill me with silent ecstasy. However, I must confess that I am not gifted by nature with a fine appreciation of the plastic arts, for very few pictures make an impression upon me. . . . To study all the art treasures of Rome conscientiously would need a whole lifetime. To-day I discovered once more how important it is to look long and carefully at a picture. I sat before Raphael's 'Annunciation,' and at first I did not see much in the picture, but the longer I looked the more profoundly was I penetrated with its beauty as a whole, and the wonder of its details. Alas! I had only just begun to really enjoy the work, when Modeste came to tell me it was three o'clock and time to go on to the Sistine Chapel. . . . I do not think I could live long in Rome. There are too many interests; it leaves no time for reflection, no time to deepen one's own nature. I should prefer Florence as a permanent place of residence; it is quieter, more peaceful. Rome is richer and grander; Florence more sympathetic.

" I agree with Goethe's characteristic opinion of Rome. . . . 'It would be a fine thing to spend a few centuries there in Pythagorean silence.'"

S. I. Taneiev to Tchaikovsky. " Moscow.

" N. Rubinstein has pointed out to me all those parts in the score of your Suite which he considers awkward.

"The difficulties are chiefly centred in the wind instruments, especially in the wood-wind. They are as follows:—

"(1) Too few pauses; the wood-wind have to play for too long at a time without opportunities for breathing. In those places where you have doubled the strings (as in the Fugue) it does not matter so much, they can make a slight break without its being observable. But it is very different when they are playing alone. For instance, in the newly added movement there is a part for three flutes which have to play triplets for twenty-two bars, without a break.

"(2) Difficult passages: these occur very often in the wood-wind and demand *virtuosi* to execute them properly. In the Andante the passages leading to the second theme are extremely difficult (where oboe and clarinet, and the

second time flute and clarinet, have triplets of semi-quavers).
This part went very badly at the rehearsals, and even at
the concert, although the musicians had practised their
parts at home. It offers such difficulties that it is impossible to render it with the expression marks indicated,
for the musicians have enough to do to get their right note
(the double flat for clarinet is particularly awkward).

"(3) The compass of all the wood-wind instruments is
too extended. The first bassoon usually plays in the tenor
register, while the second takes the lower notes. Not
only the musicians, but also their instruments, have got
accustomed to this ; the lower notes of the first bassoon
are not quite in tune; the same thing applies to the
upper notes of the second bassoon. But your Suite opens
with a unison passage for both fagotti, which employs
almost the entire range of these instruments : from

In the march the oboes have the following notes :—

which Z. played at the first rehearsal as :—

When Rubinstein asked him why he did not play the
notes as they were written, he replied that he could do so,
but it would be very bad for his lips, because they lay too
high. The French oboe players, he continued, could bring
out these high notes better, because they had different and
finer mouthpieces ; but with these mouthpieces the middle
and lower notes suffered.

"(4) Difficult rhythms which make the execution irregular.
The absence, too, of what the Germans call "Anhaltspunkt"

(punctuation)—the absence of notes on the strong beats
of the bar. Take this rhythm in the Scherzo for instance :—

the last notes come on the second crotchet, and the pause
on the third beat. In consequence, it is very difficult to
play these notes equally, they always sound a little one
on the top of the other. The same with the following
passage :—

Altogether the Scherzo requires enormous virtuosity, which
most members of the orchestra do not possess.

"Apparently some passages do not sound as you thought
they would. At the beginning of the Scherzo (where the
wood-wind enters) there is a modulation to B♭ major
through the dominant chord on F.

The superfluity of chromatic harmonies, as well as the
difficulty of executing clearly all that is written for the
wind, causes these passages to sound unintelligible and to
have the effect of a series of wrong notes. . . ."

To S. I. Taneiev.

"ROME, *January* 4*th* (16*th*), 1880.

"Nicholas Rubinstein's explanation is not at all satisfactory. From all he says, I can plainly see that he was

out of temper and visited it upon the Suite.   No one will
induce me to believe this passage

is difficult to play on the oboe or clarinet, or that the flutes
cannot play twenty-two bars of triplets in a rapid tempo.
They could easily manage to play such a passage for 220
bars.   It would be very innocent to imagine that this must
be done in one breath.   They can breathe every time.
I play the flute a little myself and am certain of it.   Difficulty is a relative matter : for a beginner it would not only
be difficult, but impossible, but for an averagely good
orchestral player it is not hard.   I do not lay myself out
to write easy things ; I know my instrumentation is almost
always rather difficult.   But you must admit that compared
with *Francesca*, or the Fourth Symphony, the Suite is child's
play.   Altogether Rubinstein's criticisms are such that—
were they accurate—I should have to lay down my pen
for ever.   What?   For ten years I have taught instrumentation at the Conservatoire (not remarkably well
perhaps, but without compromising myself), and two years
later remarks are made to me which could only be addressed to a very backward pupil !   One of two things :
either I never understood anything about the orchestra, or
this criticism of my Suite is on a par with N. R.'s remarks
upon my Pianoforte Concerto in 1875 : that it was impracticable.   What was impossible in 1875 was proved
quite possible in 1878.

"I explain the whole affair thus : the oboist Herr Z. was
in a bad temper—which not infrequently happens with
him—and this infected Rubinstein.   I like the idea that
the high notes are ruination to Herr Z.'s lips !!!   It is
a thousand pities these precious lips, from which Frau Z.
has stolen so many kisses, should be spoilt for ever by the
E in alt.   But this will not hinder me from injuring these
sacred lips by writing high notes—notes moreover that
every oboist can easily play, even without a French mouth-
piece !"

IX

To N. F. von Meck.

"ROME, *January 2nd* (14*th*), 1880.

"When I look back upon the year that has flown, I feel I must sing a hymn of thanksgiving to fate which has brought me so many beautiful days in Russia and abroad. I can say that throughout the whole year I have led a calm and cheerful life, and have been happy, so far as happiness is possible."

To P. I. Jurgenson.

"ROME, *January* 11*th* (23*rd*), 1880.

"My health is bad, and my mental condition not very good.   I have had sad news from Petersburg: my sister is ill and also her daughter.   Yesterday I heard of my father's death.   He was eighty-five, so this news did not altogether take me by surprise.   But he was such a wonderful, angelic old soul.   I loved him so much, it is a bitter grief to feel I shall never see him again."

On hearing this news, Tchaikovsky burst into tears. Afterwards he became quiet and resigned.   But the peaceful end of this venerable old man could not make a great gap in the busy life of his son, to whom, notwithstanding, he had been very dear.

To N. F. von Meck.

"ROME, *January* 12*th* (24*th*), 1880.

"This morning I received an amiable letter from Colonne, telling me my symphony[1] would be given to-morrow at the Châtelet.   This has vexed me.   If he had written a day earlier, I might have reached Paris in time. But Colonne is not to blame because, in order to preserve

[1] No. 4, dedicated to N. F. von Meck.

my incognito, I told him I could not be present at the performance of my symphony, on account of my health.

"How am I to thank you for this kindness, dear friend? I know the symphony will not have any success, but it will interest many people, and this is very important for the propaganda of my works."

Although Colonne sent a telegram of congratulation immediately after the concert, the letter which followed announced, in the politest manner, the partial failure of the symphony. *La Gazette Musicale* says the first and last movements were received with "icy coldness," and the public only showed enthusiasm for the Scherzo, and portions of the Andante.

Almost simultaneously with the performance of the Fourth Symphony in Paris, Tchaikovsky's Quartet No. 3, Op. 30, and the Serenade for violin and pianoforte were given by the Société de S. Cécile. All the newspapers were unanimously agreed as to the success of these works.

From this time Tchaikovsky's works began to make their way abroad. From New York, Leopold Damrosch sent him tidings of the great success of his First Suite; while Jurgenson wrote to tell him of the triumph of his Pianoforte Concerto in B♭ minor, which had been played twice by Bülow and once by Friedenthal in Berlin, by Breitner in Buda-Pesth, and by Rummel in New York.

To N. F. von Meck.

"ROME, *January* 16*th* (28*th*), 1880.

"What a superb work is Michel Angelo's 'Moses'! It is indeed conceived and executed by a genius of the highest order. It is said the work has some defects. This reminds me of old Fétis, who was always on the look-out for errors in Beethoven's works, and once boasted in triumph of having discovered in the *Eroica* symphony an inversion which was not in good taste.

"Do you not think Beethoven and Michel Angelo are allied by nature?"

To N. F. von Meck.

"*February 5th* (17*th*), 1880.

"Just now we are at the very height of the Carnival. At first, as I have told you, this wild folly did not suit me at all, but now I am growing used to it. Of course the character of the festival here is conditioned by climate and custom. Probably if a Roman was set down among us in our Carnival week, the crowd of tipsy people swinging and toboganning would seem to him even more barbarous!

"I am working at the sketch of an Italian Fantasia based upon folksongs. Thanks to the charming themes, some of which I have taken from collections and some of which I have heard in the streets, this work will be effective."

To N. F. von Meck.

"*February 4th* (16*th*), 1880.

"Yesterday we made the most of glorious weather and went to Tivoli. It is the loveliest spot I ever beheld. As soon as we arrived we went to lunch at the Albergo della Sybilla. Our table was near the edge of a ravine, where a waterfall splashed in the depths below; on all sides the steep banks and rocks were covered with pines and olive trees. The sun was hot as in June. After breakfast we took a long walk and visited the celebrated Villa d'Este, where Liszt spends three months every year. It is magnificent, and from the park there is a fine view over the Campagna.

"To-day we went to the gallery of the Palazzo Borghese, in which there are some masterpieces. I was most impressed by Correggio's superb picture 'Danae.'[1]

"Dear friend, leading such a life, amid all these beautiful impressions of nature and art, ought not a man to be happy? And yet a worm continually gnaws in secret at my heart. I sleep badly, and do not feel that courage and freshness which I might expect under the present conditions. Only for a moment can I conquer my mental depression. My God! What an incomprehensible and

---

[1] Removed to the Villa Borghese in 1891.

2 B

complicated machine the human organism is! We shall never solve the various phenomena of our spiritual and material existence. And how can we draw the line between the intellectual and physiological phenomena of our life? At times it seems to me as though I suffered from a mysterious, but purely physical, malady which influences my mental phases. Lately I have thought my heart was out of order; but then I remembered that last summer the doctor who examined it declared my heart to be absolutely sound. So I must lay the blame on my nerves—but what are nerves? Why, on one and the same day, without any apparent reason, do they act quite normally for a time, and then lose their elasticity and energy, and leave one incapable of work and insensible to artistic impressions? These are riddles.

"There is a lovely bunch of violets in front of me. There are quantities here. Spring is coming in to her own."

To P. I. Jurgenson.

"ROME, *February 5th* (17*th*), 1880.

"Good Lord, what a stupid idea to go and print that score!!!¹ It is not profitable, is no use to anyone, nor satisfactory in any respect—simply absurd. The moral is: when you want to prepare a little surprise for me, ask my advice first. I assure you, in spite of my well-known *naïveté*, I have more sound common sense than many clever, worthy, but too enthusiastic people—such as the person for example who suggested you should engrave this score. All the same, my unfavourable view does not prevent my being grateful—even in this case—for your friendship, which I value tremendously.

"Is it not time to lay the score of *The Maid of Orleans* before the Opera Direction? I think it is just the right moment. . . ."

To N. F. von Meck.

"ROME, *February 6th* (18*th*), 1880.

"The more I look at Michel Angelo's works the more wonderful they seem to me. Just now I was contemplat-

---

¹ *Eugene Oniegin.*

ing his 'Moses.' The church was empty, and there was nothing to disturb my meditations. I assure you I was filled with terror. You will remember that Moses is standing with his head slightly turned towards the sacrifice which is to be offered to Baal. His expression is angry and menacing; his figure majestic and commanding. One feels he has only to speak a word, for erring mortals to fall on their knees before him. It is impossible to conceive anything more perfect than this great statue. With this genius the form expresses his entire thought, there is nothing forced, no pose, such as we see, for instance, in Bernini's statues, of which Rome unfortunately possesses so many examples.

"I am so pleased with a book that has come into my hands, I cannot put it down. It is nothing less than an excellent rendering of Tacitus into French. He is a great artist."

About this time the performance of Tchaikovsky's opera *The Oprichnik* was forbidden, because the subject was considered too revolutionary in that moment of political agitation. "Je n'ai qu'à m'en féliciter," wrote the composer on receiving the news, "for I am glad of any hindrance to the performance of this ill-starred opera."

To N. F. von Meck.

"ROME, *February* 16th (28th), 1880.

"I chose the title of Divertimento for the second movement of my Suite, because it was the first which occurred to me. I wrote the movement without attaching any great importance to it, and only interpolated it in the Suite to avoid rhythmical monotony. I wrote it actually at one sitting, and spent much less time upon it than upon any other movement. As it turns out, this has not hindered it from giving more pleasure than all the rest. You are not the only one who thinks so. It proves for the thousandth time that an author never judges his own works with justice.

"I am most grateful to you for calling Colonne's attention to my new works, but I must tell you frankly: it would be very disagreeable to me if you were again to repay him in a material form for his attention. . . . The first time it was very painful that you should have spent a considerable sum of money, although I was glad to feel that, thanks to your devoted friendship, *our* symphony should be made known to the Paris public. I was grateful for this new proof of your sympathy. But now it would be painful and disgraceful to me to know that Colonne could only see the worth of my compositions by the flash-light of gold. All the same, I am grateful for your re-commendation."

To N. F. von Meck.

"ROME, *February* 18th (*March* 1st), 1880.

"The Concerto[1] of Brahms does not please me better than any other of his works. He is certainly a great musician, even a Master, but, in his case, his mastery over-whelms his inspiration. So many preparations and circum-locutions for something which ought to come and charm us at once—and nothing does come, but boredom. His music is not warmed by any genuine emotion. It lacks poetry, but makes great pretensions to profundity. These depths contain nothing: they are void. Take the opening of the Concerto, for instance. It is an introduction, a preparation for something fine; an admirable pedestal for a statue; but the statue is lacking, we only get a second pedestal piled upon the first. I do not know whether I have properly expressed the thoughts, or rather feelings, which Brahms's music awakens in me. I mean to say that he never expresses anything, or, when he does, he fails to express it fully. His music is made up of fragments of some indefinable *something*, skilfully welded together. The design lacks definite contour, colour, life.

"But I must simply confess that, independent of any definite accusation, Brahms, as a musical personality, is antipathetic to me. I cannot abide him. Whatever he does—I remain unmoved and cold. It is a purely instinctive feeling."

[1] The violin Concerto, Op. 77.

To Modeste Tchaikovsky.

"Rome, *February* 26*th* (*March* 9*th*), 1880.

"To-day I went on foot to the Vatican and sat a long while in the Sistine Chapel. Here a miracle was worked. I felt—almost for the first time in my life—an artistic ecstasy for painting. What it means to become gradually accustomed to the painter's art! I remember the time when all this seemed to me absurd and meaningless. . . ."

To Modeste Tchaikovsky.

"Berlin, *March* 4*th* (16*th*), 1880.

" In Paris I went to the 'Comédie Francaise,' and fell in love with Racine or Corneille (which of them wrote *Polyeucte ?*). The beauty and strength of these verses and, still more, the lofty artistic truth! At the first glance this tragedy seems so unreal and impossible. The last act, however, in which Felix, conscience-stricken and illumined by Christ, suddenly becomes a Christian, touched me profoundly. . . .

"After reading Toly's letter I went to Bilse's concert. The large, luxuriously decorated hall, with its smell of indifferent cigars and food, its stocking-knitting ladies and beer-drinking men, made a curious impression upon me. After Italy, where we were constantly out in the beautiful, pure air, it was quite repugnant. But the orchestra was excellent, the acoustic splendid, and the programme good. I heard Schumann's 'Genoveva,' the 'Mignon' overture, and a very sparkling *pot-pourri*, and I was very pleased with it all. How glad I shall be to hear the *Flying Dutchman* to-day!"

To Modeste Tchaikovsky.

"Berlin, *March* 5*th* (17*th*), 1880.

"To-day I went to the Aquarium, where I went into ecstasies over the chimpanzee. He lives in intimate friendship with a dog. It is delightful to see the two play together, and the chimpanzee laughs in the drollest way when he takes refuge in some place where the dog cannot get at him !

"I notice that I am making great progress in my appreciation of painting. I take the greatest delight in many things, especially in the Flemish school. Teniers, Wouvermans, and Ruysdael please me far more than the renowned Rubens, who represents even Christ as healthily robust, with unnaturally pink cheeks. One fact makes me begin to see myself as *a great* connoisseur. I recognise Correggio's brush before I see his name in the catalogue! But then Correggio has his own manner, and all his male figures and heads resemble the Christ in the Vatican, and his women the Danae in the Borghese Palace."

To N. F. von Meck.

"St. Petersburg, *March 10th (22nd)*, 1880.

" Your benevolence to poor, dying Henry Wieniawsky touches me deeply.[1] . . . I pity him greatly. In him we shall lose an incomparable violinist and a gifted composer. In this respect I think Wieniawsky very talented . . . the beautiful *Légende* and parts of the A minor Concerto show a true creative gift."

To N. F. von Meck.

"St. Petersburg, *March 20th (April 1st)*, 1880.

"Yesterday I suffered a good deal. The Grand Duke Constantine Nicholaevich has a son Constantine. This young man of two-and-twenty is passionately fond of music, and is very partial to mine. He expressed a wish to become more closely acquainted with me, and asked a relative of mine, the wife of Admiral Butakov, to arrange an evening party at which we might meet.

"As he knows my misanthropical habits, this evening was to be of an informal nature, without dress coats and white ties. It was impossible to escape. The young man is very pleasant and has musical ability. We talked music from 9 p.m. until 2 a.m. He composes very nicely,

---

[1] N. F. von Meck had given the gifted artist the wherewithal to spend his last days in comfort. Ten days after this letter was written Wieniawsky died.

but unfortunately has no time to devote himself to it seriously."

On March 25th several of Tchaikovsky's works were performed at a concert given by two singers, well known in Petersburg, V. Issakov and Madame Panaev. The First Suite and the *Romeo and Juliet* overture were played by the orchestra of the Russian Opera under Napravnik. The Suite had the greatest success, especially the "Marche Miniature." The great novelist Tourgeniev was present on this occasion.

To N. F. von Meck.

"Moscow, *April 2nd* (14*th*), 1880.

" I have come here with the intention of spending three days incognito and finishing my work. Besides, I need the rest. Imagine, my dear friend, for the last few days I have hardly ever been out of a tail coat and white tie and associating with the most august personages. It is all very flattering, sometimes touching; but fatiguing to the last degree. I feel so happy and comfortable in my room in the hotel, not being obliged to go anywhere, or do anything ! "

X

To N. F. von Meck.

"KAMENKA, *April* 18*th* (30*th*), 1880.

" To-day a cold north wind is blowing. Spring has not yet entered into possession of her own, and the nightingale is not singing yet. Still, it is beautiful in the forest.

" During the last few days I have read through two new operas : Anton Rubinstein's *Kalashnikov* and *Jean de Nivelles* by Délibes. The former is weak all through. Rubinstein is like a singer who has lost her voice, but still believes she sings charmingly. His talent has long since lost its charm. He really ought to give up composing and to be contented with his earlier works. I pray that I **may** never fall into the same error. Délibes makes just the opposite impression. His work is fresh, graceful, and very clever."

About the end of April the director of the Kiev branch of the Russian Musical Society offered to make Tchaikovsky the principal of this section, and of the musical school connected with it. Although on account of its proximity to the home of the Davidovs at Kamenka, the neighbourhood of Kiev offered many attractions to him, he declined the offer without hesitation. He had tasted the fruits of liberty and was more than ever convinced that teaching was not his vocation.

During his stay at Kamenka, Tchaikovsky finished the orchestration of his "Italian Fantasia," which he considered, apart from its musical worth, one of his most effective and brilliant orchestral works.

To P. I. Jurgenson.

"KAMENKA, *June 23rd* (*July 5th*), 1880.

"DEAR SOUL,—I believe you imagine I have no greater happiness than to compose occasional pieces to be played at forthcoming exhibitions, and that I ought to put my inspirations down post-haste upon paper, without knowing how, when, or where. I shall not stir a finger until I get a positive commission. If something vocal is required of me, I must be supplied with a suitable text (when it is a question of an order I am ready to set an advertisement of corn-plasters to music); if it is to be an instrumental work, I must have some idea of the form it should take, and what it is intended to illustrate. At the same time a definite fee must be offered, with a definite agreement as to who is responsible for it, and when I shall receive it. I do not make all these demands from caprice, but because I am not in a position to write these festival works without having some positive instructions as to what is required of me. There are two kinds of inspiration : one comes direct from the soul, by freedom of choice, or other

creative impulse; the other *comes to order.* . .   Matters of
business must be put very clearly and distinctly.   Fancy if
I had already been inspired to write a Festival Overture for
the opening of the Exhibition!   What would have come of
it?   It might have happened that the great *Anton* had also
(*An-*)*toned* something of his own.   Where should I have
been with my scribblings?

"I shall finish the corrections of the fourth act to-day.
The opera (*The Maid of Orleans*) has become a long
affair.   My poor publisher!   Well, we must live in hope!"

Early in July Tchaikovsky visited Nadejda von Meck's
estate at Brailov, for the sake of repose.   At this time a
feeling of dissatisfaction with his work seems to have taken
possession of him.   "I have written much that is beautiful,"
he wrote to his brother Modeste, "but how weak, how lacking in mastery! . . . I have made up my mind to write
nothing new for a time, but to devote myself to the correcting and re-editing of my earlier works."

A letter to Nadejda von Meck, dated Brailov, July 5th
(17th), 1880, contains some interesting comments upon
Glinka and his work.

". . . Glinka is quite an unusual phenomenon!   Reading
his *Memoirs*, which reveal a nice, amiable, but rather
commonplace man, we can hardly realise that the same
mind created that wonderful 'Slavsia,'[1] which is worthy to
rank with the work of the greatest geniuses.   And how
many more fine things there are in his other opera (*Russlan*)
and the overtures!   How astonishingly original is his
Komarinskaya, from which all the Russian composers who
followed him (including myself) continue to this day to
borrow contrapuntal and harmonic combinations directly
they have to develop a Russian dance-tune!   This is done
unconsciously; but the fact is, Glinka managed to concen-
trate in one short work what a dozen second-rate talents
would only have invented with the whole expenditure of
their powers.

[1] "Slavsia," the great national chorus in *A Life for the Tsar.*

"And it was this same Glinka who, at the height of his maturity, composed such a weak, trivial thing as the Polonaise for the Coronation (written a year before his death), or the children's polka, of which he speaks in his *Memoirs* at such length, and with such self-satisfaction, as though it had been a masterpiece.

"Mozart, too, expresses himself with great *naïveté* in his letters to his father and, in fact, all through his life. But this was a different kind of simplicity. Mozart is a genius whose childlike innocence, gentleness of spirit and virginal modesty are scarcely of this earth. He was devoid of self-satisfaction and boastfulness; he seems hardly to have been conscious of the greatness of his genius. Glinka, on the contrary, is imbued with a spirit of self-glorification; he is ready to become garrulous over the most trivial events in his life, or the appearance of his least important works, and is convinced it is all of historical importance. Glinka is a gifted Russian aristocrat of his time, and has the faults of his type: petty vanity, limited culture, intolerance, ostentatiousness and a morbid sensibility to, and impatience of, all criticism. These are generally the characteristics of mediocrity; how they come to exist in a man who ought—so it seems—to dwell in calm and modest pride, conscious of his power, is beyond my comprehension! In one page of his *Memoirs* Glinka says he had a bulldog whose conduct was not irreproachable, and his servant had to be continually cleaning the room. Kukolnik, to whom Glinka entrusted his *Memoirs* for revision, remarked in the margin, 'Why put in this?' Glinka pencilled underneath, 'Why not?' Is not this highly characteristic? Yet, all the same, he composed the 'Slavsia'"!

To N. F. von Meck.

"BRAILOV, *July 6th* (18*th*), 1880.

"To-day I went to the Orthodox, the new Catholic, and the monastery churches. There is something about the monastic singing here, as in all Russian churches, which enrages me to the last degree. It is the chord of the dominant seventh in its original position, which we misuse so terribly. There is nothing so unmusical, or so unsuitable to the Orthodox Church as this commonplace chord, which was introduced during the eighteenth century by Messrs. Galuppi, Sarti, Bortniansky and Co., and has since become so much a part of our church music that the *Gospodi pomilui*[1] cannot be sung without it.   This chord reminds me of the accordion, which only gives out two harmonies : the tonic and dominant.   It disfigures the natural progression of the parts and weakens and vulgarises our church music.   To make you clearly understand what it is that annoys me I will give you an example :—

instead of this they ought to sing

" The new Catholic church makes a pleasant impression. I much prefer our Orthodox liturgy to the Mass, especially to the so-called ' Low Mass,' which seems to me devoid of all solemnity."

To N. F. von Meck.

" BRAILOV, *July 8th (20th)*, 1880.

" Yesterday I went an expedition in the forest, where formerly there used to be wild goats, of which now only one specimen is left.   They say the others were all devoured by the wolves in winter.   It is a great pity !   But I was consoled by the beauty of the evening and a wonderful walk.   At sunset I had tea, and then wandered alone by the steep bank of the stream behind the deer-park, and drank in all the deep delight of the forest at sundown, and freshness of the evening air.   Such moments, I thought, helped us to bear with patience the many minor grievances of existence.   They make us in love with life. We are promised eternal happiness, immortal existence,

---

[1] " Lord, have mercy" (*Kyrie eleison*).

but we do not realise this, nor shall we perhaps attain to it. But if we are worthy of it, and if it is really eternal, we shall soon learn to enjoy it. Meanwhile, one wishes to live, in order to experience again such moments as those of yesterday.

"To-day I intended to leave for Simaki, but while I am writing to you a terrific storm is raging, and it is evidently going to be a wet day; so perhaps I shall remain here. I am drawn to Simaki, and yet I regret leaving Brailov. Dear friend, to-day I have committed a kind of burglary in your house, and I will confess my crime. There was no key to the bookcase in the drawing-room next to your bedroom, but I saw it contained some new books which interested me greatly. Even Marcel could not find the key, so it occurred to me to try the one belonging to the cupboard near my room, and it opened the bookcase at once. I took out Byron and Martinov's *Moscow*. Make your mind easy, all your books and music remain untouched. To quiet Marcel's conscience I gave him, when about to leave for Simaki, a memorandum of what I had taken, and before I actually depart I will return him the books and music to replace in their proper order. Pray forgive my self-justification."

To Modeste Tchaikovsky.

"SIMAKI, *July* 8*th* (20*th*), 1880.

". . . I expected a great deal from Simaki, but the reality far surpasses my expectations. What a wonderful spot this is, and how poor Brailov seems now I am here! The small house is just the same as when I saw it last year, only it has been done up a little; the furniture and upholstery are partly new; the arrangements are the ideal of comfort. But the surroundings are enchanting! The garden is a mass of flowers. I simply swim in an ocean of delightful impressions. An hour ago I was in the millet-field which lies beyond the garden, and so great was my ecstasy that I fell upon my knees and thanked God for the profound joy I experienced. I stood on rising ground; nothing was visible in the distance but the dense green which surrounds my little house; on every side the forest spreads to the hills; across the stream lay the hamlet, whence came various pleasant rural sounds; the voices of children, the bleating of sheep and the lowing of cattle, driven home from pasture. In the west the sun was setting in splendour; while in the east the crescent moon was already up. Everywhere beauty and space! What moments life holds! Thanks to these intervals, it is possible to forget everything!"

To N. F. von Meck.

"SIMAKI, *July 9th* (*21st*), 1880.

". . . The night has been glorious! At 2 a.m. I reluctantly left my place by the window. The moon shone brightly. The stillness, the perfume of the flowers, and those wondrous indefinable sounds that belong to the night—ah God, how beautiful it all is! Dear friend, I am glad you are at Interlaken, of which I am very fond; but all the same I do not envy you. It would be hard to find a place in which the conditions of life would conform better to my ideal than Simaki. All day long I feel as though I were lost in some wonderful, fantastic dream."

To N. F. von Meck.

"SIMAKI, *July 14th* (*26th*), 1880.

" I have just been playing the first act of *The Maid of Orleans*, which is now ready for the printer. Either I am mistaken, or it is not in vain, dear friend, that you have had the clock you gave me decorated with the figure of my latest operatic heroine. I do not think *The Maid of Orleans* my finest, or the most emotional, of my works, but it seems to me to be the one most likely to make my name popular. I believe *Oniegin* and one or two of my instrumental works are far more closely allied to my individual temperament. I was less absorbed in *The Maid of Orleans* than in our Symphony, for instance, or the second Quartet; but I gave more consideration to the scenic and musical effects—and these are the most important things in opera."

To N. F. von Meck.

"SIMAKI, *July* 18*th* (30*th*), 1880.

"Yesterday evening—to take a rest from my own work —I played through Bizet's *Carmen* from cover to cover. I consider it a *chef-d'œuvre* in the fullest sense of the word : one of those rare compositions which seems to reflect most strongly in itself the musical tendencies of a whole generation. It seems to me that our own period differs from earlier ones in this one characteristic : that contemporary composers *are engaged in the pursuit of charming and piquant effects,* unlike Mozart, Beethoven, Schubert, and Schumann. What is the so-called New Russian School but the cult of varied and pungent harmonies, of original orchestral combinations and every kind of purely external effect ? Musical ideas give place to this or that union of sounds. Formerly there was *composition, creation ;* now (with few exceptions) there is only research and invention. This development of musical thought is naturally purely intellectual, consequently contemporary music is clever, piquant, and eccentric ; but cold and lacking the glow of true emotion. And behold, a Frenchman comes on the scene, in whom these qualities of piquancy and pungency are not the outcome of effort and reflection, but flow from his pen as in a free stream, flattering the ear, but touching us also. It is as though he said to us : 'You ask nothing great, superb, or grandiose—you want something *pretty,* here is a *pretty opera* ' ; and truly I know of nothing in music which is more representative of that element which I call *the pretty (le joli).* . . . I cannot play the last scene without tears in my eyes ; the gross rejoicings of the crowd who look on at the bull-fight, and, side by side with this, the poignant tragedy and death of the two principal characters, pursued by an evil fate, who come to their inevitable end through a long series of sufferings.

"I am convinced that ten years hence *Carmen* will be the most popular opera in the world. But no one is a prophet in his own land. In Paris *Carmen* has had no real success."

To Modeste Tchaikovsky.

"SIMAKI, *July* 18*th* (30*th*), 1880.

" MY DEAR MODI,—How worried I am by my *Maid of Orleans,* and how glad I am to have done with her!   Now she has flown to Moscow and, until the time of performance comes, I need not bother about her any more. . . .

" Thanks (in an ironical sense) for your suggestion that I should read *L'homme qui rit.*   Do you not know the story of my relations to Victor Hugo?   Anyhow, I will tell you what came of them.   I took up *Les travailleurs de la Mer ;* I read, and read, and grew more and more irritated by his grimaces and buffoonery.   Finally, after a whole series of short, unmeaning phrases, consisting of exclamations, antitheses, and asterisks, I lost my temper, spat upon the book, tore it to pieces, stamped upon it, and wound up by throwing it out of the window.   From that moment I cannot bear the mention of Victor Hugo!   Believe me, your Zola is just such another mountebank, but more modern in spirit.   I do not dislike him quite so much as Hugo, but very nearly.   He disgusts me, as a girl would disgust me who pretended to be simple and natural, while all the time she was essentially a flirt and coquette.

" In proportion as I like modern French music, their literature and journalism seem to me revolting.

" Yesterday I wrote to you about Bizet, to-day I am enthusiastic about Massenet.   I found his oratorio, *Mary Magdalene,* at N. F.'s.   After I had read the text, which treats not only of the relations between Christ, the Magdalene, and Judas, but also of Golgotha and the Resurrection, I felt a certain prejudice against the work, because it seemed too audacious.   When I began to play it, however, I was soon convinced that it was no commonplace composition. The duet between Christ and the Magdalene is a masterpiece.   I was so touched by the emotionalism of the music, in which Massenet has reflected the eternal compassion of Christ, that I shed many tears.   Wonderful tears!   All praise to the Frenchman who had the art of calling them forth. . . . The French are really first in contemporary music.   All day long this duet has been running in my head, and under its influence I have written a song, the melody of which is very reminiscent of Massenet."

To N. F. von Meck.

"SIMAKI, *July* 24*th* (*August* 5*th*), 1880.

"Have I told you, dear friend, that I am studying English? Here I work very regularly, and with good results. I hope in six months I shall be able to read English easily. That is my sole aim ; I know that at my age it is impossible to speak it well. But to read Shakespeare, Dickens, and Thackeray in the original would be the consolation of my old age."[1]

To Modeste Tchaikovsky.

"KAMENKA, *July* 31*st* (*August* 12*th*), 1880.

"It is two days since I came to Kamenka. I was glad, very glad, to see all our people again, but I am not in high spirits. A kind of apathy has come over me; a dislike to work, to reading, and particularly to exercise, although I dutifully do my two hours a day. Apart from the people, everything here seems to me stuffy and frowsy, beginning with the air. When I think of the intoxicating charm of the gardens, the air perfumed by field and forest, at Simaki ; when I look at the poor, dusty trees, and the arid, barren soil of this place ; when instead of the clear, cold stream I have to content myself with my sitz-bath—I am overcome with a sickening sense of regret."

To P. I. Jurgenson.

"KAMENKA, *August* 12*th* (24*th*), 1880.

"If I should ever become famous, and anyone should collect materials for my biography, your letter to-day would give a very false impression of me. Anyone would suppose I had been in the habit of flattering influential people and making advances to them with the object of getting

---

[1] P. I. Jurgenson informed me that Tchaikovsky did succeed in acquiring sufficient English to read *Pickwick* and *David Copperfield* in the original. When he took to conducting, he had no time for the study of languages.

my works performed. This would be entirely untrue. I have never in my life raised a finger to win the favour of Bilse, or another. This is a sort of 'passive' pride. It is another matter if the advances are made from the other side. . . .

"As regards your advice to imitate Anton Rubinstein, I must tell you that our positions are so different that no comparison can be made between us. Take away Rubinstein's virtuosity, and he immediately falls from his greatness to the level of my nothingness. Well, I should like to see which of us has the most composer's pride! In any case I am not such a grandee that at the advances of so profitable and influential a personage as Bilse I can reply: 'this is no business of mine; apply to Jurgenson.'

"The corrected manuscripts are ready, and shall be sent to-morrow. The *Italian Capriccio* can be printed, but I should like to look through the concerto once more, and beg you to send me another revise. When I sent it to Nicholas Rubinstein in the spring, I asked him to make his criticisms to Taneiev, and to request the latter to make the necessary alterations in the piano part without changing the musical intention, of which I will not alter a single line. Taneiev replied that there were no alterations required. Consequently this must have been Rubinstein's opinion. But we can hardly assume that he will study the work."

From a letter to Jurgenson, dated some days later than the above, we see that Tchaikovsky had resolved to devote part of the current year to revising all his works published by this firm "from Opus I. to the Third Symphony."

To N. F. von Meck.

"KAMENKA, *August 13th (25th)*, 1880.

"You ask me if I share your feelings when thinking of the possibility of monumental fame? *Fame!* What contradictory sentiments the word awakes in me! On the one hand I desire and strive for it; on the other I detest it. If the chief thought of my life is concentrated upon my creative work, I cannot do otherwise than wish for fame. If I feel a continual impulse to express myself in the language of music, it follows that I need to be heard; and the larger my circle of sympathetic hearers, the better. I desire with all my soul that my music should become more widely known, and that the number of those people who derive comfort and support from their love of it should increase. In this sense not only do I love fame, but it becomes the aim of all that is most earnest in my work. But, alas! when I begin to reflect that with an increasing audience will come also an increase of interest in my personality, in the more intimate sense; that there will be inquisitive people among the public who will tear aside the curtain behind which I have striven to conceal my private life; then I am filled with pain and disgust, so that I half wish to keep silence for ever, in order to be left in peace. I am not afraid of the world, for I can say that my conscience is clear, and I have nothing to be ashamed of; but the thought that someone may try to force the inner world of my thoughts and feelings, which all my life I have guarded so carefully from outsiders—this is sad and terrible. There is a tragic element, dear friend, in this conflict between the desire for fame and the fear of its consequences. I am attracted to it like the moth to the candle, and I, too, burn my wings. Sometimes I am possessed by a mad desire to disappear for ever, to be buried alive, to ignore all that is going on, and be forgotten by everybody. Then, alas! the creative inspiration returns. . . . I fly to the flame and burn my wings once more!

"Do you know my wings will soon have to bear the weight of my opera? I shall be up to my neck in theatrical and official mire, and be suffocated in an atmosphere of petty intrigue, of microscopical, but poisonous, ambitions, and every kind of dense stupidity. What is to be done? Either do not write operas, or be prepared for all this! I believe I never shall compose another opera. When I look back upon all I went through last spring, when I was occupied with the performance of my last one, I lose all desire to write for the stage."

XI

1880–1881

To N. F. von Meck.

"KAMENKA, *September 4th* (16*th*), 1880.

" I am doing nothing whatever, only wandering through the forests and fields all day long. I want to take a change from my own work, with its eternal proof-correcting, and to play as much as possible of other people's music; so I have begun to study Mozart's *Zauberflöte*. Never was so senselessly stupid a subject set to such captivating music. How thankful I am that the circumstances of my musical career have not changed by a hair's breadth the charm Mozart exercises for me! You would not believe, dear friend, what wonderful feelings come over me when I give myself up to his music. It is something quite different from the stressful delight awakened in me by Beethoven, Schumann, or Chopin. . . . My contemporaries were imbued with the spirit of modern music from their childhood, and came to know Mozart in later years, after they had made acquaintance with Chopin, who reflects so clearly the Byronic despair and disillusionment. Fortunately, fate decreed that I should grow up in an unmusical family, so that in childhood I was not nourished on the poisonous food of the post-Beethoven music. The same kind fate brought me early in life in contact with Mozart, and thus opened up to me unsuspected horizons. These early impressions can never be effaced. Do you know that when I play Mozart, I feel brighter and younger, almost a youth again? But enough. I know that we do not agree in our appreciation of Mozart, and that my dithyramb does not interest you in the least."

To N. F. von Meck.

"KAMENKA, *September 9th* (*21st*), 1880.

"How fleeting were my hopes of a prolonged rest! Scarcely had I begun to enjoy a few days' leisure than an indefinable mood of boredom, even a sense of not being in health, came over me. To-day I began to occupy my mind with projects for a new symphony, and immediately I felt well and cheerful. It appears as though I could not spend a couple of days in idleness, unless I am travelling. I dread lest I should become a composer of Anton Rubinstein's type, who considers it his bounden duty to present a new work to the public every day in the week. In this way he has dissipated his great creative talent, and has only small change to offer instead of the sterling gold which he could have given us had he written in moderation. Lately I have been seeking some kind of occupation that would take me completely away from music for a time, and would seriously interest me. Alas, I have not discovered it! There is no guide to the history of music in Russian, and it would be a good thing if I could occupy myself with a book of this kind; I often think of it. But then I should have to give up composing for at least two years, and that would be too much. To start upon a translation—that is not very interesting work. Write a monograph upon some artist? So much has already been written about the great musicians of Western Europe. For Glinka, Dargomijsky, and Serov I cannot feel any enthusiasm, for, highly as I value their works, I cannot admire them as men. I have told you what I think of Glinka. Dargomijsky was even less cultured. As to Serov, he was a clever man of encyclopedic learning, but I knew him personally, and could not admire his moral character. As far as I understood him, he was not good-hearted, and that is sufficient reason why I do not care to devote my leisure to him. It would have been a delight to write the biography of Mozart, but it is impossible to do so after Otto Jahn, who devoted his life to the task.

"So there is no other occupation open to me but composition. I am planning a symphony or a string quartet. I do not know which I shall decide upon."

To N. F. von Meck.

"KAMENKA, *September 12th (24th)*, 1880.

" I venture to approach you, dear friend, with the following request. An employé in a counting-house, here in Kamenka, has a son who is remarkably gifted for painting. It seemed to me cruel not to give him the means of studying, so I sent him to Moscow and asked Anatol to take him to the School of Painting and Sculpture. All this was arranged, and then it turned out that the boy's maintenance would cost far more than I expected. And so I thought I would ask you whether in your house there was any corner in which this lad might live? Not, of course, without some kind of supervision. He would only need a tiny room with a bed, a cupboard, and a table where he could sleep and work. Perhaps your servants would look after him, and give him a little advice? The boy is of irreproachable character : industrious, good, obedient, clean in his person—in short, exemplary. I would undertake his meals.[1] . . .

" I have also unearthed a musical talent here, in the daughter of the local priest, and have been successful in placing her at the Conservatoire."

To N. F. von Meck.

"KAMENKA, *September 19th (October 1st)*, 1880.

"Yesterday I received an official intimation from the Imperial Opera to the effect that my opera has been accepted and will be produced in January. The libretto has been passed by the censor with one or two exceptions : the *Archbishop* must be called the *Wanderer* (?); 'every allusion to the Cross must be omitted, and no cross may be seen upon the stage.' There is nothing for it but to submit."

---

[1] Unfortunately the boy did not turn out an artist of the first rank. But his education was not wasted, for he is now drawing-master in a public school in South Russia.

To N. F. von Meck.

"KAMENKA, *September 28th (October 10th),* 1880.

"Nicholas Rubinstein has requested me to write an important work for chorus and orchestra, to be produced at the Moscow Exhibition. Nothing is more unpleasant to me than the manufacturing of music for such occasions. . . . But I have not courage to refuse. . . ."

To N. F. von Meck.

"KAMENKA, *October 10th (22nd),* 1880.

"You can imagine, dear friend, that recently my Muse has been very benevolent, when I tell you that I have written two long works very rapidly: a Festival Overture for the Exhibition and a Serenade in four movements for string orchestra. The overture[1] will be very noisy. I wrote it without much warmth of enthusiasm; therefore it has no great artistic value. The Serenade, on the contrary, I wrote from an inward impulse; I felt it, and venture to hope that this work is not without artistic qualities."

To N. F. von Meck.

"KAMENKA, *October 14th (26th),* 1880.

". . . How glad I am that my opera pleases you! I am delighted you find no 'Russianisms' in it, for I dreaded this and had striven in this work to be as objective as possible."

To N. F. von Meck.

"KAMENKA, *October 14th (26th),* 1880.

"Of course I am no judge of my own works, but I can truthfully say that—with very few exceptions—they have all been *felt* and *lived* by me, and have come straight from my heart. It is the greatest happiness to know that there is another kindred soul in the world who has such a true

---

[1] The overture entitled *The Year 1812*, op. 49, for the consecration of the Cathedral of the Saviour, Moscow. It was one of the three commissions suggested by N. Rubinstein, referred to in the previous letter.

and delicate appreciation of my music. The thought that she will discern all that I have felt, while writing this or that work, invariably warms and inspires me. There are few such souls; among those who surround me I can only point to my brothers. Modeste is very near to me in mind and sentiment. Among professional musicians I have met with the least congenial sympathy. . . .

"You ask why I have never written a trio. Forgive me, dear friend, I would do anything to give you pleasure —but this is beyond me! My acoustic apparatus is so ordered that I simply cannot endure the combination of pianoforte with violin or violoncello. To my mind the *timbre* of these instruments will not blend, and I assure you it is a torture to me to have to listen to a trio or sonata of any kind for piano and strings. I cannot explain this physiological peculiarity; I simply state it as a fact. Piano and orchestra—that is quite another matter. Here again there is no blending of tone; the piano by its elastic tone differs from all other instruments in *timbre;* but we are now dealing with two equal opponents: the orchestra, with its power and inexhaustible variety of colour, opposed by the small, unimposing, but high-mettled pianoforte, which often comes off victorious in the hands of a gifted executant. Much poetry is contained in this conflict, and endless seductive combinations for the composer. On the other hand, how unnatural is the union of three such individualities as the pianoforte, the violin and the violoncello! Each loses something of its value. The warm and singing tone of the violin and the 'cello sounds limited beside that *king* of instruments, the pianoforte; while the latter strives in vain to prove that it can sing like its rivals. I consider the piano should only be employed under these conditions: (1) As a solo instrument; (2) opposed to the orchestra; (3) for accompaniment, as the background to a picture. But a trio implies equality and relationship, and do these exist between stringed solo instruments and the piano? They do *not;* and this is the reason why there is always something artificial about a pianoforte trio, each of the three instruments being continually called upon to express what the composer imposes upon it, rather than what lies within its characteristic utterance; while the musician meets with perpetual difficulties in the distribution of the voices and grouping of the parts.   I do full justice to the inspired art with which Beethoven, Schumann, and Mendelssohn have conquered these difficulties.   I know there exist many trios containing music of admirable quality; but personally I do not care for the trio as a form, therefore I shall never produce anything sincerely inspired through the medium of this combination of sounds.   I know, dear friend, that we disagree on this point, and that you, on the contrary, are fond of a trio; but in spite of all the similarity between our artistic temperaments, we remain two separate individualities; therefore it is not surprising that we should not agree in every particular."

During the autumn of 1880 Tchaikovsky suffered greatly from neuralgic headaches.   He remained at Kamenka until early in November, when he returned to Moscow for a short time, in order to correct proofs and settle other business matters.   Towards the end of the month he wrote to Nadejda von Meck from St. Petersburg :—

"*November 27th (December 9th)*, 1880.

"The directors of the Moscow Musical Society are greatly interested in my Liturgy (St. John Chrysostom). One of their number, named Alexeiev, gave a good fee to have it studied by one of the best choirs.   This resulted in a performance of the work in the concert-room of the Moscow Conservatoire.   The choir sang wonderfully well, and it was altogether one of the happiest moments in my musical career.   It was decided to give the Liturgy at an extra concert of the Musical Society.   On the same evening my Serenade for strings was played, in order to give me an agreeable surprise.   For the moment I regard it as my best work. . . .

"Have I told you already that *Eugene Oniegin* is to be splendidly mounted at the Opera in Moscow?   I am very pleased, because it will decide the important question whether the work will become part of the repertory or not, that is to say, whether it will keep its place on the stage. As I never intended it for this purpose, I did nothing on my own initiative to get it produced."

While in St. Petersburg, Tchaikovsky undertook to make some changes in his new opera, *The Maid of Orleans*. This was in order that the part of Joan of Arc herself might be taken by Madame Kamensky, a mezzo-soprano of unusual range and quality.

To N. F. von Meck.

"Moscow, *December 14th (26th)*, 1880.

"One newspaper blames me for having dedicated my opera, *The Maid of Orleans*, to Napravnik, and considers it an unworthy action on my part to win his good graces in this way. Napravnik—one of the few thoroughly honest musicians in Petersburg—will be very much upset. They also find fault with me because my opera is not on sale.

"All this is very galling and vexatious, but I do not let it trouble me much.

"I have sworn to myself to avoid Moscow and Petersburg in future."

To N. F. von Meck.

"Moscow, *December 17th (29th)*, 1880.

"I have been very much upset the last few days. Last year I received a letter from a young man, unknown to me, of the name of Tkachenko, containing the curious proposal that I should take him as my servant and give him music lessons in return. The letter was so clever and original, and showed such a real love of music, that it affected me very sympathetically. A correspondence between us followed, from which I learnt that he was already twenty-three, and had no musical knowledge. I wrote frankly to him that at his age it was too late to begin to study music. After this, I heard no more of him for nine months. The day before yesterday I received another letter from him, returning all my previous correspondence, in order that it might not fall into strange hands after his death. He took leave of me and said he had resolved to commit suicide. The letter was evidently written in a moment of great despair, and touched me profoundly. I saw from the postmark that it was written from Voronezh, and decided to telegraph to someone there, asking them to seek Tkachenko with the help of the police and tell him —if it were not already too late—he might expect a letter from me. Fortunately, Anatol had a friend at Voronezh, to whom we telegraphed at once. Last night I heard from him that Tkachenko had been discovered *in time*. He was in a terrible condition.

"I immediately sent him some money and invited him to come to Moscow. How it will end I do not know, but I am glad to have saved him from self-destruction."

At this time Tchaikovsky's valet, Alexis, was compelled to fulfil his military service, and master and servant were equally affected at the moment of separation.

On December 6th (18th) the *Italian Capriccio* was performed for the first time under the conductorship of Nicholas Rubinstein. Its success was incontestable, although criticism varied greatly as to its merits, and the least favourable described it as being marred by "coarse and cheap" effects. In St. Petersburg, where it was given a few weeks later by Napravnik, it met with scant appreciation; Cui pronounced it to be "no work of art, but a valuable gift to the programmes of open-air concerts."

The performance of the Liturgy took place in Moscow on December 18th (30th). Thanks to the stir which had been made by the confiscation of Tchaikovsky's first sacred work, the concert was unusually crowded. At the close the composer was frequently recalled. Nevertheless, there was considerable difference of opinion as to the success of the work.

Tchaikovsky was not much affected by the views of the professional critics; but he was deeply hurt by a letter emanating from the venerable Ambrose, vicar of Moscow, which appeared in the *Rouss*. This letter complained that the Liturgy was the most sacred possession of the people, and should only be heard in church; that to use the service as a libretto was a profanation of the holy words.   It concluded by congratulating the orthodox that the text had at least been treated by a worthy musician, but what would happen if some day a " Rosenthal " or a " Rosenbluhm " should lay hands upon it?   Inevitably then " our most sacred words would be mocked at and hissed."

Fatigued by the excitement of these weeks, Tchaikovsky returned to Kamenka to spend Christmas in the restful quiet of the country.

The first performance of *Eugene Oniegin* at the Opera House in Moscow took place on January 11th (23rd), 1881. The scenery was not new and left much to be desired. The singers, with the exception of Madame Kroutikov, who took the part of Madame Larina, and Bartsal, who appeared as the Frenchman Triquet, were lacking in experience.   The costumes, however, were perfectly true to history.   The performance evoked much applause, but more for the composer than for the opera itself.   The great public allowed the best situations in the work to pass unnoticed, but the opera found an echo in the hearts of the minority, so that gradually the work gained the appreciation of the crowd and won a lasting success.

To N. F. von Meck.

" Moscow, *January* 12*th* (24*th*), 1881.

" Yesterday was the first night of *Eugene Oniegin.* I was oppressed by varied emotions, both at the rehearsals and on the night itself.   At first the public was very reserved; by degrees, however, the applause grew and at the last all went well.   The performance and mounting of the opera were satisfactory. . . .

" Tkachenko (the young man who wanted to commit suicide) has arrived.   I have seen him.   On the whole he made a sympathetic impression upon me.   His sufferings

are the outcome of the internal conflict which exists between his aspirations and stern reality. He is intelligent
and cultivated, yet in order to earn his bread he has had
to be a railway guard. He is very anxious to become
a musician. He is nervous, and morbidly modest, and
seems to be broken in spirit. Poverty and solitude have
made him misanthropical. His views are rather strange,
but he is by no means stupid. I am sorry for him and
have agreed to look after him. I have decided that he
shall go to the Conservatoire, and then it will be seen
whether he can take up music, or some other career. It
will not be difficult to make a useful and contented man
of him."

To N. F. von Meck.

"Moscow, *January* 19*th* (31*st*), 1881.

"Dear, kind friend, it has come to this: I take up my
pen to write to you unwillingly, because I feel the immediate need to pour out all the suffering and bitterness
which is heaped up in me. You will wonder how a man
who is successful in his work can still complain and rail at
fate? But my successes are not so important as they
seem; besides they do not compensate me for the intolerable sufferings I undergo when I mix in the society of my
fellow-creatures; when I have to be constantly posing
before them; when I cannot live as I wish, and as I am
accustomed to do, but am tossed to and fro like a ball in
the round of city life. . . .

"*Eugene Oniegin* does not progress. The prima donna
is seriously ill, so that the opera cannot be performed
again for some time. . . . The criticisms upon it are peculiar.
Some critics find the 'couplets' for Triquet the best thing
in the work and think Tatiana's part dry and colourless.
Others think I have no inspiration, but great cleverness.
The Petersburg papers write in chorus to rend my *Italian
Capriccio*, declaring it to be vulgar; and Cui prophesies
that *The Maid of Orleans* will turn out a commonplace
affair."

To N. F. von Meck.

"PETERSBURG, *January 27th* (*February 8th*), 1881.

"I will tell you something about Tkachenko.   He is an extraordinary being!   I had looked after him in every respect, and he began his studies with great zeal.   The day before I left Moscow he came to 'talk to me on serious business,' and the longer he talked, the more convinced I became that he is mentally and morally deranged.   He has taken it into his head that *I am not keeping him for his own sake,* but in order *to acquire the reputation of a bene-factor.*   He added that he was not disposed to be the *victim* of my desire for popularity, and absolutely refused to recognise me as his benefactor, so I was not to reckon upon his gratitude.

"I replied coldly, and advised him to devote himself to his work, without troubling himself as to my motives for assisting him.   I assured him I was quite indifferent as to his gratitude, that I was just leaving the town, and begged him not to waste his thoughts on me, but to fix them ex-clusively upon his work.

"I have entrusted him to the supervision of Albrecht, the Inspector of the Conservatoire.

"Have you heard of Nicholas Rubinstein's illness?   His condition is serious, but in spite of it he goes about and does his work.   The doctors insist upon his going away and taking rest; but he declares he could not live without the work he is used to. . . ."

On January 21st (February 2nd) Tchaikovsky's Second Symphony was given in its revised form at the Musical Society in St. Petersburg, and, according to the newspapers, met with a great success.   Not a single critic, however, observed the changes in the work, nor that the first move-ment was entirely new.

To N. F. von Meck.

"Petersburg, *February 1st (13th)*, 1881.

". . . The mounting of *The Maid of Orleans* will be very beggarly. The Direction, which has spent 10,000 (roubles) upon a new ballet, refuses to sacrifice a kopeck for the opera."

To the same.

"Petersburg, *February 7th (19th)*, 1881.

" The opera has been postponed until February 13th. I shall set off the very next day. The plan of my journey is : Vienna, Venice, Rome. The rehearsals are in progress. Most of the artists show great sympathy for my music, of which I am very proud. But the officials are doing all in their power to spoil the success of the opera. A certain Loukashevich is trying by every kind of intrigue to prevent Madame Kamensky from taking the part of Joan of Arc. When at yesterday's rehearsal—for scenic and vocal reasons—I transferred a melody from Joan's part to that of Agnes Sorel, he declared *I had no right to do such a thing without permission.* Sometimes I feel inclined to withdraw the score and leave the theatre."

The production of *The Maid of Orleans* at the Maryinsky Theatre left a very unpleasant memory in Tchaikovsky's mind. The intrigues between the prima donnas, the hostile attitude of the Direction, his dissatisfaction with some of the singers—all embittered the composer in the highest degree. His artistic vanity was exceedingly sensitive, even when his best friends told him " the plain truth." He submitted to the criticisms of Napravnik, and followed his advice regarding many details, because he was convinced of this musician's goodwill and great experience. If he got through this trying time fairly well, it was thanks to the fact that he himself, as well as the artists who were taking part in the work, did not doubt that the opera would eventually have a great success.

On the day following the performance, Tchaikovsky wrote :—

"The success of the opera was certain, even after the first act . . . the second scene of the third act was least applauded, but the fourth act was very well received. Altogether I was recalled twenty-four times. Kamenskaya was admirable; she even acted well, which she seldom does. Prianichnikov was the best among the other singers."

Tchaikovsky started for Italy under this favourable impression, and first became aware through a telegram from Petersburg in the *Neue Freie Presse* that, in spite of an ovation from the public, *The Maid of Orleans* was "poor in inspiration, wearisome, and monotonous." This was his first intimation of the attacks upon the opera which were made by the Press, and which caused the opera to be hastily withdrawn from the repertory of the Maryinsky Theatre.

Cui, as usual, led the chorus of unfavourable opinion, but all the other critics were more or less in agreement with his views.

XII

Impatient for the sunshine, Tchaikovsky broke his journey at Florence, whence he wrote to Nadejda von Meck on February 19th (March 3rd), 1881 :—

"What light! What sunshine! What a delight to sit at the open window with a bunch of violets before me, and to drink in the fresh air! I am full of sensations. I feel so well, and yet so sad—I could weep. Yet I know not why. Only music can express these feelings."

To N. F. von Meck.

"ROME, *February 22nd* (*March 6th*), 1881.

"I have just been lunching with the Grand Dukes Serge and Paul Alexandrovich. The invitation came early this morning, and I had to go out in search of a dress-coat. It was no easy matter to procure one, for, being Sunday, nearly all the shops were closed. It was with difficulty that I arrived at the Villa Sciarra in proper time. The Grand Duke Constantine introduced me to his cousins, who showed me much kindness and attention. All three are very sympathetic; but you can imagine, with my misanthropical shyness, how trying I find such meetings with strangers, especially with men of that aristocratic world. On Tuesday there is a dinner at Countess Brobinsky's, and I have also been invited to a soirée by Countess Sollogoub. I did not expect to have to lead this kind of life in Rome. I shall have to leave, for no doubt other invitations await me which I cannot refuse. Lest I should offend somebody, I am weak enough invariably to accept. I have not strength of mind to decline all such engagements."

To Modeste Tchaikovsky.

"ROME, *February* 26th (*March* 10th), 1881.

"I can just imagine how you are making fun of my worldliness! I cannot understand where I get strength to endure this senseless existence! Naturally, I am annoyed, and my visit to Rome is spoilt—but I have not altogether lost heart, and find occasional opportunities of enjoying the place. O society! What can be more appalling, duller, more intolerable? Yesterday I was dreadfully bored at Countess X.'s, but so heroically did I conceal my feelings that my hostess in bidding me good-bye said: 'I cannot understand why you have not come to me before. I am sure that after to-night you will repent not having made my acquaintance sooner.' This is word for word! She really pities me! May the devil take them all!"

To Modeste Tchaikovsky.

"NAPLES, *March* 3rd (15th), 1881.

"Yesterday I was about to write to you when Prince Stcherbatiov came to tell me of the Emperor's death,[1] which was a great shock to me. At such moments it is

---

[1] Alexander II., who was assassinated on the bank of the Catharine Canal.

very miserable to be abroad. I long to be in Russia, nearer to the source of information, and to take part in the demonstrations accorded to the new Tsar . . . in short, to be living in touch with one's own people. It seems so strange after receiving such news to hear them chattering at table d'hôte about the beauties of Sorrento, etc.

"The Grand Dukes wanted to take me with them to Athens and Jerusalem, which they intended to visit a few days hence. But this has fallen through, for all three are on their way to Petersburg by now."

To Modeste Tchaikovsky.

"*March* 13*th* (25*th*), 1881.

"DEAR MODI,—In Nice I heard by telegram from Jurgenson that Nicholai Grigorievich (Rubinstein) was very ill. Then two telegrams followed from the Grand Hotel (1) that his state was hopeless, (2) that he had already passed away. I left Nice at once. Mentally, I endured the torments of the damned during my journey. I must confess, to my shame, I suffered less from the sense of my irreparable loss, than from the horror of seeing in Paris—in the Grand Hotel too—the body of poor Rubinstein. I was afraid I should not be able to bear the shock, although I exerted all my will-power to conquer this shameful cowardice. My fears were in vain. The body had been taken to the Russian church at six o'clock this morning. At the Hotel I found only Madame Tretiakov,[1] who never left Nicholas Rubinstein during the last six days of his life. She gave me all details."[2]

To N. F. von Meck.

"PARIS, *March* 16*th* (28*th*), 1881.

"You regret having written me the letter in which you gave expression to your anger against those who have embittered your life. But I never for an instant believed

---

[1] Wife of S. Tretiakov, the wealthy art patron, afterwards chief burgomaster of Moscow.

[2] These details, in the form of a long letter, were communicated by Tchaikovsky to the *Moscow Viedomosti.*

that you could really *hate* and *never forgive,* whatever might happen. It is possible to be a Christian in life and deed without clinging closely to dogma, and I am sure that un-Christian feelings could only dwell in you for a brief moment, as an involuntary protest against human wickedness. Such really good people as you do not know what *hate* means in the true sense of the word. What can be more aimless and unprofitable than hate? According to Christ's words, our enemies only injure us from *ignorance.* O, if only men could only be Christians in truth as well as in form! If only everyone was penetrated by the simple truths of Christian morality! That can never be, for then eternal and *perfect* happiness would reign on earth; and we are imperfect creations, who only understand goodness and happiness as the opposites of evil. We are, as it were, specially created to be eternally reverting to evil, to perpetually seek the ideal, to aspire to everlasting truth—and never to reach the goal. At least we should be indulgent to those who, in their blindness, are attracted to evil by some inborn instinct. Are they to be blamed because they exist only to bring the chosen people into stronger relief? No, we can only say with Christ, 'Lord, forgive them, they know not what they do.' I feel I am expressing *vague* thoughts *vaguely*—thoughts which are wandering through my mind, because a man who was good and dear to me has just vanished from this earth. But if I think and speak vaguely, I *feel* it all clearly enough. My brain is obscured to-day. How could it be otherwise in face of those enigmas—*Death, the aim and meaning of life, its finality or immortality?* Therefore the light of *faith* penetrates my soul more and more. Yes, dear friend, I feel myself increasingly drawn towards this, the one and only shield against every calamity. I am learning to love God, as formerly I did not know how to do. Now and then doubts come back to me; I still strive at times to conceive the inconceivable with my feeble intellect; but the voice of divine truth speaks louder within me. I sometimes find an indescribable joy in bowing before the Inscrutable, Omniscient God. I often pray to Him with tears in my eyes (where He is, what He is, I know not; but I know He exists), and implore Him to grant me love and peace, to pardon and enlighten me; and it is sweet to say to Him, 'Lord, Thy will be done,' because I know His will is *holy*. Let me also tell you that I see clearly the finger of God in my own life, showing me the way and upholding me in all danger. Why it has been God's will to shield me I cannot say. I wish to be *humble*, and not to regard myself as one of the elect, for God loves all His creatures equally. I only know He really cares for me, and I shed tears of gratitude for His eternal goodness. That is not enough. I want to accustom myself to the thought that all trials are good in the end. I want to love God always, not only when He sends me good, but when He proves me; for somewhere there must exist that kingdom of eternal happiness, which we seek so vainly upon earth. The time will come when all the questionings of our intellects will be answered, and we shall know why God sends us these trials. I want to believe that there is another life. When this desire becomes a fact, I shall be happy, in so far as happiness is possible in this world.

"To-day I attended the funeral service in the church, and afterwards I accompanied the remains to the Gare du Nord, and saw that the leaden coffin was packed in a wooden case and placed in a luggage van. It was painful and horrible to think that our poor Nicholai Grigorievich should return thus to Moscow. Yes, it was intensely painful. But faith has now taken root in me, and I took comfort from the thought that it was God's *inscrutable* and *holy* will."

To Modeste Tchaikovsky.

"PARIS, *March* 17*th* (29*th*), 1881.

"Modi, we shall soon meet again, so I will say nothing now about the last sad days. My present trip has been altogether unfortunate and calculated to weaken my love of going abroad. Once more I am face to face with changes which will affect my whole future life. First, the death of Nicholas Rubinstein, which is of great importance to me, and, secondly, the fact that Nadejda von Meck is on the verge of bankruptcy. I heard this talked about in Moscow, and begged her to tell me the truth. From her reply I see it is actually so. She writes that the sum I receive from her is nothing as compared to the millions that have been lost, and that she wishes to continue to pay it as before, but begs me not to mention it to anyone. But you see that this allowance is no longer a certainty, and therefore sooner or later I must return to my teaching. All this is far from cheerful."

To Nadejda von Meck.

"KAMENKA, *April 29th (May 11th)*, 1881.

"I only stayed a few days in Moscow, where I was forced to collect all my strength in order to decline most emphatically the directorship of the Conservatoire. I arrived here to-day."

To P. Jurgenson.

"KAMENKA, *May 7th (19th)*, 1881.

"As my sister is ill and has gone away with her husband, I am playing the part of the head of the family and spend most of my time with the children. This would be a nuisance if I did not care for them as though they were my own. . . . I have no inclination to compose. I wish you would commission something. Is there really nothing you want? Some external impulse might perhaps reawaken my suspended activity. Perhaps I am getting old and all my songs are sung."

To Nadejda von Meck.

"KAMENKA, *May 8th (20th)*, 1881.

"I think I have now found a temporary occupation. In my present religious frame of mind it will do me good to dip into Russian church music. At present I am studying the 'rites,' that is to say, the root of our church tunes, and I want to try to harmonise them.

"Every day I pray that God may preserve and uphold you for the sake of so many people."

To P. Jurgenson.

"KAMENKA, *May 9th (21st)*, 1881.

" I beg you to send me the following :—

"(1) I want to write a Vesper service and require the words in full.   If there is a book on sale, a kind of 'short guide to the Liturgy for laymen,' please send it to me.

"(2) I have begun to study the rites and ceremonials of the Church, but to acquire sufficient information on the subject I need Razoumovsky's *History of Church Music.* I send thanks in anticipation."

Tchaikovsky describes his condition at this time as "grey, without inspiration or joy," but "physically sound." He often felt that the spring of inspiration had run dry, but consoled himself with the remembrance that he had passed through other periods "equally devoid of creative impulse."

To E. Napravnik.

"KAMENKA, *June 17th (29th)*, 1881.

"Last winter, at N. Rubinstein's request, I wrote a Festival Overture for the concerts of the Exhibition, entitled *The Year 1812.*   Could you possibly manage to have this played?   If you like I will send the score for you to see.   It is not of any great value, and I shall not be at all surprised or hurt if you consider the style of the music unsuitable to a symphony concert."

To Modeste Tchaikovsky.

"KAMENKA, *June 21st (July 3rd)*, 1881.

"My Vesper music compels me to look into many service books, with and without music.   If you only knew how difficult it is to understand it all!   Every service contains some chants that may be modified and others that may not.   The latter—such as *Khvalitey* and *Velikoe slavoslovie* —do not present any great difficulties; but those that change—such as the canonical verses to *Gospodi vozzvakh* —are a science in themselves, for which a lifetime of study

would hardly suffice.   I should like at least to succeed in
one Canon, the one relating to the Virgin.   Imagine that,
in spite of all assistance, I can arrive neither at the words
nor the music.   I went to ask our priest to explain it to me,
but he assured me that he himself did not know anything
about it and went through the routine of his office without
referring to the Typikon.   I am swallowed up in this sea
of Graduals, Hymns, Canticles, Tropaires, Exapostelaires,
etc., etc.   I asked our priest how his assistant managed,
and how he knew how, when, and where, to sing or read (for
the Church prescribes to the smallest detail on what days,
with what voice, and how many times things have to be
read).   He replied: 'I do not know; before every service
he has to look out something for himself.'   If the initiated
do not know, what can a poor sinner like myself expect?"

To P. Jurgenson.

"KAMENKA, *June* 21*st* (*July* 3*rd*), 1881.

"I have received Bortniansky's works and looked them
through.   To edit them would be a somewhat finicking
and wearisome task, because the greater number of his
compositions are dull and worthless.   Why do you want to
issue a 'Complete Edition'?   Let me advise you to give
up this plan and only bring out a 'Selection from the
works of Bortniansky.' . . . 'Complete Edition'?   An imposing word, but out of place in connection with a man of
no great talent, who has written a mass of rubbish, and
only about a dozen good things.   I am doubtful whether
I should lend my name to such a publication . . . on the
other hand I am a musician, and live by my work; consequently there is nothing derogatory in my editing this
rubbish for the sake of what I can earn.   My pride, however, suffers from it.   Think it over and send me a reply."

To N. F. von Meck.

"KAMENKA, *July* 3*rd* (15*th*), 1881.

"I am very glad, my dear, you like my songs and duets.
I will take this opportunity of telling you which of these
vocal compositions I care for most.   Among the duets

I prefer 'Thränen' ('Tears'), and among the songs: (1) the one to Tolstoi's words, (2) the verses of Mickievicz, and (3) 'War ich nicht der Halm.' The 'Schottische Ballade' is also one of my favourites, but I am convinced it will never be so popular as I fancied it would. It should not be so much sung, as declaimed, but with the most impassioned feeling.

To P. Jurgenson.

"KAMENKA, *July* 31*st* (*August* 12*th*), 1881.

"I am working intensely hard at Bortniansky to get this dreadful work done as soon as possible. His works as a rule are quite antipathetic to me. I shall finish the job, for I always complete anything I have begun. But some day I shall actually burst with rage. . . ."

To N. F. von Meck.

"KAMENKA, *August* 24*th* (*September* 5*th*), 1881.

"I wish with all my heart you could hear my Serenade properly performed. It loses so much on the piano, and I think the middle movements—played by the violins— would win your sympathy. As regards the first and last movements you are right. They are merely a play of sounds, and do not touch the heart. The first movement is my homage to Mozart; it is intended to be an imitation of his style, and I should be delighted if I thought I had in any way approached my model. Do not laugh, dear, at my zeal in standing up for my latest creation. Perhaps my paternal feelings are so warm because it is the youngest child of my fancy. . . .

"As regards Balakirev's songs, I am quite of your opinion. They are actually little masterpieces, and I am passionately fond of some of them. There was a time when I could not listen to 'Selim's Song' without tears in my eyes, and now I rank 'The Song of the Golden Fish' very highly."

To S. I. Taneiev.

"*August 25th (September 6th),* 1881.

" I am almost certain my Vespers will not please you. I see nothing in them which would win your approval. Do you know, Sergei Ivanovich, I believe I shall never write anything good again, I am no longer in a condition to compose. What form should I choose?—none of them appeal to me. Always the same indispensable *remplissage,* the same routine, the same revolting methods, the same conventions and shams. If I were young, this aversion from composition might be explained by the fact that I was gathering my forces, and would suddenly strike out some new path of my own making. But, alas! the years are beginning to tell. To write in a naïve way, as the bird sings, is no longer possible, and I lack energy to invent something new. I do not tell you this because I hope for your encouraging denial, but simply as a fact. I do not regret it. I have worked much in my time, in a desultory way, and now I am tired. It is time to rest. . . .

" Do not speak to me of coming back to the Conservatoire ; at present this is impossible. I cannot answer for the future. You, on the contrary, seem made to carry on Rubinstein's work."

XIII

1881–1882

In one of his letters to Nadejda von Meck, written in 1876, Tchaikovsky says : " I no longer compose anything —a sure indication of an agitated mind."

From November, 1880, until September, 1881, Tchaikovsky wrote nothing—from which we may conclude that during this time he again underwent a period of spiritual and mental disturbance.

It is not surprising that during the time he spent in Moscow and Petersburg (November to February) he should not have written a note. We know that town life—to which was added at this time the anxieties attendant upon the production of two operas—stifled all his inclination for composing. His visit to Rome, with its many social obligations, was also unfavourable to creative work.

That Tchaikovsky continued to be silent even after his return to Kamenka cannot, however, be attributed to unsuitable surroundings or external hindrances. It points rather to a restless and unhappy frame of mind.

There were numerous reasons to account for this condition.

In the first place he was touched to the quick by the loss of Nicholas Rubinstein. In spite of their many differences he had loved him with all his heart, and valued him as "one of the greatest virtuosi of his day." He had also grown to regard him as one of the chief props of his artistic life. Nicholas Rubinstein was always the first, and best, interpreter of his works for pianoforte and orchestra. Whenever Tchaikovsky wrote a symphonic work, he already heard it in imagination as it would sound in the concert-room in Moscow, and knew beforehand that under Rubinstein's direction he would experience no disappointment. The great artist had the gift of discovering in Tchaikovsky's works beauties of which the composer himself was hardly conscious. There was the sonata, for instance, which Tchaikovsky "did not recognise" when he heard it played by N. Rubinstein. And now this sure and subtle interpreter of all his new works was gone for ever.

Apart from personal relations, Rubinstein's intimate connection with the Conservatoire had its influence upon Tchaikovsky. Although the latter had resigned his position there, he had not ceased to take an interest in the musical life of Moscow. After his friend's death Tchaikovsky was aware that everyone was waiting for him to decide whether he would take over Rubinstein's work. To accept this duty meant to abandon his career as a composer. There was no mental conflict, because he never hesitated for a moment in deciding that nothing in the world would make him give up his creative work. At the same time he felt so keenly the helpless position of the Conservatoire that he could not avoid some self-reproach; and thus the calm so needful for composition was constantly disturbed.

Another reason for his sadness was of a more intimate character. After many years of unclouded happiness, a time of severe trial had come to the numerous Davidov family, which was not without its influence upon Tchaikovsky. Kamenka, formerly his refuge from all the tempests of life, was no longer so peaceful a harbour, because his ever-increasing attachment to his sister's family made him more sensible of their joys and sorrows. At this time the shadows prevailed, for Alexandra Ilinichna was confined to bed by a long and painful illness, which eventually ended in her death.

Finally, Tchaikovsky suffered much at this time from the loss of his faithful servant Alexis Safronov, who had been in his service from 1873 to 1880, when he was called upon to serve his time in the army.

Tchaikovsky spent most of September, 1881, in Moscow, in the society of his brother Anatol. This visit was comparatively agreeable to him, because the greater part of Moscow society had not yet returned from their summer holidays, and he felt free.

He left Moscow on October 1st (13th).

To P. Jurgenson.

"KAMENKA, *October 8th* (*20th*), 1881.

" I inhabit the large house where my sister's family used to live, but at present there are no other human beings but myself and the woman who looks after me. I have laid myself out to complete the arrangements of Bortniansky's works for double chorus in a month. Good Lord, how I loathe Bortniansky! Not himself, poor wretch, but his wishy-washy music! Yet if I had not undertaken this work I should find myself in a bad way financially. Were I to tell you how much money I got through in Moscow, without knowing why or wherefore, you would be horrified and give me a good scolding. . . ."

To P. Jurgenson.

"KAMENKA, *October* 11*th* (23*rd*), 1881.

" DEAR FRIEND,—I know you will laugh at me when you read this letter. . . . There is a young man here of eighteen or nineteen who is very clever and capable, but dislikes his present occupation because his domestic circumstances are miserable, and he longs for a wider sphere and experience of life. He has the reputation of being honest and industrious, and knows something of the book-trade. . . . Could you make him useful in your publishing house, or in the country? Dear friend, do look after him! What can I do for him? This is ' my fate' over again. In any case I shall not abandon him, for I am sure he would come to grief here.

"Laugh if you like, but have compassion and answer me." [1]

To Nadejda von Meck.

"KIEV, *November* 9*th* (21*st*), 1881.

" Because I am deeply interested in Church music just now, I go to the churches here very frequently, especially to the ' Lavra.' [2] On Sunday the bishop celebrated services in the monasteries of Michael and the Brotherhood. The singing in these churches is celebrated, but I thought it very poor, and pretentious, with a repertory of commonplace concert pieces. It is quite different in the ' Lavra,' where they sing in their own old style, following the traditions of a thousand years, without notes and without any attempts at concert-music. Nevertheless it is an

---

[1] P. Jurgenson took this young man into his business, where he remained some time. Like Tkachenko, he was nervous and peculiar, and gave Tchaikovsky much trouble and anxiety.

[2] Monasteries of the first rank.

original and grand style of sacred singing. The public think the music of the 'Lavra' is bad, and are delighted with the sickly-sweet singing of other churches. This vexes and enrages me. It is difficult to be indifferent to the matter. My efforts to help our church music have been misunderstood. My Liturgy is forbidden. Two months ago the ecclesiastical authorities in Moscow refused to let it be sung at the memorial service for Nicholas Rubinstein. The Archbishop Ambrose pronounced it to be a *Catholic* service. . . . The authorities are pig-headed enough to keep every ray of light out of this sphere of darkness and ignorance.

"To-morrow I hope to leave for Rome, where I expect to meet my brother Modeste."

To N. F. von Meck.

"ROME, *November* 26th (*December 8th*), 1881.

"The day before yesterday I was at the concert in honour of Liszt's seventieth birthday. The programme consisted exclusively of his works. The performance was worse than mediocre. Liszt himself was present. It was touching to witness the ovation which the enthusiastic Italians accorded to the venerable genius, but Liszt's works leave me cold. They have more poetical intention than actual creative power, more colour than form—in short, in spite of being externally effective, they are lacking in the deeper qualities. Liszt is just the opposite of Schumann, whose vast creative force is not in harmony with his colourless style of expression. At this concert an Italian celebrity played; Sgambati is a very good pianist, but exceedingly cold."

To N. F. von Meck.

"ROME, *November* 27th (*December 9th*), 1881.

"I cannot take your advice to publish my opera with a French title-page. Such advances to foreign nations are repugnant to me. Do not let us go to them, let them rather come to us. If they want our operas then—not the title-page only, but the full text can be translated, as in the case of the proposed performance at Prague. So long as an opera has not crossed the Russian frontier, it is not necessary—to my mind—that it should be translated into the language of those who take no interest in it."

To N. F. von Meck.

"ROME, *December 4th* (*16th*), 1881.

"Yesterday I received sad news from Kamenka. In the neighbourhood lies a little wood, the goal of my daily walk. In the heart of the wood lives a forester with a large and lovable family. I never saw more beautiful children. I was particularly devoted to a little girl of four, who was very shy at first, but afterwards grew so friendly that she would caress me prettily, and chatter delightful nonsense, which was a great pleasure to me. Now my brother-in-law writes that this child and one of the others have died of diphtheria. The remaining children were removed to the village by his orders, but, he adds, 'I fear it is too late.' Poor Russia! Everything there is so depressing, and then this terrible scourge which carries off children by the thousand."

The violin concerto was the only one of Tchaikovsky's works which received its first performance outside Russia. This exceptional occurrence took place in Vienna. The originality and difficulty of this composition prevented Leopold Auer, to whom it was originally dedicated, from appreciating its true worth, and he declined to produce it in St. Petersburg.[1] Two years passed after its publication, and still no one ventured to play it in public. The first to recognise its importance, and to conquer its difficulties, was Adolf Brodsky. A pupil of Hellmesberger's, he held a post at the Moscow Conservatoire for a time, but relinquished it in the seventies in order to tour in Europe. For two years he considered the concerto without, as he himself says, being able to summon courage to learn it.

---

[1] Some years later Auer changed his opinion and became one of the most brilliant interpreters of this work.

Finally, he threw himself into the work with fiery energy, and resolved to try his luck with it in Vienna. Hans Richter expressed a wish to make acquaintance with the new concerto, and finally it was included in the programme of one of the Philharmonic Concerts, December 4th, 1881. According to the critics, and Brodsky's own account, there was a noisy demonstration at the close of the performance, in which energetic applause mingled with equally forcible protest. The former sentiment prevailed, and Brodsky was recalled three times. From this it is evident that the ill-feeling was not directed against the executant, but against the work. The Press notices were very hostile. Out of ten criticisms, two only spoke quite sympathetically of the concerto. The rest, which emanated from the pens of the best-known musical critics, were extremely slashing. Hanslick, the author of the well-known book, *On the Beautiful in Music*, passed the following judgment upon this work :—

" Mozart's youthful work (the *Divertimento*) would have had a more favourable position had it been played after, instead of before, Tchaikovsky's Violin Concerto ; a drink of cold water is welcome to those who have just swallowed brandy. The violinist, A. Brodsky, was ill-advised to make his first appearance before the Viennese public with this work. The Russian composer, Tchaikovsky, certainly possesses no commonplace talent, but rather one which is forced, and which, labouring after genius, produces results which are tasteless and lacking in discrimination. Such examples as we have heard of his music (with the exception of the flowing and piquant Quartet in D) offer a curious combination of originality and crudeness, of happy ideas and wretched affectations. This is also the case as regards his latest long and pretentious Violin Concerto. For a time it proceeds in a regular fashion, it is musical and not without inspiration, then crudeness gains the upper hand and reigns to the end of the first movement. The violin is no longer played, but rent asunder, beaten black and blue. Whether it is actually possible to give clear effect to these hair-raising difficulties I do not know, but I am sure Herr Brodsky in trying to do so made us suffer martyrdom as well as himself. The Adagio, with its tender Slavonic sadness, calmed and charmed us once more, but it breaks off suddenly, only to be followed by a finale which plunges us into the brutal, deplorable merriment of a Russian holiday carousal. We see savages, vulgar faces, hear coarse oaths and smell fusel-oil. Friedrich Fischer, describing lascivious paintings, once said there were pictures 'one could see stink.' Tchaikovsky's Violin Concerto brings us face to face for the first time with the revolting idea: May there not also be musical compositions which we can hear stink?"

Hanslick's criticism hurt Tchaikovsky's feelings very deeply. To his life's end he never forgot it, and knew it by heart, just as he remembered word for word one of Cui's criticisms dating from 1866. All the deeper and more intense therefore was his gratitude to Brodsky. This sentiment he expressed in a letter to the artist, and in the dedication of the Concerto he replaced Auer's name by that of Brodsky.

While Tchaikovsky was touched by Brodsky's courage in bringing forward the Concerto, he was unable to suppress his sense of injury at the attitude of his intimate friend Kotek, who weakly relinquished his original intention of introducing the work in St. Petersburg. Still more did he resent the conduct of Auer, who, he had reason to believe, not only declined to produce the Concerto himself, but advised Sauret not to play it in the Russian capital.

To N. F. von Meck.
                                    ROME, 1881.

"Do you know what I am writing just now? You will be very much astonished. Do you remember how you once advised me to compose a trio for pianoforte, violin, and violoncello, and my reply, in which I frankly told you that I disliked this combination? Suddenly, in spite of this antipathy, I made up my mind to experiment in this form, which so far I have never attempted. The beginning of the trio is finished. Whether I shall carry it through, whether it will sound well, I do not know, but I should like to bring it to a happy termination. I hope you will believe me, when I say that I have only reconciled myself to the combination of piano and strings in the hope of giving you pleasure by this work. I will not conceal from you that I have had to do some violence to my feelings before I could bring myself to express my musical ideas in a new and unaccustomed form. I wish to conquer all difficulties, however; and the thought of pleasing you impels me and encourages my efforts."

To N. F. von Meck.

"ROME, *December 22nd*, 1881 (*January 3rd*, 1882).

"Things are well with me in the fullest sense of the word. . . . If everything were well in Russia, and I received good news from home, it would be impossible to conceive a better mode of life. But unhappily it 'is not so. Our dear, but pitiable, country is passing through a dark hour. A vague sense of unrest and dissatisfaction prevails throughout the land; all seem to be walking at the edge of a volcanic crater, which may break forth at any moment. . . .

"According to my ideas, now or never is the time to turn to the people for counsel and support; to summon us all together and to let us consider in common such ways and means as may strengthen our hands. The Zemsky Sobor—this is what Russia needs. From us the Tsar could learn the truth of things; we could help him to suppress rebellion and make Russia a happy and united country. Perhaps I am a poor politician, and my remarks are very naive and inconsequential, but whenever I think the matter over, I see no other issue, and cannot understand why the same thought does not occur to him, in whose hands our salvation lies. Katkov, who describes all parliamentary discussions as talkee-talkee, and hates the words *popular representation* and *constitution*, confuses the idea of the Zemsky Sabor, which was frequently summoned in old days when the Tsar stood in need of counsel, with the Parliaments and Chambers of Western Europe. A Zemsky Sobor is probably quite opposed to a constitution in the European sense; it is not so much a question of giving us at once a responsible Ministry, and the whole routine of English parliamentary procedure, as of revealing the true state of things, giving the Government the confidence of the people, and showing us some indication of where and how we are being led.

"I had no intention of turning a letter to you into a political dissertation. Forgive me, dear friend, if I have bored you with it. I only meant to tell you the Italian sun is beautiful, and I am enjoying the glory of the South; but I live the life of my country, and cannot be completely at rest here so long as things are not right with us. Nor is the news I receive from my family in Russia very cheerful just now."

To P. Jurgenson.

"ROME, *January 4th* (*16th*), 1882.

"This season I have no luck. *The Maid of Orleans* will not be given again; *Oniegin* ditto; Auer intrigues against the Violin Concerto; no one plays the Pianoforte Concerto (the second); in short, things are bad. But what makes me furious, and hurts and mortifies me most, is the fact that the Direction, which would not spend a penny upon *The Maid of Orleans*, has granted 30,000 roubles for the mounting of Rimksy-Korsakov's *Sniegourochka*. Is it not equally unpleasant to you to feel that 'our subject' has been taken from us, and that Lel will now sing new music to the old words? It is as though someone had forcibly torn away a piece of myself and offered it to the public in a new and brilliant setting. I could cry with mortification."

To N. F. von Meck.

"ROME, *January 13th* (*25th*), 1882.

"The trio is finished. . . . Now I can say with some conviction that the work is not bad. But I am afraid, having written all my life for the orchestra, and only taken

2 E

late in life to chamber music, I may have failed to adapt the instrumental combinations to my musical thoughts. In short, I fear I may have arranged music of a symphonic character as a trio, instead of writing directly for my instruments. I have tried to avoid this, but I am not sure whether I have been successful."

To N. F. von Meck.

"ROME, *January* 16*th* (28*th*), 1882.

" I have just read the pamphlet you sent me (*La Vérité aux nihilistes*) with great satisfaction, because it is written with warmth, and is full of sympathy for Russia and the Russians. I must observe that it is of no avail as an argument against Nihilism. The author speaks a language which the Nihilists cannot understand, since no moral persuasion could change a tiger into a lamb, or induce a New Zealand cannibal to love his neighbour in a true Christian spirit. A Nihilist, after reading the pamphlet, would probably say: ' Dear sir, we know already from innumerable newspapers, pamphlets, and books, all you tell us as to the uselessness of our murders and dynamite explosions. We are also aware that Louis XVI. was a good king, and Alexander II. a good Tsar, who emancipated the serfs. Nevertheless we shall remain assassins and dynamiters, because it is our vocation to murder and blow up, with the object of destroying the present order of things.'

" Have you read the last volume of Taine's work upon the Revolution? No one has so admirably characterised the unreasoning crowd of anarchists and extreme revolutionists as he has done. Much of what he says respecting the French in 1793, of the degraded band of anarchists who perpetrated the most unheard-of crimes before the eyes of the nation, which was paralysed with astonishment, applies equally to the Nihilists. . . . The attempt to convince the Nihilists is useless. They must be exterminated ; there is no other remedy against this evil."

At the end of January Tchaikovsky sent the Trio to Moscow with a request that it might be tried by Taneiev,

Grjimali, and Fitzenhagen.   His letter to Jurgenson concludes as follows :—

"The Trio is dedicated to Nicholas G. Rubinstein.   It has a somewhat plaintive and funereal colouring.   As it is dedicated to Rubinstein's memory it must appear in an *édition de luxe*.   I beg Taneiev to keep fairly accurately to my metronome indications.   I also wish him to be the first to bring out the Trio next season. . . ."

To P. Jurgenson.

"ROME, *February 5th* (17*th*), 1882.

" MY DEAR FRIEND,—Your letters always bring me joy, comfort, and support.   God knows I am not lying !   You are the one regular correspondent through whom I hear all that interests me in Moscow—and I still love Moscow with a strange, keen affection.   I say 'strange,' because in spite of my love for it I cannot live there.   To analyse this psychological problem would lead me too far afield."

To A. Tchaikovsky.

"ROME, *February 7th* (19*th*), 1882.

" Toly, my dearest, I have just received your letter with the details of your engagement.   I am heartily glad you are happy, and I think I understand all you are feeling, although I never experienced it myself.   There is a certain kind of yearning for tenderness and consolation that only a wife can satisfy.   Sometimes I am overcome by an insane craving for the caress of a woman's touch.   Sometimes I see a sympathetic woman in whose lap I could lay my head, whose hands I would gladly kiss.   When you are quite calm again—after your marriage—read *Anna Karenina*, which I have read lately for the first time with an enthusiasm bordering on fanaticism (*sic*).   What you are now feeling is there wonderfully expressed with reference to Levin's marriage."

To P. Jurgenson.

"NAPLES, *February* 11*th* (23*rd*), 1882.

"Are you not ashamed of trying to 'justify' yourself of the accusation brought against you by my protégé Klimenko? I know well enough that you cannot be unjust. I know, on the other hand, that Klimenko is a crazy fellow who loses his head over Nekrassov's poetry and vague echoes of Nihilism. Nevertheless he is not stupid, and it would be a pity to discharge him. I feel unless he can make himself an assured livelihood in Moscow he will do no good elsewhere. I beg you to be patient a little longer, in the hope he will come to himself, and see where his own interests lie."

To N. F. von Meck.

"NAPLES, *February* 13*th* (25*th*), 1882.

"What a blessing to feel oneself safe from visitors—to be far from the noise of large hotels and the bustle of the town! What an inexhaustible source of enjoyment to admire this incomparable view, which stretches in all its beauty before our windows! All Naples, Vesuvius, Castellammare, Sorrento, lie before us. At sunset yesterday it was so divinely beautiful that I shed tears of gratitude to God. . . . I feel I shall not do much work in Naples. It is clearly evident that this town has contributed nothing to art or learning. To create a book, a picture, or an opera, it is necessary to become self-concentrated and oblivious of the outer world. Would that be possible in Naples? . . .

"Even the sun has spots, therefore it is not surprising that our abode, about which I have been raving, should gradually reveal certain defects. I suffer from a shameful weakness: I am mortally afraid of mice. Imagine, dear friend, that even as I write to you, a whole army of mice are probably conducting their manœuvres across the floor overhead. If a solitary one of their hosts strays into my room, I am condemned to a night of sleeplessness and torture. May Heaven protect me!"

Shortly afterwards, the landlord of this mouse-infested residence—the Villa Postiglione—turned out "an impudent thief," and Tchaikovsky, with his brother Modeste, returned to an hotel in the town.

To N. F. von Meck.

"NAPLES, *March 7th* (*19th*), 1882.

" To-day I finished my Vespers. . . . It is very difficult to work in Naples.   Not only do its beauties distract one, but there is also the nuisance of the organ grinders.   These instruments are never silent for an instant, and sometimes drive me to desperation.   Two or three are often being played at the same time; someone will also be singing, and the trumpets of the Bersaglieri in the neighbourhood go on unceasingly from 8 a.m. until midday.

" In my leisure hours I have been reading a very interesting book, published recently, upon Bellini.   It is written by his friend, the octogenarian Florimo.   I have always been fond of Bellini.   As a child I often cried under the strong impression made upon me by his beautiful melodies, which are impregnated with a kind of melancholy.   I have remained faithful to his music, in spite of its many faults : the weak endings of his concerted numbers, the tasteless accompaniments, the roughness and vulgarity of his recitatives.   Florimo's book contains not only Bellini's life, but also his somewhat extensive correspondence.   I began to read with great pleasure the biography of this composer, who for long years past had been surrounded in my imagination with an aureole of poetical feeling.   I had always thought of Bellini as a childlike, naïve being, like Mozart. Alas ! I was doomed to disillusion.   Bellini, in spite of his talent, was a very commonplace man.   He lived in an atmosphere of self-worship, and was enchanted with every bar of his own music.   He could not tolerate the least contradiction, and suspected enemies, intrigues, and envy in all directions ; although from beginning to end of his career success never left him for a single day.   Judging from his letters, he loved no one, and, apart his own interests, nothing existed for him.   It is strange that the author of the book does not seem to have observed that these letters show

Bellini in a most unfavourable light, otherwise he would surely not have published them. Another book which I am enjoying just now is Melnikov's *On the Hills*. What an astonishing insight into Russian life, and what a calm objective attitude the author assumes to the numerous characters he has drawn in this novel! Dissenters of various kinds (*Rasskolniki*), merchants, moujiks, aristocrats, monks and nuns—all seem actually living as one reads. Each character acts and speaks, not in accordance with the author's views and convictions, but just as they would do in real life. In our day it is rare to meet with a book so free from ' purpose.'

10 *p.m.*

". . . One thing spoils all my walks here—the beggars, who not only beg, but display their wounds and deformities, which have a most unpleasant and painful effect upon me. But to sit at the window at home, to gaze upon the sea and Mount Vesuvius in the early morning, or at sunset, is such heavenly enjoyment that one can forgive and forget all the drawbacks of Naples."

Tchaikovsky spent a few days at Sorrento before going to Florence, whence he returned to Moscow about the middle of April.

XIV

To M. Tchaikovsky.

"KAMENKA, *May* 10*th* (*22nd*), 1882.

"Modi, I am writing at night with tears in my eyes. Do not be alarmed—nothing dreadful has happened. I have just finished *Bleak House*, and shed a few tears, first, because I pity Lady Dedlock, and find it hard to tear myself away from all these characters with whom I have been living for two months (I began the book when I left Florence), and secondly, from gratitude that so great a writer as Dickens ever lived. . . . I want to suggest to you a capital subject for a story. But I am tired, so I will leave it until to-morrow.

" Subject for a Story.

" The tale should be told in the form of a diary, or letters to a friend in England. Miss L. comes to Russia. Everything appears to her strange and ridiculous. The family into which she has fallen please her—especially the children —but she cannot understand why the whole foundation of family life lacks the discipline, the sense of Christian duty, and the good bringing-up which prevail in English homes. She respects this family, but regards them as belonging to a different race, and the gulf between herself and them seems to grow wider. She draws into herself and remains there. Weariness and oppression possess her. The sense of duty, and the need of working for her family, keep her from despair. She is religious, in the English way, and finds the Russian Church, with its ritual, absurd and repugnant. Some of the family and their relations with her must be described in detail.

" A new footman appears upon the scene. At first she does not notice him at all. One day, however, she becomes aware that he has looked at her in particular—and love steals into her heart. At first she does not understand what has come over her. Why does she sympathise with him when he is working—others have to work too? Why does she feel so ill at ease when he waits on her? Then the footman begins to make love to the laundrymaid. In her feeling of hatred for this girl she realises she is jealous, and discovers her love. She gives the man all the money she has saved to go on a journey for his health, etc. She begins to love everything Russian. . . . She changes her creed. The footman is dismissed for some fault. She struggles with herself—but finally goes with him. One fine day he says to her : ' Go to the devil and take your ugly face with you ! What do you want from me ? ' I really do not know how it all ends. . . ."

To N. F. von Meck.

" KAMENKA, *May 29th (June 10th),* 1882.

" . . . You ask me why I chose the subject of *Mazeppa.* About a year ago K. Davidov (Director of the Petersburg

Conservatoire) passed on this libretto to me. It is arranged by Bourenin from Poushkin's poem *Poltava*. At that time it did not please me much, and although I tried to set a few scenes to music, I could not get up much enthusiasm, so put it aside. For a whole year I sought in vain for some other book, because the desire to compose another opera increased steadily. Then one day I took up the libretto of *Mazeppa* once more, read Poushkin's poem again, was carried away by some of the scenes and verses —and set to work upon the scene between Maria and Mazeppa, which is taken without alteration from the original text. Although I have not experienced as yet any of the profound enjoyment I felt in composing *Eugene Oniegin*; although the work progresses slowly and I am not much drawn to the characters—I continue to work at it because I have started, and I believe I may be successful. As regards Charles XII. I must disappoint you, dear friend. He does not come into my opera, because he only played an unimportant part in the drama between Mazeppa, Maria, and Kochoubey.'

The first symphony concert in the hall of the Art and Industrial Exhibition took place on May 18th (30th), 1882, under the direction of Anton Rubinstein. On this occasion Taneiev played Tchaikovsky's Second Pianoforte Concerto for the first time in public. It was received with much applause, but it was difficult to determine whether this was intended for the composer, or the interpreter.

To N. F. von Meck.

"GRANKINO, *June 9th* (21st), 1882.

" The quiet and freedom of this place delight me. This is true country life! The walks are very monotonous; there is nothing but the endless, level Steppe. The garden is large, and will be beautiful, but at present it is new. In the evening the Steppe is wonderful, and the air so exquisitely pure; I cannot complain. The post only comes once a week, and there are no newspapers. One lives here in complete isolation from the world, and that has a great fascination for me. Sometimes I feel—to a certain extent —the sense of perfect contentment I used always to experience in Brailov and Simaki. O God, how sad it is to think that those moments of inexpressible happiness will never return!"[1]

To N. F. von Meck.

"GRANKINO, *July* 5*th* (17*th*), 1882.

"The news about Skobeliev only reached us a week after the sad catastrophe. It is long since any death has given me a greater shock than this. In view of the lamentable lack of men of mark in Russia, what a loss is this personality, on whom so many hopes depended!"

To P. Jurgenson.

"KAMENKA, *July* 26*th* (*August* 7*th*), 1882.

"My sister has just returned from Carlsbad, having stopped at Prague on the way to hear my *Maid of Orleans*, or *Panna Orleanska*, as she is called there. It appears the opera was given in the barrack-like summer theatre, and both the performance and staging were very poor."

This first appearance of one of Tchaikovsky's operas upon the stage of a West-European theatre passed almost unnoticed. The work had a *succès d'estime* and soon disappeared from the repertory of the Prague opera house. The Press were polite to the well-known symphonist Tchaikovsky, and considered that as regarded opera he deserved respect, sympathy, and interest, although he was not entitled to be called a dramatic composer "by the grace of God."

The programme of the sixth symphony concert (August 8th (20th) 1882) of the Art and Industrial Exhibition was made up entirely from the works of Tchaikovsky, and included: (1) *The Tempest;* (2) Songs from *Sniegourochka;* (3) the Violin Concerto (with Brodsky as

---

[1] Nadejda von Meck had sold Brailov.

soloist); (4) the *Italian Capriccio*; (5) Songs; (6) the Overture "1812." The last-mentioned work was now heard for the first time, and the Violin Concerto—although it had already been played in Vienna, London, and New York—for the first time in Russia. The success of these works, although considerable, did not equal that which has since been accorded them. Among many laudatory criticisms, one was couched in an entirely opposite spirit. Krouglikov said that the three movements of the Violin Concerto were so "somnolent and wearisome that one felt no desire to analyse it in detail." The "1812" Overture seemed to him "much ado about nothing." Finally, he felt himself obliged to state the "lamentable fact" that Tchaikovsky was "played out."

To Modeste Tchaikovsky.

"Moscow, *August 15th (27th),* 1882.

"DEAR MODI,—I found your letter when I came home an hour ago; but I have only just read it, because my mental condition was such that I had to collect myself first. What produces this terrible state?—I do not understand it myself. . . . Everything has tended to make to-day go pleasantly, and yet I am so depressed, and have suffered so intensely, that I might envy any beggar in the street. It all lies in the fact that life is impossible for me, except in the country or abroad. Why this is so, God knows—but I am simply on the verge of insanity.

"This undefinable, horrible, torturing malady, which declares itself in the fact that I cannot live a day, or an hour, in either of the Russian capitals without suffering, will perhaps be explained to me in some better world. . . . I often think that all my discontent springs from my own egoism, because I cannot sacrifice myself for others, even those who are near and dear to me. Then comes the comforting thought that I should not be suffering martyrdom except that I regard it as a kind of duty to come here now and then, for the sake of the pleasure it gives others. The devil knows! I only know this: that unattractive as

Kamenka may be, I long for my corner there, as one longs for some inexpressible happiness. I hope to go there to-morrow."

To N. F. von Meck.

" KAMENKA, *August 23rd (September 4th),* 1882.

" DEAR, INCOMPARABLE FRIEND,—How lovely it is here! How freely I breathe once more! How delighted I am to see my dear room again! How good to live once more as one pleases, not as others order! How pleasant to work undisturbed, to read, to play, to walk, to be oneself, without having to play a different part a thousand times a day! How insincere, how senseless, is social life!"

XV

1882–1883

To N. F. von Meck.

" KAMENKA, *September 14th (26th),* 1882.

" Never has any important work given me such trouble as this opera (*Mazeppa*). Perhaps it is the decadence of my powers, or have I become more severe in self-judgment? When I remember how I used to work, without the least strain, and knowing no such moments of doubt and uncertainty, I seem to be a totally different man. Formerly I wrote as easily, and as much in obedience to the law of nature, as a fish swims in water or a bird flies. Now I am like a man who carries a precious, but heavy, burden, and who must bear it to the last at any cost. I, too, shall bear mine to the end, but sometimes I fear my strength is broken and I shall be forced to cry halt!"

To Modeste Tchaikovsky.

" KAMENKA, *September 20th (October 2nd),* 1882.

" I am writing on a true autumnal day. Since yesterday a fine rain has been falling like dust, the wind howls, the green things have been frost-bitten since last week—yet I am not depressed. On the contrary, I enjoy it. It is only in this weather that I like Kamenka ; when it is fine, I always long to be elsewhere.

" I have begun the instrumentation of the opera. The introduction, which depicts Mazeppa and the galloping horse, will sound very well ! . . ."

To E. Napravnik.

" KAMENKA, *September 21st (October 3rd)*, 1882.

" Kamenskaya tells me that in case of the revival of *The Maid of Orleans* she would be glad to undertake the part again, if I would make the cuts, changes, and transpositions which you require. Apart from the fact that it is very desirable this opera should be repeated, and that I am prepared to make any sacrifice for this end, your *advice* alone is sufficient to make me undertake all that is necessary without hesitation. . . . Yet I must tell you frankly, nothing is more unpleasant than the changing of modulations, and the transposition of pieces which one is accustomed to think of in a particular tonality, and I should be *very glad* if the matter could be arranged without my personal concurrence. At the same time, I repeat that I am willing to do whatever you advise."

To P. Jurgenson.

" KAMENKA, *October 20th (November 1st)*, 1882.

" The copy of the Trio which you sent me gave me the greatest pleasure. I think no other work of mine has appeared in such an irreproachable edition. The title-page delighted me by its exemplary simplicity."

The Trio was given for the first time at one of the quartet evenings of the Musical Society in Moscow, October 18th (30th). Judging from the applause, the public was very much pleased with the work, but the critics were sparing in their praise.

In a letter to the composer Taneiev says :—

" I have studied your Trio for more than three weeks, and worked at it six hours a day. I ought long since to have written to you about this glorious work. I have never had greater pleasure in studying a new composition. The majority of the musicians here are enchanted with the Trio. It also pleased the public. Hubert has received a number of letters asking that it may be repeated."

To S. I. Taneiev.

" KAMENKA, *October 29th* (*November 10th*), 1882.

" My best thanks for your letter, dear Serge Ivanovich. Your approval of my Trio gives me very great pleasure. In my eyes you are a great authority, and my artistic vanity is as much flattered by your praise, as it is insensible to the opinions of the Press, for experience has taught me to regard them with philosophical indifference. . . .

" *Mazeppa* creeps along tortoise-fashion, although I work at it daily for several hours. I cannot understand why I am so changed in this respect. At first I feared it was the loss of power that comes with advancing years, but now I comfort myself with the thought that I have grown stricter in self-criticism and less self-confident. This is perhaps the reason why it now takes me three days to orchestrate a thing that I could formerly have finished in one."

To N. F. von Meck.

" KAMENKA, *November 3rd* (*15th*), 1882.

". . . I think—if God grants me a long life—I shall never again compose an opera. I do not say, with you and many others, that opera is an inferior form of musical art. On the contrary, uniting as it does so many elements which all serve the same end, it is perhaps the richest of musical forms. I think, however, that personally I am more inclined to symphonic music, at least I feel more free and independent when I have not to submit to the requirements and conditions of the stage."

To N. F. von Meck.

"KAMENKA, *November* 10*th* (22*nd*), 1882.

"Napravnik sends me word that *The Maid of Orleans* will be remounted in Prague, and Jurgenson writes that he would like to go there with me. I, too, would like to see my opera performed abroad. Very probably we shall go direct to Prague next week, and afterwards I shall return with him to Moscow, where I must see my brother. . . ."

To N. F. von Meck.

"Moscow, *November* 23*rd* (*December* 5*th*), 1882.

"I have made the acquaintance of Erdmannsdörfer, who has succeeded Nicholas Rubinstein as conductor of the Symphony Concerts. He is a very gifted man, and has taken the hearts of the musicians and the public by storm. The latter is so fickle: it received Erdmannsdörfer with such enthusiasm, one would think it valued him far more highly than Rubinstein, who never met with such warmth. Altogether Moscow is not only reconciled to the loss of Rubinstein, but seems determined to forget him.

"I am torn to pieces as usual, so that I already feel like a martyr, as I always do in Moscow or Petersburg. It has gone to such lengths that to-day I feel quite ill with this insane existence, and I am thinking of taking flight."

To N. F. von Meck.

"Moscow, *December* 5*th* (17*th*) 1882.

"To the many fatigues of the present time, one more has been added; every day I have to sit for some hours to the painter Makovsky. The famous art collector, P. Tretiakov, commissioned him to paint my portrait, so that I could not very well refuse. You can fancy how wearisome it is to me to have to sit for hours, when I find even the minutes necessary for being photographed simply horrible. Nevertheless the portrait seems very successful.[1]

[1] This portrait was one of the least successful of Makovsky's efforts. A far better portrait of the composer was made some years later by Kouznietsov. See frontispiece.

I forget if I have already told you that at the last concert but one my Suite was given with great success. Erdmannsdörfer proved a good conductor, although I think the Moscow Press and public greatly overrate his capabilities. . . . My work is not yet finished, so I shall hardly be able to leave before next week."

Tchaikovsky left Moscow on December 28th (January 9th, 1883), travelling by Berlin to Paris, where he met his brother Modeste, who was to accompany him to Italy.

To N. F. von Meck.

"BERLIN, *December* 31*st*, 1882 (*January* 12*th*, 1883).

"I broke my journey to rest here. Yesterday *Tristan and Isolde* (which I had never seen) was being given at the Opera, so I decided to remain another day. The work does not give me any pleasure, although I am glad to have heard it, for it has done much to strengthen my previous views of Wagner, which—until I had seen all his works performed—I felt might not be well grounded. Briefly summed up, this is my opinion : in spite of his great creative gifts, in spite of his talents as a poet, and his extensive culture, Wagner's services to art—and to opera in particular—have only been of a negative kind. He has proved that the older forms of opera are lacking in all logical and æsthetic *raison d'être*. But if we may no longer write opera on the old lines, are we obliged to write as Wagner does? I reply, *Certainly not.* To compel people to listen for four hours at a stretch to an endless symphony which, however rich in orchestral colour, is wanting in clearness and directness of thought ; to keep singers all these hours singing melodies which have no independent existence, but are merely notes that belong to this symphonic music (in spite of lying very high these notes are often lost in the thunder of the orchestra), this is certainly not the ideal at which contemporary musicians should aim. Wagner has transferred the centre of gravity from the stage to the orchestra, but this is an obvious absurdity, therefore his famous operatic reform— —viewed apart from its negative results—amounts to nothing. As regards the dramatic interest of his operas, I find them very poor, often childishly naïve. But I have never been quite so bored as with *Tristan and Isolde*. It is an endless void, without movement, without life, which cannot hold the spectator, or awaken in him any true sympathy for the characters on the stage. It was evident that the audience—even though Germans—were bored, but they applauded loudly after each act. How can this be explained? Perhaps by a patriotic sympathy for the composer, who actually devoted his whole life to singing the praise of Germanism."

To A. Merkling.

"PARIS, *January* 10*th* (22*nd*), 1882.

"I have seen a few interesting theatrical performances, among others Sardou's *Fedora*, in which Sarah Bernhardt played with *arch-genius*, and would have made the most poignant impression upon me if the play—in which a clever but cold Frenchman censures our Russian customs—were not so full of lies. I have finally come to the conclusion that Sarah is really a woman of genius.[1] I also enjoyed Musset's play, *On ne badine pas avec l'amour*. After the theatre I go to a restaurant and drink punch (it is bitterly cold in Paris). . . ."

To N. F. von Meck.

"PARIS, *January* 11*th* (23*rd*), 1883.

"I have just come from the Opera Comique, where I heard *Le Nozze di Figaro*. I should go every time it was given. I know my worship of Mozart astonishes you, dear friend. I, too, am often surprised that a broken man, sound neither in mind nor spirit, like myself, should still be able to enjoy Mozart, while I do not succumb to the depth and force of Beethoven, to the glow and passion of Schumann, nor the brilliance of Meyerbeer, Berlioz, and Wagner. Mozart is not oppressive or agitating. He captivates, delights and comforts me. To hear his

---

[1] It is interesting to know that this opinion was in direct opposition to that of Tourgeniev, who made some harsh criticisms upon the celebrated French actress.—R. N.

music is to feel one, has accomplished some good action.
It is difficult to say precisely wherein this good influence
lies, but undoubtedly it is beneficial ; the longer I live and
the better I know him, the more I love his music.

"You ask why I never write anything for the harp.
This instrument has a beautiful timbre, and adds greatly
to the poetry of the orchestra. But it is not an independent instrument, because it has no *melodic* quality, and
is only suitable for harmony. True, artists like Parish-
Alvars have composed operatic fantasias for the harp,
in which there are melodies ; but this is rather forced.
Chords, arpeggios—these form the restricted sphere of the
harp, consequently it is only useful for accompaniments."

Before Tchaikovsky left Moscow he had been approached
by Alexeiev, the president of the local branch of the
Russian Musical Society, with regard to the music to be
given at the Coronation festivities, to take place in the
spring of 1883. A chorus of 7,500 voices, selected from
all the educational institutions in Moscow, was to greet
the Emperor and Empress with the popular ' Slavsia,' from
Glinka's opera, *A Life for the Tsar.* The arrangement of
this chorus, with accompaniment for string orchestra, was
confided to Tchaikovsky. In January he accomplished
this somewhat uncongenial task, and sent it to Jurgenson
with the following remarks :—

"There are only a few bars of 'original composition' in
the work, besides the third verse of the text, so if—as you
say—I am to receive a fee from the city of Moscow, my
account stands as below :—

"For the simplification of six-
    teen bars of choral and
    instrumental music, to be
    repeated three times   . 3 r.
"For the composition of eight
    connecting bars   .   . 4 r.
"For four additional lines to
    the third verse, at forty
    kopecks per line   .   . 1 r. 60 k.
                Total .   . 8 r. 60 k. (16/11½)

2 F

"This sum I present to the city of Moscow. Joking apart, it is absurd to speak of payment for such a work, and, to me, most unpleasant. These things should be done gratuitously, or not at all."

To N. F. von Meck.

"PARIS, *February 5th* (*17th*), 1883.

"I have not read Daudet's *L'Evangéliste*, although I have the book. I cannot conquer a certain prejudice; it is not the author's fault, but all these sects, the Salvation Army—and all the rest of them—are antipathetic to me, and since in this volume Daudet (whom I like as much as you do) deals with a similar subject, I have no wish to read it.

"As regards French music, I will make the following remarks in justification of my views. I do not rave about the music of the new French school as a whole, nor about each individual composer, so much as I admire the influence of the novelty and freshness which are so clearly discernible in their music. What pleases me is their effort to be eclectic, their sense of proportion, their readiness to break with hard-and-fast routine, while keeping within the limits of musical grace. Here you do not find that ugliness in which some of our composers indulge, in the mistaken idea that *originality* consists in treading under foot all previous traditions of beauty. If we compare modern French music with what is being composed in Germany, we shall see that German music is in a state of decadence, and that apart from the eternal fluctuation between Mendelssohn and Schumann, or Liszt and Wagner, nothing is being done. In France, on the contrary, we hear much that is new and interesting, much that is fresh and forceful. Of course, Bizet stands head and shoulders above the rest, but there are also Massenet, Délibes, Guirand, Lalo, Godard, Saint-Saëns. All these are men of talent, who cannot be compared with the dry *routinier* style of contemporary Germans."

To P. Jurgenson.

"PARIS, *February 6th* (18*th*), 1883.

"DEAR FRIEND,—To-day I received a telegram from Bartsal,[1] asking if my Coronation Cantata is ready, and for what voices it is written. I am replying that I have never composed such a Cantata. Apparently it is some absurdity which does not demand serious attention, and yet I am really somewhat agitated. The matter stands as follows. Early in December I met an acquaintance whom I have regarded for many years as a commonplace fool. But this fool was suddenly put upon the Coronation Commission. One day, after lunch, he took me aside and inquired: 'I trust you are not a Nihilist?' I put on an air of surprise, and inquired why he had to ask such a question. 'Because I think it would be an excellent thing if you were to compose something suitable for the Coronation—something in a festival way—something patriotic—in short, write something. . . .' I replied that I should be very pleased to compose something, but I could not supply my own text, that would have to be commissioned from Maikov, or Polonsky, then I should be willing to write the music. Our conversation ended here. Afterwards I heard that this man was saying all over Petersburg that he had commissioned me to write a Cantata. I had forgotten the whole story until the telegram came this morning. I am afraid the story may now be grossly exaggerated, and the report be circulated that I refused to compose such a work. I give you leave to use all possible means to have the matter put in the true light, and so to exonerate me."

To N. F. von Meck.

"PARIS, *February 24th* (*March 8th*), 1883.

"*Henry VIII.*, by Saint-Saëns, was recently given at the Grand Opéra. I did not go, but, according to the papers, the work had no signal success. I am not surprised, for I know his other operas, *Samson et Dalila*,

---

[1] A. I. Bartsal, chief manager of the Imperial Opera, in Moscow.

Etienne Màrcel, and *La Princesse Jaune*, and all three have strengthened my conviction, that Saint-Saens will never write a great dramatic work. Next week I will hear the opera, and tell you what I think of it.

" In consequence of his death, Wagner is the hero of the hour with the Parisian public. At all three Sunday concerts (Pasdeloup, Colonne and Lamoureux) the programmes have been devoted to his works, with the greatest success. Curious people ! It is necessary to die in order to attract their attention. In consequence of the death of Flotow, there was a vacancy in the *Académie des Beaux Arts*. Gounod put me forward as one of the five candidates, but I did not attain to this honour. The majority of votes went to the Belgian composer Limnander."

XVI

At this time two unexpected and arduous tasks fell to Tchaikovsky's lot. The city of Moscow commissioned him to write a march for a fête, to be given in honour of the Emperor in the Sokolniky Park, and the Coronation Committee sent him the libretto of a lengthy cantata, with a request that the music might be ready by the middle of April. These works he felt it his duty to undertake. For the march he declined any payment, for reasons which he revealed to Jurgenson, under strict pledges of secrecy. When, two years earlier, his financial situation had been so dark that he had undertaken the uncongenial task of editing the works of Bortniansky, he had, unknown to all his friends, applied for assistance to the Tsar. After the letter was written, he would gladly have destroyed it, but his servant had already taken it to the post. Some days later he received a donation of 3,000 roubles (£300). He resolved to take the first opportunity of giving some return for this gift, and the Coronation March was the outcome of this mingled feeling of shame and gratitude.

His projected journey to Italy was abandoned, and he decided to remain some weeks longer in Paris.

To P. Jurgenson.

"PARIS, *March 9th (21st)*, 1883.

"About the middle of August I received, in Moscow, the manuscript of the *Vespers*, with the Censor's corrections. You then requested me to carry out these corrections. I altered what was actually essential. As regards the rest, I sent you an explanation to be forwarded to the Censor. . . . What has become of it? Either you have lost it, or the Censor is so obstinate and dense that one can do nothing with him. The absurdity is that I have not *composed* music to the words of the Vesper Service, but taken it from a book published by the Synodal Press. I have only harmonised the melodies as they stood in this book. . . . In short, I have improved everything that was capable of improvement. I will not endure the caprices of a drivelling pedant. He can teach me nothing, and the Synodal book is more important than he is. I shall have to complain about him. There . . . he has put me out for a whole day!"

To P. Jurgenson.

"PARIS, *April 14th (26th)*, 1883.

"You reproach me because the pieces Rubinstein played belong to Bessel.[1] I am very sorry, but I must say in self-justification that had I had any suspicion twelve years ago that it would be the least deprivation to you *not* to possess anything of mine, I would on no account have been faithless to you. . . . In those days I had no idea that I could wound your feelings by going to Bessel. Now I would give anything to get the pieces back again. A curious man Anton Rubinstein! Why could he not pay some attention to these pieces ten years ago? Why did he never play a note of my music then? That would indeed have been a service! I am grateful to him, even now, but it is a very different matter."

---

[1] Six pianoforte pieces, Op. 21.

To Modeste Tchaikovsky.

"PARIS, *April* 14*th* (26*th*), 1883
" (*Thursday in Passion Week*).

"DEAR MODI,—I am writing in a café in the Avenue Wagram. This afternoon I felt a sudden desire to be—if not actually in our church — at least somewhere in its vicinity. I am so fond of the service for to-day. To hold the wax-taper and make little pellets of wax after each gospel ; at first, to feel a little impatient for the service to come to an end, and afterwards to feel sorry it is over! But I arrived too late, only in time to meet the people coming out and hear them speak Russian."

To N. F. von Meck.

"PARIS, *May* 3*rd* (15*th*), 1883.

" Loewenson's article, with its flattering judgment of me, does not give me much pleasure. I do not like the repetition of that long-established opinion that I am not a *dramatic musician*, and that I *pander* to the public. What does it mean — to have dramatic capabilities? Apparently Herr Loewenson is a Wagnerian, and believes Wagner to be a great master in this sphere. I consider him just the reverse. Wagner has genius, but he certainly does not understand the art of writing for the stage with breadth and simplicity, keeping the orchestra within bounds, so that it does not reduce the singers to mere speaking *puppets*. As to his assertion that I aim at effects to catch the taste of the great public, I can plead not guilty with a clear conscience. I have always written, and always shall write, with feeling and sincerity, never troubling myself as to what the public would think of my work. At the moment of composing, when I am aglow with emotion, it flashes across my mind that all who will hear the music will experience some reflection of what I am feeling myself. Then I think of someone whose interest I value—like yourself, for instance—but I have never deliberately tried to lower myself to the vulgar requirements of the crowd. If opera attracts me from time to time, it signifies that I have as much capacity for this as for any other form. If I have had many failures in this branch of music, it only proves that I am a long way from perfection, and make the same mistakes in my operas as in my symphonic and chamber music, among which there are many unsuccessful compositions. If I live a few years longer, perhaps I may see my *Maid of Orleans* suitably interpreted, or my *Mazeppa* studied and staged as it should be; and then possibly people may cease to say that I am incapable of writing a good opera. At the same time, I know how difficult it will be to conquer this prejudice against me as an operatic composer. This is carried to such lengths that Herr Loewenson, who knows nothing whatever of my new work, declares it will be a *useless sacrifice* to the Moloch of opera. . . ."

To N. F. von Meck.

"BERLIN, *May 12th (24th)*, 1883.

". . . A report has been circulated in many of the Paris papers that Rubinstein had refused to compose a Coronation Cantata because he was not in sympathy with the *central figure of the festivities.* As Rubinstein's children are being educated in Russia, and this might be prejudicial to his interests—for even the most baseless falsehood always leaves some trace behind it—I sent a brief *dementi* to the *Gaulois* the day I left Paris. I cannot say if it will be published.[1]

"To-day *Lohengrin* is being given. I consider it Wagner's best work, and shall probably go to the performance. To-morrow I leave for Petersburg."

In April, 1883, *Eugene Oniegin* was heard for the first time in St. Petersburg, when it was performed by the Amateur Dramatic and Musical Society in the hall of the Nobles' Club. It was coolly received, and the performance made so little impression that it was almost ignored by the Press. Soloviev, alone, wrote an article of some length in the St. Petersburg *Viedomosti,* in which he said :—

[1] The letter appeared on May 23rd (June 4th), 1883.

"Tchaikovsky's opera—apart from the libretto and stage effects—contains much that is musically attractive. Had the composer paid more attention to Poushkin's words and shown greater appreciation of their beauty; had he grasped the simplicity and naturalness of Poushkin's forms—the opera would have been successful. Having failed in these requirements, it is not surprising that the public received the work coldly. . . ."

Nevertheless the opera survived several performances. The lack of success—apart from the quality of the music, which never at any time aroused noisy demonstrations of applause—must be attributed to the performance, which was excellent for amateurs, but still left much to be desired from the artistic point of view.

To N. F. von Meck.

"PETERSBURG, *May 24th (June 5th)*, 1883.

"I hear the Cantata was admirably sung and won the Emperor's approval."

To N. F. von Meck.

"PODOUSHKINO, *June 15th (27th)*, 1883.

"In my youth I often felt indignant at the apparent injustice with which Providence dealt out happiness and misfortune to mankind. Gradually I have come to the conviction that from our limited, earthly point of view we cannot possibly comprehend the aims and ends towards which God guides us on our way through life. Our sufferings and deprivations are not sent blindly and fortuitously; they are needful for our good, and although the good may seem very far away, some day we shall realise this. Experience has taught me that suffering and bitterness are frequently for our good, even in this life. But after this life *perhaps* there is another, and—although my intellect cannot conceive what form it may take—my heart and my instinct, which revolt from death in the sense of complete annihilation, compel me to believe in it.

Perhaps we may then understand the things which now appear to us harsh and unjust. Meanwhile, we can only pray, and thank God when He sends us happiness, and submit when misfortune overtakes us, or those who are near and dear to us. I thank God who has given me this conviction. Without it life would be a grievous burden. Did I not know that you, the best of human beings, and above all deserving of happiness, were suffering so much, not through an insensate blow aimed by a blind destiny, but for some divine end which my limited reason cannot discern—then, indeed, there would remain for me in life nothing but despair and loathing. I have learnt not to murmur against God, but to pray to Him for all who are dear to me."

To Modeste Tchaikovsky.

"PODOUSHKINO,[1] *July 3rd* (15*th*), 1883.

"My incapacity for measuring time correctly is really astonishing! I believed I should find leisure this summer for everything—for reading, correspondence, walks ; and suddenly I realise that from morning to night I am tormented with the thought that I have not got through all there was to do. . . . Added to which, instead of resting from composition, I have taken it into my head to write a Suite. Inspiration will not come ; every day I begin something and lose heart. Then, instead of waiting for inspiration, I begin to be afraid lest I am played out, with the result that I am thoroughly dissatisfied with myself. And yet the conditions of life are satisfactory : wonderful scenery and the society of those I love. . . ."

During this visit to Podoushkino, Tchaikovsky wrote to Jurgenson concerning their business relations. Actually, this connection remained unbroken to the end of the composer's life, but at this moment it suffered a temporary strain. Tchaikovsky acknowledged that his publisher had often been most generous in his payments, but as

[1] From Petersburg Tchaikovsky went on a visit to his brother Anatol, who had taken summer quarters at Podoushkino, near Moscow.

regards his new opera *Mazeppa* he felt aggrieved at the small remuneration proposed by Jurgenson. This work, he said, ought, logically speaking, to be worth ten times as much as ten songs, or ten indifferent pianoforte pieces. He valued it at 2,400 roubles (£240). On the other hand, he asked no fee for his Coronation Cantata.

To N. F. von Meck.

"PODOUSHKINO, *August 10th (22nd),* 1883.

"Yesterday a council was held by the Opera Direction to consider the staging of *Mazeppa.* Everyone connected with the Opera House was present. I was astonished at the zeal—I may say enthusiasm—which they showed for my opera. Formerly what trouble I had to get an opera accepted and performed! Now, without any advances on my part, Petersburg and Moscow contend for my work. I was told yesterday that the direction at St. Petersburg had sent the scenic artist Bocharov to Little Russia, in order to study on the spot the moonlight effect in the last act of *Mazeppa.* I cannot understand the reason of such attentions on the part of the theatrical world—there must be some secret cause for it, and I can only surmise that the Emperor himself must have expressed a wish that my opera should be given as well as possible in both capitals.[1]

"The corrections are now complete, and I am sending you the first printed copy. Dear friend, now I must take a little rest from composition, and lie fallow for a time. But the *cacoethes scribendi* possesses me, and all my leisure hours are devoted to a Suite. I hope to finish it in a day or two, and set to work upon the instrumentation at Kamenka.

"My health is better. I have gone through such a terrible attack of nervous headache, I thought I must have died. I fell asleep so worn out, I had not even strength to undress. When I awoke I was well."

[1] This agreeable change in the attitude of the authorities towards Tchaikovsky was due to the influence of I. Vsievolojsky, who had recently been appointed Director of the Opera House.

XVII

1883–1884

To N. F. von Meck.

"VERBOVKA, *September* 10*th* (22*nd*), 1883.

"With regard to my opera, you have picked out at first sight the numbers I consider the best. The scene between Mazeppa and Maria will, thanks to Poushkin's magnificent verses, produce an effect even off the stage. It is a pity you will not be able to see a performance of *Mazeppa*. Allow me, dear friend, to point out other parts of the opera which can easily be studied from the pianoforte score: In Act I. (1), the duet between Maria and Andrew; (2), Mazeppa's *arioso*. Act II. (1), the prison scene; (2), Maria's scene with her mother. Act III., the last duet."

To M. Tchaikovsky.

"VERBOVKA, *September* 12*th* (24*th*), 1883.

". . . I bought Glazounov's Quartet in Kiev, and was pleasantly surprised. In spite of the imitations of Korsakov, in spite of the tiresome way he has of contenting himself with the endless repetition of an idea, instead of its development, in spite of the neglect of melody and the pursuit of all kinds of harmonic eccentricities—the composer has undeniable talent. The form is so perfect, it astonishes me, and I suppose his teacher helped him in this. I recommend you to buy the Quartet and play it for four hands. I have also Cui's opera, *The Prisoner of the Caucasus*. This is utterly insignificant, weak, and childishly naïve. It is most remarkable that a critic who has contended throughout his days against routine, should now, in the evening of his life, write a work so shamefully conventional."

To Modeste Tchaikovsky.

"VERBOVKA, *September* 19*th* (*October* 1*st*), 1883.

". . . On my arrival here I found a parcel from Tkat-chenko at Poltava. It contained all my letters to him. As on a former occasion, when he thought of committing suicide, he sent me back two of my letters, I understood at once that he wished by this means to intimate his immediate intention of putting an end to his existence. At first I was somewhat agitated; then I calmed myself with the reflection that my Tkatchenko was certainly still in this world. In fact, to-day I received a letter from him asking for money, but without a word about my letters. His, as usual, is couched in a scornful tone. He is a man to be pitied, but not at all sympathetic." [1]

To M. Tchaikovsky.

"VERBOVKA, *September* 26*th* (*October* 8*th*), 1883.

" My Suite progresses slowly; but it seems likely to be successful. I am almost sure the Scherzo (with the Har-monica) and the Andante ('Children's Dreams') will please. My enthusiasm for *Judith* has made way for a passion for *Carmen*. I have also been playing Rimsky-Korsakov's *Night in May*, not without some enjoyment."

To Frau von Meck.

"VERBOVKA, *September* 28*th* (*October* 10*th*), 1883.

" I will tell you frankly, dear friend, that, although I gladly hear some operas—and even compose them myself —your somewhat paradoxical view of the untenability of operatic music pleases me all the same. Leo Tolstoi says the same with regard to opera, and strongly advised me to give up the pursuit of theatrical success. In *Peace and War* he makes his heroine express great astonishment and dissatisfaction with the falseness and limitations of operatic action. Anyone who, like yourself, does not live in society and is not therefore trammelled by its conven-

---

[1] This was the end of all relations between Tchaikovsky and Tkatchenko.

tions, or who, like Tolstoi, has lived for years in a village, and only been occupied with domestic events, literature, and educational questions, must naturally feel more intensely than others the complete falseness of Opera. I, too, when I am writing an opera feel so constrained and fettered that I often think I will never compose another. Nevertheless, we must acknowledge that many beautiful things of the first order belong to the sphere of dramatic music, and that the men who wrote them were directly inspired by the dramatic ideas. Were there no such thing as opera, there would be no *Don Juan*, no *Figaro*, no *Russlan and Lioudmilla*. Of course, from the point of view of the sane mind, it is senseless for people on the stage—which should reflect reality—to sing instead of speaking. People have got used to this absurdity, however, and when I hear the sextet in *Don Giovanni* I never think that what is taking place before me is subversive of the requirements of artistic truth. I simply enjoy the music, and admire the astonishing art of Mozart, who knew how to give each of the six voices its own special character, and has outlined each personality so sharply that, forgetful of the lack of *absolute truth*, I marvel at the depth of *conditional truth*, and my intellect is silenced.

"You tell me, dear friend, that in my *Eugene Oniegin* the musical pattern is more beautiful than the canvas on which it is worked. I must say, however, that if my music to *Eugene Oniegin* has the qualities of warmth and poetic feeling, it is because my own emotions were quickened by the beauty of the subject. I think it is altogether unjust to see nothing beautiful in Poushkin's poem but the versification. Tatiana is not merely a provincial ' Miss,' who falls in love with a dandy from the capital. She is a young and virginal being, untouched as yet by the realities of life, a creature of pure feminine beauty, a dreamy nature, ever seeking some vague ideal, and striving passionately to grasp it. So long as she finds nothing that resembles an ideal, she remains unsatisfied but tranquil. It needs only the appearance of a man who—at least externally—stands out from the commonplace surroundings in which she lives, and at once she imagines her ideal has come, and in her passion becomes oblivious of self.

Poushkin has portrayed the power of this virginal love with such genius that—even in my childhood—it touched me to the quick. If the fire of inspiration really burned within me when I composed the 'Letter Scene,' it was Poushkin who kindled it; and I frankly confess, without false modesty, that I should be proud and happy if my music reflected only a tenth part of the beauty contained in the poem. In the 'Duel Scene' I see something far more significant than you do. Is it not highly dramatic and touching that a youth so brilliant and gifted (as Lensky) should lose his life because he has come into fatal collision with a false code of mundane 'honour'? Could there be a more dramatic situation than that in which that 'lion' of town-life (Oniegin), partly from *sheer boredom*, partly from petty annoyance, but without purpose—led by a fatal chain of circumstances—shoots a young man to whom he is really attached? All this is very simple, very ordinary, if you like, but poetry and the drama do not exclude matters of simple, everyday life."

To N. F. von Meck.

"KAMENKA, *October* 11*th* (*23rd*), 1883.

"My work is nearly finished. Consequently, so long as I have no fresh composition in view, I can quietly enjoy this glorious autumn weather.

"My Suite has five movements: (1) Jeux de sons, (2) Valse, (3) Scherzo burlesque, (4) Rêves d'enfants, (5) Danse baroque."

To N. F. von Meck.

"*October* 25*th* (*November* 6*th*), 1883.

"Every time I finish a work I think rapturously of a season of complete idleness. But nothing ever comes of it; scarcely has the holiday begun, before I weary of idleness and plan a new work. This, in turn, takes such a hold on me that I immediately begin again to rush through it with unnecessary haste. It seems my lot to be always hurrying to finish something. I know this is equally bad for my nerves and my work, but I cannot control myself. I only rest when I am on a journey;

that is why travelling has such a beneficial effect on my health. Probably I shall never settle anywhere, but lead a nomadic existence to the end of my days. Just now I am composing an album of 'Children's Songs,' an idea I have long purposed carrying out. It is very pleasant work, and I think the little songs will have a great success."

To Frau von Meck.

"KAMENKA, *November 1st (13th)*, 1883.

" I should feel quite happy and contented here, were it not for the morbid, restless need of hurrying on my work, which tires me dreadfully, without being in the least necessary. . . .

" I had a fancy to renew my study of English. This would be harmless, were I content to devote my leisure hours quietly to the work. But no : here again, I am devoured by impatience to master enough English to read Dickens easily, and I devote so many hours a day to this occupation that, with the exception of breakfast, dinner, and the necessary walk, I literally spend every minute in hurrying madly to the end of something. This is certainly a disease. Happily, this feverish activity will soon come to an end, as my summons to the rehearsals in Moscow will shortly be due."

XVIII

Towards the end of November Tchaikovsky left Kamenka for Moscow, where, after a lapse of sixteen years, his First Symphony was given at a concert of the Musical Society. He was greatly annoyed to find that the preparations for *Mazeppa* were proceeding with exasperating slowness. " It is always the way with a State theatre," he wrote at this time to Nadejda von Meck. " Much promised, little performed." While at Moscow, he played his new Suite to some of the leading musicians, who highly approved of the work.

A few days later he went to meet Modeste in Petersburg. He left the dry cold of a beautiful Russian winter in Moscow, and found the more northern capital snowless, but windy, chilly, and "so dark in the morning that even near the window I can hardly see to write."

The journeys to and fro involved by the business connected with *Mazeppa*, and all the other difficulties he had to encounter in connection with it, were very irksome to Tchaikovsky. At this time he vowed never to write another opera, since it involved the sacrifice of so much time and freedom.

To N. F. von Meck.

"Moscow, *December* 11th (23rd), 1883.

"How can you think me capable of taking offence at anything you may say, especially with regard to my music? I cannot always agree with you, but to be offended because your views are not mine would be impossible. On the contrary, I am invariably touched by the warmth with which you speak of my compositions, and the originality and independence of your judgment pleased me from the first. For instance, I am glad that, in spite of my having composed six operas, when you compare Opera with Symphony or Chamber music, you do not hesitate to speak of it as a lower form of art. In my heart I have felt the same, and intend henceforth to renounce operatic music; although you must acknowledge opera possesses the advantage of touching the musical feeling of the *masses;* whereas symphony appeals only to a smaller, if more select, public. . . ."

Christmas and the New Year found Tchaikovsky still in Moscow, awaiting the rehearsals for *Mazeppa*. As usual, when circumstances detained him for any length of time in town, he suffered under the social gaieties which he had not the strength of will to decline. Laroche was staying in the same hotel as Tchaikovsky, and was in a hypochondriacal condition. "He needs a *nurse*," says Tchaikovsky in one of his letters, "and I have undertaken the part, having no work on hand just now. When I depart, he will relapse into the same apathetic state."

At last, on January 15th (27th), the rehearsals for the opera began, and with them a period of feverish excitement. The preparations for *Mazeppa* had been so long postponed that they now coincided with the staging of the work in Petersburg. Tchaikovsky declined the invitation to be present at the rehearsals there, feeling he could safely entrust his opera to the experienced supervision of Napravnik.

The first performance of *Mazeppa* in Moscow took place on February 3rd (15th), under the direction of H. Altani. The house was crowded and brilliant. The audience was favourably disposed towards the composer, and showed it by unanimous recalls for him and for the performers. Nevertheless, Tchaikovsky felt instinctively that the ovations were accorded to him personally, and to such of the singers who were favourites with the public, rather than to the opera itself. The ultimate fate of *Mazeppa*, which attracted a full house on several occasions, but only kept its place in the repertory for a couple of seasons, confirmed this impression. The failure may be attributed in some degree to the quality of the performance. Some of the singers had no voices, and those who were gifted in this respect lacked the necessary musical and histrionic training, so that not one number of the opera was rightly interpreted. Only the chorus was irreproachable. As regards the scenery and dresses, no opera had ever been so brilliantly staged. The Moscow critics were fairly indulgent to the opera and to its composer. To Nadejda von Meck, Tchaikovsky wrote: "The opera was successful in the sense that the singers and myself received ovations. . . . I cannot attempt to tell you what I went through that day. I was nearly crazed with excitement."

2 G

To E. Pavlovskaya.[1]

"Moscow, *February 4th* (16*th*), 1884.

"DEAR AND SUPERB EMILIE KARLOVNA,—I thank you heartily, incomparable Maria, for your indescribably beautiful performance of this part. God give you happiness and success. I shall never forget the deep impression made upon me by your splendid talent."

After informing a few friends of his intended journey— amongst them Erdmannsdórfer—Tchaikovsky left Moscow just at the moment when the public had gathered in the Concert Hall to hear his new Suite.

The Suite (No. 2 in C) had such a genuine and undisputed success under Erdmannsdorfer's excellent direction on February 4th (16th), that it had to be repeated by general request at the next symphony concert, a week later. The Press was unanimous in its enthusiasm, and even the severe Krouglikov was moved to lavish and unconditional praise.

The Petersburg performance of *Mazeppa*, under Napravnik, took place on February 7th (19th). The absence of the composer naturally lessened its immediate success, but the impression was essentially the same as in Moscow: the opera obtained a mere *succès d'estime*. As regards acting, the performance of the chief parts (Mazeppa and Maria) was far less effective than at its original production. On the other hand, the staging and costumes excelled in historical fidelity and brillancy even those of the Moscow performance. Comparing the reception of *Mazeppa* in the two capitals, we must award the palm to the Petersburg critics for the unanimity with which they "damned" the work.

[1] The singer who created the part of Maria in the Moscow performance of *Mazeppa*.

To N. F. von Meck.

"BERLIN, *February 7th (19th)*, 1884.

"Early this morning I received a telegram from Modeste, who informs me that the performance of *Mazeppa* in Petersburg yesterday was a complete success, and that the Emperor remained to the end and was much pleased.[1] To morrow I continue my journey to Paris and from thence to Italy, where I might possibly join Kolya and Anna,[2] unless I should disturb their *tête-à-tête*. I dread being alone. . . ."

To M. Tchaikovsky.

"PARIS, *February 18th (March 1st)*, 1884.

"Modi, I can well imagine how difficult it must have been for you to lie to me as to the '*grand succès*' of *Mazeppa* in Petersburg. But you did well to tell a lie, for the *truth* would have been too great a blow, had I not been prepared for it by various indications. Only yesterday did I learn the worst in a letter from Jurgenson, who not only had the cruelty to blurt out the plain truth, but also to reproach me for not having gone to Petersburg. It came as a thunderbolt upon me, and all day I suffered, as though some dreadful catastrophe had taken place. Of course, this is exaggeration, but at my age, when one has nothing more to hope in the future, a slight failure assumes the dimensions of a shameful fiasco. Were I different, could I have forced myself to go to Petersburg, no doubt I should have returned crowned with laurel wreaths. . . ."

To P. Jurgenson.

"PARIS, *February 18th (March 1st)*, 1884.

"It is an old truth that no one can hurt so cruelly as a dear friend. Your reproach is very bitter. Do you not understand that I know better than anyone else how

---

[1] On account of Tchaikovsky's nervous condition the account of the success of *Mazeppa* was slightly overdrawn.

[2] Nicholas and Anna von Meck, *née* Davidov (Tchaikovsky's niece), who were on their wedding tour.

much I lose, and how greatly I injure my own success, by my unhappy temperament? As a card-sharper, who has cheated all his life, lifts his hand against the man who has made him realise what he is, so nothing makes me so angry as the phrase: 'You have only yourself to blame.' It is true in this case; but can I help being what I am? The comparative failure of *Mazeppa* in Petersburg, of which your letter informed me, has wounded me deeply— very deeply. I am in a mood of darkest despair."

To N. F. von Meck.

"PARIS, *February* 27*th* (*March* 10*th*), 1884.

"You have justly observed that the Parisians have become Wagnerites. But in their enthusiasm for Wagner, which is carried so far that they neglect even Berlioz— who, a few years ago, was the idol of the Paris public —there is something insincere, artificial, and without any real foundation. I cannot believe that *Tristan and Isolde*, which is so intolerably wearisome on the stage, could ever charm the Parisians. . . . It would not surprise me that such excellent operas as *Lohengrin, Tannhäuser,* and the *Flying Dutchman* should remain in the repertory. These, originating from a composer of the first rank, must sooner or later become of general interest. The operas of the later period, on the contrary, are false in principle; they renounce artistic simplicity and veracity, and can only live in Germany, where Wagner's name has become the watch-word of German patriotism. . . ."

To N. F. von Meck.

"PARIS, *February* 29*th* (*March* 12*th*), 1884.

". . . Napravnik writes that the Emperor was much astonished at my absence from the first performance of *Mazeppa*, and that he showed great interest in my music; he has also commanded a performance of *Eugene Oniegin*, his favourite opera. Napravnik thinks I must not fail to go to Petersburg to be presented to the Emperor. I feel if I neglect to do this I shall be worried by the thought that the Emperor might consider me ungrateful, and so I have decided to start at once. It is very hard, and I have to make a great effort to give up the chance of a holiday in the country and begin again with fresh excitements. But it has to be done."

XIX

The official command to appear before their Imperial Majesties was due to the fact that on February 23rd (March 6th), 1884, the order of St. Vladimir of the Fourth Class had been conferred upon Tchaikovsky. The presentation took place on March 7th (19th), at Gatchina. Tchaikovsky was so agitated beforehand that he had to take several strong doses of bromide in order to regain his self-possession. The last dose was actually swallowed on the threshold of the room where the Empress was awaiting him, in agony lest he should lose consciousness from sheer nervous breakdown.

To Anatol Tchaikovsky.

"PETERSBURG, *March* 10*th* (22*nd*), 1884.

" I will give you a brief account of what took place. Last Saturday I was taken with a severe chill. By morning I felt better, but I was terribly nervous at the idea of being presented to the Emperor and Empress. On Monday at ten o'clock I went to Gatchina. I had only permission to appear before His Majesty, but Prince Vladimir Obolensky had also arranged an audience with the Empress, who had frequently expressed a wish to see me. I was first presented to the Emperor and then to the Empress. Both were most friendly and kind. I think it is only necessary to look once into the Emperor's eyes, in order to remain for ever his most loyal adherent, for it is difficult to express in words all the charm and sympathy of his manner. She is also bewitching. Afterwards I had to visit the Grand Duke Constantine Nicholaevich, and yesterday I sat with him in the Imperial box during the whole of the rehearsal at the Conservatoire."

To N. F. von Meck.

"PETERSBURG, *March* 13th (25th), 1884.

"What a madman I am! How easily I am affected by the least shadow of ill-luck! Now I am ashamed of the depression which came over me in Paris, simply because I gathered from the newspapers that the performance of *Mazeppa* in Petersburg had not really had the success I anticipated! Now I see that in spite of the ill-feeling of many local musicians, in spite of the wretched performance, the opera really pleased, and there is no question of reproach, as I feared while I was so far away. There is no doubt that the critics, who unanimously strove to drag my poor opera through the mire, were not expressing the universal opinion, and that many people here are well disposed towards me. What pleases me most is the fact that the Emperor himself stands at the head of this friendly section. It turns out that I have no right to complain; on the contrary, I ought rather to thank God, who has shown me such favour.

"Have you seen Count Leo Tolstoi's *Confessions*, which were to have come out recently in the *Russkaya Myssl* ('Russian Thought'), but were withdrawn by order of the Censor? They have been privately circulated in manuscript, and I have just succeeded in reading them. They made a profound impression upon me, because I, too, know the torments of doubt and the tragic perplexity which Tolstoi has experienced and described so wonderfully in the *Confessions*. But *enlightenment* came to me earlier than Tolstoi; perhaps because my brain is more simply organised than his; and perhaps it has been due to the continual necessity of work that I have suffered less than Tolstoi. Every day, every hour, I thank God for having given me this faith in Him. What would have become of me, with my cowardice, my capacity for depression, and—at the least failure of courage—my desire for *non-existence*, unless I had been able to believe in God and submit to His will?"

About the end of the seventies Tchaikovsky kept an accurate diary. Ten years later he relaxed the habit, and only made entries in his day-book while abroad, or on important occasions. Two years before his death the composer burnt most of these volumes, including all those which covered the years between his journeys abroad in 1873 and April, 1884.

The following are a few entries from the later diaries:—

"*April* 13*th* (25*th*), 1884.

". . . After tea I went to Leo's,[1] who soon went out, while I remained to strum and think of something new. I hit upon an idea for a pianoforte Concerto [afterwards the Fantasia for pianoforte, op 56], but it is poor and not new. . . . Played Massenet's *Hérodiade*. . . read some of Otto Jahn's *Life of Mozart*."

On April 16th (28th) Tchaikovsky began his third orchestral Suite, and we can follow the evolution of this work, as noted from day to day in his diary.

"*April* 16*th* (28*th*), 1884.

" In the forest and indoors I have been trying to lay the foundation of a new symphony . . . but I am not at all satisfied. . . . Walked in the garden and found the germ, not of a symphony, but of a future Suite."

"*April* 17*th* (29*th*).

". . . Jotted down a few ideas."

" *April* 19*th* (*May* 1*st*).

" Annoyed with my failures. Very dissatisfied because everything that comes into my head is so commonplace. Am I played out?"

April 24*th* (*May* 6*th*).

" I shall soon be forty-four. How much I have been through, and—without false modesty—how little I have accomplished ! In my actual vocation I must say—hand on heart—I have achieved nothing perfect, nothing which can serve as a model. I am still seeking, vacillating.

---

[1] His brother-in-law, Leo Davidov.

And in other matters? I read nothing, I know nothing. . . . The period of quiet, undisturbed existence is over for me. There remain agitation, conflict, much that I, such as I am, find hard to endure. No, the time has come to live by *oneself* and in *one's own way !*"

"*April 26th (May 8th)*.

"This morning I worked with all my powers at the Scherzo of the Suite. Shall work again after tea."

"*April 30th (May 12th)*, 1884.

"Worked all day at the Valse (Suite), but without any conviction of success."

Extracts from a Letter to Anna Merkling.

"KAMENKA, *April 27th (May 9th)*, 1884.

"Many thanks, dear Anna, for your thought of me on the 25th (May 7th). . . . Without bitterness, I receive congratulations upon the fact that I am a year older. I have no wish to die, and I desire to attain a ripe old age; but I would not willingly have my youth back and go through life again. Once is enough! The past, of which you speak with regret, I too regret it, for no one likes better to be lost in memories of old days, no one feels more keenly the emptiness and brevity of life—but I do not wish to be young again. . . . I cannot but feel that the sum total of good which I enjoy at present is far greater than that which stood to my credit in youth: therefore I do not in the least regret my forty-and-four years. Nor sixty, nor seventy, provided I am still sound mentally and physically! At the same time one ought not to fear death. In this respect I cannot boast. I am not sufficiently penetrated by religion to regard death as the beginning of a new life, nor am I sufficiently philosophical to be satisfied with the prospect of *annihilation*. I envy no one so much as the religious man. . . ."

Diary.
"*May 2nd (14th)*.

"The Valse gives me infinite trouble. I am growing old. . . ."

"*May 6th* (18*th Sunday*).

"Went to church. I was very susceptible to religious impressions, and felt the tears in my eyes. The simple, healthy, religious spirit of the poorer classes always touches me profoundly. The worn-out old man, the little lad of four, who goes to the holy water of his own accord."

"*May 8th* (20*th*), 1884.

"Worked all morning. Not without fatigue, but my Andante progresses, and seems likely to turn out quite nice ... finished the Andante. I am very pleased with it."

At this time Tchaikovsky resolved to take a small country house on his own account. "I want no land," he wrote to Nadejda von Meck, "only a little house, with a pretty garden, *not too new*. A *stream* is most desirable. The neighbourhood of a forest (which belonged to some-one else) would be an attraction. The house must stand alone, not in a row of country villas, and, most important of all, be within easy reach of a station, so that I can get to Moscow at any time. I cannot afford more than two to three thousand roubles."

Diary.
"*May* 11*th* (23*rd*), 1884.

"The first movement of the Suite, which is labelled 'Contrasts,' and the theme :

has grown so hateful since I tormented myself about it all day long that I resolved to set it aside and invent some-thing else. After dinner I squeezed the unsuccessful movement out of my head. What does it mean? I now work with such difficulty! Am I really growing old?"

"*May 12th (24th).*"

"After tea I took up the hateful 'Contrasts' once more. Suddenly a new idea flashed across me, and the whole thing began to flow."

"*May 17th (29th).*"

"Played Mozart, and enjoyed it immensely. An idea for a Suite from Mozart."

"*May 18th (30th).*"

"I am working too strenuously, as though I were being driven. This haste is unhealthy, and will, perhaps, reflect upon the poor Suite. My work (upon the variations before the finale) has been very successful. . . .'"

"*May 21st (June 2nd).*"

"Worked well. Four variations completed."

"*May 23rd (June 4th).*"

". . . . The Suite is finished."

To P. Jurgenson.

"GRANKINO, *June 20th (July 2nd),* 1884.

"I live here in a very pleasant way, a quiet, countrified existence, but I work hard. A work of greater genius than the new Suite never was!!! My opinion of the new-born composition is so optimistic; God knows what I shall think of it a year hence. At least it has cost me some pains."

To S. I. Taneiev.

"GRANKINO, *June 30th (July 12th),* 1884.

". . . . Although it was interesting to hear your opinion of my songs, I was rather angry with you for saying nothing whatever about your own work, plans, etc.

"Your criticisms of the songs—the end of the 'Legend,' and the abuse of the minor in the 'Lied vom Winter'— are very just. . . . I should like to say your praise was equally well deserved, but modesty forbids. So I will not say you are right, but that I am pleased with your commendations. . ."

" At the present moment I am composing a third Suite. I wanted to write a Symphony, but it was not a success. However, the title is of no consequence. I have composed a big symphonic work in four movements: (1) Andante ; (2) another Valse ; (3) Scherzo ; (4) Theme and Variations. It will be finished by the end of the summer, for I am working regularly and with zeal. Besides this, I am planning a concert-piece for pianoforte in two movements. It would be a fine thing if the work could be played during the coming season ! "

To N. F. von Meck.

"GRANKINO, *July* 14*th* (26*th*), 1884.

" I shall not set to work upon the pianoforte Concerto, of which I wrote to you, before autumn or early winter. Of course, it will be difficult ever again to find such an ideal interpreter as Nicholas Rubinstein, but there is a pianist whom I had in my mind when I thought of a second Concerto. This is a certain young man, called d'Albert, who was in Moscow last winter, and whom I heard several times in public and at private houses. To my mind he is a pianist of *genius*, the legitimate successor of Rubinstein. Taneiev—whom I value very highly as musician, teacher, and theorist—would also be a suitable interpreter, if he had just that *vein of virtuosity* wherein lies the secret of the magic spell which great interpreters exercise over the public."

To Modeste Tchaikovsky.

"SKABEIEVKA, *July* 28*th* (*August* 9*th*), 1884.

" The coachman will have told you our adventures. All went well as far as Kochenovka. There I had supper, and read *Sapho* by the mingled light of the moon and a lantern, keeping an anxious eye upon the lightning that was flashing all around. At 11.30 p.m. we resumed our journey. The storm came nearer and nearer, until it broke over our heads. Although the constant flashes were mild, and the rain wetted us through, my nerves were overstrained. I was convinced we should miss the train. . . . Fortunately it was late. Here we had an appalling storm. The sight of it at the hour of sunset, which still glowed here and there through the clouds, was so grand that, forgetful of my fears, I stood by the door to watch it. The rest of the journey was comfortable. I read *Sapho*, which I do not like."

To N. F. von Meck.

"SKABEIEVKA, *July 25th (August 6th)*, 1884.

". . . You ask my opinion upon Daudet's *Sapho* . . . in spite of his great talent, this author has long since dropped out of favour with me. If Daudet had not dedicated the book to his sons in order to display the fact that it contained a lesson and a warning, I should say that he had described the sensuality and depravity of the hero and heroine very simply and picturesquely, with considerable sympathy. But in view of this dedication I feel indignant at the Pharisaism and false virtuousness of the author. In reality he wants to tickle the depraved taste of his public, and describes with cynical frankness the immorality of Parisian life, while pretending to deliver a sermon to his sons. He would have us believe him to be pursuing a moral aim, actuated by the noble aspiration of saving the young from evil ways. In reality his only aim was to produce a book which would please the immoral Parisian public, and to make money by it. One must own that he has attained his object. The book will have a great success, like Zola's *Pot-Bouille*, the novels of Guy de Maupassant, and similar works of the new French school. When we reflect upon the group of people, and their way of life, as depicted by the author, we come to the conclusion that under the cloak of verisimilitude and realism the novel is fundamentally false. Sapho is an impossible being; at least I never came across a similar combination of honourable feeling and baseness, of nobility and infamy. Yet the author always sympathises with his heroine, and although, judging from the dedication, she is intended to inspire his sons with horror and repulsion, she must really seem very attractive to them. On the other hand, the virtuous characters in the book could not appeal sympathetically either to Daudet's sons, or to anyone else; the tiresome Divonne, the hero's impossible sister, and the rest of

them—all these people are quite artificial. Sapho is an
overdrawn type of a Parisian cocotte, but there is something true to nature in her. The others are not alive.
Most insipid of all is Irène. Any young man reading the
book must realise why Sapho succeeded in supplanting
her in the heart of her husband Jean. It is here that
Daudet's hypocrisy is so evident, for while we ought to
sympathise with Irène as greatly as we despise Sapho, in
reality we involuntarily take the part of the depraved
heroine. At the same time we cannot deny the great
talent and mastery displayed in the book. Two or three
dozen pages are wonderfully written."

XX

Early in September, 1884, Tchaikovsky went to stay at
Plestcheievo, a country property which Nadejda von Meck
had purchased after circumstances compelled her to sell
Brailov. Here he led the kind of life which suited him
best—reading, composing, and studying the works of other
musicians, in undisturbed quiet and freedom from social
duties.

To N. F. von Meck.

"PLESTCHEIEVO, *September 8th (20th),* 1884.

"I have realised two intentions since I came here—the
study of two works hitherto unknown to me—Moussorgsky's *Khovanstchina* and Wagner's *Parsifal.* In the first
I discovered what I expected : pretensions to realism,
original conceptions and methods, wretched technique,
poverty of invention, occasionally clever episodes, amid
an ocean of harmonic absurdities and affectations. . . .
Parsifal leaves an entirely opposite impression. Here we
are dealing with a great master, a genius, even if he has
gone somewhat astray. His wealth of harmony is so
luxuriant, so vast, that at length it becomes fatiguing,
even to a specialist. What then must be the feelings of an
ordinary mortal who has wrestled for three hours with this

flow of complicated harmonic combinations? To my mind Wagner has killed his colossal creative genius with *theories.* Every preconceived theory chills his incontestable creative impulse. How could Wagner abandon himself to inspiration, while he believed he was grasping some particular theory of music-drama, or musical truth, and, for the sake of this, turned from all that, according to his predecessors, constituted the strength and beauty of music? If the singer may not *sing*, but—amid the deafening clamour of the orchestra—is expected to declaim a series of set and colourless phrases, to the accompaniment of a gorgeous, but disconnected and formless symphony, is that opera?

"What really astounds me, however, is the seriousness with which this philosophising German sets the most inane subjects to music. Who can be touched, for instance, by *Parsifal*, in which, instead of having to deal with men and women similar in temperament and feeling to ourselves, we find legendary beings, suitable perhaps for a ballet, but not for a music drama? I cannot understand how anyone can listen without laughter, or without being bored, to those endless monologues in which Parsifal, or Kundry, and the rest bewail their misfortunes. Can we sympathise with them? Can we love or hate them? Certainly not; we remain aloof from their passions, sentiments, triumphs, and misfortunes. But that which is unfamiliar to the human heart should never be the source of musical inspiration. . . ."

To N. F. von Meck.

"PLESTCHEIEVO, *October 3rd* (15*th*), 1884.

"This is my last evening here, and I feel both sadness and dread. After a month of complete solitude it is not easy to return to the vortex of Petersburg life. To-day I put all the bookshelves and music-cases in order. My conscience is clear as to all your belongings. But I must confess to one mishap: one night I wound the big clock in my bedroom with such energy that the weights fell off, and it now wants repairing. Dear and incomparable friend, accept my warmest thanks for your hospitality. I shall keep the most agreeable memories of Plestcheievo.

How often, when I am in Petersburg, will my thoughts stray back to this dear, quiet house! Thank you again and again."

To N. F. von Meck.

"PETERSBURG, *October 12th (24th)*, 1884.

"DEAR FRIEND,—When a whole week passes without my finding time to write to you, you may conclude what a busy life I am leading. . . . The first night[1] of *Eugene Oniegin* is fixed for Friday, October 19th (31st)."

Thanks to Napravnik, this was by far the finest performance of *Eugene Oniegin* that had hitherto been seen. Never had this complicated score received so perfect an interpretation, both as a whole and as regards detail, because never before had a man so gifted, so capable and sympathetic, stood at the head of affairs. Yet even this first performance was by no means irreproachable. Since then, the St. Petersburg public has heard finer interpretations of the parts of Tatiana, Eugene, and others, and has seen more careful staging of the work. The soloists gave a thoughtful rendering of their parts, but nothing more. Not one of them can be said to have "created" his or her part, or left a traditional reading of it.

The success of the opera was great, but not phenomenal. There was no hissing, but between the acts, mingled with expressions of praise and appreciation, many criticisms and ironical remarks were audible.

These unfavourable views came to light in the Press. Cui thought the mere choice of the libretto of *Eugene Oniegin* proved that Tchaikovsky was lacking in "discriminating taste," and was not capable of self-criticism. The chief characteristic of the opera was its "wearisome monotony." Tchaikovsky, he considered, was too fond of airing his troubles in his music. Finally, he pronounced the work to be "still-born, absolutely valueless and weak."

Most of the other critics agreed with this view.

---

[1] At the Imperial Opera.

Tchaikovsky himself was "satisfied." He had not realised, any more than the critics, that the crowded theatre signified the first great success of a Russian opera since Glinka's *A Life for the Tsar*. In spite of the Press notices, it was not merely a success, but a triumph ; a fact which became more and more evident. Dating from the second performance, *Eugene Oniegin* drew a long series of packed audiences, and has remained the favourite opera of the Russian public to this day.

This success did not merely mark an important event in the history of Russian opera, it proved the beginning of a new era in the life of Tchaikovsky himself. Henceforward his name, hitherto known and respected among musicians and a fairly wide circle of musical amateurs, was now recognised by the great public, and he acquired a popularity to which no Russian composer had ever yet attained in his own land. Together with his increase of fame, his material prospects improved. *Eugene Oniegin* transformed him from a needy into a prosperous man, and brought him that complete independence which was so necessary to his creative work.

It is instructive to observe that all this was the outcome of an opera which was never intended to appeal to the masses ; but written only to satisfy the composer's enthusiasm for Poushkin's poem, without any hope—almost without any desire—of seeing it performed on a large stage.

In spite of its success, this performance of *Eugene Oniegin* was a great strain upon the composer's nerves. He felt bound to stay for the second performance, after which he left St. Petersburg for Davos, having in view a twofold object : to take a short rest, and to visit his friend Kotek, of whose condition he had just received disquieting intelligence. Tchaikovsky broke his journey in Berlin, where he saw Weber's *Oberon* at the Opera. Instead of being bored by this work, as he expected, he enjoyed it very much. "The music is often enchanting," he wrote to his brother, "but the subject is absurd, in the style of *Zauberflöte*. However, it is amusing, and I roared with laughter in one place, where at the sound of the magic horn the entire *corps de ballet* fall flat on the stage and writhe in convulsions. . . . I also went to Bilse's and heard the Andante from my own quartet. This everlasting Andante ; they want to hear no other work of mine ! "

On November 12th (24th) he arrived at Davos. He expected to find a wilderness, in which neither cigarettes nor cigars were to be had, and the civilised aspect of the place, the luxurious hotels, the shops, and the theatre made upon him the fantastic impression of a dream. He had dreaded the meeting with Kotek, lest his friend should be changed beyond recognition by the ravages of consumption. He was agreeably surprised to find him looking comparatively well. But this was only a first impression ; he soon realised that Kotek's condition was serious. He remained a few days at Davos, rejoiced his friend's heart by his presence, had a confidential interview with the doctor, and left for Paris on November 17th (29th), after having provided liberally for the welfare of the invalid.

To P. Jurgenson.

"ZURICH, *November* 18*th* (30*th*), 1884.

" . . . I have received a letter from Stassov urging me to present the following manuscripts to the Imperial Public Library :

(1) ' Romeo and Juliet,'
(2) ' The Tempest,'
(3) ' Francesca,'
(4) ' The String Quartet, No. 3,'

and any others I like to send. Of the above works you do not possess the first two (' The Tempest' was lost long ago !), but please send him the others. . . . Be so good as to reply personally, or simply to send such scores as you can spare."

2 H

To M. Tchaikovsky.

"Paris, *December 3rd* (15*th*), 1884.

" I can scarcely tell you, dear Modi, how wearisome the last few days have been—although I cannot say why.   It proceeds chiefly from home-sickness, the desire for a place of my own ; and even the knowledge that I start for Russia to-morrow brings no satisfaction, *because I have no home anywhere.*   Life abroad no longer pleases me. . . . I must have a *home*, be it in Kamenka, or in Moscow.   I cannot go on living the life of a wandering star. . . . Where will my *home* be ? "

With the year 1884 closes the second period in Tchaikovsky's artistic career.   To distinguish it from the "Moscow period," which was inseparably connected with his teaching at the Conservatoire, it might be described as the "Kamenka period."   Not only because from 1878–84 Kamenka was his chief place of residence, but still more because the life there answered to the whole sum of his requirements, to all which characterised his spiritual condition during these years.   After the terrible illness in 1877 he found in Kamenka, far more than in San Remo, Clarens, or France, all he needed for his recovery ; during these seven years, it was at Kamenka that he gathered force and recuperated for the life which was becoming infinitely more strenuous and many-sided.

Those who have been at death's door often speak of their return to health as the happiest time in their lives. Tchaikovsky could say the same of the first years of the Kamenka period.   Happy in the friendship of Nadejda von Meck and surrounded by his sister's family, who loved him, and whom he loved, his whole life shows no gladder days than these.

But with a gradual return to a normal state of mind Tchaikovsky's relations to his environment underwent a change.   As the years went on, Kamenka became too

narrow a circle for him ; he felt the want of " social intercourse"; the sympathy of his relations ceased to be the
one thing indispensable ; the conditions of the family life
palled, and sometimes he grumbled at them. By the
middle of the eighties, he was so much stronger that he
was possessed by a desire for complete independence and
liberty of action. He no longer dreaded either *absolute
solitude, or the society of those whose interests were identical
with his own.* By *absolute solitude* we do not mean that
solitary leisure which he enjoyed during his visits to
Brailov and Simaki, during which he was cared for, as
in a fairy tale, by the invisible hand of the truest of
friends, but rather that independence and freedom in every
detail of existence which constitutes the solitude of the
typical bachelor's life.

In 1878 Tchaikovsky's dread of this kind of solitary
existence, like his fear of social intercourse, was a symptom
of his terrible mental suffering. Now his desire for both
independence and society must be regarded as a sign of
complete recovery. Hence his increasing disposition in
his letters to grumble at Kamenka, and his final decision
to leave it. This resolve—like so many important decisions
in Tchaikovsky's life—was not the result of mature reflection. As usual, he allowed himself to be guided by
negative conclusions. . . . He knew well enough that he
must and would change his manner of life; he knew the
kind of life that would suit him for the time being—that it
must be in the country ; he observed with surprise his increasing need of social intercourse—but he had no definite
idea how he should reconcile these contradictory requirements and, on the very eve of his new departure in life, he
asks the question: " Where will my home be made ? "

The answer to this question is contained in the following period of his life and work.

Part VI

I

STRONG and energetic, fearing neither conflict nor effort, the Tchaikovsky who entered upon this new phase of life in no way resembled the man we knew in 1878.

The duties connected with his public career no longer dismayed him ; on the contrary, they proved rather attractive, now he had strength to cope with them. At the same time interests stirred within him such as could not have been satisfied in his former restricted existence. Thanks to the enormous success of *Eugene Oniegin*, his fame had now reached every class in educated Russia, and he was compelled to accept a certain rôle which—at least, in these first days of success—was not unpleasant to him. He was glad to pay attentions to others, to help everyone who came his way, because by this means he could show his gratitude to the public for the enthusiastic reception accorded to his work. He was no longer a misanthropist, rather he sought those to whom he was dear, not only as a man, but as a personage. Amongst these, his old and faithful friends in Moscow took the first place. These intimacies were now renewed, and every fresh meeting with Laroche, Kashkin, Jurgenson, Albrecht, Hubert, and Taneiev gave him the keenest delight. Although death had separated him from Nicholas Rubinstein, he showed his devotion to the memory of his friend by taking the deepest interest in his orphaned children.

468

In February, 1885, Tchaikovsky was unanimously elected Director of the Moscow branch of the Russian Musical Society.

As the most popular musician in Russia, he no longer avoided intercourse with his fellow-workers. He was ready with advice, assistance and direction, and regarded it as a duty to answer every question addressed to him. His correspondence with his "colleagues" would fill a book in itself.

He received letters not only from professional musicians, but from amateurs, male and female, students, enthusiastic girls, officers, and even occasionally from priests. To all these letters he replied with astonishing conscientiousness and strove, in so far as he could, to fulfil all their requests, which often led to touching, or sometimes grotesque, expressions of gratitude from the recipients of his favours.

As a composer Tchaikovsky no longer stood aloof, leaving the fate of his compositions to chance; nor did he regard it as *infra dig.* to make them known through the medium of influential people. After a convalescence which had lasted seven years, Tchaikovsky returned to all these activities with vigour and enjoyment, although after a time his courage flagged, and all his strength of will had to be requisitioned to enable him " to keep up this sort of existence." Enthusiasm waned, and there succeeded—in his own words—"a life-weariness, and at times an insane depression ; something hopeless, despairing, and final— and (as in every Finale) a sense of triviality."

The new conditions of his life are reflected in his constantly increasing circle of acquaintances. In every town he visited he made new friends, who were drawn to him with whole-hearted affection. With many of them he entered into brisk correspondence. In some cases this was continued until his death ; in other instances the exchange of letters ceased after a year or two, to make way for a fresh correspondence.

The most important and interesting of Tchaikovsky's correspondents during this time are: Julie Spajinsky, wife of the well-known dramatist (1885–1891); Emilie Pavlovskaya, the famous singer, with whom Tchaikovsky became acquainted during the rehearsal for *Mazeppa* in 1884, and continued to correspond until 1888; the Grand Duke Constantine Constantinovich; the composer Ippolitov-Ivanov and his wife, the well-known singer, Zaroudna; Vladimir Napravnik, son of the conductor: the pianists Sapellnikov and Siloti. With Glazounov, Désirée Artôt, Brodsky, Hubert, his cousin Anna Merkling, and many others, there was an occasional exchange of letters.

The greater part of these communications, notwithstanding the intimate style and frankness of the writer's nature, bear signs of effort, and give the impression of having been written for duty's sake. Taken as a whole, they are not so important, or so interesting, as the letters to Nadejda von Meck, and to Tchaikovsky's own family, belonging to the Moscow period.

The same may be said of the majority of new acquaintances made during the later years of his life, of which no epistolary record remains. These were so numerous that it would be impossible to speak of them individually. They included such personalities as Liadov, Altani, Grieg, Sophie Menter, Emil Sauer, Louis Diemer, Colonne, Carl Halir. Besides these, he was in touch with a vast number of people belonging to the most varied strata of social life. Among them was Legoshin, valet to his friend Kondratiev. Tchaikovsky got to know this man by the death-bed of his master, and valued his purity of heart and integrity more and more as years went by. Another unprofessional friend was the celebrated Russian general, Dragomirov. While travelling to France by sea, he made the acquaintance of an extraordinarily gifted boy, the son of Professor Sklifasskovsy. The friendship was brief as it was touching, for the youth died a year later. Tchaikovsky was deeply affected by his loss, and dedicated to his memory the *Chant Elégiaque*, op. 72.

All these new friendships served to surround the composer with that atmosphere of affection and appreciation which was as indispensable to him as his daily bread. But none of them were as deep and lasting as the ties of old days, none so close and intimate ; nor did they contribute any new element to his inner life. . . .

One word as to the dearest of all his later affections. His sister, A. Davidov, had three sons. The second of these, Vladimir, had always been Tchaikovsky's favourite from childhood. Up to the age of eighteen, however, these pleasant relations between uncle and nephew had not assumed any deep significance. But as Vladimir Davidov grew up, Tchaikovsky gradually felt for him a sentiment which can only be compared to his love for the twins, Toly and Modi, in their youth. The difference of age was no hindrance to their relations. Tchaikovsky preferred the companionship of his nephew ; was always grieved to part with him ; confided to him his inmost thoughts, and finally made him his heir, commending to this young man all those whom he still desired to assist and cherish, even after his death.

II

To N. F. von Meck.

"Moscow, *January 1st* (*13th*), 1885.

"It is so long since I wrote, dear friend ! Two events have interrupted my correspondence with you : on Christmas Eve I received a telegram announcing the death of Kotek. Not only was I much upset by this intelligence, but the sad duty of breaking the news to his parents devolved upon me. . . . I have also had to make the difficult corrections in my new Suite myself. Hans von Bülow is shortly to conduct in Petersburg, and all must be ready four or five days hence. While I was away nothing was done here. I was furious, rated Jurgenson and the engravers, and worked till I was worn out; therefore I have had no time to lament for poor Kotek."

To N. F. von Meck.

"MOSCOW, *January 5th* (*17th*), 1885.

"All my thoughts are now directed towards taking up my abode in some village near Moscow. I am no longer satisfied with a nomadic existence, and am determined to have a *home of my own* somewhere. As I am sure I am not in a position to buy a country house, I have decided to rent one."

The first performance of the Third Suite, which took place at a symphony concert in Petersburg, on January 12th (24th), 1885, under Von Bülow's direction, was a veritable triumph for Tchaikovsky. Never before had any of his works been received with such unanimous enthusiasm. Doubtless this was partly owing to the accessible and attractive character of the music, but far more to the admirable way in which it was interpreted.

Hans von Bülow was a great pianist, yet in this sphere he had rivals who almost overshadowed his fame. As a conductor, however, he ranked, after Richard Wagner, as the first man of his day. In spite of his years he was as enthusiastic as a youth, highly strung, receptive, and a fine all-round musician. He knew how to bring out every detail in a work, and thus infused his own virtuoso-inspiration into each individual player. Under him—in spite of his mannerisms and ungraceful movements—the orchestra performed wonders, and threw new light upon the most hackneyed works (such as the overture to *Freischütz*), holding the attention of the audience from the opening phrase to the last chord.

Quick, restless, and continually under the influence of some inspiration, he was as extreme and pitiless in his dislikes as he was sentimental and enthusiastic in his sympathies. He could not merely like or dislike. He hated or adored.

After having been in turn a passionate partisan of the classical masters, of Wagner and of Brahms, he became in the seventies a great admirer of Russian music, and was devoted to Tchaikovsky's works. His devotion was then at its zenith, consequently he put into his interpretation of the Third Suite not merely his accustomed experience, but all the fire of his passing enthusiasm. I say "passing," because some ten years later this enthusiasm had somewhat cooled, and he had begun to rave over the works of Richard Strauss, who at that time had scarcely entered upon his career as a composer.

To N. F. von Meck.

"Moscow, *January* 18*th* (30*th*), 1885.

"DEAR, KIND FRIEND,—Forgive me my indolence, and for so seldom writing. To-day I returned from Petersburg, where I spent a week of feverish excitement. The first few days were taken up by the rehearsals for the concert at which my new Suite was to be performed. I had a secret presentiment that it would please the public. I experienced both pleasure and fear. But the reality far surpassed my expectations. I have never had such a triumph; I could see that the greater part of the audience was touched and grateful. Such moments are the best in an artist's life. . . . On the 15th (27th) *Oniegin* was performed in the presence of the Emperor and Empress, and other members of the Tsar's family. The Emperor desired to see me. We had a long and friendly conversation, in the course of which he asked all about my life and musical work, and then took me to the Empress, who paid me the most touching attention. The following evening I returned to Moscow."

On January 16th (28th), the new Suite was given in Moscow, under Erdmannsdörfer. It met with considerable success, but not with such appreciation as in Petersburg. Erdmannsdörfer's interpretation was fine, but lacked the inspiration by means of which Hans von Bülow had electrified his audience. At this time Tchaikovsky was in search of an operatic subject. Just then, says his brother Modeste, "I was in Moscow, and remarked one day that certain scenes from Shpajinsky's play, *The Enchantress*, would make an effective opera without using the whole drama as a libretto." The following day Tchaikovsky wrote to the author, asking permission to use the play for musical setting. Shpajinsky replied that he would be pleased to co-operate with the composer.

When the time came for Tchaikovsky to find a residence in his native land, or to go abroad according to his usual custom, he was seized with an inexplicable fear of the journey, and sent his servant Alexis to take a furnished house, in the village of Maidanovo, near Klin. "The house," he wrote to Nadejda von Meck, "contains many beautifully furnished rooms, and has a fine view. Apparently it is a pleasant place to live in, but the number of rooms gives me some anxiety, because they must be heated in winter." Finally he decided to take it for a year, and should it prove beyond his means, to look out for something more suitable in the meanwhile.

The village of Maidanovo lies close to the town of Klin. The manor house stands upon a high bank, overlooking the river Sestra, and is surrounded by a large park. Once it belonged to an aristocratic Russian family, but had gradually fallen into decay. Nevertheless, it bore many traces of its former splendour : the remains of a rosary in front of the façade, arbours, lakes, little bridges, rare trees, an orangery and a marble vase, placed in a shady spot in the park. In 1885 this property was already spoilt by the numerous country houses built by rich owners in the immediate neighbourhood. But Tchaikovsky was so enamoured of the scenery of Great Russia that he was quite satisfied with a birch or pine wood, a marshy field, the dome of a village church and, in the far distance, the dark line of some great forest. The chief motive, however, for his choice of this neighbourhood, where he lived to the end of his days, was not so much the charm of scenery as its situation between the two capitals. Klin lies near Moscow, and is also easily accessible from Petersburg, so that Tchaikovsky was within convenient distance from either city; while at the same time he was beyond the reach of accidental visitors, who now frequently molested him.

The first glimpse of Maidanovo disappointed Tchaikovsky. All that seemed splendid and luxurious to his man Alexis appeared in his eyes tasteless and incongruous. Nevertheless, he felt it would be pleasant as a temporary residence. The view from the windows, the quiet and sense of being *at home*, delighted him. The cook was good and inexpensive. The only other servants he employed were a moujik and a washerwoman. " In spite of my disappointment," he writes to his brother, " I am contented, cheerful, and quiet. . . . I am now receiving the newspapers, which makes life pleasanter. I read a great deal, and am getting on with English, which I enjoy. I eat, walk, and sleep when—and as much as—I please—in fact I live."

III

To E. Pavlovskaya.

" MAIDANOVO, *February 20th* (*March 4th*), 1888.

" DEAR EMILIE KARLOVNA,—I rather long for news of you. Where are you now? I have settled down in a village. My health is not good . . . in Carnival week I suffered from the most peculiar nervous headaches. . . . As I felt sure my accursed and shattered nerves were to blame, and I only wanted rest, I hurried into the country. . . . My *Vakoula* will be quite a respectable opera, you can feel sure of that. I always see you as Oxana, and so you dwell in my company without suspecting it. I have made every possible alteration which could retrieve the work from its unmerited oblivion. I hope it will be quite ready by Easter. I intend to begin a new opera in spring, so I shall once more have an opportunity of spending all my time with my 'benefactress.'"[1]

In February Taneiev played the new Fantasia for pianoforte in Moscow. Its immediate success was very great, but probably the applause was as much for the favourite pianist as for the work itself, for neither in Moscow nor yet in Petersburg — where Taneiev played it a year later—did this composition take any lasting hold upon the public.

To N. F. von Meck.

"MAIDANOVO, *March 5th (17th)*, 1885.

"DEAR FRIEND,—Your letter gave me food for reflection. You are quite right : property is a burden, and only he who owns nothing is quite free. But, on the other hand, one must have a *home*. If I could live in Moscow, I should rent a house there. But it is not sufficient to *rent* a place in the country if one wants to feel at home. Here in Maidanovo, for instance, I have already found it very unpleasant to have my landlady living close by. I cannot plant the flowers I like, nor cut down a tree that obstructs my view. I cannot prevent people from walking in front of my windows, because there are other houses let in the park. I think, with my reserved character and nature, it would be better to have a little house and garden of my own. . . .

"The Russian solitudes of which you speak do not frighten me. One can always take a great store of books and newspapers from town, and, moreover, I am very simple in my tastes.

"I do not at all agree with your idea that in our country

---

[1] Tchaikovsky addressed Emilie Pavlovskaya by this term in gratitude for her splendid interpretation of the heroine in *Mazeppa*.

it must always be *horrid, dark, marshy*, etc. Even as
the Esquimaux, or the Samoyede, loves his icy northern
land, I love our Russian scenery more than any other,
and a Russian landscape in winter has an incomparable
charm for me. This does not hinder me in the least from
liking Switzerland or Italy, in a different way. To-day
I find it particularly difficult to agree with you about
the poverty of our Russian scenery : it is a bright, sunny
day, and the snow glistens like millions of diamonds. A
wide vista lies before my window. . . . No ! it is beautiful
here in this land of ours, and one breathes so easily under
this boundless horizon.

"It seems to me you think too gloomily, too despair-
ingly, of Russia. Undoubtedly there is much to be
wished for here, and all kinds of deceit and disorder
do still exist. But where will you find perfection? Can
you point out any country in Europe where everyone
is perfectly contented? There was a time when I was
convinced that for the abolishment of autocracy and
the introduction of law and order, political institutions,
such as parliaments, chambers of deputies, etc., were indispensable, and that it was only necessary to introduce
these reforms with great caution, then all would turn
out well, and everyone would be quite happy. But now,
although I have not yet gone over to the camp of the
ultra-conservatives, I am very doubtful as to the actual
utility of these reforms. When I observe what goes on in
other countries, I see everywhere discontent, party conflict and hatred ; everywhere—in a greater or less degree
—the same disorder and tyranny prevails. Therefore
I am driven to the conclusion that there is no ideal
government, and, until the end of the world, men will have
to endure in patience many disappointments with regard
to these things. From time to time great men—bene-
factors of mankind—appear, who rule justly and care more
for the common welfare than for their own. But these are
very exceptional. Therefore I am firmly convinced that
the welfare of the great majority is not dependent upon
principles and *theories*, but upon those individuals who, by
the accident of their birth, or for some other reason, stand
at the head of affairs. In a word, mankind serves man.

not a personified principle. Now arises the question :
Have we a *man* upon whom we can stake our hopes?
I answer, Yes, and this man is the Emperor. His personality fascinates me ; but, apart from personal impressions, I
am inclined to think that the Emperor is a good man.
I am pleased with the caution with which he introduces
the new and does away with the old order. It pleases
me, too, that he does not seek popularity ; and I take
pleasure also in his blameless life, and in the fact that
he is an honourable and good man. But perhaps my
politics are only the *naïveté* of a man who stands aloof
from everyday life and is unable to see beyond his
own profession."

To E. K. Pavlovskaya.

"MAIDANOVO, *March 14th (26th)*, 1885.

"I am now arranging the revised score of *Vakoula*,
orchestrating the new numbers and correcting the old.
I hope to have finished in a few weeks. The opera will
be called *Cherevichek*,[1] to distinguish it from the numerous
other *Vakoulas :* Soloviev's and Stchourovsky's for instance.
The authorities have promised to produce the opera in
Moscow ; it will hardly be possible in Petersburg, as they
have already accepted two new operas there.

"As to *The Captain's Daughter*,[2] if only I could find a
clever librettist, capable of carrying out such a difficult task,
I would begin the work with pleasure. Meanwhile I have
made a note of *The Enchantress*, by Shpajinsky. The
latter has already started upon the libretto. He will make
many alterations and, if I am not mistaken, it will make a
splendid background for the music. You will find it
your most suitable rôle. If *Les Caprices d'Oxane* should
be produced, you will continue to play the part of my
'benefactress,' for you give me incredibly more than
I give you. But if, with God's help, I achieve *The Enchantress*, I hope I may become your benefactor in some
degree. Here you shall have a fine opportunity to display
your art."

[1] This means *The Little Shoes*, but the opera has since been republished as
Les Caprices d'Oxane.   [2] A tale by Poushkin.

To N. F. von Meck.

"MAIDANOVO, *April 3rd* (15*th*), 1885.

"MY DEAREST FRIEND,—I am once more back in Maidanovo, after a week and a half of travelling hither and thither. I worked almost without a break through the whole week before Palm Sunday and the whole of Passion Week, in order to be ready for the Easter festival. By Saturday everything was finished, and (although not well) I arrived in Moscow in time for the early service. I did not pass my holidays very pleasantly, and at the end of Easter Week I went to Petersburg, where I had to see Polonsky, author of the libretto of *Vakoula*, about the printing of the opera in its new form. I stayed four days in Petersburg, and spent them with my relations in the usual running about, which I found as wearisome as it was fatiguing. On Monday I travelled to Moscow in order to attend the reception of the Grand Duke Constantine Nicholaevich, who was to be present at the performance of the opera at the Conservatoire. As a member of the Musical Committee, I could not avoid taking part in the official reception to the Grand Duke, which I found a great bore. The performance went very well. Many thanks for sending me the articles in the *Novoe Vremya*. I had already seen them, and was very pleased with their warmth of tone. I am never offended at frank criticism, for I am well aware of my faults, but I feel very bitterly the cold and inimical note which pervades Cui's criticisms. It is not very long since the Russian Press (principally the Petersburg organs) began to notice me in a friendly spirit. Ivanov, the author of the articles in the *Novoe Vremya*, had formerly no good opinion of me, and used to write in a cold and hostile manner, although in Moscow I taught him theory for three years, and did not in the least deserve his enmity, as everyone knows. I can never forget how deeply his criticism of *Vakoula* wounded me ten years ago."

To Rimsky-Korsakov.

"MAIDANOVO, *April 6th* (18*th*), 1885.

"DEAR NICHOLAS ANDREIEVICH,—Since I saw you last I have had so much to get through in a hurry that I could not spare time for a thorough revision of your primer. But now and again I cast a glance at it, and jotted down my remarks on some loose sheets. To-day, having finished my revision of the first chapter, I wanted to send you these notes, and read them through again. Then I hesitated: should I send them or not? All through my criticism of your book[1] ran a vein of irritation, a grudging spirit, even an unintentional suspicion of hostility towards you. I was afraid the mordant bitterness of my observations might hurt your feelings. Whence this virulence? I cannot say. I think my old hatred of teaching harmony crops up here; a hatred which partly springs from a consciousness that our present theories are untenable, while at the same time it is impossible to build up new ones; and partly from the peculiarity of my musical temperament, which lacks the power of imparting conscientious instruction. For ten years I taught harmony, and during that time I loathed my classes, my pupils, my text-book, and myself as teacher. The reading of your book reawakened my loathing, and it was this which stirred up all my acrimony and rancour. . . . Now I am going to lay a serious question before you, which you need not answer at once, only after due consideration and discussion with your wife.

"Dare I hope that you would accept the position of Director of the Moscow Conservatoire should it be offered you? I can promise you beforehand so to arrange matters that you would have sufficient time for composing, and be spared all the drudgery with which N. Rubinstein was overwhelmed. You would only have the supervision of the musical affairs.

"Your upright and ideally honourable character, your distinguished gifts, both as artist and as teacher, warrant my conviction that in you we should find a splendid

---

[1] A course of harmony.

Director. I should consider myself very fortunate could I realise this ideal.

"So far, I have not ventured to speak of it to anyone, and beg you to keep the matter quiet for the present.

"Think it over, dear friend, and send me your answer.[1] ..."

To E. K. Pavlovskaya.

"MAIDANOVA, *April 12th (24th)*, 1885.

"MY DEAR EMILIE KARLOVNA,—Your exceedingly malicious criticism of *The Enchantress* not only failed to annoy me, but awoke my gratitude, for I wanted to know your opinion. I had even thought of asking you if you would go to see the play itself and give me your impressions. My conception and vision of the type of Natasha differs entirely from yours. Of course, she is a licentious woman ; but her spell does not consist merely in the fact that she can win people with her fine speeches. This spell might suffice to draw customers to her inn—but would it have power to change her sworn enemy, the Prince, into a lover ? Deep hidden in the soul of this light woman lies a certain moral force and beauty which has never had any chance of development. *This power is love.* Natasha is a strong and womanly nature, who can only love once, and she is capable of sacrificing all and everything to her love. So long as her love has not yet ripened, Natasha dissipates her forces, so to speak, in current coin ; it amuses her to make everyone fall in love with her with whom she comes in contact. She is merely a sympathetic, attractive, undisciplined woman; she knows she is captivating, and is quite contented. Lacking the enlightenment of religion and culture—for she is a friendless orphan—she has but one object in life—to live gaily. Then appears *the* man destined to touch the latent chords of her better nature, and she is transfigured. Life loses all worth for her, so long as she cannot reach her goal; her beauty, which, so far, had only possessed an instinctive and elementary power of attraction, now becomes a strong weapon in her hand, by which, in a single moment, she shatters the oppos-

---

[1] Rimsky-Korsakov courteously, but decidedly, declined the offer.

2 I

ing forces of the Prince—his hatred. Afterwards they
surrender themselves to the mad passion which envelops
them and leads to the inevitable catastrophe of their
death; but this death leaves in the spectator a sense of
peace and reconciliation. I speak of what is going to be
in my opera; in the play everything is quite different.
Shpajinsky quite understands my requirements, and will
carry out my intentions in delineating the principal characters. He will soften down the hardness of Natasha's
manières d'être, and will give prominence to the power of
her moral beauty. *He and I—you* too, later, if only you
will be reconciled to this rôle—will so arrange things that
in the last act there shall not be a dry eye in the audience.
This is my own conception of this part, and I am sure it
must please you, and that you will not fail to play it
splendidly. My enthusiasm for *The Enchantress* has not
made me unfaithful to the desire, so deeply rooted in my
soul, to illustrate in music those words of Goethe's: 'The
eternal feminine draws us onward.' The fact that the
womanly power and beauty of Natasha's character remain
so long hidden under a cloak of licentiousness, only
augments the dramatic interest. Why do you like the part
of Traviata or of Carmen? Because power and beauty
shine out of these two characters, although in a somewhat
coarser form. I assure you, you will also learn to like
The Enchantress."

To M. Tchaikovsky.

"MAIDANOVO, *April 26th* (*May 8th*), 1885.

"The business connected with *Cherevichek* has ended
very well. Vsievolojsky put an end to the irresolution of
the so-called management and ordered the opera to be produced in the most sumptuous style. I was present at a
committee at which he presided, when the mounting was
discussed. They will send Valetz, the scene-painter, to
Tsarskoe-Selo, so that he may faithfully reproduce some of
the rooms in the palace. I am very pleased."

To P. Jurgenson.

"MAIDANOVO, *April 26th* (*May 8th*), 1885.

" The position of my budget is as follows: I possess (together with the Moscow royalty which I have not yet received) 6,000 roubles. From Petersburg and Moscow there must still be about 800 or 1,000 roubles to come in; the honorarium from the church music, 300 roubles; the honorarium from the Moscow Musical Society, 300 roubles.

" Total : 6000 + 800 + 300 + 300 = 7,500 (*sic !*).

" Up to the present I have not received more than 3,000 roubles from you.

" Consequently the capital which you have in hand amounts to 4,500–5000 roubles. A nice little sum."

To N. F. von Meck.

"Moscow, *May 26th* (*June 7th*), 1885.

" . . . I am completely absorbed in the affairs of the Conservatoire, and have decided that the position of Director shall be offered to Taneiev. If I do not succeed in this, I shall retire from the Committee. Finally, I can tell you what, so far, I have said to no one here : I hate every public office more than ever. Oh, God ! how many disappointments have I experienced and how many bitter truths I have learnt! No! next year I must get right away."

Tchaikovsky actually succeeded in getting Taneiev chosen as Director of the Conservatoire. Through him Hubert, who had long been absent from the Conservatoire, was once more reinstated as a teacher. To support Taneiev's authority Tchaikovsky determined to resume his place upon the teaching staff, and undertook the gratuitous class for composition. This only necessitated his attendance once a month to supervise the work of the few (two to three) students of which the class was composed.

To S. I. Taneiev.

"MAIDANOVO, *June* 13*th* (25*th*), 1885.

"Alexeiev has told me that according to the rules of the Conservatoire it is not permissible for me to be both teacher and member of Committee. Of course, I will not go back on my word, and I leave it to you to decide which would be the most useful—to remain on the Committee, or undertake the somewhat honorary post of professor. I think it would be best to remain on the Committee, but just as you like. In any case I will do my duty conscientiously, on the condition that my freedom is not curtailed and that I may travel whenever I please. . . .

"So, my dear chief, my fate lies in your hands.

"After some hesitation I have made up my mind to compose *Manfred*, because I shall find no rest until I have redeemed my promise, so rashly given to Balakirev in the winter. I do not know how it will turn out, but meantime I am very discontented. No! it is a thousand times pleasanter to compose without any programme. When I write a programme symphony I always feel I am not paying in sterling coin, but in worthless paper money."

IV

Tchaikovsky began the composition of *Manfred* in June. The following letter from Balakirev, dated 1882, led him to choose this subject for a symphonic work.

M. Balakirev to P. Tchaikovsky.

"PETERSBURG, *October* 28*th* (*November* 9*th*), 1882.

"Forgive me for having left your last letter so long unanswered. I wanted to write to you in perfect peace and quiet, but many things hindered me. You are more fortunate than we are, for you do not need to give lessons, and can devote your whole time to art. I first offered the subject about which I spoke to you to Berlioz, who declined my suggestion on account of age and ill-health.

Your *Francesca* gave me the idea that you were capable of treating this subject most brilliantly, provided you took great pains, subjected your work to stringent self-criticism, let your imagination fully ripen, and did not hurry. This fine subject—Byron's *Manfred*—is no use to me, for it does not harmonise with my intimate moods.

"Let me tell you first of all that your Symphony—like the Second Symphony of Berlioz—must have an *idée fixe* (the *Manfred* theme), which must be carried through all the movements. Now for the programme :—

"*First Movement.* Manfred wandering in the Alps. His life is ruined. Many burning questions remain unanswered ; nothing is left to him but remembrance. The form of the ideal Astarte floats before his imagination ; he calls to her in vain : the echo of the rocks alone repeats her name. Thoughts and memories burn in his brain and prey upon him ; he implores the forgetfulness that none can give him (F ♯ minor, second theme D major and F ♯ minor).

"*Second Movement.* In complete contrast to the first. Programme : The customs of the Alpine hunters : patriarchal, full of simplicity and good humour. Adagio Pastorale (A major). Manfred drops into this simple life and stands out in strong contrast to it. Naturally at the beginning a little hunting theme must be introduced, but in doing this *you must take the greatest care not to descend to the commonplace.* For God's sake avoid copying the common German fanfares and hunting music.

"*Third Movement.* Scherzo fantastique (D major). Manfred sees an Alpine fairy in the rainbow above a waterfall.

"*Fourth Movement.* Finale (F ♯ minor). A wild Allegro representing the caves of Ariman, whither Manfred has come to try and see Astarte once more. The appearance of Astarte's wraith will form the contrast to these infernal orgies (the same theme which was employed in the first movement in D major now reappears in D♭ major; in the former it dies away like a fleeting memory, and is immediately lost in Manfred's phase of suffering—but now it can be developed to its fullest extent). The music must be light, transparent as air, and ideally virginal. Then comes the repetition of Pandemonium, and finally the sunset and Manfred's death.

" Is it not a splendid programme? I am quite convinced that if you summon up all your powers it will be your *chef-d'œuvre*.

" The subject is not only very deep, but in accordance with contemporary feeling; for all the troubles of the modern man arise from the fact that he does not know how to preserve his ideals. They crumble away and leave nothing but bitterness in the soul. Hence all the sufferings of our times."

To N. F. von Meck.

" MAIDANOVO, *June 13th (25th)*, 1885.

" DEAR FRIEND.—I can at last congratulate you on the beautiful weather. I should enjoy it twice as much if Maidanovo were more congenial to me. But alas! the lovely park, the beautiful views, and the splendid bath, are all alike spoiled by the *summer visitors*. I cannot take a step in the park without coming across some neighbour. It was beautiful in the winter, but I ought to have thought of the summer and the summer tourist.

" I am deep in the composition of a new symphonic work. Shpajinsky could not send me the first act of *The Enchantress* at the date agreed upon, so without losing any time, in April I set to work upon the sketches for a programme Symphony, upon the subject of Byron's *Manfred*. I am now so deep in the composition of this work that the opera will probably have to be laid aside for some time. The Symphony gives me great trouble. It is a very complicated and serious work. There are times when it seems to me it would be wise to cease from composing for a while; to travel and rest. But an unconquerable desire for work gains the upper hand and chains me to my desk and piano."

To E. K. Pavlovskya.

" MAIDANOVO, *July 20th (August 1st)*, 1885.

" . . . I have been playing through some numbers from *Harold*. A very interesting work and a clever one, well thought out and full of talent. But are you not surprised that Napravnik, who is so against Wagner, should have

written a genuine Wagnerian opera? I was filled with
astonishment."

To N. F. von Meck.

"MAIDANOVO, *August 3rd* (15*th*), 1885.

"The horizon has been shrouded for days in thick mist,
caused, they say, by forest fires and smouldering peat-
mosses. This mist gets thicker and thicker, and I begin
to fear we shall be suffocated. It has a very depressing
effect. In any case my mental condition has been very
gloomy of late. The composition of the *Manfred* Symphony—a work highly tragic in character—is so difficult
and complicated that at times I myself become a Manfred.
All the same, I am consumed with the desire to finish it as
soon as possible, and am straining every nerve: result—
extreme exhaustion. This is the eternal *cercle vicieux* in
which I am for ever turning without finding an issue. If I
have no work, I worry and bore myself; when I have it,
I work far beyond my strength."

To N. F. von Meck.

"MAIDANOVO, *August 31st* (*September 12th*), 1885.

". . . My fate, that is to say the question of my future
home, is at last decided. After a long and unsuccessful
search I have agreed to my landlady's proposal to remain
at Maidanovo. I shall not stay in the uncomfortable and
unsuitable house in which I have been living, but in one
which she herself has occupied. This house stands somewhat apart from the others, and a large piece of the garden
is to be fenced in and kept for my especial use; the house
itself was thoroughly done up last summer. Although the
neighbourhood is not what I could wish, yet, taking into
consideration the proximity of a large town with station,
shops, post, telegraph office, doctor and chemist—and also
my dislike for searching further—I have decided to take
this place for two years. It is pleasant and comfortable,
and I think I shall feel happy there. I am now starting
to furnish, and shall enter on my tenancy on September
15th. If during the next two years I feel comfortably
settled, I shall not search any more, but remain there to

the end of my days.   It is indeed time that I had a settled home."

V

1885–1886

All the important epochs in Tchaikovsky's life were preceded by a transition period in which he tried, as it were, whether the proposed change would be feasible or not.   From 1861–2, before he became a student at the Conservatoire, he was half-musician, half-official; in 1866, before he became a professor at the Conservatoire, and entirely a Muscovite, he was for eight months half-Petersburger and half-Muscovite; in 1877, before he gave up his professorship and started on what he called "the nomadic life" of the last seven years, he was half-professor and half-tourist; now, from February to September, 1885, he was rather a summer visitor than an inhabitant of the village of Maidanovo, but he had proved the firmness of his decision to remain there.   It was only in the beginning of September that he became the true "hermit of Klin," who, alas, was often compelled to leave his hermitage.   As he had now decided to settle down in a home of his own, he proceeded to make it comfortable. . . . With a school-girl's *naïveté* in all practical questions of life, Tchaikovsky could not do much himself towards furnishing his little home, and handed over the task to his servant Alexis. He himself only helped by purchasing the most un-necessary things (for example, he bought two horses, which he sold again with great difficulty, also an old English clock, which proved quite useless), or by furnishing his library with books and music.   He was as pleased as a child, and was never tired of talking of "my cook," "my washerwoman," "my silver," "my tablecloths," and "my dog."   He considered all these to be of the very best, and praised them to the skies. With the exception of some portraits and ikons, all the remainder of Tchaikovsky's movable property dates its existence from this time.

In comparison with the luxurious houses of other men in his position, painters, writers, and artists, Tchaikovsky's home was very modest. It contained only what was absolutely necessary. He did not possess beautiful or luxurious things, because his means were decidedly smaller than those of his colleagues in Western Europe, and also because he paid but little attention to outward appearances. If tables, cupboards, or curtains fulfilled their purpose fairly well, he was quite content. Workmanship and material were matters of indifference to him. He also troubled very little about "style" (he could not distinguish one style from another); even if a table was shaky, or the door of a cupboard refused to close, he took it all quite calmly. He would not surround himself with luxury, because his money belonged less to himself than to others, and because, even at the close of his life, when his income was 20,000 roubles a year, he remained free from all pretentious notions.

Little as Tchaikovsky troubled about buying furniture, he cared still less about the placing of it. He entrusted the matter entirely to the will of his servant, who, knowing and taking into consideration his little fancies and habits, arranged everything just as "his master liked it," without paying any heed to beauty or tastefulness. Tchaikovsky preferred that nothing should be altered in his surroundings; he found it most disagreeable to have to accustom himself to anything new, still more to miss any of his old friends. Henceforth a certain tradition which surrounded every piece of furniture was always considered, if possible, at each removal, so that wherever Tchaikovsky might be, the appearance of his room remained the same. The division of his time in Klin was never changed to the end of his life.

Tchaikovsky rose between seven and eight a.m. Took tea (generally without anything to eat) between eight and nine, and then read the Bible. After which he occupied himself with the study of the English language, or with reading such books as provided not only recreation, but instruction. In this way he read Otto Jahn's *Life of Mozart* in the original, the philosophical writings of Spinoza, Schopenhauer, and many others. He next took a walk for about three-quarters of an hour. If Tchaikovsky talked while taking his morning tea, or took his walk in company with a visitor, it signified that he did not intend to compose that day, but would be scoring, writing letters, or making corrections. During his life at Klin, when engaged on a new work, he could not endure company, not only in the morning, but also during the day. In earlier days in Moscow, abroad, or in Kamenka, he had to content himself with the solitude of his room during his hours of active work. The presence of his servant Alexis did not in any way disturb him. The latter, the sole witness of the creative process of the majority of his master's works, did not even appear to hear them, and only once unexpectedly gave expression to his enthusiasm for the Chorus of Maidens in the third scene of *Eugene Oniegin*, to the great astonishment and perturbation of his master. To his "perturbation," because he feared in future to be continually overheard and criticised. But this was fortunately the only flash of enlightenment which penetrated Safronov's musical darkness.

Manfred was the last work Tchaikovsky composed in anything but complete isolation, and this is probably the reason why the task proved so difficult, and cost him such moments of depression. The principal advantage of his new surroundings was the enjoyment of complete solitude during his hours of work.

We may mention that his reserve as to his compositions dates from this time. In the earlier days of his musical

life Tchaikovsky had been very communicative about his
work ; even before his compositions were finished he was
ready to discuss them.   In the evening he would ask the
opinion of those with whom he lived upon what he had
composed in the morning, and was always willing to let
them hear his work.   In course of time, however, the circle
of those to whom he communicated the fruits of his inspiration became ever smaller, and when he played any of
his compositions he begged his hearers to keep their
opinions to themselves.   From 1885 he ceased to show
his works to anyone.   The first to make acquaintance
with them was the engraver at Jurgenson's publishing
house.

Tchaikovsky never wasted time between 9.30 and 1 p.m.,
but busied himself in composing, orchestrating, making
corrections, or writing letters.   Before he began a pleasant
task he always hastened to get rid of the unpleasant ones.
On returning from a journey he invariably began with his
correspondence, which, next to proof-correcting, he found
the most unpleasant work.   In the nineties his correspondence had attained such volume that Tchaikovsky
was frequently engaged upon it from morning till night,
and often answered thirty letters a day.

Tchaikovsky dined punctually at 1 p.m., and, thanks
to his excellent appetite, always enjoyed any fare that was
set before him, invariably sending a message of thanks to
the cook by Safronov.   As he was always very abstemious
and plain in his meals, it often happened that his guests,
instead of complimenting the cook, felt inclined to do just
the contrary.   Wet or fine, Tchaikovsky always went for
a walk after dinner.   He had read somewhere that, in
order to keep in health, a man ought to walk for two hours
daily.   He observed this rule with as much conscientiousness and superstition as though some terrible catastrophe
would follow should he return five minutes too soon.
Solitude was as necessary to him during this walk as

during his work. Not only a human being, but even a favourite dog was a bother.

Every witness of his delight in nature spoilt his enjoyment; every expression of rapture destroyed the rapture itself, and in the very moment when he said to his companion, " How beautiful it is here ! " it ceased to be beautiful in his eyes.

Most of the time during these walks was spent in composition. He thought out the leading ideas, pondered over the construction of the work, and jotted down fundamental themes. In Klin there are carefully preserved many little exercise books, which he had used for this purpose. If in absence of mind Tchaikovsky had left his note-book at home, he noted down his passing thoughts on any scrap of paper, letter, envelope, or even bill, which he chanced to have with him. The next morning he looked over these notes, and worked them out at the piano. With the exception of two scenes in *Eugene Oniegin*, some piano pieces, and songs, he always worked out his sketches at the piano, so that he should not trust entirely to his indifferent memory. He always wrote out everything very exactly, and here and there indicated the instrumentation. In these sketches the greater part of a work was generally quite finished. When it came to the orchestration he only copied it out clearly, without essentially altering the first drafts. When he was not busy with music during his walks, he recited aloud or improvised dramatic scenes (almost always in French). Sometimes he occupied himself by observing insects. In the garden at Grankino was an ant-hill, to which he played the part of benefactor, providing it with insects from the steppe.

During the first year of his life at Maidanovo Tchaikovsky himself ruined the charm of these walks. Like every good-hearted summer visitor he had given tips lavishly to the village children. At first it was a pleasure, but afterwards turned into a veritable nuisance. The children waited for him at every corner, and when they noticed that he began to avoid them, they surprised him in the most unexpected places in the forest. This quest of pennies spread from the children to the young people of the village, nay, even to the men and women, so that at last he could hardly take a step without being waylaid by beggars. There was nothing left for Tchaikovsky but to keep within the precincts of his park.

About 4 p.m. Tchaikovsky went home to tea, read the papers if he was alone, but was very pleased to talk if he had visitors. At five he retired once more and worked till seven. Before supper, which was served at 8 p.m., Tchaikovsky always took another constitutional. This time he liked to have company, and generally went into the open fields to watch the sunset. In the autumn and winter he enjoyed playing the piano either alone, or arrangements for four hands if Laroche or Kashkin were there. After supper he sat with his guests till 11 p.m., playing cards or listening while one of them read aloud. Laroche was his favourite reader, not because he showed any particular talent that way, but because at every phrase his face expressed his enjoyment, especially if the author of the book happened to be Gogol or Flaubert. When there were no visitors, Tchaikovsky read a number of historical books dealing with the end of the eighteenth or beginning of the nineteenth century, or played patience—and was a little bored. At 11 p.m. he went to his room, wrote up his diary, and read for a short time. He never composed in the evening after the summer of 1866.

Unexpected guests were treated most inhospitably, but to invited guests he was amiability itself, and often gave himself the pleasure of gathering together his Moscow friends—Kashkin, Hubert, Albrecht, Jurgenson, and Taneiev. But those who stayed with him longest and most frequently were Laroche, Kashkin, and myself.

VI

In the beginning of the eighties Tchaikovsky's fame greatly increased in Europe and America, not only without any co-operation on his part, but even without his being aware of it. More and more frequently came news of the success of one or other of his works, and letters from various celebrated artists who had played his compositions, or wished to do so. The Committees of the Paris " Sebastian Bach Society " and the Association for the National Edition of Cherubini's works both elected him an honorary member. Nevertheless it surprised him greatly to learn that a Paris publisher (Félix Mackar) had proposed to P. Jurgenson to buy the right of bringing out his works in France. The sum which Jurgenson received was not indeed excessive, but it testified to the fact that Tchaikovsky's fame had matured and reached the point when it might bring him some material advantage. Incidentally it may be mentioned that P. Jurgenson, without any legal obligation, handed over to Tchaikovsky half the money he received from F. Mackar, so that the former became quite suddenly and unexpectedly a capitalist, although at the end of the year he was not a single kopek to the good. After F. Mackar had become the representative of Tchaikovsky's interests in Paris he pushed his works with great zeal. First of all he induced him to become a member of the Society of Composers and Publishers, the aim of which was to enforce a certain fee for every work by one of its members performed in public. The yearly sum which Tchaikovsky now began to draw from France can be taken as an authentic proof of the growth of his popularity in that country. This sum increased every year until 1893. After Tchaikovsky's death it suddenly decreased in a very marked manner. Elsewhere I will give some explanation of this curious fact.

Mackar also started his gratuitous *Auditions* of Tchai-kovsky's works.   These *Auditions*, in spite of the free admission, were not very well patronised by the Paris public, who were satiated with music.   But they produced one very important result.   The best artists (Marsick, Diemer, and others) willingly took part in them, and henceforth Tchaikovsky's name appeared more often in the programmes of the Paris concerts.

To E. K. Pavlovskaya.

"MAIDANOVO, *September 9th (21st),* 1885.

". . . *Manfred* is finished, and I have set to work upon the opera without losing an hour. . . . The first act (the only one in hand) is splendid: life and action in plenty. If nothing prevents me I hope to have the sketch ready by the spring: so that I may devote next year to the instrumentation and working out.   The opera can then be produced in the season 1887–8.   Dear E. K., do please say a good word on every possible occasion for *The Enchantress.*"

To A. P. Merkling.

"MAIDANOVO, *September 13th (25th),* 1885.

". . . Annie, first of all I am going to flatter you a little and then ask you to do something for me.   After much searching and trouble I have rented a very pretty house here in Maidanovo. . . . I am now furnishing this house . . . now . . . some good people . . . have promised . . . if I am not mistaken . . . that is, how shall I express myself? . . . to sew . . . woollen *portières* . . . or cur-tains . . . that is, I would like to know . . . perhaps at once . . . if you would . . . I, in a word . . . oh! how ashamed I am . . . write please, how what . . . now, I hope, I have made myself understood. . . ."[1]

[1] Anna Petrovna kept her promise, and made the curtains which ornament the dining-room at Klin till this day.

To A. S. Arensky.

" MAIDANOVO, *September* 25*th* (*October* 7*th*), 1885.

" DEAR ANTON STEPANOVICH,—Pardon me if I force my advice upon you.   I have heard that 5/4 time appears twice in your new Suite.   It seems to me that the mania for 5/4 time threatens to become a habit with you.   I like it well enough if it is indispensable to the musical idea, that is to say if the time signature and rhythmic accent respectively form no hindrance.   For example, Glinka, in the chorus of the fourth act of *A Life for the Tsar*, clearly could not have written in anything else but 5/4 time : here we find an actual 5/4 rhythm that is a continual and uni-form change from 2/4 to 3/4 :

"It would be curious, and certainly 'an effort to be original,' to write a piece with a simple rhythm of 2/4 or 3/4 time in 5/4 time.   You will agree with me that it would have been very stupid of Glinka to have written his music thus:

" It would be the same to the ear whether 2/4 or 3/4 : it would not be a mathematical blunder, but a very clumsy musical one.

" You have made just such a mistake in your otherwise beautiful *Basso ostinato.*   I made the discovery yesterday that in this instance 5/4 time was not at all necessary. You must own that a series of three bars of 5/4 is mathe-matically equal to a similar series of 3/4 time ;[1] in music, on the contrary, the difference between them is quite as sharp as between 3/4 and 6/8.

[1] A series of five bars of 3/4 is evidently meant.

" In my opinion, your *Basso ostinato* should be written in 3/4 or 6/4 time, but not in 5/4.

" I cannot imagine a more distinct five-bar rhythm in 3/4 time. What do you think?"

To N. F. von Meck.

" MAIDANOVO, *September 27th (October 9th),* 1885.

" The first act of *The Enchantress* lies finished before me, and I am growing more and more enthusiastic over the task in prospect.

" Dear friend, I like your arrogant views upon my opera. You are quite right to regard this insincere form of art with suspicion. But for a composer opera has some irresistible attraction; it alone offers him the means of getting into touch with the great public. My *Manfred* will be played once or twice, and then disappear; with the exception of a few people who attend symphony concerts, no one will hear it. Opera, on the contrary—and opera alone—brings us nearer to our fellows, inoculates the public with our music, and makes it the possession, not only of a small circle, but—under favourable circumstances—of the whole nation. I do not think this tendency is to be condemned; that is to say, Schumann, when he wrote *Genoveva,* and Beethoven, when he wrote *Fidelio,* were not actuated by ambition, but by a natural desire to increase the circle of their hearers and to penetrate as far as possible into the heart of humanity. Therefore we must not only pursue what is merely effective, but choose subjects of artistic worth which are both interesting and touching."

2 K

To M. Tchaikovsky.

" MAIDANOVO, *October 1st* (*13th*), 1885.

" What a wretch Zola is!! A few weeks ago I accidentally took up his *Germinal,* began to read it, got
interested, and only finished it late at night. I was so
upset that I had palpitations, and sleep was impossible.
Next day I was quite ill, and now I can only think of the
novel as of some fearful nightmare. . . ."

To P. Jurgenson.

" MAIDANOVO, *October 9th* (*21st*), 1885.

" DEAR FRIEND,—Hubert tells me you do not think it
possible to publish *Manfred* this season. Is this true?
The question is this, I cannot allow two opportunities to
slip: (1) Bülow is conducting in Petersburg; (2) Erdmannsdorfer is conducting in Moscow—perhaps his last
season—and, in spite of all, he is one of the few people on
whom I can depend. On the other hand, I am not in a
position to spend an incredible amount of trouble on a
work which I regard as one of my very best, and then wait
till it is played *some time.* As far as I am concerned, it is
all the same to me whether it is played from written or
printed notes—so long as it is done. I believe it might be
ready by February. But if you think that this is quite
impossible, then I propose that you decline *Manfred*
altogether (this will not offend me at all, for I know you
cannot do the impossible for the sake of my whims). Only
understand that I cannot on any account wait till next
season, and cost what it may, I will see *Manfred* produced. Do not take my caprice (if it is a caprice) amiss,
and answer me at once."

To N. F. von Meck.

" MAIDANOVO, *October 11th* (*23rd*), 1885.

" . . . As regards the lofty significance of symphony
and chamber music in comparison with opera, let me only
add that to refrain from writing operas is the work of a

hero, and we have one such hero in our time—Brahms. Cui has justly remarked in one of his recent articles that Brahms, both as man and artist, has only followed the highest ideals—those which were worthy of respect and admiration. Unfortunately his creative gift is poor, and does not correspond to his great aspirations. Nevertheless he is a hero. This heroism does not exist in me, for the stage with all its glitter attracts me irresistibly."

VII

To N. F. von Meck.

"MAIDANOVO, *November* 19*th* (*December* 1*st*), 1885.

". . . I spent a week in Moscow, and was present at three concerts. The first, given by Siloti, who has just returned from abroad to serve his time in the army. He has made great progress. Then the Musical Society gave a concert and quartet-matinée, at which the celebrated Paris violinist, Marsick, played. All three concerts gave me great pleasure, as I have not heard any good music for so long. For a musician who writes as much as I do it is very necessary and refreshing to hear foreign music from time to time. Nothing inspires me more than listening to a great foreign work: immediately I want to write one equally beautiful.

"I have also been once or twice to the Conservatoire, and was very pleased to notice that Taneiev is just the Director we wanted under the circumstances. His work shows resolution, firmness, energy, and also capability. I hear nothing about *Les Caprices d'Oxane*, and begin to fear the work will not be produced this season."

The following letter was written after Ippolitov-Ivanov had communicated the success of *Mazeppa* in Tiflis.

To M. M. Ippolitov-Ivanov.[1]

"*December 6th* (18*th*), 1885.

". . . As to *Mazeppa*, accept my warmest thanks. My brother and his wife, who live in Tiflis, and had seen the opera in Moscow and Petersburg, tell me it went splendidly.

"For some time I have been longing to find a subject—not too dramatic—for an opera, and then to write a work suitable to the resources of the provincial stage. Should God grant me a long life, I hope to carry out this plan, and thus to obliterate the unpleasant recollections of the immeasurable trouble which the rehearsals of *Mazeppa* must have left with you. But the harder your task, the warmer my thanks."

To Modeste Tchaikovsky.

"MAIDANOVO, *December* 9*th* (21*st*), 1885.

"I am going to Moscow on December 14th (26th), principally to decide the fate of *Les Caprices d'Oxane*. I shall make heroic efforts to have my opera produced. I am advised to conduct it myself, and it is possible I may decide to do so. In any case, I shall spend the holidays in Petersburg. . . . I am working very hard at the corrections of *Manfred*. I am still convinced it is my best work. Meanwhile *The Enchantress* is laid aside, but the first act is quite finished. The libretto is splendid. In this I am lucky."

To N. F. von Meck.

"MAIDANOVO, *December* 11*th* (23*rd*), 1885.

". . . My Third Suite was played at the last concert. The public gave me an enthusiastic ovation. . . . Lately we have had such lovely moonlight nights, without a breath of wind. O God, how beautiful they are! The Russian winter has a particular charm for me, but that does not prevent me from planning a journey to Italy in

---

[1] The present Professor of Composition at the Moscow Conservatoire and Director of the Private Opera in Moscow.

the spring. I am thinking of going by sea from Naples to Constantinople, then to Batoum, and thence by train to Tiflis to visit my brother Anatol, who is already expecting me."

To S. I. Taneiev.

"MAIDANOVO, *December* 11*th* (23*rd*), 1885.

". . . Imagine! I am rejoicing at the thought of hearing Beethoven's First Symphony. I had no suspicion that I liked it so much. The reason is perhaps that it is so like my idol, Mozart. Remember that on October 27th, 1887, the centenary of *Don Juan* will be celebrated."

To P. Jurgenson.

"*December* 22*nd* (*January* 3*rd*), 1885.

". . . I have only just now been able to consider this question of *Manfred*, of Mackar, and the fee, and this is my decision: Even were *Manfred* a work of the greatest genius, it would still remain a symphony which, on account of its unusual intricacy and difficulty, would only be played once in ten years. This work cannot therefore bring any profit either to you or Mackar. On the other hand, I value it highly. How is the material value of such a work to be decided? I may be wrong, but it seems to me my best composition, and a few hundred roubles would not repay me for all the work and trouble I have put into it. If you were very rich, I would unhesitatingly demand a very large sum, on the grounds that you could recover your outlay on other things—but you are not at all rich. As for Mackar—to speak frankly—I am greatly touched by his cheerful self-sacrifice, for certainly he can have made very little out of my works in France. After having just received 20,000 francs from him, we must not show ourselves too grasping, especially as we know that there is not much to be made out of *Manfred*."

"In short, I have made up my mind to claim nothing from Mackar, or from you, and have already told him this. I tell you also, so that you should not demand the promised thousand francs from him. The demanding of payment for restoration of his copy—is your affair."

To N. F. von Meck.

"MAIDANOVO, *January* 13th (25th), 1886.

"DEAR FRIEND,— . . . This time I have not brought back any pleasant impressions with me from Petersburg. My operas—I do not know why—have not been given lately, and I feel this the more bitterly because, owing to the unusual success of *Oniegin*, it appears that the Direction has been urging that it should be given with greater frequency. The new symphony *Manfred* is completely ignored, for no preparations for its production are being made. In all this I do not recognise any enmity towards me personally, for in truth I have no enemies, but a kind of contempt which is a little wounding to my artistic vanity. Certainly this is an unfavourable year for me. They have decided not to give *Les Caprices d'Oxane* in Moscow this season, and I had been expecting it so impatiently!

" I have a piece of news for you to-day, which pleased me very much. I had observed that here in Maidanovo the village children are constantly idle and run about without any occupation, which induced me to consult with the local priest about the founding of a school. This has proved to be possible, so long as I assure them an annual sum. I have consented to do so, and the priest began to take the necessary steps about two months ago. The official permission to open a school has arrived and the instruction can begin this week. I am very glad."

To N. F. von Meck.

"MAIDANOVO, *January* 14th (26th), 1886.

" . . . The priest came to see me to-day, and brought me an invitation to the opening of the school on the 19th. I am proud to have initiated this work. I hope some good will come of it. In spite of the greatest care and moderation, I suffer from dyspepsia. It is not serious, and I have no doubt a cure at Vichy will completely set me up."

To N. F. von Meck.

" Moscow, *February 4th* (16*th*), 1886.

" How difficult it is after receiving your money to say in the baldest way, ' Money received, many thanks ! ' If only you had an inkling of all the happiness I owe you, and the whole meaning of that ' independence and freedom ' which are the result of my liberty. Life is an unbroken chain of little unpleasantnesses and collision with human egoism and pride, and only he can rise above these things who is free and independent. How often do I say to myself: *Well that it is so, but how if it were otherwise ?*

" Just lately I had some very unpleasant frictions which only just fell short of open quarrels, but failed to upset me because I could appear to ignore the wrong inflicted upon me. Yes, in the last few years of my life there have been many occasions on which I have sincerely felt the debt of gratitude I owe to you. And yet I usually send you the receipt as if it were a matter of course. My gratitude has no limits, my dear."

To N. F. von Meck.

" MAIDANOVO, *February 6th* (18*th*), 1886.

" . . . . To-day I returned from Moscow, where I have been attending Rubinstein's concerts once a week. Were it only a question of listening to that marvellous pianist, I should not have found the journeys at all tedious, in spite of my dislike of leaving home. But I had to go to all the dinners and suppers which were held in his honour, which I generally found intolerably wearisome and most injurious to my health. At the last concert Rubinstein played pieces by Henselt, Thalberg, Liszt, and others. There was very little artistic choice, but the performance was indeed astonishing."

To N. F. von Meck.

" MAIDANOVO, *February 14th* (26*th*), 1886.

" . . . . The festival which the town of Moscow held in Rubinstein's honour was a great success. He was visibly touched by the energy and warmth with which the Muscovites expressed their affection for him. Indeed, everyone must recognise that Rubinstein is worthy of all such honour. He is not only a gifted artist, but also a most honourable and generous man."

Diary.

"MAIDANOVO, *February 22nd* (*March 8th*), 1886.

"What an unfathomable gulf lies between the Old and the New Testament! Read the psalms of David, and at first it is impossible to understand why they have taken such a high place from an artistic point of view; and, secondly, why they should stand beside the Gospels. David is altogether *of this* world. He divides the whole of humanity into two unequal portions: sinners (to which belong the greatest number) and the righteous, at whose head he places himself. In every psalm he calls down God's wrath upon the sinner and His praise upon the righteous; yet the reward and the punishment are both worldly. The sinners shall be undone, and the righteous shall enjoy all the good things of this earthly life. How little that agrees with Christ's teaching, who prayed for His enemies, and promised the good no earthly wealth, but rather the kingdom of heaven! What touching love and compassion for mankind lies in these words: 'Come unto Me, all ye that labour and are heavy laden'! In comparison with these simple words all the psalms of David are as nothing."

Diary.

"*February 28th* (*March 12th*), 1886.

". . . . At tea I read through Alexis Tolstoi's *St. John Chrysostom* and *The Sinner*, which reduced me to tears. While in this agitation of spirit, into which any strong artistic enjoyment throws me, I received a telegram from the Conservatoire: 'The Grand Duke is coming.' So all plans go to the devil! Despair, irresolution, and even terror at the prospect of the journey. Went in and fed my landlady's hungry dog. In the twilight I was overcome with insane depression. Played through my

Second Suite, and was glad to find it not so bad as I had imagined."

Diary.

"*March 1st* (13*th*), 1886.

". . . . Played through *Nero*, and cannot sufficiently marvel at the audacious coolness of the composer. The very sight of the score makes me fume. However, I only play this abomination because the sense of my superiority —at least, as regards conscientiousness—strengthens my energy. I believe I compose badly, but when I come across such an atrocity, written in all earnestness, I feel a certain relief. I am ashamed to show so much anger over such a publication—but there is no need to disguise one's feelings in a diary."

To N. F. von Meck.

"MAIDANOVO, *March* 13*th* (25*th*), 1886.

" DEAR FRIEND,—I have not written to you for a long time owing to a ten days' visit to Moscow. . . . I devoted two days to the rehearsal of *Manfred*, and attended the concert at which it was played. I am quite satisfied ; I am sure it is my best symphonic work. The performance was excellent, but it seemed to me the public were un-intelligent and cold, although they gave me quite an ovation at the end. . . ."

The very short and sparse Press notices of *Manfred* add nothing essential to Tchaikovsky's words. They merely confirm the fact that the Symphony received an excellent rendering, but the author's high opinion of his work only held good as regards the first two movements ; later on he came to reckon the other movements, the Pastorale, Ariman's Kingdom, and Manfred's Death, as being on a level with *The Oprichnik*, one of the least favoured of his works.

Although out of chronological order, I may mention here that on the occasion of a performance of this work in Petersburg (December, 1886) Cui gave it the most enthusiastic and unreserved praise. Everything pleased him, especially the Scherzo, and his criticism closed with these words : "We must be grateful to Tchaikovsky for having enriched the treasury of our national symphonic music."

VIII

To M. Tchaikovsky.

"TIFLIS, *April 1st* (*13th*), 1886.

". . . I left Moscow on March 23rd (April 4th), and travelled direct to Taganrog to Hyppolite, whose guest I was for two days, so as to arrive in Vladikavkas on the 28th.

"Early on Sunday (30th) I started in a four-horse post-carriage, accompanied by a guard, whose sole duty is to look after the requirements and comforts of the travellers. I had not slept the preceding night on account of the horrible bed and the insects (when I think of the *best* hotel in Vladikavkas I feel quite sick), and thought therefore that the beauties of the Georgian Road would make but little impression on me. The road is, however, so grand, so astonishingly beautiful, that I never thought of sleeping the whole day long. The variety of impressions did not allow my interest to flag for a moment. At first the approach to the mountains was slow, although they appeared to be quite close to us, and yet we still drove on and on. Then the valley of the Terek became narrower, and we reached the wild and gloomy Darjal Gorge. Afterwards we ascended into the region of snow. Shortly before I started on my journey there had been an avalanche, and hundreds of miserable-looking natives were busy shovelling away the snow. At last we were driving higher and higher between great snow walls, and it was necessary to put on our furs. By six o'clock we were descending into the Aragva Valley, and spent the night in Mlety. I occupied the *imperial rooms*. After the dirt of the Vladikavkas hotel I found the clean rooms, good beds, and daintily-set table very delightful. I dined, took a little walk by moonlight in the gallery, and went to bed at nine o'clock.   Next morning I started off again. Already we could feel the breath of the south in the air ; the sides of the mountains were cultivated, and constantly there came in sight picturesque *aouli*[1] and all kinds of dwellings.   The descent was made at a terrific pace, considering the curves of the road.   Not far from Dushet such a wonderful view came in sight that I almost wept with delight.   The further we descended, the more the influence of the south wind was felt.   At last we reached Mtskhet (noted for the ruins of its castle and the celebrated cathedral), and at half-past five we reached Tiflis. Toly and his wife were not there ; they had not expected me till later, and had gone to meet me at Mtskhet.   They did not arrive till eight o'clock.   Meanwhile I had had time to wash, dress, and see something of the town.   It is delightful.   The trees are not yet all green ; the fruit trees are in full blossom ; a mass of flowers in the gardens.   It is as warm as in June—in a word, really spring—just as it was four years ago when we left Naples.   The chief streets are very lively ; splendid shops, and quite a European air. But when I came to the native quarters I found myself in entirely new surroundings.   The streets mean and narrow, as in Venice; on both sides an endless row of small booths and all kinds of workshops, where the natives squat and work before the eyes of the passers-by. . . ."

To N. F. von Meck.

"TIFLIS, *April 6th* (18th), 1886.

"I begin to know Tiflis quite well already, and have seen the sights.   I have been in the baths, built in Oriental style.   Visited the celebrated churches, amongst others the Armenian church, where I was not only very much interested in the peculiarities of the service, but also in the singing ; I also visited David's monastery on the hill, where Griboiedov[2] lies buried.   One evening I went to a concert given by the Musical Society, where a very poor, thin orchestra played Beethoven's Third Symphony,

---

[1] Caucasian villages.
[2] The celebrated Russian dramatist.

Borodin's *Steppes*, and my Serenade for strings, to a public which was conspicuous by its absence. Many excellent musicians live in Tiflis; the most prominent are the talented composer Ippolitov-Ivanov and the pianist Eugene Korganov, an Armenian, and a former student of the Moscow Conservatoire. They show me every attention, and although I should much prefer to remain incognito, I am much touched by this proof of the love and sympathy of my fellow-workers. I had certainly not expected to find my music so widely known in Tiflis. My operas are played oftener here than anywhere else, and I am pleased that *Mazeppa* is such a great favourite."

Diary.

"Tiflis, *April 11th (23rd)*, 1886.

"While waiting for Korganov I busied myself with looking through his works. He came first, then Ippolitov-Ivanov. The poor Armenian (a very nice man and a good musician) was very grieved at my criticism. Then Ivanov played his things : very good."

To M. Tchaikovsky.

"Tiflis, *April 23rd (May 5th)*, 1886.

"Modi,—I only remain a few days longer in Tiflis. I could count this month the happiest in my life, if it were not for the visitors, and for my social existence. I do not think I have yet written to you of the honour paid me on the 19th. It was simply splendid. At eight o'clock, accompanied by Pani,[1] I entered the Director's box, which was decorated with flowers and foliage. The whole theatre rose, and amid great applause I was presented with a silver wreath and many others. A deputation from the Musical Society read an address. Then the concert began, which consisted entirely of my works. There were endless cheers! I have never experienced anything like it before. After the concert, a subscription supper, with many toasts. A most exhausting evening, but a glorious remembrance."

[1] Anatol's wife.

This was the first great honour in Tchaikovsky's life, and made a most agreeable impression on him, as proving the recognition of his merit by the Russian nation. Tchaikovsky, in the depths of his heart, was well aware that fame would eventually come, and that he would be worthy of it. He did not realise, however, that what he had already created was as worthy of fame as what he should create in the future. He knew, indeed, that the popularity of his name had greatly increased in the last few years, but he was still far from suspecting the truth. The honour paid him in Tiflis revealed to him his real relation to the Russian public. This revelation was so pleasing to his artistic vanity that it overcame for a moment his characteristic timidity and his dislike of posing before the public.

IX

Just at this time Tchaikovsky had to travel to Paris on important family business. He wished also to take this opportunity of making acquaintance with his Paris publisher, Mackar. To avoid the fatigue of the wearisome railway journey, he thought of taking the steamer from Batoum to Italy, thence by train to France. But owing to cholera at Naples, the French steamer belonging to the Batoum-Marseilles line did not call at the Italian port. Tchaikovsky therefore gave up his idea of visiting Italy, and took a through ticket for Marseilles by one of the steamers of the " Packet Company."

To A. Tchaikovsky.

"STEAMSHIP 'ARMENIA,' *May 3rd* (15*th*), 1886.

" . . . I am feeling less home-sick to-day, and better able to enjoy the sea, the mountains, and the sun . . . but how stupid it is, that one can only be alone in one's cabin ! On deck, scarcely a quarter of an hour passes without someone beginning a conversation. I know all the passengers already, but have not taken to anyone. The captain talks to me about music, and enrages me by his stupid opinions. A Frenchman, a doctor from Trebizond, also sets up to be a lover of music, and thinks it his duty —now he has discovered I am a musician—to talk to me about this detestable art, which seems to possess the quality of interesting everybody. . . ."

To A. Tchaikovsky.

"ARCHIPELAGO, *May 6th* (18*th*), 1886.

"The day before yesterday, about midday, we reached the Bosphorus in the most glorious weather. It is wonderfully beautiful, and the further one goes the more beautiful it becomes. About three o'clock we arrived at Constantinople. The motion was very great during the passage into the harbour. About five o'clock we got into a boat, and were rowed over to the town. The captain had made up his mind to stay twenty-four hours in Constantinople, so I thought I would spend the night at an hotel. The next day I visited the places of interest. The cathedral of St. Sophia delighted and astonished me. But, on the whole, I do not much care for Constantinople, and the famous Constantinople dogs simply make me feel sick. By 5 p.m. we were once more on board, and started immediately. New passengers had joined the ship. I preferred to remain in my own snug little cabin ; the whole evening I watched the water and the moonlight, and absorbed all the poetry of a sea journey. To-day is a little rougher. Many are ill—even men. I am quite well, and find a certain pleasure in the motion, and in watching the foaming blue waves. No trace of fear. I am quite accustomed to my surroundings, and have made friends with everyone, especially a Turkish officer, who is travelling to Paris."

To M. Tchaikovsky.

"'ARMENIA,' *May 8th* (20*th*), 1886.

" . . . To-day the sea is just like a mirror. So far we have been very lucky, and it is impossible to imagine anything more beautiful than such a journey. Of course there are some wearisome moments, especially when they begin to talk of music. The chief offender is an Englishman, who continually bothers me with questions as to whether I like this or that song by Tosti, Denza, etc. Also a French doctor, who has invented a new piano in which every sign for transposition ($\sharp$, $\flat$, $\times$, $\flat\flat$) has its own keynote. He talks incessantly of his awful invention, and gives me long pamphlets on the subject. We have already passed Sicily and the heel of the Italian boot. Etna is smoking a little, and to the left there is a horrible pillar of smoke and fire which excites us all very much. The captain cannot say for certain what it means, and seems somewhat disturbed by it. Consequently I, too, feel a little afraid."

To A. Tchaikovsky.

"'ARMENIA,' *May 9th (21st)*, 1886.

"The pillar of smoke and fire about which I wrote yesterday proves to be a terrible eruption of Mount Etna, not at the top, but at the side. This eruption was distinctly visible at a distance of three hundred versts, and the nearer we came the more interesting was the sight. Alexis woke me at two in the morning, that I might see this unique spectacle. We were in the Straits of Messina; the sea, which had been quite calm all day, was now very rough; I cannot describe the beauties of the moonlight, the fire from Mount Etna, and the swelling waves. At 3 a.m. I went back to bed and at five the captain sent a sailor to wake me, so that I might see the town of Messina, the sunrise, and the eruption on the other side. Later we passed between the volcano Stromboli and a new little island giving forth smoke; at least, the captain, who knows these parts well, has never suspected a volcano here and thinks it may portend a serious eruption. To-day the weather is splendid and the sea much quieter."

Diary.

"PARIS, *May 21st (June 2nd)*, 1886.

" I decided to go and see Mackar. What I suffered, and how excited I was, passes description. Ten times I tried to go in, and always turned away again—even a large glass of absinthe did not help me. At last I went. He was expecting me. I had pictured him a little man like Wuchs. He is astonishingly like Bessel. We talked a little (some-one near me was buying my works), and then I left. Naturally I felt a weight off my heart."

To P. V. Tchaikovsky.[1]

"PARIS, *June 1st (13th)*, 1886.

" . . . Yesterday I had breakfast with old Madam Viar-dot. She is such a stately and interesting woman ; I was quite enchanted. Although seventy, she only looks about forty. She is very lively, amiable, gay, and sociable, and knew how to make me feel at home from the very first moment."

Later Tchaikovsky wrote the following details to Na-dejda von Meck concerning his acquaintance with Madame Viardot :—

" . . . Madame Viardot often speaks about Tourgeniev, and described to me how he and she wrote 'The Song of Love Triumphant' together. Have I already told you that I was with her for two hours while we went through the *original score* of Mozart's *Don Juan*, which thirty years ago her husband had picked up very cheaply and quite by accident? I cannot tell you what I felt at the sight of this musical relic. I felt as if I had shaken Mozart by the hand and spoken to him ! . . ."

To Modeste Tchaikovsky.

"*June 23rd (11th)*, 1886.

"Yesterday, at the invitation of Ambrose Thomas, I visited the Conservatoire during the examination of the

[1] Anatol's wife.

pianoforte class. He is a very nice, friendly old man. A certain Madame Bohomoletz, a rich lady (half Russian), gave a dinner in my honour, followed by a musical evening, at which my quartet was played (Marsick and Brandoukov) and my songs were sung. . . . Leo Délibes has visited me; this touched me very deeply. Certainly it seems I am not as unknown in Paris as I thought. . . ."

I will add to this short and disjointed account that Tchaikovsky was received in a most friendly manner by Professor Marmontel, a warm admirer of his works, also by the composers Lalo, Lefèbre, Fauré, and others. The meeting with Colonne and Lamoureux is described by Tchaikovsky himself in a later letter :—

". . . I saw Colonne several times. He was very friendly, and expressed a wish to give a concert of my compositions. He asked me to send him some of my new scores to Aix-les-Bains, so that he could arrange a programme during the course of the summer. He continually lamented his *poverty* and the '*terrible* Concurrence Lamoureux.' As to Lamoureux, he was amiability itself, and made me a thousand promises."

Tchaikovsky was thrown into close contact with many other artists, several of whom, like the well-known pianist Diemer, for instance, remained his devoted friends to the end.

X

To N. F. von Meck.

"MAIDANOVO, *June* 18*th* (30*th*), 1886.

"How glad I am to be at home once more! How dear and cosy is my little house which, when I left, lay deep in snow, and is now surrounded by foliage and flowers! The three months I spent abroad were lost time as regards work, but I feel I have gained in strength, and can now devote my whole time to it without exhausting myself."

Diary.　"*July* 8*th* (20*th*), 1886.

"... Worked atrociously again. And yet people say I am a genius! Nonsense!"

To P. Jurgenson.

"MAIDANOVO, *July* 19*th* (31*st*), 1886.

"DEAR FRIEND,—I completely understand the difficulties of your situation. One of my letters to you is wanted for publication. You possess hundreds of my letters, but not one suitable to the case. Very natural; our correspondence was either too business-like, or too intimate. How can I help you? I cannot commit forgery, even for the pleasure of appearing in Mme. La Mara's book;[1] I cannot write a letter especially for her collection and take this lucky opportunity of displaying myself in the most favourable light as musician, thinker, and man. Such a sacrifice on the altar of European fame is repugnant to me, although, on the other hand, it would be false to say that Mme. La Mara's wish to place me among the prominent musicians of our time did not flatter me in the least. On the contrary, I am very deeply touched and pleased by the attention of the well-known authoress, and openly confess I should be very glad to be included in the company of Glinka, Dargomijsky, and Serov. If she were not in such a hurry, it would be better to send to one of my musical friends, such as Laroche, who could not fail to find among all my letters some with detailed effusions about my musical likes and dislikes; in short, a letter in which I speak quite candidly as a musician. But there is no time, and Laroche is away. Is it not curious that it should be difficult to find a suitable letter from a man who has carried on—and still carries on—the widest correspondence, dealing not only with business matters, but with artistic work? I am continually exchanging letters with four brothers, a sister, several cousins, and many friends, besides a quantity of casual correspondence

---

[1] The authoress of the well-known works, *Musikalische Studienköpfe* and *Musik Briefe aus funf Jahrhunderten.* Tchaikovsky's letter appears in the second volume of the latter.

with people often unknown to me. The necessity of sacrificing so much of my time to letter-writing is such a burden to me that, from the bottom of my heart, I curse all the postal arrangements in the world. The post often causes me sad moments, but it also brings me the greatest joy. One person plays the chief part in the story of the last ten years of my life: she is my good genius; to her I owe all my prosperity and the power to devote myself to my beloved work. Yet I have never seen her, never heard her voice; all my intercourse with her is through the post. I can certainly say I flood the world with my correspondence, and yet I am not in a position to help you out of your difficulty.

"There is nothing to be done, but to send this letter itself to Mme. La Mara. If it does not represent me in the least as a musician, it will at any rate give the authoress a chance of satisfying her flattering wish to place me among the prominent musicians of the day."

Diary.
"*August 1st* (13*th*), 1886.

". . . Played *Manon* at home. It pleased me better than I expected. I spent moments of longing and loneliness."

"*August 2nd* (14*th*).

". . . Played *Manon*. To-day Massenet seems to cloy with sweetness."

"*August 4th* (16*th*).

". . . Played Massenet at home. How stale he has grown! The worst of it is, that in this staleness I trace a certain affinity to myself."

To N. F. von Meck.
"MAIDANOVO, *August 4th* (16*th*), 1886.

". . . I feel at my best when I am alone; when trees, flowers, and books take the place of human society. O God, how short life is! How much I have yet to accomplish before it is time to leave off! How many projects!

When I am quite well—as I am at present—I am seized with a feverish thirst for work, but the thought of the shortness of human life paralyses all my energy. It was not always so. I used to believe I could, and must, carry out all my ideas to completion; therefore my impulses towards creative work were then more lasting and more fruitful. In any case I hope to have the outline of the opera (*The Enchantress*) ready in a month's time, and then to begin the orchestration."

Diary.

"*August 6th* (18th), 1886.

"Played the conclusion of the sickly *Manon* and Lefèbre's inanities to the end."

"*August 15th* (27th).

". . . Worked a little before and after supper. Kouma's Arioso is finished. Read Loti's *Pêcheurs d'Islande.* Not very pleased with it. The tone of the descriptions remind me of that . . . Zola and . . ."

"*August 18th* (30th).

"Walked in the garden. Worked and completely finished the rough sketches for the opera. Thank God!"

To M. Tchaikovsky.

"MAIDANOVA, *September,* 9th (21st), 1886.

". . . I have been all through Vietinghov-Scheel's opera. Good heavens! what a weak piece of work! He is a child, and no mature artist. It is a shame such a work should be given at the Imperial Opera. However, in this way the Direction have done Rubinstein a great service. His *Demon* appears a masterpiece in comparison with that little Scheel affair. To tell the truth, at present the best operas in the world are composed by P. I. Tchaikovsky, and *The Enchantress* is the most beautiful of them all. A gem all round. At least so it appears to me at this moment. Probably it appears to Vietinghov that his *Tamara* is far more beautiful; and God alone knows which of us is right."

Diary.

"*September 20th (October 2nd)*, 1886.

" Tolstoi never speaks with love and enthusiasm of any prophet of Truth (with the exception of Christ), but rather with contempt and hatred.   We do not know how he regards Socrates, Shakespeare, or Gogol.   We do not know if he cares for Michael Angelo and Raphael, Tourgeniev, George Sand, Dickens and Flaubert.   Perhaps his sympathies and antipathies in the sphere of philosophy and art are known to his intimates, but this inspired talker has never openly let fall a word which could enlighten us as to his attitude towards those great spirits who are on an equality with him.   For instance, he has told me that Beethoven had no talent (as compared with Mozart), but he has never expressed himself in writing either on music or any kindred subject.   Truly I think this man inclines only before God or the people, before humanity as a whole.   There is no individual before whom he would bow down.   Suitaiev was not an individual in Tolstoi's eyes, but the people itself, the personified wisdom of the people.   It would be interesting to know what this giant liked or disliked in literature.

" Probably after my death it will be of some interest to the world to hear of my musical predilections and prejudices, the more so that I have never expressed them by word of mouth.

" I will begin by degrees, and when touching upon contemporary musicians I shall also speak of their personalities.

" To begin with Beethoven, whom I praise unconditionally, and to whom I bend as to a god.   But what is Beethoven to me?   I bow down before the grandeur of some of his creations, but I do not love Beethoven.   My relationship to him reminds me of that which I felt in my childhood to the God Jehovah.   I feel for him—for my sentiments are still unchanged—great veneration, but also fear.   He has created the heaven and the earth, and although I fall down before him, I do not love him. Christ, on the contrary, calls forth exclusively the feeling of *love*. He is God, but also Man. He has suffered like ourselves. We pity Him and love in Him the ideal side of man's nature. If Beethoven holds an analogous place in my heart to the God Jehovah, I love Mozart as the musical Christ. I do not think this comparison is blasphemous. Mozart was as pure as an angel, and his music is full of divine beauty.

"While speaking of Beethoven I touch on Mozart. To my mind, Mozart is the culminating point of all beauty in the sphere of music. He alone can make me weep and tremble with delight at the consciousness of the approach of that which we call the ideal. Beethoven makes me tremble too, but rather from a sense of fear and yearning anguish. I do not understand how to analyse music, and cannot go into detail. . . . Still I must mention two facts. I love Beethoven's middle period, and sometimes his first; but I really hate his *last*, especially the latest quartets. They have only brilliancy, nothing more. The rest is chaos, over which floats, veiled in mist, the spirit of this musical Jehovah.

"I love everything in Mozart, for we love everything in the man to whom we are truly devoted. Above all, *Don Juan*, for through that work I have learnt to know what music is. Till then (my seventeenth year) I knew nothing except the enjoyable *semi-music* of the Italians. Although I love everything in Mozart, I will not assert that every one of his works, even the most insignificant, should be considered a masterpiece. I know quite well that no single example of his Sonatas is a great creation, and yet I like each one, because it is his, because he has breathed into it his sacred breath.

"As to the forerunner of both these artists, I like to play Bach, because it is interesting to play a good fugue; but I do not regard him, in common with many others, as a great genius. Handel is only fourth-rate, he is not even interesting. I sympathise with Glück in spite of his poor creative gift. I also like some things of Haydn. These four great masters have been surpassed by Mozart. They are rays which are extinguished by Mozart's sun."

To the Grand Duke Constantine Constantinovich.

"*September*, 1886.

"YOUR IMPERIAL HIGHNESS,—Permit me to thank you cordially for your valued present and your sympathetic letter. Very highly do I esteem the attention of which you have thought me worthy.

"I only regret, your Highness, that while looking for poems for my songs which are to be dedicated to her Majesty, I had not as yet the pleasure of possessing that charming little book which, thanks to your flattering attention, is now in my hands. How many of your poems glow with that warm and sincere feeling which makes them suitable for musical setting! When I read your collection of verses I determined at once to select some for my next song-cycle, and to dedicate them, with your gracious permission, to your Highness. I should be much pleased if you would accept this dedication as the expression of my sincere devotion."

To N. F. von Meck.

"MAIDANOVO, *October 5th (17th)*, 1886.

". . . What you say about *my conducting* is as balm to my wounded heart. The consciousness of my inability to conduct has been a torment and a martyrdom to me all my life. I think it is contemptible and shameful to have so little self-control that the mere thought of stepping into the conductor's desk makes me tremble with fright. This time too—although I have already promised to conduct myself—I feel when the time comes my courage will vanish and I shall refuse."

Diary.

"MAIDANOVO, *October 7th (19th)*, 1886.

"Played Brahms. It irritates me that this self-conscious mediocrity should be recognised as a genius. In comparison with him, Raff was a giant, not to speak of Rubinstein, who was a much greater man. And Brahms is so chaotic, so dry and meaningless!"

XI

At the end of October Tchaikovsky went to Petersburg, to be present at the first performance of Napravnik's opera, *Harold.* But as the performance was constantly postponed, he finally returned to Maidanovo without waiting for it.   Nevertheless, the journey was not without results, for Vsievolojsky, Director of the Imperial Opera, commissioned Tchaikovsky for the first time to compose a ballet.   Joukovsky's *Undiné* was chosen as a subject.

Judging from all accounts, this visit to Petersburg must have convinced Tchaikovsky of his great popularity there. Not only did he meet with a very friendly reception from the composers, with Rimsky-Korsakov at their head, but he received from an anonymous well-wisher, through the medium of Stassov, a premium of 500 roubles, usually bestowed on the best musical novelty of the season, judged in this instance to be *Manfred.*   He was also honoured by a brilliant gathering on the occasion of his election as honorary member of the St. Petersburg Chamber Music Society.

To Rimsky-Korsakov.

" *October* 30*th* (*November* 11*th*), 1886.

"DEAR NICHOLAS ANDREIEVICH,—I have a favour to ask.   Arensky is now quite recovered, although I find him somewhat depressed and agitated.   I like him so much and wish you would sometimes take an interest in him, for, as regards music, he venerates you more than anyone else.   The best way of doing this would be to give one of his works at one of your next concerts.   There, where all Russian composers find a place, should be a little room for Arensky, who, at any rate, is as good as the rest. But as you would not like to offend anyone, I propose that you should put one of Arensky's works in the programme of your fourth concert instead of my *Romeo* overture. He needs stirring up; and such an impulse given by you would count for so much with him, because he loves and respects you. Please think it over and grant my wish. Thereby you will make your deeply devoted pupil (Arensky) very happy.

"In conclusion, I must add that your 'Spanish Capriccio' is a *colossal masterpiece of instrumentation*, and you may regard yourself as the greatest master of the present day."

To M. Tchaikovsky.

"Moscow, *November 19th (December 1st)*, 1886.

". . . I arrived in Moscow early to-day. There has already been a rehearsal. I was ill again after my last letter to you. This time I was so bad that I decided to send for the doctor. It seemed to me that I was about to have a strange illness. Suddenly I received a telegram saying that I must be at the rehearsal.[1] I answered that the rehearsal was not to be thought of, for I could not travel. But at the end of half an hour I suddenly felt so well that—in spite of terrible disinclination—I went to Moscow. Every trace of headache, which for ten days had so affected me, vanished. Is not this a curious pathological case?"

To A. S. Arensky.

"*November 24th (December 6th)*, 1886.

"Dear Friend Anton Stepanovich,—I only received your welcome letter yesterday; I knew already from Taneiev that you had composed *Marguerite Gautier* and dedicated it to me. Thank you cordially for this dedication. The attention and honour you have shown me touch me deeply. *Marguerite* lies beside me on the table, and—in my free moments, which are not many—I cast a glance at it here and there, with much interest and pleasure. Please do not feel hurt that I did not write you my impressions at once. At the first glance I found the work very interesting, because you have entirely departed from your accustomed style. *Marguerite* has so little resemblance to the Suite and the Symphony that one could

---

[1] Of *Cherevichek*, "The Little Shoes."

easily suppose it came from the pen of a different man. The elegance of form, harmony, and orchestration are the same, but the character of the theme and its working out are quite different. Naturally the question arises: Is it better than the Symphony and the Suite? At present I cannot answer."

Although somewhat anticipating my narrative, I will insert here an extract from a later letter of Tchaikovsky's, in which he gives Arensky his opinion of *Marguerite Gautier*.

To A. Arensky.

"MAIDANOVO, *April 2nd* (14*th*), 1887.

"DEAR ANTON STEPANOVICH,—I wrote to you in August that I would pronounce judgment on *Marguerite Gautier* as soon as I had heard the work and had leisure to study the score. I held it all the more my duty to wait because, although I value your talent very highly, I do not like your Fantasia. It is very easy to praise a man who is highly esteemed. But to say to him: 'Not beautiful; I do not like it,' without basing one's judgment on a full explanation, is very difficult. . . .

"I must state my opinion briefly. First the choice of subject. It was very painful and mortifying to me, and to all your friends, that you had chosen *La Dame aux Camelias* as the subject of your Fantasia. How can an educated musician—when there are Homer, Shakespeare, Gogol, Poushkin, Dante, Tolstoi, Lermontov, and others—feel any interest in the production of Dumas *fils*, which has for its theme the history of a demi-mondaine adventuress which, even if written with French cleverness, is in truth false, sentimental, and vulgar? Such a choice might be intelligible in Verdi, who employed subjects which could excite people's nerves at a period of artistic decadence; but it is quite incomprehensible in a young and gifted Russian musician, who has enjoyed a good education, and is, moreover, a pupil of Rimsky-Korsakov and a friend of S. Taneiev.

"Now for the music: (1) *The Orgies.*—If we are to realise in these orgies a supper after a ball at the house of a light woman, in which a crowd of people participate, eat mayonnaise with truffles, and afterwards dance the *cancan*, the music is not wanting *in realism*, fire, and brilliancy. It is, moreover, saturated with Liszt, as is the whole Fantasia. Its beauty—if one looks at it closely—is purely on the surface; there are no enthralling passages. Such beauty is not *true* beauty, but only a forced imitation, which is rather a fault than a merit. We find this superficial beauty in Rossini, Donizetti, Bellini, Mendelssohn, Massenet, Liszt, and others. But they were also masters in their own way, though their chief characteristic was not the Ideal, after which we ought to strive. For neither Beethoven, nor Bach (who is wearisome, but still a genius), nor Glinka, nor Mozart, ever strove after this surface beauty, but rather the ideal, often veiled under a form which at first sight is unattractive.

"(2) *Pastorale in Bougival.*—Oh God! If you could only understand how unpoetical and unpastoral this Bougival is, with its boats, its inns, and its *cancans!* This movement is as good as most conventional pastoral ballets that are composed by musicians of some talent.

"(3) *The Love Melody*

is altogether beautiful. It reminds me of Liszt. Not of any particular melody, but it is in his style, after the manner of his semi-Italian melodies, which are wanting in the plasticity and simplicity of the true Italian folk airs. Moreover, the continuation of your theme:

is not only beautiful, but wonderful; it captivates both the ear and the heart.

"No one can ever reproach you with regard to the technical part of your work, which deserves unqualified praise."

To Modeste Tchaikovsky.

"Moscow, *December* 4th (16th), 1886.

"MY DEAR MODI,—Something very important happened to-day. I conducted the first orchestral rehearsal in such style that all were astonished (unless it were mere flattery), for they had expected I should make a fool of myself. The nearer came the terrible day, the more unbearable was my nervousness. I was often on the point of giving up the idea of conducting. In the end I mastered myself, was enthusiastically received by the orchestra, found courage to make a little speech, and raised the bâton. Now I know I *can* conduct, I shall not be nervous at the performance."

To N. F. von Meck.

"Moscow, *January* 14th (26th), 1887.

"MY VERY DEAR FRIEND,—I have been enjoying your hospitality for a week.[1] I live in your house as if under the wing of Christ. Your servants are so careful of my welfare that I cannot praise them enough. I only regret that I can be so little at home. Daily rehearsals. I take a walk every morning, and by eleven o'clock I am waiting in the conductor's desk. The rehearsal is not over till four o'clock, and then I am so tired that when I return home I have to lie down for a while. Towards evening I feel better and take some food.

"The conducting gives me great anxiety and exhausts my whole nervous system. But I must say it also affords me great satisfaction. First of all, I am very glad to have conquered my innate, morbid shyness; secondly, it is a good thing for a composer to conduct his own work, instead of having constantly to interrupt the conductor to draw his attention to this, or that, mistake; thirdly, all my colleagues have shown me such genuine sympathy that I am quite touched by it, and very pleased. Do you know I feel much less agitation than when I sit at the rehearsal doing nothing. If all goes well, I believe that not only will my nerves be none the worse, but it will have a beneficial effect on them."

---

[1] Tchaikovsky was staying in N. F. von Meck's house at this time.

The first performance of *Les Caprices d'Oxane* took place at Moscow on January 19th (31st), 1887, and had a far-reaching influence on Tchaikovsky's future, because he then made his first successful attempt at conducting. The great interest which the production of a new opera always awakens was thereby doubled, and all the places were taken before the opening night. The singers did their work conscientiously; there was no fault to be found, but no one made a memorable "creation" of any part. The mounting and costumes were irreproachable.

The public greeted the composer-conductor with great enthusiasm. Gifts of all kinds showed plainly that it was Tchaikovsky himself who was honoured, not the new conductor and composer of *Les Caprices d'Oxane*. The opera was a success; four numbers had to be repeated *da capo*.

The Press criticisms on this occasion were all favourable, even the *Sovremenny Izvesty*, in which Krouglikov, as we know, generally criticised Tchaikovsky's works so severely. In short, the opera really had a brilliant success; far greater than that achieved by *Eugene Oniegin* in Petersburg. Neverthess this opera only remained in the repertory for two seasons.

But little can be said about that which interests us most—the impression made by Tchaikovsky's conducting. The severest judge and critic, Tchaikovsky himself, was satisfied. We know in what an objective spirit he criticised the success of his works, so we can safely believe him when he says he fulfilled his task satisfactorily. He describes this memorable evening as follows :—

To E. K. Pavlovskaya.

"Moscow, *January 20th* (*February 1st*), 1887.

" I did not expect to be very excited on the day of the performance, but when I awoke, quite early, I felt really ill, and could only think of the approaching ordeal as of a horrible nightmare. I cannot describe what mental agonies

I suffered during the course of the day. Consequently, at the appointed hour, I appeared half dead at the theatre. Altani accompanied me to the orchestra. Immediately the curtain went up and, amid great applause, I was presented with many wreaths from the chorus, orchestra, etc. While this took place, I somewhat recovered my composure, began the Overture well, and by the end felt quite master of myself. There was great applause after the Overture. The first Act went successfully, and afterwards I was presented with more wreaths, among them yours, for which many thanks. I was now quite calm, and conducted the rest of the opera with undivided attention. It is difficult to say if the work really pleased. The theatre was at least half-full of my friends. Time and future performances will show if the applause was for me personally (for the sake of past services), or for my work. Now the question is, how did I conduct? I feel some constraint in speaking about it. Everyone praised me; they said they had no idea I possessed such a gift for conducting. But is it true? Or is it only flattery? I shall conduct twice more, and after the third time I ought to know for certain how much truth there is in all this."

I have seldom seen Tchaikovsky in such a cheerful frame of mind as on that evening. We did not reach home till after five o'clock in the morning, and he immediately sank into a deep sleep. After so many days of anxiety and excitement he really needed rest! No one was more unprepared than he for the sad news which reached us next morning.

About seven o'clock I was aroused by a telegram which announced the death of our niece Tatiana, the eldest daughter of Alexandra Davidov. She had died quite suddenly at a masked ball in Petersburg. Not only was she a near relative, but also a highly gifted girl of great beauty. It required considerable resolution on my part to break the sad news to my brother when he awoke at eleven o'clock, happy and contented, and still under the pleasant impressions of the previous evening.

In spite of this heavy blow, Tchaikovsky did not alter his decision to conduct *Les Caprices d'Oxane* for two nights longer. The constant activity, and anxiety of a different nature, helped to assuage the violence of his grief.

XII

To N. F. von Meck.

"MAIDANOVO, *February 2nd* (14*th*), 1887.

"I have now been at home five days, yet there is no question of rest; on the contrary, I am working with such feverish haste at *The Enchantress* that I feel quite exhausted. I cannot live without work, but why do circumstances always compel me to be in a hurry, to have to overtax my strength? I see such an endless pile of work before me to which I am pledged that I dare not look into the future. How short life is! Now that I have probably reached that last step which means the full maturity of my talent, I look back involuntarily and, seeing so many years behind me, glance timidly at the path ahead and ask: Shall I succeed? Is it worth while? And yet it is only now that I begin to be able to compose without self-doubt, and to believe in my own powers and knowledge."

To N. F. von Meck.

"MAIDANOVO, *February 9th* (21*st*), 1887.

"I am already dreaming of a time when I shall give concerts abroad. But of what does one not dream? If only I were twenty years younger!!! One thing is certain: my nerves are much stronger, and things which formerly were not to be thought of are now quite possible. Undoubtedly I owe this to my free life, relieved from all anxiety of earning my daily bread. And who but you, dear friend, is the author of all the good things fate has brought me?

"The concert will take place in Petersburg on March 5th."

On February 23rd (March 7th) Tchaikovsky went to Petersburg to attend the rehearsals for the Philharmonic Concert, at which the St. Petersburg public was to make his acquaintance as a conductor, from which dated the commencement of a whole series of similar concerts which made his name known in Russia, Europe and America.

On February 28th (March 12th) the first rehearsal took place, and Tchaikovsky writes in his diary in his customary laconic style: "Excitement and dread." Henceforth, to the very end of his life, it was not the concert itself so much as the first rehearsal which alarmed him. By the second rehearsal he had usually recovered himself. Abroad, he found it particularly painful to stand up for the first time before an unknown orchestra.

All the important musical circles in Petersburg showed a lively interest in Tchaikovsky's début as a concert conductor. The three rehearsals attracted a number of the first musicians, who encouraged him by their warm words of sympathy. No début could have been made under more favourable conditions.

The concert itself, which took place on March 5th (17th), in the hall of the Nobles' Club, went off admirably. The programme consisted of: (1) Suite No. 2 (first performance in St. Petersburg), (2) Aria from the opera *The Enchantress*, (3) the "Mummers' Dance" from the same opera, (4) Andante and Valse from the Serenade for strings, (5) *Francesca da Rimini*, (6) Pianoforte solos, (7) Overture "*1812*."

The hall was full to overflowing, and the ovations endless. The Press criticisms of the music, as well as of Tchaikovsky's conducting, proved colourless and commonplace, but on the whole laudatory. Even Cui expressed some approbation for Tchaikovsky as a conductor, although he again found fault with him as a composer.

Tchaikovsky's diary contains the following brief account of the concert: "My concert. Complete success. Great enjoyment—but still, why this drop of gall in my honey-pot?"

In this question lie the germs of that weariness and suffering which had their growth in Tchaikovsky's soul simultaneously with his pursuit of fame, and reached their greatest intensity in the moment of the composer's greatest triumphs.

To N. F. von Meck.

"MAIDANOVO, *March 12th (24th)*, 1887.

"The Empress has sent me her autograph picture in a beautiful frame.[1] This attention has touched me deeply, especially at a time when she and the Emperor have so many other things to think about."

Diary.

"Ippolitov-Ivanov and his wife came very late, about ten o'clock. I met them out walking. At first I felt annoyed to see them, and vexed at my work being interrupted; but afterwards these good people (she is extremely sympathetic) made me forget everything, except that it is the greatest pleasure to be in the society of congenial friends. Ivanov played, and she sang beautiful fragments from his opera *Ruth* (the duet especially charmed me). They left at six. Worked before and after supper."

To Modeste Tchaikovsky.

"MAIDANOVO, *March 15th (27th)*, 1887.

"*Ruth* pleases me more and more. I believe Ippolitov-Ivanov will come to the front, if only because he has something original about him, and this 'something' is also very attractive."

Diary.

"*March 16th (28th)*, 1887.

"I will not conceal it: all the poetry of country life and solitude has vanished. I do not know why. *Nowhere do I feel so miserable as at home.* If I do not work, I torment

---

[1] In return for the dedication of the twelve songs.

myself, am afraid of the future, etc. Is solitude really necessary to me? When I am in town, country life seems a paradise; when I am here, I feel no delight whatever. To-day, in particular, I am quite out of tune."

"*March* 19*th* (31*st*).

"Have just read through my diary for the last two years. Good heavens! how could my imagination have been so deceived by the melancholy bareness of Maidanovo? How everything used to please me!"

"*March* 26*th* (*April* 7*th*).

"Read through Korsakov's 'Snow-Maiden,' and was astonished at his mastery. I envy him and ought to be ashamed of it."

"*March* 30*th* (*April* 11*th*).

"After supper I read the score of *A Life for the Tsar*. What a master! How did Glinka manage to do it? It is incomprehensible how such a colossal work could have been created by an amateur and—judging by his diary— a rather limited and trivial nature."

"*April* 16*th* (*28th*).

"Played through *The Power of the Evil One*.[1] An almost repulsive musical monstrosity; yet, at the same time, talent, intuition, and imagination."

To N. F. von Meck.

"MAIDANOVO, *April* 24*th* (*May* 6*th*), 1887.

"MY VERY DEAR FRIEND,—I wished to leave Maidanovo a month ago, and yet I am still here. My work (the orchestration of the opera) detains me. This work is not really difficult, but it takes time. I notice that the older I grow, the more trouble my orchestration gives me. I judge myself more severely, am more careful, more critical with regard to light and shade. In such a case the country is a real boon. Saint-Saëns has invited me to be present at both his concerts at Moscow, but I have courteously refused. Poor Saint-Saëns had to play to an

---

[1] Opera by Serov.

empty room. I knew it would be so, and that the poor Frenchman would take it deeply to heart, so I did not wish to be a witness of his disappointment. But also I did not want to interrupt my work."

Tchaikovsky stayed at Maidanovo to complete the instrumentation of the whole score of *The Enchantress,* and left on May 9th to visit his sick friend, Kondratiev, before starting on his journey to the Caucasus.

XIII

To N. F. von Meck.

"THE CASPIAN SEA, *May 28th* (*June 9th*), 1887.

" I left Moscow on the 20th. At Nijni-Novogorod I had great trouble in securing a second-class ticket for the steamer, *Alexander II.* This steamer is considered the best, and is therefore always full. My quarters were very small and uncomfortable, but I enjoyed the journey down the Volga. It was almost high tide, and therefore the banks were so far away that one could almost imagine oneself at sea. Mother Volga is sublimely poetical. The right bank is hilly, and there are many beautiful bits of scenery, but in this respect the Volga cannot compare with the Rhine, nor even with the Danube and Rhône. Its beauty does not lie in its banks, but in its unbounded width and in the extraordinary volume of its waters, which roll down to the sea without any motion. We stopped at the towns on the way just long enough to get an idea of them. Samara and the little town of Volsk pleased me best, the latter having the most beautiful gardens I have ever seen. We reached Astrakhan on the fifth day. Here we boarded a little steamer, which brought us to the spot where the mouth of the Volga debouches into the open sea, where we embarked on a schooner, on board which we have been for the last two days. The Caspian Sea has been very treacherous. It was so stormy during the night that I was quite frightened. Every moment it seemed as if the trembling ship must break up beneath the force of the waves; so much so that I could not close an eye all night. But in spite of this I was not sea-sick. We reached Baku to-day. The storm has abated. I shall not be able to start for Tiflis until to-morrow morning, for we cannot catch the train to-day."

On the journey between Tsaritsin and Astrakhan, Tchaikovsky had a very droll experience. He had managed so cleverly that no one on board knew who he was. One day a little musical entertainment was got up, and Tchaikovsky offered to undertake the accompanying. It so happened that a lady amateur placed one of his own songs before him and explained to him the manner in which he was to accompany it. On his timidly objecting, the lady answered that she must know best, as Tchaikovsky himself had gone through the song in question with her music-mistress. The same evening a passenger related how Tchaikovsky had been so delighted with the tenor Lody in the rôle of Orlik in *Mazeppa*[1] that after the performance "he fell on Lody's neck and wept tears of emotion."

To N. F. von Meck.

"TIFLIS, *May* 30*th* (*June* 11*th*), 1887.

"Baku, in the most unexpected fashion, has turned out to be an altogether beautiful place, well planned and well built, clean and very characteristic. The Oriental (especially the Persian) character is very prevalent, so that one could almost imagine oneself to be on the other side of the Caspian Sea. It has but one drawback: the complete lack of verdure. . . .

"On the day after my arrival I visited the neighbourhood of the naphtha wells, where some hundred boring-towers throw up a hundred thousand *pouds* of naphtha every minute. The picture is grand but gloomy. . . .

"The road between Baku and Tiflis runs through a stony, desolate country."

[1] Orlik's part is written for a bass, and Lody has a tenor voice.

The end of this journey was Borjom, where he intended to pass the whole summer in the family of his brother Anatol. He reached there on June 11th. He only learnt to appreciate by degrees the enchanting beauty of the neighbourhood. The horizon, shut in by lofty mountains, the sombre flora, their luxuriance, and the depth of the shadows, made an unpleasant impression upon him at first. Only after he had learnt to know the inexhaustible number and variety of the walks did he begin to like this country more and more. When, ten days later, his brother Modeste arrived at Borjom he was already full of enthusiasm and ready to initiate him into all the beauties of the place.

Tchaikovsky worked very little while at Borjom, only spending an hour a day at the instrumentation of the "Mozartiana" Suite.

At the commencement of July Tchaikovsky left Borjom in response to a telegram from his friend Kondratiev, who had been removed to Aix-la-Chapelle, in the hopes that the baths might prolong his life for a few months. Kondratiev's condition was so critical that Tchaikovsky could not do less than interrupt his own cure and join his friend as soon as possible.

To Modeste Tchaikovsky.

"Aix-la-Chapelle, *July* 16th (28th), 1887.

"I do not dislike Aix—that is all I can say. What is really bad here is the atmosphere, saturated as it is with smells of cooking, cinnamon, and other spices. I think sorrowfully of the air in Borjom, but I try to dwell upon it as little as possible. However, I feel more cheerful here than I did on the journey. I see that my arrival has given much pleasure to Kondratiev and Legoshin, and that I shall be of use to them."

Diary.

"AIX, *July 22nd* (*August 3rd*), 1887.

"I sit at home full of remorse. The cause of my remorse is this : life is passing away and draws near to its end, and yet I have not fathomed it. Rather do I drive away those disquieting questions of our destiny when they intrude themselves upon me, and try to hide from them. Do I live truly ? Do I act rightly ? For example, I am now sitting here, and everyone admires my *sacrifice*. Now there is no question of sacrifice. I lead a life of ease, gormandise at the *table d'hôte*, do nothing, and spend my money on luxuries, while others want it for absolute necessities. Is not that the veriest egoism ? I do not act towards my neighbours as I ought."

To P. Jurgenson.

"AIX, *July 29th* (*August 10th*), 1887.

"DEAR FRIEND,—To-day I am sending you my Mozart Suite, registered. Three of the borrowed numbers in the Suite are pianoforte pieces (Nos. 1, 2, 4); one (No. 3) is the chorus ' Ave Verum.' Of course, I should be glad if the Suite could be played next season. That is all."

Tchaikovsky's " heroic act " of friendship consumed more than a month of his time. While paying full tribute to the generosity of his undertaking, we must confess that he failed to grasp the relation between wishing and doing. Tchaikovsky, filled with real and self-denying compassion for the sufferings of his neighbour, was wanting—as in all practical questions of life—in the necessary ability, self-control, and purpose. In the abstract, no one had more sympathy for his neighbour than he ; but in reality no one was less able to do much for him. Anyone who could ask the trivial question : " Where wadding, needles, and thread could be bought ? " would naturally lose his head at the bedside of a dying man. The consciousness of his helplessness and incapacity to lessen his friend's suffering

in the least, his irresolution in face of the slightest difficulty, rendered Tchaikovsky's useless visit to Aix all the
more painful. He suffered for the dying man and for
himself. The result was that he did "too much" for
friendship and "too little" for his sick friend ; at least, in
comparison to the extraordinary sacrifice of strength
which his generous action demanded. When, at the end
of August, the dying man's nephew came to relieve him,
Tchaikovsky fled from Aix, deeply grieved at parting from
his friend "for ever," humbled at his own mental condition,
and angry at his inability "to see the sad business through
to the end." Exhausted, and wrathful with himself, he
arrived at Maidanovo on August 30th (September 11th),
where the news of Kondratiev's death reached him a fortnight later.

Diary.

"*September 21st (October 3rd),* 1887.

"How short is life! How much I have still to do, to
think, and to say! We keep putting things off, and meanwhile death lurks round the corner. It is just a year since
I touched this book, and so much has changed since
then. How strange! Just 365 days ago I was afraid
to confess that, in spite of the glow of sympathetic feeling which Christ awoke in me, I dared to doubt His
divinity. Since then my *religion* has become more clearly
defined, for during this time I have thought a great deal
about God, life, and death. In Aix especially I meditated
on the fatal questions : why, how, for what end? I should
like to define my religion in detail, if only I might be
quite clear, once for all, as to my faith, and as to the
boundary which divides it from speculation. But life and
its vanities are passing, and I do not know whether I shall
succeed in expressing the *symbol* of that faith which has
arisen in me of late. It has very definite forms, but I do
not use them when I pray. I pray just as before ; as
I was taught. Moreover, God can hardly require to know
how and why we pray. God has no need of prayers.
But we have."

On October 20th (November 1st) *The Enchantress* was produced under the bâton of the composer, and the performance was altogether most brilliant and artistic.

On this first night Tchaikovsky does not appear to have observed that the opera was a failure. He thought, on the contrary, that it pleased the public. After the second performance (on October 23rd), which—notwithstanding that it went better than the first—still failed to move the audience to applause, he first felt doubts as to its success. The indifference of the public was clearly apparent after the third and fourth representations, when his appearance in the conductor's desk was received in chilling silence. It was only then that he realised that *The Enchantress* was a failure. On the fifth night the house was empty.

Tchaikovsky, as we shall see, ascribed this failure to the ill-will of the critics. After I had read through all the notices—says Modeste—it seemed to me that, in the present instance, my brother had done them too much honour. In none of the eleven criticisms did I trace that tone of contempt and malicious enjoyment with which his other operas had been received. No one called *The Enchantress* a " still-born nonentity," as Cui had said of *Eugene Oniegin;* no one attempted to count up the deliberate thefts in *The Enchantress,* as Galler had done with *Mazeppa.* The reason for the failure of *The Enchantress* must be sought elsewhere : possibly in the defective interpretation of both the chief parts ; but more probably in the qualities of the music, which still awaits its just evaluation at the hands of a competent critic.

To N. F. von Meck.

" Moscow, *November* 13*th* (25*th*), 1887.

" MY DEAR FRIEND,—Please forgive me for so seldom writing. I am passing through a very stirring period of my life, and am always in such a state of agitation that it is impossible to speak to you from my heart as I should wish. After conducting my opera four times, I returned here, about five days ago, in a very melancholy frame of mind. In spite of the ovation I received on the opening night, my opera has not taken with the public, and practically met with no success. From the Press I have encountered such hatred and hostility that, even now, I cannot account for it. On no other opera have I expended so much labour and sacrifice; yet never before have I been so persecuted by the critics. I have given up the journey to Tiflis, for I shall scarcely have time to get sufficient rest in Maidanovo before I have to start on my concert tour abroad. I conduct first in Leipzig, and afterwards in Dresden, Hamburg, Copenhagen, Berlin, and Prague. In March I give my own concert in Paris, and from there I go to London, as I have received an invitation from the Philharmonic Society. In short, a whole crowd of new and strong impressions are awaiting me."

The Symphony Concert of the Russian Musical Society, November 14th (26th), was the first concert ever conducted by Tchaikovsky in Moscow. The programme consisted exclusively of his own works, including " Mozartiana " (first time), *Francesca da Rimini*, the Fantasia for pianoforte, op. 56 (Taneiev as soloist), and the Arioso from *The Enchantress*. On the following day the same programme was repeated by the Russian Musical Society at a popular concert. The " Mozartiana " Suite was a great success (the " Ave Verum " was encored), and the Press—in contradistinction to that of St. Petersburg—spoke with great warmth and cordiality of the composer and conductor.

To P. Jurgenson.

" *November 24th (December 6th)* 1887.

" In to-day's paper I accidentally saw that the eighth performance of *The Enchantress* was given before a half-empty house. It is an undoubted *fiasco*. This failure has wounded me in my inmost soul, for I never worked with greater ardour than at *The Enchantress*.   Besides, I feel ashamed when I think of you, for you must have sustained a terrible loss.   I know well enough that some day the opera will be reinstated, but when?   Meanwhile it makes me very bitter. So far I have always maintained that the Press could not influence one's success or failure; but now I am inclined to think that it is only the united attack of these hounds of critics which has ruined my opera.   The devil take them!   Why this spite?   Just now, for example, in to-day's number of the *Novosti*, see how they rail at our Musical Society and at me, because of this Popular Concert!   Incomprehensible!"

Part VII

I

1888

WITH December, 1887, began a new and last period in the life of Tchaikovsky, during which he realised his wildest dreams of fame, and attained to such prosperity and universal honour as rarely fall to the lot of an artist during his lifetime. Distrustful and modest (from an excess of pride), he was now in a perpetual state of wonder and delight to find himself far more appreciated in Russia and abroad than he had ever hoped in the past. Physically neither better nor worse than in former years, possessing the unlimited affections of those whom he loved in return, —he was, to all appearance, an example of mortal happiness, yet in reality he was less happy than before.

Those menacing blows of fate—like the opening of Beethoven's Fifth Symphony—had sounded, although muffled and distant, even on the day of Tchaikovsky's first concert (March 5th); while that intangible and groundless sense of bitterness—that "touch of gall," as he himself calls it—was present even in that triumphant moment when he found himself master of the orchestra and all its tempestuous elements, as though prophetic of those sufferings which overshadowed the last years of his life. At the time he did not understand this vague warning; afterwards, when it came back to him, he realised it had been a friendly caution, not to continue the chase for fame; not to take up occupations that went against his nature, nor to spend his strength upon the attainment of things which would come of themselves; finally, to cling to his true vocation, lest disappointment should await him in the new path he had elected to follow. In February he wrote to Nadejda von Meck: " New and powerful impressions continually await me. Probably my fame will increase, but would it not be better to stay at home and work? God knows! I can say this : I regret the time when I was left in peace in the solitude of the country." And this regret grew keener, as his weariness grew more intolerable. The more he accustomed his temperament to unsuitable occupations, the further he advanced his reputation, the more complete was his disenchantment with the prize. Radiant and glittering as it had appeared from afar, seen closer, it proved insignificant and tarnished. Hence the profound disillusionment, " the insane depression," the something " hopeless and final " which make so dark a background to the picture of his brilliant success at home and abroad.

Tchaikovsky left Russia on December 15th (27th) and arrived in Berlin two days later. Here he was to meet Herr N—— who was acting as his concert agent during this tour. He had no sooner settled in his hotel than, picking up a newspaper, his eye fell upon a paragraph to the effect that: " To-day, December 29th, the Russian composer Tchaikovsky arrives in Berlin. To-morrow his numerous friends (?) and admirers (?) will meet to celebrate his arrival by a luncheon at the —— restaurant, at one o'clock. Punctual attendance is requested." " No words could describe my horror and indignation," wrote Tchaikovsky. " At that moment I could cheerfully have murdered Herr N——. I went out to breakfast at a café in the Passage, and afterwards to the Museum, walking in fear and trembling lest I should meet Herr N—— or some of my numerous *friends and admirers*."

The following morning the dreaded interview with his agent took place. Tchaikovsky found him not altogether unsympathetic, but during the entire tour he realised that he was dealing with a very peculiar and eccentric man, whom he never really understood.

To Modeste Tchaikovsky.

" LEIPZIG, *December 21st,* 1887 (*January 2nd,* 1888).

" I have made acquaintance with Scharwenka and a number of other people. I also met Artôt.[1] Everyone was astonished to see me with N——, who follows me like my own shadow. At three o'clock I left for Leipzig, luckily without N—— for once, and was met by Brodsky, Siloti, and two of my admirers. I had supper with Brodsky. There was a Christmas-tree. His wife and sister-in-law are charming—really good Russian women. All the time the tears were in my eyes. Next day I took a walk (it was New Year's Day), and went back to dine with Siloti at Brodsky's. He was just trying a new trio by Brahms. The composer himself was at the piano. Brahms is a handsome man, rather short and stout.[2] He was very friendly to me. Then we sat down to table. Brahms enjoys a good drink. Grieg, fascinating and sympathetic, was there too.[3] In the evening I went to

---

[1] Their first meeting since 1869.

[2] In an account of his visit to Leipzig, which Tchaikovsky afterwards published as the *Diary of My Tour in 1888,* he characterises the German composer more fully : "Brahms is rather a short man, suggests a sort of amplitude, and possesses a very sympathetic appearance. His fine head—almost that of an old man—recalls the type of a handsome, benign, elderly Russian priest. His features are certainly not characteristic of German good looks, and I cannot conceive why some learned ethnographer (Brahms himself told me this after I had spoken of the impression his appearance made upon me) chose to reproduce his head on the first page of his books as being highly characteristic of German features. A certain softness of outline, pleasing curves, rather long and slightly grizzled hair, kind grey eyes, and a thick beard, freely sprinkled with white—all this recalled at once the type of pure-bred Great Russian so frequently met with among our clergy. Brahms's manner is very simple, free from vanity, his humour jovial, and the few hours spent in his society left me with a very agreeable recollection."

[3] In the same series of articles appeared the following sketch of Grieg : " There entered the room a very short, middle-aged man, exceedingly fragile

the Gewandhaus, when Joachim and Hausmann played the new Double Concerto of Brahms for violin and 'cello, and the composer himself conducted. I sat in the Directors' box, and made acquaintance with such numbers of people that I could not keep pace with them all. The Directors informed me that my rehearsal was fixed for the next day. What I suffered during the evening—in fact the whole time—cannot be described. If Brodsky and Siloti had not been there, I think I should have died. I spent a terrible night. The rehearsal took place early this morning. I was formally introduced to the orchestra by Carl Reinecke. I made a little speech in German. The rehearsal went well in the end. Brahms was there, and yesterday and to-day we have been a good deal together. We are ill at ease, because we do not really like each other, but he takes great pains to be kind to me. Grieg is charming. Dined with Siloti. Quartet concert at night. The new trio of Brahms. Home-sick. Very tired.

"You cannot imagine a finer room than at the Gewand-haus. It is the best concert-room I ever saw in my life."

To P. I. Jurgenson.

"Leipzig, *December 24th*, 1887 (*January 5th*, 1888).

"Yesterday the public rehearsal took place. I was very nervous, but my success was unusually flattering. . . . To-night, however, all may be reversed, for it is by no means certain that I shall not make a fool of myself. I have seen a good deal of Brahms. He is by no means a total abstainer, but he is very pleasant, and not so vain as I expected. But it is Grieg who has altogether won my heart. He is most taking and sympathetic, and his wife

in appearance, with shoulders of unequal height, fair hair brushed back from his forehead, and a very slight, almost boyish, beard and moustache. There was nothing very striking about the features of this man, whose exterior at once attracted my sympathy, for it would be impossible to call them hand-some or regular ; but he had an uncommon charm, and blue eyes, not very large, but irresistibly fascinating, recalling the glance of a charming and candid child. I rejoiced in the depths of my heart when we were mutually introduced to each other, and it turned out that this personality, which was so inexplicably sympathetic to me, belonged to a musician whose warmly emotional music had long ago won my heart. It was Edvard Grieg."

equally so. Reinecke is very amiable. At the first
rehearsal he introduced me to the band, and I made the
following speech: 'Gentlemen, I cannot speak German,
but I am proud to have to do with such a . . . such a
. . . that is to say . . . I am proud . . . I cannot.' The
band is splendid; I could not have believed that our
musicians—good as they are—were still so far behind a
first-rate German orchestra."

"December 25th (January 6th).

" The concert has gone off well. The reception of the
Suite was good, but not to be compared with that at the
public rehearsal, when the audience consisted almost
entirely of students and musicians. After the concert
I went to a banquet arranged in my honour by Reinecke.
He related much that was interesting about Schumann
and, generally speaking, I felt very much at ease with him.
Afterwards I had to go on to a fête given by the Russian
students, and I did not get home until very late. Now
I am just off to a Tchaikovsky Festival held by the Liszt-
Verein. It begins at 11 a.m."

The Press notices upon Tchaikovsky's début in Leipzig
as conductor and composer were numerous and lengthy.
Keeping in view the importance of this occasion, and the
influence it exercised on his future career, it has been
thought well to give some extracts from the most interesting of these criticisms, which will be found in the
Appendix.[1]

At the Tchaikovsky Festival given by the Liszt-Verein,
his Quartet, op. 11, Trio, and some of his smaller compositions were included in the programme. The following day
the composer returned to Berlin, where he arranged with
the Directors of the Philharmonic Society to give a concert
of his works on February 8th. He then left for Hamburg
in the company of Adolf Brodsky, where the latter was
to take part in a concert conducted by Hans von Bülow.
As Tchaikovsky had the prospect of a few days' leisure,

[1] See Appendix C, p. 762.

he decided to spend them in Lübeck, whence he wrote to his brother Modeste on December 30th, 1887 (January 11th 1888):—

"What joy! I do so enjoy finding myself in a strange town, in a capital hotel, with the prospect of five peaceful days before me! I arrived in Hamburg with Brodsky at 6 a.m. The rehearsal for Bülow's concert began at ten o'clock. Bülow was delighted to see me. He has altered and aged. He seems, too, calmer, more subdued, and softer in manner. . . . I went to the concert in the evening. Bülow conducted with inspiration, especially the 'Eroica.' I came on here to-day. It is very pleasant. What a blessing to be silent! To feel that no one will be coming, that I shall not be dragged out anywhere!"

To Modeste Tchaikovsky.

"*January 1st (13th), 1888.*

" . . . At last January (old style) has come. Now at any rate I can reckon four months to my return to Russia. I went to the theatre yesterday. Barnay was the star in *Othello.* He is sometimes astounding, quite a genius, but what an agonising play! Iago is too revolting—such beings do not exist."

On January 1st, 1888, a piece of good fortune fell to Tchaikovsky's lot. Thanks to the efforts of Vsievolojsky, Director of the Imperial Opera, the Emperor bestowed upon him a life pension of 3,000 roubles (£300) per annum.

To Modeste Tchaikovsky.

"HAMBURG, *January 10th (22nd), 1888.*

"On my appearance I was enthusiastically received by the orchestra, and their applause was supported by the public, which was not the case in Leipzig. I conducted without agitation, but towards the end I grew so tired I was afraid I could not hold out. Sapellnikov[1] played

---

[1] Pupil of Brassin and Madame Sophie Menter at the St. Petersburg Conservatoire, and, later on, an intimate friend of Tchaikovsky.

splendidly. After the concert there was a large party at the house of Bernuth, the Director of the Philharmonic. About a hundred guests were present, all in full-dress. After a long speech from Bernuth, I replied in German, which created a *furore*. Then we began to eat and drink. Yesterday was terrible ; I cannot describe how I was torn to pieces, nor how exhausted I felt afterwards. In the evening there was a gala in my honour, at which my compositions were exclusively performed. The Press was very favourable.

" After the *soirée* followed a fearful night of it, in company with many musicians, critics, and amateurs, admirers of my music. I feel befogged. To-day I start for Berlin. Bülow is very amiable."

The programme of the concert at which Tchaikovsky made his first appearance in Hamburg was as follows : Tchaikovsky's Serenade for strings, Pianoforte Concerto in B♭ minor (Sapellnikov), the Theme and Variations from his Third Suite, and Haydn's " Oxford " Symphony.[1]

Between the Hamburg and Berlin concerts Tchaikovsky was anxious for a little repose, and decided to spend a few days at Magdeburg. On the one day spent in Berlin *en passant* he heard, for the first time, a work by Richard Strauss. " Bülow has taken him up just now," he wrote to his brother, " as formerly he took up Brahms and others. To my mind such an astounding lack of talent, united to such pretentiousness, never before existed."

Tchaikovsky now began to receive invitations from many musical centres to conduct his own works. Colonne had engaged him for two concerts in Paris on March 11th and 18th. Several other offers, including Weimar and the Dresden Philharmonic, had to be refused because the dates did not fit in with his plans.

On the advice of Bülow, Wolf, and other friends he decided to alter the programme of the forthcoming concert at Berlin, for which he had put down his *Francesa da Rimini*.

---

[1] For Press notices see Appendix C, p. 764.

2 N

"Perhaps they are right," he says in a letter to his brother. "The taste of the German public is quite different to ours. Now I understand why Brahms is idolised here, although my opinion of him has not changed. Had I known this sooner, perhaps I, too, might have learnt to compose in a different way. Remind me later to tell you about my acquaintance with the venerable Ave-Lallemant,[1] which touched me profoundly.

"Sapellnikov made quite a sensation in Hamburg. He really has a great talent. He is also a charming and good-hearted young man."

To V. Napravnik.

"MAGDEBURG, *January*, 12th (24th), 1888.

"The newspapers have published long articles about me. They 'slate' me a good deal, but pay me far more attention than our own Press. Their views are sometimes funny. A critic, speaking of the variations in the Third Suite, says that one describes a sitting of the Holy Synod and another a dynamite explosion."

---

[1] Chairman of the Committee of the Philharmonic Society. In the *Diary of My Tour* Tchaikovsky says: "This venerable old man of over eighty paid me great attention. . . . In spite of his age and his infirmity, he attended two rehearsals, the concert, and the party at Dr. Bernuth's. Herr Lallemant candidly confessed that many of my works which had been performed in Hamburg were not at all to his mind; that he could not endure my noisy instrumentation and disliked my use of the instruments of percussion. For all that he thought I had in me the making of a really good German composer. Almost with tears in his eyes he besought me to leave Russia and settle permanently in Germany, where classical conventions and traditions of high culture could not fail to correct my faults, which were easily explicable by the fact of my having been born and educated in a country so un-enlightened and so far behind Germany. . . . I strove my best to overcome his prejudice against our national sentiments, of which, moreover, he was quite ignorant, or only knew them through the speeches of the Russophobist section. We parted good friends."

To Modeste Tchaikovsky.

"LEIPZIG, *January 20th (February 1st)*, 1888.

". . . How shall I describe all I am experiencing just now? Continual home-sickness, some well-nigh intolerable hours, and a few very pleasant moments. I intended to spend a few quiet days here, instead of which I am whirled along in a stream of gaiety: dinners, visits, concerts, suppers, the theatre, etc. My sole comfort is the society of Siloti, Brodsky (I am quite in love with his wife and sister-in-law), and Grieg and his wife. But besides these, every day I make new and sympathetic acquaintances. I take Sapellnikov with me wherever I go, and have introduced him to many people in the musical world. Wherever he plays he creates a sensation. I am more and more convinced of his superb talent. . . . I went to a Quartet Concert, at which I heard a quartet by an exceedingly gifted Italian, Busoni. I quickly made friends with him. At an evening given by Brodsky I was charmed with a new sonata by Grieg. Grieg and his wife are so quaint, sympathetic, interesting, and original that I could not describe them in a letter. I regard Grieg as very highly gifted. To-day I dine with him at Brodsky's. To-night is the extra concert in aid of the funds for the Mendelssohn Memorial, and to-morrow the public rehearsal of the Gewandhaus Concert, at which Rubinstein's symphony will be given. Afterwards I am giving a dinner to my friends at a restaurant, and start for Berlin at five o'clock. How tired I am!"

"*January 23rd (February 4th).*

". . . to-day I got rid of N——. We parted in peace, but my purse was lighter by five hundred marks in consequence. I do not regret it in the least; I would have given a good deal more to see the last of this gentleman."

To Modeste Tchaikovsky.

"BERLIN, *January 23rd (February 4th).*

". . . I have made great progress in my conducting. . . . Wolf gave a large dinner-party at my desire, in order that all the great lights here might hear Sapellnikov. All the critics were there. Sapellnikov created a *furore*. For the last three weeks we have been inseparable. I have grown so fond of him, and he so attached and good to me—just as though he were a near relation. Since Kotek's days I have never cared for anyone so much. It is impossible to imagine anyone more sympathetic, gentle, kindly ; more delicate-minded and distinguished. On his return I beg you not only to be friendly to him, but to introduce him to all our relatives. I consider him—and I am not alone in my opinion—a future genius as regards the piano. Yesterday Bock had a party. Artôt was there. I was inexpressibly glad to see her again ; we made friends at once, without a word as to the past. Her husband, Padilla, embraced me heartily. To-morrow she gives a dinner. As an elderly woman she is just as fascinating as twenty years ago."

To N. F. von Meck.

"LEIPZIG, *January* 30*th* (*February* 11*th*), 1888.

"MY DEAR FRIEND,—My concert in Berlin was a great success.[1] I had a splendid orchestra to deal with and musicians who were in sympathy with me from the very first rehearsal. The programme was as follows :—

"(1) Overture, *Romeo and Juliet ;* (2) Pianoforte Concerto, played by Siloti ; (3) Introduction and Fugue from the First Suite ; (4) Andante from the First Quartet ; (5) Songs, sung by Fräulein Friede ; (6) Overture, "*1812.*"

"The public gave me a most enthusiastic reception. Of course, all this is very pleasant, but at the same time I feel so worn out I hardly know how I am to get through all that lies before me. . . . Can you recognise in this Russian musician, touring all over Europe, the man who, a few years ago, fled from life and society, and lived in solitude abroad, or in the country ?

"A real triumphal festival awaits me in Prague. The programme of my week's visit there is already arranged, and has been sent to me. It includes any number of ovations and receptions. The idea is to give my concert

---

[1] For Press notices see Appendix C, p. 767.

there a certain patriotic and anti-German character. This puts me in an awkward position, because I have been received in a very friendly way in Germany."

In spite of the applause of the public and the flattering notices in the Press, Tchaikovsky's visit made less impression in Berlin than in Leipzig and Hamburg. Whereas in the latter towns his concerts were the great events of the day, in the capital the début of a Russian composer passed comparatively unnoticed amid a thousand other interests. A brief entry in his diary on January 28th about "a bucket of cold water" seems to point to a certain disillusionment as to the character of his reception in Berlin. Possibly he had heard rumours that the concert-room had been liberally "papered," and in this way a certain amount of artificial enthusiasm spread through the audience.

In any case, it was Leipzig, rather than Berlin, that showed the greater interest in Tchaikovsky during this tour, and he was glad to return there for a few days before leaving Germany. "I have come back to Leipzig," he wrote to a relative on January 30th (February 11th), 1888, "as I had promised to be present at the concert given in my honour by the Liszt-Verein. The concert could not come off, so yesterday, at my request, Wagner's *Meistersinger* was performed at the theatre instead. I had never heard this opera. Early this morning I was awakened by the strains of the Russian hymn. An orchestra was serenading me. They played for nearly an hour under my windows, and the whole hotel ran out to see and hear."

The marvellous performance of *Meistersinger* under Nikisch, and the touching ovation in the form of a serenade, were the closing events of Tchaikovsky's first concert tour in Germany. In Bohemia and France far more brilliant receptions awaited him, but these were of quite a different nature.

II

On January 31st (February 12th) Tchaikovsky, accompanied by Siloti, arrived at the frontiers of Bohemia. The triumphal character of the reception which awaited him was soon made apparent by the extraordinary attentions of the railway officials. At one of the last stations before Prague, a deputation of members of various societies had assembled to welcome him. At Prague a representative of the "Russian Club" awaited him on the platform, having come expressly from Vienna to pay him this compliment. He presented Tchaikovsky with an address in Russian. This was followed by a speech in Czech, delivered by Dr. Strakaty, the representative of the "Umclecká Beseda,"[1] after which children presented him with flowers, and he was hailed with prolonged cries of "Slava!" (Hurrah!). The carriage which awaited him, and the suite of rooms at the Hotel de Saxe, were provided for him at the expense of the Artists' Club.

In the evening he was invited to hear Verdi's *Otello*, and a box was reserved for him at the Opera House. Rieger, "the leader of the Czech people," was the first to greet the guest, after which followed many of the most prominent men in Bohemia.

The following day Tchaikovsky received a visit from Dvořák, and the two composers quickly made friends with each other.

It is impossible to give in detail the programme drawn up for each day of the composer's visit to Prague. He made an almost royal progress to all the chief places of interest. On one occasion, entering the "Rathaus" while

---

[1] The Artists' Club.

a session was being held, the entire body of members rose
to greet him. One evening he was serenaded by the
famous Choral Union " Hlahol." He listened to the songs
from his balcony, and afterwards came down to thank the
singers in person. An offer, made in the course of his
speech, to compose something expressly for the Society
was received with loud cheering. On February 6th (18th)
he was invited to the Students' Union and presented to
the students. In his diary he speaks of this as " a very
solemn and touching ceremony." Accompanied by cries
of " Slava!" and " Na Sdrava!" he was next led off to the
public rehearsal of the concert. The evening wound up
with a brilliant *soirée* at the Town Club (Meschtschanska
Beseda).

The first concert itself took place on February 7th (19th),
in the " Rudolfinum." The programme consisted entirely
of Tchaikovsky's music, and included: (1) Overture,
Romeo and Juliet; (2) Concerto for Pianoforte (B♭ minor),
played by Siloti; (3) Elégie from the Third Suite;
(4) Violin Concerto, played by Halir; (5), Overture,
" *1812*." Of all these works the last-named excited the
greatest applause. Tchaikovsky sums up his impressions
as follows: " Undoubtedly it was the most eventful day
of my life. I have become so attached to these good
Bohemians . . . and with good reason! Heavens, what
enthusiasm! Such as I have never known, but in my own
dear Russia!"

Two days later, on February 9th (21st), the second
concert was given in the *foyer* of the Opera House. This
time the programme comprised: (1) Serenade for strings;
(2) Variations from the Third Suite; (3) Pianoforte Solos
(Siloti); (4) Overture, " *1812*." The ovations were even
more hearty, and the gifts more costly, than at the first
concert. "An overwhelming success," says Tchaikovsky
in his diary. " A moment of absolute bliss. But only one
moment."

On the evening of February 10th (22nd), sped by farewell addresses, and smothered in flowers, the composer took leave of the festive city of Prague.

Although the chief object of Tchaikovsky's tour was to make his works more widely known in Europe, and to carry them beyond the confines of his native land, he combined with this aim—although in a lesser degree—the desire to see for himself the extent of his reputation and to reap some profit by it. Distrustful and modest as he was, he made no great demands in this respect, and even the appreciation he received in Germany quite surpassed his expectations. The honour done him in Prague far outstripped his wildest dreams. These ten days were the culminating point of Tchaikovsky's fame during his lifetime. Allowing that nine-tenths of the ovations lavished on him were really intended for Russia, even then, he could not fail to be flattered that he was the chosen recipient of the sympathy of the Czechs for the Russians, since it proved that he was already famous as a composer. It was flattering, too, to feel that he was honoured by a nation which could be regarded as one of the most musical in the world. It pleased him that Prague—the first place to recognise the genius of Mozart—should pay him honour, thus uniting his fate with that of the illustrious German. It touched Tchaikovsky deeply to feel that those who gave him one "moment of absolute happiness" were descendants of the same race which, long ago, had given a portion of joy to him who was his teacher and model, both as man and as musician. This strange coincidence was the most flattering event of his life—the highest honour to which he had ever ventured to aspire.

Simultaneously with this climax of his renown, came one of the bitterest experiences of his life. The Russian Press did not give a line to this triumph of a native composer in Prague. He felt this to be a profound injury, which surprised and mortified him the more, because all these triumphs in his life were regarded as important events even by the Czechs themselves. It was most painful to realise that Russia, for whom the greater part of these honours were intended, knew nothing whatever about them; that on account of the attitude of the Press towards him, personally, this warm sympathy, meant for his countrymen as a whole, would never be known to them, nor evoke any response.

Quite another kind of ovation awaited Tchaikovsky in Paris. Here, too, his success surpassed his expectations; but the sympathy of the French capital differed as widely in character from that which was shown him in Prague as the Czechs differ from the French in their musical tastes and their relations towards the Russians. There is no country in which music is better loved, or more widely understood, than in Bohemia. Nor is there any other nation which feels such appreciation for all that is Russian; not merely as a matter of passing fashion, but on account of actual kinship between the Eastern and Western Slav. In Bohemia, therefore, both as a musician and a native of Russia, Tchaikovsky had been received with a warmth and sincerity hardly to be expected from France. It is true a little political feeling influenced his reception in Paris; it was just the beginning of the Franco-Russian *rapprochement*, so that everything Russian was the fashion of the hour. Many French people, who were not in the least musical, regarded it as their duty to express some appreciation of Tchaikovsky—simply because he was a Russian. All this, like the French sympathy itself, had no solid foundation of national affinity, but merely sprang from an ephemeral political combination. The enthusiastic, explosive, but fleeting, craze of the French for all that was Russian showed itself in hats *à la* Kronstadt, in shouting the Russian national anthem simultaneously with the " Marseillaise," in ovations to the clown Durov, and in a "patronising" interest for our art and literature—as species of curiosities—rather than in the hearty relations of two countries drawn together by true affinity of aims and sympathies. Naturally the festivities of Kronstadt, Toulon, and Paris led to no real appreciation of Poushkin, Gogol, Ostrovsky, Glinka, Dargomijsky, or Serov, only, at the utmost, to a phase of fashion, thanks to which Tolstoi and Dostoievsky found a certain superficial vogue, without being understood in their fullest value. Tchaikovsky was also a modern, and this lent a kind of brilliance to his reception in Paris ; but it was purely external. . . . It may truly be said that all Prague welcomed the composer ; whereas in Paris only the musicians and amateurs, a few newspapers in favour of the Franco-Russian alliance, and that crowd which is always in pursuit of novelty, were interested in Tchaikovsky's visit.

Time has proved the respective value of these ovations. Although it is now fifteen years since Tchaikovsky visited Prague, his operas still hold their own in the repertory of the theatre, and his symphonic music is still as well known there and as much loved as in Russia. In Paris, on the contrary, not only are his works rarely given, either on the stage or in the concert-room, but his name— although it has gained in renown all over Europe—is not considered worthy of inclusion among those which adorn the programmes of the Conservatoire concerts. And yet those who are at the head of this institution are the same men who honoured him in 1888. Is not this a proof of that hidden but smouldering antipathy which the French really feel for the Russian spirit—that spirit which Tchaikovsky shares in common with his great predecessors in music, and with the representatives of all that Russia has produced of lofty and imperishable worth?

Tchaikovsky arrived in Paris on February 12th (24th), and went almost straight from the station to the rehearsal of his Serenade for strings, which—conducted by the composer—was to be played by Colonne's orchestra at a *soirée* given by M. N. Benardaky.

N. Benardaky had married one of the three sisters Leibrock, operatic artists well known to the Russian public. He had a fine house in Paris, frequented by the *élite* of the artistic world. As a wealthy patron of art—and as a fellow-countryman—he inaugurated the festivities in Tchaikovsky's honour by this musical evening.

Over three hundred guests were present, and, besides his Serenade for strings, Tchaikovsky conducted the Andante from his Quartet and presided at the piano. The composer was grateful to his kindly host for the unexpected and—according to Parisian custom—absolutely indispensable *réclame* which this entertainment conferred upon him. To ensure the success of the evening, and in return for the service done him, Tchaikovsky felt himself obliged to run from rehearsal to rehearsal, from musician to musician. To appear as a conductor before this assemblage of amateurs—more distinguished for vanity than for love of art—and to earn their languid approval, seemed to him flattering and important. But when we reflect what far greater trouble and fatigue this entailed upon him than his appearance before the Gewandhaus audience—whose opinion was really of weight and value—we cannot but regret the waste of energy and the lowering of the artist's dignity. When we think of him, exhausted and out of humour, amid this crowd of fashionably attired strangers, who to-morrow would be "consecrating" the success of the latest chansonette singer, or the newest dance of a Loie Fuller—we cannot but rebel against fate, who took him from his rural quiet, from the surroundings to which he was attached, in which—sound in body and mind—it was his pleasure to plan some new composition in undisturbed solitude. Thank God, my brother comforted himself with the belief that it was necessary to suffer this martyrdom cheerfully, and that he did not live to realise that it was indeed useless, for nowhere did he make a greater sacrifice for popularity's sake with smaller results than in Paris.

Those musicians who had been absent during Tchaikovsky's visit to Paris in 1886 now made his acquaintance for the first time. All of them, including Gounod, Massenet, Thomé and others, received him with great cordiality and consideration. The sole exception was Reyer, the composer of *Salammbô*, whose indifference was the less hurtful to Tchaikovsky because he did not esteem him greatly as a musician. Of the *virtuosi* with whom he now became acquainted, Paderewski made the most impression upon him.

Among the brilliant Parisian gatherings held in Tchaikovsky's honour must be mentioned the memorable evening at Colonne's; the *soirée* given by the aristocratic amateur, Baroness Tresderne, at whose house in the Place Vendôme Wagner's Trilogy had been heard for the first time in Paris ("Marchionesses, duchesses—bored," is Tchaikovsky's laconic entry in his diary the day after this entertainment); the fête at the Russian Embassy; a reception at Madame Pauline Viardot's; and an entertainment arranged by the *Figaro*.

Tchaikovsky made two public appearances in the double capacity of composer and conductor; both these were at the Châtelet concerts. At the first, half the programme was devoted to his works, including the Serenade for strings, Fantasia for pianoforte (Louis Diemer), Songs (Madame Conneau), pieces for violoncello (Brandoukov), and Theme and Variations from the Third Suite.

On ascending to the conductor's desk he was received with a storm of applause, intended as much for his nationality as for his personality. Of his orchestral works, the Valse from the Serenade won most success, and had to be repeated in order to satisfy the audience.

The second concert, which took place a week later, consisted almost exclusively of Tchaikovsky's works. The

Variations from the Third Suite, the Elégie, and Valse from the Serenade, and the pieces for violoncello were repeated; to which were added the Violin Concerto (Marsick) and *Francesca da Rimini*. The applause was as vociferous as on the first occasion, although comparatively little of it fell to the lot of *Francesca*.

As long as they dealt with the private performances in the houses of Benardaky, Colonne, Madame Tresderne, or at the *Figaro*, the representatives of the Paris Press spoke with enthusiasm of the composer, of his works, and his nationality. After the public concerts, however, there was a sudden change of tone, and their fervour waned. It seemed they had most of them studied Cui's book, *La Musique en Russie*, to good purpose, for, without quoting their source of information, they discovered that Tchaikovsky "was not so Russian as people imagined," that he did not display "much audacity or a strong originality," wherein lay the chief charm of the great Slavs: Borodin, Cui, Rimsky-Korsakov, Liadov, etc.

The Western cosmopolitanism of Tchaikovsky's works was made a subject of reproach. "The German dominates and absorbs the Slav," says one critic, who had looked for "impressions exotiques" at the Châtelet—perhaps for something in the style of the music of Dahomey, which had created such a sensation at the Jardin d'Acclimatation.

The remaining critics, who had not read Cui's book, disapproved of the length of Tchaikovsky's works, and held up to him as models, Saint-Saens and other modern French composers. His own sense of disappointment appears in a letter addressed to P. Jurgenson towards the end of his visit :—

"I have expended a great deal of money, and even more health and strength," he writes.[1] "In return I have

---

[1] In a later letter to Jurgenson he says: "One has to choose between never travelling, or coming home with empty pockets. I had hardly decided

gained some celebrity, but every hour I ask myself—
Why? Is it worth while? And I come to the conclusion
it is far better to live quietly without fame."

From Paris Tchaikovsky crossed to England.

"The journey to London was terrible," he wrote to
Nadejda von Meck. "Our train was brought to a standstill in the open country in consequence of a snowstorm
On the steamer it was alarming, for the storm was so
severe that every moment we dreaded some catastrophe."

Tchaikovsky only spent four days in London. No one
welcomed him, no one paid him special attention, or
worried him with invitations. Except for a complimentary
dinner given to him by Berger, the Secretary of the
Philharmonic Society, he spent his time alone, or in the
society of the violinist Ondricek and his wife. Yet, in
spite of appearances, his visit to London had brilliant
results for his future reputation. Next to Russia and
America his music at present is nowhere more popular
than in England.

He conducted the Serenade for strings and the Variations from the Third Suite. "The success was great,"
he wrote, in the letter quoted above. "The Serenade
pleased most, and I was recalled three times, which means
a good deal from the reserved London public. The Variations were not so much liked, but all the same they
elicited hearty applause."

The leading London papers mostly gave Tchaikovsky
the credit of a signal success. The *Musical Times*

to throw up everything and fly home, when paid engagements were offered
me on all sides; at Angers, with a fee of £40; the same at Geneva, in
London (at the Crystal Palace) for a sum not stated; but I gave them all up.
You are mistaken in your calculations as to the result of my journey. For
London I received £25 instead of £20 (thanks to my great success, the
Directors of the Philharmonic were moved to add an extra £5), and you
omitted the £25 from Hamburg. My journey was certainly not a financial
success; but I did not undertake it for the sake of the money."

only regretted that he had not chosen some more serious work for his début before the London public. "The Russian composer was received with signs of unanimous approbation," said the *Times*, while the *Daily Chronicle* felt convinced that Tchaikovsky must have been fully satisfied with the extraordinarily warm welcome accorded him by the Londoners.

"Thus ended the torments, fears, agitations, and—to speak the truth—the joys of my first concert tour abroad." In these words Tchaikovsky concludes his letter to N. F. von Meck, from which the above extracts have been quoted.

III

After a long journey—six nights in the train—Tchaikovsky reached Tiflis on March 26th (April 7th), 1888. Here he stayed with his brother Hyppolite, whom he had not seen for two years. About the end of April he travelled north to take possession of the country house at Frolovskoe, which had been prepared for him during his absence by his servant Alexis. He describes it as a highly picturesque spot, lying on a wooded hill on the way from Moscow to Klin. It was simpler and not so well furnished as Maidanovo. There was no park planted with lime trees, there were no marble vases; but its unpretentiousness was an added recommendation in Tchaikovsky's eyes. Here he could be alone, free from summer excursionists, to enjoy the little garden (with its charming pool and tiny islet) fringed by the forest, behind which the view opened out upon a distant stretch of country—upon that homely, unassuming landscape of Central Russia which Tchaikovsky preferred to all the sublimities of Switzerland, the Caucasus, and Italy. Had not the forest been gradually exterminated, he would never have quitted Frolovskoe, for although he only lived there for three years, he became greatly attached to the place. A month before his death, travelling from Klin to Moscow, he said, looking out at the churchyard of Frolovskoe: "I should like to be buried there."

To Modeste Tchaikovsky.

"KLIN, *May 15th (27th)*, 1888.

"I am in love with Frolovskoe. The neighbourhood is a paradise after Maidanovo. It is, indeed, so beautiful that when I go out for half an hour's walk in the morning, I feel compelled to extend it to two hours. . . . I have not yet begun to work, excepting at some corrections. To speak frankly, I feel as yet no impulse for creative work. What does this mean? Have I written myself out? No ideas, no inclination? Still I am hoping gradually to collect material for a symphony.

"To-day we were to have sown seeds and planted flowers in the beds in front of the house. I was looking forward to it with such pleasure, but the rain has hindered us. By the time you arrive all our seeds will be in."

To the Grand Duke Constantine Constantinovich.

"FROLOVSKOE, *May 30th (June 11th)*, 1888.

"YOUR HIGHNESS,—I am very glad you were not offended by my remarks, and thank you most heartily for your explanations in reference to them.[1] In matters of versification I am only an amateur, but have long wished to become thoroughly acquainted with the subject. So far, I have only reached the stage of inquiry. Many questions interest me to which no one seems able to give a clear and decided reply. For instance, when I read Joukovsky's translation of the *Odyssey*, or his *Undine*, or Gniedich's version of the *Iliad*, I suffer under the intolerable monotony of the Russian hexameter as compared with the Latin (I do not know the Greek), which has strength, beauty, and variety. I know that the fault lies in the fact that we do not use the spondee, but I cannot

[1] The Grand Duke Constantine had sent Tchaikovsky a volume of his verses.

understand why this should be. To my mind we ought
to employ it. Another question that greatly occupies me
is why, as compared with Russian poetry, German verse
should be less severe in the matter of regular rhythm and
metre. When I read Goethe I am astonished at his
audacity as regards metrical feet, the cæsura, etc., which
he carries so far that, to an unpractised ear, many of his
verses scarcely seem like verse. At the same time, the
ear is only taken by surprise—not offended. Were a
Russian poet to do the same, one would be conscious
of a certain lameness. Is it in consequence of the
peculiar qualities of our language, or because tradition
allows greater freedom to the Germans than to us? I do
not know if I express myself correctly ; I only state that,
as regards regularity, refinement, and euphony, much
more is expected from the Russian than from the German
poet. I should be glad to find some explanation of
this. . . ."

To N. F. von Meck.

"FROLOVSKOE, *June* 1*st* (13*th*), 1888.

" . . . . Just now I am busy with flowers and flower-
growing. I should like to have as many flowers as possible
in my garden, but I have very little knowledge or experience. I am not lacking in zeal, and have indeed taken
cold from pottering about in the damp. Now, thank
goodness, it is warmer weather ; I am glad of it, for you,
for myself, and for my dear flowers, for I have sown
a quantity, and the cold nights made me anxious for
them. . . . ."

To N. F. von Meck.

"FROLOVSKOE, *June* 10*th* (22*nd*), 1888.

" . . . . Now I shall work my hardest. I am dreadfully
anxious to prove not only to others, but also to myself,
that I am not yet *played out* as a composer. . . . Have I
already told you that I intend to write a symphony? The
beginning was difficult ; now, however, inspiration seems
to have come. We shall see ! "

2 O

To the Grand Duke Constantine Constantinovich.

"FROLOVSKOE, *June 11th (23rd),* 1888.

"YOUR IMPERIAL HIGHNESS,—I am the more glad to hear your favourable verdict upon my songs, because I was afraid you would think them weak. . . . I composed them at a time when my state of mind was anything but promising for good work. At the same time, I did not wish to postpone the setting of your words, as I had informed you long ago of my intention with regard to them. . . .

"I am not at all astonished that you should write beautiful verses without being an adept in the science of versification. Several of our poets—Plestcheiev for one—have told me the same. All the same, I think it would be better if some of our gifted Russian poets were more interested in the technique of their art. 'I am sick of four iambic feet,' said Poushkin, and I would add that sometimes his readers get weary of it too. To discover new metres and rare rhythmic combinations must be very interesting. Were I a poet, I should certainly try to write in varied rhythms like the Germans. . . ."

To N. F. von Meck.

"FROLOVSKOE, *June 22nd (July 4th),* 1888.

". . . . Lately I have been in frequent correspondence with the Grand Duke Constantine Constantinovich, who sent me his poem, 'St. Sebastian,' with the request that I would say what I thought of it. On the whole I liked it, but I criticised a few details very freely. He was pleased with this, but defended himself, and thus a brisk exchange of letters has taken place. He is not only gifted, but surprisingly modest, devoted to art, and ambitious to excel in it rather than in *the service.* He is also an excellent musician—in fact, a rare and sympathetic nature.

"It is well that the political horizon is clearer, and if it be true that the German Emperor is to visit Russia, we may say with some certainty that the horrors of war will not break out for many years to come. . . ."

Diary.

"*June 27th (July 9th),* 1888.

" It seems to me letters are not perfectly sincere—I am judging by myself. No matter to whom I am writing, I am always conscious of the effect of my letter, not only upon the person to whom it is addressed, but upon any chance reader. Consequently I embroider. I often take pains to make the tone of a letter simple and sincere—at least to make it *appear* so. But apart from letters written at the moment when I am worked upon, I am never quite myself in my correspondence. These letters are to me a source of repentance, and often of agonising regret. When I read the correspondence of great men, published after their death, I am always disturbed by a vague sense of insincerity and falsehood.

" I will go on with the record of my musical predilections which I began some time ago. What are my feelings towards the Russian composers?

GLINKA.

" An unheard-of and astonishing apparition in the world of art. A dilettante who played the violin and the piano a little; who concocted a few insipid quadrilles and fantasias upon Italian airs; who tried his hand at more serious musical forms (songs, quartets, sextets, etc.), but accomplished nothing which rose superior to the jejune taste of the thirties; suddenly, in his thirty-fourth year, creates an opera, which for inspiration, originality, and irreproachable technique, is worthy to stand beside all that is loftiest and most profound in musical art! We are still more astonished when we reflect that the composer of this work is the author of the *Memoirs* published some twenty years later. The latter give one the impression of a nice, kind, commonplace man, with not much to say for himself. Like a nightmare, the questions continually haunt me : How could such colossal artistic force be united to such emptiness? and how came this average amateur to catch up in a single stride such men as Mozart and Beethoven? Yes, for he *has* overtaken them. One may say this without exaggeration of the composer of the

'Slavsia.' This question may be answered by those who are better fitted than myself to penetrate the mysteries of the artistic spirit which makes its habitation in such fragile and apparently unpromising shrines. I can only say no one loves and appreciates Glinka more than I do. I am no indiscriminate worshipper of *Russlan*; on the contrary, I am disposed to prefer *A Life for the Tsar*, although *Russlan* may perhaps be of greater musical worth. But the elemental force is more perceptible in his earlier opera ; the 'Slavsia' is overwhelming and gigantic. For this he employed no model. Neither Glück nor Mozart composed anything similar. Astounding, inconceivable ! *Kamarinskaya* is also a work of remarkable inspiration. Without intending to compose anything beyond a simple, humorous trifle, he has left us a little masterpiece, every bar of which is the outcome of enormous creative power. Half a century has passed since then, and many Russian symphonic works have been composed ; we may even speak of a symphonic school. Well ? The germ of all this lies in *Kamarinskaya*, as the oak tree lies in the acorn. For long years to come Russian composers will drink at this source, for it will need much time and much strength to exhaust its wealth of inspiration. Yes ! Glinka was a true creative genius !"

To N. F. Von Meck.

"FROLOVSKOE, *July 17th (29th)*, 1888.

" . . . . My name-day was a great interruption to my work, for my visitors arrived the day before and only left yesterday evening. My guests were Laroche and his wife, Jurgenson, Albrecht, Siloti, and Zet,[1] who arrived quite unexpectedly from Petersburg. The last named (who has been highly recommended to me) has been my concert agent since May. . . . He is a great admirer of my work, and cares less to make money out of his position than to forward my interests in Europe and America. . . . "

---

[1] Julius Zet had been secretary to Sophie Menter, and so became acquainted with Tchaikovsky. Their friendship lasted until the latter's death, but their business relations were of brief duration. Zet was not sufficiently calculating. Rather an enthusiast than a man of business, he was unpractical and inaccurate.

At this time Tchaikovsky received an offer from an American impresario offering him a three months' concert tour at a fee of 25,000 dollars. The sum appeared to the Russian composer fabulous in its amount. "Should this really come off," he says, "I could realise my long-cherished wish to become a landowner."

Diary.

"*July* 13*th* (25*th*), 1888.

"Dargomijsky? Certainly he was a gifted man. But never was the type of amateur musician more strikingly realised than in him. Glinka, too, was a dilettante, but his immense inspiration served him as a defence from amateurishness. Except for his fatal *Memoirs*, we should not have realised his dilettantism. It is another matter with Dargomijsky: his amateurishness lies in his creative work, in his very forms themselves. To possess an average talent, to be weak in technique and yet to pose as an *innovator*—is pure amateurishness. When, at the close of his life, Dargomijsky composed *The Stone Guest*, he seriously believed he had overturned the old foundations and erected something new and colossal in their place. A piteous error; I saw him in this last period of his life, and in view of his suffering condition (he had a heart disease) there could be no question of a discussion. But I have never come in contact with anything more anti-pathetic and false than this unsuccessful attempt to drag *truth* into this sphere of art, in which everything is based upon falsehood, and "truth," in the everyday sense of the word, is not required at all. Dargomijsky was no *master* (he had not a tenth part of Glinka's mastership). He possessed a certain originality and piquancy. He was most successful in *curiosities*. But artistic beauty does not lie in this direction, as so many of us think.

"I might speak personally of Dargomijsky (I frequently saw him in Moscow at the time of his success there), but I prefer not to recall my acquaintance. He was very cutting and unjust in his judgments (when he raged against the brothers Rubinstein, for instance), but was pleased to talk of himself in a tone of self-laudation. During his fatal illness he became far more kindly disposed, and showed much cordial feeling to his younger colleagues. I will only keep this memory of him. Unexpectedly he showed me great sympathy (in respect of my opera *The Voyevode*).[1] Apparently he did not believe the report that I had hissed at the first performance of his *Esmeralda* in Moscow."

To N. F. von Meck.

"FROLOVSKOE, *July 25th (August 6th)*, 1888.

" . . . The real summer weather has not lasted long, but how I enjoyed it! My flowers, which I feared would die, have nearly all recovered, and some have blossomed luxuriantly. I cannot tell you what a pleasure it has been to watch them grow and to see daily—even hourly—new blossoms coming out. Now I have as many as I want. When I am quite old, and past composing, I shall devote myself to growing flowers. I have been working with good results, and half the symphony is orchestrated. My age—although not very advanced—begins to tell. I get very tired now, and can no longer play or read at night as I used. Lately I miss the chance of a game of *vint*[2] in the evenings; it is the one thing that rests and distracts me."

To N. F. von Meck.

"FROLOVSKOE, *August 14th (26th)*, 1888.

"Again I am not feeling well . . . but I am so glad to have finished the Symphony (No. 5) that I can forget all physical ailments. I have made no settled plans for the winter. There is a prospect of a tour in Scandinavia and also in America. But nothing is decided as to the first, and the second seems so fantastic that I can hardly give it a serious thought. I have promised to conduct at Dresden, Berlin, and Prague. . . . In November I am to conduct a whole series of my works in Petersburg (at the Philharmonic), including the new Symphony. They also want me in Tiflis, but I do not know if it will come off."

[1] Unfortunately it will always remain unknown in what way this sympathy was shown to Tchaikovsky.

[2] A favourite game of cards in Russia.

IV

1888–1889

The winter season 1888–1889 opened with much arduous work and personal anxiety. Tchaikovsky's niece, Vera, the second daughter of his sister Alexandra Davidov, was in a dying condition, and his old friend Hubert was suffering from a terrible form of intermittent fever. One gleam of joy shone through the darkness. His Moscow friends, Taneiev in particular, were delighted with the Fifth Symphony, a work which had filled Tchaikovsky himself with gloomy misgivings. At this time he was engaged in an active correspondence upon music and poetry with the Grand Duke Constantine.

To the Grand Duke Constantinovich.

"FROLOVSKOE, *September 21st* (*October 3rd*), 1888.

" . . . Fet[1] is quite right in asserting, as you say he does, that 'all which has no connection with the leading idea should be cast aside, even though it is beautiful and melodious.' But we must not deduce from this that only what is terse can be highly artistic; therefore, to my mind, Fet's rule that an exemplary lyric must not exceed a certain limit is entirely wrong. All depends upon the nature of the leading idea and the poet who expresses it. Of two equally inspired poets, or composers, one, by reason of his artistic temperament, will show greater breadth of treatment, more complexity in the development of the leading idea, and a greater inclination for luxuriant and varied elaboration; while the other will express himself concisely. All that is good, but superfluous, we call 'padding.' Can we say we find this padding in Beethoven's works? I think most decidedly we do not. On the contrary, it is astonishing how equal, how significant and forceful, this giant among musicians always remains, and

---

[1] A well-known Russian poet.

how well he understands the art of curbing his vast inspiration, and never loses sight of balanced and traditional form.   In his last quartets, which were long regarded as the productions of an insane and deaf man, there seems to be some padding, until we have studied them thoroughly. But ask someone who is well acquainted with these works, a member of a quartet who plays them frequently, if there is anything superfluous in the C♯ minor Quartet. Unless he is an old-fashioned musician, brought up upon Haydn, he would be horrified at the idea of abbreviating or cutting any portion of it.   In speaking of Beethoven I was not merely thinking of his latest period.   Could anyone show me a bar in the *Eroica*, which is very lengthy, that could be called superfluous, or any portion that could really be omitted as padding?   So everything that is long is not *too long;* many words do not necessarily mean empty verbiage, and terseness is not, as Fet asserts, the essential condition of beautiful form.   Beethoven, who in the first movement of the *Eroica* has built up a superb edifice out of an endless series of varied and ever new architectural beauties upon so simple and seemingly poor a subject, knows on occasion how to surprise us by the terseness and exiguity of his forms.   Do you remember the Andante of the Pianoforte Concerto in B flat? I know nothing more inspired than this short movement ; I go cold and pale every time I hear it.

"Of course, the classical beauty of Beethoven's predecessors, and their art of keeping within bounds, is of the greatest value.   It must be owned, however, that Haydn had no occasion to limit himself, for he had not an inexhaustible wealth of material at command.   As to Mozart, had he lived another twenty years, and seen the beginning of our century, he would certainly have sought to express his prodigal inspiration in forms less strictly classical than those with which he had to content himself.

"While defending Beethoven from the charge of long-windedness, I confess that the post - Beethoven music offers many examples of prolixity which is often carried so far as to become mere padding. That inspired musician who expresses himself with such breadth, majesty, force, and even brusqueness, has much in common with Michael

Angelo. Just as the Abbé Bernini has flooded Rome with his statues, in which he strives to imitate the style of Michael Angelo, without possessing his genius, and makes a caricature of what is really powerful in his model, so Beethoven's musical style has been copied over and over again. Is not Brahms in reality a caricature of Beethoven? Is not this pretension to profundity and power detestable, because the content which is poured into the Beethoven mould is not really of any value? Even in the case of Wagner (who certainly has genius), wherever he oversteps the limits it is the spirit of Beethoven which prompts him.

"As regards your humble servant, I have suffered all my life from my incapacity to grasp form in general. I have fought against this innate weakness, not—I am proud to say —without good results; yet I shall go to my grave without having produced anything really perfect in form. There is frequently *padding* in my works; to an experienced eye the stitches show in my seams, but I cannot help it. As to *Manfred*, I may tell you—without any desire to pose as being modest—that this is a repulsive work, and I hate it, with the exception of the first movement. I intend shortly, with the consent of my publisher, to destroy the remaining three movements and make a symphonic poem out of this long-winded symphony. I am sure my *Manfred* would then please the public. I enjoyed writing the first movement, whereas the others were the outcome of strenuous effort, in consequence of which—as far as I remember—I felt quite ill for a time. I should not think of being offended at what your Highness says about *Manfred*. You are quite right and even too indulgent."

To the Grand Duke Constantine Constantinovich.

"FROLOVSKOE, *October 2nd* (14*th*), 1888.

"YOUR IMPERIAL HIGHNESS,—Just returned from Moscow, where I have seen my poor friend Hubert laid in his grave, and still depressed by my painful experiences, I hasten to answer your letter. . . . Your Highness must bear in mind that although one art stands in close relationship to the other, at the same time each has its peculiarities. As such we must regard the "verbal repetitions" which are only possible to a limited extent in literature, but are a necessity in music. Beethoven never repeats an entire movement without a special reason, and, in doing so, rarely fails to introduce something new; but he has recourse to this characteristic method in his instrumental music, knowing that his idea will only be understood after many statements. I cannot understand why your Highness should object to the constant repetition of the subject in the Scherzo of the Ninth Symphony. I always want to hear it over and over again. It is so divinely beautiful, strong, original, and significant! It is quite another matter with the prolixity and repetitions of Schubert, who, with all his genius, constantly harps upon his central idea—as in the Andante of the C major Symphony. Beethoven develops his first idea fully, in its entirety, before repeating it; Schubert seems too indolent to elaborate his first idea, and—perhaps from his unusual wealth of thematic material—hurries on the beginning to arrive at something else. It seems as though the stress of his inexhaustible inspiration hindered him from the careful elaboration of the theme, in all its depth and delicacy of workmanship.

"God grant I may be in Petersburg to hear the performance of Mozart's *Requiem* in the Marble Palace. I hope your Highness will permit me to be present at this concert. The *Requiem* is one of the most divine creations, and we can but pity those who are unable to appreciate it.

"As regards Brahms, I cannot at all agree with your Highness. In the music of this master (it is impossible to deny his mastery) there is something dry and cold which repulses me. He has very little melodic invention. He never speaks out his musical ideas to the end. Scarcely do we hear an enjoyable melody, than it is engulfed in a whirlpool of unimportant harmonic progressions and modulations, as though the special aim of the composer was to be unintelligible. He excites and irritates our musical senses without wishing to satisfy them, and seems ashamed to speak the language which goes straight to the heart. His depth is not real: *c'est voulu*. He has set before himself, once and for all, the aim of trying to be profound, but he has only attained to an appearance of profundity. The gulf is void. It is impossible to say that the music of Brahms is weak and insignificant. His style is invariably lofty. He does not strive after mere external effects. He is never trivial. All he does is serious and noble, but he lacks the chief thing—beauty. Brahms commands our respect. We must bow before the original purity of his aspirations. We must admire his firm and proud attitude in the face of triumphant Wagnerism; but to love him is impossible. I, at least, in spite of much effort, have not arrived at it. I will own that certain early works (the Sextet in B♭) please me far more than those of a later period, especially the symphonies, which seem to me indescribably long and colourless. . . . Many Brahms lovers (Bülow, among others) predicted that some day I should see clearer, and learn to appreciate beauties which do not as yet appeal to me. This is not unlikely, for there have been such cases. I do not know the *German Requiem* well. I will get it and study it. Who knows?—perhaps my views on Brahms may undergo a complete revolution."

To Ippolitov-Ivanov.

" *October* 27th (*November 8th*), 1888.

" I cannot possibly give you any definite news as to my journey to Tiflis. It will be two or three weeks, at the earliest, before I know when I shall have to go abroad. . . . I only know that *I will come to Tiflis, even if I am dying.* As to my fee, we will not speak of it. Before I take anything from you, something must be there. Let us see how the concert succeeds, and then we can settle how much you shall give me as ' a tip.' If it is not a success, I shall accept nothing."

To N. F. von Meck.

" FROLOVSKOE, *October* 27th (*November 8th*), 1888.

" Now we are having sharp frosts, without snow, and fine, sunny days. It depresses me to think that I must

soon leave my quiet home, my regular life, and daily con-
stitutionals.   Three days hence I go to Petersburg, where
my concert takes place on November 5th (17th).   On the
12th (24th) I take part in the Musical Society's concert,
and leave for Prague the next day to attend the rehearsals
for *Eugene Oniegin*.   I have been working very hard lately.
The orchestration of the *Hamlet* overture is now finished.
I have made innumerable corrections in the Symphony,
and have been preparing everything I have to conduct at
the forthcoming concerts.

"I hope to spend December here, for I have to return
direct from Prague in order to conduct the new Symphony in Moscow, and then I shall hasten to my harbour
of refuge."

The Philharmonic concert in St. Petersburg was apparently a great success, but the Press notices of the
new Symphony (No. 5) were far from satisfactory.   On
November 12th (24th) Tchaikovsky conducted it once
more at the Musical Society, and on this occasion the
fantasia-overture *Hamlet* was heard for the first time.   Both
works were well received by the public.

V

On this occasion Prague received Tchaikovsky less
hospitably than on his first visit.   "The rehearsal," he
wrote to Nadejda von Meck, "took place the very day I
arrived.   Last year, if you remember, I conducted two
grand patriotic concerts, without a fee.   To show their
gratitude for my having come to the performance of
the opera here, the management of the Prague Theatre
organised a concert, of which I was to receive half the
profits.   But they chose such a bad day, and arranged
everything so stupidly, that the concert only realised
three hundred florins.   After being received like a prince

last year, when the enthusiasm which greeted me almost amounted to a frenzy, I felt somewhat hurt at this meagre offering on the part of the Prague public. I therefore declined the money, and made it over to the Musicians' Pension Fund. This was soon made public, and the Theatre Direction was overwhelmed with reproaches. The whole Press took up the matter, and thanks to this, the performance of *Oniegin*, which I conducted the evening before last, gave rise to a series of enthusiastic ovations. Yesterday I left Prague, crowned with laurels; but, alas! my laurel wreaths were all I carried away. I do not know how to look after my pecuniary interests."

The success of *Oniegin* in Prague was extraordinary, and the opera has kept its place in the repertory up to the present time.

Amid the chorus of praise, in which both the public and the Press united, one voice was especially valued by Tchaikovsky—that of his famous colleague, Anton Dvořák.

A. Dvořák to P. Tchaikovsky.

"PRAGUE, *January 2nd* (14*th*), 1889.

"DEAR FRIEND,—When you were lately with us in Prague I promised to write to you on the subject of your opera *Oniegin*. I am now moved to do so, not only in answer to your request, but also by my own impulse to express all I felt on hearing your work. I confess with joy that your opera made a profound impression on me— the kind of impression I expect to receive from a genuine work of art, and I do not hesitate to tell you that not one of your compositions has given me such pleasure as *Oniegin*.

"It is a wonderful creation, full of glowing emotion and poetry, and finely elaborated in all its details; in short, this music is captivating, and penetrates our hearts so deeply that we cannot forget it. Whenever I go to hear it I feel myself transported into another world.

"I congratulate both you and ourselves upon this work. God grant you may give us many another like it.

"I embrace you, and remain your sincerely devoted

"ANTON DVOŘÁK."

On his way home from Prague to Vienna, Tchaikovsky heard of the death of his niece, Vera Rimsky-Korsakov, *née* Davidov. Although he had long since given up all hope of her recovery, this news affected him deeply.

From Prague he returned to Frolovskoe for a short time. On December 10th (22nd) he conducted his new works at a Symphony Concert in Moscow. These included the new Symphony (No. 5, E minor) and the second Pianoforte Concerto, with Sapellnikov as soloist; both works achieved great success.

December 17th (29th) found him again in Petersburg, where, at the fourth of Belaiev's "Russian Symphony Concerts," he conducted his *Tempest* overture, and on the following day was present at a performance of the *Oprichnik* given by the pupils of the Petersburg Conservatoire. Tchaikovsky was interested to renew his impressions of this work, and to prove whether his prejudice against it was well founded. In spite of a very good performance, his opinion of the opera remained unaltered.

The next work which Tchaikovsky took in hand after his return from Prague was the music of the ballet, *The Sleeping Beauty*, the programme of which had been prepared by Vsievolojsky, Director of the Imperial Opera. Tchaikovsky was charmed with the subject and the proposed mounting of the work, and retired to Frolovskoe late in December, in order to devote himself to the task.

In view of the great popularity to which his Fifth Symphony has since attained, it is interesting to read the composer's own judgment of the work, recorded within a few weeks of its first performance. Writing to Nadejda von Meck, in December, 1888, he says :—

" . . . After two performances of my new Symphony in Petersburg, and one in Prague, I have come to the conclusion that it is a failure. There is something repellent, something superfluous, patchy, and insincere, which the public instinctively recognises. It was obvious to me that the ovations I received were prompted more by my earlier work, and that the Symphony itself did not really please the audience. The consciousness of this brings me a sharp twinge of self-dissatisfaction. Am I really played out, as they say? Can I merely repeat and ring the changes on my earlier idiom? Last night I looked through *our* Symphony (No. 4). What a difference! How immeasurably superior it is! It is very, very sad!"

Such attacks of pessimism as to his creative powers were often, as we have already seen, the forerunner of a new tide of inspiration. This was now the case. Since *Eugene Oniegin* Tchaikovsky had never worked at anything with the ease and enthusiasm which inspired him in the first four tableaux of this ballet, *The Sleeping Beauty*, the sketch of which was completely finished by January 18th (30th).

The monotony of these six weeks' work was relieved by news of the success of the Fifth Symphony in Moscow, and also by the kindness of his friend, Peter Jurgenson, who surprised him at Christmas with a beautiful and valuable gift—the complete edition of Mozart's works. These he commissioned Alexis to present to his master, together with a tiny Christmas-tree.

On January 24th (February 5th), 1889, Tchaikovsky started on his second concert tour abroad. He experienced "the usual feelings of home-sickness," and began to anticipate the joy of his return. He remained three days in Berlin, and arrived in Cologne on January 29th (February 10th), where he was to make his first appearance as composer and conductor, with his Third Suite (in G), at a so-called "Gürzenich" concert.

To M. Tchaikovsky.

"COLOGNE, *January 30th* (*February 11th*), 1889.

". . . To-day was my first rehearsal. It went very well, and the orchestra is excellent, so that the three hours passed very pleasantly, excepting for the agitation at the start. Hardly had I got back to my hotel before I was seized with home-sickness and a wild longing for April 8th. . . ."

Tchaikovsky made his début at Cologne on January 31st (February 12th). He thus describes his impressions to Glazounov :—

"I arrived shortly before the first of the three rehearsals. One hardly expects to find a first-class orchestra in a town of secondary importance, and I was convinced it would only be a very poor one. The local conductor, Wullner, has, however, worked with such care and energy that he has succeeded in organising a magnificent orchestra, which filled me with astonishment and admiration from the very opening of my Third Suite. Twenty first violins! And such violins! The wind, too, is admirable. They read the Scherzo, which is particularly difficult, as if they were playing it for the tenth time. With such an orchestra and three rehearsals, it was easy to achieve an admirable performance. The concert-hall is also excellent; the audience equally so, and not so stupidly conservative as in many German towns. The success was great, and when I was recalled the musicians greeted me with a fanfare.

"Early on February 1st (13th)," the letter continues, "I started for Frankfort. Here the orchestra is equally large and excellent. The violins did not seem to me quite as good as those in Cologne, although they consist mostly of leaders from the neighbouring towns—so I was told—who come here to play at the great concerts. There are twelve 'cellos. One of them, Kossmann, the celebrated virtuoso, was once professor at Moscow. My Overture "*1812*" was in the programme. At the first rehearsal, however, the managers of the concert took fright at the noisy Finale, and timidly requested me to choose another piece. Since, however, I had no other piece at hand, they decided to confine themselves to the Suite. The success here was as great as it was unexpected, for the Frankfort public is very classical, and I am regarded in Germany as a notorious revolutionary."

Of those in Frankfort whose society Tchaikovsky most enjoyed, he mentions in his diary the family of the celebrated music publisher, pianist, and composer, Otto Neitzel, and Ivan Knorr, Professor at the Frankfort Conservatoire, besides the 'cellist Kossmann.

Tchaikovsky reached Dresden on February 4th (16th). Here disappointment awaited him. The orchestra proved to be only "third-rate," to use his own words, and the work he had to rehearse made even greater technical demands than the Third Suite; it was his favourite composition—the Fourth Symphony. The *Dresdner Zeitung* spoke of "a very poor rendering of several passages, the result of insufficient rehearsal." The concert took place on February 8th (20th). The first Pianoforte Concerto (Emil Sauer) was included in the programme. According to Tchaikovsky's account, "the first movement pleased the audience a little, the Andante pleased better, the Scherzo still more, while the Finale had a real success. The musicians honoured me with a fanfare. Sauer played incomparably."

To P. Jurgenson.

"DRESDEN, *February 5th* (17*th*), 1889.

"DEAR FRIEND,—I had forgotten to answer you about Paris. Please remember that it is impossible to give a concert there unless support is guaranteed by the French. I hear that Slaviansky, Bessel, and others want to have a finger in the pie. I have not the least wish to associate myself with them. You can simply say that, without a

2 P

guarantee, we are not in a position to undertake anything.[1] Heavens, how tired I am, and how bored by all this!

"... I expect soon to hear decisively from Klindworth and Dvořák. A letter to hand from Massenet. He accepts with enthusiasm, but begs to keep the date open for the present, as it depends on the fate of his new opera."

To N. F. von Meck.

"BERLIN, *February* 11th (23rd), 1889.

"After an exhausting tour I arrived here yesterday. In one week I had three concerts and nine rehearsals. I cannot conceive whence I draw strength for all this. Either these fresh exertions will prove injurious, or this feverish activity will be an antidote to my troubles, which are chiefly the result of the constant sitting my work entails. There is no medium; I must return to Russia *'either with my shield or upon it.'* I am inclined to think that, in spite of hard moments and the continual self-conflict, all this is good for me."

To A. Glazounov.

"BERLIN, *February* 15th (27th), 1889.

"... If my whole tour consisted only of concerts and rehearsals, it would be very pleasant. Unhappily, however, I am overwhelmed with invitations to dinners and suppers. ... I much regret that the Russian papers have said nothing as to my victorious campaign. What can I do? I have no friends on the Russian Press. Even if I had, I should never manage to advertise myself. My Press notices abroad are curious: some find fault, others flatter; but all testify to the fact that Germans know very little about Russian music. There are exceptions, of course. In Cologne and in other towns I came across people who took great interest in Russian music and were well acquainted with it. In most instances Borodin's E flat Symphony is well known. Borodin seems to be a special favourite in Germany (although they only care for this symphony). Many people ask for information about you.

---

[1] Thus ended the plan for sending Tchaikovsky as musical representative of Russia to the Paris Exhibition of 1889.

They know you are still very young, but are amazed when I tell them you were only fifteen when you wrote your Symphony in E flat, which has become very well known since its performance at the festival. Klindworth intends to produce a Russian work at his concert in Berlin. I recommended him Rimsky-Korsakov's *Caprice Espagnol* and your *Stenka Razin.*"

To P. Jurgenson.

"LEIPZIG, *February* 17*th* (*March* 1*st*), 1889.

"Klindworth says that I am an 'excellent conductor.' First-rate, isn't it?

"Klindworth is prepared to appear next season at our concerts for anything we like to offer. He will give a Wagner programme. Dvořák promises to conduct a whole concert; but he cannot travel alone, and brings his wife, so he asks a higher fee. Never mind. In the spring it would be well to get out an advertisement with such names as Massenet, Dvořák, Klindworth. I shall make an attempt to invite Brahms. That would be grand!

"When in Berlin, Artôt and dear Hugo Bock were my great comfort"

To N. F. von Meck.

"GENEVA, *February* 21*st* (*March* 5*th*), 1889.

"I am engaged to give a concert of my own compositions here. It takes place on Saturday, March 9th. The orchestra is very small, only third-rate. Had I known, I never would have come, but the theatrical Director (he is no musician) probably believes that the quality and number of an orchestra are of no importance to a wandering musician. How I shall get through with this small provincial band, I really do not know. However, I must confess that they showed great zeal at yesterday's rehearsal. . . ."

After all, this concert was a success. The room was crowded, and the Russian colony presented Tchaikovsky with a gilt laurel-wreath.

On February 27th (March 11th) Tchaikovsky arrived in

Hamburg. Brahms was at his hotel, occupying the room next his own. Peter Ilich felt greatly flattered on learning that the famous German composer was staying a day longer on purpose to hear the rehearsal of his Fifth Symphony. Tchaikovsky was very well received by the orchestra. Brahms remained in the room until the end of the rehearsal. Afterwards, at luncheon, he gave his opinion of the work "very frankly and simply." It had pleased him on the whole, with the exception of the Finale. Not unnaturally, the composer of this movement felt "deeply hurt" for the moment; but happily the injury was not incurable, as we shall see. Tchaikovsky took this opportunity to invite Brahms to conduct one of the Symphony Concerts in Moscow, but the latter declined. Nevertheless Tchaikovsky's personal liking for the composer of the *German Requiem* was increased, although his opinion of his compositions was not changed. Tchaikovsky played no part in the conflict between Brahms and Wagner, which divided all musical Germany into two hostile camps. Brahms's personality as man and artist, his purity and loftiness of aim, and his earnestness of purpose won his sympathy. Wagner's personality and tendencies were antipathetic to him; but while the inspired music of the latter found an echo in his heart, the works of Brahms left him cold.

At the second rehearsal all went "excellently," and at the third Tchaikovsky observed that the Symphony pleased the musicians. At the public rehearsal "there was real enthusiasm," and although the demonstration at the concert on March 3rd (15th) was less noisy, the success of the Symphony was no less assured.

The pleasant impressions of the evening were slightly marred by the absence—on account of illness—of Ave-Lallemant, to whom the Symphony is dedicated.

To V. Davidov.

"HANOVER *March 5th* (*17th*), 1889.

" . . . The concert at Hamburg has taken place, and I may congratulate myself on a great success. The Fifth Symphony was magnificently played, and I like it far better now, after having held a bad opinion of it for some time. Unfortunately the Russian Press continues to ignore me. With the exception of my nearest and dearest, no one will ever hear of my successes. In the daily papers here one reads long telegrams about the Wagner performances in Russia. Certainly I am not a second Wagner, but it would be desirable for Russia to learn how I have been received in Germany."

To M. Tchaikovsky.

" . . . Success is very pleasant at the time, but when there is neither rehearsal nor concert, I immediately relapse into my usual state of depression and boredom. Only one concert remains, the one in London, but not for another month. How on earth shall I kill time till then? Possibly I may go straight to Paris. Rushing about there ought to drive away *ennui*. How one wastes time!"

The three days' visit to Hanover only differed from Tchaikovsky's sojourn in other towns in that he missed the only thing that could help him to conquer his chronic home-sickness—concerts and rehearsals.

"Curious fact," he remarks in his diary, "I seek solitude, and suffer when I have found it." In this state of fluctuation between *bad* and *worse* Tchaikovsky had spent his time since he left Russia; but the *worst* was reserved for Hanover, where he experienced "extreme loneliness."

On March 8th (20th) he arrived in Paris, and remained there until the 30th (April 11th).

As his present visit to the French capital was not undertaken in a public capacity, it was neither so brilliant, nor so fatiguing, as that of the previous year. At the same time he came in contact with many people and received a number of invitations. On March 19th (31st) he was present at one of Colonne's concerts, when three numbers from his Third Suite were played.

During this holiday in Paris Tchaikovsky had only two aims in view: to secure Massenet for one of the Moscow Symphony Concerts and to use his influence in favour of Sapellnikov, whose gifts as a pianist he valued very highly.

To P. Jurgenson.

"*March 21st (April 2nd)*, 1889.

"I have seen Massenet several times; he is very much flattered and prepared to come. The spring will suit him best. I have engaged Paderewski, who has had a colossal success in Paris. He is not inferior to D'Albert, and one of the very first pianists of the day.

"The Third Suite had a splendid success at Colonne's concert."

To Modeste Tchaikovsky.

"Paris, *April 7th (19th)*, 1889.

"Modi,—Vassia[1] played to Colonne yesterday evening. After the Chopin Polonaise Colonne was astonished, and said he would engage him next year and do '*les choses en grand.*' . . . Vassia has made a *furore.*"

To V. Davidov.   "London, 1889.

" . . . The evening before I left Paris I went to Madame Viardot's. I heard an opera which she composed twenty years ago to a libretto by Tourgeniev.[2] The singers were her two daughters and her pupils, among whom was a Russian, who danced a national dance to the delight of all the spectators. I have seen the celebrated Eiffel Tower quite near. It is very fine . . . I very much enjoyed hearing the finest of Berlioz's works, *La Damnation de Faust.* I am very fond of this masterpiece, and wish you knew it.

---

[1] Vassily Sapellnikov.
[2] The opera is entitled *Le Dernier Sorcier.*

Lalo's opera, *Le Roi d'Ys*, also pleased me very much. It has been decided that I shall compose an opera to a French book, *La Courtisane*.[1] I have made acquaintance with a number of the younger French composers;[2] they are all the most rabid Wagnerites. But Wagnerism sits so badly on the French! With them it takes the form of a childishness which they pursue in order to appear earnest."

To the same.

"LONDON, *March 30th (April 11th)*, 1889.

". . . Before all else, let me inform you that I have made acquaintance with London fog. Last year I enjoyed the fog daily, but I never dreamt of anything like the one we had to-day. When I went to rehearsal this morning it was rather foggy, as it often is in Petersburg. But when at midday I left St. James's Hall with Sapellnikov and went into the street, it was actually night—as dark as a moonless, autumn night at home. It made a great impression upon us both. I felt as though I were sitting in a subterranean dungeon. Now at 4 p.m. it is rather lighter, but still gloomy. It is extraordinary that this should happen half-way through April. Even the Londoners are astonished and annoyed.

"Ah, Bob, how glad I shall be to get back to Frolovskoe! I think I shall never leave it again.

"The rehearsal went off very well to-day; the orchestra here is very fine. Sapellnikov has not played yet. To-morrow he will certainly make a sensation among the musicians. . . ."

At the London Philharmonic Tchaikovsky conducted his first Pianoforte Concerto (with Sapellnikov as soloist) and the Suite No. 1. Both works had a brilliant success. This was evident from the opinions of the Press, although the lion's share of praise fell to the lot of Sapellnikov. *The Musical Times* regretted that one of Tchaikovsky's

---

[1] This work, the libretto of which was by Galée and Detroyat, was never actually begun.

[2] In his diary Tchaikovsky only mentions V. d'Indy and Chaminade.

symphonies had not been given instead of the Suite, and considered this work was not sufficiently characteristic to give a just idea of the composer's talent.

Tchaikovsky left London very early on the morning of March 31st (April 12th), and arrived at Marseilles on the following day, where he embarked for Batoum by the Messageries Maritimes.

To Modeste Tchaikovsky.

"CONSTANTINOPLE, *April 8th* (20th), 1889.

". . . We left Marseilles a week ago. The ship is a good one, the food excellent. It was sometimes very rough. Between Syra and Smyrna there was quite a storm, to which I cannot look back without horror. Both these places pleased me very much. I got to know two Russians on board: a lad of fourteen, Volodya Sklifassovsky (son of the celebrated surgeon), and Hermanovich, a student at the Moscow University, who was travelling with him. Both were charming beings, with whom I made fast friends. They were going to Odessa—I to Batoum. We spent the whole of the evening together in the town, but slept on board. I shall miss them very much. . . ."

When Tchaikovsky parted from his new friends he returned to his cabin and "cried bitterly," as though he had some premonition that he should never again see this lovable and highly gifted boy on earth. Volodya Sklifassovsky died in January, 1890.

To N. F. von Meck.

"TIFLIS, *April 20th* (*May 2nd*), 1889.

". . . A glorious land, the Caucasus! How indescribably beautiful is the valley of the Rion, for instance, with its rich vegetation, through which runs the railway from Batoum to this place! Imagine, my dear, a wide valley, shut in on either side by rocks and mountains of fantastic form, in which flourish rhododendrons and other spring flowers, besides an abundance of trees, putting forth their fresh green foliage; and, added to this, the noisy, winding, brimming waters of the Rion. . . . In Tiflis, too, it is wonderful just now; all the fruit trees are in blossom. The weather is so clear that all the distant snow-peaks are visible, and the air is full of the feeling of spring, fragrant and life-giving. After the London fog it seems so beautiful, I can find no words to express it. . . ."

By May 7th (19th) Tchaikovsky was back in Moscow. The following letter throws some light on the musical life of that town.

To Anatol Tchaikovsky.

"Moscow, *May 12th (24th)*, 1889.

". . . All were glad to see me again. Since my return I have attended the committee meetings of the Musical Society every day. There is a great accumulation of business. A *coup d'état* has taken place in the Conservatoire. Taneiev has resigned the direction, and Safonov is prepared to take his place, on condition that Karl Albrecht gives up the post of inspector. I backed Karl persistently and energetically, and finally declared that I would retire from the Board of Direction if he were allowed to leave without any decoration for long service. . . ."

From Moscow Tchaikovsky went to Petersburg for a few days, returning to Frolovskoe, where he remained for the next four months.

The summer of 1889 passed in peaceful monotony. Tchaikovsky was engaged in composing and orchestrating his ballet, *The Sleeping Beauty*. . . . The little parties he occasionally gave—when Jurgenson, Mme. A. Hubert, and Siloti were his usual guests—were the sole "events" of this period of his life. But no account of this summer — uneventful as it was — would be complete without some mention of Legoshin's[1] daughter, a child of three.

---

[1] The servant of his friend Kondratiev.

Tchaikovsky was altogether fascinated by her prettiness, her clear, bell-like voice, her charming ways, and clever little head. He would spend hours romping with the child, listening to her chatter, and even acting as nurse-maid.

At this time Tchaikovsky's correspondence had not decreased, but many of his business letters are not forth-coming, and those of a more private nature which date from this summer are for the most part short and un-interesting.

To Edward Napravnik.

"KLIN, *July 9th (21st)*, 1889.

". . . You have not forgotten your promise to conduct one of the concerts of the Moscow Musical Society, dear friend ? . . .

"Now for the programme. It rests entirely with you both as regards the choice of music and of the soloists. . . . We beg you to lay aside your modesty, and to in-clude at least two important works of your own. I implore you *most emphatically* not to do any of my com-positions. As I am arranging this concert, it would be most unseemly were the conductor I engaged to perform any work of mine. I would not on any account have it suspected that I was looking after my own interests. But people would be sure to put this interpretation upon the matter, if the conductor invited for the occasion were to include any of my music in the programme. I think Dvořák will only bring forward his own works, so I will ask you as a Russo-Bohemian to give us something of Smetana's, *Vishergrad*, or *Moldava*. . . ."

To N. F. von Meck.

"FROLOVSKOE, *July 25th (August 6th)*, 1889.

". . . My ballet will be published in November or December. Siloti is making the pianoforte arrangement. I think, dear friend, that it will be one of my best works. The subject is so poetical, so grateful for musical setting, that I have worked at it with all that enthusiasm and goodwill upon which the value of a composition so much depends. The instrumentation gives me far more trouble than it used to do ; consequently the work goes slowly, but perhaps all the better. Many of my earlier compositions show traces of hurry and lack of due reflection."

VI

1889–1890

At the close of September, 1889, Tchaikovsky went to Moscow, where very complicated business in connection with the Russian Musical Society awaited his attention. For each symphony concert during the forthcoming season a different conductor was to be engaged.[1] Besides this, he had to superintend the rehearsals for *Eugene Oniegin*. This opera was to be newly and sumptuously remounted on September 18th (30th), when the composer had undertaken to conduct his own work.

From Moscow Tchaikovsky went to Petersburg for a few days, to attend a meeting of the committee appointed to arrange the Jubilee Festival for Anton Rubinstein. Tchaikovsky had undertaken to compose two works for this occasion.

While he was in Petersburg, Alexis prepared the new quarters in Moscow, which he had taken for the whole winter.

The lack of society in the evening, and the heavy duties which awaited him in connection with the Musical Society, were Tchaikovsky's sole reasons for wintering in Moscow rather than in the neighbourhood of Klin.

---

[1] Massenet and Brahms having declined their invitations, the following conductors were engaged for 1889-90 :—Rimsky - Korsakov, Tchaikovsky, Siloti, Arensky, Klindworth, A. Rubinstein, Slatin, Dvořák, Altani, Ippolitov-Ivanov, Napravnik, and Colonne.

During the summer the idea of trying town life once more seemed to attract him, and he spoke with enthusiasm of his new apartment, and took the greatest interest in getting it ready ; but, as the day of departure drew near, he felt less and less inclined to leave his country home.

Two circumstances contributed to make the first days after his arrival in Moscow depressing : first, he greatly missed the society of Laroche, who had gone to live in Petersburg ; and, secondly, his friend, the 'cellist Fitzenhagen, was on his death-bed.

His winter quarters were small, but comfortable. The work to which he looked forward with most apprehension was the direction of the two festival concerts for Rubinstein's jubilee. For two and a half years he had been conducting his own compositions, but had comparatively little experience of other music. Therefore these long and heavy programmes, including as they did several of Rubinstein's own works, filled him with anxious foreboding.

To N. F. von Meck.

" Moscow, *October 12th* (*24th*), 1889.

" I am very glad you are at home, and I envy you. By nature I incline *very, very* much to the kind of life you lead. I long to live completely away from society, as you do, but during recent years circumstances have made it impossible for me to live as I please. I consider it my duty, while I have strength for it, to fight against my destiny and not to desert my fellow-creatures so long as they have need of me. . . .

" But, good God, what I have to get through this winter ! It frightens me to think of all that lies before me, here and in Petersburg. Directly the season is over I shall go to Italy for a rest. I have not been there since 1882."

To Modeste Tchaikovsky.

"*October 16th (28th)*, 1889.

"Just think: I have heard from Tchekov.[1] He wants to dedicate his new stories to me. I have been to thank him. I am very proud and pleased."

Tchaikovsky first became acquainted with Tchekov's works in 1887. His enthusiasm was such that he felt impelled to write to the author, expressing his delight at having come across a talent so fresh and original. His first personal acquaintance with his literary favourite probably dated from the autumn of the same year. At any rate, they had known each other previous to 1889.

To the Grand Duke Constantine Constantinovich.[2]

"MOSCOW, *October 29th* (*November 10th*), 1889.

"YOUR IMPERIAL HIGHNESS,—I feel a certain pride in knowing that your admirable poem is partly the outcome of my letter to you last year. I cannot think why you should fancy that the idea of your poem does not please me. On the contrary, I like it very much. I cannot say that I have sufficient love and forbearance in my own nature always to love 'the hand that chastises.' Very often I want to parry the blows, and play the rebellious child in my turn. Nevertheless, I cannot but incline before the strength of mind and lofty views of such rare natures as Spinoza, or Tolstoi, who make no distinction between good and bad men, and take the same attitude towards every manifestation of human wickedness that you have expressed in your poem. I have never read Spinoza, so I speak of him from hearsay ; but as regards Tolstoi, I have read and re-read him, and consider him the greatest writer in the world, past or present. His writings awake in me— apart from any powerful artistic impression — a peculiar

---

[1] A celebrated Russian novelist and writer of short stories.
[2] The Grand Duke had dedicated his last volume of verse to Tchaikovsky.

emotion. I do not feel so deeply touched when he describes anything really emotional, such as death, suffering, separation, etc., so much as by the most ordinary, prosaic events. For instance, I remember that when reading the chapter in which Dolokhov plays cards with Rastov and wins, I burst into tears. Why should a scene in which two characters are acting in an unworthy manner affect me in this degree? The reason is simple enough. Tolstoi surveys the people he describes from such a height that they seem to him poor, insignificant pigmies who, in their blindness, injure each other in an aimless, purposeless way —and he pities them. Tolstoi has no malice; he loves and pities all his characters equally, and all their actions are the result of their own limitations and naïve egotism, their helplessness and insignificance. Therefore he never punishes his heroes for their ill-doings, as Dickens does (who is a great favourite of mine), because he never depicts anyone as absolutely bad, only blind people, as it were. His humanity is far above the sentimental humanity of Dickens; it almost attains to that view of human wickedness which is expressed in the words of Christ: 'they know not what they do.'

"Is not your Highness's poem an echo of this lofty feeling of humanity which so dominates me, and how can I therefore fail to admire the fundamental idea of your verses?

"The news that the Emperor has deigned to inquire after me gives me great pleasure. How am I to understand the Emperor's question about little pieces? If it is an indirect incitement to compose something in this style, I will take the first opportunity of doing so. I should immensely like to compose a great symphony, which should be, as it were, the crown of my creative work, and dedicate it to the Tsar. I have long since had a vague plan of such a work in my mind, but many favourable circumstances must combine before I can realise my idea. I hope I shall not die before I have carried out this project. At present I am entirely absorbed in the concerts here and the preparations for Rubinstein's jubilee."

In the same year in which my brother began to study

with Zaremba, in 1861 (or perhaps the previous year—I cannot remember for certain), he took Anatol and myself to an amateur performance in aid of some charity, given in the house of Prince Bieloselsky. Anton Rubinstein, already at the height of his fame, was among the audience. Peter Ilich pointed him out to me for the first time, and I still remember the excitement, rapture and reverence with which the future pupil gazed on his future teacher. He entirely forgot the play, while his eyes followed his "divinity," with the rapt gaze of a lover for the unattainable beauty of his fancy. During the intervals he stood as near to him as possible, strove to catch the sound of his voice, and envied the fortunate mortals who ventured to shake hands with him.

This feeling (I might say "infatuation" had it not been based upon a full appreciation of Rubinstein's value as a man and artist) practically lasted to the end of Tchaikovsky's life. Externally he was always "in love" with Rubinstein, although—as is always the case in love affairs—there were periods of coolness, jealousy, and irritation, which invariably gave place in turn to a fresh access of that sentiment which set me wondering in Prince Bieloselsky's reception-room. In Rubinstein's presence Tchaikovsky became quite diffident, lost his head, and seemed to regard him as a superior being. When at a supper, given during the pianist's jubilee, someone, in an indelicate and unseemly way, requested Rubinstein and Tchaikovsky to drink to each other "as brothers," the latter was not only confused and indignant, but, in his reply to the toast, protested warmly, saying that his tongue would never consent to address the great artist in the second person singular—it would be entirely against the spirit of their relations. He would be happy if Rubinstein addressed him by the familiar "thou," but for his own part, the more ceremonious form better expressed a sense of reverence from the pupil to his teacher, from

the man to the embodiment of his ideal. These were no
empty words. Rubinstein had been the first to give the
novice in his art an example of the untiring devotion and
disinterested spirit which animates the life of the true
artist. In this sense Tchaikovsky was far more the pupil
of Rubinstein than in questions of orchestration and composition. With his innate gifts and thirst for knowledge,
any other teacher could have given him the same instruction. It was in his character as an energetic, irreproach-
ably clean-minded and inspired artist, as a man who never
compromised with his conscience, who had all his life
detested every kind of humbug and the successes of
vulgarity, as an indefatigable worker, that Rubinstein left
really deep traces upon Tchaikovsky's artistic career. The
latter, writing to the well-known German journalist,
Eugen Zabel, said : "Rubinstein's personality shines before
me like a clear, guiding star."

But there were times when clouds obscured this "guiding
star." While recognising Rubinstein's great gifts as a
composer, and valuing some of his works very highly—
such as the "Ocean Symphony," *The Tower of Babel*,
the Pianoforte Concerto, *Ivan the Terrible*, the violoncello sonatas, and many of the pieces for pianoforte—
Tchaikovsky grew angry and impatient over the vast
majority of the virtuoso's mediocre and empty creations.
He frequently expressed himself so sarcastically on this
subject that I have cut out certain passages in his letters,
lest they might give the reader a false impression of his
attitude towards Rubinstein. But he soon forgot and
forgave these momentary eclipses of "his star," and always
returned to his old spirit of veneration.

The deepest, keenest, and most painful aspect of their
relations—and here artistic self-esteem doubtless played
a part—was the knowledge of Rubinstein's antipathy to
him as a composer, which he never conquered to the end
of his life. The virtuoso never cared for Tchaikovsky's

music.   Many of Rubinstein's intimate friends, and also his wife, maintained the reverse.   But in that case it was the love of Wotan for the Wälsungs.   Secretly rejoicing in the success of Tchaikovsky-Siegmund, and sympathising in his heart with Tchaikovsky-Siegfried, Wotan-Rubinstein never did anything to forward the performance of his works, nor held out a helping hand. . . . From the earliest exercises at the Conservatoire, to the "Pathetic Symphony," he never praised—and seldom condemned—a single work of Tchaikovsky's.   All of them, without exception, were silently ignored—together with all the music which came after Schumann—as unworthy of serious attention.

The legend of Rubinstein's envy, which had absolutely no foundation in fact, always annoyed Tchaikovsky and aroused his wrath.   Even if it might be to a certain extent true as regards the eighties, when my brother was recognised and famous, it could not apply to the attitude of a teacher towards a pupil who—although undoubtedly gifted—had a doubtful future before him.   To the composer of the "Ocean Symphony" Tchaikovsky's earliest essays in composition were as antipathetic as *Eugene Oniegin* and the Fifth Symphony.   Envy can only exist between two equally matched rivals, and could not have influenced a giant—as Rubinstein was in the sixties—in his relations with anyone so insignificant as the Tchaikovsky of those days.

The feeling was simply the same which Tchaikovsky himself cherished for the works of Chopin and Brahms; a sentiment of instinctive and unconquerable antipathy. Rubinstein felt like this, not only towards Tchaikovsky's music, but to all musical works which came after Chopin and Schumann.

In any case, however much Tchaikovsky may have been wounded by Rubinstein's indifference, he remained loyal to his enthusiasm for his former teacher.   When the

2 Q

Duke of Mecklenburg-Strelitz requested him to take part in organising the celebration of Rubinstein's jubilee, he expressed himself willing to put himself at the disposal of the committee. It was decided that he should conduct the jubilee concerts and compose a chorus *a capella* to words by Polonsky. The chorus was to be sung at the festival given in the hall of the Nobles' Club, November 18th (30th), 1889. In addition he undertook to contribute something to the album which Rubinstein's former pupils at the Petersburg Conservatoire were going to present him on the same occasion.

The second half of his task was easily fulfilled. In a few days both compositions—the chorus and an Impromptu for pianoforte—were ready. The conducting of the concerts was another matter. The labour it involved, and the difficulties in connection with it, made real demands upon Tchaikovsky's devotion for his old teacher.

The programme of the first concert consisted entirely of symphonic works, including the Konzertstück (op. 113), with Rubinstein himself at the piano, and the Symphony No. 5 (op. 107). At the second concert, besides the dances from *Feramors* and the *Roussalka* songs, the chief item was the Biblical opera, *The Tower of Babel*.

This programme would have made very heavy demands upon the most experienced conductor; it was a still heavier task for one who—only a month previously—had conducted for the first time any works other than his own.

"There were moments," he wrote to Nadejda von Meck, "when I experienced such a complete loss of strength that I feared for my life. The working up of *The Tower of Babel*, with its chorus of seven hundred voices, gave me the most trouble. On the evening of November 10th (22nd), just before the oratorio began, I had an attack of nerves, which they feared might prevent my returning to the conductor's desk. But—perhaps thanks to this crisis—I pulled myself together in time, and all went well to the end. You will learn all details about the festival from the newspapers. I will only add that from the 1st to the 19th of November I endured martyrdom, and I am still marvelling how I lived through it all."

To the period between the end of October, 1889, to the middle of January, 1890, belong but twelve letters, only two of which have any biographical interest. The rest are merely short notes of no importance. Such a decrease in Tchaikovsky's correspondence is a symptom of the highly nervous and distracted phase which he was now passing through. For a long time past letter-writing had ceased to be a pleasant duty; still, it remained a *duty*, which he could only neglect under special circumstances, such as overwhelmed him at the commencement of this season.

He had scarcely got over the jubilee concerts, when he had to return to Moscow to conduct Beethoven's Ninth Symphony at an extra Symphony Concert, given in aid of the fund for the widows and orphans of musicians.

Only two published notices of this concert are in existence at Klin. Both emanate from staunch admirers of Tchaikovsky: Kashkin and Konius, who, in spite of all their justice, probably show some partisanship in their praise.

On the same occasion Brandoukov played Tchaikovsky's Pezzo Capriccioso for violoncello with great success.

It was unfortunate that after all this strain and anxiety the composer was not able to return to his country retreat, where the peaceful solitude invariably restored him to health and strength. In spite of all precautions, he was overrun with visitors; and his Moscow quarters were so small that he sighed perpetually for his roomy home at Frolovskoe. Added to which, Alexis Safronov's wife was dying of consumption. We know Tchaikovsky's attitude to those who served him. He never regarded them as subordinates, mere machines for carrying out his wishes, but rather as friends, in whose joys and sorrows he felt the keenest sympathy. The illness of his servant's young wife caused him great sorrow ; the more so that he saw no way of saving her life. The knowledge that he was of no use, but rather a hindrance to the care of the invalid—for Alexis was the poor soul's only nurse—made Tchaikovsky anxious to save his man all the personal services with which he could possibly dispense. For this reason he cut short his stay in Moscow and returned to Petersburg at the end of November, where his ballet, *The Sleeping Beauty*, was already in rehearsal.

To N. F. von Meck.

"PETERSBURG, *December* 17*th* (29*th*), 1889.

" MY DEAR, KIND, INCOMPARABLE FRIEND,—Where are you now ? I do not know. But I have such a yearning to talk to you a little that I am beginning this letter with the intention of posting it to you in Moscow, as soon as I can find your address. For three weeks I have been doing nothing in Petersburg. I say 'doing nothing' because my real business is to compose; and all this conducting, attending rehearsals for my ballet, etc., I regard as something purposeless and fortuitious, which only shortens my days, for it needs all my strength of will to endure the kind of life I have to lead in Petersburg. . . . On January 6th I must be back in Moscow to conduct a concert of the Musical Society, at which Anton Rubinstein will play his new compositions, and on the 14th I have a popular concert here; after that I shall be at the end of my forces. I have made up my mind to refuse all engagements at home and abroad, and perhaps to go to Italy for four months to rest and work at my future opera, *Pique Dame*. I have chosen this subject from Poushkin. It happened in this way : three years ago my brother Modeste undertook to make a libretto for a certain Klenovsky, and gradually put together a very successful book upon this subject.

"Moscow, *December 26th* (*January 7th*), 1889.

" I continue my letter. The libretto of *Pique Dame* was written by Modeste for Klenovsky, but for some reason he declined to set it to music. Then Vsievolojsky, the Director of the Opera, took it into his head that I should write a work on this subject and have it ready by next season. He communicated his wish to me, and as the business fitted in admirably with my determination to escape from Russia for a time and devote myself to composition, I said ' yes.' A committee meeting was improvised, at which my brother read his libretto, its merits and demerits were discussed, the scenery planned, and even the parts distributed. . . . I feel very much inclined to work. If only I can settle myself comfortably in some corner abroad, I should be equal to my task, and could let the Direction have the pianoforte score in May. In the course of the summer the orchestration would be finished."

On January 1st (13th) Tchaikovsky was back in St. Petersburg, and on the following day attended a gala rehearsal of *The Sleeping Beauty*, at which the Imperial Court was present.

Practically it was the first night, for while the *parterre* was reserved for the Imperial party, the boxes on the first tier were crowded with aristocratic spectators. The Imperial family were pleased, but not enthusiastic in their appreciation of the music, although afterwards they grew very fond of this Ballet. " Very nice " was the only expression of opinion Tchaikovsky received from the Emperor's lips. This scanty praise—judging from the entry in his diary—greatly mortified the composer.

It is interesting to observe that at the first public performance, on the following day, the public seems to have shared the Emperor's opinion, for the applause, which was lacking in warmth, seemed to pronounce the same lukewarm verdict, "Very nice." The composer was still further depressed and embittered. " Embittered," because, during the rehearsals, Tchaikovsky had learnt to appreciate the splendour and novelty of the scenery and costumes, and the inexhaustible taste and invention of M. Petipa, and expected that all this talent and taste, combined with his music—which came only second to *Oniegin* in his affections—would arouse a storm of enthusiasm in the public.

This was not the case, because the novelty of the programme and the dazzling wealth of detail blinded the public to the musical beauties of the work. They could not appreciate the Ballet at the first performance, as they afterwards learnt to do. Its success was immense, and was proved in the same way as that of *Eugene Oniegin*—not by frantic applause during the performance, but by a long series of crowded houses.

On January 4th (16th) Tchaikovsky went to Moscow, where he conducted on the 6th. Convinced that no repose was possible in that town, he decided to start abroad immediately, and to take his brother Modeste's servant, Nazar, in place of Alexis, who remained by his wife's death-bed. Tchaikovsky left Petersburg on January 14th (26th) without any plans as to his destination.

VII

Not until he reached Berlin did Tchaikovsky decide in favour of Florence, where he arrived early on January 18th (30th), 1890, Italy did not interest him at the moment. He was actuated only by one motive—to get away. Soon he was at work upon *Pique Dame*. His surroundings were favourable, and he made rapid progress. His condition of mind was not cheerful, however, as may he gathered from the following letter to Glazounov, dated January 30th (February 11th), 1890.

"DEAR ALEXANDER CONSTANTINOVICH,—Your kind letter touched me very much. Just now I am sadly in need of friendly sympathy and intercourse with people who are intimate and dear. I am passing through a very enigmatical stage on my road to the grave. Something strange, which I cannot understand, is going on within me. A kind of life-weariness has come over me. Sometimes I feel an insane anguish, but not that kind of anguish which is the herald of a new tide of love for life ; rather something hopeless, final, and—like every *finale*— a little commonplace. Simultaneously a passionate desire to create. The devil knows what it is ! In fact, sometimes I feel my song is sung, and then again an unconquerable impulse, either to give it fresh life, or to start a new song. . . . As I have said, I do not know what has come to me. For instance, there was a time when I loved Italy and Florence. Now I have to make a great effort to emerge from my shell. When I do go out, I feel no pleasure whatever, either in the blue sky of Italy, in the sun that shines from it, in the architectural beauties I see around me, or in the teeming life of the streets. Formerly all this enchanted me, and quickened my imagination. Perhaps my trouble actually lies in those fifty years to which I shall attain two months hence, and my imagination will no longer take colour from its surroundings?

"But enough of this ! I am working hard. Whether what I am doing is really good, is a question to which only posterity can give the answer.

"I feel the greatest sympathy for your misgivings as to the failure of your ' Oriental Fantasia.' There is nothing more painful than such doubts. But all evil has its good side. You say your friends did not approve of the work, but did not express their disapproval at the right time— at a moment when you could agree with them. It was wrong of them to oppose the enthusiasm of the author for his work, before it had had time to cool. But it is better that they had the courage to speak frankly, instead of giving you that meaningless, perfunctory praise some friends consider it their duty to bestow, to which we listen, and which we accept, because we are only too glad to believe. You are strong enough to guard your feelings as composer in those moments when people tell you the truth. . . . I, too, dear Alexander Constantinovich, have sometimes wished to be quite frank with you about your work. I am a great admirer of your gifts. I value the earnestness of your aims, and your artistic sense of honour. And yet I often think about you. I feel that, as an older friend who loves you, I ought to warn you against certain exclusive tendencies, and a kind of one-sidedness. Yet how to tell you this I do not quite know. In many respects you are a riddle to me. You have genius, but something prevents you from broadening out and penetrating the depths. . . . In short, during the winter you may expect a letter from me, in which I will talk to you after due reflection. If I fail to say anything apposite, it will be a proof of my incapacity, not the result of any lack of affection and sympathy for you."

To Modeste Tchaikovsky.

"FLORENCE, *February 2nd* (14*th*), 1890.

"You have arranged the death scene of *The Queen of Spades* very well, and suitably for musical setting. I am very pleased with you as a librettist, only keep conciseness in view and avoid prolixity. As to the scene on the bridge, I have thought it over. You and Laroche are quite opposed, and in spite of my wish to have as few scenes as possible, and to be concise, I fear the whole of Act III. will be without any women actors, and that would be dull. Lisa's part cannot be finished in the fourth scene ; the audience must know what becomes of her."

To Modeste Tchaikovsky.

"FLORENCE, *February 6th* (18*th*), 1890.

". . . . To-day, for the first time, I enjoyed my visit to Italy. So far I have felt indifferent—even hostile to it. But to-day the weather was so divine, and it was such a joy to gather a few violets in the Cascine! At Kamenka they only appear in April.

"Now to return to *Pique Dame*. How can we manage to make the part lighter for poor Figner? Seven scenes, in which he has to sing without intermission! Do think it over.

"I am anxiously awaiting the ball scene. For Heaven's sake lose no time, Modi, or I shall find myself without any text to set."

To A. P. Merkling.

"FLORENCE, *February* 7*th* (19*th*), 1890.

"To-day I wrote the scene in which Hermann goes to the old *Queen of Spades*. It was so gruesome that I am still under the horrible spell of it."

To Modeste Tchaikovsky.

"FLORENCE, *February* 12*th* (24*th*), 1890.

"If, God willing, I finish the opera, it will be something *chic*. The fourth scene will have an overwhelming effect."

Meanwhile, on February 4th (16th), *The Enchantress* had been produced in Moscow for the first time. Kashkin wrote of it as follows :—

"That the opera had been very superficially studied was evident from the entire performance, which was most unsatisfactory. I will not blame the artists, who did what they could, while some of them were very good ; but the ensemble was bad, in consequence of insufficient rehearsal. All went in a more or less disconnected way. The orchestra accompanied very roughly, without light or shade, the brass playing *ff* throughout and drowning everything else with their monotonous noise. Madame Korovina, who took the chief part, was ill, and should not have been allowed to sing. We see from the repertory published in the newspapers that *The Enchantress* will not be put on again before Lent. Thank goodness! The repetition of such a performance is most undesirable. An opera should be studied before it is put on the stage."

The Enchantress, however, was not repeated, even after Lent. With this solitary performance its career came to an end as regards the Imperial Opera House.

Diary.

"*February 21st* (*March 5th*), 1890.

" This morning I had a letter from Alexis. He says Theklousha (his wife) prays God to take her soon. Poor, poor sufferer!

" Began the fifth scene, and in imagination I finished it yesterday, but in reality only got through it early to-day."

"*February 24th* (*March 8th*), 1890.

" Heard from Alexis. Theklousha is dead. I wept. Altogether a sad morning. . . . In the evening an act from *Puritani*. With all his glaring defects, Bellini is fascinating!"

"*March 3rd* (*15th*), 1890.

" *Finished everything* this morning. God be praised, Who has let me bring my work to an end."

To Modeste Tchaikovsky.

"FLORENCE, *March 3rd* (*15th*), 1890.

" Yesterday I set your own closing scene to music. When I came to Hermann's death and the final chorus, I was suddenly overcome by such intense pity for Hermann that I burst out crying. Afterwards I discovered the reason for my tears (for I was never before so deeply moved by the sorrows of my hero, and I tried to explain to myself why it should be so now). I came to the conclusion that Hermann was to me not merely a pretext for writing this or that kind of music, but had been all the while an actual, living, sympathetic human being. Because I am very fond of Figner, and I always see Hermann in the form of Figner, therefore I have felt an intimate realisation of his fate.[1] Now I hope my warm and lively feeling for the hero of my opera may be happily reflected in my music. In any case, I think *Pique Dame* by no means a bad opera. We shall see. . . .

" Laroche writes that he and Napravnik do not approve of my having composed an opera in so short a time. They

---

[1] For the story of *Pique Dame* see Appendix B, p. 759.

will not realise that to rush through my work is an essential feature of my character. I only work quickly. I took my time over *The Enchantress* and the Fifth Symphony, and they were failures, whereas I finished the Ballet in three weeks, and *Oniegin* was written in an incredibly short time. The chief thing is to love the work. I have certainly written with love. How I cried yesterday when they sang over my poor Hermann!"

Tchaikovsky had decided to leave Florence early in March for Rome. But failing to find rooms in any of the hotels, he stayed on in Florence for two or three weeks longer.

To Anna Merkling.

"FLORENCE, *March 5th* (17*th*), 1890.

". . . Heavens, what charming creatures children are! But little dogs are even more beautiful. They are simply the pearls of creation! . . . There is a breed here, almost unknown with us, called 'Lupetto.' You can often buy puppies of this kind on the Lungarno. If my Alexis did not hate dogs (they have a wretched life when the servants dislike them), I could not resist buying one of them."

To Modeste Tchaikovsky.

"FLORENCE, *March 19th* (31*st*), 1890.

"Just two months ago I began the composition of the opera. To-day I finished the pianoforte score of the second act. This is to me the most dreadful and nerve-exasperating occupation. I composed the opera with pleasure and self-oblivion; I shall orchestrate with delight; but to make an arrangement! All the time one has to keep undoing what is intended for orchestra. I believe my ill-health is simply the result of this confounded work. Nazar says I have very much altered the last week or two, and have been in a dreadful state of mind. Whether it is that the worst and most wearisome part of my work is nearing an end, or that the weather is finer, I cannot say, but since yesterday I feel much better. . . . Modi, either I am greatly mistaken or *Pique Dame* is a masterpiece. At one place in the fourth scene, which I was arranging to-day, I felt such horror, such gruesome thrills, that surely the listeners cannot escape the same impressions.

"Understand, that I shall certainly spend my fiftieth birthday in Petersburg. Besides yourself, Anatol, and Jurgenson, I shall write to no one."

On March 27th (April 8th), Tchaikovsky completed the pianoforte arrangement of *Pique Dame*, and resolved to move on to Rome. "I am going there chiefly for Nazar's sake," he writes, "I want him to see the place." For the first time, after nine weeks of continuous work, the composer enjoyed a little leisure, and spent one of his last days in the Uffizi and Pitti galleries. "In spite of my efforts," he says, "I cannot acquire any appreciation of painting, especially of the older masters—they leave me cold."

To Modeste Tchaikovsky.

"ROME, *March 27th (April 8th).*

". . . The cheerful feelings that came over me to-day as soon as I stepped into the streets, breathed the well-known air of Rome, and saw the old familiar places, made me realise how foolish I had been not to come here first of all. However, I must not blame poor Florence, which for no particular reason grew so detestable to me, since I was able to compose my opera there unmolested. Rome is much changed. Parts of it are unrecognisable. Yet, in spite of these alterations, it is a joy to be back in the dear place. I think of the years that have dropped into eternity, of the two Kondratievs, gone to their rest. It is very sad and yet it has a melancholy pleasure. . . . Nazar is enchanted with Rome. I seem to see you and Kolya at every turn. I shall stay here three weeks."

To P. Jurgenson.

"ROME, *March 28th (April 9th),* 1890.

"All I hear about Safonov[1] does not surprise me in the least. But in any case it must be confessed that he may

---

[1] He had succeeded Taneiev as Director of the Moscow Conservatoire.

be useful at this critical juncture. A man of such child-like guilelessness and rectitude as Taneiev can hardly uphold the prestige of the Conservatoire. A Safonov is useful when there is no longer a Rubinstein. Such a man as Nicholas Rubinstein, who had furious energy, and at the same time could quite forget himself in the work he loved, is rare indeed."

To N. F. von Meck.

"ROME, *April 7th* (*19th*), 1890.

"DEAR FRIEND,—I am forced to flee from Rome. I could not preserve my incognito. A few Russians have already called to ask me to dinners, soirées, etc. I have refused every invitation, but my liberty is done for, and all pleasure in my visit at an end. Sgambati, the leading musician here, having heard from the Russians that I was in Rome, put my First Quartet into the programme of his chamber concert, and came to request my attendance. I could not possibly be ungracious, so I had to sacrifice one of my working hours in order to sit in a stuffy room and listen to a second-rate performance of my work; while all the time I was an object of curiosity to the audience, whom Sgambati had informed of my presence, and who seemed very curious to see what a Russian musician could be like. It was most unpleasant. As these occurrences are certain to be repeated, I have decided to return to Russia in two or three days by way of Venice and Vienna.

"You cannot imagine how I long for Russia, and with what joy I look forward to my rural solitude. Just now something wrong is going on in Russia. But nothing hinders my passionate love of my own land. I cannot imagine how formerly I was contented to stay so long away from it, and even to take some pleasure in being abroad."

To Modeste Tchaikvosky.

"ROME, *April 7th* (*19th*), 1890.

". . . . The Quartet had a tremendous success; the papers praise it to the skies. But the papers here praise everything. Home, quick, quick, home!"

VIII

To Modeste Tchaikovsky.

"FROLOVSKOE, *May 5th (17th)*, 1890.

" I have been back four days. The house is almost unrecognisable: the parlour (it is also the dining-room) has become a beautiful apartment, thanks to the addition of Siloti's furniture to mine.[1] . . . But outside the house, O horror! *The whole—literally every stick—of the forest has been cut down!* Only the little thicket behind the church is left. Where is one to walk? Heavens, how entirely the disappearance of a wood changes the character of a place, and what a pity it is! All those dear, shady spots that were there last year are now a bare wilderness. Now we are sowing our flowering seeds. I am doing double work, that is to say, out of working hours I am correcting proofs. . . ."

To Ippolitov-Ivanov.

"FROLOVSKOE, *May 5th (17th)*, 1890.

" My visit abroad brought forth good fruit. I composed an opera, *Pique Dame,* which seems to me a success, that is why I speak of 'good fruit'. . . . My plans for the future are as follows: to finish the orchestration of the opera, to sketch out a string sextet, to go to my sister at Kamenka for the end of the summer, and to spend the whole autumn with you at Tiflis. Is your opera *Asra* finished? I saw none of the musical world in Moscow, and know nothing of what is going on. Safonov is a capable director, but—— However, we will talk this over when we meet."

---

[1] Siloti had taken a smaller house, and made over part of his furniture to Tchaikovsky, thinking it would be a kindness to him, for the composer's household lacked many comforts. Siloti did not reclaim the furniture after Tchaikovsky's death, and it stands at present in the house at Klin.

To the Grand Duke Constantine Constantinovich.

"FROLOVSKOE, *May* 18*th* (30*th*), 1890.

"YOUR IMPERIAL HIGHNESS,—. . . I should be delighted to meet Maikov[1] at your house to discuss the relations between art and craftsmanship. Ever since I began to compose I have endeavoured to be in my work just what the great masters of music—Mozart, Beethoven, and Schubert—were in theirs; not necessarily to be as great as they were, but to work as they did—as the cobbler works at his trade; not in a gentlemanly way, like Glinka, whose genius, however, I by no means deny. Mozart, Beethoven, Schubert, Mendelssohn, Schumann, composed their immortal works just as a cobbler makes a pair of boots—by daily work; and more often than not because they were ordered. The result was something colossal. Had Glinka been a cobbler, rather than a gentleman, besides his two (very beautiful) operas, he would have given us perhaps fifteen others, and ten fine symphonies into the bargain. I could cry with vexation when I think what Glinka might have left us, if he had not been born into an aristocratic family before the days of the Emancipation. He showed us what he could have done, but he never actually accomplished a twentieth part of what it was in him to do For instance, in symphonic music (*Kamarinskaya*, and the two Spanish overtures) he simply played about like an amateur—and yet we are astonished at the force and originality of his gifts. What would he not have accomplished had he worked in the same way as the great masters of Western Europe?

"Although I am convinced that if a musician desires to attain to the greatest heights to which his inspiration will carry him he must develop himself as a craftsman, I will not assert that the same thing applies to the other arts. For instance, in the sphere you have chosen I do not think a man can force himself to create. For a lyrical poem, not only the mood, but the idea, must be there. But the idea will be evoked by some fortuitous phe-

[1] One of the most eminent of Russian poets.

nomenon. In music it is only necessary to evoke a certain general mood or emotion. For example, to compose an elegy I must tune myself to a melancholy key. But in a poet this melancholy must take some concrete expression so to speak; therefore in his case an external impulse is indispensable. But in all these things the difference between the various creative temperaments plays a great part, and what is right for one would not be permissible for another. The majority of my fellow-workers, for instance, do not like working to order; I, on the other hand, never feel more inspired than when I am requested to compose something, when a term is fixed and I know that my work is being impatiently awaited."

At the beginning of June, Ippolitov-Ivanov wrote to Tchaikovsky that the usual opera season would take place at Tiflis, and that, besides works by Tchaikovsky, his own opera *Asra* would be performed there. At the same time, he seems to have sounded his friend as to his prospects of succeeding to Altani's post in Moscow.

" The rumours of Altani's resignation were false," replied Tchaikovsky, "and the work of his enemies. . . . But you have no notion of all the disagreeables and annoyances you would have to endure. A more suitable position for you would be a professorship at the Moscow Conservatoire. But Safonov, it appears, makes no propositions. Write to me: yes or no."

To N. F. von Meck.

" FROLOVSKOE, *June 30th* (*July 12th*), 1890.

" . . . I find more and more delight in the cultivation of flowers, and comfort myself with the thought of devoting myself entirely to this occupation when my powers of composition begin to decay. Meanwhile I cannot complain. Scarcely was the opera finished before I took up a new work, the sketch of which is already completed. I hope you will be pleased to hear I have composed a sextet for strings. I know your love of chamber music, and I am glad you will be able to hear my sextet; that will not necessitate your going to a concert, you can easily arrange a performance of it at home. I hope the work will please you: I wrote it with the greatest enthusiasm and without the least exertion."

To Modeste Tchaikovsky.

"FROLOVSKOE, *June* 30*th* (*July* 12*th*), 1890.

"Yesterday was my name-day. I had eleven guests to dinner, which was served in the garden. The peasants came again to get their money, and brought cracknels, etc. The summer is wonderful. My flowers have never been so luxuriant. Quantities of everything. Yesterday morning I had hardly left the house before I came upon two splendid white mushrooms."

To N. F. von Meck.

"FROLOVSKOE, *July* 2*nd* (14*th*), 1890.

"DEAR, KIND FRIEND,—At the same time as your letter yesterday, the composer Arensky came to see me, which delayed my immediate reply. I am afraid I did not fully express my thanks. But then, words are wanting to tell you of my eternal gratitude, and to say how deeply touched I am by your care and attention. Acting upon your advice, I have paid two-thirds of the sum to my current account. I have firmly resolved to begin to put by this year, so that in time I may buy a small landed property—perhaps Frolovskoe itself, since I am very fond of it, in spite of the demolition of the woods.

"Arensky has written an opera,[1] which Jurgenson has published. I had gone through it carefully and felt I must tell him exactly what I thought of this fine work. My letter touched him so deeply that he came here to thank me in person. Arensky is a man of remarkable gifts, but morbidly nervous and lacking in firmness—altogether a strange man."

[1] *A Dream on the Volga.*

To P. Jurgenson.

"*July 2nd* (14*th*), 1890.

"DEAR FRIEND,—The manuscript of the cantata is in the Petersburg Conservatoire. I cannot consent to its publication, because it is an immature work, for which there is no future. Besides, it is written to Schiller's *Ode to Joy*. It is not seemly to enter into competition with Beethoven.

"As to the fate of *The Little Shoes* (*Les Caprices d'Oxane*), I fully believe it will come to have a place in the repertory, and regard it, musically speaking, as my best operatic work.

"Arensky was here yesterday, and showed me a book of theory. It is admirably put together, and would be very useful for teaching purposes. I strongly recommend you to buy it."

To the Grand Duke Constantine Constantinovich.

"FROLOVSKOE, *August* 3*rd* (15*th*), 1890.

"YOUR IMPERIAL HIGHNESS,—Your kind and charming letter has reached me on the eve of my departure for a long journey, so forgive me if I do not answer it as fully as I ought. But I have much to say in answer to your remarks about *Pique Dame*. . . . Your criticisms of my sins as regards declamation are too lenient. In this respect I am past redemption. I do not think I have perpetrated many blunders of this kind in recitative and dialogue, but in the lyrical parts, where my mood has carried me away from all just equivalents, I am simply unconscious of my mistakes—you must get someone to point them out to me. . . .

"As regards the repetition of words and phrases, I must say that my views differ entirely from those of your Imperial Highness. There are cases in which such repetitions are quite natural and in accordance with truth of expression. . . . But even were it not so, I should not hesitate for an instant to sacrifice the literal to the artistic truth. These truths differ fundamentally, and I could not forget the second in pursuit of the first, for, if we aimed at pushing realism in opera to its extreme limits, we should finally have to abandon opera itself. To sing instead of speaking—that is the climax of falsehood in the accepted sense of the word. Of course, I am the child of my generation, and I have no wish to return to the worn-out traditions of opera ; at the same time I am not disposed to submit to the despotic requirements of realistic theories. I should be most grieved to think that any portions of *Pique Dame* were repellent to you—for I hoped the work might please you—and I have made a few changes in the scene where the governess scolds the girls, so that all the repetitions have some good reason. . . ."

IX

1890–1891

On December 13th (25th), 1890, Tchaikovsky received a letter from Nadejda von Meck, informing him that in consequence of the complicated state of her affairs she was on the brink of ruin, and therefore no longer able to continue his allowance.

In the course of their correspondence, which extended over thirteen years, Nadejda Filaretovna had referred more than once to her pecuniary embarrassments and to her fears of becoming bankrupt. But each time she had added that the allowance made to Tchaikovsky could be in no way affected, since she had assured it to him for life, and that the sum of 6,000 roubles a year was of no consequence to her one way or the other. In November, 1889, she had spoken again of her business anxieties, but, as usual, without any reference to Tchaikovsky's pension. On the contrary, in the summer of 1890 she showed her willingness to help him still further by advancing him a considerable sum. Consequently this news fell upon the composer like a bolt from the blue, and provoked the following reply :—

To N. F. von Meck.

" Tiflis, *September 22nd (October 4th),* 1890.

" DEAREST FRIEND,—The news you communicated to me in your last letter caused me great anxiety ; not on my account, however, but on your own. It would, of course, be untrue were I to say that such a radical change in my budget did not in any way affect my financial position. But it ought not to affect me so seriously as you apparently fear. In recent years my earnings have considerably increased, and there are indications that they will continue to do so. Therefore, if I am accountable for any fraction of your endless cares and anxieties, I beg you, for God's sake, to be assured that I can think of this pecuniary loss without any bitterness. Believe me, this is the simple truth ; I am no master of empty phraseology. That I shall have to economise a little is of no importance. What really matters is that you, with your requirements and large ways of life, should have to retrench. This is terribly hard and vexatious. I feel as though I wanted to lay the blame on someone (you yourself are certainly above reproach), but I do not know who is the real culprit. Besides, not only is my indignation quite useless, but I have no right to interfere in your family affairs. I would rather ask Ladislaw Pakhulsky to tell me what you intend to do, where you will live, and how far you will be straitened as to means. I cannot think of you except as a wealthy woman. The last words of your letter have hurt me a little,[1] but I do not think you meant them seriously. Do you really think me incapable of remembering you when I no longer receive your money? How could I forget for a moment all you have done for me, and all for which I owe you gratitude? I may say without exaggeration that you saved me. I should certainly have gone out of my mind and come to an untimely end but for your friendship and sympathy, as well as for the material assistance (then my safety anchor), which enabled me to rally my forces and take up once more my chosen vocation. No, dear friend, I shall always remember and bless you with my last

---

[1] " Do not forget, and think of me sometimes."

breath. I am glad you can now no longer spend your means upon me, so that I may show my unbounded and passionate gratitude, which passes all words. Perhaps you yourself hardly suspect how immeasurable has been your generosity. If you did, you would never have said that, now you are poor, I am to think of you '*sometimes.*' I can truly say that I have never forgotten you, and never shall forget you for a moment, for whenever I think of myself my thoughts turn directly to you.

" I kiss your hands, with all my heart's warmth, and implore you to believe, once and for all, that no one feels more keenly for your troubles than I do.

" I will write another time about myself and all I am doing. Forgive my hasty, badly written letter : I am too much upset to write well."

To the above letter we need only add that Tchaikovsky, with his usual lack of confidence, greatly exaggerated to himself the consequences of this loss. A few days later he wrote to Jurgenson :—

" Now I must start quite a fresh life, on a totally different scale of expenditure. In all probability I shall be compelled to seek some occupation in Petersburg which will bring me in a good salary. This is very, very humiliating—yes, humiliating is the word ! "

But this " humiliation " soon passed away. About this time his pecuniary situation greatly improved, and the success of *Pique Dame* more than covered the loss of his pension.

Soon, too, he was relieved as to the fate of Nadejda Filaretovna, for he learnt that her fears of ruin had been unfounded, and her financial difficulties had almost completely blown over. But with this relief—strange as it may appear—came also a sense of injury which Tchaikovsky carried to the grave. No sooner was he assured that his friend was as well off as before, than he began to persuade himself that her last letter had been nothing

"but an excuse to get rid of him on the first opportunity";
that he had been mistaken in idealising his relations with
his "best friend"; that the allowance had long since
ceased to be the outcome of a generous impulse, and that
Nadejda Filaretovna was no longer as grateful to him for
his ready acceptance of her help, as he was to receive it.

"Such were my relations with her," he wrote to Jurgenson, "that I never felt oppressed by her generous gifts;
but now they weigh upon me in retrospect. My pride is
hurt; my faith in her unfailing readiness to help me, and
to make any sacrifice for my sake is betrayed."

In his agony of wounded pride Tchaikovsky was driven
to wish that his friend had really been ruined, so that he
"might help her, even as she had helped him." To these
painful feelings was added all the bitterness involved in
seeing their ideal connection shattered and dissolved. He
felt as though he had been roughly awakened from some
beautiful dream, and found in its stead "a commonplace,
silly joke, which fills me with disgust and shame."

But the worst blow was yet to come. Shortly after
receiving Nadejda von Meck's letter, Tchaikovsky's circumstances—as we have already said—improved so
greatly that it would not have been difficult for him to
have returned her the sum she had allowed him. He
believed, however, that this would have hurt her feelings,
and he could not bring himself to mortify in the smallest
degree the woman who had actually been his saviour at
the most critical moment of his life. The only way out
of this painful situation seemed the continuance of his
correspondence with her, as though nothing had happened. His advances, however, met with nothing but
silent opposition on the part of Nadejda Filaretovna, and
this proved the unkindest cut of all. Her indifference to
his fate, her lack of interest in his work, convinced him
that things had never been what they seemed, and all the
old ideal friendship now appeared to him as the whim of

a wealthy woman—the commonplace ending to a fairy tale; while her last letter remained like a blot upon the charm and beauty of their former intercourse. Neither the great success of *Pique Dame*, nor the profound sorrow caused by the death of his beloved sister, in April, 1891, nor even his triumphs in America, served to soften the blow she had inflicted.

On June 6th (18th), 1891, he wrote from Moscow to Ladislaw Pakhulsky:—

" I have just received your letter. It is true Nadejda Filaretovna is ill, weak, and her nerves are upset, so that she can no longer write to me as before. Not for the world would I add to her sufferings. I am grieved, bewildered, and—I say it frankly—deeply hurt that she has ceased to feel any interest in me. Even if she no longer desired me to go on corresponding directly with her, it could have been easily arranged for you and Julia Karlovna to have acted as links between us. But she has never once inquired through either of you how I am living, or what I am doing. I have endeavoured, through you, to re-establish my correspondence with Nadejda Filaretovna, but not one of your letters has contained the least courteous reference to my efforts. No doubt you are aware that in September last she informed me that she could no longer pay my pension. You must also know how I replied to her. I *wished* and *hoped* that our relations might remain unchanged. But unhappily this seemed impossible, because of her complete estrangement from me. The result has been that all our intercourse was brought to an end *directly I ceased to receive her money*. This situation lowers me in my own estimation; makes the remembrance of the money I accepted from her wellnigh intolerable; worries and weighs upon me more than I can say. When I was in the country last autumn I reread all her letters to me. No illness, no misfortune, no pecuniary anxieties could ever—so it seemed to me—change the sentiments which were expressed in these letters. And yet they have changed. Perhaps I idealised Nadejda Filaretovna because I did not know her personally. I could not conceive change in anyone so *half-divine*. I would sooner have believed that the earth could fail beneath me than that our relations could suffer change. But the inconceivable has happened, and all my ideas of human nature, all my faith in the best of mankind, have been turned upside down. My peace is broken, and the share of happiness fate has allotted me is embittered and spoilt.

" No doubt Nadejda Filaretovna has dealt me this cruel blow unconsciously and unintentionally. Never in my life have I felt so lowered, or my pride so profoundly injured as in this matter. The worst is that, on account of her shattered health, I dare not show her all the troubles of my heart, lest I should grieve or upset her.

" I may not speak out, which would be my sole relief. However, let this suffice. Even as it is, I may regret having said all this—but I felt the need of giving vent to some of my bitterness. Of course, I do not wish a word to be said to her.

" Should she ever inquire about me, say I returned safely from America and have settled down to work in Maidanovo. You may add that I am well.

" Do not answer this letter."

Nadejda Filaretovna made no response to this communication. Pakhulsky assured Tchaikovsky that her apparent indifference was the result of a serious nervous illness, but that in her heart of hearts she still cared for her old friend. He returned the above letter to Tchaikovsky, because he dare not give it to Nadejda Filaretovna during her illness, and did not consider himself justified in keeping it.

This was Tchaikovsky's last effort to win back the affection of his " best friend." But the wound remained unhealed, a cause of secret anguish which darkened his life to the end. Even on his death-bed the name of Nadejda Filaretovna was constantly on his lips, and in the broken phrases of his last delirium these words alone were intelligible to those around him.

Before taking leave of this personality who played so

benevolent a part in Tchaikovsky's existence, let it be said, in extenuation of her undeserved cruelty, that from 1890 Nadejda von Meck's life was a slow decline, brought about by a terrible nervous disease, which changed her relations not only to him, but to others. The news of his end reached her on her death-bed, and two months later she, too, passed away, on January 13th (25th), 1894.

X

Early in September, 1890, Tchaikovsky spent a day or two in Kiev on his way to Tiflis. In the former town he learnt that Prianichnikov, a favourite singer and theatrical impresario, was anxious to produce *Dame de Pique*. The idea pleased Tchaikovsky, for, thanks to Prianichnikov's energy, the opera at Kiev almost surpassed that of Moscow as regards *ensemble* and the excellence of the staging in general.

On October 20th (November 1st) Tchaikovsky conducted a concert given by the Tiflis branch of the Musical Society, the programme of which was drawn exclusively from his own works. The evening was a great success for the composer, who received a perfect ovation and was "almost smothered in flowers," besides being presented with a bâton.

Tiflis was the first town to welcome Tchaikovsky with cordiality and enthusiasm ; it was also the first to accord him a warm and friendly farewell, destined, alas ! to be for eternity.

On his return to Frolovskoe he busied himself with the collected edition of his songs, which Jurgenson proposed to issue shortly. The composer stipulated that the songs should be reprinted in their original keys, for, as he writes to Jurgenson : " I have neither strength nor patience to look through all the transpositions, which have been very badly done, and are full of the stupidest mistakes."

From Frolovskoe Tchaikovsky went to Petersburg, about the middle of November, to attend the rehearsals for his latest opera, *Pique Dame*. During his stay at the Hôtel Rossiya he arranged an *audition* of his newly composed sextet. The instrumentalists were : Albrecht, Hildebrandt, Wierzbilowicz, Hille, Kouznietsov and Heine. As audience, he invited Glazounov, Liadov, Laroche, and a few friends and relatives. Neither his hearers, nor the composer himself, were equally pleased with all the movements of the sextet, so that he eventually resolved to rewrite the Scherzo and Finale. Apart from this one disappointment, the rest of his affairs—including the rehearsals —went so well that his prevailing mood at this time was cheerful ; although the numerous festivities given in his honour hindered him from keeping up his correspondence during this visit to Petersburg. Not a single letter appears to exist dating from these weeks of his life.

On December 6th (18th) a rehearsal of the opera was given before their Imperial Majesties and many leaders of society in the capital. The success of the work was very evident ; yet Tchaikovsky had an idea that the Emperor did not care for it. As we shall see, later on, he was quite mistaken in coming to this conclusion.

The first public representation took place on December 7th (19th), 1890, just a year after the commencement of the work. Not one of Tchaikovsky's operas had a better caste than *Pique Dame*. The part of Hermann was taken by the celebrated singer Figner, while the heroine was represented by his wife. The rôles of the old Countess and Paulina were respectively allotted to Slavina and Dolina. Each of these leading singers distinguished themselves in some special quality of their art. Throughout the entire evening artists and audience alike experienced a sense of complete satisfaction, rarely felt during any operatic performance. Napravnik as conductor, and Figner in the part of hero, surpassed themselves, and did most to ensure the success of the opera. The scenery and dresses, by their beauty and historical accuracy, were worthy of the fine musical interpretation.

The applause increased steadily to the end of the work, and composer and singers were frequently recalled. At the same time, no one would have ventured to predict that the opera would even now be holding its own in the repertory, for there was no question of a great ovation.

The critics not only unanimously condemned the libretto, but did not approve of the music. One remarked: "As regards instrumentation, Tchaikovsky is certainly a great poet; but in the actual music *he not only repeats himself, but does not shrink from imitating other composers.*" Another thought this "the weakest of all his efforts at opera." A third called the work "a card problem," and declared that, musically speaking, "the accessories prevailed over the essential ideas, and external brilliance over the inner content."

A few days after the first performance of *Pique Dame* in St. Petersburg, Tchaikovsky went through the same experience in Kiev, with this difference, that the reception of the opera in the southern city far surpassed in enthusiasm that which had been accorded to it in the capital.

"It was indescribable," he wrote to his brother on December 21st (January 2nd, 1891). "I am very tired, however, and in reality I suffer a great deal. My uncertainty as to the immediate future weighs upon me. Shall I give up the idea of wandering abroad or not? Is it wise to accept the offer of the Opera Direction,[1] for the sextet seems to point to the fact that I am going downhill? My brain is empty; I have not the least pleasure in work. *Hamlet*[2] oppresses me terribly."

---

[1] To compose an opera in one act and a ballet for the season 1891-2.
[2] Incidental music to the tragedy *Hamlet*, for Guitry's benefit.

To Ippolitov-Ivanov.

"KAMENKA, *December 24th,* 1890 (*January 5th,* 1891).

"In Petersburg I frequently saw the Intendant of the Opera, and tried to throw out a bait with regard to your *Asra.* I shall be able to go more closely into the matter in January, but I can tell you already there is little hope for next year. Rimsky-Korsakov's *Mlada* is being considered, and I am commissioned to write a one-act opera and a ballet. . . . In this way I am involuntarily a hindrance to the younger composers, who would be glad to see their works performed at the Imperial Opera. This troubles me, but the temptation is too great, and I am not yet convinced that the time has come for me to make room for the younger generation. . . . As I have also asked Kondratiev—at Arensky's request—to persuade the Direction into giving a performance of his *Dream on the Volga,* I must warn you that you will meet with great difficulties in gaining your end. . . . No one knows better than I do how important it is for a young composer to get his works performed at a great theatre, therefore I would be willing to make some sacrifice, if I were sure it would be of any use. But supposing I were to relinquish my commission to compose an opera and a ballet. What would be the result? They would rather put on three foreign operas than risk a new Russian one by a young composer."

To Modeste Tchaikovsky.

"KAMENKA, *January 1st* (*13th*), 1890.

"Do you sometimes give a thought to *King René's Daughter?*[1] It is very probable that I shall end by going to work in Italy. In that case the libretto ought to be in my hands by the end of January. And the ballet? I shall spend a fortnight at Frolovskoe."

The time Tchaikovsky now spent at Frolovskoe was devoted to the *Hamlet* music, which he had promised Guitry should be ready in February.

---

[1] An opera in one act, afterwards known as *Iolanthe.*

Not one of his works inspired him with less enthusiasm than this. As a rule he rather enjoyed working to order, but he took up this task with great repugnance, because he had to begin by arranging the existing *Hamlet* overture, originally written for full orchestra, for the small band of the Michael Theatre. At his request the orchestra of twenty-nine was increased by seven musicians, but there was no room to accommodate a larger number. In spite of his disinclination for the work, Tchaikovsky succeeded in composing several numbers which delighted the public; while one movement (*The Funeral March*) became exceedingly popular.

Tchaikovsky arrived at Frolovskoe on January 6th (18th), and immediately telegraphed to the concert agent, Wolf, that he would be unable to fulfil the engagements made for him at Mainz, Buda-Pesth, and Frankfort.

It was not merely the composition of the *Hamlet* music which caused him to relinquish these engagements; at this time he was suffering from a nervous affection of the right hand, which made conducting a matter of considerable difficulty.

To S. I. Taneiev.

"*January* 14*th* (26*th*), 1891.

"The question: How should opera be written? is one I answer, have answered, and always shall answer, in the simplest way. Operas, like everything else, should be written just as they come to us. I always try to express in the music as truthfully and sincerely as possible all there is in the text. But truth and sincerity are not the result of a process of reasoning, but the inevitable outcome of our inmost feelings. In order that these feelings should have warmth and vitality, I always choose subjects in which I have to deal with real men and women, who share the same emotions as myself. That is why I cannot bear the Wagnerian subjects, in which there is so little human interest. Neither would I have chosen your subject, with its supernatural agencies, its inevitable crimes, its Eumenides and Fates as *dramatis personæ*. As soon as I have found a subject, and decided to compose an opera, I give free rein to my feelings, neither trying to carry out Wagner's principles, nor striving after originality. At the same time I make no conscious effort to go against the spirit of my time. If Wagner had not existed, probably my compositions would have been different to what they are. I may add that even the 'Invincible Band' has had some influence on my operas. Italian music, which I loved passionately from my childhood, and Glinka, whom I idolised in my youth, have both influenced me deeply, to say nothing of Mozart. But I never invoked any one of these musical deities and bade him dispose of my musical conscience as he pleased. Consequently I do not think any of my operas can be said to belong to a particular school. Perhaps one of these influences may occasionally have gained the upper hand and I have fallen into imitation; but whatever happened came of itself, and I am sure I appear in my works just as God made me, and such as I have become through the action of time, nationality, and education. I have never been untrue to myself. What I am, whether good or bad, others must judge for me. . . .

"Arensky's opera[1] did not please me much when he played me fragments of it in Petersburg after his illness. I liked it a little better when he played it to you at Altani's; far more when I went through it myself this summer; and now, having seen it actually performed, I think it one of the best of Russian operas. It is very elegant and equal throughout; only the end lacks something of inspiration. It has one defect: a certain monotony of method which reminds me of Korsakov. . . . Arensky is extraordinarily clever in music; everything is so subtly and truly thought out. He is a very interesting musical personality."

To P. Jurgenson.

"*January* 15th (27th), 1891.

"DEAR FRIEND,—Wolf has sent me the letter from that American gentleman who has arranged for my en-

---

[1] *A Dream on the Volga* (the Voyevode).

gagement. It is so easy and profitable that it would be foolish to lose this opportunity of an American tour, which has long been one of my dreams. This explains my telegram to you yesterday. In America, the news that I could not go, because my right hand was disabled, reached them by cable, and they were very much upset. Now they are awaiting an answer—yes or no."

To the same.

"January 17*th* (29*th*), 1891.

"DEAR SOUL,—Send me immediately my *Legend* for chorus, and the *Liturgy* and other church works, with the exception of the Vespers. I must make a selection for the American festival.[1] Have you the *Children's Songs* in Rahter's edition? I want the German text for the *Legend.*"

At the close of January Tchaikovsky went to St. Petersburg. Early in February he had to conduct at a concert in aid of the school founded by the Women's Patriotic League. This annual concert drew a fashionable audience, who only cared for the singing of such stars as Melba and the De Reszkes. Consequently Tchaikovsky's Third Suite merely served to try their patience.

His reception on the 9th, at the performance of *Hamlet* (at the Michael Theatre), was equally poor. But he was agreeably surprised at the individual criticisms of his music which reached his ears. "I am not averse from your idea of publishing the *Hamlet* music," he wrote to Jurgenson, "for it pleased, and everyone is delighted with the March."

Meanwhile the Direction of the Imperial Opera were discussing the opera and ballet which Tchaikovsky had been commissioned to compose. For the former, Herz's play, *King René's Daughter*—translated into Russian by Zvanstiev—was chosen; and for the ballet, *Casse-Noisette*

---

[1] The opening ceremony of the new Carnegie Hall in New York.

("The Nut-cracker"). Neither of these subjects awoke in Tchaikovsky that joy of creation he had experienced while composing *The Sleeping Beauty* and *Pique Dame*. There were several reasons for this. The *Casse-Noisette* subject did not at all please him. He had chosen *King René's Daughter* himself, but he did not know as yet how the libretto would suit him. He was also annoyed with the Direction because they had engaged foreign singers, and were permitting them to sing in French and Italian at the Russian Opera. Thirdly, in view of the American tour, he did not feel master of his time, and really had no idea how he should get through so much music by December, 1891. Finally, he was very deeply mortified.

The source of his vexation lay in the fact that after its thirteenth performance *Pique Dame* was unexpectedly withdrawn until the autumn, although almost all the tickets had been secured beforehand for at least another ten performances. No definite reason was assigned for this action, which was the outcome of mere caprice on the part of some unknown person. Tchaikovsky's anxiety was aggravated by the fear that his favourite work might disappear altogether from the repertory. He suspected that its withdrawal was ordered at the desire of the Emperor, who—so he fancied—did not like the opera. Anyone else would have discovered the real reason by the medium of inquiry, but Tchaikovsky was prevented from speaking of it in Petersburg "by pride and fear," as he wrote to Jurgenson, "lest people should think I was regretting the royalty; and, on their part, the members of the operatic Direction carefully avoided mentioning the subject to me." After a while he poured out his heart in a letter to Vsievolojsky, who, in reply, entirely reassured him as to his fears. The Emperor, he said, was very pleased with *Pique Dame*, and all that Tchaikovsky composed for the opera in Petersburg awakened a lively interest in the Imperial box. "Personally, I need not 'lay floral tributes' before you," he concludes, "for you know how greatly I admire your talents. . . . In *Pique Dame* your dramatic power stands out with startling effect in two scenes: the death of the Countess and Hermann's madness. I think you should keep to intimate drama and avoid grandiose subjects. *Jamais, au grand jamais, vous ne m'avez impressioné comme dans ces deux tableaux d'un réalisme saisissant.*"

Comforted by this letter, Tchaikovsky set to work upon his new ballet, *Casse-Noisette.* "I am working with all my might," he wrote to his brother from Frolovskoe, "and I am growing more reconciled to the subject. I hope to finish a considerable part of the first act before I go abroad."

Early in March he left Frolovskoe and travelled to Paris, *viâ* St. Petersburg.

To Vladimir Davidov.

"BERLIN, *March 8th (20th),* 1891.

"Against this form of home-sickness, that you have hardly experienced as yet, which is more agonising than anything in this world, there is but one remedy—to get drunk. Between Eydkuhnen and Berlin I consumed an incredible amount of wine and brandy; consequently I slept, though badly. . . . To-day I am less home-sick, yet all the while I feel as though some vampire were sucking at my heart. I have a headache, and feel weak, so I shall spend the night in Berlin. . . . After the midday meal I shall take a long walk through the town and go to a concert where my '*1812*' overture is being played.

"It is great fun to sit incognito among a strange audience and listen to one's own works. I leave to-morrow, and my next letter will be written from Paris. Bob, I idolise you! Do you remember how I once told you that the happiness your presence gave me was nothing compared to all I suffered in your absence? Away from home, with the prospect of long weeks and months apart, I feel the full meaning of my affection for you."

2 S

" I had already been in Paris a month when my brother arrived on March 10th (22nd)," says Modeste Tchaikovsky. " This was the first time I had seen him abroad, except in a very intimate circle. Now I saw him as the artist on tour. This period has left an unpleasant impression on my memory. He had not told me the hour of his arrival, and I only knew of it when I returned one evening to my hotel. He was already asleep, and the servants told me he did not wish to be aroused. This, in itself, was a symptom of an abnormal frame of mind. As a rule he was eager for the first hour of meeting. We met the next morning, and he evinced no sign of pleasure, only wondered how I—who was under no obligation—could care to stay so long away from Russia. A chilling and gloomy look, his cheeks flushed with excitement, a bitter laugh upon his lips—this is how I always remember Peter Ilich during that visit to Paris. We saw very little of each other ; he was continually occupied either with Colonne, or Mackar, or somebody. Or he sat in his room surrounded by visitors of all kinds. The real Peter Ilich only reappeared in the evening when, in the society of Sophie Menter, Sapellnikov, and Konius—a young violinist in Colonne's orchestra, formerly his pupil in Moscow—he rested after the rush and bustle of the day."

The concert which Tchaikovsky was to conduct in Paris on March 24th (April 5th) was the twenty-third of Colonne's series, and the French conductor had relinquished his place for the occasion because he himself was engaged in Moscow. The colossal programme included : (1) the Third Suite, (2) Pianoforte Concerto No. 2 (Sapellnikov), (3) *Sérénade Mélancolique* (Johann Wolf), (4) Songs, (5) Andante from the First Quartet (arranged for string orchestra), (6) Symphonic Fantasia, *The Tempest*, (7) Slavonic March. The room was crowded, and all the works met with notable success. The Press was also unanimous in its favourable verdict.

But nothing could appease Tchaikovsky's home-sickness. There still remained twelve days before he sailed from Havre for America. Partly to work at his opera and ballet, partly to have a little rest and freedom, he decided to spend ten days at Rouen. On April 4th Sophie Menter, Sapellnikov, and myself were to meet him there, and see him off the following day from Havre.

This plan was not carried out, however, for on March 29th I received a telegram informing me of the death of our sister Alexandra Davidov.

For some years past, in consequence of a serious illness, which gradually cut her off from her relations with others, this sister had not played so important a part in the life of Peter Ilich. Continually fighting against her malady, sorely tried by the death of her two elder daughters, she could not keep up the same interest as of old in her brother's existence. Yet he loved her dearly, and she was as essential to his happiness as ever. She, who had been to him a haven and a refuge from all the troubles of life, was still the holiest reliquary of his childhood, his youth, and the Kamenka period of his life; for, together with Nadejda von Meck, she had been his chief support, making him welcome, and bestowing upon him the most affectionate attention.

I was aware that the news of her death would come as a crushing blow to my brother, and felt it imperative to break it to him in person. The same day I set out for Rouen. Peter Ilich was as delighted to see me as though we had not met for ages. It was not difficult to guess at the overwhelming loneliness which he had experienced during his voluntary exile. Apart from the fact that I found it hard to damp his cheerful mood, I became more and more preoccupied with the idea: was it wise to tell him of our loss under the present circumstances? I knew it was too late for him to give up his journey to America. He had already taken his ticket to New York. What would he have done during the long voyage alone, which he already dreaded, had he been overweighted with this grief? In America, distracted by the anxieties of his concerts, the sad news would not come as so great a shock. Therefore, in answer to his question, why had I come, I did not reveal the truth, but simply said that I, too, felt home-sick, and had come to say good-bye before starting for Russia the next day. He seemed almost pleased at my news. . . . Incomprehensible to others, I understood his satisfaction. He had often said: "Modeste is too closely akin to myself." In Paris, it vexed him to realise that I did not yearn for our native land. Now that he believed I was content to cut short my stay abroad, he forgave me, and our meeting was as hearty as though we had come together after a long separation. This made it all the more difficult to tell him what had happened, and I returned to Paris after a touching farewell, without having broken the news to him. I had warned our friends in Paris, and there were no Russian newspapers to be had in Rouen. All letters from home were to be addressed to the Hôtel Richepanse, whence I requested that they should be forwarded straight to America.

Firmly convinced that my brother would not receive the melancholy news until he reached New York, I started for St. Petersburg.

But no sooner had his brother left Rouen than Tchaikovsky's depression reached a climax. First of all he wrote to Vsievolojsky that he could not possibly have the ballet and opera ready before the season of 1892–3; and then he resolved to return to Paris for a couple of days, to distract his anxiety as to the approaching journey.

On his arrival the truth became known to him, and he wrote the following letter to his brother :—

"Modi, yesterday I went to Paris. There I visited the reading-room in the Passage de l'Opéra, took up the

Novoe Vremya and read the announcement of Sasha's death. I started up as though a snake had stung me. Later on I went to Sophie Menter's and Sapellnikov's. What a fortunate thing they were here! I spent the night with them. To-day I start, *vià* Rouen and Le Havre. At first I thought it was my duty to give up America and go to Petersburg, but afterwards I reflected that this would be useless. I should have had to return the 5,000 francs I had received, to relinquish the rest, and lose my ticket. No, I must go to America. Mentally I am suffering much. I am very anxious about Bob, although I know from my own experience that at his age we easily recover from such blows.

". . . . For God's sake write all details to New York. To-day, even more than yesterday, I feel the absolute impossibility of depicting in music the ' Sugar-plum Fairy.' "

XI

To Modeste Tchaikovsky.

"S.S. 'LA BRETAGNE,' ATLANTIC OCEAN,
"*April 6th* (18*st*), 1891.

" During the voyage I shall keep a diary, and send it to you when I get to New York. Please take care of it, for I mean to write an article later on, for which my diary will serve as material. . . . The ship is one of the largest and most luxurious. I dined in Le Havre, walked about a little, and at 10 p.m. made myself comfortable in my cabin. . . . There I suddenly felt more miserable than ever. Principally because I had received no answer to my telegram to Petersburg. I cannot think why. Probably the usual telegraphic blunder, but it is very hard to leave without any news. . . . I curse this voyage.

" The ship is superb. A veritable floating palace. There are not a great number of passengers, about eighty in the first class. . . . At dinner I sit at a little table with an American family. Very uncomfortable and wearisome.

" At five o'clock there was a tragic occurrence, which had a depressing effect upon me and all the other passengers.

I was below, when suddenly a whistle was heard, the ship hove to, and everyone was greatly excited. A boat was lowered. I went on deck and heard that a young man, a second-class passenger, had suddenly taken out his pocket-book, scribbled a few words in haste, thrown himself overboard and disappeared beneath the waves. A life-belt was flung to him, and a boat was lowered immediately, which was watched with the greatest anxiety by all of us. But nothing was to be seen on the surface of the sea, and after half an hour's search we continued our course. In his pocket-book was found thirty-five francs, and on a sheet of paper a few words hardly decipherable. I was the first to make them out, for they were written in German, and all the passengers were French or Americans. '*Ich bin unschuldig, der Bursche weint* . . .' followed by a few scrawls no one could read. Afterwards I heard that the young man had attracted attention by his strange conduct, and was probably insane.

"The weather is beautiful, and the sea quite calm. The ship moves so quietly that one can hardly believe oneself on the water. We have just seen the lighthouse at the Lizard. The last sight of land before we reach New York."

To Modeste Tchaikovsky.

"*April 7th* (19*th*), 1891.

"Early this morning the tossing began, and grew gradually worse, until at times I felt horribly nervous. It was a comfort that most of the passengers had made the voyage very often, and were not in the least afraid of going down, as I was, only of being sea-sick. I was not afraid of that, for I felt no symptoms whatever. The steward to whom I spoke called it '*une mer un peu grosse*.' What must '*une mer très grosse*' be like? The aspect of the sea is very fine, and when I am free from alarm I enjoy watching the grand spectacle. I am interested in three huge sea-gulls which are following us. They say they will go with us to Newfoundland. When do they rest, and where do they spend the night? I read all day, for there is nothing else to do. Composition goes against the grain. I am very depressed. When I opened my heart to my acquaintance, the commercial traveller in the second class, he replied, 'Well, at your age it is very natural,' which hurt my feelings. . . . I would rather not say what I feel. . . . It is for the last time. . . . When one gets to my years it is best to stay at home, close to one's own folk.   The thought of being so far from all who are dear to me almost kills me.   But otherwise I am quite well, thank God.   A 'miss' has been singing Italian songs the whole evening, and her performance was so abominable, such an effrontery, that I was surprised no one said anything rude to her."

To M. Tchaikovsky.

"*April* 8*th* (20*th*), 1891.

" I had a good night.   When everyone had gone to bed I walked for a long time on deck.   The wind went down, and it was quite calm by the time I went to my cabin. To-day it is sunny, but the wind has been getting up since midday.   There is now a head sea instead of the waves coming broadside on.   But the ship is so big that very few have been sea-sick.   My friendship with the commercial traveller and his companions grows more intimate.   They are very lively, and entertain me more than the correct and respectable first-class passengers. . . . The most interesting of these is a Canadian bishop with his secretary, who has been to Europe to receive the Pope's blessing.   Yesterday he celebrated mass in a private cabin, and I chanced to be present.   While I am writing, the ship is beginning to pitch more, but now I realise it must be so in mid-ocean, and I am getting used to it."

"*April* 9*th* (21*st*), 1891.

" In the night the ship pitched so that I awoke, and had palpitations and almost nervous fever.   A glass of brandy soon picked me up and had a calming effect.   I put on my overcoat and went on deck.   It was a glorious moonlight night.   When I saw that everything was going on as usual, I realised that there was no cause for fear. . . . By morning the wind had dropped.   We were in the Gulf

Stream. This was evident, because suddenly it became much warmer. There are about a hundred emigrants on board, mostly Alsatians. As soon as the weather improves they give a ball, and it is amusing to see them dancing to the strains of their concertinas. These emigrants do not appear at all unhappy. The unsympathetic lady who sits near me at table is the wife of a member of the Boston orchestra. Consequently to-day the conversation turned upon music. She related some interesting things about the Boston concerts and musical life there.

" To-day we passed a few sailing vessels, and a huge whale which sent up a spout of water into the air."

To Modeste Tchaikovsky.

"April 10th (22nd), 1891.

" I believed I was quite immune from sea-sickness. It appears that I am not. Last night the weather got worse and worse. When I got up at seven a.m. it was so bad, and the sea so rough, that I enjoyed watching it, in spite of the huge ocean waves. It continued to blow until two o'clock, when it was so terrible that I expected every moment the ship would go down. Of course there was really no question whatever of our sinking. Not only the captain, but the sailors and all the stewards took it as a matter of course. But to me, who only know the sea from the Mediterranean, it was like hell let loose. Everything cracked and groaned. One minute we were tossed up to the clouds, the next we sank into the depths. It was impossible to go on deck, for the wind almost blew one overboard—in short, it was terrible. Most of the passengers were ill, but some enjoyed it, and even played the piano, arranged card-parties, etc. I had no appetite for breakfast, afterwards I felt *very uncomfortable*, and at dinner I could not bear the sight of the food. I have not really been ill, but I have experienced disagreeable sensations. It is impossible to sleep. *Brandy* and *coffee* are the only nourishment I have taken to-day."

To Modeste Tchaikovsky.

"*April* 12*th* (24*th*), 1891.

"The night was horrible. Towards morning the weather improved, and remained bearable until four o'clock. Then came a fresh misery. As we approached the 'sand banks' of Newfoundland we passed into a belt of dense fog—which seems the usual experience here. This is the thing most dreaded at sea, because a collision, even with a small sailing vessel, may sink the ship. Our speed was considerably slackened, and every few seconds the siren was heard; a machine which emits a hideous roar, like a gigantic tiger. It gets terribly on one's nerves. . . . Now the people on board have discovered who I am, and amiabilities, compliments, and conversations have begun. I can never walk about by myself. Besides, they press me to play. I refuse, but apparently it will never end until I have played something on the wretched piano. . . . The fog is lifting, but the rolling is beginning again."

To Modeste Tchaikovsky.

"*April* 12*th* (24*th*), 1891.

"I absolutely cannot write. Since yesterday evening I have been a martyr. It is blowing a fearful gale. They say it was predicted by the Meteorological Observatory. It is horrible! Especially to me, a novice. They say it will last till we get to New York. I suffer as much mentally as physically ; simply from fright and anxiety."

"*April* 13*th* (25*th*), 1891.

"After writing the above lines I went into the smoking-room. Very few passengers were there, and they sat idle, with gloomy, anxious faces. . . . The gale continually increased. There was no thought of lying down. I sat in a corner of the sofa in my cabin and tried not to think about what was going on; but that was impossible, for the straining, creaking, and shivering of the vessel, and the howling of the wind outside, could not be silenced. So I sat on, and what passed through my mind I cannot describe to you. Unpleasant reflections. Presently I noticed that the horrible shocks each time the screw was lifted out of the water came at longer intervals, the wind howled less. Then I fell asleep, still sitting propped between my trunk and the wall of the cabin. . . . In the morning I found we had passed through the very centre of an unusually severe storm, such as is rarely experienced. At two o'clock we met the pilot who had long been expected. The whole bevy of passengers turned out to see him waiting for us in his tiny boat. The ship hove to, and we took him on board. There are only about twenty-four hours left. In consequence of the gale we are a few hours late. I am very glad the voyage is nearing its end: I simply could not bear to remain any longer on board ship. I have decided to return from New York by a German liner on April 30th (May 12th). By May 10th (22nd), or a little later, I shall be in Petersburg again, D.V."

XII

To Modeste Tchaikovsky.

"NEW YORK, *April* 15*th* (27*th*), 1891.

"The remainder of the journey was happily accomplished. The nearer we came to New York, the greater grew my fear and home-sickness, and I regretted ever having undertaken this insane voyage. When all is over I may look back to it with pleasure, but at present it is not without suffering. Before we reached New York— endless formalities with passports and Customs. A whole day was spent in answering inquiries. At last we landed at 5 p.m. I was met by four very amiable gentlemen and a lady, who took me straight to the Hotel Normandie. Here I explained to Mr. Morris Reno[1] that I should leave on the 12th. He said that would not be feasible, because an extra concert had been fixed for the 18th, of which Wolf had not said a word to me. After all these people had gone, I began to walk up and down my

---

[1] President of the Music Hall Company of New York, upon whose initiative Tchaikovsky had been engaged in America.

rooms (I have two) and shed many tears. I declined their invitations to dinner and supper, and begged to be left to myself for to-night.

"After a bath, I dressed, dined against my inclination, and went for a stroll down Broadway. An extraordinary street! Houses of one and two stories alternate with some nine-storied buildings. Most original. I was struck with the number of nigger faces I saw. When I got back I began crying again, and slept like the dead, as I always do after tears. I awoke refreshed, but the tears are always in my eyes."

Diary.

"*Monday, April 15th (27th).*

"Mayer[1] was my first visitor. The cordial friendliness of this pleasant German astonished and touched me. For, being the head of a pianoforte firm, he had no interest in paying attentions to a musician who is not a pianist. Then a reporter appeared, and I was very thankful for Mayer's presence. Many of his questions were very curious. Reno next arrived, bringing an interesting friend with him. Reno told me I was expected at the rehearsal. After we had got rid of the interviewer we went on foot to the music hall.[2] A magnificent building. We got to the rehearsal just at the end of Beethoven's Fifth Symphony. Damrosch[3] (who was conducting without his coat) appeared very pleasant. I wanted to speak to him at the finish of the Symphony, but had to wait and answer the cordial greetings of the orchestra. Damrosch made a little speech. More ovations. I could only rehearse the first and third movements of the First Suite. The orchestra is excellent. After the rehearsal I breakfasted with Mayer, who then took me up Broadway, helped me to buy a hat, presented me with a hundred cigarettes, showed me the very

[1] The head of the Knabe Pianoforte Manufactory.

[2] This hall was built principally with the help of Mr. Carnegie. Tchaikovsky was invited to the opening festivities.

[3] Walter Damrosch, son of the founder of the "Symphony Society" in New York, one of the directors of the Music Hall Company of New York, and conductor of the Symphony Concerts and of the opera.

interesting Hoffman Bar, which is decorated with the most beautiful pictures, statues and tapestries, and finally brought me home. I lay down to rest, completely exhausted. Later on I dressed, for I was expecting Reno, who soon turned up. I tried to persuade him to let me give up Philadelphia and Baltimore, but he did not seem inclined to grant my request. He took me to his house and introduced me to his wife and daughters, who are very nice. Afterwards he went with me to Damrosch's. A year ago Damrosch married the daughter of a very rich and distinguished man. They are a very agreeable couple. We sat down three to dinner. Then Damrosch took me to visit Carnegie,[1] the possessor of 30,000,000 dollars, who is very like our dramatist Ostrovsky. I was very much taken with the old man, especially as he is an admirer of Moscow, which he visited two years ago. Next to Moscow, he admires the national songs of Scotland, a great many of which Damrosch played to him on a magnificent Steinway grand. He has a young and pretty wife. After these visits I went with Hyde[2] and Damrosch to see the Athletic Club and another, more serious in tone, which I might perhaps compare with our English Club. The Athletic Club astonished me, especially the swimming bath, in which the members bathe, and the upper gallery, where they skate in winter. We ordered drinks in the serious club. I reached home about eleven o'clock. Needless to say, I was worn out.

"*April 16th (28th).*

"Slept very well. A messenger came from * * * * to know if I wanted anything. These Americans strike me as very remarkable, especially after the impression the Parisians left upon me : there politeness or amiability to a stranger always savoured of self-interest ; whereas in this country the honesty, sincerity, generosity, cordiality, and readiness to help you without any *arrière-pensée*, is

---

[1] A. Carnegie, the greatest ironmaster in America, perhaps in the world ; orator, author, politician ; a most generous benefactor and founder of many schools, libraries and museums.

[2] Francis Hyde, Director of the Trust Company, and President of the New York Philharmonic Society.

very pleasant. I like this, and most of the American ways and customs, yet I enjoy it all in the same spirit as a man who sits at a table laden with good things and has no appetite. My appetite will only come with the near prospect of my return to Russia.

"At eleven a.m. I went for a walk, and breakfasted in a very pretty restaurant. Home again by one o'clock and reflected a little. Reinhard,[1] an agreeable young man, came to take me to Mayer's. On the way we turned into the Hoffman Bar. Saw Knabe's warehouse. Mayer took me to a photographic studio. We went up by the lift to the ninth or tenth floor, where a little old man (the owner of the studio) received us in a red nightcap. I never came across such a droll fellow. He is a parody of Napoleon III. (very like the original, but a caricature of him). He turned me round and round while he looked for the *best* side of my face. Then he developed rather a tedious theory of the *best side of the face* and proceeded to experiment on Mayer. Finally I was photographed in every conceivable position, during which the old man entertained me with all kinds of mechanical toys. But, with all his peculiarities, he was pleasant and cordial in the American way. From the photographer I drove with Mayer to the park, which is newly laid out, but very beautiful. There was a crowd of smart ladies and carriages. We called for Mayer's wife and daughter and continued our drive along the high bank of the Hudson. It became gradually colder, and the conversation with these good German-Americans wearied me. At last we stopped at the celebrated Restaurant Delmonico, and Mayer invited me to a most luxurious dinner, after which he and the ladies took me back to my hotel. I hurried into my dress-coat and waited for Mr. Hyde. Then, together with him and his wife, Damrosch, and Mr. and Mrs. Reno, we all went to a somewhat tedious concert at the great Opera House. We heard an oratorio, *The Captivity*, by the American composer Max Wagrich. Most wearisome. After this I wanted to go home, but the dear Hydes carried me off to supper at Delmonico's. We ate oysters with a sauce of small turtles (! ! !), and cheese. Champagne, and an

---

[1] A representative from the firm of Knabe.

iced peppermint drink, supported my failing courage. They brought me home at twelve o'clock. A telegram from Botkin summoning me to Washington.

"April 17*th* (29*th*).

" Passed a restless night. After my early tea I wrote letters. Then I sauntered through Fifth Avenue. What palaces! Breakfasted alone at home. Went to Mayer's. The kindness and attentiveness of this man are simply wonderful. According to Paris custom, I try to discover what he wants to get out of me. But I can think of nothing. Early this morning he sent Reinhard to me again, in case I wanted anything, and I was very glad of his help, for I did not know what to do about the telegram from Washington. By three o'clock I was at home, waiting for William de Sachs, a very amiable and elegant gentleman, who loves music and writes about it. He was still here when my French friends from the steamer arrived. I was very glad to see them and we went out together to have some absinthe. When I got back I rested for a while. At seven o'clock Hyde and his wife called for me. What a pity it is that words and colours fail me to describe this most original couple, who are so extremely kind and friendly! The language in which we carry on our conversation is very amusing ; it consists of the queerest mixture of English, French and German. Every word which Hyde utters in our conversation is the result of an extraordinary intellectual effort : literally a whole minute passes before there emerges, from an indefinite murmur, some word so weird-sounding that it is impossible to tell to which of the three languages it belongs. All the time Hyde and his wife have such a serious, yet good-natured air. I accompanied them to Reno's, who was giving a big dinner in my honour. The ladies—all in full evening dress. The table decorated with flowers. At each lady's place lay a bunch of flowers, while the men had lilies-of-the-valley, which we put in our buttonholes as soon as we were seated at table. Each lady had also a little picture of myself in a pretty frame. The dinner began at half-past seven, and was over at eleven. I am not exaggerating when I say this, for it is the custom here.

It is impossible to describe all the courses.   In the middle
of the dinner ices were served in little cases, to which were
attached small slates with pencils and sponges, on which
fragments from my works were beautifully inscribed. I
had to write my autograph on these slates. The conversation was very lively. I sat between Mrs. Reno and
Mrs. Damrosch. The latter is a most charming and graceful woman. Opposite to me sat Carnegie, the admirer
of Moscow, and the possessor of forty million dollars.
His likeness to Ostrovsky is astonishing. Tormented by
the want of a smoke, and almost ill with over-eating, I
determined about eleven o'clock to ask Mrs. Reno's
permission to leave the table. Half an hour later we
all took our leave."

To V. Davidov.

"New York, *April* 18*th* (30*th*), 1891.

"Have just received my letters. It is impossible to
say how precious these are under the present circumstances. I was unspeakably glad. I make copious entries
every day in my diary and, on my return, you shall each
have it to read in turn, so I will not go into details now.
New York, American customs, American hospitality—all
their comforts and arrangements—everything, in fact, is
to my taste. If only I were younger I should very much
enjoy my visit to this interesting and youthful country.
But now, I just tolerate everything as if it were a slight
punishment mitigated by many pleasant things. All my
thoughts, all my aspirations, tend towards Home, Home!!!
I am convinced that I am ten times more famous in
America than in Europe. At first, when others spoke
about it to me, I thought it was only their exaggerated
amiability. But now I see that it really is so. Several of
my works, which are unknown even in Moscow, are
frequently played here. I am a much more important
person here than in Russia. Is not that curious?"

Diary.   "*April* 18*th* (30*th*).

"It is becoming more and more difficult to find time
for writing. Breakfasted with my French friends. Inter-

view with de Sachs. We went to see the Brooklyn Bridge. From there we went on to see Schirmer, who owns the largest music business in America; the warehouse—especially the metallography—resembles Jurgenson's in many respects. Schirmer begged to be allowed to publish some of my compositions. On reaching home, I received the journalist, Ivy Ross, who asked me for a contribution for her paper. When she had gone, I sank on the sofa like a log and enjoyed a little rest and solitude. By 8.30 I was already at the Music Hall for the first rehearsal. The chorus greeted me with an ovation. They sang beautifully. As I was about to leave, I met the builder of the hall in the doorway; he presented to me a pleasant, rather stout, man, his chief assistant, whose talent and cleverness he could not sufficiently praise. This man was—as it turned out—a pure-blooded Russian, who had become a naturalised American. The architect told me he was an anarchist and socialist. I had a little conversation with my fellow-countryman, and promised to visit him. After a light supper I took a walk. Read over and over again the letters I had received and, naturally, shed a few tears.

" April 19*th* (*May* 1*st*).

"Awoke late and sat down to write a little article for Miss Ross. Reno appeared, with the news that he had engaged a cabin for me on board the *Furst Bismarck*, which sails on May 2nd (14th). Oh God, what a long way off it still seems! I called for my good friend Mayer and breakfasted with him in an excellent little Italian restaurant, after which we went down town. Here I saw for the first time what life means at certain hours on Broadway. So far I had only been able to judge this street from the neighbourhood of the hotel, where there is little traffic. But this is only a very small portion of this street, which is seven versts (over four miles) long. The houses down town are simply colossal; I cannot understand how anyone can live on the thirteenth floor. Mayer and I went out on the roof of one such house. The view was splendid, but I felt quite giddy when I looked down into Broadway. Then Mayer obtained permission for me to visit the cellars of the mint, where hundreds of millions of gold and silver coins, as well as paper money, are kept. Very good-natured, but fussy and important, officials conducted us round these cellars, and opened monumental doors with mysterious keys and no less mysterious pressings of various springs and knobs. The sacks of gold, which look just like sacks of corn in a granary, are kept in clean, tidy rooms lit by electric light. I was allowed to hold in my hand a packet of new shining coins worth about 10,000,000 dollars.[1] Then I understood why so little gold and silver are in circulation. The Americans prefer dirty, unpleasant paper notes to metal, because they find them so much more practical and useful. Therefore, these paper notes—quite the reverse to our country—thanks to the vast amount of metals kept in the mint, are valued far more than gold and silver. From the mint we visited the scene of activity of good Mr. Hyde. He is a director of one of the banks, and took me round his strong-rooms, in which mountains of paper money are stored away. We also visited the Exchange, which struck me as quieter than the Paris Bourse. Hyde treated us to lemonade at a café. On my return home I had to finish my newspaper article on Wagner for Miss Ross, and at five o'clock I was ready to visit William de Sachs. He lives in a very large house, where rooms are let to bachelors only. Ladies are only admitted as guests into this curious American monastery. I found a small gathering, which gradually grew larger. It was "five o'clock tea." The pianist, Miss Wilson (who called on me yesterday, and is a staunch adherent of Russian music), played Borodin's beautiful Serenade. After refusing several invitations I spent the evening alone. How pleasant it was! Dined in the Restaurant Hoffmann, as usual, without any enjoyment. During my walk further along Broadway I came upon a meeting of Socialists in red caps. Next morning I learnt from the newspapers that about five thousand men had assembled, carrying banners and huge lanterns, on which were inscribed these words : 'Comrades! We are slaves in free America. We

---

[1] This would have been an impossible athletic feat, probably the equivalent in notes is intended.—R. N.

2 T

will no longer work more than eight hours!' The whole demonstration seemed to me a farce; I think the inhabitants also look on it as such, for very few people had the curiosity to stand and watch; the others walked about as usual. I went to bed bodily tired, but mentally refreshed.

"*April 20th (May 2nd)*.

"By 10.30 a.m. I was at the rehearsal in the Music Hall. It was held in the large hall, where several workmen were hammering, shouting, and running hither and thither. The orchestra is placed across the whole breadth of the huge platform; consequently the sound is bad and unequal, This got on my nerves until, in my rage, I was several times on the point of making a scene, leaving everything in the lurch and running away. I played through the Suite and the March very carelessly, and stopped the Pianoforte Concerto at the first movement, as the parts were in confusion and the musicians exhausted. The pianist, Adèle Aus-der-Ohe, came at five o'clock and played over the Concerto, which had gone so badly at rehearsal.

"*April 21st (May 3rd)*.

"Telegram from Jurgenson: 'Christos vosskresse.'[1] Rain outside. Letters from Modi and Jurgenson. 'Nur wer die Sehnsucht kennt'—realises what it means to receive letters in a strange country. I have never before experienced similar sensations. Mr. N. and his wife came to call upon me. He—a tall, bearded man, with iron-grey hair, very elegantly dressed, always bewailing his spinal complaint, speaking very good Russian and abusing the Jews (although he himself looks very like one); she—a very plain Englishwoman (not American), who càn speak nothing but English. She brought a great pile of newspapers with her, and showed me her articles. I cannot make out what these people want. He asked me if I had composed a fantasia on the *Red Sarafan*. On my replying in the negative, he was very much astonished, and added: 'I will send you Thalberg's fantasia; pray copy his style.' I had great trouble in politely getting rid of this

---

[1] " Christ is risen "—a Russian Easter greeting.

curious couple. De Sachs came to fetch me at twelve o'clock. We walked into the park. Then we went up by the lift to the fourth floor of an immense house where Schirmer lives. Besides myself and Sachs, there were at table the conductor Seidl, a Wagnerian and well known in this country, his wife, the pianist Adèle Aus-der-Ohe, who is going to play at my concert, her sister, and the Schirmer family. Seidl told me that my *Maid of Orleans* would be produced next season. I had to be at rehearsal by four o'clock. De Sachs accompanied me to the Music Hall in the Schirmers' carriage. It was lit up and in order for the first time to-day. I sat in Carnegie's box, while an oratorio, *The Shulamite*, by the elder Damrosch, was being rehearsed. Before my turn came they sang a wearisome cantata by Schütz, *The Seven Words*. My choruses[1] went very well. After it was over, I accompanied Sachs very unwillingly to the Schirmers', as he had made me promise to come back. We found a number of people there who had come merely to see me. Schirmer took us on the roof of his house. This huge, nine-storied house has a roof so arranged that one can take quite a delightful walk on it and enjoy a splendid view from all sides. The sunset was indescribably beautiful. When we went downstairs we found only a few intimate friends left, with whom I enjoyed myself most unexpectedly. Aus-der-Ohe played beautifully. Among other things, we played my Concerto together. We sat down to supper at nine o'clock. About 10.30 we, that is, Sachs, Aus-der-Ohe, her sister, and myself, were presented with the most splendid roses, conveyed downstairs in the lift and sent home in the Schirmers' carriage. One must do justice to American hospitality; there is nothing like it—except, perhaps, in our own country.

"*April 22nd (May 4th).*

"Received letters. A visit from Mr. Romeike, the proprietor of the bureau for newspaper cuttings. Apparently, he, too, is one of our Anarchists, like those mysterious Russians who spoke to me yesterday at the rehearsal. Wrote letters and my diary. Called for Mayer, and went

---

[1] "Legend" and "Our Father."

with him to see Hyde, who invited us to breakfast at the Down Town Club. After a most excellent breakfast I walked down Broadway, alas—still with Mayer. Then we went to the concert given by the celebrated English singer Santley. The celebrated singer turned out to be an elderly man, who sang arias and songs in a fairly rhythmic manner, but without any tone, and with truly English stiffness. I was greeted by several critics, among them Finck, who had written to me last winter so enthusiastically about *Hamlet*. I went home without waiting for the end of the concert, as I had to go through my Pianoforte Concerto with Adèle Aus-der-Ohe. She came with her sister, and I showed her various little nuances and delicate details, which—after yesterday's rehearsal—I considered necessary, in view of her powerful, clean, brilliant, but somewhat rough, style of playing. Reno had told me some interesting facts about Aus-der-Ohe's American career. Four years ago she obtained an engagement at one of the Symphony Concerts to play a Concerto by Liszt (she was one of his pupils), and came over without a penny in her pocket. Her playing took with the public. She was engaged everywhere, and was a complete success. During these four years she has toured all over America, and now possesses a capital of over £20,000!!! Such is America! After they had left, I hurried into my evening clothes and went to dinner at the Renos'. This time it was quite a small family party. Damrosch came in after dinner. I played duets with charming Alice Reno. The evening passed very pleasantly. Reno saw me to the tramway. It has suddenly turned very cold.

"April 23rd (May 5th).

" The waiter Max, who brings me my tea in the morning, spent all his childhood in Nijni-Novogorod and went to school there. Since his fifteenth year he has lived partly in Germany, partly in New York. He is now twenty-three, and has so completely forgotten his native tongue that he can only mangle it, although he still remembers the most common words. I find it very pleasant to talk a little Russian with him. At eleven a.m. the pianist Rummel (an old acquaintance from Berlin) came to ask me again if I would conduct his concert on the 17th; he has been once before. Next came a very pleasant and friendly journalist, who asked how my wife liked New York. I have been asked this question before. One day, shortly after my arrival, it was announced in some of the newspapers that I had arrived with a young and pretty wife. This arose from the fact that two reporters on the pier had seen me get into a carriage with Alice Reno. At 7.30 Reno's brother-in-law came. We drove to the Music Hall in a carriage, filled to overflowing. The appearance of the hall in the evening, lit up and crowded with people, was very fine and effective. The ceremony began with a speech by Reno (this had caused the poor fellow much perturbation all the day before). After this the National Anthem was sung. Then a clergyman made a very long and wearisome speech, in which he eulogised the founders of the Hall, especially Carnegie. The Leonore Symphony was then beautifully rendered. Interval. I went downstairs. Great excitement. I appeared, and was greeted with loud applause. The March went splendidly. Great success. I sat in Hyde's box for the rest of the concert. Berlioz's *Te Deum* is somewhat wearisome; only towards the end I began to enjoy it thoroughly. Reno carried me off with him. An improvised supper. Slept like a log.

" April 24th (May 6th), 1891.

"'Tchaikovsky is a man of ample proportions, with rather grey hair, well built, of a pleasing appearance, and about sixty years of age (!!!). He seemed rather nervous, and answered the applause with a number of stiff little bows. But as soon as he had taken up the bâton he was quite master of himself.' I read this to-day in the *Herald.*[1] It annoys me that, not content with writing about my music, they must also write about my personal appearance. I cannot bear to think that my shyness is noticeable, or that my 'stiff little bows' fill them with astonishment. I went to rehearsal at 10.30. I had to get a workman to show me the entrance to the Hall. The rehearsal went very well. After the Suite the musicians called out something which

[1] *The New York Herald*, 6th May, 1891.

sounded like 'hoch.' Simply bathed in perspiration, I had to go and talk to Mme. Reno, her eldest daughter and two other ladies. Went to see Reno. The steamboat ticket. Instructions for the journey to Philadephia and Boston. Then I hurried over to Mayer's, where Rummel had already been waiting half an hour to play me the Second Concerto. But we did not play it. I practised my powers of eloquence instead. I tried to prove to him that there was no reason why I should accede to his proposal—to conduct his concert gratuitously on the 17th. Breakfasted with Mayer at the Italian Restaurant. P. Botkin[1] from Washington turned up quite unexpectedly about seven o'clock. He has come on purpose to be at the concert. Hyde and his wife fetched me about 7.30. The second concert. Mendelssohn's oratorio, *Elijah*, was given. A splendid work, but rather too long. During the interval, I was dragged the round of the boxes of various local magnates.

"*April 25th (May 7th).*

"I am fifty-one to-day. I feel very excited. The concert begins at two o'clock, with the Suite. This curious fright I suffer from is very strange. How many times have I already conducted the Suite, and it goes splendidly. Why this anxiety? I suffer horribly, and it gets worse and worse. I never remember feeling so anxious before. Perhaps it is because over here they pay so much attention to my outward appearance, and consequently my shyness is more noticeable. However that may be, after getting over some painful hours (the last was worst of all, for before my appearance I had to speak to several strangers) I stepped into the conductor's desk, was received most enthusiastically, and made a sensation—according to to-day's papers. After the Suite I sat in Reno's private room, and was interviewed by several reporters. (Oh, these reporters!) Among others, the well-known journalist, Jackson. I paid my respects to Mrs. Reno in her box; she had sent me a quantity of flowers in the morning, almost as if she had guessed it was my birthday. I felt

---

[1] Son of the celebrated scientist, S. Botkin, and Secretary to the Russian Embassy in Washington.

I must be alone, so refused Reno's invitation, pushed my way through a crowd of ladies, who were standing in the corridor to stare at me, and in whose eyes I read with involuntary pleasure signs of enthusiastic sympathy—and hastened home. I wrote Botkin a card, telling him that I could not keep my promise to dine with him. Relieved and—in a measure—happy, I went out to stroll about, to eat my dinner, and lounge in a café, to enjoy silence and solitude.

"*April 26th* (*May 8th*).

" I can scarcely find time to keep up my diary and correspondence. I am simply overrun with visitors—reporters, composers, and librettists. Among the latter was one who brought me the text of an opera, *Vlasta*, and touched me very deeply by the account of the death of his only son. Moreover, from every part of America I receive a heap of letters asking for my autograph; these I answer most conscientiously. Went to the rehearsal of the Pianoforte Concerto. Damrosch annoyed me very much by taking up the best of the time for himself and leaving the rest of the rehearsal to me. However, all went well. Went to Knabe's to thank him for the beautiful present (a statue of Freedom) which he sent me yesterday. Shall I be allowed to take it into Russia? Then I hastened home. Visitors without end, among others two Russian ladies. One of them was Mrs. MacMahan, widow of the celebrated war correspondent of 1877, and herself the correspondent of the *Russky Viedomosti* and the *Severny Vestnik*. This was the first time I had had the pleasure of talking to a Russian lady; consequently I made a fool of myself. Suddenly the tears came into my eyes, my voice broke, and I could not suppress my sobs. I fled into the next room, and could not show myself again for a long time. I blush with shame to think of this unexpected episode. . . . Rested a little before the concert. The chorus went well, but might have gone better if I had not been so upset. Sat in the box with Reno and Hyde during the beautiful oratorio, *The Shulamite*. Walked with Reno and Carnegie to sup with Damrosch. This archmillionaire is very kind to me, and constantly talks of an engagement for next year. . . . A good deal of champagne was drunk. I sat between the host and the conductor, Dannreuther. While I was talking to him about his brother he must have had the impression, for at least two hours, that I was either a madman or an impudent liar. He sat with his mouth open, and looked quite astonished. It seems that I had confused the pianist Dannreuther with the pianist Hartvigson. My absent-mindedness is becoming almost unbearable, and is a sign of advancing age. However, everyone was surprised to learn that I was only fifty-one yesterday. Carnegie especially was very much astonished. They all thought, except those who knew something of my life, that I was much older. Probably I have aged very much in the last few years. I feel I have lost vitality. I returned in Carnegie's carriage. This talk about my age resulted in dreadful dreams; I thought I slipped down a tremendously steep wall into the sea, and then climbed on to a little rocky projection. Probably this was the result of our conversation yesterday.

" Every day Romeike sends me a heap of newspaper cuttings about myself. All, without exception, are written in terms of the highest praise. The Third Suite is praised to the skies, and, what is more, my conducting also. Am I really such a good conductor, or do the Americans exaggerate?

" *April 27th (May 9th).*

" The manager of the Composers' Club called upon me and wished to arrange an evening for my compositions. Mrs. White[1] sent me such a quantity of lovely flowers that, owing to lack of room and vases, I had to give some to Max, who was highly delighted, as his wife is passionately fond of them. Ritzel, the violinist, also called upon me. He would like to have my portrait, and told me that the members of the orchestra were quite delighted with me. This touched me very much. I changed my things, and took Mayer my large portrait. From there I went to Schirmer's, and then hurried to the Music Hall, where I was to make my last appearance before the public. All

---

[1] Schirmer's married daughter.

these visits made before the concert show how calm I was at this time. Why, I do not know. In the artists' room I made the acquaintance of a singer who sang one of my songs yesterday. A very fine artist and a charming woman. My Concerto went magnificently, thanks to Aus-der-Ohe's brilliant interpretation. The enthusiasm was far greater than anything I have met with, even in Russia. I was recalled over and over again ; handkerchiefs were waved, cheers resounded—in fact, it is easy to see that I have taken the Americans by storm. But what I valued most of all was the enthusiasm of the orchestra. Owing to the heat and my exertions, I was bathed in perspiration, and could not, unfortunately, listen to the scenes from *Parsifal.* At the last evening concert of the Festival I sat alternately in the boxes of Carnegie, Hyde, and Reno. The whole of Handel's oratorio, *Israel in Egypt,* was given. During the course of the evening the architect of the Hall received an ovation. Afterwards I had supper with Damrosch at the Sachs'. . . .

"*April* 28*th* (*May* 10*th*).

" This has been a very heavy day. In the morning I was besieged by visitors. The interesting Korbay, the young, good-looking composer Klein, the pianist F.— with gold-stopped teeth—and others I do not remember. I went out at one o'clock to call on the nihilist Starck-Stoleshnikov, but he lives so far away, and the heat was so oppressive, that I gave it up. I hastened instead to Dr. N.'s, and arrived there in good time. Dr. N. is a Russian—at least he was brought up in Russia. His wife, as I finally discovered, is Countess G. They have lived in America since 1860, and often go to Europe, but never visit Russia. I did not like to ask their reason for avoiding it. They are both ardent patriots, and have a genuine love of Russia. In speaking of our country he seems to think that despotism and bureaucracy hinder it from becoming a leading nation. It strikes me that he is a freethinker who has at some time brought down the wrath of the Government on himself, and fled just at the right moment. But his liberalism is not in the least akin to Nihilism or Anarchism. Both frequently asserted that they had nothing to do with the nihilists in this country. I lunched with them about three o'clock, and then rushed off to B. MacMahan's (owing to a lack of cabs one has to walk everywhere). While the N.s' house is almost luxuriously furnished, this Russian correspondent lives quite in the student style. Somewhat later the celebrated sculptor Kamensky came in; he has lived in America for the last twenty years, but I do not know why. He is an old, somewhat invalidish-looking man, with a deep scar on his forehead. He confused me very much by asking me to tell him *everything* that I knew about the Russia of to-day. I did not quite know how to accomplish such a vast undertaking, but Barbara Nikolaevna (Mrs. MacMahan) began to talk about my music, and I soon took my departure, as I had to go home and dress before dining with Carnegie. All the cafés are closed on Sundays. This English Puritanism, which shows itself in such senseless trivialities (for instance, one can only obtain a glass of whisky or beer on Sunday by means of some fraud), irritates me very much. It is said that the men who brought this law into force in the State of New York were themselves heavy drinkers. I had scarcely time to change and drive to Carnegie's in a carriage, which had to be fetched from some distance, and was very expensive. This millionaire really does not live so luxuriously as many other people. Mr. and Mrs. Reno, Mr. and Mrs. Damrosch, the architect of the Music Hall and his wife, an unknown gentleman and a stout friend of Mrs. Damrosch's were at dinner. I sat beside this aristocratic and evidently distinguished lady. This singular man, Carnegie, who rapidly rose from a telegraph apprentice to be one of the richest men in America, while still remaining quite simple, inspires me with unusual confidence, perhaps because he shows me so much sympathy. During the evening he expressed his liking for me in a very marked manner. He took both my hands in his, and declared that, though not crowned, I was a genuine king of music. He embraced me (without kissing me: men do not kiss over here), got on tiptoe and stretched his hand up to indicate my greatness, and finally made the whole company laugh by imitating my conducting. This he did so solemnly, so well, and so like me, that I myself was quite delighted. His wife is also an extremely simple and charming young lady, and showed her interest in me in every possible way. All this was very pleasant, but still I was glad to get home again at eleven, as I felt somewhat bored.

"*April 29th* (*May 11th*).

"Mayer fetched me at a quarter-past eight. How should I have got on without Mayer? I got a seat in a saloon carriage. . . . We reached Buffalo at 8.30. I was met by two gentlemen whom Mayer had instructed to look after me, as I had to change here, and it is very difficult to find one's way in this labyrinth of lines. I reached Niagara fifty minutes after leaving Buffalo, and went to the hotel in which a room—also thanks to Mayer—was reserved for me. The hotel is quite unpretentious—after the style of the small Swiss inns—but very clean and convenient, as German is spoken. I went to bed early. The roaring of the waterfall is very audible in the stillness of the night.

"NIAGARA, *April 30th* (*May 12th*).

"The carriage was here at nine o'clock. There was no guide, which was very pleasant. I will not try to describe the beauties of the Falls; it is hard to find words for these things. In the afternoon I walked again to the Falls and round the town. During this walk—as in the morning—I could not get rid of a curious—probably entirely nervous—lassitude, which prevented my full enjoyment of this beautiful scenery. I started again at a quarter-past six in a special sleeping-carriage.

"NEW YORK, *May 1st* (*13th*).

"At five o'clock I awoke, my mind full of anxious thoughts about the approaching week, which I dread so much. I was home by 8 a.m., and very glad to see Max again. The news of the attempt on the Tsarevich made me feel very sad. I was also grieved to find that there were no letters from home—and I had hoped to find a number. Many visitors. I hired a carriage from the hotel, on account of the great distances which I had to get over to-day.   First I went to say good-bye to Damrosch, as he is going to Europe.   He asked me to take him as a pupil.   Of course I refused, but am afraid involuntarily I showed far too plainly my horror at the idea of Damrosch arriving at my country home to study with me.   From there I hastened to lunch at the Renos'.   The coachman was quite drunk, and would not understand where I wanted him to drive.   It was lucky I knew the way myself.   The Renos received me as cordially as ever.   Afterwards I went to Mayer's.   Then the same drunken coachman drove Mayer and myself to the great steam-ferry which conveys carriages, horses, and foot-passengers over the East River. Thence we went by train to Mayer's summer residence.   I felt so tired, so irritable and unhappy, I could hardly restrain my tears.   His family is good and kind, but all the same I was bored, and longed to get away.   In the afternoon we walked along the shore ; the sea was rather rough.   The air is so fresh and pure here that my walk really gave me pleasure and did me good.   I stayed the night at Mayer's, but slept badly.

"May 2nd (14*th*).

"I got up at six o'clock.   Went down to the sea, and was delighted.   After breakfast we drove into the town. I should have liked to be alone.   Miss Ross came to see me.   My letter on Wagner has been published, and created quite a sensation.   Anton Seidl, the celebrated conductor and Wagnerian, had published a lengthy reply, in which he attacked me, but in quite a friendly tone.   Miss Ross came to ask me to write an answer to Seidl's reply.   I set to work upon it, but was interrupted by X., who stayed an endless time, and told me all kinds of uninteresting musical gossip, which I had heard a hundred times before. The next to come was the correspondent of a Philadelphia newspaper, who is one of my most fervent admirers.   I had to speak English with him : I have made progress, and can say a few phrases very well.   Wrote letters. Breakfasted alone in my hotel.   Wandered through the Central Park.   According to my promise, I went over to Z.'s to write a testimonial for the * * * pianofortes. Was this the object of all Z.'s attentions?   All these

presents, all this time and money spent on me, all these
unaccountable kindnesses, were these intended as a premium for a future puff? I proposed that Z. himself
should write the testimonial. He sat for a long time, but
could not think of anything; so we put it off until our
next meeting. Then I paid a call on Tretbar, Steinway's
representative, for whom I had a letter of introduction
from Jurgenson. He had waited till now without calling
upon me because he did not wish to make the first
advances. I had purposely delayed my visit from similar
motives. Home to pack. Shortly afterwards a messenger
from Z. brought me the testimonial to sign. It read as
follows: '*I consider the* * * * *pianofortes without doubt the
best in America.*' Now as I do *not* think so at all, but value
some other makers' far more highly, I declined to have
my opinion expressed in this form. I told Z., that notwithstanding my deep gratitude to him, I could not tell a
lie. The reporter from the *Herald* came to see me—a very
interesting man. Drove to Hyde's. I wish I could find
words to describe all the charm and originality of this
interesting couple. Hyde greeted me with these words:
'Kak vasche sdorovie? sidite poschaljust.'[1] Then he
laughed like a lunatic, and his wife and I joined in. He had
bought a guide to Russian conversation, and learnt a few
phrases as a surprise to me. Mrs. Hyde immediately invited me to smoke a cigarette in her drawing-room—the
climax of hospitality in America. After the cigarette we
went to dinner. The table was most exquisitely decorated
with flowers; everyone received a bouquet. Then, quite
unexpectedly, Hyde became very solemn, closed his eyes
and said the Lord's Prayer. I did the same as the
others: lowered my eyes and gazed on the ground.
Then began an endlessly long dinner. . . . At ten o'clock
I withdrew. At home a messenger from Knabe was
waiting for me. We drank a glass of beer together, took
my trunk, and went down town. We went over the Hudson in the steam ferry, and finally reached the station.
Knabe's messenger (without whose help I should certainly
have been lost) engaged a comfortable *coupé* for me; the
friendly negro made the bed, I threw myself on it just as

---

[1] Broken Russian. "How are you? Please sit down."

I was, for I really had not the strength to undress, and sank at once into a deep sleep. I slept soundly, but not for long. The negro woke me an hour before my arrival at Baltimore.

"BALTIMORE, *May* 3*rd* (15*th*).

"As usual, I was received at the hotel with cool contempt. Sitting alone in my room, I suddenly felt so unhappy, chiefly because everyone around me speaks only English. I slept a little. Then I went into a restaurant for breakfast, and was quite annoyed because the waiter (a negro) would not understand that I wished for tea and bread-and-butter only. I had to go to the desk, where they did not understand me any better. At last a gentleman knowing a little German kindly came to my help. I had hardly sat down when Knabe, a stout man, came in. Very shortly after, Adèle Aus-der-Ohe and her sister joined us, too. I was very glad to see them, for they seem like connections, at least as regards music. We went to the rehearsal together. This was held on the stage of the Lyceum Theatre. The orchestra was small, only four first violins, but not bad. But the Third Suite was not to be thought of. It was decided to put the Serenade for strings in its place. The orchestra did not know this work. The conductor had not even played it through, although Reno had promised that this should be done. The Concerto with Adèle Aus-der-Ohe went very smoothly, but the Serenade needs many rehearsals. The orchestra was impatient. The young leader behaved in rather a tactless way, and made it too clearly evident that he thought it time to stop. It is true—this unhappy touring orchestra must be wearied by their constant travelling. After the rehearsal I went home with Adèle Aus-der-Ohe, dressed, and went immediately to the concert. I conducted in my frock-coat. Happily everything went very well, but there was little enthusiasm in comparison with New York. After the concert we both drove home to change. Half an hour later Knabe called for us. His hospitality is on the same colossal scale as his figure. This beardless giant had arranged a festivity in my honour at his own house. I found a number of people there. The dinner was endlessly long, but very tasteful and good, as were also the wines with which Knabe kept filling up our glasses. During the second half of the dinner I felt quite worn out. A terrible hatred of everything seemed to come over me, especially of my two neighbours. After dinner I conversed a little with everyone, and smoked and drank ceaselessly. At half-past twelve Knabe brought me home, and also the sisters Aus-der-Ohe.

"WASHINGTON, 4th (16th).

" I woke early, breakfasted downstairs, wrote my diary, and waited, rather in fear and trembling, for Knabe, who wanted to show me the sights of the town. At last he came and, together with the sisters Aus-der-Ohe, we drove round Baltimore. Weather bad and inclined to rain. Baltimore is a pretty, clean town. Then the good-natured giant helped me to pack my box, invited Aus-der-Ohe and myself to a champagne lunch, and finally put me in the carriage that was to take me to my destination. He him-self was travelling to Philadelphia, while I was going to Washington. The journey lasted about three-quarters of an hour. I was met by Botkin, who accompanied me to the hotel, where a room was engaged for me. This was delightfully comfortable, and at the same time tastefully and simply furnished. I declined to receive Rennen, begged Botkin to call for me before the dinner, took a bath, and hurried into my dress clothes. The dinner was given in the Metropolitan Club, of which Botkin and his colleagues are members. The dinner was very gay, and I was so delighted to talk Russian once more, although this happiness was a little dimmed by the sad fact that my 's,' ' sch,' ' tsch,' are beginning to sound rather indistinct from age. During the dinner we heard, first by telegram and then through the telephone, that the Ambassador Struve had returned from a journey to New York solely on my account. At ten o'clock we all repaired to the Embassy, where Botkin had arranged a musical evening. About a hundred persons were invited. The Ambassador also arrived, an old man, very cordial and also interesting. The company at the Embassy belonged principally to the diplomatic circle. There were ambassadors with their wives and daughters, and personages belonging to the highest class of the diplomatic service. Most of the ladies spoke French, so things were not so difficult for me. The programme consisted of my Trio and a Quartet by Brahms. Hausen, the Secretary to our Embassy, was at the piano, and he proved quite a respectable pianist. My Trio he played decidedly well. The violinist was only middling. I was introduced to everyone. After the music there was an excellent cold supper. When most of the guests had left, ten of us (the Belgian Ambassador and the Secretaries to the Swedish and Austrian Embassies, besides the Russians) sat for some time longer at a large round table, before an excellent flagon. Struve enjoys a glass of wine. He gave me the impression of a broken and unhappy man who finds it a consolation. It was three o'clock before I went home, accompanied by Botkin and Hausen.

"*May 5th* (*17th*).

"Awoke with pleasant memories of yesterday. I always feel well in Russian society when I am not obliged to speak a foreign tongue. At twelve o'clock Botkin called for me to lunch with the Ambassador, Struve. Afterwards I went with Botkin and Hausen to see the sights of Washington.

"PHILADELPHIA, *May 6th* (*18th*).

"I reached Philadelphia at three o'clock. Breakfasted downstairs. A very importunate Jew from Odessa called and got some money out of me. Went for a walk. The concert at eight p.m. The enormous theatre was filled to overflowing. After the concert, according to long-standing promise, I went to the club. The return journey to New York was very wearisome.

"*May 7th* (*19th*).

"Feel quite stupid from exhaustion and constant travelling. I could stand no more, if it were not for the thought of my departure to-morrow, which buoys me up. I am inundated with requests for my autograph. At 12.30 I went over to Z.'s and wrote the testimonial, omitting the phrase which ranks these pianos as the first. Went home and waited for the composer Brummklein. He came and played me some very pretty things.

" *May 8th* (*20th*).

" The old librettist came. I was very sorry to have to tell him I could not compose an opera to his libretto. He seemed very sad. Scarcely had he gone before Dannreuther came in to take me to the rehearsal of the Quartets and Trios to be played this evening at the Composers' Club. It was rather a long distance. The Quartet was indifferently played and the Trio really badly, for the pianist, a shy, nervous man, was no good : he could not even count. I had no time to make any preparations for the journey. Drove to Renos'. They received me with more kindness and cordiality than ever, especially Madame Reno and her three daughters. The eldest (Anna, who is married) gave me a beautiful cigar-case, M. Reno a quantity of scent, and Alice and her sister cakes for the journey. Then I hurried to Hyde's. Mrs. Hyde was already expecting me. Here too I was received with great kindness and sincere enthusiasm. At last I got home to pack my box. Hateful business, which gave me a dreadful pain in my back. Tired out, I went over to Mayer's, and invited him to dinner at Martelli's. At eight o'clock I was taken to the Composers' Club. This is not a club of composers, as I first thought, but a special musical union which arranges, from time to time, evenings devoted to the works of one composer. Yesterday was devoted to me, and the concert was held in the magnificent Metropolitan House. I sat in the first row. They played the Quartet (E flat minor) and the Trio ; some songs were very well sung, but the programme was too long. In the middle of the evening I received an address ; I answered shortly, in French ; of course an ovation. One lady threw an exquisite bouquet of roses straight in my face. I was introduced to a crowd of people, among others our Consul-General. At the conclusion I had to speak to about a hundred people and distribute a hundred autographs. ·I reached home half dead with fatigue. As the steamer left at five o'clock in the morning, I had to go on board that night, so I dressed with all speed, and packed my things while Reno and Mayer waited for me. Downstairs we drank two bottles of champagne. I said good-bye to the servants of the hotel and drove off to the steamer. The drive was very long. The steamer is quite as fine as the *Bretagne ;* I have an officer's cabin. On this ship the officers are allowed to let their cabins, but they ask an exorbitant price. I had to pay 300 dollars (1,500 francs) for mine. . . . But it is really nice and very roomy. I said good-bye to my dear American friends and went straight to bed. I slept badly and heard all the noise when the steamer started at five o'clock. I came out of my cabin as we passed the statue of Freedom."

Altogether Tchaikovsky gave six concerts in America: four in New York, one in Baltimore, and one in Philadelphia. The following works were performed: (1) The Coronation March, (2) Third Suite, (3) two Sacred Choruses: the Lord's Prayer and the Legend, (4) Pianoforte Concerto No. 1, and (5) Serenade for string instruments.

I have before me sixteen American Press notices of Tchaikovsky, and all are written in a tone of unqualified praise ; the only difference lies in the degree of enthusiasm expressed. According to some he is " the first of modern composers after Wagner " ; according to others, " one of the first." His talent as a conductor is equally praised. Everywhere he had an unprecedented success, and many spoke of his interesting appearance. The interviews (especially those in *The New York Herald*) are reproduced with astonishing fidelity. As we read them we can almost fancy we can hear the voice of Tchaikovsky himself.

XIII

"'Prince Bismarck,' *May 9th* (21*st*).

" On account of the maddening pain in my back, I dressed with great difficulty, went below for my morning tea, and then walked about the ship to make myself better acquainted with the various quarters. A host of passengers, but of totally different appearance to those who travelled with me on the *Bretagne*. The most perceptible difference lies in the fact that there are no emigrants. At eight a.m. I was called to breakfast. My place had already been allotted to me. I had a middle-aged man for my neighbour, who immediately began to converse. Slept the whole morning. The sight of the sea leaves me indifferent. I think with horror of the rest of the journey, but also with longing: may it soon be over. This is a very fast ship; it is the magnificent new *Prince Bismarck*, and is making its first passage. Last week it only took six days and fourteen hours from Hamburg to New York. I trust we shall get over the horrible distance as quickly. The motion is not so smooth as that of the *Bretagne*. The weather is splendid just now. At breakfast I became better acquainted with my vis-à-vis. It is difficult to say to what nationality he belongs, as he speaks all languages wonderfully well; perhaps he is a Jew, so I told him on purpose the story of the importunate Jew. He lives in Dresden, and is a wholesale tobacco dealer. He has already discovered who I am. If he speaks the truth, he heard me conduct in New York; anyway, he improves on acquaintance. I have got so accustomed to talking in New York that, in spite of my preference for silence, I can stand his society without being bored. I am astonished to find I sleep so much. In the evening, soon after dinner, I was so overcome that I went to bed at ten o'clock and slept straight on until seven the next morning. Nothing particular happened during the day. A Mr. Aronson and his young wife introduced themselves to me. He is the proprietor of the Casino Theatre (favoured by Von Bülow), as I discovered by means of an autograph album which was sent to me that I might write my name and a few lines in it. Schröder, the man who attends to my cabin, is a good-natured young German; at table also there are two nice German stewards—this is very important for me. I am pleased with the ship, the cabin, and the food. As there are no emigrants I can walk on the lower deck; this is very pleasant, as I meet no first-class passengers there and can be quiet.

" May 11th (23rd).

" I keep very much to myself and, thanks to my splendid cabin, in which there is plenty of room to move about, I feel much freer than on the *Bretagne*. I only use the drawing-room in the morning when no one is there. There is a nice Steinway grand, and not at all a bad musical library, including a few of my own productions. The day is divided as follows : Dress, ring my bell, and Schröder brings me a cup of tea ; first breakfast, eight o'clock ; walk on the lower deck, work, read. By work I mean the sketches for my next Symphony. At twelve o'clock the gong sounds for second breakfast. . . . I am reading a book by Tatistchev, *Alexandre et Napoléon*.

" May 11th (23rd).

" In New York they so often assured me that the sea was calm at this time of year that I believed them. But what a disenchantment ! Since early morning the weather has been getting worse : rain, wind, and towards evening quite a gale. A dreadful night, could not sleep, so sat on the sofa. Towards morning dozed a little.

" May 12th (24th).

" A detestable day. The weather is frightful. Sea-sickness, could eat nothing but an orange.

" May (13th) 25th.

" I feel quite unnerved from exhaustion and sickness. Yesterday evening I fell asleep in my clothes on my sofa and slept there the whole night. To-day the motion is less, but the weather is still dreadful. My nerves are inexpressibly strained and irritated by this ceaseless noise and horrible cracking. Shall I ever make up my mind to endure such torment again ?

" During the course of the day the motion grew still less and the weather improved. I have taken such a dislike to the society of my fellow-passengers that the very sight of them annoys and irritates me. I constantly sit in my own cabin.

"*May 14th (26th).*

"The moon was magnificent to-night. I read in my cabin till I was tired, and then went out for a stroll on deck. Everyone, without exception, was asleep, and I was the only one of the 300 first-class passengers who had come out to enjoy the lovely night. It was beautiful beyond all words. It was strange to think of the terrible night on Sunday, when everything in my cabin, even my trunk, was hurled from one side to the other, and the vessel seemed to be fighting for life against the storm; when one was racked with terror, and, added to all, the electric lamp and bell fell with a crash on the floor and was smashed to pieces. That night I vowed never to make another sea-voyage. But Schröder, my steward, says he resolves to give up his place every time the weather is bad, but no sooner is he in harbour than he longs for the sea again. Perhaps it may be the same with me. The passengers are getting up a concert, and want me to play. Quite the worst part of a sea-voyage is having to know all the passengers.

"*May 15th (27th).*

"As we neared the Channel it became more lively. Hundreds of little ships came in sight. About two o'clock the English coast was visible; sometimes rocky and picturesque, sometimes flat and green with spring grass. . . . Soon afterwards we entered Southampton.

"*May 16th (28th).*

"After passing Southampton and the Isle of Wight, I went to sleep and awoke feeling rather chilly. . . . Enjoyed the views of the English coast and the sight of the many steamers and sailing vessels which enliven the Channel. We saw Folkestone and Dover. The North Sea is very lively. We passed Heligoland in the night.

"*May 17th (29th).*

"Arrived early this morning at Cuxhaven. . . . At 8 a.m. we went on board a small steamer that took us to the Custom House. Long wait and examination. Arrived at Hamburg by midday."

Tchaikovsky spent one day in Hamburg and one in Berlin ; then travelled direct to Petersburg.

During his short stay there he was in a cheerful frame of mind. This was partly the result of his reunion with his friends and relatives, and partly the delightful impression of the early spring in Petersburg, which he always enjoyed. This time he was so charmed with the city that he had a great wish to settle in the neighbourhood, and commissioned us to look out for a suitable house, or a small country property.

Since Frolovskoe was becoming more and more denuded of its forests, and the demands of the landlord steadily increased, Tchaikovsky decided to leave. After many vain attempts to find a suitable country house, or to acquire a small property, he resolved to return to Maidanovo. While he was abroad, Alexis Safronov had moved all his belongings into the house he formerly occupied, and arranged it just as in 1886. Although Tchaikovsky was fond of this house and its surroundings, and looked forward to working there under the old conditions, his return somewhat depressed him. There was an air of decay about house and park ; the walks did not please him ; and then there was the prospect of an inroad of summer visitors.

Soon after settling in Maidanovo he was visited by his brother, Modeste Tchaikovsky, and his nephews, Vladimir Davidov and Count A. Litke. All four travelled to Moscow together, where he was greatly interested by the Franco-Russian Exhibition, and enjoyed acting as cicerone to his favourite nephews.

The chief musical works upon which he was engaged at this time were : the second act of the Ballet, *The Nutcracker ;* the completion of the opera, *King René's Daughter ;* the remodelling of the Sextet and the instrumentation of a symphonic poem, *The Voyevode*, composed the previous autumn while he was staying at Tiflis.

To P. Jurgenson.

"MAIDANOVO, *June 3rd* (15*th*), 1891.

"I have discovered a new instrument in Paris, something between a piano and a *glockenspiel*, with a divinely beautiful tone. I want to introduce this into the ballet and the symphonic poem. The instrument is called the 'Celesta Mustel,' and costs 1,200 francs. You can only buy it from the inventor, Mustel, in Paris. I want to ask you to order one of these instruments. You will not lose by it, because you can hire it out to the concerts at which *The Voyevode* will be played, and afterwards sell it to the Opera when my ballet is put on. . . . Have it sent direct to Petersburg; but no one there must know about it. I am afraid Rimsky-Korsakov and Glazounov might hear of it and make use of the new effect before I could. I expect the instrument will make a tremendous sensation."

To J. Konius.

"*June* 15*th* (27*th*), 1891.

" . . . The news that you are engaged (for America) with Brodsky rejoices me. Brodsky is one of the most sympathetic men I ever met. He is also a fine artist and the best quartet player I ever heard, not excepting Laub, who was so great in this line."

To V. Davidov.

"*June* 25*th* (*July* 7*th*), 1891.

" According to my promise, I write to let you know that I finished the sketch of the ballet yesterday. You will remember my boasting when you were here that I should get it done in about five days. But I have taken at least a fortnight. Yes, the old fellow is getting worn out. Not only is his hair turning white as snow and beginning to fall, not only is he losing his teeth, not only do his eyes grow weaker and get tired sooner, not only do his feet begin to drag—but he is growing less capable of accomplishing anything. This ballet is far weaker than *The Sleeping Beauty*—no doubt about it. We shall see how the opera turns out. Once I feel convinced that I can only contribute 'warmed-up' dishes to the musical bill of fare, I shall give up composing."

The following is quoted from a letter to Arensky, who had been consulting Tchaikovsky as to the advisability of taking the post of Director of the Tiflis branch of the Musical Society :—

"I hardly know how to advise you, dear Anton Stepano-vich. I would prefer not to do so. If you had some private means, I could only rejoice in the prospect of your going to the Caucasus for a time. But it saddens me to think of you in the provinces, remote from musical centres, overburdened with tiresome work, solitary and unable to hear good music. You cannot imagine how it depresses me to think of men like Rimsky-Korsakov, Liadov, and yourself being obliged to worry with teaching. But how can it be helped? I think if you bear it for another two years, and work hard, little by little, you may manage to live by composition only. I know in my own case this is not impossible. I earn enough now to keep a large family, if need were. I may tell you in conclusion, that Tiflis is a fascinating town, and life there is pleasant."

To Anatol Tchaikovsky.

"MAIDANOVO, *July* 8*th* (20*th*), 1891.

". . . Do not be vexed that I stayed so long in Peters-burg without coming to see you in Reval.[1] . . . From your letter I gather that you are pretty comfortable there, although you mention many difficulties you have to con-tend with. I think one must be very politic and tactful in these things, then we can get over most difficulties. In the diplomatic service we must often *faire bonne mine au mauvais jeu*. There is nothing for it! I think you would find Valoniev's diary interesting. He was governor of one of the Baltic provinces, and relates a great deal that is

---

[1] Anatol was then Vice-Governor of Estland.

interesting. At that time Souvarov, the extreme Liberal, ruled in these provinces. In the long run the spirit of Pobiedonostsiev is better than the spirit of Souvorov."

Towards the end of July a misfortune befell Tchaikovsky which was the cause of much subsequent anxiety. While he was taking his afternoon constitutional, and Alexis was resting in his room, a thief, who probably entered through the window, carried off the clock which had been given to him by Nadejda von Meck in 1888. This clock, which was beautifully decorated with a figure of Joan of Arc on one side, and on the other with the Apollo of the Grand Opéra, upon a background of black enamel, had been specially made in Paris, and cost 10,000 francs. For years Tchaikovsky had hardly consented to be parted from this gift, even for the necessary cleaning and repairs. It was his chief souvenir of his relations with his friend and benefactress. The police of Moscow and Klin were communicated with at once, but to no purpose : the clock was never recovered.

To V. Davidov.

"*August 1st (13th)*, 1891.

". . . I am now reading your " Chevrillon on Ceylon,"[1] and thinking of you. I do not altogether share your enthusiasm. These modern French writers are terribly affected ; they have a kind of affectation of simplicity which disgusts me almost as much as Victor Hugo's high-sounding phrases, epithets, and antitheses. Everything that your favourite recounts in such a clever and lively style might be told in very simple and ordinary language, neither in such brief and broken sentences, nor yet in long periods with the subject and predicate in such forced and unnatural positions. It is very easy to parody this gentleman :—

"Une serviette de table négligemment attachée à son cou, il dégustait. Tout autour des mouches, avides, grouil-

---

[1] In the *Revue des Deux Mondes*, 1891.

lantes, d'un noir inquiétant volaient. Nul bruit sinon un claquement de machoirs énervant. Une odeur moite, fétide, écœurante, lourde, répandait un je ne sais quoi d'animal, de carnacier dans l'air. Point de lumière. Un rayon de soleil couchant, pénétrant comme par hasard dans la chambre nue et basse, éclairait par-ci, par-là tantôt la figure blême du maître engurgitant sa soupe, tantôt celle du valet, moustachue, à traits kalmouks, stupide et rampante. On devinait un idiot servi par un idiot. 9 heures. Un morne silence régnait. Les mouches fatiguées, somnolentes, devenues moins agitées, se dispersaient. Et là-bas, dans le lointain, par la fenêtre, on voyait une lune, grimaçante, enorme, rouge, surgir sur l'horizon embrasé. Il mangeait, il mangeait toujours. Puis l'estomac bourré, la face écarlate, l'œil hagard, il se leva et sortit, etc., etc., etc. I have described my supper this evening. I think Zola was the discoverer of this mode of expression."

To A. Alferaki.

"*August 1st (13th),* 1891.

". . . I have received your letter and the songs, and played through the latter. I have nothing new to add to what I have already said as to your remarkable creative gifts. It is useless to lament that circumstances have not enabled you to go through a course of strict counterpoint, which you specially needed. This goes without saying. Your resolve to confine yourself entirely to song-writing does not please me. A true artist, even if he possesses only a limited creative capacity, which hinders him from producing great works in certain spheres of art, should still keep the highest aim in view. Neither age, nor any other obstacle, should check his ambition. Why should you suppose one needs less than a complete all-round technique in order to compose a perfect song? With an imperfect technique you may limit your sphere of work as much as you please—you will never get beyond an elegant amateurism. . . . I dislike the system of putting the date of composition on each song. What is the use of it? What does it matter to the public when and where a work was composed?"

About August 20th Tchaikovsky left home for Kamenka, from whence he went on to stay with his brother Nicholas. Here he met his favourite poet, A. Fet, and became very friendly with him. Fet wrote a poem, "To Peter Ilich Tchaikovsky," an attention which touched the musician very deeply. At the end of August he returned to Moscow in a very contented frame of mind.

XIV

1891–1892

Through September, and the greater part of October, Tchaikovsky remained at Maidanovo, working uninterruptedly upon the opera *Iolanthe* and the orchestration of *The Voyevode*. The work went easily, and his health was good. The evenings, which during the last years of his life brought home to him a sense of his loneliness, were enlivened by the presence of Laroche, who was staying in the house. The friends played arrangements for four hands, or Laroche read aloud. Everything seemed so ordered as to leave no room for dissatisfaction with his lot ; and yet his former contentment with his surroundings had vanished.

The theft of his clock was still a matter of anxiety. He might have partially forgotten it, had not the police announced the capture of the criminal. "I am living in the atmosphere of one of Gaboriau's novels," he wrote to his brother. "The police have caught the criminal, and he has confessed. But nothing will induce him to reveal where he has hidden the clock. To-day he was brought to me in the hopes that I might persuade him to tell the truth. . . . He said he would confess all, if he was left alone with me. We went into the next room. There he flung himself at my feet and implored forgiveness. Of course I forgave him, and only begged him to say where the clock was. Then he became very quiet and afterwards declared he had never stolen it at all! . . . You can imagine how all this has upset me, and how it has set me against Maidanovo."

Another cause of his passing discontent was wounded pride. So far he believed himself to have scored a great success in America ; he was convinced that his return was anxiously waited, and that his popularity had greatly increased. One day, however, he received a letter from Morris Reno, who had originally engaged him, offering him a three months' tour with twenty concerts at a fee of 4,000 dollars. Seeing that on the first occasion he had received 2,400 dollars for four concerts, Tchaikovsky immediately concluded that he had greatly overrated the importance of his previous visit, and was deeply mortified in consequence. He telegraphed in reply to Reno two words only : "Non. Tchaikovsky." Afterwards he came to recognise that there was nothing offensive in the proposal made to him, and that it in no way denoted any falling off in the appreciation of the Americans. But the desire to return was no longer so keen ; only a very substantial pecuniary advantage would have induced him to undertake the voyage.

Finally, he had another reason for feeling somewhat depressed at this moment. The will which he made in the month of September involuntarily caused him to think of that "flat-nosed horror," which was sometimes his equivalent for death. He had hitherto been under the impression that the law which existed before the accession of Alexander III. was still in force, and that at his death all his rights in his operas would pass into the hands of the Theatrical Direction. The discovery that he had more than a life interest in them was the reason for making a will. It proves how much attention Tchaikovsky must have given to his contracts for *Eugene Oniegin*, *Mazeppa*, and the later operas before signing them, since the clause relating to his hereditary rights was prominent in them all. When his brother Modeste called his attention to the fact, he would not believe him until he had inquired from the Direction, when he found himself agreeably mistaken. He was always anxious as to the fate of certain people whom he suppported during his lifetime, and was thankful to feel that this assistance would be continued after his death.

The number of those he assisted continually increased. " I was the most expensive pensioner," says Modeste Tchaikovsky, " for he allowed me about two thousand roubles a year." But he always met every request for money half-way. Here are a few specimens of his generosity, quoted from letters to Jurgenson and others :—

" DEAR FRIEND,—I want to help X. in some way. You are selling the tickets for his concert. Should they go badly, take fifteen or twenty places on my behalf and give them to whomsoever you please. Of course, X. must know nothing about it."

" If you are in pecuniary difficulties," he wrote to Y., "come to your sincere friend (myself), who now earns so much from his operas and will be delighted to help you. I promise not a soul shall hear of it ; but it will be a great pleasure to me."

" Please write at once to K., that he is to send Y. twenty-five roubles a month. He may pay him three months in advance."

There would be no difficulty in multiplying such instances. Not only his neighbour's need, but the mere whim of another person, awoke in Tchaikovsky the desire of fulfilment. He always wished to give all and receive nothing. It is not surprising, therefore, that there were occasionally periods—as in September and October, 1891

—when he found himself penniless and felt the shortness of funds, chiefly because he was unable to help others.

His correspondence with concert agents, publishers and all kinds of applicants had become a great burden to him in those days.

All these things conduced to that mood of melancholy which is reflected in the letters written at this time.

At the end of October he went to Moscow, to be present at the first performance of *Pique Dame*, and to conduct Siloti's concert, at which his Symphonic Fantasia, *The Voyevode*, was brought out.

To the Grand Duke Constantine Constantinovich.

"Moscow, *October 31st* (*November 12th*), 1891.

"It is difficult to say how deeply your precious lines touched and delighted me. Naturally I felt in my heart of hearts that you had not forgotten me—but it is pleasant to have some clear evidence that amid all your varied and complicated occupations, and while under the impression of a profound family sorrow, you still found time to think of me.

"I was very pleased to make Fet's acquaintance. From his 'Reminiscences,' which were published in the *Russky Viestnik*, I fancied it would not be very interesting to converse with him. On the contrary, he is most agreeable company, full of humour and originality. If your Highness only knew how enchanting his summer residence is! The house and park—what a cosy retreat for a poet in his old age! Unluckily, as his wife complained to me, the poet does not enjoy life in these poetical surroundings at all. He sits at home all day, dictating verses, or his translation of Martial, to his lady secretary. He read me many new poems, and I was surprised at the freshness and youthfulness of his inspiration. We both regretted your Highness could not devote yourself entirely to poetry. If only you could repose in summer in just such a solitary spot! But, alas! it is not possible. . . .

"When I have finished my opera and ballet I shall give

up that kind of work for a time and devote myself to Symphony. . . . I often think it is time to shut up shop. A composer who has won success and recognition stands in the way of younger men who want to be heard. Time was when no one wanted to listen to my music, and if the Grand Duke, your father, had not been my patron, not one of my operas would ever have been performed. Now I am spoilt and encouraged in every way. It is very pleasant, but I am often tormented by the thought that I ought to make room for others."

The first performance of *Pique Dame* in Moscow took place on November 4th (16th), 1891, under Altani's bâton. It was merely a fair copy of the Petersburg performance, and presented no "special" qualities as regards musical rendering or scenery.

The opera met with a warmer and more genuine welcome than in the northern capital. Nevertheless the Press was not very pleased with the music. The *Moscow Viedomosti* thought "Tchaikovsky possessed a remarkable talent for imitation, sometimes going so far as to borrow wholesale from the older masters, as in his Suite *Mozartiana*." Another newspaper considered the opera "more pleasing than inspired." The only serious and intelligent criticism of the work appeared in the *Russky Viedomosti*, from Kashkin's pen.

Siloti's concert, two days later, was marked by one of the most painful episodes in the composer's career. Kashkin, in his 'Reminiscences,' says that, even at the rehearsals, Tchaikovsky had shown a kind of careless indifference in conducting his latest orchestral work, the Symphonic Ballade, *The Voyevode*. After the rehearsal he asked several people for their opinion upon the work, among others Taneiev, who seems to have replied that the chief movement of the Ballade—the love episode—was not equal to similar episodes in *The Tempest*, *Romeo and Juliet*, or *Francesca*. Moreover, he considered that

Tchaikovsky had treated it wrongly, and that Poushkin's words could be *sung* to this melody, so that it was more in the style of a vocal than an orchestral work.

At the concert *The Voyevode* made little impression, notwithstanding the enthusiastic reception given to the composer. This was due to some extent to Tchaikovsky's careless rendering of the work.

Siloti relates that during the interval the composer came into the artists' room and tore his score to pieces, exclaiming: "Such rubbish should never have been written." To tear a thick score in pieces is not an easy feat, and possibly Siloti's memory may have been at fault. It is more probable that Tchaikovsky *wished* to destroy the score on the spot than that he actually did so. Besides, he himself wrote to V. Napravnik: "*The Voyevode* turned out such wretched stuff that I tore it up the day *after* the concert."

Siloti carefully concealed the parts of *The Voyevode*, so that after Tchaikovsky's death the score was restored from these and published by M. Belaiev, of Leipzig. When it was given for the first time in Petersburg, under Nikisch, it made a very different impression upon Taneiev, and he bitterly regretted his hasty verdict delivered in 1891.

Tchaikovsky remained two days longer in Moscow, in order to be present at a dinner given in his honour by the artists who had taken part in *Pique Dame*, and returned to Maidanovo worn out with the excitement he had experienced.

On December 17th (29th) he started upon his concert tour, which included not only foreign, but Russian towns. He was pledged to conduct in Kiev and Warsaw, as well as at the Hague and in Amsterdam,[1] and to attend the first performance of *Oniegin* in Hamburg and of *Pique Dame* in Prague.

[1] In July of this year he had been made a corresponding member of the "Maatschappij tot Bevordering van Toonkunst."

At the time of the first performance of *Pique Dame* in Kiev, Tchaikovsky had become intimately acquainted with Prianichnikov, whose services to art he valued very highly. Not only the attitude of this artist towards him, but that of the entire opera company, had touched him very deeply. He was aware that the affairs of this company—one of the best in Russia—were not very flourishing, and he wanted to show his sympathy in some substantial form. He proposed, therefore, that the first performance of his *Iolanthe* should be transferred from Petersburg to Kiev, provided the Imperial Direction made no objections to the plan. Naturally they objected very strongly, and Tchaikovsky, by way of compensation, offered to conduct a concert for the benefit of Prianichnikov's company. The local branch of the Musical Society, which had made overtures to the composer on several occasions, was offended at his preference for the artists of the opera, and immediately engaged him for a concert of their own. In view of his former connection with the Society, Tchaikovsky could not refuse this offer. Both concerts were a great success, and evoked immense enthusiasm from the public and the Press.

From Kiev he went to Kamenka for a few days, but a feeling of sadness came over him at the sight of his old dwelling-place, so inseparably connected with the memory of the sister he had lost.

. . . At Warsaw, where he arrived on December 29th (January 10th), he was overcome with that terrible, despairing nostalgia, which, towards the close of his life, accompanied him like some sinister travelling companion whenever he left Russia. "I am counting—just as last year—the days, hours, and minutes till my journey is over," he wrote to Vladimir Davidov. "You are constantly in my thoughts, for at every access of agitation and homesickness, whenever my spiritual horizon grows dark, the thought that you are there, that I shall see you sooner or

2 X

later, flashes like a ray of sunlight across my mind. I am not exaggerating, upon my honour! Every moment this sun-ray keeps breaking forth in these or similar words: " Yes, it is bad, but never mind, Bob lives in the world "; " Far away in ' Peter '[1] sits Bob, drudging at his work "; " In a month's time I shall see Bob again."

To N. Konradi.

"Warsaw, *December* 31*st* (*January* 12*th*).

" I have been three days in Warsaw. I do not find this town as agreeable as many others. It is better in summer. The rehearsals are in progress, but the orchestra here is worse than second-rate. I spend my time with my former pupil, the celebrated violinist Barcewicz, and with the Friede[2] family. I shall stay here over the New Year. In the evening I generally go to the theatre. The opera is not bad here. Yesterday I saw the famous *Cavalleria Rusticana*. This opera is really very remarkable, chiefly for its successful subject. Perhaps Modi could find a similar libretto. Oh, when will the glad day of return be here!"

To Modeste Tchaikovsky.

"Warsaw, *January* 3*rd* (15*th*), 1892.

" . . . I have only time for a few lines. Yesterday my concert took place in the Opera House, and went off brilliantly in every respect. The orchestra, which took a great liking to me, played admirably. Barcewicz played my Concerto with unusual spirit, and Friede[3] sang beautifully. The day before yesterday Grossmann[4] arranged a grand soirée in my honour. The Polish countesses were fascinatingly amiable to me. I have been fêted everywhere. Gurko[5] is the only person who has not shown me

---

[1] Diminutive of Petersburg.

[2] A. Friede, General of Infantry.

[3] Daughter of General A. Friede and a prima donna at the Maryinsky Theatre, St. Petersburg.

[4] The representative of the firm of Bechstein.

[5] The celebrated general.

the least attention. . . . Three weeks hence I go to Hamburg. I shall conduct *Oniegin* there myself; Pollini has made a point of it."

To A. Merkling.

"BERLIN, *January 4th* (16th), 1892.

". . . At Grossman's grand evening I observed that the Polish ladies (many very aristocratic women were there) are amiable, cultivated, interesting, and sympathetic. The farewell at the station yesterday was very magnificent. There is some talk of giving one of my operas in Polish next season. I am spending a day in Berlin to recover from the exciting existence in Warsaw. To-morrow I leave for Hamburg, where I conduct *Oniegin* on January 7th (19th). On the 29th (February 10th) my concert takes place in Amsterdam, and on the 30th (February 11th), at the Hague. After that—full steam homewards. I can only look forward with fearful excitement and impatience to the blessed day when I shall return to my adored Mother Russia."

Tchaikovsky arrived in Hamburg to find *Oniegin* had been well studied, and the preparations for its staging satisfactory on the whole. "The conductor here," he wrote to his favourite nephew, "is not merely passable, but actually has genius, and he ardently desires to conduct the first performance. Yesterday I heard a wonderful rendering of *Tannhäuser* under his direction. The singers, the orchestra, Pollini, the managers, and the conductor—his name is Mahler [1]—are all in love with *Oniegin;* but I am very doubtful whether the Hamburg public will share their enthusiasm." Tchaikovsky's doubts as to the success of *Eugene Oniegin* were well founded. The opera was not much applauded.

---

[1] Gustav Mahler, afterwards conductor at the Vienna Opera, also produced *Eugene Oniegin* and *Iolanthe* in the Austrian capital.

To Vladimir Davidov.

"PARIS, *January* 12*th* (24*th*), 1892.

". . . I am in a very awkward position. I have a fortnight in prospect during which I do not know how to kill time. I thought this would be easier in Paris than anywhere else—but it was only on the first day that I did not feel bored. Since yesterday I have been wondering how I could save myself from idleness and ennui. If Sapellnikov and Menter would not be offended at my not going to Holland, how gladly I should start homewards! If the Silotis had not been here, I do not think I could have stayed. Yesterday I was at the 'Folies-Bergères,' and it bored me terribly. The Russian clown Durov brings on 250 dressed-up rats. It is most curious in what forms the Parisians display their Russophile propensities. Neither at the Opera, nor at any of the more serious theatres, is anything Russian performed, and while *we* are giving *Esclarmonde, they* show their goodwill towards Russian art by the medium of Durov and his rats! Truly, it enrages me—I say it frankly—partly on account of my own interests. Why cannot Colonne, who is now the head of the Opera, give my *Pique Dame*, or my new Ballet? In autumn he spoke of doing so, and engaged Petipa with a view to this. But it was all empty talk. . . . You will say : 'Are you not ashamed to be so envious and small-minded?' I am ashamed. Having nothing to do, I am reading Zola's *La bête humaine.* I cannot understand how people can seriously accept Zola as a great writer. Could there be anything more false and improbable than the leading idea of this novel? Of course, there are parts in which the truth is set forth with realism and vitality. But, in the main, it is so artificial that one never for a moment feels any sympathy with the actions or sufferings of the characters. It is simply a story of crime *à la* Gaboriau, larded with obscenities."

His increasing nostalgia and depression of spirits finally caused Tchaikovsky to abandon the concerts in Holland and return to Petersburg about the end of January. There he spent a week with his relatives, and went back to Maidanovo on the 28th (February 9th).

While in Paris, Tchaikovsky completed the revision of his Sextet, and on his return to Russia devoted himself to the orchestration of the *Nut-cracker* Ballet.   He was in haste to finish those numbers from this work, which, in the form of a Suite, were to be played in St. Petersburg on March 7th (19th), instead of the ill-fated ballade, *The Voyevode.*

To Anatol Tchaikovsky.

" MAIDANOVO, *February 9th* (*21st*), 1892.

" I am living very pleasantly here and enjoying the most beautiful of all the winter months.   I love these clear, rather frosty days, when the sun sometimes begins to feel quite warm.   They bring a feeling of spring. . . . Volodya Napravnik is staying with me just now, and has turned out to be excellent company.   He is very musical, and that is a great pleasure.   I often play pianoforte duets with him in the evening, or simply listen while he plays my favourite pieces.   I have taken a house at Klin which will be my future home. . . . Later on I may buy it. Thank God, my financial position is excellent.   *Pique Dame* was given nineteen times in Moscow, and the house was always sold out.   Besides, there are the other operas. There is a good deal due to me from Petersburg."

Late in February Tchaikovsky went to St. Petersburg for a short visit.   Here he received news which made a startling impression upon him.   He had long believed his old governess Fanny to be dead.   Suddenly he was informed that not only was she still alive, but had sent him her greetings.   The first effect of these glad tidings came upon him as a kind of shock.   In his own words, " he felt as though he had been told that his mother had risen from the dead, that the last forty-three years of existence were nothing but a dream, and that he had awakened to find himself in the upstairs rooms of the house at Votinsk." He dreaded, too, lest his dear teacher should now be only the shadow of her old self, a feeble and senile creature to whom death would be a boon. Nevertheless, he wrote to her at once, a kindly letter in which he asked if he could serve her in any way, and enclosed his photograph. Her reply, written in a firm handwriting, in which he recognised her old clearness of style, and the absence of all complaint, greatly assured him. Thus, between teacher and pupil the old affectionate relations were again renewed.

At the Symphony Concert of the Musical Society, on March 7th (19th), Tchaikovsky conducted his *Romeo and Juliet* Overture and the *Nut-cracker* Suite. The new work must have had an unprecedented success, since five out of the six movements had to be repeated.

At a concert given by the School of Jurisprudence, on March 3rd (15th), the composer had the honour of being introduced to the Tsarevich, now the reigning Emperor of Russia.

He returned to Maidanovo on March 9th.

To J. Konius.

"*March 9th (21st)*, 1892.

"In Petersburg I heard a very interesting violinist named (César) Thomson. Do you know him? He has a most remarkable technique; for instance, he plays passages of octaves with a rapidity to which no one has previously attained. I am telling you this on the assumption that you, too, will attempt this artistic feat. It makes a tremendous effect."

To P. Jurgenson.

"*March 18th (30th)*, 1892.

". . . I have no recollection of having promised you that I would never give away any of my manuscripts. I should have been very unwilling to make any such promise, because there are cases in which I could only be very pleased to present one of my scores to the Opera Direction—or in a similar instance.[1] . . . Your reproach that I give them away 'right and left' is without foundation. The Opera Direction, to which I owe my prosperity, is surely worthy to possess one of my scores in its superb library; and the same applies to the Russian Musical Society, from which originated the Conservatoire where I studied, and where I was invariably treated with kindness and indulgence. If you are really going to make it a *sine quâ non* that all my manuscripts must be your property, we must discuss the question . . . and should you convince me that your interests really suffer through the presentation of my scores, I will promise not to do it again. I have so rarely deprived you of the priceless joy of possessing my autograph scrawls! You have so many to the good! I cannot understand why you should be so annoyed!"

At the end of March Tchaikovsky spent a week with his relatives in Petersburg—now a very reduced circle— and afterwards went to Moscow. During the month Tchaikovsky spent in this city Alexis moved all his master's belongings from Maidanovo to the new house at Klin.

To Anatol Tchaikovsky.

"Moscow, *April 23rd (May 5th)*, 1892.

"Moscow is unbearable, for there is scarcely a human being who does not bother me with visits or invitations; or ask me to look at an opera or songs, or—most unpleasant of all—try to get money out of me in one form or another. I shall look back upon this month spent in Moscow as upon a horrid nightmare. So far, I have conducted *Faust* and Rubinstein's *Demon; Oniegin* has yet to come.[2] But what are all these small inconveniences

---

[1] Tchaikovsky presented several autograph scores to the Imperial Public Library, Petersburg.

[2] Tchaikovsky was conducting for the benefit of Prianichnikov and the Kiev Opera Company, then in Moscow.

compared to what you have to do?[1] I have read your last letter with the greatest interest, and felt glad for your sake that you have such a fine opportunity of helping your fellow-creatures. I am sure that you will always cherish the memory of your mission to the famine-stricken Siberians."

XV

After the month's uncongenial work in Moscow, Tchaikovsky rested a few days in Petersburg, until Alexis had everything ready for him in the new home—which was destined to be his last. The house at Klin stood at the furthest end of the little town, and was completely surrounded by fields and woods; two-storied and very roomy. It particularly pleased Tchaikovsky, because—quite an unusual thing in a small country house in Russia—the upper rooms were large, and could be turned into an excellent bedroom and study for a guest. This was perhaps the only improvement upon Maidanovo and Frolovskoe. A small garden, the usual outlook across the country, the neighbourhood of endless kitchen-gardens on the one hand, and of the high-road to Moscow on the other, deprived the spot of all poetic beauty, and only Tchaikovsky, with his very modest demands for comfort or luxury, could have been quite satisfied—even enthusiastic—about the place.

After the composer's death, this house was purchased by his servant, Alexis Safronov, who sold it in 1897 to Modeste Tchaikovsky and his nephew, Vladimir Davidov. At the present moment—in so far as possible—every relic, and all documents connected with the composer, are preserved in the house.

---

[1] Anatol was one of the nine commissioners chosen by the Tsarevich to inquire into the failure of the crops and the sufferings of the starving peasants in Siberia.

To Modeste Tchaikovsky.

"KLIN, *May 20th (June 1st)*, 1892.

" I have spent so much money lately (of course not upon myself alone) that all my hopes of laying aside something for George[1] have vanished."

To Eugen Zabel.

"KLIN, NEAR MOSCOW, *May 24th (June 5th)*, 1892.

" I have just received your esteemed letter, and feel it a pleasant duty to send you an immediate answer, but as I write German very badly I must have recourse to French. I doubt if you will find anything new, interesting, or of any value for your biography in the following lines; but I promise to say quite frankly all that I know and feel about Rubinstein.

" It was in 1858 that I heard the name of Anton Rubinstein for the first time. I was then eighteen, and I had just entered the higher class of the School of Jurisprudence, and only took up music as an amateur. For several years I had taken lessons on Sundays from a very distinguished pianist, M. Rodolphe Kundinger. In those days, never having heard any other virtuoso than my teacher, I believed him, in all sincerity, to be the greatest in the world. One day Kundinger came to the lesson in a very absent-minded mood, and paid little attention to the scales and exercises I was playing. When I asked this admirable man and artist what was the matter, he replied that, the day before, he had heard the pianist Rubinstein, just come from abroad; this man had impressed him so profoundly that he had not yet recovered from the experience, and everything in the way of virtuosity now seemed to him so poor that it was as unbearable to listen to my scales as to hear himself play the piano.

" I knew what a noble and sincere nature Kundinger possessed. I had a very high opinion of his taste and knowledge—and this caused his words to excite my

---

[1] George, the son of Nicholas Tchaikovsky, to whom the composer left his real estate and a life annuity of 1,200 roubles per annum.

imagination and my curiosity in the highest degree.   In
the course of my scholastic year I had the opportunity of
hearing Rubinstein—and not only of *hearing* him, but of
seeing him play and conduct.   I lay stress upon this first
visual impression, because it is my profound conviction
that Rubinstein's prestige is based not only upon his rare
talent, but also upon an irresistible charm which emanates
from his whole personality; so that it is not sufficient to hear
him in order to gain a full impression—one must see him
too.   I heard and saw him.   Like everyone else, I fell
under the spell of his charm.   All the same, I finished my
studies, entered the Government service, and continued to
amuse myself with a little music in my leisure hours.   But
gradually my true vocation made itself felt.   I will spare
you details which have nothing to do with my subject, but
I must tell you that about the time of the foundation of
the St. Petersburg Conservatoire, in September, 1862, I
was no longer a clerk in the Ministry of Justice, but a
young man resolved to devote himself to music, and ready
to face all the difficulties which were predicted by my
relatives, who were displeased that I should voluntarily
abandon a career in which I had made a good start.   I
entered the Conservatoire.   My professors were: Zaremba
for counterpoint and fugue, etc., Anton Rubinstein
(Director) for form and instrumentation.   I remained three
and a half years at the Conservatoire, and during this
time I saw Rubinstein daily, and sometimes several times
a day, except during the vacations.   When I joined the
Conservatoire I was—as I have already told you—an enthusiastic worshipper of Rubinstein.   But when I knew
him better, when I became his pupil and we entered into
daily relations with each other, my enthusiasm for his
personality became even greater.   In him I adored not
only a great pianist and composer, but a man of rare
nobility, frank, loyal, generous, incapable of petty and
vulgar sentiments, clear and right-minded, of infinite goodness—in fact, a man who towered far above the common
herd.   As a teacher, he was of incomparable value.   He
went to work simply, without grand phrases or long dis-
sertations; but always taking his duty seriously.   He was
only once angry with me.   After the holidays I took him

an overture entitled 'The Storm,' in which I had been guilty of all kinds of whims of form and orchestration. He was hurt, and said that it was not for the development of imbeciles that he took the trouble to teach the art of composition.   I left the Conservatoire full of gratitude and admiration for my professor.

"For over three years I saw him daily.   But what were our relations?   He was a great and illustrious musician— I a humble pupil, who only saw him fulfilling his duties, and had no idea of his intimate life.   A great gulf lay between us.   When I left the Conservatoire I hoped that by working courageously, and gradually making my way, I might look forward to the happiness of seeing this gulf bridged over.   I dared to aspire to the honour of becoming the friend of Rubinstein.

"It was not to be.   Nearly thirty years have passed since then, but the gulf is deeper and wider than before. Through my professorship in Moscow I came to be the intimate friend of Nicholas Rubinstein; I had the pleasure of seeing Anton from time to time; I have always continued to care for him intensely, and to regard him as the greatest of artists and the noblest of men, but I never became, and never shall become, his friend.   This great luminary revolves always in my heaven, but while I see its light I feel its remoteness more and more.

"It would be difficult to explain the reason for this. I think, however, that my *amour propre* as a composer has a great deal to do with it.   In my youth I was very impatient to make my way, to win a name and reputation as a gifted composer, and I hoped that Rubinstein—who already enjoyed a high position in the musical world— would help me in my chase for fame.   But painful as it is, I must confess that he did nothing, *absolutely nothing*, to forward my plans or assists my projects.   Certainly he never injured me—he is too noble and generous to put a spoke in the wheel of a comrade—but he never departed from his attitude of reserve and kindly indifference towards me.   This has always been a profound regret. The most probable explanation of this mortifying luke-warmness is that Rubinstein *does not care for my music, that my musical temperament is antipathetic to him.*   Now

I still see him from time to time, and always with pleasure, for this extraordinary man has only to hold out his hand and smile for us to fall at his feet. At the time of his jubilee I had the happiness of going through much trouble and fatigue for him ; his attitude to me is always exceedingly correct, exceedingly polite and kind—but we live very much apart, and I can tell you nothing about his way of life, his views and aims—nothing, in fact, that could be of interest to the future readers of your book.

"I have never received letters from Rubinstein, and never wrote to him but twice in my life, to thank him for having, in recent years, included, among other Russian works in his programmes, one or two of my own.

"I have made a point of fulfilling your wish and telling you all I could about Rubinstein. If I have told too little, it is not my fault, nor that of Anton, but of fatality.

"Forgive my blots and smudges. To-morrow I have to leave home, and have no time to copy this.

"Your devoted

"P. T."

The sole object of the journey mentioned in this letter was to take a cure at Vichy. The catarrh of the stomach from which he suffered had been a trouble to Tchaikovsky for the last twenty years. Once, while staying with Kondratiev at Nizy, the local doctor had recommended him *natron* water. From that time he could not exist without it, and took it in such quantities that he ended by acquiring a kind of taste for it. But it did not cure his complaint, which grew worse and worse, so that in 1876 he had to undergo a course of mineral waters. The catarrhal trouble was not entirely cured, however, but returned at intervals with more or less intensity. About the end of the eighties his condition grew worse. Once during the rehearsals for *Pique Dame*, while staying at the Hôtel Rossiya in St. Petersburg, he sent for his brother Modeste, and declared he "could not live through the night." This turned his thoughts more and more to the "hateful but health-giving Vichy." But the periods of rest after his various tours, and of work in his "hermit's cave" at Klin, were so dear to him that until 1892 he could not make up his mind to revisit this watering-place. This year he only decided to go because the health of Vladimir Davidov equally demanded a cure at Vichy. He hoped in this congenial company to escape his usual home-sickness, and that it might even prove a pleasure to take his nephew abroad.

To Modeste Tchaikovsky.

"VICHY, *June* 19*th* (*July* 1*st*), 1892.

"We have been here a week. It seems more like seven months, and I look forward with horror to the fortnight which remains. I dislike Vichy as much as I did sixteen years ago, but I think the waters will do me good. In any case I feel sure Bob will benefit by them."

To P. Jurgenson.

"VICHY, *July* 1*st* (13*th*), 1892.

"I only possess one short note from Liszt, which is of so little importance that it is not worth your while to send it to La Mara. Liszt was a good fellow, and ready to respond to everyone who paid court to him. But as I never toadied to him, or any other celebrity, we never got into correspondence. I think he really preferred Messrs. Cui and Co., who went on pilgrimages to Weimar, and he was more in sympathy with their music than with mine. As far as I know, Liszt was not particularly interested in my works."

By July 9th (21st) Tchaikovsky and his nephew were back in Petersburg, from whence he travelled almost immediately to Klin, where he busied himself with the new Symphony (No. 6) which he wished to have ready in August.

At the outset of his career Tchaikovsky was somewhat indifferent as to the manner in which his works were

published. He troubled very little about the quality of
the pianoforte arrangements of his operas and symphonic
works, and still less about printers' errors. About the end
of the seventies, however, he entirely changed his attitude,
and henceforth became more and more particular and
insistent in his demands respecting the pianoforte arrangements and correction of his compositions. Quite half his
correspondence with Jurgenson is taken up with these
matters. . . . His requirements constantly increased. No
one could entirely satisfy him. The cleverest arrangers,
such as Klindworth, Taneiev, and Siloti did not please
him, because they made their arrangements too difficult
for amateurs. He was also impatient at the slowness
with which they worked.

Now that for a year and a half Tchaikovsky has been
in his grave, it is easy to attribute to certain events in his
life (which passed unnoticed at the time) a kind of
prophetic significance. His special and exclusive care as
to the editing and publishing of his works in 1892 may,
however, be compared to the preparations which a man
makes for a long journey, when he is as much occupied
with what lies before him as with what he is leaving
behind. He strives to finish what is unfinished, and to
leave all in such a condition that he can face the unknown
with a quiet conscience.

The words Tchaikovsky addressed to Jurgenson with
reference to the Third Suite—"If all my best works were
published in this style I might depart in peace"—offer
some justification for my simile.

In the autumn of 1892 he undertook the entire correction of the orchestral parts of *Iolanthe* and the *Nut-
cracker* Ballet; the improvements and corrections of the
pianoforte arrangement (two hands) of *Iolanthe;* the
corrections of the pianoforte score of the Opera and
Ballet, and a simplified pianoforte arrangement of the
latter.

Tchaikovsky so often speaks in his letters of his dislike to this kind of work that he must have needed extraordinary self-abnegation to take this heavy burden upon his shoulders.

As with the spirits in Dante's *Inferno*, the dread of their torments by the will of divine justice "*si volge in disio*,"[1] so the energy with which Tchaikovsky attacked his task turned to a morbid, passionate excitement. "Corrections, corrections! More, more! For Heaven's sake, corrections!" he cries in his letters to Jurgenson, so that the casual reader might take for an intense desire that which was, in reality, only a worry to him, as the following letter shows.

To S. Taneiev.

"KLIN, *July* 13*th* (25*th*), 1892.

"Just now I am busy looking through the pianoforte score of *Iolanthe*. It bothers and annoys me indescribably. Before I went abroad in May I had sketched the first movement and finale of a Symphony. Abroad it did not progress in the least, and now I have no time for it."

To Anna Merkling.

"KLIN, *July* 17*th* (29*th*), 1892.

"DEAREST ANNA,—I have received your letter with the little additional note from dear Katy.[2] What extraordinary people you are! How can you imagine it would be a great pleasure for you if I were to come on a visit? If I were cheerful and pleasant company that would be a different matter. But I am no use for conversational purposes, and am often out of spirits, nor have I any resources in myself. I cannot help thinking that if I came you might afterwards say to yourselves: 'This old fool, we awaited him with such impatience, and he is not a bit nice after all!' Anna, I really do want to come to

---

[1] "Is changed to desire."

[2] Katharine Oboukhov, a second cousin of Tchaikovsky.

the Oboukhovs', but I cannot positively say 'yes' at present. . . . It will be sad to part from Bob, who is dearer to me than ever, since we have been inseparable companions for the last six weeks."

To Modeste Tchaikovsky.

"KLIN, *July* 17*th* (29*th*), 1892.

". . . I am sorry your comedy is ineffective and not suitable for the stage. Why do you think so? Authors are never good judges of their own work. Flaubert's letters—which I enjoy very much at present—are very curious in this respect. I think there is no more sympathetic personality in all the world of literature. A hero and martyr to his art. And so wise! I have found some astonishing answers to my questionings as to God and religion in his book."

At the end of July Russian art suffered a great loss in the death of the connoisseur and wealthy patron, S. M. Tretiakov, who had been Nicholas Rubinstein's right hand in the founding of the Moscow Conservatoire. To Tchaikovsky, Tretiakov's somewhat sudden end came as a severe blow, and he immediately travelled to Moscow to be present at the funeral of his friend.

A pleasanter incident during this summer of hard work came in the form of an invitation to conduct a concert at the Vienna Exhibition. "It is an advantage," he wrote to his brother Modeste, "because so far—on account of Hanslick—Vienna has been hostile to me. I should like to overcome this unfriendly opinion."

At last, at the very end of August, the vast accumulation of proof-correcting was finished, which, as he himself said, would have almost driven him out of his mind, but for his regular and healthy way of life. "Even in dreams," he wrote to Vladimir Davidov, "I see corrections, and flats and sharps that refuse to do what they are ordered. . . . I should like to see you at Verbovka after Vienna, but Sophie Menter, who is coming to my concert there, has given me a pressing invitation to her castle. Three times already I have broken my promise to go to Itter. I am really interested to see this 'marvel,' as everyone calls the castle."

In the course of this year, at the suggestion of the Grand Duke Constantine Constantinovich, President of the Academy of Sciences, Tchaikovsky was invited by the academician Y. K. Grote to contribute to the new *Dictionary of the Russian Language*, then appearing in a second edition. Tchaikovsky's duties were limited to the superintendence of musical words, but he was flattered by his connection with such an important scientific work.

XVI

1892–1893

Tchaikovsky never travelled so much as during the foregoing season. It is true he was always fond of moving about. He could not remain long in one spot; but this was chiefly because it always seemed to him that "every place is better than the one in which we are." Paris, Kamenka, Clarens, Rome, Brailov, Simaki, Tiflis—all in turn were his favourite resorts, which he was delighted to visit and equally pleased to quit. But apart from the ultimate goal, travelling in itself was an enjoyment rather than a dread to Tchaikovsky.

From 1885, when he resolved "no longer to avoid mankind, but to keep myself before the world so long as it needs me," his journeys became more frequent. When he began to conduct his own compositions in 1887, his journeys were undertaken with a fresh object : the propagation of his works abroad. As his fame increased, so also did the number of those who wished to hear him

interpret his own music, and thus it was natural that by
1892 the number of his journeys was far greater than it
had been ten years earlier.

When Tchaikovsky started upon his first concert tour
he undoubtedly did violence to his "actual self," and did
not look forward with pleasure, but rather with dread, to
what lay before him. At the same time he was full of the
expectation of happy impressions and brilliant results,
and was firmly convinced of the importance of his undertaking, both for his own fame and for the cause of Russian
art in general.

The events of his first tour would not have disappointed
even a man less modest than Tchaikovsky. He had many
consoling experiences, beginning with the discovery that
he was better known abroad than he had hitherto suspected. His reception in Prague, with its "moment of
absolute happiness," the sensation in Paris, the attention
and respect with which he was received in Germany, all
far surpassed his expectations. Nevertheless, he returned
disillusioned, not by what had taken place, but by the price
he had paid for his happiness.

But no sooner home again, than he forgot all he had
gone through, and was planning his second tour with
evident enjoyment.

This inexplicable discontent and disenchantment may,
he thought, have been the result of a passing mood. The
worst of his fears—the appearance before a crowd of
foreigners—was over. He believed his second appearance
would be far less painful, and expected even happier
impressions than on his first tour. He was mistaken.
He merely awoke to the "uselessness" of the sacrifice he
was making for popularity's sake, and he asked himself
whether it would not be better to stay at home and work.
His belief in the importance of the undertaking vanished,
and with it the whole reason for doing violence to his
nature. In the early part of 1890 he declined all engage-

ments to travel, and devoted himself to composition. But
by the end of the year Tchaikovsky seems to have forgotten all the lessons of his two concert tours, for he
began once more to conduct in Russia and abroad.
Every journey cost him keener pangs of home-sickness,
and each time he vowed it should be the last. Yet no
sooner had he reached home again, than he began planning
yet another tour. It seemed as though he had become
the victim of some blind force which drove him hither and
thither at will. This power was not merely complaisance
to the demands of others, nor his old passion for travelling, nor the fulfilment of a duty, nor yet the pursuit of
applause; still less was it the outcome of a desire for
material gain. This mysterious force had its source in an
inexplicable, restless, despondent condition of mind, which
sought appeasement in any kind of distraction. I cannot
explain it as a premonition of his approaching death;
there are no grounds whatever for such a supposition.
Nor will I, in any case, take upon myself to solve the
problem of my brother's last psychological development.
I will only call attention to the fact that he passed
through a similar phase before every decisive change in
his life. As at the beginning of the sixties, when he
chose a musical career, and in 1885, when he resolved to
" show himself in the eyes of the world," so also at this
juncture, we are conscious of a feeling *that things could
not have gone on much longer;* we feel on the brink of a
change, as though something had come to an end, and was
giving place to a new and unknown presence.

His death, which came to solve the problem, seemed
fortuitous. Yet it is clear to me that it came at a moment
when things could not have gone on much longer; nor can I
shake off the impression that the years 1892 and 1893
were the dark harbingers of a new and serene epoch.

An unpleasant surprise awaited Tchaikovsky in Vienna.
The concert, in connection with the Exhibition, which he

had been engaged to conduct was to be given, so he discovered, in what was practically a large restaurant, reeking
of cookery and the fumes of beer and tobacco. The composer immediately declined to fulfil his contract, unless the
tables were removed and the room converted into something approaching a concert-hall. Moreover, the orchestra,
though not very bad, was ridiculously small. Tchaikovsky's friends—Door, Sophie Menter, and Sapellnikov
—were indignant at the whole proceeding, and realising
the unpleasantness of his position, he decided to disregard
his contract, and started with Mme. Menter for her castle
at Itter.

Professor Door has related his reminiscences of Tchaikovsky's unlucky visit to Vienna,[1] when he met his old
friend again after a long separation. " I was shocked at
his appearance," he writes, " for he had aged so much that
I only recognised him by his wonderful blue eyes. A man
old at fifty! His delicate constitution had suffered terribly
from his incessant creative work. We spoke of old days,
and I asked him how he now got on in Petersburg. He
replied that he was so overwhelmed with all kinds of
attentions that he was perpetually embarrassed by them,
and had but one trouble, which was that he never saw anything of Rubinstein, whom he had loved and respected
from his student days. ' Do what I will,' he said, ' I can
get no hold on him; he escapes me like an eel.' I laughed
and said : ' Do not take the great man's ways too much to
heart; he has his weaknesses like other mortals. Rubinstein, a distinctly lyrical temperament, has never had any
great success in dramatic music, and avoids everyone who
has made a name in this sphere of art. Comfort yourself,
dear friend; he cut Richard Wagner and many others
besides.' ' But,' he broke in with indignation, ' how can
you compare me with Wagner and many others who have

---

[1] *Neue Freie Presse*, March 30th, 1901. The above is quoted from the
German edition of *The Life and Letters of Tchaikovsky.*

created immortal works?' 'Oh, as to immortality,' I replied, ' I will tell you a good story about Brahms. Once when this question was being discussed, Brahms said to me: 'Yes, immortality is a fine thing, if only one knew how long it would last.' Tchaikovsky laughed heartily over this ' bull,' and his cheerfulness seemed quite restored. . . . After three hours' rehearsal he was greatly exhausted. He descended with great difficulty from the conductor's desk, the perspiration stood in beads on his forehead, and he hurried into his fur-lined coat, although it was as warm as a summer's day. He rested for a quarter of an hour, and then left with Sophie Menter and Sapellnikov."

During this short visit to Vienna, Tchaikovsky stayed in the same hotel as Pietro Mascagni, and their rooms actually adjoined. The Italian composer was then the most fêted and popular man in Vienna. As we have already mentioned, Tchaikovsky admired *Cavalleria Rusticana*. The libretto appealed to him in the first place, but he recognised much promising talent in the music. The rapidity with which the young musician had become the idol of the Western musical world did not in the least provoke Tchaikovsky's envy ; on the contrary, he was interested in the Italian composer, and drawn to him. Accident having brought him into such near neighbourhood, it occurred to him to make the acquaintance of his young colleague. But when he found himself confronted in the passage with a whole row of admirers, all awaiting an audience with the *maestro*, he resolved to spare him at least one superfluous visitor.

The Castle of Itter, which belongs to Madame Sophie Menter, is situated in Tyrol, a few hours from Munich. Besides its wonderfully picturesque situation, it has acquired a kind of reflected glory, not only from the reputation of its owner, but because Liszt often stayed there.

To Modeste Tchaikovsky.

"ITTER, *September* 15*th* (27*th*), 1892.

"... Itter deserves its reputation. It is a devilish pretty nest. My rooms—I occupy a whole floor—are very fine, but a curious mixture of grandeur and bad taste: luxurious furniture, a wonderful inlaid bedstead and—some vile oleographs. But this does not affect me much. The great thing is the exquisite, picturesque neighbourhood. Peace and stillness, and not a trace of any other visitors. I am fond of Sapellnikov and Menter, and, altogether, I have not felt more comfortable for a long while. I shall stay five days longer and return to 'Peter' by Salzburg (where I want to see the Mozart Museum) and Prague (where I stay for the performance of *Pique Dame*). On the 25th (October 7th) I hope to put in an appearance upon the Quay Fontanka. The chief drawback here is that I get neither letters nor papers and hear nothing about Russia or any of you."

The performance of *Pique Dame* in Prague did not take place until October 8th. The opera, judging from the accounts of those present, had a brilliant success, and the composer was repeatedly recalled. Between 1892–1902 *Pique Dame* was given on forty-one occasions. When we bear in mind that opera is only given three times a week at the National Theatre in Prague, and that the chief object of this enterprise is to forward the interests of Czechish art, this number of performances points to the fact that the success of *Pique Dame* has proved as lasting as it was enthusiastic.

Tchaikovsky returned to Klin about the first week in October (Russian style), and was soon busy with preparations for the performance of *Iolanthe* in St. Petersburg. On the 28th (November 9th) he left home for the capital, in order to superintend the rehearsals of the new opera. Soon after his arrival he received two interesting communications. The first informed him that he had been elected a Corresponding Member of the French Academy; the second, from the University of Cambridge, invited him to accept the title of Doctor of Music, *honoris causa*, on condition that he attended in person to receive the degree at the hands of the Vice-Chancellor.

Tchaikovsky acknowledged the first honour, and expressed his readiness to conform to the conditions of the second.

At the same time he had a further cause for congratulation in the success of his Sextet, *Souvenir de Florence*, which was played for the first time in public at the St. Petersburg Chamber Music Union, on November 25th (December 7th). The players were : E. Albrecht, Hille, Hildebrandt, Heine, Wierzbilowiez, and A. Kouznietsov. This time all were delighted : the performers, the audience, and the composer himself. The medal of the Union was presented to Tchaikovsky amid unanimous applause. During this visit the composer sat to the well-known sculptor, E. Günsburg, for a statuette which, in spite of its artistic value, is not successful as a likeness.

To Anatol Tchaikovsky.

" PETERSBURG, *November 24th (December 6th)*, 1892.

" . . . Modeste's play was given yesterday.[1] It was a complete failure, which does not surprise me in the least, for it is much too subtle for the public at the Alexander Theatre. It does not matter : may it be a lesson to Modeste. The pursuit of the unattainable hinders him from his real business—to write plays in the accepted form. The rehearsals for *Iolanthe* and the Ballet are endlessly dragged out. The Emperor will be present on the 5th, and the first public performance will take place the following day."

During this visit to the capital Tchaikovsky did his utmost to forward the interests of his friends, Taneiev

---

[1] *A Day in St. Petersburg.*

and Arensky, as will be seen from the following extract from a letter to the former, respecting the performance of his *Orestes* :—

" Vsievolojsky (Director of the Opera) took Napravnik aside and consulted him as to the advisability of proposing *Orestes* to the Emperor for next season. . . . I suggested that you should be sent for, in order to play over the work in their presence. Vsievolojsky was afraid if you were put to this trouble you might feel hurt should the matter fall through. I ventured to say that, as a true philosopher, you would not lose heart if nothing came of it. . . . I spoke not less eloquently of Arensky, but so far without success."

On December 5th (17th) *Iolanthe* and the *Nut-cracker* Ballet were given in the presence of the Imperial Court. The opera was conducted by Napravnik. The Figners distinguished themselves by their admirable interpretations of the parts of Vaudemont and Iolanthe. The scenery and costumes were beautiful. Nevertheless the work was only accorded a *succès d'estime*. The chief reason for this —according to Modeste Tchaikovsky—was the prolixity of the libretto and its lack of scenic interest.

The Ballet—admirably conducted by Drigo—was brilliantly staged, and received with considerable applause ; yet the impression left by the first night was not wholly favourable. The subject, which differed greatly from the conventional ballet programme, was not entirely to blame. The illness of the talented ballet-master, Petipa, and the substitution of a man of far less skill and imagination, probably accounted for the comparative failure of the work. The delicate beauty of the music did not appeal to the public on a first hearing, and some time elapsed before the *Nut-cracker* became a favourite item in the repertory.

The attitude of the Press appears from the following letter from the composer to Anatol, dated Petersburg, December 10th (22nd), 1892 :—

"This is the fourth day on which all the papers have been cutting up both my latest creations. . . . It is not the first time. The abuse does not annoy me in the least, and yet—as always under these circumstances—I am in a hateful frame of mind. When one has lived in expectation of an important event, as soon as it is over there comes a kind of apathy and disinclination for work, while the emptiness and futility of all our efforts becomes so evident. . . . The day after to-morrow I leave for Berlin. There I shall decide where to go for a rest (most probably to Nice). On December 29th I shall be in Brussels. From thence I shall go to Paris, and afterwards to see Mlle. Fanny at Montbeillard. About the 10th January I have to conduct the concerts at Odessa. At the end of the month I shall be in Petersburg. Later I shall spend some time in Klin, and go to you in Lent."

To *Vladimir Davidov.*

"BERLIN, *December* 16*th* (28*th*), 1892.

"Here I am, still in Berlin. To-day I have given myself up to serious reflections, which will have important results. I have been carefully, and as it were objectively, analysing my Symphony, which luckily I have not yet orchestrated and given to the world. The impression was not flattering : the work is written for the sake of writing, and is not interesting or moving. I ought to put it aside and forget it. . . . Am I done for and dried up? Perhaps there is yet some subject which could inspire me ; but I ought to compose no more absolute music, symphony or chamber works. To live without work would weary me. What am I to do? Fold my hands as far as composition is concerned and try to forget it? It is difficult to decide. I think, and think, and do not know how to settle the question. In any case, the outlook has not been cheerful the last three days."

To *Modeste Tchaikovsky.*

"BÂLE, *December* 19*th* (31*st*), 1902.

" . . . I have nothing to write about but fits of weeping. Really it is surprising that this phenomenal, deadly

home-sickness does not drive me mad. Since this psychological phase grows stronger with every journey abroad, in
future I shall never travel alone, even for a short time. To-
morrow this feeling will give place to another (scarcely?)
less painful emotion. I am going to Montbeillard, and I
must confess to a morbid fear and horror, as though I were
entering the kingdom of the dead and the world of those
who had long since vanished."

To his brother, Nicholas Ilich Tchaikovsky.

" PARIS, *December 22nd (January 3rd)*, 1892.

" . . . I wrote to Mlle. Fanny from Bâle to let her know
the time of my arrival, so that she should not be upset by
my unexpected appearance. I reached Montbeillard at
3 p.m. on January 1st (new style), and went straight to
her house. She lives in a quiet street in this little town,
which is so quiet that it might be compared to one of our
own Russian 'district' towns. The house contains but
six rooms—two on each floor—and belongs to Fanny and
her sister. Here they were born, and have spent their
whole lives. Mlle. Fanny came to the door, and I knew
her at once. She does not look her seventy years, and,
curiously enough, has altered very little on the whole.
The same high-coloured complexion and brown eyes,
and her hair is not very grey. She has grown much
stouter. I had dreaded tears and an affecting scene,
but there was nothing of the sort. She greeted me
as though we had not met for a year—joyfully and
tenderly, but quite simply. It soon became clear to me
why our parents, and we ourselves, were so fond of her.
She is a remarkably clever, sympathetic creature, who
seems to breathe an atmosphere of kindliness and integrity.
Naturally we started upon reminiscences, and she recalled a number of interesting details from our childhood.
Then she showed me our copybooks, my exercises, your
letters and mine, and—what was of the greatest interest to
me—a few dear, kind letters from our mother. I cannot
tell you what a strange and wonderful feeling came over
me while listening to her recollections and looking over
these letters and books. The past rose up so clearly before

me that I seemed to inhale the air of Votinsk and hear my mother's voice distinctly. . . . When she asked me which of my brothers I loved best, I replied evasively that I was equally fond of them all. At which she was a little indignant, and said that, as my playmate in childhood, I ought to care most for you. And truly at that moment I felt I loved you intensely, because you had shared all my youthful joys. I stayed with her from three until eight o'clock, without noticing how time went. I spent the whole of the next day in her society. . . .

" She gave me a beautiful letter from my mother, in which she writes of you with special tenderness. I will show it to you. The two sisters do not live luxuriously— but comfortably. Fanny's sister also lived a long time in Russia, and does not speak the language badly. Both of them still teach. They are known to the whole town, for they have taught all the educated people there, and are universally loved and respected. In the evening I embraced Fanny when I took leave of her, and promised to return some day. . . ."

To Modeste Tchaikovsky.

"PARIS, *January 4th* (16th), 1892.

". . . After my brilliant concert in Brussels I returned here yesterday. The orchestra was very good, but not highly disciplined. I was very cordially received, but this did not make things any easier for me. I suffered equally from agitation and the anguish of home-sickness. During the interval Gevaert, as President of the Artists' Benevolent Association, made a speech before the assembled orchestra, in which he thanked me on behalf of this society. As the concert was given in aid of a charity, I declined to accept any fee, which touched the artists very deeply."

The programme of the Brussels concert included, among other compositions by Tchaikovsky, the Pianoforte Concerto, op. 23 (Rummel as soloist), the *Nut-cracker* Suite, and the Overture " *1812.*"

On January 12th (24th), 1893, Tchaikovsky arrived in Odessa, where for nearly a fortnight he was fêted with such enthusiasm that even the Prague festivities of 1888 dwindled into insignificance compared with these experiences.

The ovations began the day after his arrival, when, on his appearance at the rehearsal of *Pique Dame*, he was welcomed by the theatrical direction and the entire opera company. Not contented with vociferous cheering, he was "chaired" and borne around in triumph, much to his discomfort. On the 16th he conducted the following works at the concert of the Musical Society: *The Tempest*, the Andante cantabile from the Quartet, op. 11, and the *Nutcracker* Suite. The local section of the Musical Society presented him with a bâton, and the musicians gave him a laurel wreath. Some numbers on the programme had to be repeated three times in response to the vociferous applause.

This triumph was followed by a series of others: the first performance of *Pique Dame*, a soirée in his honour at the English Club, a charity concert, given by the Slavonic Association, and a second concert of the Musical Society, at which the Overture "*1812*" had to be repeated *da capo*.

Tchaikovsky left Odessa on January 25th (February 6th), and returned to Klin to recover from the strain and fatigue of his visit.

Among the many occupations which overwhelmed him there, he found time to sit to Kouznietsov for his portrait. "Although the artist knew nothing of Tchaikovsky's inner life," says Modeste, "he has succeeded, thanks to the promptings of inspiration, in divining all the tragedy of that mental and spiritual phase through which the composer was passing at that time, and has rendered it with profound actuality. Knowing my brother as I do, I can affirm that no truer, more living likeness of him exists. There are a few slight deviations from strict truth in the delineation of the features; but they do not detract from the portrait as a whole, and I would not on any account have them corrected. Perhaps the vitality which breathes from the picture has been purchased at the price of these small defects."

Kouznietsov presented the portrait to Tchaikovsky, who, however, declined to accept it, partly because he could not endure a picture of himself upon his own walls, but chiefly because he did not consider himself justified in preventing the artist from making something out of his work. The portrait is now in the Tretiakov Gallery, Moscow.

To Modeste Tchaikovsky.

"KLIN, *February* 5*th* (17*th*), 1893.

"... My journey from Kamenka here was not very propitious. I was taken so ill in the carriage that I frightened my fellow-passengers by becoming delirious, and had to stop at Kharkov. After taking my usual remedies, and a long sleep, I awoke quite well in the morning. . . .

"Next week I must pay a visit to Vladimir Shilovsky. The prospect fills me with fear and agitation. Tell me, has he greatly changed? How is the dropsy? I am afraid of a scene, and altogether dread our meeting. Is there really no hope for him? Answer these questions."

Vladimir Shilovsky, who had played an important part in my brother's life some twenty years earlier, had very rarely come in contact with his old teacher since his marriage with the only remaining child of Count Vassiliev. There had been no breach between them, but their lives had run in opposite directions. In January, 1893, I heard that Vladimir Shilovsky was seriously ill. I informed Peter Ilich, who visited his old pupil in Moscow, and was touched by the joy he showed at their reunion, and by the calm self-control with which he spoke of his hopeless condition. The old intimacy was renewed, and only ended with the Count's death in June, 1893.

XVII

Tchaikovsky's life moved in spiral convolutions. At every turn his way seemed to lie through the same spiritual phases. The alternations of light and shade succeeded each other with a corresponding regularity. When speaking of the depression which darkened his last years, I emphasised the fact that he had gone through a similar condition of mind before every decisive change in his existence. The acute moral tension which preceded his retirement from the Ministry of Justice was followed by the calm and happy summer of 1862. To his glad and hopeful mood at the beginning of 1877 succeeded the crisis which compelled him to go abroad for rest and change. So, too, this year, 1893, opened with a period of serene content, for which the creation of his Sixth, or so-called "Pathetic," Symphony was mainly accountable. The composition of this work seems to have been an act of exorcism, whereby he cast out all the dark spirits which had possessed him in the preceding years.

The first mention of this Symphony occurs in a letter to his brother Anatol, dated February 10th (22nd), 1893, in which he speaks of being completely absorbed in his new project. The following day, writing to Vladimir Davidov, he enters into fuller particulars :—

"I must tell you how happy I am about my work. As you know, I destroyed a Symphony which I had partly composed and orchestrated in the autumn. I did wisely, for it contained little that was really fine—an empty pattern of sounds without any inspiration. Just as I was starting on my journey (the visit to Paris in December, 1892) the idea came to me for a new Symphony. This time with a programme; but a programme of a kind which remains an enigma to all—let them guess it who can. The work will be entitled "A Programme Symphony" (No. 6). This programme is penetrated by subjective sentiment. During my journey, while composing it in my mind, I frequently shed tears. Now I am home again I have settled down to sketch out the work, and it goes with such ardour that in less than four days I have completed the first movement, while the rest of the Symphony is clearly outlined in my head. There will be much that is novel as regards form in this work. For instance, the Finale will not be a great Allegro, but an Adagio of considerable dimensions. You cannot imagine what joy I feel at the conviction that my day is not yet over, and that I may still accomplish much. Perhaps I may be mistaken, but it does not seem likely. Do not speak of this to anyone but Modeste."

After an interval of three years Tchaikovsky once more conducted a concert of the Moscow Musical Society on February 14th (26th). This was in response to a letter from Safonov begging him to make up their former personal differences and to take part again in the work of Nicholas Rubinstein, of imperishable memory. The Overture-Fantasia *Hamlet* was played at this concert for the first time in Moscow.

About the end of February Tchaikovsky again returned to Moscow to hear a new Suite *From Childhood's Days*, by George Konius, which pleased him very much. Through the influence of the Grand Duke Constantine, Tchaikovsky succeeded in getting an annual pension of 1,200 roubles (£120) for the struggling young composer.

At this time he suffered from a terrible attack of headache, which never left him, and threatened to become a chronic ailment. It departed, however, with extraordinary suddenness on the fourteenth day after the first paroxysm.

On March 11th (23rd) he visited Kharkov, where he remained till the 16th (28th), and enjoyed a series of triumphs similar to those he had experienced in Odessa earlier in the year.

By March 18th (30th) Tchaikovsky was back in Klin. Here he received news that Ippolitov-Ivanov was leaving

Tiflis to join the Moscow Conservatoire. In his answer, which is hardly a letter of congratulation, Tchaikovsky refers to his last Symphony, which he does not *intend to tear up*, to the sketch of a new Pianoforte Concerto, and to several pieces for piano which he hopes to compose in the near future.

He spent the Easter holidays in the society of his relatives and intimate friends in Petersburg, and, but for the hopeless illness of his oldest friend, the poet Apukhtin, this visit would have been a very quiet and cheerful interlude in his life.

To Vladimir Davidov.

"KLIN, *April* 15*th* (27*th*), 1893.

"I am engaged in making musical pancakes.[1] To-day I have tossed the tenth. It is remarkable ; the more I do, the easier and pleasanter the occupation grows. At first it was uphill work, and the first two pieces are the outcome of a great effort of will; but now I can scarcely fix the ideas in my mind, they succeed each other with such rapidity. If I could spend a whole year in the country, and my publisher was prepared to take all I composed, I might—if I chose to work *à la* Leikin—make about 36,000 roubles a year!"

To Modeste Tchaikovsky.

"MOSCOW, *April* 22*nd* (*May* 4*th*), 1893.

"Ah, dear Modi, I do not believe I shall get the thirty pieces written! I have finished eighteen in fifteen days and brought them with me to Moscow. But now I must stay here four days (the performance at the Conservatoire, one morning with the Synodal singers, and my birthday with old friends), then go on to Nijny and return here in time for the first performance of Rakhmaninov's *Aleko*. I

---

[1] Jurgenson had commissioned Tchaikovsky to send him as many songs and pianoforte pieces as he liked, and while awaiting at Klin the day of his departure for London, the composer determined to write one number every day.

shall not be home before the 30th (May 12th), and I start on the 10th (22nd) of May, . . . but perhaps I may knock off a few songs very quickly."

To P. Jurgenson.

" KLIN, *May 2nd,* 1893.

" I intended to ask my old fee—100 roubles for each number. Now, in consequence of the number of paying propositions made to me (I swear it is true), I must put up my prices a little. But I will not forget that you have also published my greater works, from which you will not derive any profit for a long time to come. So let it stand at the old fee. . . . It is a pity I had not more time for writing.

" Should anything happen to Karl,[1] and the family be in need, do not hesitate to help them out of my present, or future, funds. . . ."

To P. Jurgenson.

" PETERSBURG, *May 6th* (18*th*), 1893.

". . . . As regards my fee, I must tell you that Gutheil has never made me any proposals, because all Russian publishers know that I am not to be caught by any bait they may offer. But abroad my relations with you are not understood, therefore I often receive advances from other countries. Many of them (André of Offenbach) have offered me far higher fees than I get from you (of course, I am only speaking of short compositions). . . . I cannot lose sight of the fact that many of my symphonies and operas have cost you more than they bring in. Of course, they will sell better some day, but at present I do not like to bleed you. You are not as rich as an Abraham, a Schott, or a Simrock. . . . If (on your honour) you do not consider it too much to give me another fifty, I will agree to it. Naturally I shall be very glad, for this has been a heavy year.

" I want nothing for the Mozart,[2] because I have not put much of myself into it."

---

[1] Karl Albrecht, who was on his death-bed.
[2] The Quartet *Night.*

2 Z

To Vladimir Davidov.

"BERLIN, *May* 15*th* (27*th*), 1893.

". . . . This time I wept and suffered more than ever, perhaps because I let my thoughts dwell too much on our last year's journey. It is purely a psychophysical pheno- menon! And how I loathe trains, the atmosphere of railway carriages, and fellow-travellers! . . . I travel too much, that is why I dislike it more and more. It is quite green here, and flowers blooming everywhere—but it does not give me any pleasure, and I am only conscious of an incredible and overwhelming home-sickness."

To Modeste Tchaikovsky.

"LONDON, *May* 17*th* (29*th*), 1893.

"I arrived here early this morning. I had some difficulty to find a room—all the hotels are packed. The concert takes place on May 20th (June 1st), after which I must rush around for about a week, for the Cambridge ceremony does not come off until the 11th or 12th, and on the 13th —our 1st of June—I begin my homeward journey. I am continually thinking of you all. I never realise all my affection for you so much as when away from home, and oppressed with loneliness and nostalgia."

To Vladimir Davidov.

"LONDON, *May* 17*th* (29*th*), 1893.

"Is it not strange that of my own free will I have elected to undergo this torture? What fiend can have suggested it to me? Several times during my journey yesterday I resolved to throw up the whole thing and turn tail. But what a disgrace to turn back for no good reason! Yesterday I suffered so much that I could neither sleep nor eat, which is very unusual for me. I suffer not only from torments which cannot be put into words (there is one place in my new Symphony—the Sixth—where they seem to me adequately expressed), but from a dislike to strangers, and an indefinable terror— though of what the devil only knows. This state makes itself felt by internal pains and loss of power in my legs. However, it is for the last time in my life. Only for a heap of money will I ever go anywhere again, and never for more than three days at a time. And to think I must kick my heels here for another fortnight!! It seems like eternity. I arrived early this morning, *viâ* Cologne and Ostend. The crossing took three hours, but it was not rough. . . . On the steps of my hotel I met the French pianist Diemer, and to my great astonishment found myself delighted to see him. He is an old acquaintance, and very well disposed towards me. In consequence of our meeting I had to go to his 'Recital.' Saint-Saens also takes part in the concert at which I am conducting."

Profiting by the presence in England of the composers who were about to receive the honorary degree at Cambridge, the Philharmonic Society gave two concerts in which they took part. At the first of these Tchaikovsky conducted his Fourth Symphony with brilliant success. According to the Press notices, none of his works previously performed had pleased so well, or added so much to his reputation in England.

To Modeste Tchaikovsky.

"LONDON, *May 22nd (June 3rd)*, 1893.

" . . . The concert was brilliant. It was unanimously agreed that I had a real triumph, so that Saint-Saens, who followed me, suffered somewhat from my unusual success. Of course, this is pleasant enough, but what an infliction London life is during the 'season'! Luncheons and dinners which last an interminable time. Yesterday the directors of the Philharmonic gave a dinner at the Westminster Club in honour of Saint-Saens and myself. It was very smart and luxurious; we sat down to table at seven and rose at 11.30 p.m. (I am not exaggerating). Besides this I am invited to concerts daily and cannot refuse to go. To-day, for instance, I went to Sarasate's concert. He is most kind and amiable to me. Last time I was here in the winter and in bad weather, so that I got no idea of what the town is really like. The devil knows Paris is a mere village compared to London! Walking in Regent Street and Hyde Park, one sees so many carriages, so much splendid and luxurious equipment, that the eye is fairly dazzled. I have been to afternoon tea at the Embassy. Our secretary at the Embassy here, Sazonov, is a charming man. What a number of people I see, and how tired I get! In the morning I suffer a great deal from depression, and later I feel in a kind of daze. I have but one thought: to get it all over. . . . At Cambridge I will keep a full diary. It seems to me it will be a very droll business. Grieg is ill. All the other recipients will come. . . ."

To Modeste Tchaikovsky.

"LONDON, *May 29th (June 10th)*, 1893.

"This letter will not be in time to reach you in 'Peter.' . . . I have not had a chance of writing. This is an infernal life. Not a moment's peace: perpetual agitation, dread, home-sickness, fatigue. However, the hour of escape is at hand. Besides which, I must say I find many excellent folks here, who show me every kind of attention. All the doctors designate have now arrived except Grieg, who is too ill. Next to Saint-Saens, Boito appeals most to me. Bruch is an unsympathetic, inflated sort of personage. I go to Cambridge the day after to-morrow, and do not stay at an hotel, but in the house of Dr. Maitland, who has written me a very kind letter of invitation. I shall only be there one night. On the day of our arrival there will be a concert and dinner, and on the following day—the ceremony. By four o'clock it will be all over."

In 1893, in consequence of the fiftieth anniversary of the Cambridge University Musical Society, the list of those who received the Doctor's degree, *honoris causa*, was distinguished by an unusual number of musicians: Tchaikovsky, Saint-Saëns, Boito, Max Bruch and Edvard Grieg.

The festivities at Cambridge began on June 12th (new

style) with a concert, the programme of which included a work by each of the five recipients of the musical degree, and one by Dr. Stanford,[1] the director of the society.

The programme was as follows : (1) Fragment from *Odysseus* for soli, chorus, and orchestra (Max Bruch); (2) Fantasia for pianoforte and orchestra, *Africa*, the composer at the piano (Saint-Saëns); (3) Prologue from *Mefistofele* for solo, chorus, and orchestra (Boïto); (4) Symphonic poem, *Francesca da Rimini* (op. 32), (Tchaikovsky); (5) *Peer Gynt* Suite (op. 46) (Grieg); (6) Ode, *The East to the West*, for chorus and orchestra (op. 52) (Stanford).

The various numbers were conducted by the respective composers, with the exception of Grieg's Suite and the Fantasia *Africa*, which were given under the bâton of Dr. Stanford.

The singers were Mr. and Mrs. Henschel, Mme. Marie Brema, and Plunket Green.

In his *Portraits et Souvenirs* Saint-Saens has given the following description of this concert, and I cannot refrain from interrupting my narrative in order to quote what the French composer says of my brother's *Francesca*.

" Piquant charms and dazzling fireworks abound in Tchaikovsky's *Francesca da Rimini*, which bristles with difficulties, and shrinks from no violence of effect. The gentlest and kindest of men has let loose a whirlwind in this work, and shows as little pity for his interpreters and hearers as Satan for sinners. But the composer's talent and astounding technique are so great that the critic can only feel pleasure in the work. A long melodic phrase, the love-song of Paola and Francesca, soars above this tempest, this *bufera infernale*, which attracted Liszt before Tchaikovky, and engendered his Dante Symphony. Liszt's Francesca is more touching and more Italian in character than that of the great Slavonic composer ; the whole work is so typical that we seem to see the profile of Dante

---

[1] This was before Sir Charles Villiers Stanford was knighted.

projected in it. Tchaikovsky's art is more subtle, the out-lines clearer, the material more attractive ; from a purely musical point of view the work is better. Liszt's version is perhaps more to the taste of the poet or painter. On the whole, they can fitly stand side by side ; either of them is worthy of Dante, and as regards noise, both leave nothing to be desired."[1]

The concert was followed by a banquet in the hall of King's College, at which a hundred guests sat down to table. As it was purely a musical festivity, only those who were to receive the honorary musical degree were invited to this banquet. The place of honour, next to the chairman, was given to Saint-Saëns, the eldest of the guests. Never had Tchaikovsky greater reason to con-gratulate himself upon his comparative youth, for, together with the honour, the difficult task of replying to a toast on behalf of his colleagues fell to the lot of Saint-Saëns.

After the dinner came a brilliant reception to the com-posers in the hall of the Museum.

Besides the musicians, there were several other recipients of the honorary degree, including the Maharajah of Bohon-ager, Lord Herschel, Lord Roberts, Dr. Julius Stupitza, Professor of English Philology in the University of Berlin, and the Irish scholar, Standish O'Grady.

On the morning of June 13th all the future doctors assembled in the Arts School and attired themselves in their splendid doctors' robes of red and white ; after which they took up their positions, and the procession started. Saint-Saëns, in the volume already quoted, says :

" We were attired in ample robes of silk, parti-coloured scarlet and white, with full sleeves, and on our heads college-caps of black velvet with gold tassels. Thus decked out, we walked in procession through the town, under a tropical sun. At the head of the group of doctors went the King of Bohonager in a turban of cloth of gold,

[1] *Portraits et Souvenirs*, Saint-Saëns, p. 141.

sparkling with fabulous jewels and a diamond necklace. Dare I confess that, as the enemy of the commonplace, and of the neuter tints of our modern garb, I was enchanted with the adventure?

" The people stood on each side of the railings, and cheered us with some enthusiasm, especially Lord Roberts."

" Meanwhile the Senate House, in which the degrees were conferred, had become crowded with undergraduates and guests. The former were not merely spectators, but —as we afterwards discovered—participated in the event. When the Vice-Chancellor and other members of the Senate had taken their places, the ceremony began. Each recipient rises in turn from his seat, while the public orator recounts his claims to recognition in a Latin oration. Here the undergraduates begin to play their part. According to ancient tradition, they are allowed to hiss, cheer, and make jokes at the expense of the new doctors. At every joke the orator waits until the noise and laughter has subsided, then continues to read aloud. When this is done, the recipient is led up to the Vice-Chancellor, who greets him as doctor *in nomine Patri, Filii et Spiritus Sancti.* This formula was not used in the case of the Maharajah."

The oration delivered in honour of Tchaikovsky ran as follows :—

" Russorum ex imperio immenso hodie ad nos delatus est viri illustris, Rubinsteinii, discipulus insignis, qui neque Italiam neque Helvetiam inexploratam reliquit, sed patriae carmina popularia ante omnia dilexit. Ingenii Slavonici et ardorem fervidum et languorem subtristem quam feliciter interpretatur ! Musicorum modorum in argumentis animo concipiendis quam amplus est ! in numeris modulandis quam distinctus ! in flexionibus variandis quam subtilis ! in orchestrae (ut aiunt) partibus inter se diversis una componendis quam splendidus ! Talium virorum animo grato admiramur ingenium illud facile et promptum, quod, velut ipsa rerum natura, nulla, necessitate coactum sed quasi sua sponte pulcherrimum quidque in luminis oras quotannis submittit.

" Audiamus Propertium :

> " ' aspice quot submittit humus formosa colores ;
> et veniunt hederae sponte sua melius.'

" Etiam nosmet ipsi hodie fronti tam felici hederae nostrae corollam sponte imponimus.

" Duco ad vos Petrum Tchaikovsky."

After the ceremony there was a breakfast given by the Vice-Chancellor, at which all attended in their robes. At the end of the meal, in obedience to the tradition of centuries, a loving-cup was passed round.

The breakfast was .followed by a garden - party, the hostess being the wife of the Vice-Chancellor.

By evening Tchaikovsky was back in London, where he gave a farewell dinner to some of his new friends. Among these I must mention the fine baritone, Eugene Oudin.   Tchaikovsky was soon very sincerely attached to him, both as a man and an artist.   Upon his initiative Oudin was invited to sing at the Symphony Concerts in Moscow and Petersburg.

The following day Tchaikovsky left for Paris.

To P. Jurgenson.

" PARIS, *June 3rd* (15*th*), 1893.

" Cambridge, with its peculiar customs which retain much that is medieval, with its colleges that resemble monasteries, and its buildings recalling a remote past, made a very agreeable impression upon me."

To N. Konradi.

" PARIS, *June 3rd* (15*th*), 1893.

" At Cambridge I stayed with Professor Maitland. This would have been dreadfully embarrassing for me, if he and his wife had not proved to be some of the most charming people I ever met ; and Russophiles into the bargain, which is the greatest rarity in England. Now all is over, it is pleasant to look back upon my visit to England, and to remember the extraordinary cordiality shown to me everywhere, although, in consequence of my peculiar temperament, while there, I tormented and worried myself to fiddle-strings."

XVIII

Tchaikovsky's home-coming was by no means joyful. The shadow of death was all around him. Hardly had he heard of the death of his old friend Karl Albrecht than a letter from the Countess Vassiliev-Shilovsky informed him that her husband had passed away. Besides this, Apukhtin lay dying in Petersburg, and in Moscow another valued friend, Zvierev, was in an equally hopeless condition.

A few years earlier one such grief would have affected Tchaikovsky more keenly than all of them taken together seemed to do at this juncture. Now death appeared to him less enigmatical and fearful. Whether his feelings were less acute, or whether the mental sufferings of later years had taught him that death was often a deliverance, I cannot say. I merely lay emphasis on the fact that, in spite of the discomforting news which met him in all directions, from the time of his return from England to the end of his life, Tchaikovsky was as serene and cheerful as at any period in his existence.

He looked forward with joy to meeting his nephew Vladimir Davidov at Grankino, in the government of Poltava. He always felt well in the glorious air of the steppes.

From Grankino he went to stay with his brother Nicholas at Oukolovo.

To Vladimir Davidov.

"*July* 19*th* (31*st*), 1893.

"I spent two very pleasant days in Moscow. Tell Modi I was very ill the day after he left. They said it was from drinking too much cold water at dinner and supper. . . . The day after to-morrow I start upon the Symphony again. I must write letters for the next two days."

To Modeste Tchaikovsky.

"*July* 22*nd* (*August* 3*rd*), 1893.

"I am up to my eyes in the Symphony. The further I go, the more difficult the orchestration becomes. Twenty years ago I should have rushed it through without a second thought, and it would have turned out all right. Now I am turning coward, and have lost my self-confidence. I have been sitting all day over two pages, yet they will not come out as I wish. In spite of this, the work makes progress, and I should not have done so much anywhere else but at home.

"Thanks to Alexis' exertions, my house has a very coquettish appearance. All is in order ; a mass of flowers in the garden, good paths, and a new fence with gates. I am well cared for. And yet I get terribly bored unless I am working. . . ."

To Vladimir Davidov.

"*August* 3*rd* (15*th*), 1893.

"The Symphony which I intended to dedicate to you—although I have now changed my mind[1]—is progressing. I am very well pleased with its contents, but not quite so satisfied with the orchestration. It does not realise my dreams. To me, it will seem quite natural, and not in the least astonishing, if this Symphony meets with abuse, or scant appreciation at first. I certainly regard it as quite the best—and especially the 'most sincere'—of all my works. I love it as I never loved any one of my musical offspring before."

[1] This was merely a playful threat because his nephew had neglected to answer his letters.

To P. Jurgenson.

"KLIN, *August* 12*th* (24*th*), 1893.

"DEAR FRIEND,—I have finished the orchestration of the new Symphony. . . . I have made the arrangement for four hands myself, and must play it through, so I have asked the youngest Konius to come here, that we may try it together.   As regards the score and parts, I cannot put them in order before the first performance, which takes place in Petersburg on October 16th (28th). . . . On my word of honour, I have never felt such self-satisfaction, such pride, such happiness, as in the consciousness that I am really the creator of this beautiful work."

To the same.

"KLIN, *August* 20*th* (*September* 1*st*), 1893.

"I shall take the Symphony with me to Petersburg to-day.   I promise not to give away the score.   The arrangement for four hands needs a thorough revision. I have entrusted this to Leo Konius.   I wished him to receive a fee of at least 100 roubles, but he refused. . . ."

Tchaikovsky spent two days with Laroche in Petersburg.   Even the prospect of his journey to Hamburg did not suffice to damp his cheerful frame of mind.   He does not appear to have written any letters during his absence from Russia, which was of very brief duration.

"On his return from Hamburg he met me in St. Petersburg," says Modeste, "and stayed with me a day or two. I had not seen him so bright for a long time past.   He was keenly interested in the forthcoming season of the Musical Society, and was preparing the programme of the fourth concert, which he was to conduct.

"At this time there was a change in the circumstances of my own life.   Having finished the education of N. Konradi, I decided to set up housekeeping with my nephew Vladimir Davidov, who had completed his course at the School of Jurisprudence and was now an independent man.   My brother was naturally very much interested in all the arrangements of our new home.

"At this time we discussed subjects for a new opera. Peter Ilich's favourite author in later life was George Eliot. Once during his travels abroad he had come across her finest book, *The Mill on the Floss*, and from that time he considered she had no rival but Tolstoi as a writer of fiction. *Adam Bede, Silas Marner*, and *Middlemarch* stirred him to the greatest enthusiasm, and he read them over and over again. He cared less for *Romola*, but was particularly fond of *Scenes from Clerical Life*. For a time he seriously contemplated founding the libretto of his next opera upon *The Sad Fortunes of the Rev. Amos Barton*. He wished me to read the tale and give him my opinion : I must confess that, from his own account of it, I persuaded him to give up the idea.

"I do not know if I actually convinced him, or whether he lost interest in it himself, but he never referred to this tale again when he spoke of other subjects for a libretto.

"We separated early in September, and he went to our brother Anatol, who was spending the summer and autumn with his family at Mikhailovskoe."

Here he enjoyed a very happy visit. "It is indescribably beautiful," he wrote to Modeste. "It is altogether pleasant and successful. The weather is wonderful. All day long I wander in the forest and bring home quantities of mushrooms."

His high opinion of the new Symphony was still unchanged, for he wrote to the Grand Duke Constantine Constantinovich on September 21st (October 3rd), "Without exaggeration I have put my whole soul into this work." Yet in spite of his cheerful attitude, a momentary cloud of depression passed over him at this time. Writing to Modeste from Moscow, a few days later, he says : "Just lately I have been dreadfully bored and misanthropical. I do not know why. I sit in my room and see no one but the waiter. I long for home, work, and my normal existence."

On September 25th he returned to Klin for the last time.

To Anna Merkling.

"*September 29th (October 11th),* 1893.

"I am now very busy with the orchestration of the Pianoforte Concerto. I shall soon appear on the banks of the Neva. You will see me about the 10th."

On October 7th (19th) Tchaikovsky left Klin never to return. The following day he intended to be present at the memorial service for his friend Zvierev and then to go on to Petersburg. As the train passed the village of Frolovskoe, he pointed to the churchyard, remarking to his fellow-travellers: "I shall be buried there, and people will point out my grave as they go by." He repeated this wish to be buried at Frolovskoe while talking to Taneiev at the memorial service for Zvierev. Beyond these two references to his death, prompted no doubt by the sad ceremony with which he was preoccupied, Tchaikovsky does not appear to have shown any symptoms of depression or foreboding.

Kashkin has given the following account of his friend's last visit to Moscow :—

"We met at the memorial service in the church, and afterwards Peter Ilich went to Zvierev's grave. On October 9th (21st) he had promised to go to the Conservatoire to hear the vocal quartet ('Night') which he had arranged from Mozart's pianoforte Fantasia. The master's music had not been altered, Tchaikovsky had only written words to it. . . . Madame Lavrovsky had promised that her pupils should learn the work. We assembled in the concert hall of the Conservatoire, and I sat with Tchaikovsky. The quartet was beautifully sung . . . Tchaikovsky afterwards told me this music had the most indescribable charm for him, but he could not explain, even to himself, why this simple melody gave him such pleasure. . . .

"At that time Pollini, the Director of the Hamburg Opera, was staying in Moscow. He was an ardent admirer of Tchaikovsky, and had given some of his operas in Hamburg. When—as invited—I went to supper with Tchaikovsky at the Moscow Restaurant, I met Pollini, Safonov, and two foreign guests. We talked over Pollini's idea of making a great concert tour through Russia, with a German orchestra under a Russian conductor . . . Tchaikovsky was to conduct his own works and Safonov the rest of the programme. . . . After the others had gone, and Peter Ilich and I were left to ourselves, he told me all about Cambridge, and spoke very warmly of the Professor in whose house he had stayed, and of one of the other recipients of the honorary degree—Arrigo Boïto, who had charmed him with his intellect and culture. . . . Unconsciously the talk turned to our recent losses : to the death of Albrecht and Zvierev. We thought of the gaps time had made in our circle of old friends and how few now remained. Involuntarily the question arose : Who will be the next to take the road from which there is no return ? With complete assurance of its truth, I declared that Tchaikovsky would outlive us all. He disputed the probability, but ended by saying he had never felt better or happier in his life. He had to catch the night mail to Petersburg, where he was going to conduct his Sixth Symphony, which was still unknown to me. He said he had no doubt as to the first three movements, but the last was still a problem, and perhaps after the performance in Petersburg he should destroy the Finale and replace it by another. The concert of the Musical Society in Moscow was fixed for October 23rd (November 4th). We arranged, if we should not see each other there, to meet at the Moscow Restaurant, for Tchaikovsky was anxious to introduce the singer Eugene Oudin to the musical circle in Moscow. Here our conversation ended. Tchaikovsky went to the station. It never occurred to me to see him off, for neither of us cared for that kind of thing ; besides, we should meet again in a fortnight. We parted without the least presentiment that it was for the last time."

XIX

Tchaikovsky arrived in Petersburg on October 10th (22nd). He was met by his brother Modeste and his favourite nephew. He was delighted with their new abode and his spirits were excellent—so long as his arrival remained unknown and he was master of his time.

One thing only depressed him : at the rehearsals the Sixth Symphony made no impression upon the orchestra. He always set store by the opinion of the musicians. Moreover, he feared lest the interpretation of the Symphony might suffer from their coldness. Tchaikovsky only conducted his works well when he knew they appealed to the players. To obtain delicate *nuances* and a good balance of tone he needed his surroundings to be sympathetic and appreciative. A look of indifference, a coolness on the part of any of the band, seemed to paralyse him ; he lost his head, went through the work perfunctorily, and cut the rehearsal as short as possible, so as to release the musicians from a wearisome task. Whenever he conducted a work of his own for the first time, a kind of uncertainty—almost carelessness—in the execution of details was apparent, and the whole interpretation lacked force and definite expression. The Fifth Symphony and *Hamlet* were so long making their way merely because the composer had failed to make them effective. The same reason accounts for the failure of the orchestral ballade, *The Voyevode*.

Tchaikovsky was easily disenchanted with his work by the adverse opinion of others. But on this occasion his judgment remained unshaken, and even the indifference of the orchestra did not alter his opinion that this Symphony was " the best thing I ever composed or ever shall compose." He did not, however, succeed in convincing the public or the performers. At the concert on the 16th (28th) the work fell rather flat.   It was applauded and the composer was recalled; but the enthusiasm did not surpass what was usually shown for one of Tchaikovsky's new works. The Symphony produced nothing approaching to that powerful and thrilling impression it made shortly afterwards (November 6th (18th), 1893) under Napravnik, which has since been repeated in so many other cities.

The Press did not speak of the new Symphony with as much admiration as Tchaikovsky had expected, but on the whole the notices were appreciative.   The *St. Petersburg Viedomosti* thought "the thematic material of the work was not very original, the leading subjects were neither new nor significant.   The last movement, Adagio Lamentoso, was the best."   The *Syn Otechestva* discovered a phrase in the first movement which recalled Gounod's *Romeo and Juliet*, while Grieg was reflected in the Finale. The *Novoe Vremya* said: "The new Symphony is evidently the outcome of a journey abroad ; it contains much that is clever and resourceful as regards orchestral colour, besides grace and delicacy (in the two middle movements), but *as far as inspiration is concerned it stands far below Tchaikovsky's other Symphonies.*   Only one newspaper, *The Birjevya Viedomosti*, spoke of the work in terms of unqualified praise, while finding fault with the composer's conducting of the work.

The morning after the concert I found my brother sitting at the breakfast-table with the score of the Symphony before him.   He had agreed to send it to Jurgenson in Moscow that very day, and could not decide upon a title.   He did not wish to designate it merely by a number, and had abandoned his original intention of calling it "a programme Symphony."   "Why programme," he said, "since I do not intend to expound any meaning?" I suggested "tragic Symphony" as an appropriate title. But this did not please him either.   I left the room while Peter Ilich was still in a state of indecision.   Suddenly the word "pathetic" occurred to me, and I returned to suggest it. I remember, as though it were yesterday, how my brother exclaimed: "Bravo, Modeste, splendid! *Pathetic!*" Then and there, in my presence, he added to the score the title by which the Symphony has always been known.[1]

I do not relate this incident in order to connect my name with this work. Probably I should never have mentioned it but for the fact that it serves to illustrate in a simple way how far the conjectures of the most enlightened commentators may wander from the truth.

Hugo Riemann, in his thematic analysis of the Sixth Symphony, sees the solution of this title in "the striking resemblance between the fundamental idea of this work and the chief subject of Beethoven's *Sonata Pathétique,*" of which Tchaikovsky never dreamed:

After having despatched the score to Moscow with this title, Tchaikovsky changed his mind, as may be seen from the following letter to Jurgenson:—

"*October* 18*th*, 1893.

"Be so kind as to put on the title page what stands below.

To Vladimir Lvovich
Davidov

(No. 6)

Composed by P. T.

"I hope it is not too late.

---

[1] There was no other witness of this incident but myself. But it is clear from the programme of the concert of October 16th (28th) that this title had not then been given to the work. Moreover, anyone can see by a glance at the title-page that this name was written later than the rest.

"It is very strange about this Symphony. It was not exactly a failure, but was received with some hesitation. As far as I am concerned, I am prouder of it than of any of my previous works. However, we can soon talk it over together, for I shall be in Moscow on Saturday."

At this time he talked a great deal about the re-modelling of *The Oprichnik* and *The Maid of Orleans*, which he had in view for the immediate future. He did not confide to me his intentions as to the former opera; but as regards *The Maid of Orleans*, we discussed the alteration of the last scene, and I made a point of his arranging this, like so many other parts of the opera, from Schiller's poem. The idea seemed to interest him, but it was not permitted to him to come to a definite conclusion on the subject.

During these last days he was neither very cheerful, nor yet depressed. In the circle of his intimate friends he was contented and jovial; among strangers he was, as usual, nervous and excited and, as time went on, tired out and dull. But nothing gave the smallest hint of his approaching end.

On Tuesday, October 19th (31st), he went to a private performance of Rubinstein's *The Maccabees*. On the 20th (November 1st) he was still in good health and dined with his old friend Vera Boutakov (*née* Davidov). Afterwards he went to see Ostrovsky's play, *A Warm Heart*, at the Alexander Theatre. During the interval he went with me to see the actor Varlamov in his dressing-room. The conversation turned upon spiritualism. Varlamov described in his own humorous style—which cannot be transferred to paper—his loathing for "all those abominations" which reminded one of death. Peter Ilich laughed at Varlamov's quaint way of expressing himself.

"There is plenty of time," said Tchaikovsky, "before we need reckon with this snub-nosed horror; it will not come to snatch us off just yet! I feel I shall live a long time."

From the theatre, Tchaikovsky went with his nephews, Count Litke and Baron Buxhovden, to the Restaurant Leiner. I joined them an hour later, and found one or two other visitors—of whom Glazounov was one. They had already had their supper, and I was afterwards told my brother had eaten macaroni and drunk, as usual, white wine and soda water. We went home about two a.m. Peter Ilich was perfectly well and serene.

On the morning of Thursday, October 21st (November 2nd), Tchaikovsky did not appear as usual at the early breakfast-table. His brother went to his room and found him slightly indisposed. He complained of his digestion being upset and of a bad night. About eleven a.m. he dressed and went out to see Napravnik. Half an hour later he returned, still feeling unwell. He absolutely declined to send for a doctor. His condition gave no anxiety to Modeste, who had often seen him suffer from similar derangements.

He joined his brother and nephew at lunch, although he ate nothing. But this was probably the fatal moment in his indisposition for, while talking, he poured out a glass of water and drank a long draught. The water had not been boiled, and they were dismayed at his imprudence. But he was not in the least alarmed, and tried to calm their fears. He dreaded cholera less than any other illness. After this his condition grew worse; but he attributed all his discomfort to a copious dose of Hunyadi which he had taken earlier in the day, and still declined to send for his favourite doctor, Bertenson. Towards evening Modeste grew so anxious that he sent for the doctor on his own account. Meanwhile Tchaikovsky was tended by his brother's servant Nazar, who had once travelled with him to Italy.

About eight p.m. Bertenson arrived. He saw at once that the illness was serious, and sent for his brother in consultation. The sufferer had grown very weak, and complained of terrible oppression on his chest. More than once he said, " I believe this is death."

After a short consultation the brothers Bertenson, the two leading physicians in Petersburg, pronounced it to be a case of cholera.

All night long those who nursed him in turn fought against the cramps ; towards morning with some hope of success. His courage was wonderful, and in the intervals between the paroxysms of pain he made little jokes with those around him. He constantly begged his nurses to take some rest, and was grateful for the smallest service.

On Friday his condition seemed more hopeful, and he himself believed he had been " snatched from the jaws of death." But on the following day his mental depression returned. "Leave me," he said to his doctors, "you can do no good. I shall never recover."

Gradually he passed into the second stage of the cholera, with its most dangerous symptom—complete inactivity of the kidneys. He slept more, but his sleep was restless, and sometimes he wandered in his mind. At these times he continually repeated the name of Nadejda Filaretovna von Meck in an indignant, or reproachful, tone. Consciousness returned at longer intervals, and when his servant Alexis arrived from Klin he was no longer able to recognise him. A warm bath was tried as a last resource, but without avail, and soon afterwards his pulse grew so weak that the end seemed imminent. At the desire of his brother Nicholas, a priest was sent for from the Isaac Cathedral. He did not administer the sacrament, as Tchaikovsky was now quite unconscious, but prayed in clear and distinct tones, which, however, did not seem to reach the ears of the dying man.

At three o'clock on the morning of October 25th (November 6th) Tchaikovsky passed away in the presence of his brothers Nicholas and Modeste, his nephews Litke, Buxhövden, and Vladimir Davidov, the three doctors, and his faithful servant Alexis Safronov.   At the last moment an indescribable look of clear recognition lit up his face— a gleam which only died away with his last breath.

My work is finished. With this account of Tchaikovsky's last moments my task, which was to express the man, is accomplished.

To characterise the artist in every phase of his development, and to determine his position in the history of music, is beyond my powers.   If all the documental and authentic evidence I have collected in this book should serve as fundamental material for another writer capable of fulfilling such a task, the most cherished aim of all my efforts will have been attained.

MODESTE TCHAIKOVSKY

ROME, 1902

APPENDIX A

CHRONOLOGICAL LIST OF TCHAIKOVSKY'S COMPOSITIONS FROM 1866–1893

First Season, 1866–1867

1. Op. 15. Festival Overture upon the Danish National Hymn; completed October, 1866. Published by Jurgenson.

2. Op. 13. Symphony in G minor, No. 1, "Winter Dreams." Begun in March, completed in November, 1866. Jurgenson.

3. Op. 1. Russian Scherzo and Impromptu. Composed early in 1867. The first of these compositions was originally entitled "Capriccio." It is based on the first theme of the Andante in the quartet in B major, which Tchaikovsky composed while still at the Conservatoire in 1865. The theme itself is a Malo-Russian folksong, heard at Kamenka. The Impromptu—a still earlier work—was never intended for publication. It chanced to be in the same manuscript-book as the Capriccio, which was given to Jurgenson by Rubinstein, without any intimation that the Impromptu was not to be published. The Russian Scherzo was performed at Rubinstein's concert in 1867. Both these works—like the *First Symphony*—were dedicated to Nicholas Rubinstein, and published by Jurgenson.

4. Op. 2. *Souvenir de Hapsal*—three pianoforte pieces: (*a*) "The Ruin," (*b*) "Scherzo," (*c*) "Chant sans Paroles." June and July, 1867. Hapsal. Only the first and third of these pieces were composed at Hapsal; the second dates back to the days of the Conservatoire. This *opus* number is dedicated to Vera Davidov. Jurgenson. Besides these works, Tchaikovsky was engaged from the beginning of 1867 upon his opera, *The Voyevode*.

1867–1868

The Voyevode was the sole work of this season.

In a letter dated November 25th (December 7th) Tchaikovsky speaks of having completed the third act, which is as good as saying that he had finished the whole opera, because he rarely broke through his custom of working straight through a composition. The instrumentation remained, and this was finished in Paris during the summer.

The Voyevode, or *A Dream on the Volga*, is a play in five acts, with a prologue, by A. N. Ostrovsky. The opera libretto is condensed into three acts, the prologue being omitted.

The chief beauty of the play, the scenes from national life, so charmingly depicted by Ostrovsky, had been ruthlessly cut out of the libretto, and only an insipid and uninteresting story left. The charm of national colour, the characteristic details of the secondary *dramatis personæ*, such as Nedviga, the apparition of the Domovoi, or "house spirit," the gloomy figure of Mizgir— of all these things the libretto had been completely denuded.

But it was not so much Ostrovsky as Tchaikovsky who was to blame, for it is evident from the manuscript which the latter used while composing the music that he eliminated every episode which did not bear directly upon the tale. A few years later Tchaikovsky would not have missed so many good opportunities of effective musical illustration.

Ostrovsky's collaboration was practically limited to Act I., which is also the best, and to a portion of Act II. The remainder is almost entirely of Tchaikovsky's own writing.

Of this opera only the "Dances of the Serving Maids" and the "Entr'acte" were published as Op. 3. Jurgenson. The rest of the score was destroyed by the composer during the seventies. The orchestral and choral parts and some of the solos—unfortunately not the principal ones—are still preserved in the library of the Imperial Opera House in Moscow.

1868–1869

1. Op. 77. Symphonic Poem, *Fatum*. Begun about the middle of September, 1868. Sketch completed on October 21st

(November 2nd). Orchestrated in November and December. Produced for the first time by the Musical Society in Moscow, February 25th (March 9th), 1869, conducted by N. Rubinstein. This work is dedicated to M. A. Balakirev. During the seventies Tchaikovsky destroyed the score, but the orchestral parts remained intact, and the work was reconstructed from these, and published in 1896, by Belaiev, in Leipzig.

2. Op. 4. Valse Caprice for pianoforte. Composed in October, 1868. Dedicated to Anton Door. Jurgenson.

3. Op. 5. Romance for pianoforte. November, 1868. Dedicated to Désirée Artôt. Jurgenson.

4. Twenty-five Russian folksongs, arranged for pianoforte, four hands. These were probably finished during the autumn months, and printed in November, 1868.

5. Recitatives and choruses for *Le Domino Noir*, by Auber. This work has entirely disappeared; it cannot be found in the library of the Petersburg or Moscow Opera.

6. *Undine*, an opera in three acts, begun in January and completed in July, 1869. The text by Count Sollogoub.

The libretto of *Undine* contained scenes more interesting and grateful for musical treatment than *The Voyevode*, but was so unskilfully put together and so lacking in logical sequence that it is even inferior to the dry, uninteresting, but literary verse of the latter. The music—judging from the fragments that have been preserved—seems to have possessed a certain vitality.

The composer destroyed the score of *Undine* in 1873. All that remains of the music is Undine's aria, "The spring is my brother," which was afterwards utilised in *Sniegourochka*, and the Wedding March in the last act, which Tchaikovsky employed in the Andantino Marziale of his Second Symphony. Besides these two fragments, Kashkin says an Adagio in the ballet, "The Swan Lake," was originally the love-duet between Gulbrand and Undine.

Part of this opera was produced at a concert given by the Capellmeister Merten, March 16th (28th), 1870. Laroche wrote:—

"Unfortunately, I was not able to attend the concert itself, but I had heard these fragments from *Undine* at the rehearsals, and observed not only the careful and delicate orchestration for which Tchaikovsky's music is remarkable, but picturesque suggestions of the fantastic realms of the water sprites. Other parts—notably the finale—appeared to me lacking in spontaneity. On the whole, however, the new score is worthy of attention."

1869–1870

1. Twenty-five Russian folksongs, arranged for pianoforte, four hands. Completed September 25th, 1869. Published, together with the twenty-five of the previous year, by Jurgenson, Moscow.

2. *Romeo and Juliet*. Overture-Fantasia for orchestra, founded on Shakespeare's tragedy. Begun September 25th (October 7th); sketch completed by October 7th (19th), and orchestrated by November 15th (27th), 1869. During the summer of 1870 the work was completely revised. According to Kashkin, the Introduction was entirely new; the funeral march at the close of the work was omitted and a fresh ending substituted for it, while many alterations were made in the orchestration as a whole. The overture is dedicated to Mily Alexandrovich Balakirev, and was performed for the first time at Moscow, under the bâton of N. Rubinstein, March 4th (16th), 1870. Published by Bote and Bock, Berlin, 1871.

3. Pianoforte arrangement for four hands of the overture *Ivan the Terrible*, by Anton Rubinstein. Bessel, St. Petersburg.

4. Op. 6. Six songs.[1] Written between November 15th (27th) and December 19th (31st), 1869. (1) "Glaub' nicht mein Freund," words by Count A. Tolstoi, dedicated to A. G. Menshikov. (2) "Nicht Worte," words by Plestcheiev, dedicated to N. Kashkin. (3) "Wie wehe, wie süss," words by Countess Rostopchin, dedicated to A. D. Kochetov. (4) "Die Thräne bebt," words by Count A. Tolstoi, dedicated to P. Jurgenson. (5) "Warum," words by Mey, dedicated to I. Klimenko. (6) "Nur wer die Sehnsucht kennt," words by Mey (from Goethe), dedicated to Madame Khvostova. P. Jurgenson, Moscow.

5. "Chorus of Insects," from the unfinished opera *Mandragora*,

---

[1] As several English versions exist of many of Tchaikovsky's songs, and some of these so-called translations have not even titles in common with the original texts, it is less misleading to keep to the German titles.—R. N.

January 13th (25th), 1870. The score of this work has been entirely lost. The pianoforte arrangement is preserved by Jurgenson. In 1898 Glazounov orchestrated it.

6. Op. 7. Valse Scherzo (A major) for pianoforte, dedicated to Alexandra Ilinichna Davidov. P. Jurgenson.

7. Op. 8. Capriccio (G flat) for piano, dedicated to K. Klindworth. P. Jurgenson. Both these pieces were completed about February 3rd (15th), 1870.

Besides the above, Tchaikovsky began his opera, *The Oprichnik*, about the end of January, 1870.

1870–1871

1. Op. 9. Three pianoforte pieces. (1) "Rêverie," dedicated to N. Murometz. (2) "Polka de Salon," dedicated to A. Zograf. (3) "Mazurka de Salon," dedicated to A. L. Dubuque.

2. Song, "So schnell vergessen," words by Apukhtin. This and the above works were composed before October 26th (November 7th), 1870, and published by Jurgenson, Moscow.

3. "Nature and Love." Trio for two sopranos and one contralto, with chorus and pianoforte accompaniment; dedicated to Madame Valzek. It was composed in December expressly for this lady's pupils, and performed for the first time at Tchaikovsky's concert on March 16th (28th), 1871. It was published by Jurgenson after the composer's death.

4. Op. 11. Quartet No. 1 (D major), for two violins, viola, and violoncello. Dedicated to Serge Rachinsky. Composed during February, 1871, and first performed at the composer's concert, March 16th (28th), 1871. The Andante of this quartet is based on a Russian folksong which Tchaikovsky wrote down at Kamenka in the summer of 1869. It was sung in Great Russian by a man who was working outside the room in which he was engaged in orchestrating his *Undine*.

5. A Course of Harmony, completed during the summer at Nizy. Jurgenson.

Besides the above, Tchaikovsky was working during the whole of this period on his opera, *The Oprichnik*.

1871–1872

1. Op. 10. Two pianoforte pieces : "Nocturne" and "Humoresque." Probably composed in December, 1871, during his stay at Nice. Part of the second piece consists of a French popular song. These pieces are both dedicated to Vladimir Shilovsky.

2. Cantata for chorus, orchestra, and tenor solo. Text by Polonsky. Composed during February and March, 1872. Performed May 31st (June 12th), 1872, under the conductorship of K. Davidov. The manuscript of the score is in the library of the Imperial Opera House, Moscow.

3. *The Oprichnik*, an opera in four acts. Begun at the end of January, 1870, completed in April, 1872. Dedicated to His Imperial Highness the Grand Duke Constantine Nicholaevich. Published by Bessel, St. Petersburg.

Without entering into a detailed criticism of Lajetnikov's tragedy, I must call attention to some of its features which are calculated to make it an easy subject for the librettist to handle; these special features lie in its admirable plot The interest of the love-intrigue, which is well sustained, a whole series of effective situations, the dark yet poetic colouring of its sinister period (Ivan the Terrible), the variety of episodes well suited to musical illustration (such as the love-duet in the first act, the scenes with the populace, the picturesque figures of the Oprichniks, the pathos of the oath scene, "The Terrible" himself, and the death of Andrew), all contribute to make an effective and moving opera.

But it did not fulfil these expectations. The most serious hindrance came from the Censor. The striking figure of Ivan the Terrible, which seemed so well adapted to musical representation, was not permitted to appear. For an outline of the plot of this opera, see Appendix B.

1872–1873

1. Op. 17. Symphony No. 2 (C minor), composed during June, July, and August, 1872. Orchestrated in September and October of the same year, and completed early in November.

Dedicated to the Moscow section of the Imperial Russian Musical Society. First performed, under N. Rubinstein, in Moscow, January 26th (February 7th), 1873. Published by V. Bessel, St. Petersburg. The second movement, Andantino Marziale, is taken from the opera *Undine*. Speaking of this work, Kashkin says, "It may be called 'The Little Russian' Symphony, because its chief themes are Little Russian folksongs."[1] Later on the composer made considerable alterations, and entirely rewrote the first movement.

2. Op. 16. Six songs. (1) "Wiegenlied," words by Maikov, dedicated to Frau N. N. Rimsky-Korsakov. (2) "Warte noch," words by Grekov, dedicated to N. A. Rimsky-Korsakov. (3) "Erfass nur einmal," words by Maikov, dedicated to G. A. Laroche. (4) "Oh, mochtest du einmal noch singen," words by Plestcheiev, dedicated to N. A. Hubert. (5) "Was nun?" Words by the composer, dedicated to N. Rubinstein. (6) "Neugriechisches Lied," words by Maikov, dedicated to K. Albrecht. The precise date of these songs is not known. Probably they were written in December, 1872. Published by V. Bessel, St. Petersburg.

3. Op. 12. Music to *Sniegourochka, a Legend of Springtide*, by A. N. Ostrovsky. Composed during March and April, 1873. First performed at the Opera, Moscow, May 11th (23rd), 1873. Jurgenson, Moscow. One or two numbers of this work are transferred from *Undine*.

4. "Perpetuum mobile," from a sonata by Weber, arranged for the left hand only. Dedicated to Madame Zograf. Published 1873, by Jurgenson.

Besides the above, Tchaikovsky worked at the symphonic fantasia, *The Tempest*, between August 7th–17th (19th–29th), 1873.

His literary work comprised seventeen articles, in which he reviewed the chief musical events of the season in Moscow.

---

[1] The Introduction is the Malo-Russian variant of "Down by Mother Volga," the Finale is based upon a popular tune called "The Crane."—R.N.

1873–1874

1. Op. 18. *The Tempest*, symphonic fantasia for full orchestra upon a Shakespearean programme. Composed between 7th (19th) and 17th (29th) August, 1873; orchestrated by October 10th (22nd). Dedicated to Vladimir Vassilievich Stassov. First performed December 7th (19th), 1873, under N. Rubinstein. Jurgenson.

2. Op. 21. Six pianoforte pieces upon a theme. (1) Prelude, (2) Fugue, (3) Impromptu, (4) Funeral March, (5) Mazurka, (6) Scherzo. Dedicated to Anton Rubinstein. Composed before October 30th (November 11th), 1873. Bessel.

3. Op. 22. Quartet No. 2 (F major), for two violins, viola, and violoncello. Dedicated to the Grand Duke Constantine. Commenced at the end of December, 1873, or early in January, 1874, and finished by the 26th of that month. Shortly afterwards it was played at a musical evening at N. Rubinstein's, and probably Tchaikovsky afterwards made some changes in it, as he was still engaged upon the work in the middle of February. First public performance March 10th (22nd), 1874. Jurgenson.

4. Op. 14. *Vakoula the Smith* (Kouznetz Vakoula, known also as *Cherevichek* and *Les Caprices d'Oxane*), opera in three acts and seven scenes. The libretto is taken from a tale by Gogol and set to verse by J. Polonsky. Dedicated to the memory of the Grand Duchess Helena. Composed and orchestrated during the summer of 1874. Partially remodelled about 1885. Published by Jurgenson.

1874–1875

1. Op. 25. Six songs : (1) "Herz, o lass dich von Schlummer umfangen," words by Scherbin, dedicated to A. P. Kroutikov. (2) "Wie hier die Schrift in Aschengluth," words by Tioutchev, dedicated to D. Orlov. (3) "Mignon's Lied," words by Goethe, dedicated to M. Kamenskaya. (4) "Der Kanarienvogel," words by Mey, dedicated to V. Raab. (5) "Mit ihr ein Wort gesprochen hab' ich nie," words by Mey, dedicated to I. Melnikov. (6) "Einst zum Narren Jemand spricht," words by Mey. These

songs were probably composed in September, 1874. Published by V. Bessel.

2. Op. 19. Six pianoforte pieces : (1) "Rêverie," dedicated to N. D. Kondratiev. (2) "Scherzo-humoristique," dedicated to Vera Timanov. (3) "Feuillet d'album," dedicated to A. Abramov. (4) "Nocturne," dedicated to Frau Terminsky. (5) Capriccio, dedicated to E. Langer. (6) "Thème avec Variations," dedicated to H. Laroche. The manuscript is dated October 27th (November 8th), 1873. Jurgenson.

3. Op. 23. Concerto for pianoforte and orchestra (in B♭ minor). Composed in November and December, 1874. The orchestration was completed, according to a note on the score, February 9th (21st), 1875. Dedicated to Hans von Bülow. Published by Jurgenson. In a letter to Frau von Meck, Tchaikovsky says he took as the principal subject of the first movement a phrase sung by Malo-Russian blind beggars at a village fair at Kamenka.

Besides the example just quoted, he also borrowed another air, the chansonette, "Il faut s'amuser, danser, et rire," which the twins used to hum early in the seventies, in remembrance of a certain charming singer.

4. Op. 26. Serenade for violin, with orchestral accompaniment (B minor). Composed January, 1875. Dedicated to L. Auer. Jurgenson.

5. Op. 27. Six songs : (1) "An den Schlaf," words by Ogariev. (2) "Ob sich die Wolke dort," words by Grekov. (3) "Geh' nicht von mir," words by Fet. (4) "Abend," words by Chevchenko. (5) "Klage," words by Mickiewicz. (6) "Dem Voglein gleich," words by Mickiewicz. All six dedicated to Madame Lavrovskaya. The date of composition not precisely known. Jurgenson.

6. Op. 28. Six songs : (1) "Nein, wen ich liebe," words from de Musset, dedicated to A. Nikholaev. (2) "Die rothe Perlenschnur," words by Syrokomli, dedicated to D. Dodonov. (3)

"Warum im Traume," words by Mey, dedicated to Frau Ilina. (4) " Er liebte mich so sehr," words by Apukhtin, dedicated to E. Marsini. (5) " Kein Wort von Dir," words by Alexis Tolstoi, dedicated to B. Korsov. (6) " Ein einzig Wörtchen," text by P. Tchaikovsky, dedicated to Frau E. Kadmina. The date of completion is given on the manuscript as April 11th (23rd), 1875, in Moscow. Jurgenson.

7. Op. 29. Symphony No. 3 (in D major) in five movements. The score bears the following note in the composer's own writing: "Commenced June 5th (17th) at Ussovo, completed August 1st (13th), 1875, at Verbovka." Published by Jurgenson. Played for the first time in Moscow, November 7th (19th), 1875.

Besides the above works, Tchaikovsky was engaged during part of August, 1875, upon the Ballet, *The Swan Lake*.

His literary activity was very considerable. Between September, 1874, and April, 1875, he wrote not less than fifteen articles.

1875–1876

1. Op. 30. Quartet No. 3 in E flat major, for two violins, viola, and 'cello, dedicated to the memory of F. Laub. The first sketch dates from the beginning of January, 1876, in Paris. Finished, according to date upon the manuscript, February 18th (March 1st), 1876. Performed for the first time March 18th (30th) of the same year at Grijimaly's concert. Published by Jurgenson.

2. Op. 20. *The Swan Lake.* Ballet in four acts. Begun August, 1875, finished at the end of March, 1876. Published by Jurgenson. First performance at the Opera House, Moscow, February 20th (March 4th), 1877.

3. Op. 37. *The Seasons,* twelve pieces for piano. These were written in the course of the year, one piece each month, and were commissioned by the publisher of a St. Petersburg musical journal. Kashkin tells us that Tchaikovsky did not consider this a very important work, but in order not to miss sending each number at the right time, he ordered his servant to remind him

when a certain date came round in each month. The man carried out his master's order, coming at the right day with the reminder: "Peter Ilich, is it not time to send to St. Petersburg?" upon which Tchaikovsky would sit down at once and write the required piece without a pause. Later the pieces were collected and republished by Jurgenson.

4 The translation of the libretto and arrangement of the recitatives of Mozart's *Figaro*, which Tchaikovsky undertook (at the desire of N. Rubinstein) for a performance of this opera by the students of the Conservatoire.

This season Peter Ilich brought his literary work to an end. His last criticisms dealt with Wagner's Trilogy, and remained unfinished.

1876–1877

1. Op. 31. Slavonic March for full orchestra. First performance in November, 1877, under N. Rubinstein's bâton, at a symphony concert in Moscow. Jurgenson.

2. Op. 32. *Francesca da Rimini* (after Dante), symphonic fantasia for full orchestra. Dedicated to S. I. Taneiev. Tchaikovsky sketched the plan of this work during his visit to Paris in the summer of 1876. He did not actually work at the composition until the end of September. The sketch was finished October 14th (26th), the orchestration November 5th (17th). First performance, under N. Rubinstein, at a symphony concert, Moscow, February 26th (March 10th), 1877. Jurgenson.

3. Op. 33. *Variations on a Rococo Theme*, for violoncello and orchestra. Dedicated to G. Fitzenhagen. Composed December, 1876. Jurgenson.

4. Op. 34. Valse Scherzo, for violin and orchestra. Dedicated to Joseph Kotek. Composed early in January, 1877. Jurgenson.

During this season Tchaikovsky sketched out his Fourth Symphony and two-thirds of his opera, *Eugene Oniegin*.

1877–1878

1. Op. 36, Symphony No. 4 (F minor), in four movements. Dedicated to "My best friend." The first sketch was finished in

May, 1877. On August 11th (23rd) Tchaikovsky began the instrumentation of the work, and completed the first movement on September 12th (24th). After an interval of two months he returned to the Symphony, about the end of November. The Andante was finished on December 15th (27th), the Scherzo on the 20th (January 1st) 1878, and the Finale on the 26th (January 7th, 1878). The first performance of the Symphony took place February 10th (22nd), 1878, at a concert of the Russian Musical Society, conducted by N. Rubinstein.

2. Op. 24, *Eugene Oniegin*, lyric scenes, in three acts and seven scenes. The libretto is freely arranged from Poushkin by the composer himself and K. S. Shilovsky. The idea of this opera originated with the celebrated singer, Madame E. A. Lavrovsky.

On May 18th (30th), 1877, Tchaikovsky sketched the plan for a libretto.

On June 6th (18th) the second scene of the first act (the Letter Scene) was finished, and by June 15th (27th) the entire act was complete. By June 23rd (July 5th), two-thirds of the opera were ready. After a month's respite, Tchaikovsky returned to the work at Kamenka, in August, and completed the opera. Here he also began the instrumentation. During September and the first half of October he did not work upon it at all; afterwards he continued the instrumentation, finishing the whole of the first act and despatching it to Moscow by the 23rd (November 4th). In November Tchaikovsky orchestrated the first scene of the second act. The whole of December was devoted to the Fourth Symphony. On January 2nd (14th) he took up the opera once more, at San Remo, and, completed it by the 20th (February 1st) of this month. In the summer of 1880, at the request of the Director of the Imperial Opera, Tchaikovsky added an *écossaise* to the first scene of Act II. and made some slight changes in the Finale.

The first performance of the opera took place on March 17th (29th), 1879, by the students of the Moscow Conservatoire, in the Small Theatre. For an account of the plot, see Appendix B.

3. Op. 38. Six songs, dedicated to A. Tchaikovsky. (1) "Don Juan's Serenade," words by Count A. Tolstoi; (2) "Das war im

3 B

ersten Lenzesstrahl" (A. Tolstoi); (3) "Im erregenden Tanze"
(A. Tolstoi); (4) "Ach wenn du könntest" (A. Tolstoi); (5)
"Aus dem Jenseits" (Lermontov); (6) "Pimpinella" (Florentine
song). Published by P. I. Jurgenson, Moscow.

4. Op. 40. Twelve pieces for pianoforte (medium difficulty),
dedicated to M. Tchaikovsky. (1) "Etude," (2) "Chanson triste,"
(3) "Marche funèbre," (4) "Mazurka in C major," (5) "Mazurka in
D major," (6) "Chant sans paroles," (7) "Au village," (8) "Valse in
A major," (9) "Valse in A major," (10) "Danse russe," (11)
"Scherzo in F major," (12) "Rêverie interrompue." Of these
pieces, No. 12 was composed first. The middle section of this
piece is a Venetian song, which was sung almost every evening
under his window in Venice. The other pieces date from various
times, the "Danse russe" from 1876, having been originally intended as a number for the Ballet, *The Swan Lake*. Jurgenson,
Moscow.

5. Op. 37. Sonata for pianoforte (G major), in four movements. Dedicated to Carl Klindworth. Commenced early in
March, 1878, at Clarens, and completed on April 30th (May
12th). First performed in public by Nicholas Rubinstein, in
Moscow, October 21st (November 2nd), 1879.

6. Op. 35. Concerto for violin and orchestra. Originally
dedicated to L. Auer. Tchaikovsky afterwards substituted the
name of A. Brodsky. Begun early in March, 1878, at Clarens,
and the sketch finished by the 16th (28th) of the same month.
The original Andante did not satisfy the composer, who wrote a
new one. The instrumentation was completed by the end of April.
First performance by A. Brodsky, in Vienna (1879). Jurgenson.

7. Op. 42. "Souvenir d'un lieu cher," three pieces for violin
and pianoforte accompaniment. No. 1 is the original Andante of
the Violin Concerto. The other two pieces were composed at
Brailov about the end of May. Jurgenson.

8. Op. 41. The Liturgy of St. John Chrysostom, for four-part
mixed chorus. Commenced May, 1878, at Kamenka, and finished
on the 27th (June 8th) at Brailov. Jurgenson.

9. Op. 39. Kinderalbum, twenty-four easy pieces for pianoforte (*à la* Schumann). Dedicated to Volodya Davidov. P. I.
Jurgenson.

10. "Skobeliev March," composed by "Sinopov." Tchaikovsky concealed the authorship of this piece, because he considered it of no value. It was commissioned by Jurgenson at the end of April, and composed at Kamenka.

Besides these works, Tchaikovsky translated in December, 1877, the Italian words of six songs by Glinka, and wrote the text of a vocal quartet, also by Glinka.

The greater part of his First Suite was also completed during August, 1878.

1878–1879

1. Op. 43. First Suite, for full orchestra, in six movements.

The first sketches were made at Verbovka between August 15th and 25th, 1878. Originally the Suite was intended to have five movements only: Introduction and Fugue, Scherzo, Andante, Intermezzo ("Echo du bal"), and Rondo. Of these, three movements were completed, the fourth sketched out, and the fifth projected, when Tchaikovsky laid it aside, only to return to it in November while in Florence. On the 13th (25th) of this month it was finished. The last two movements, however, received different titles, "March Miniature" (4th) and "Giants' Dance" (5th). In August, 1879, the composer added a sixth movement, Divertimento. The work was first performed in Moscow, under Nicholas Rubinstein. Published by Jurgenson.

2. *The Maid of Orleans*, an opera in four acts and six scenes, dedicated to E. Napravnik.

The libretto of this work was written by Tchaikovsky himself. It is chiefly based upon Joukovsky's translation of Schiller's *Maid of Orleans*, but some ideas were also derived from Wallon, Barbier's play, and the libretto of Mermet's opera on the same subject. It is a pity the composer did nor confine himself to Schiller's work, and more especially as regards the uninteresting and gloomy ending. Shortly before his death Tchaikovsky frequently spoke of altering the last scene and substituting Schiller's close. With this intention, he purchased the works of the German poet, but unfortunately he was not destined to read the tragedy again. For the plot of *The Maid of Orleans*, see Appendix B.

1879–1880

1. Op. 44. Second Concerto, for pianoforte and orchestra, in three movements. Dedicated to N. Rubinstein. Played for the first time in public on May 22nd (June 3rd), 1882, by S. I. Taneiev. Jurgenson.

2. The revised edition of the Second Symphony. Published by Bessel.

3. The "Italian Capriccio," for full orchestra. Dedicated to K. Davidov. The opening fanfare in this work is a bugle call of the Italian cavalry, which Tchaikovsky heard every evening while living in the Hôtel Constanzi, next to the barracks of the Royal Cuirassiers. Jurgenson.

4. Music for a *tableau vivant:* "Montenegro at the moment of receiving the news of war between Russia and Turkey. A village elder reading out the manifesto." This music was never performed, as the projected entertainment fell through. The manuscript has entirely disappeared.

5. Six vocal duets, with pianoforte accompaniment. Dedicated to Tatiana Davidov: (*a*) "Der Abend," (*b*) "Ballade," (*c*) "Thränen," (*d*) "Im Garten," (*e*) "Leidenschaft," (*f*) "Dämmerung." Jurgenson.

6. Op. 47. Seven songs, with pianoforte accompaniment. Dedicated to A. V. Panaiev: (*a*) "Wenn ich das gewusst," (*b*) "Durch die Gefilde des Himmels," (*c*) "Der Dammerung Schleier sank," (*d*) "Schlaf ein, betrubtes Lieb," (*e*) "Gesegnet sei mir Wald und Au," (*f*) "Ob Heller Tag," (*g*) "War ich nicht ein Halm." Jurgenson.

Besides the above, Tchaikovsky revised the overture, *Romeo and Juliet.*

1880–1881

1. Serenade for string orchestra, in four movements. Dedicated to Carl Albrecht. First performance January 16th (28th), under the direction of Erdmannsdörfer. Published by Jurgenson.

2. Op. 49. *The Year 1812*, festival overture for full orchestra. Composed for the consecration of the Cathedral of the Saviour, Moscow. Jurgenson.

Besides the above, an attempt to harmonise the Vesper Service and the first sketch of the opera, *Mazeppa*.

1881–1882

1. Op. 50. Trio for pianoforte, violin, and violoncello. Dedicated to the memory of a great artist (N. G. Rubinstein). The variation theme of the second movement is a reminiscence of an excursion made in company with Nicholas Rubinstein, and other colleagues from the Moscow Conservatoire, shortly after the first performance of *Sniegourochka* (*The Snow Maiden*), in the spring of 1873. The Trio was played for the first time in public on October 18th (30th), 1882, by Taneiev, Grijimaly, and Fitzenhagen. Published by Jurgenson.

2. An attempt to harmonise Divine Service. Setting for mixed chorus. Seventeen numbers. Jurgenson.

From June to October Tchaikovsky was occupied in editing the works of Bortniansky.

During this year he began the sketch of the opera, *Mazeppa*. By the middle of July two acts were completed.

1882–1883

1. Op. 51. Six pieces for pianoforte : (1) " Valse de Salon," (2) " Polka peu dansante," (3) " Menuetto scherzoso," (4) " Natha —Valse," (5) " Romance," (6) " Valse sentimentale."

These pieces were commissioned by the brothers Jurgenson and composed at Kamenka about the end of August.

2. Verses upon the theme of the " Slavsia," from Glinka's *A Life for the Tsar,* winding up with the Russian National Anthem, for chorus and orchestra.

This chorus was sung by 7,500 students in Moscow, May 10th (22nd), 1883, at the moment when the Emperor Alexander III. appeared at the Red Staircase upon his solemn entry to the Kremlin. (Manuscript only.)

3. Festal Coronation March for orchestra. Commissioned by the city of Moscow, first performed at Sokolinky, on May 23rd (June 4th), at a fête in honour of the Coronation. Jurgenson.

4. *Mazeppa*, an opera, in three acts and six scenes. The

subject is taken from Poushkin's poem, *Poltava*, arranged by Bourenin and the composer himself.

The opera was first performed at the Imperial Opera, Moscow, February 3rd (15th), 1884. Jurgenson. For the plot, see Appendix B.

Besides the above, Tchaikovsky began his Second Suite for orchestra during the summer of 1883.

1883 TO JANUARY, 1885

1. Op. 53. Suite No. 2, in four movements, for full orchestra. Dedicated to Madame P. W. Tchaikovsky. First performed at an extra concert of the Russian Musical Society, February 4th (16th), 1884, in Moscow, under the direction of Max Erdmanns-dörfer. Published by Jurgenson.

2. Op. 54. Sixteen Children's Songs, with pianoforte accompaniment. Published by Jurgenson.

3. Op. 55. Suite No. 3, in four movements, for full orchestra. Dedicated to M. Erdmannsdörfer. First performance in Petersburg, in January, 1885, under the direction of Hans von Bülow. Published by Jurgenson.

4. Op. 56. Fantasia Concerto, in two movements, for pianoforte, with orchestral accompaniment. Originally dedicated to Madame A. Essipoff; afterwards to Madame Sophie Menter. Played for the first time by S. Taneiev, February 22nd (March 6th), 1885, in Moscow. Published by Jurgenson.

5. Impromptu Capriccio for pianoforte. Dedicated to Madame S. Jurgenson. Originally published in the "Subscribers' Album" of Paris *Gaulois*. Was taken over later by Jurgenson.

6. Elegy for string orchestra. Composed in memory of the actor, I. Samarin. Published by Jurgenson.

7. Three church anthems. Published by Jurgenson.

8. Op. 57. Six songs, with pianoforte accompaniment. (1) "O, sprich, wovon die Nachtigall," (2) "Auf's bleiche Herbstgefild," (3) "O, frage nicht," (4) "Schlaf' ein," (5) "Der Tod," (6) "Nur du allein." Published by Jurgenson. Besides the above, Tchaikovsky had been working, in November, 1884, at the reconstruction of his opera, *Vakoula the Smith*.

1. Remodelling the opera *Vakoula the Smith* as *Les Caprices d'Oxane.* Besides simplifying the orchestration and harmony and cutting down the work, as he first proposed, Tchaikovsky also introduced some entirely new numbers: (1) the duet between Vakoula and Oxane and the Finale of the second scene in first act, (2) the Schoolmaster's song, (3) the quintet in the first scene of the second act, (4) the couplets in third act. Published by Jurgenson.

2. Hymn in honour of Saints Cyril and Methodius. This hymn is an old Slavonic melody arranged for a choir :—

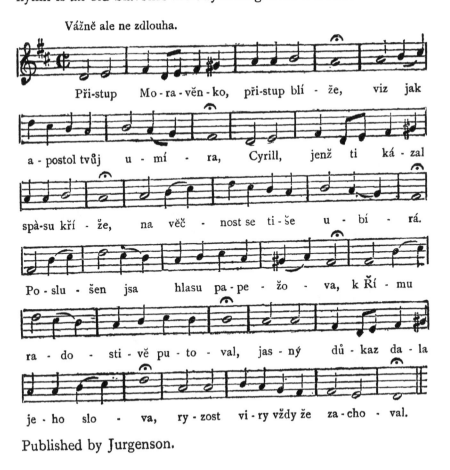

Published by Jurgenson.

3. Five church hymns. Published by Jurgenson.

4. " Ecossaise," for the sixth scene in the opera *Eugene Oniegin*. Tchaikovsky composed and orchestrated this piece in Maidanovo and sent it to St. Petersburg all in one day.

5. Op. 58. *Manfred*. A Symphony in four scenes for full orchestra, from a dramatic poem by Lord Byron. Dedicated to Mily Balakirev. The first sketches for this work were made in April, 1885. According to the note on the score, it was finished December 12th (24th), 1885, and played for the first time March 11th (23rd), 1886, under the direction of Erdmanns-dörfer, in Moscow. Published by Jurgenson.

1885–1886

1. Text and music of a chorus for the fiftieth anniversary of the foundation of the Imperial School of Jurisprudence. Composed at Maidanovo, September, 1885. Manuscript.

2. " Jurists' March," for full orchestra. Composed at Kamenka, October, 1885. Published by Jurgenson.

3. The " Domovoi " (" House Spirit "), from a scene in Ostrovsky's play, *The Voyevode*. Composed January, 1886. Manuscript.

4. Op. 59. " Dumka." Russian village scene for the pianoforte. Dedicated to the Principal of the Paris Conservatoire, A. Marmontel. Composed at Maidanovo end of February. Published by Jurgenson. Besides these unimportant works, Tchaikovsky was engaged during the whole season upon his opera, *The Enchantress*.

1886–1887

(FROM SEPTEMBER 1ST, 1886, TO JANUARY 1ST, 1888)

1. Op. 60. Twelve songs, with pianoforte accompaniment. Dedicated to Her Majesty the Empress Maria Feodorovna. (1) " Die gestrige Nacht," (2) " Verschwiegenheit," (3) " O, wüsstest Du," (4) " Die Nachtigall," (5) " Schlichte Worte," (6) " Die Schlaflose Nächte," (7) " Lied der Zigeunerin," (8) " Lebewohl," (9) " Die Nacht," (10) " Lockung," (11) " Heldenmut," (12) " Sternennacht." Published by Jurgenson.

2. *The Enchantress*, opera in four acts. The libretto by

I. V. Shpajinsky, author of the drama of the same name. First performed on October 20th (November 1st), 1887, at the Maryinsky Theatre, St. Petersburg, and conducted by the composer. Jurgenson. For plot, see Appendix B.

3. Op. 61. *Mozartiana.* Suite No. 4, in four movements, arranged from various works of Mozart and orchestrated for full orchestra. In his short preface to the score Tchaikovsky gives the following reasons which prompted this work : " A large number of the most beautiful of Mozart's smaller works are, for some reason, little known, not only to the public, but to musicians. The composer's object in arranging this Suite was to bring more frequently before the public works which, however modest in form, are gems of musical literature." First performed at Moscow, November 14th (26th), 1887, under the direction of the composer. Jurgenson.

4. Op. 62. "Pezzo Capriccioso," for violoncello, with orchestral accompaniment. Dedicated to A. Brandoukov. Played by him for the first time, November 25th (December 7th), 1889. Jurgenson.

5. Op. 63. Six songs. Dedicated to the Grand Duke Constantine Constantinovich. (1) "Nicht sogleich," (2) "Am offenen Fenster," (3) "Fahrt hin, ihr Träume," (4) Wiedersehen," (5) "Kein Lichtlein glänzt," (6) "Serenade." Jurgenson.

6. A chorus for men's voices *a capella*. Dedicated to the Students' Choir of the Moscow University. Published by Jurgenson.

1888 (FROM JANUARY 1ST TO SEPTEMBER 1ST)

1. Op. 64. Symphony No. 5 (E minor), in four movements, for full orchestra Dedicated to Herr Theodor Ave-Lallemant of Hamburg. First performance in Petersburg, November, 1888, conducted by the composer. Published by Jurgenson.

2. Op. 65. Six songs to French words, with pianoforte accompaniment. Dedicated to Désirée Artôt. (1) "Où vas-tu souffle d'aurore?" (2) "Déception," (3) "Sérénade," (4) "Qu'importe que l'hiver," (5) "Les larmes," (6) "Rondel." Composed in the course of the summer. Jurgenson.

3. "Die Nachtigall," chorus *a capella*. Dedicated to the

mixed choir of the Petersburg Imperial Opera House.   Exact
date of composition unknown.   Jurgenson.

Besides the above, Tchaikovsky completed the sketches for the
overture-fantasia, *Hamlet.*

1888–1889

1. Orchestration of an overture by Laroche.   Manuscript.

2. Op. 67.   *Hamlet,* overture-fantasia for full orchestra.
Dedicated to Edvard Grieg.   Jurgenson.

3. Valse Scherzo, for pianoforte.   Jurgenson.

4. Op. 66.   *Dornröschen* (Sleeping Beauty).   Ballet in three
acts, with a prologue.   Dedicated to I. A. Vsievolojsky.   The
subject is taken from Perrault's fairy tale of the same name.

The first performance of the Ballet took place January 3rd
(15th), 1890, in the Maryinsky Theatre, Petersburg.   Jurgenson.

1889–1890

1. Impromptu for pianoforte.   Dedicated to A. Rubinstein.
Jurgenson.

2. "Greeting to A. G. Rubinstein," chorus *a capella.*
Jurgenson.

3. *Pique Dame.*   Opera in three acts and seven scenes.
Libretto by Modeste Tchaikovsky.   The subject is taken from
Poushkin's novel of the same name.   The first performance
took place in the Maryinsky Theatre, in Petersburg, December
7th (19th), 1890.   Published by Jurgenson.   For plot, see Appendix B.

Besides the above, on June 13th Tchaikovsky began to compose a Sextet for Strings, of which the sketches were finished by
June 30th.

1890–1891

1. Op. 67a.   Music to Shakespeare's *Hamlet.*   Overture,
melodramas, fanfares, marches, and entr'actes for small orchestra.
Seventeen numbers in all, of which, however, some are transferred from earlier works.   Jurgenson.

2. Three choruses *a capella.*   Composed at Frolovskoe, and

dedicated to I. A. Melnikov's "Gratuitous Choral Class." Published in Melnikov's *Collection of Russian Choruses.*

Besides the above, Tchaikovsky finished the sketches of the *Nut-cracker* Ballet and of the opera of *Iolanthe.*

1891–1892

1. Op. 78. *The Voyevode*, symphonic ballad, for full orchestra (after Poushkin). First performance under the direction of the composer, at a concert given by Siloti, November 6th (18th), 1891. The following day Tchaikovsky himself destroyed the score of this work, the band parts remaining in Siloti's keeping. After the composer's death the score was restored from the parts and published by Belaiev.

2. Op. 69. *Iolanthe.* Lyrical opera in one act. The subject founded on the drama, *King René's Daughter*, by the Danish poet, Henrik Herz. The libretto by Modeste Tchaikovsky. First performed in Petersburg in the Maryinsky Theatre, December 6th (18th), 1892. Published by Jurgenson. See Appendix B.

3. Op. 70. "Souvenir de Florence." Sextet for two violins, two violas, and two violoncellos, in four movements. Dedicated to the Petersburg Chamber Music Society. First performance by this society November 25th (December 7th), 1892. Published by Jurgenson.

4. Op. 71. *The Nut-cracker.* Fairy Ballet in two acts and three scenes. The subject is borrowed from A. Dumas' version of Hoffman's fairy tale. The following programme was suggested to Tchaikovsky by the gifted ballet-master, Petipa :—

No. 1. Soft music. Sixty-four bars.

No. 2. The tree is lit up. Sparkling music. Eight bars.

No. 3. Enter the children. Animated and joyous music. Twenty-four bars.

No. 4. A moment of surprise and admiration. A few bars of tremolo.

No. 5. A march. Sixty-four bars.

No. 6. Entrée des Incroyables. Sixteen bars, rococo (tempo menuet).

No. 7. Galop.

No. 8. Enter Drosselmeyer. Awe-inspiring but comic music. A broad movement, sixteen to twenty-four bars.

The music gradually changes character—twenty-four bars. It becomes less serious, lighter, and finally gay in tone.

Grave music for eight bars, then pause.

Repeat the eight bars—pause.

Four bars which express astonishment.

No. 9. Eight bars in mazurka rhythm. Eight more. Sixteen still in mazurka rhythm.

No. 10. A piquant, spicy valse, strongly rhythmic. Forty-eight bars.

1892–1893

1. Military march. Dedicated to the 98th Infantry Regiment. Tchaikovsky's cousin, Andrew Petrovich Tchaikovsky, colonel of this regiment, asked him in February, 1893, to compose this march.

2. Op. 72. Eighteen pieces for pianoforte. (1) "Impromptu," (2) "Berceuse," (3) "Tendres reproches," (4) " Danse caractéristique," (5) "Méditation," (6) "Mazurque pour danser," (7) "Polacca de Concert," (8) "Dialogue," (9) "Un poco di Schumann," (10) "Scherzo-Fantaisie," (11) "Valse-Bluette," (12) "L'Espiègle," (13) "Echo rustique," (14) "Chant élégiaque," (15) "Un poco di Chopin," (16) "Valse à cinq temps," (17) "Passé lointain," (18) "Scène dansante. Invitation au trépak." Published by Jurgenson.

3. Op. 73. Six songs, with pianoforte accompaniment. Words by D. Rathaus. Dedicated to N. Figner. (1) "An den schlummernden Strom," (2) "Nachts," (3) "O, du mondhelle Nacht," (4) "Sonne ging zur Ruhe," (5) "In Truber Stunde," (6) "Weil ich wie einstmals." Published by Jurgenson.

4. "Night." Quartet for soprano, alto, tenor, and bass, with pianoforte accompaniment. Words by P. Tchaikovsky. The music is founded on Mozart's Pianoforte Fantasia No. 4.

In 1892 Vladimir Napravnik, who was staying with Tchaikovsky at Maidanovo, played to him very frequently. This pleased his host, and on one occasion Napravnik's clever rendering of Mozart's fantasia roused him to so much enthusiasm that he resolved to make a quartet from the middle movement. He carried out this intention in May, 1893. Jurgenson.

5. Op. 74. Symphony No. 6, in four movements, for full orchestra. Dedicated to V. Davidov. Performed for the first time in Petersburg, October, 16th (28th), 1893. Conducted by the composer. Jurgenson.

6. Op. 75. Concerto No. 3, for pianoforte and orchestra. Dedicated to Louis Diemer. This Concerto was taken from a Symphony which Tchaikovsky began in May, 1892, and all but completed. He afterwards destroyed the Symphony. The Concerto was first played in Petersburg by Taneiev. Published by Jurgenson.

Besides the above, the following works were found at Klin after Tchaikovsky's death :—

1. *Momento lirico.* A piece, nearly completed, for the pianoforte. Taneiev only pieced together the separate sketches. Published by Jurgenson.

2. Duet, " Romeo and Juliet." In this work Taneiev had more to amplify, as he had to supply the entire accompaniments of the solo parts. He borrowed these from Tchaikovsky's orchestral fantasia on the same subject.

3. Andante and Finale, for pianoforte and orchestra. Both movements were arranged by Tchaikovsky himself from sketches for the Symphony planned in 1892. The orchestration is by Taneiev, who was the first to play the work in public at Belaiev's first Russian Symphony Concert, February 8th (20th), 1896. Thus Taneiev accomplished his rôle as the original interpreter of all Tchaikovsky's pianoforte works (excepting the Concerto in B flat minor, which was played for the first time by Kross). Published by Belaiev.

APPENDIX B

1. *The Oprichnik.* The Oprichniks were a band of dissolute young noblemen, the chosen body-guard of Ivan the Terrible, who swore by fearful and unnatural oaths to carry out every command of the despot they served. Sometimes they masqueraded as monks and celebrated "black mass." In reality they were robbers and murderers, hated and feared by the people whom they oppressed. Andrew Morozov, the descendant of a noble, but impoverished, house, and the only son of the widowed Lady Morozova, is in love with the beautiful Natalia, daughter of Prince Jemchoujny. His poverty disqualifies him as a suitor. Natalia's father promises her hand to the elderly boyard Mitkov. While desperately in need of money, Andrew falls in with Basmanov, a young Oprichnik, who persuades him to join their community, telling him that an Oprichnik can always fill his own pockets Andrew consents, believing it to be his only chance of revenging himself upon Prince Jemchoujny. The Lady Morozova is a high-minded, religious woman. Andrew, anxious to relieve her poverty, takes her money which he has borrowed from Basmanov. His mother refuses to touch what she knows to be the fruit of robbery and murder, and implores her son not to associate with the hated Oprichniks. Andrew, who is devoted to his mother, promises to respect her wishes. Afterwards the desire for power and vengeance prevails, and he consents to take the oath of the Oprichnik band. The first sacrifice demanded of him is the complete renunciation of his mother and Natalia. Lady Morozova is now heart-broken, deserted by her son and hated by the populace, who insult her in the public square as the "mother of an Oprichnik." She is about to take refuge in the

church, when Natalia flies to her for protection. She has escaped from her father and her middle-aged suitor Mitkov. Prince Jemchoujny appears on the scene and orders his rebellious daughter to return to her home. His chidings are interrupted by the arrival of the Oprichniks, awakening terror and hatred among the people. Andrew catches sight of his mother, whom he has not seen for many days, and rushes to embrace her, when the sinister theme of the Oprichniks is heard in the orchestra, reminding him of his vows. Lady Morozova turns from her son, disowns him, and solemnly curses him as an Oprichnik. In the last act Andrew, unable to abandon Natalia to her fate, resolves to marry her in spite of his vows. But Prince Viazminsky, the leader of the Oprichniks, cherishes an old grudge against the family of Morozov, and works for Andrew's downfall. He breaks in upon the wedding-feast with a message from the Tsar. Ivan the Terrible has heard of the bride's beauty, and desires her attendance at the royal apartments. Andrew, with gloomy forebodings in his heart, prepares to escort his bride, when Viazminsky, with a meaning smile, explains that the invitation is for the bride *alone*. Andrew refuses to let his wife go into the royal presence without his protection. Viazminsky proclaims him a traitor to his vows. Natalia is carried off by force, and the Oprichniks lead Andrew into the market-place to suffer the death penalty at their hands. Meanwhile Lady Morozova, who has relented, comes to bless her son on his wedding-day. She enters the deserted hall, where Viazminsky, alone, is gloating over the success of his intrigue. She inquires unsuspectingly for Andrew, and he leads her to the window. Horror-stricken, she witnesses the execution of her son, and falls dead at the feet of her triumphant enemy.

2. *Vakoula the Smith*, afterwards known as *Cherevichek* (" The Little Shoes "), and finally republished as *Les Caprices d'Oxane*. Christmas Eve. A moonlight night, in the village of Dikanka. Solokha, the witch, comes out of one of the huts, and is joined by the devil. They decide to fly off together. The witch goes to fetch a broomstick, and the devil in his monologue sings of his hatred of Vakoula the Smith, because the latter has drawn a caricature of him upon the church wall. He invokes a snowstorm. Solokha reappears, and they elope together, stealing the moon and

stars as they go, and leaving the village plunged in darkness. Vakoula is making love to the beautiful daughter of Choub the Cossack. To-night Choub is going to supper with the sacristan, and Vakoula will take the opportunity of visiting his sweetheart, who, however, remains deaf to all his entreaties. Meanwhile Choub loses his way in the darkness, and after wandering round in a circle finds himself at his own hut. Vakoula mistakes him for a rival lover, and drives him away from his own threshold.

The second act shows the interior of the witch's hut, where Solokha is making herself smart after her ride through space on a broomstick. The devil comes out of the stove and makes love to her. They dance the *Gopak*, while little imps emerge from every nook and cranny in the form of crickets and beetles. A knock is heard, and the devil hides himself in an empty sack. Enter the Headman of the village. Another knock, and the Headman, who does not want to be caught with Solokha, disposes of himself in another sack. This time the sacristan comes in, and the same ruse is enacted; and, finally, Choub appears on the scene and, at a fourth knock, he too takes refuge in a sack. The last comer is the witch's son Vakoula. He is so wrapped up in his love troubles, that he picks up the sacks in an absent-minded way and carries them off to the smithy. In the scene that follows the villagers are singing Christmas carols in the village street. The moon has returned to its place. Oxana, who is among the singers, catches sight of Vakoula and cannot refrain from teazing him a little more. She tells him she will marry him if he will bring her the Tsaritsa's own shoes. Vakoula goes off in a temper, taking the sack containing the devil and leaving the others ·in the road. The children peep inside and discover the Headman, the sacristan, and Choub.

In the third act Vakoula goes to drown himself in the forest pool. He puts the sack containing the devil at the edge of the water. The evil spirit offers to give Oxana to the smith in exchange for his soul. Vakoula consents, and will sign the contract in his blood. The devil lets him go for a moment, and Vakoula overpowers him in turn. He makes the devil promise to take him to the Tsaritsa, and they take flight for St. Petersburg. A room in the Palace: the herald announces a victory of the Russian army. The Zaparogue Cossacks are summoned before the Tsar. The Cossacks dance a *Gopak*. Vakoula takes the opportunity of begging for the Tsaritsa's shoes, which are granted to him. The devil takes him back to his native village. Christmas morning: Vakoula finds Oxana bewailing his supposed loss. He consoles her with the shoes, and she consents to become his wife.

3. *Eugene Oniegin*. Madame Lerin and the old nurse are making preserves in the garden of a Russian country house. From indoors a duet is heard. Tatiana and her sister Olga are singing to the accompaniment of a harp. The peasants appear on the scene, carrying the last sheaf from the harvest fields. National songs and dances. The announcement of guests creates a considerable commotion in the quiet country household. They prove to be Lensky, a young neighbour, fresh from a German university, and Oniegin, a dandy from the capital, on a visit to his friend. Madame Lerin and the nurse retire to prepare supper. The young people saunter in the garden, Lensky with Olga, Tatiana with Oniegin. Tatiana is shy at first, then falls in love with the stranger. In the second scene Tatiana is sitting in her room by moonlight. The old nurse comes to scold her for not being asleep. There follows a long, confidential talk between them (recitative with soft accompaniment based on Tatiana's theme). When her nurse has gone, Tatiana sits dreaming of her love for Oniegin. How will he guess her secret, unless she reveals it herself? In her innocence of the world she resolves to write him a love letter. She begs the nurse to convey it to Oniegin. The old woman hesitates, but cannot refuse anything to the child of her heart. Reluctantly she departs on her errand. The third scene takes us back to the garden. Oniegin meets Tatiana. He cannot appreciate the directness and sweetness of the girl's nature. Jaded and world-worn, Tatiana seems to him insipid and provincial, while at the same time he finds her forward. He thanks her coldly for her letter, assures her he is not a marrying man, and gives her some cynical advice as to the wisdom of acting with more maidenly reserve in future. Then he leaves her, crushed with shame and disappointment.

3 C

The second act opens upon a ballroom scene. It is Tatiana's birthday. Oniegin, whom Lensky has dragged to the dance against his will, amuses himself by flirting with Olga. The complimentary couplets sung to Tatiana by the elderly Frenchman Triquet are a favourite number in this scene. As the ball progresses Lensky, mad with jealousy, loses his self-control and insults Oniegin. The latter now feels some qualms of conscience, but the hot-headed youth forces a challenge upon him, and he consents to fight. The party breaks up in consternation. The second scene is devoted to the duel in which Oniegin kills Vladimir Lensky.

Some years are supposed to elapse between the second and third acts. A reception at a fashionable house in Petersburg. Oniegin is seen standing apart from the guests, in gloomy reflection. He has returned home after a self-imposed exile. Remorse for Lensky's death haunts him, and he can find no satisfaction in love or folly. All the guests are impatient for the arrival of the acknowledged belle of society, Princess Gremin. When she comes on the scene, Oniegin recognises Tatiana, transformed into a stately, gracious woman of the world. Her husband is elderly, but distinguished, handsome, and devoted to his beautiful young wife. Oniegin's chilly egotism is thawed, and he falls passionately in love with the woman he once despised. The last scene takes place in the boudoir of the Princess Gremin. She is reading a letter from Oniegin, in which he declares his love. This communication throws her into a state of agitation, and, before she can recover herself, Oniegin breaks in upon her in person. In a long, impassioned duet he implores her to have pity and to fly with him. With some of the rake's vanity still left in his nature, he cannot at first realise that she can resist him. Tatiana respects and honours her husband. At first she tries to punish Oniegin for the past. Then she struggles between duty and reawakened love. Finally, with a supreme effort, she breaks away from him at the very moment when she has confessed her true feelings. When the curtain falls, Oniegin, baffled and despairing, is left alone on the stage.

4. *The Maid of Orleans.* A village festival at Domrémy. Thibaut, Joan's father, and Raimond, her lover, appear upon the scene.

Thibaut says it is no time for dancing and singing; a maid needs a man to protect her, and therefore he wishes Joan to marry Raimond. She is silent, but finally confesses that she has chosen another destiny. Her father is angry and reproachful. A fire is seen on the horizon, and the tocsin is heard. Old Bertrand comes in. He speaks of the desperate state of the country and the approach of the English army. Suddenly Joan rises up and speaks with prophetic inspiration. She feels the hour for action has come, and bids farewell to her birthplace. The angels appear to Joan and incite her to heroic deeds.

Third act. A field near Rheims. The meeting of Joan and Lionel. They fight. Joan overcomes him, and stands above him with her drawn sword. At this moment she catches sight of his face, and falls in love with him. He returns her passion. Dunois comes upon the scene, and Lionel tells him that he wishes to join the French army. Dunois is delighted that such a great leader should come over to France. He leads him away in the King's name. Joan collapses, and discovers she is wounded. Second scene. The coronation of Charles VII. The King announces to the people that Joan has saved the country. Her father declares that she has been supported by the powers of hell, rather than the angels of heaven. No one believes him. Lionel and Dunois are ready to do combat on her behalf. The Archbishop of Rheims asks her if she is "pure." She believes herself a sinner in intention, and will not reply. All leave her. Lionel comes to console her in her abandonment. She turns from him in indignation, as from "her worst enemy."

Fourth act. The forest. Lionel pursues Joan. At first she flees from him, then suddenly yields to their mutual passion. They hear the English trumpets in the distance. Joan refuses to escape. She is taken prisoner, and Lionel is slain. Second scene. Rouen. Joan is led to the stake. For a moment she loses courage, but is sustained by a chorus of angels. She is bound to the stake. A priest offers her a wooden crucifix. The faggots are lighted.

5. *Mazeppa.*—First act. First scene. Kochoubey's garden, where his daughter Maria, after parting with her girl friends, sings of her love for her father's guest, Mazeppa. Enter Andrew,

a young Cossack, who has loved Maria from childhood. He knows her secret passion for Mazeppa. Kochoubey and his wife come into the garden with their guests, including Mazeppa and Iskra. The former asks Kochoubey's consent to his marriage with Maria. Songs and dances take place during the discussion. Mazeppa insinuates that Maria cannot marry anyone but himself, and her father indignantly orders him to leave the house. He does so, but first wrings from Maria the confession that she cares for him more than for her parents. Second scene. Kochoubey's house. Maria has fled with Mazeppa. His wife bemoans the loss of her child, and instigates her husband to vengeance. He promises to denounce Mazeppa to the Tsar. Andrew undertakes to lay his complaint at the foot of the throne.

Second act. A dungeon in the castle of Bielotserkovsky. Kochoubey is imprisoned there, because Mazeppa has treacherously impeached him at Court before he had time to lay his own grievances before the Tsar. This scene contains a dramatic moment, in which Kochoubey is confronted with Mazeppa's tool —Orlik. In the second scene Mazeppa gives orders to Orlik for the execution of Kochoubey on the following day. Then Maria appears. Love scene with Mazeppa. She does not know the full extent of his cruelty and treachery, and still cares for him, in spite of her vague forebodings. Her mother appears on the scene, and reveals the terrible destiny which awaits Maria's father. Mother and daughter hurry away to try if they can save Kochoubey. Third scene. The place of execution. The populace are waiting to see the death of Kochoubey and Iskra. Dance of a drunken Cossack. Procession to the scaffold. Maria and her mother arrive at the moment when the axe falls, and the former loses consciousness when she realises that it is too late to effect a rescue.

Third act. Symphonic sketch, "The Battle of Poltava." The deserted garden and homestead of the Kochoubeys. Andrew appears. All day in the battle he has striven to meet Mazeppa, and slay him in single combat, but in vain. Now he has come to take a last leave of the spot where he and Maria spent their happy childhood. Enter Mazeppa and Orlik. Andrew reproaches the former for all the misery he has brought upon Maria, and challenges him to fight. Andrew is mortally wounded. Then Maria wanders in. Her misfortunes have upset her reason. Mazeppa tells her to follow him, but she refuses, and he abandons her to her fate. She sees Andrew, but does not fully recognise him. She takes the dying Cossack in her arms, and sings him to his last sleep with a childish lullaby. The peasantry, attracted by the noise of the fight between Mazeppa and Andrew, now arrive upon the scene. Maria starts up suddenly, and, with a mad laugh, throws herself into the stream.

6. *The Enchantress* ("Charodeika"). First act. The banks of the Oka, near Nijny-Novgorod. National customs. Kouma Nastasia appears outside her inn and welcomes her customers. A boat comes down the river. The Prince—son of the Governor of Nijny—is returning from the chase. He drifts by, and Kouma remains pensive at the river's edge. She is in love with the Prince. The Governor and his Counsellor, Prince Mamirov, suddenly appear on the scene. The latter, who is the representative of respectability and decency, detests Kouma. He has compelled the Governor to come and see for himself what a gang of disorderly characters meet in Nastasia's inn. The people are very agitated at this arrival, and wish to remain near Kouma in order to protect her from violence. But she begs them to retire. Then she puts on her best attire and goes out to meet the unexpected guests. The Prince immediately falls a victim to her charms. He accepts a cup of wine from the beautiful innkeeper, and gives her his ring in return. Kouma, not contented with her victory over the two men, is seized with a desire to humiliate Mamirov, and asks him to join in the mummers' dance. He refuses, but the Governor— now completely under the spell of Kouma Nastasia's beauty— orders him to do so. Mamirov dances amid the laughter of the spectators.

Second act. The garden of the Governor's house. His wife is discovered, deep in thought. Her maid Nenila is near at hand. The Governor's wife is jealous, because her husband now spends all his days with Kouma. She vows to revenge herself. Mamirov fans her smouldering wrath. Enter the Prince, who perceives that his mother is in trouble and tries to console her. They enter the house together. The Wanderer comes upon the scene, and Mamirov orders him to report upon everything that takes place in Kouma's inn. Then the Governor himself arrives. He is full of his passion for Kouma Nastasia. There follows a stormy scene between husband and wife. The Governor returns to Kouma. The Wanderer reveals to the Prince the real reason of the quarrel between the Governor and his wife, the son swears to avenge his mother's wrongs and to kill Kouma, whom he has never seen.

Third act. Kouma's house. Evening. The Governor tells Kouma he loves her, but she does not respond. He threatens her, but she declares she would sooner lose her life than yield to him. He goes away in anger. Kouma's uncle warns her that the young Prince has sworn to avenge his mother, and is coming to kill her that very night. She sends all her friends away and remains alone. She would rather die by the Prince's hand than accept the Governor as her lover. She puts out the light, lies down on her bed, and awaits the end. The Prince comes, creeps to the bedside, draws the curtain aside, and drops his dagger, spell-bound by the beauty of the woman. A lengthy duet. The Prince becomes wholly entranced by Kouma's charms.

Fourth act. A dark forest on the banks of the Oka. The cave of Koudma the Wizard. The Prince comes on the scene, attired as for hunting. He inquires of Koudma whether all is now ready for his flight with Kouma. He departs with his huntsmen. Enter the Wanderer, bringing the Governor's wife, disguised as a beggar-woman. She has come to ask the wizard for some fatal spell to destroy Kouma. The Wanderer flees in terror, and the Governor's wife enters the cave alone. A boat arrives containing Kouma and her friends. They land, leaving her alone to wait for the Prince. The revengeful wife approaches Kouma and offers her a refreshing drink, into which she drops the fatal poison. Kouma drinks. The Prince returns and rushes to embrace her. All is ready for their flight, but the poison has already done its work—Kouma dies in her lover's arms. The Governor's wife confesses her guilt, and the Prince in despair repulses her. Enter the Governor in search of the fugitives. He cannot see Kouma, and believes she is being hidden from him

Maddened with jealousy, he hurls himself upon his son and kills him. His wife curses him as a murderer. The body of the Prince is borne away and the Governor remains alone. A terrible storms breaks over his head. Overcome with remorse and terror, he falls down in a mortal swoon.

7. *Pique Dame.* First act. First scene. The Summer Garden in Petersburg. Spring. Chorus of nurses and governesses. Some of the "golden youth" of the capital appear on the scene. They speak of Hermann's extraordinary passion for gambling. Enter Hermann and Tomsky. The former talks of his love for a distinguished girl with whose name he is not acquainted, although he often meets her in the street, accompanied by an old lady of forbidding appearance. Enter Prince Yeletsky, who announces his engagement to the very girl in whom Hermann is interested. Hermann is depressed because his poverty is a hindrance to his suit. While the sight of Liza always awakens his best feelings, that of her grandmother fills him with a vague horror. Tomsky tells him a tale to the effect that the old Countess possesses the secret combination of three cards, which accounts for her extraordinary luck at the gaming tables. Hermann, in his morbid mental condition, believes himself destined to acquire this secret at any price. A terrible thunderstorm still further upsets his mind, and he begins to realise with horror that he is capable of committing a murder. He resolves to put an end to himself, but not until he has declared his love to Liza.

Second scene. Liza and her young friends are amusing themselves with singing and dancing. The governess appears on the scene, and the merry party is broken up. Liza is left alone. She is not in love with her fiancé, for her imagination is entirely occupied with the mysterious young man whom she so often meets out of doors. Suddenly Hermann appears before her. He threatens to kill himself on the spot if she will not listen to him. Just as she has gathered courage to drive him away, the old Countess comes in, alarmed by the commotion in her granddaughter's apartment. Liza conceals Hermann. The sight of the old Countess brings back his *idée fixe* of the three cards. When Liza has succeeded in calming her grandmother, and has induced her to return to her room, she goes back to Hermann with the intention of dismissing him; but in the end his passion prevails over her scruples.

Second act. Third scene. A fancy-dress ball. Prince Yeletsky pays his addresses to Liza, who does not respond. Hermann is among the guests. At the sight of the Countess the insane longing to possess the secret of her luck comes over him again. In a *tête-à-tête* with Liza he implores her to let him visit her that night. She tells him how he may gain access to her room unperceived.

Fourth scene. The Countess's bedroom. Hermann appears through the secret door. He hears steps, and hides himself again. The old Countess returns from the ball. She goes into her boudoir, and presently reappears in her night attire. She is tired and cross, and complains that in her youth parties were more amusing than they are now. She dismisses her maid, and falls asleep humming to herself an air from an old-fashioned opera. Hermann awakes her. She is so terrified that she dies suddenly, without having revealed her secret. Liza appears, and can no longer conceal from herself that Hermann only made love to her in order to carry out his mad scheme.

Third act. Fifth scene. Evening. The barracks. Hermann alone in his quarters is haunted by remorse. In his terror he rushes from the room, but is met on the threshold by the apparition of the Countess showing him the three cards. Sixth scene. Liza is waiting for Hermann near the Winter Canal. Midnight strikes, and Liza in despair is about to do away with herself when he appears on the scene. At the sight of her his madness subsides, and he thinks only of his love for her. But he soon begins to rave about the three cards, and no longer recognises Liza. In despair she throws herself into the Neva. Seventh scene. Hermann at the gambling tables. He wins on the first two cards shown him by the ghost of the Countess. When it comes to the third card no one will venture to stake against him except Prince Yeletsky. Instead of the expected ace, Hermann turns up the queen of spades, and loses all his winnings. The apparition of the Countess appears to him once more, and he stabs himself in a fit of madness.

8. *Iolanthe.* The blind daughter of King René of Provence

lives among the Vosges Mountains under the care of her nurse
Martha and her husband Bertrand. In order that she may not
realise her blindness, the King has forbidden the word "light" to
be used in her presence. The girl is sad without knowing why.
Her friends bring her flowers and try to amuse her, but in vain.
She falls asleep in the garden, and is carried into the castle by
her nurse. The King arrives, accompanied by the famous
Moorish physician, Ebn-Khakya. The latter says he must see
Iolanthe, even in her sleep, before he can pronounce an opinion
as to her sight. After a time he informs the King that she can
only be cured by a great desire to see; therefore she must be
made conscious of her condition. The King refuses to follow
this advice. Robert, Duke of Burgundy, and the Knight, de
Vaudemont, come by accident to the castle. The former has
been betrothed from childhood to Iolanthe, and is now on his
way to King René's court in order to woo his future bride. He
has never seen her, and is in no hurry to wed. They see the
notice which warns them that it is death to enter the castle
grounds. But Vaudemont catches a glimpse of the maiden
asleep on the terrace, and is spell-bound. Robert tries to make
him leave these haunts of witchcraft, but he refuses, and the
Duke goes to summon his men in order that he may carry off his
friend by force. A duet between Vaudemont and Iolanthe. He
does not realise her blindness until she asks him, "What is
light?" He breaks through the atmosphere of secrecy in which
she lives. She knows she is blind and longs for light. King
René is horror-stricken, but Ebn-Khakya reminds him that now
her sight may be restored. To stimulate her desire, René
declares Vaudemont must be put to death unless her blindness
is cured. Iolanthe is prepared to undergo any pain to save
Vaudemont, whom she loves. The physician leads her away.
Robert of Burgundy returns with his men. He recognises King
René, and begs to be freed from his obligation to marry his
daughter. The King consents, and promises Iolanthe's hand to
Vaudemont. Her girl friends arrive on the scene and announce
that the cure is successful. Iolanthe appears with bandaged
eyes. Ebn-Khakya takes off the handkerchief, and her sight is
restored. The opera concludes with a hymn of thanksgiving.

APPENDIX C

EXTRACTS FROM GERMAN PRESS NOTICES DURING TCHAIKOVSKY'S TOURS ABROAD IN 1888 AND 1889

LEIPZIG "SIGNALE"

"January, 1888.

"So far we have only become acquainted with three or four works by Peter Tchaikovsky, a follower of the Neo, or young, Russian school of 'storm and stress' composers, and these works, to speak frankly, have not won our sympathies; not because the composer is lacking in talent and skill, but because the manner in which he employs his gifts is repellent to us. Equally frankly we are ready to confess that we went to hear the Suite (op. 43) included in this programme, somewhat in fear and trembling, being prepared for all kinds of monstrosities, distortions, and repulsiveness. But it turned out otherwise. . . . The Fugue and Introduction at the beginning of the Suite bore honourable witness to the composer's contrapuntal science; of the other movements—the Divertimento, Intermezzo, Marche miniature, and Gavotte—the march seems least worthy of praise, for it merely recalls the tea-caddy-decoration style of art applied to music, and rather spoils than enhances the work.

"The composer, who conducted his Suite, must have been equally pleased with the way in which it was played and the reception accorded by the public. For the Gewandhaus audience, in recalling him *twice*, paid Herr Tchaikovsky a compliment rarely bestowed on any but a few of the most prominent composers of the day. He will carry away the impression that there is no question of Russophobia among *musical* people in Leipzig.

"E. BERNSDORF."

762

"MUSIKALISCHES WOCHENBLATT," NO. 3, JAHRGANG XIX

"January 12th, 1888.

"*Leipzig.* The first week of the New Year was really rich in interesting musical events. At the twelfth Subscription Concert Herr Tchaikovsky conducted his orchestral Suite (op. 43). . . . Undoubtedly the choice of this work was not calculated to display the composer to the Gewandhaus audience in his full creative strength. The Suite opens with a very promising Fugue, cleverly and effectively worked out, and continues very passably well with a Divertimento and an Intermezzo, two movements which are not profound, but possess much charm of sonority. The last two movements—Marche miniature and Gavotte—deteriorate so distinctly into a mere pattern of sounds, that it is impossible to derive from them any real artistic enjoyment. The sister work, of which Siloti gave several movements last season, is far stronger and more original. Still less can op. 43 be compared with the two chamber works played at the concert of the Liszt-Verein : the deeply reflective Trio dedicated to the memory of Nicholas Rubinstein, and the Quartet, delightful in every movement, but wonderful as regards the Andante. . . . The Liszt-Verein presented Herr Tchaikovsky with a splendid laurel-wreath."

"NEUE ZEITSCRIFT FUR MUSIK," NO. 2

" LEIPZIG, January 11th, 1888.

"Besides the exhaustively developed Fugue, which displays great contrapuntal skill and sureness, all the rest is of second-rate musical interest. We feel this the more strongly because the composer has been impolitic enough to pad out his fleeting ideas into pretentious movements of a quarter of an hour's duration. What is the use of a monotonous *fugato* which comes into the Introduction *before* the Fugue itself ? In the remaining movements we are conscious that the music has a ' society tone,' which finds expression in a pleasant conversational style : it has an aroma of Bizet, Délibes, and Co., and is sometimes reminiscent of the heroes of French Grand Opera and sometimes of Wagner. Naturally such methods only produce a frivolous eclecticism that can lead to no lasting results. Besides its aimless length—forty-five minutes—this Suite impresses us most by its evidences of submission to the shallow tastes of the hour. Here Tchaikovsky is posing too much in the part of Proteus; consequently he is not all that he *can be.*

"A far happier and more sympathetic view of Tchaikovsky is presented by his great Trio in A minor (op. 50)—also of extraordinary length—and the String Quartet (op. 11). . . . These works are of far superior quality and finer material; they have intellect, temperament, and imagination; here the composer never descends to the commonplace. The Trio—especially the *Pezzo elegiaco*—bears the imprint of a profound seriousness, impregnated with sorrow and lamentation. The Quartet, which was composed much earlier, shows chiefly a pleasing *naïveté.* The Andante is our favourite movement; we might compare it to a slumbering lily of the valley.   "BERNHARD VOGEL."

"LEIPZIGER TAGEBLATT"

"LEIPZIG, *January 6th,* 1888.

"We give decided preference to the first movement of the Suite (op. 43), especially as regards the Fugue, the subject of which, being full of energy and easily grasped, offers material for sustained and interesting development, in which, one after another, all the instruments. take part, until the movement is steadily worked up to a brilliant and effective close. The Introduction pleased us less, partly on account of its being spun out, but also because its contents are only of mediocre quality. The Divertimento treats a folk melody, which is interesting in itself, and is also very effective, thanks to variety of instrumentation. The same may be said of the Intermezzo, in which the 'cellos have a pleasing, but in no way remarkable, melody. This movement suffers equally from its prolixity. The little March, given to the wood wind and violins, is in the national style, and owes its effect chiefly to the orchestration. Here the flageolet tones of the violins produce a most original effect. The Gavotte, which forms the last movement, cannot lay claim to great appreciation; its effect is rather superficial. The hearty applause after each movement was intended rather for the composer than for his work."

"HAMBURG CORRESPONDENT"
"SIXTH PHILHARMONIC CONCERT

"HAMBURG, *January 20th,* 1888.

"We cannot deny to Tchaikovsky originality, temperament, or a bold flight of fancy, although when he is possessed by the spirit of his race he overthrows every limitation. All logic is then thrown to the winds, and there begins a Witches' Sabbath of sound which offends our sight and hearing, especially the latter. Flashes of genius mingle with musical banalities; delicate and intellectual touches with effects which are often ugly. There is something uncompromising, restless, and jerky about his work. In spite of all his originality, and the unrestrained passion of his emotions, Tchaikovsky is too eclectic in his tendencies ever to attain to independence in the highest meaning of the word. An artist's originality does not lie in the fact that he brings us what is strange and unusual. What deludes the senses is far from sufficient to satisfy the intellect. Tchaikovsky is a gifted, highly cultured, interesting artist. An artist who knows how to excite us by his ideas, but whom we should not venture to describe as a creative force in the highest sense. His music is too deeply rooted in a one-sided national tendency; but when he passes these limits the eclectic becomes prominent, who uses all the influences he has assimilated, although in his own original way. It is not what Tchaikovsky says that is new, but his manner of saying it. He likes to take wild and sudden leaps, allows himself to be carried away by the mood of the moment, and spins these moods out as much as possible, padding them largely with pathos and concealing the lack of really great thoughts by means of dazzling colour, unusual harmonic combinations, and lively, exotic rhythms. "SITTARD."

"FREMDENBLATT"

"SIXTH PHILHARMONIC CONCERT

"HAMBURG, *January* 20*th*, 1888.

"The Serenade was given to the public about 1883. The first and third movements are the most important, yet, even at its weightiest, it is not worthy to be placed beside the works of our latest German composers. This movement shows some similarity in form to the old French overture, as appears from its division into three parts and the Introduction in slow time. The second movement, a Valse Tempo in the dominant, is as out of keeping with the leading emotion of the opening movement as is the Finale—which is not always very lofty in conception. Undoubtedly the highest recognition would be accorded to the Elégie (third movement) if it, too, had more in common with the first movement. This sense of unity is lacking, in spite of the admirable development of the parts, while the key of D major, and the second sequence of dominants leading to C, is not calculated to give coherence to the whole.   From the point of view of instrumentation the Serenade is admirably worked out, and the means selected are so well handled that it is worthy to rank with numerous other serenades for strings which have been turned out by skilled artists in recent years.   If in the Serenade many fundamental principles of form have been violated, this method of procedure, which might be attributed to an effort after novelty, stands in no approximate relationship to the music of the Pianoforte Concerto (op. 23), a work which will hardly please German musicians in its entirety.   This music bears so essentially the Russian stamp that we must be able to view it entirely from a national standpoint in order to find it interesting.   The Concerto, in three extended movements, consists of an endless chain of phrases, and offers only a superficial development of the themes.   Each phrase stands by itself, and has no connection with the next.   It is not lacking in noisy passages, which cost the pianist enormous efforts, but none of these are the outcome of logical necessity.   It is true that the work is not lacking in clever-ness, but how regrettable that such an eminent talent should go so far astray ! . . . The Theme and Variations from the Third Suite for orchestra brought the Tchaikovsky performance to a close.   Here the composer gives us something clever and skilful, at least as regards the first half of the work ; but our pleasure in these welcome, solid tone-structures only lasts until the violin solo in B minor.   After this number the work runs a superficial course, culminating in a very commonplace *Tempo di Polacca*. If this is really Russian, and justified as such, Tchaikovsky's music may have its special qualities for Russian artists.   German composers, however, are not likely to derive from it any satis-factory results which could forward the development of their art. . . .   " EMIL KRAUSE "

" HAMBURGER NACHRICHTEN "

" *January* 20*th*, 1888.

" Yesterday Tchaikovsky's Serenade (op. 48), his Pianoforte Concerto op. 23, and Theme and Variations from op. 55 were given at the Philharmonic Concert.   In all these works we observed the same half-popular (*volkstümlich*), half-trivial element as regards the melodic invention.   We need not, however, lay stress upon this in referring to the individual movements, since the absence of what seems indispensable to a German audience is not a fault in the composer.   The Concerto is least calculated

to convince the hearer of Tchaikovsky's power of logical development and perfection of form. The first movement conceals its
very primitive formal structure under an overpowering rush of
harmonic effects, of dazzling kaleidoscopic passages, of intricate
treatment of the subjects and of orchestral colour. . . . The
Serenade is more lucid in design and far clearer in expression.
Its sonority is full and satisfying, and it displays much variety of
colouring. By the divisions of the violins, the skilful employment of violas and 'cellos, and the judicious combination and
alternation of bowed and pizzicato passages, the composer
succeeds in producing many picturesque effects. Interrupted
cadences and frequent changes of rhythm break the flow of the
work as a whole, but it leaves a general impression of freshness,
animation, and attractiveness. The subjects of the fluently
handled first Allegro have a piquant quality. The second movement is a slow Valse. Far more distinctive is the first subject of
the third movement—with its old-world colouring—which resembles the introduction to the Finale, and is treated, moreover,
in the genuine Russian folk-style, being heard first in C major
and E flat major. In the Variations from the Third Suite the
composer gives us a convincing proof of his musical science and
fruitful imagination. The theme itself is only of mediocre quality,
musically speaking, but, as the movement proceeds, it increases
in importance, in depth, and complexity of the parts, until in the
Finale it is worked up to a somewhat obtrusive apotheosis of
elemental strength, the outcome of the mere rhythm. This was
regarded as a signal for departure by a large section of the
audience, who were too much concerned in safeguarding their
own tympanums to feel compunction for the disturbance they
caused to the more strong-minded, who sat it out to the end."

"VOSSICHE ZEITUNG," NO. 68

"BERLIN, *February 9th*, 1888.

" Not only among the new school of his compatriots, but
among all contemporary composers Tchaikovsky is now reckoned
as one of the most gifted. He possesses intellect, originality, and
invention, and is master alike of the old and the more modern
forms. Compared with his fellow-countryman Rubinstein,
through whose nature runs a vein of greater amplitude and
warmth—Tchaikovsky has more charm and judgment. Both
have in common—what we find in every Russian composer with
whom we are acquainted—a tendency to exaggeration of form and
expression; but here again, Tchaikovsky seems to possess the

most artistic refinement   The songs which Frl. Friede sang yesterday, and the String Quartet, are remarkable for delicacy of invention and beauty of form.   The overture to *Romeo and Juliet*, and the Pianoforte Concerto, played by Herr Siloti, are full of characteristic animation and originality of rhythm, harmony, and instrumentation.   But here also the defects to which we have alluded are clearly perceptible.   The overture becomes wearisome by the spinning out of the same idea ; while, according to our conception of the play which inspired this work, the use of the big drum seems rather a coarse effect.

" In the first movement of the Concerto we cannot reconcile ourselves to the noisy, somewhat common-place, principal subject, nor to the frequent and violent interruptions of the musical flow of the work.   On the other hand, the Andante, which is a delightful combination of poetry and humour, and the ebullient Finale, in the national style, offer only fresh and undisturbed enjoyment.   A clever and animated Fugue from one of the Suites bore witness, by its admirable technical treatment, to the composer's mastery of polyphonic forms."

"BERLINER BÖRSEN-COURIER," NO. 5

"February 9th, 1888.

" The concert—long awaited with great excitement—at which Tchaikovsky, the leading representative of the modern Russian school, was to conduct a series of his own works, took place yesterday. . . . Among the orchestral works the Solemn Overture, "*1812*," was given for the first time.   The *Romeo and Juliet* overture is already known here ; it is a symphonic poem which describes more or less the tragic fate of the two lovers.   The Introduction shows deep emotion, while the Fugue displays great contrapuntal skill (of which the modern Russian composers give astonishing evidence) and force of ideas.   The Andante from op. 11, a charming cabinet picture, most tenderly elaborated, appeals directly to the heart, and is beautiful in its sonority. . . . The overture "*1812*" is a characteristic tone-picture of strife and victory, more ideally than realistically depicted, especially the former.   But by far the most weighty and lasting impression was made by the Pianoforte Concerto, which Alexander Siloti played with taste and brilliant virtuosity upon a fine full-toned Bluthner.   It is one of Tchaikovsky's best works, fresh in invention, glowing with passion, beautiful as regards its themes and admirable in its development. . . ."   "O. E."

"Kölnische Zeitung," No. 45

"The Eighth Gürzenich Concert.

"February 14th, 1889.

" Tchaikovsky's Third Suite made a striking impression upon all who heard it. Although the German public do not possess the key to many incidents in this work—because we know so little of Russia and its people, and what we know is not founded upon accurate observation—yet the music is so inspired, masterly and original, that it cannot fail to make a lasting impression upon any educated and progressive audience. . . .

" It is a question whether Tchaikovsky would not have done well to further elucidate the titles of the various movements—Elégie, Valse mélancolique, Scherzo, etc.—by the addition of a programme. But however desirable this may sometimes seem to listeners who are not Russians, it is doubtful whether the pleasant and stirring character of this work, which we may best define as a play of moods, would not have suffered in being tied down by any precise definition. . . .

" This music is of the kind which is pre-eminently calculated to stir our feelings by its richness of colour, its peculiarities of tonality—in one variation the Phrygian mode is successfully employed—and by its clever workmanship, which betokens an unusual skill in the working out of the parts. If an ingenious development of a theme, or an unusual effect of orchestration, occasionally predominates over the rest, on the whole it is the voice of the heart which is heard throughout the work, lending even an undertone to the glitter and hum of the Scherzo. The composer attains to this highest of all qualities by means of the wealth and charm of his melodic inspiration, the simplicity of his musical idiom, and the freshness of his invention. . . . Tchaikovsky not only possesses the gift of melodic invention, he pays due honour to Melody itself, and makes all the other elements of music hold their breath when Melody is speaking. . . . Simplicity is still the sign of profound truth, and of the promptings of inspiration. Tchaikovsky's creative power prevents this quality from degenerating into superficiality."

" General-Anzeiger "

" Frankfort, February 16th, 1889.

" A novelty headed the programme : the Third Suite, op. 55, by Peter Tchaikovsky, who is generally spoken of as the head of the young Russian school of musicians. . . . As the last notes of the Suite died away, there followed a burst of applause so hearty and so continuous, that nothing equal to it has been accorded to any novelty during recent years, except perhaps when Richard Strauss conducted his First Symphony. . . . The impression made by Tchaikovsky's work was dazzling rather than profound ; strictly speaking, it was not so much the Suite as a whole that won this recognition, as the bright, fresh, brilliantly orchestrated Polonaise with which it comes to an end. The second and third movements, Valse mélancolique and Scherzo, only evoked moderate applause : both numbers are in the minor, and seem to be stamped with a peculiar, national, Sarmatian character, they are so strange and gloomy. After the Valse mélancolique, which is quite in keeping with its title, a real Scherzo would have followed better ; a Scherzo in the sense of the classical symphonists, rather than a number of this kind, which is rich in rhythmic devices, but poor in that true gaiety which we expect to find in a piece entitled Scherzo. In this number the combination of 6/8 and 2/4 has an unfortunate effect, for the wind instruments always seem to come in a little too late. The variations are most of them very interesting, and one or two appeal direct to the heart. The Fugue is strong, effective, and most skilfully worked out."

" Dresdner Nachrichten "

" February 22nd, 1889.

" . . . The first number on the programme—Tchaikovsky's Fourth Symphony in F minor—acted like some magic spell upon the audience, somewhat disappointed at the non-appearance of the singer Frl. Leisinger. The Russian master—now undoubtedly the first composer of his nation—not only impressed us as a personality, but proved himself to be such in his Symphony, then given for the first time in Dresden. The work is planned upon large and bold lines and carried out in the same spirit. The ideas are clear-cut and concise ; the melody and harmony distinctive and strikingly characteristic. Occasionally, as in the first and last movements, the composer

indulges in an orgy of sound, for which he evokes all the resources of the modern orchestra. At these moments he produces
with true orchestral virtuosity the most piquant and unusual
effects, while always remaining master of the situation; saying
precisely what he has to say, and avoiding all empty phrases and
rambling statements. What he expresses, however, is spirited,
and full of elemental strength and weight. With all this, Tchaikovsky knows how to strike a note of tenderness. The third
movement of his Symphony—the Scherzo 'pizzicato ostinato'—
is a masterly invention, which stands alone in musical literature.
The vein of national feeling which runs throughout the work
accords admirably with its style and beauty. Here and there
it echoes the melancholy and sadness of some solemn, wailing
folksong, but so inspired and perfect is the treatment that both
heart and intellect are completely satisfied.

"An equally fine impression was made by his Pianoforte Concerto (op. 23). This impression would have been still more
profound if the Symphony had not come first; it was a case in
which *le mieux est l'ennemi du bien*. The Concerto is symphonic
in structure, and the piano part is indissolubly welded with the
orchestration. Nor for a moment can we fail to recognise great
mastery of form, inspiration, and emotion; but these qualities do
not impress the hearer so strongly as in the Fourth Symphony. . . .

" DRESDNER-ANZEIGER "

" February 22nd, 1889.

"Tchaikovsky may congratulate himself upon the complete
success of his Fourth Symphony (F minor), which opened the
programme of the Fifth Philharmonic Concert. This Symphony
proved to be irreproachable as regards form: a virtue not to be
underrated in a modern production. This original work is not
lacking in vital and stirring material which corresponds to its
nobility of form, although it is so saturated with national colour
that it affects us strangely at first. These melodies, harmonies,
and rhythms, derived from the spirit of the Russian folksongs
and dances, unlike other attempts of the kind, possess sufficient
weight and character to be used as symphonic material. . . .
Equally good and artistic is his Pianoforte Concerto in B♭ minor,
which is more of the new German school. This Concerto is
a gigantic work of its kind, which demands for its execution the
most perfect technique and extraordinary physical strength. . . .

"FERDINAND GLEICH."

"Vossiche Zeitung"

"*February 27th*, 1889.

"The interest of yesterday's Popular Concert given by the Philharmonic Orchestra was enhanced by the presence of Herr Tchaikovsky, who conducted two of his own works : a Serenade for strings and the symphonic poem, *Francesca da Rimini*. The Serenade is a cheerful composition, fluent, pleasing, and not without a touch of humour. It is not remarkable for originality, so much as for a skilful and artistic treatment of the thematic material, particularly noticeable in the last movement of the work. The valse section, which is especially full of charm and graceful in the elaboration of the melodies, had to be repeated. We had already heard the symphonic poem at Bilse's concerts. This time the work did not impress us more favourably, Sometimes it repels by its violence; sometimes it wearies by the constant repetition of an insignificant subject. A few clever episodes and occasional moments in which it keeps within the limits of the beautiful make the general effect of this work not too intolerable. . . ."

"Berliner Tageblatt"

"*February* 27, 1889.

". . . . Tchaikovsky's Serenade for strings consists of a series of charming little pieces, in the subjects of which we seem to recognise now and again a well-known face from some operetta. But these reminiscences are so delightfully decked out that we are very pleased to meet them again. . . . Musically speaking, the last movement is the most important. Here the composer has evolved a number of clever variations from a Russian theme. The symphonic poem, *Francesca da Rimini*, displays much interesting, but glaring, tone-colour. What Dante has described in ten lines is reproduced with effort in innumerable bars of music; we are endlessly wallowing in the harshest discords, until the attentive hearer undergoes a martyrdom scarcely less painful than the poor souls who are blown hither and thither in Dante's Whirlwind. Tchaikovsky is a gifted tone-poet, whom we have often recognised as such; but this symphonic poem exceeds all limits of what is acceptable. . . ."

ALPHABETICAL INDEX OF NAMES

Adamov, 25
Aertel, 25
Albert D', 459
Albrecht, Karl (Constantine), 6, 258, 260, 564, 705, 713
Alferaki, Achilles, 666
Alexandrov, Elizabeth M., 58
Alexis. *See* Safronov
Alexeiev, E. A., 23
Alexeiev, Nich., 392, 433
Altani, 449, 470, 608
Ambrose, 397, 412
Apukhtin, Alex, 25, 26, 713
Arensky, Anton S., 496, 520, 521–3, 609, 610, 620, 622, 664
Artôt, Desirée, 95–101, 470, 548, 579
Asantchevsky, M., 128, 150
Assier, Alexandra. *See* Tchaikovsky
Assier, Michael, 2
Auer, Leopold, 413, 415
Aus-der-Ohe, Adèle, 642–4, 649, 654, 655
Ave-Lallemant, 546, 580

Bach, J. S., 518
Bachmetiev, N., 347
Balakirev, Mily A., 81, 104–5, 107–11, 252, 407, 484
Barcewicz (Bartzevich), 318, 674
Bartsal, 395, 435
Beethoven, 311, 517, 567–9, 570
Begichev, 79, 93
Bellini, 421
Beresovsky, 298

Berger, Francesco, 558
Berlioz, Hector, 87, 88, 296, 330 335
Bernadaky, 555
Bernhardt, Sarah, 432
Bernuth, 545
Bertenson (the brothers), 723
Bessel, V., 145–6, 360, 437
Bevignani, 134
Bilse, 319, 334, 373, 385
Bizet, 253, 329, 382
Boito, Arrigo, 708
Borodin, 81, 252, 578
Bortniansky, 298, 406–7, 410
Botkin, P. S., 638, 646, 655
Brahms, Joh., 240–1, 319, 372, 499, 519, 541–2, 569, 570, 571 580
Brandoukov, A., 513
Breitner, 368
Brema, Marie, 709
Brodsky, Adolf, 413–15, 470, 451, 547, 663
Bruch, Max, 287, 320, 708
Bülow, Hans von, 157, 167, 175, 291, 320, 334, 347, 368, 471–3, 544, 545
Busoni, 547

Carnegie, Andrew, 636, 639, 643, 645–9, 650
Carnegie, Mrs., 650
Chopin, 296
Colonne, 193, 335, 340, 347, 354, 367, 372, 470, 513, 545

Constantine, Constantinovich, Grand Duke, 374, 470, 519, 560, 562, 567-71, 589, 590, 607, 610, 670

Constantine, Nicholaevich, Grand Duke, 145, 159, 177, 352, 374, 435, 479

Cui, Cæsar, 81, 148, 151, 173, 251-2, 358, 443, 463, 479, 557

Damrosch, Leo, 368, 643
Damrosch, Mrs., 639
Damrosch, Walter, 635, 636, 637, 651
Dannreuther, 648
Dargomijsky, 81, 388, 565-6
Daudet, A., 434, 460
Davidov, Alexandra I. (b. Tchaikovsky), 29, 40, 71, 72, 74, 83, 113, 122, 172, 189, 201, 367, 410, 672
Davidov, A. I., 56
Davidov, Elizabeth, 56, 76
Davidov, Karl, 128
Davidov, Leo V., 29, 56
Davidov, Nich., 58, 59
Davidov, Tatiana, 526
Davidov, Vera (m. Boutakov), 76, 83
Davidov, Vera (m. Rimsky-Korsakov), 567, 574
Davidov, Vladimir (Bob), 471, 581, 582, 583, 625, 662-3, 665, 673, 674, 676, 685, 688, 697, 702-4, 713, 714-15, 721, 724
Délibes, 241, 253, 375, 434, 513
Dickens, Charles, 384, 422, 590
Diemer, Louis, 470, 513, 707
Door, Anton, 78, 692
Dostoievsky, 55
Dubuque, 78
Dürbach, Fanny, 5-9, 17, 677, 698
Dütsch, 45
Dvořák, Anton, 550, 573, 579

Eliot, George, 715
Erdmannsdörfer, Max, 430, 431, 450, 473

Fet, 567, 667, 670
Figner, Medea, 618
Figner, N., 600, 602, 618
Finck, H. T., 644
Fitzenhagen, 347, 588
Flaubert, 493
Friede, 548, 674
Friedenthal, 368

Galitsin, Alexis, Prince, 57
Gerhard, V., 25
Gerke, A., 48
Gevaert, 59
Glazounov, Alex., 443, 470, 576, 578, 599, 723
Glinka, 54, 308, 311, 377-8, 388, 530, 563-4, 576, 607
Gluck, 518
Gogol, 72, 493
Goldmark, 287, 333
Gounod, 556
Green, Plunket, 709
Grieg, Edward, 470, 541-2, 547, 708
Grijimal, 148, 180

Halir, Carl, 470
Hanslick, 191, 414-15
Hausen, 656
Haydn, 518
Helena Pavlovna, Grand Duchess 155, 156
Henschel, Mr. and Mrs., 709
Hubert, Nich. A., 55, 165-6, 323 470, 483, 567, 569
Hugo, Victor, 383
Hyde, Mr. and Mrs., 636-8, 641 643, 645, 646, 649, 653

Ippolitov-Ivanov, M. M., 470, 500 508, 529, 571, 606, 608, 620
"Invincible Band, The," 90-3, 104 105, 134, 358, 622
Issakov, V., 375
Ivanov, 479

Jahn, Otto, 388
Joachim, 320
Joukovsky, 299, 331
Jurgenson, Peter I., 67, 68, 265, 286,
313, 325, 332, 334, 335, 344, 351,
357, 361, 370, 376, 384, 404-7,
410, 411, 417, 419, 420, 425, 428,
435, 437, 458, 483, 498, 501, 514,
534, 537, 542, 557, 564, 575, 577,
579, 582, 604, 610, 617, 622, 623,
663, 678, 685, 687, 705, 712, 715,
721

Kadmina, E., 145
Kamensky (Kamenskaya), E., 393,
398-9, 428
Kashkin, Nich., 68, 127, 201, 493,
601, 671, 717-8
Katkov, M., 127, 416
Klein, 649
Klimenko, I. A., 86, 116, 121, 132,
202
Klimenko, P., 420
Klindworth, Karl, 119, 120, 319,
579, 686
Knabe (see Mayer), 654-5
Knorr, Ivan, 577
Kondratiev, G., 146, 159, 620
Kondratiev, Nich., 124, 168-9, 243-4,
531, 533
Konius, Julius, 626, 663
Konius, George, 703
Konius, Leo, 715
Konradi, G. K., 245
Konradi, Nich., 177, 164, 712-13
Korbay, 649
Korganov, 508
Kossman, 78, 576
Kotek, Joseph, 204, 205, 240-1, 356,
415, 464, 471
Kross, Gustave, 55, 174
Kündinger, Rudolf, 30, 31, 681

Lagroua, 28
Lalo, 280, 326-9, 434, 513
Lamara, Mme., 514, 685

Lamoureux, 513
Laroche, Hermann, 42, 43, 62, 63,
102, 127, 151, 163, 330, 448, 493,
514, 564, 588, 667
Laub, Ferd., 78, 148, 168, 288
Lavrovsky (Lavrovskaya) Eliz., 123,
202, 717
Lefèbre, G., 513
Legoshin, 333, 470, 585
Lermontov, 268
Leschetizky, T., 45, 48, 128
Limnander, 436
Liszt, 52, 181, 241, 356, 412, 685
Litolff, H., 52
Liadov, 470
Löwenson, 438
Lomakin, 30, 45
Litke, A., Count, 662, 723

Mackar, Félix, 494, 501, 512
MacMahan, Mrs., 647, 650
Mahler, Gustave, 675
Maitland, Professor, 708, 712
Maleziomov, Sophia, 160
Marcel, 300, 345, 380
Maslov, T., 25
Massenet, 326, 333, 385, 515, 556,
582
Mayer (Knabe and Mayer), 635,
637-8, 640, 651, 657
Meck, Nadejda Filaretovna von, 143,
165, 204-16, 217, 219, 221-3, 225-
54, 260, 261, 263, 266-92, 295-9,
301-4, 305-13, 314-16, 322, 323,
325, 326-31, 333, 334, 335, 338,
340, 341, 342, 344, 345-8, 349,
350, 352, 353, 357, 363, 367-72,
374, 377-99, 401-4, 406, 407, 411
-13, 415-18, 420-5, 427, 429-36,
439, 448, 452, 454 459-63, 471-3,
476-9, 483, 486, 487, 497-500, 502
-4, 505, 507, 513, 515, 519, 524,
527, 529, 530-2, 536, 548, 558,
561, 562, 564, 566, 571, 572, 574,
578, 579, 584, 586, 588, 596, 597,
605, 608, 609, 611-17, 724

Melnikov, 422
Menter, Sophie, 470, 626
Merkling, Anna (*b.* Tchaikovsky),
    432, 456, 470, 495, 601, 603, 675,
    687, 717
Merten, 114
Metzdorf, Richard, 55
Michael Angelo, 237, 368, 371, 568
Milioukov, A. I. (Tchaikovsky), 217,
    219
Mozart, W. A., 287-9, 296, 378, 387,
    432, 518, 552, 622, 717
Musset, A. de, 315-16, 432
Moussorgsky, 252, 358, 461

Napravnik, Edward, 134, 147, 148,
    159, 188, 352, 375, 393, 405, 463,
    486, 520, 586, 618
Napravnik, V., 470, 546, 677
Neitzel, Otto, 577
Nikisch, Arthur, 549
Nikonov, Sophia, 106
Nilsson, 133

Obolensky, Prince, 453
Odoevsky, Prince, 78, 87, 88
Osberg, 71,
Ostrovsky, 79, 85
Oudin, Eugene, 712

Paderewski, 556
Padilla, 101, 548
Palchikov, Marie, 13
Panaev, 375
Pasdeloup, 191-2
Pavlovsky (Pavlovskaya),   Emilie,
    450, 470, 475, 478, 481, 486, 495,
    525
Philipov, 15
Piccioli, 32, 33
Plestcheiev, A., 72
Pollini, 675
Polonsky, 155, 479
Poushkin, 424, 445, 596
Prianichnikov, 399, 617, 673

Rachinsky, S., 103, 112, 113
Razoumovsky, D., 405
Reinecke, Carl, 542-43
Reno, Alice, 644-45, 657
Reno, Morris, 634, 635, 636-37
    638-40, 645-50, 652, 657, 668
Richter, Hans, 191, 290, 414
Rieger, 550
Riemann, Hugo, 721
Rimsky-Korsakov, Nat. N. (*b.* Pour
    gold), 111, 134, 137
Rimsky - Korsakov, Nich. A., 81,
    89, 172, 175, 177, 187, 251, 480,
    520
Ristori, Adelaide, 28
Ritzel, 648
Rioumin, C., 115
Romeike, 643, 648
Ross, Ivy, 640, 641, 652
Rousseau, J. J., 340
Rubinstein, Anton G., 45, 47, 48,
    49, 62, 81, 291, 342-3, 375, 385,
    388, 437, 439, 503, 587, 591-5,
    681-4
Rubinstein, Nicholas G., 61, 64, 67,
    165-8, 225-6, 231, 254, 262, 342,
    335, 397, 401, 403, 419
Rummel, 368, 644, 646

Sachs, William de, 368, 640, 641,
    642, 643, 649
Sadovsky, 79
Safonov, V., 604, 608
Safronov, Alexis, 162, 324, 394, 410,
    488, 490, 595, 602, 662, 680, 714,
    728
Saint-Saens, C., 176, 193, 434, 435,
    707-10
Sand, George, 314
Sapellnikov, 470, 544, 546-8, 582-3,
    626
Sarasate, 707
Sardou, 432
Sauer, Emil, 470, 577
Sauret, 415
Schobert, Eliz., 27

Schirmer, 640, 643
Schopenhauer, 266, 269, 270, 273
Schubert, Franz, 570
Schumann, Robert, 412
Seidl, Anton, 643, 652
Serov, 54, 55, 155, 282-4, 388
Sgambati, 412, 605
Shilovsky, C., 79, 180
Shilovsky, Count Vassiliev-, 79, 93, 117, 713
Shpajinsky, 474, 478, 482
Stanford, Charles Villiers, 709
Siloti, Alex., 470, 499, 541, 547, 550, 564, 670, 686
Sklifasskovsky, 470
Skobeliev, 425
Slaviansky, 55
Smetana, 586
Soloviev, V., 354
Spinoza, 589
Stassov, V. V., 81, 134-7, 161, 194, 465, 520
Strakaty, Dr., 550
Strauss, Richard, 473, 545

Taneiev, Serge, 149, 175-6, 191, 192, 193, 255-8, 292-5, 323, 363, 366, 408, 429, 458, 476, 483, 484, 501, 537, 621, 671, 687
Tarnovsky, Eliz., 73
Tchaikovsky, Alexandra A., 3-4, 19, 20, 22
Tchaikovsky, Alexandra I. (*see* Davidov), 5
Tchaikovsky, Anatol, 17, 35, 69-75, 85, 86, 94, 96, 100, 107, 112, 114, 115, 121, 122, 147, 154, 162, 164, 168, 186, 216, 223, 224, 351, 352, 354, 356, 410, 419, 453, 507, 509, 554, 664, 677, 679, 696, 702
Tchaikovsky, Anna P. *See* Merkling
Tchaikovsky, George, 679
Tchaikovsky, Hyppolite, 5, 506, 559
Tchaikovsky, Ilia Petrovich, 2 3, 4, 9, 27, 95-9, 122, 133, 138, 150, 217, 220, 367

Tchaikovsky, Modeste, 17, 35, 69-75, 86, 94, 97, 112, 114, 115, 118, 132, 133, 146, 154, 160, 163, 168, 177-181, 184, 186, 200, 203, 245, 299-301, 304, 317, 330, 337, 338-9, 348, 351, 373, 380, 383, 384, 400, 401, 403, 405, 422, 426, 427, 438, 441, 443, 444, 451, 459, 466, 482, 493, 498, 500, 506-8, 510, 512, 516, 521, 524, 529, 533, 541, 544, 547, 560, 576, 581, 582, 584, 589, 600-6, 609, 626-8, 629-35, 662, 674, 681, 685, 688, 694, 697, 701, 704, 706, 707, 708, 714, 716
Tchaikovsky, Nich., 4, 15, 33, 124, 698, 724
Tchaikovsky, Peter P., 27, 123
Tchaikovsky, P. V. (Anatol's wife), 512
Tchaikovsky, Zinaïda, 3, 9, 15, 21
Tchekov, 589
Thackeray, W. M., 244
Thomas, Ambroise, 512
Thomé, 556
Thomson, César, 678
Tkachenko, 393-94, 395-97, 444
Tolstoi, A. Count, 284, 504
Tolstoi, Leo, Count, 194, 200, 336, 444, 454, 517, 589
Tourgeniev, I. S., 123, 375, 512
Tretiakov, Helen, 401
Tretiakov, P. M., 430, 688

Vakar, Plato, 19, 21
Viardot, Pauline, 512, 582
Vietinghov-Scheel, 516
Volkmann, R., 303
Vsievolojsky, I., 442, 482, 520, 544, 574, 624

Wagner, Richard, 181-5, 238-39, 344-5, 431-2, 436, 438, 452, 461-2, 581, 622
Weber, 464
White, Mrs., 648

Wieniawsky, Henry, 45, 374
Wieniawsky, Joseph, 78, 357
Würst, Richard, 319

Zabel, Eugen, 592, 681–4

Zaremba, 40, 41, 45–9
Zet, Julius, 564
Zola, 383, 498, 676
Zvantsiev, 180, 623
Zveriev, 713

ALPHABETICAL INDEX OF TCHAIKOVSKY'S WORKS

Andante from *Quartet* in D, Op. 11 (1872), arranged for String Orchestra, 626, 700

Articles on *Music* (1871–6), 90, 127, 131, 138, 181

Barcarole for pianoforte, Op. 37ª, No. 6 (1876), 289

Cantata, Schiller's "Ode to Joy," for chorus and orchestra (1866), 62

Cantata, written for the opening of the Polytechnic Exhibition (1872), 128, 129, 390

Cantata, Coronation, "Moscow" (1883), 435, 436, 440, 442

Caprices d'Oxane, Les, Opera (1885). *See also* "Vakoula the Smith" and "Cherevichek," 155–8, 162, 171, 177, 188–91, 193, 194, 247, 306, 323, 355, 359, 475, 478, 482, 499, 500, 502, 521, 525, 526, 610

Casse-Noisette Suite, Op. 71ª, taken from the Ballet, *The Nut-cracker*, 677, 678, 699, 700

Chant sans Paroles. *See* "Souvenir de Hapsal"

Chant Elégiaque, Op. 72, 471

Cherevichek (The Little Shoes). *See* "Les Caprices d'Oxane"

Children's Album, twenty-four easy pieces for pianoforte, Op. 39 (1878), 298

Children's Songs, sixteen, Op. 54 (1883), 447, 623

Chorus of Insects, from unfinished opera *Mandragora* (1870), 112, 113

Cinderella, Ballet, 122

Concerto for pianoforte, No. 1, B flat minor, Op. 23 (1875), 162, 165–7, 171, 174–6, 313, 318, 347, 368, 545, 548, 551, 577, 583, 642–4, 649, 654, 699

Concerto for pianoforte, No. 2, Op. 44 (1880), 360, 424, 574, 626, 646

Concerto for pianoforte, No. 3, Op. 75, 717

Concerto for violin, Op. 35 (1878), 282, 286, 413, 415, 425, 426, 557

Concert-Fantasia. *See* "Fantasia"

Dance of Serving-Maids, from the opera *Voyevode*, 54, 58, 61, 86, 87, 89

Domino Noir. *See* "Recitatives"

Duets, six, Op. 46 (1881), 407

Enchantress, The, Opera (1887), 478, 481, 482, 495, 497, 500, 516, 527, 528, 530, 536–8, 601, 603

Eugene Oniegin, Opera, Op. 24 (1878), 202, 203, 217, 225, 231, 255, 257, 260, 293, 295, 304, 312, 334, 355, 381, 392, 395, 396, 417, 424, 439, 445, 452, 463, 464, 468, 490, 502, 572, 573, 587, 598, 603, 672, 675, 679

Fantasia, Concert—for pianoforte and orchestra, Op. 56 (1884), 459, 476, 537, 556
Fatum (Destiny), Symphonic Poem, Op. 77 (1868), 79, 92, 97, 103–5, 329.
Festival-Overture on the Danish National Hymn, Op. 15 (1866), 79, 80, 329
Festival-Overture " 1812," Op. 49 (1880), 390, 405, 426, 528, 551, 576, 699
Folksongs, Russian, twenty-five for pianoforte, four hands, 97
Francesca da Rimini, Fantasia on Dante's poem, Op. 32 (1876), 180, 188, 193, 201, 212, 313, 319, 320, 366, 465, 528, 537, 709

Gevaert, Translation of his " Course of Instrumentation," 59

Hamlet, Overture-Fantasia, Op. 67ª (1885), 572, 621, 644, 703, 719
Hamlet (Incidental music to the Tragedy), Op. 67ᵇ (1891), 619, 620, 621, 623

Iolanthe (King René's Daughter), Opera, Op. 69 (1891), 623, 624, 662, 667, 673, 686, 687, 694–6
Italian Capriccio, Op. 45 (1880), 376, 385, 394, 396, 426
Ivan the Terrible. Arrangement of A. G. Rubinstein's overture for pianoforte, four hands (1869), 112

Legend. See " Children's Songs "
Liturgy of St. John Chrysostom, Op. 41 (1878), 299, 313, 347, 348, 392, 394, 412, 623

Maid of Orleans, The, Opera (1879), 325, 331, 332, 334, 346, 348, 355, 359, 370, 377, 381, 383, 389, 393, 396, 398, 399, 412, 417, 425, 428, 430, 722
Mandragora. See " Chorus of Insects "
Manfred, Symphony, Op. 58 (1885), 484–7, 490, 495, 497, 498, 520
March, Coronation, 436, 658
March, Slav or Russo-Serbian, Op. 31 (1876), 201, 626
March, Funeral, from " Hamlet," Op. 67ᵇ (1891), 621, 623
Mazeppa, Opera (1883), 423, 424–9, 441–3, 447–52, 454, 470, 499, 500–2, 505
Mozartiana, Suite No. 4, Op. 61 (1817), 533, 534, 537

Night, vocal quartet from Mozart's Fantasia, No. 4, 717
Nut-cracker, The, Ballet, Op. 71 (1892), 623–5, 662–4, 686, 696
Nut-cracker, Suite. *See* " Casse-Noisette "

Oprichnik, The, Opera (1872), 113, 115, 116, 128, 129, 132, 134, 138, 145–52, 154, 158, 162, 163, 171–4, 212, 359, 371, 505, 574, 722
Overture, C minor (1866), 70, 76

Overture, F major (1865), 61, 73, 76
Overture, Romeo and Juliet. *See* " Romeo and Juliet "
Overture, Hamlet. *See* " Hamlet"

Pezzo Capriccioso, for violoncello, Op. 62 (1887), 556, 595
Pianoforte Pieces, three, Op. 9 (1871), 121
Pianoforte Pieces, twelve, Op. 40 (1878), 298, 305
Pianoforte Pieces, eighteen, Op. 72 (1893), 704
Pique Dame (The Queen of Spades), Opera, Op. 68 (1890), 598, 600, 601–4, 611, 613, 615, 617–19, 624, 625, 670–3, 677, 694, 700

Quartet, No. 1, D major, Op. 11 (1871), 123, 124, 196, 201, 289, 319, 543, 548, 605
Quartet, No. 2, F major, Op. 22 (1874), 147, 148, 160, 355
Quartet, No. 3, E flat major, Op. 30 (1876), 179, 180, 188, 289, 368, 465, 657
Quartet, No. 4, B flat major (1865), 61

Recitatives and Choruses for Auber's Opera, "Le Domino Noir," 96, 101
Romeo and Juliet, Overture-Fantasia (1870), 92, 107, 114–16, 119–22, 135, 157, 174, 191–3, 241, 289, 316, 320, 375, 465, 548, 551, 678
Russian Scherzo and *Impromptu*, Op. 61 (1867), 59

Serenade, for strings, Op. 48 (1880), 390, 508, 528, 545, 551, 555–8, 634
Sérénade Mélancolique, for violin and orchestra, B flat minor, Op. 26 (1875), 626
Sextet, "Souvenir de Florence," 606, 609, 618, 662, 677
Sleeping Beauty, The, Ballet, Op. 66 (1889), 574, 585, 586, 596, 597, 624
Sniegourotchka (The Snow-Maiden), Incidental music to Ostrovsky's "Legend of the Spring," 138, 426
Sonata, G major, for pianoforte, Op. 37 (1879), 298, 313, 355
Song, "So schnell vergessen," 121
Songs, seven, Op. 47 (1881), 407
Songs, six, Op. 73 (1893), 704
Souvenir de Florence. *See* "Sextet"
Souvenir de Hapsal, three pianoforte pieces, Op. 2 (1867), 83, 318
Storm, The, Overture to Ostrovsky's play of same name, Op. 76 (1865), 50, 57
Suite, No. 1, in D, for orchestra, Op. 43 (1879), 316, 324, 356, 361, 363–6, 368, 371, 375, 543, 546, 583, 635, 642, 645
Suite, No. 2 in C, for orchestra, Op. 53 (1883), 441, 444, 446, 450, 528
Suite, No 3 in G, for orchestra, Op. 55 (1884), 455–9, 471–3, 545, 551, 556, 557, 558, 575, 576, 582, 626, 645, 646
Suite, No. 4 ("Mozartiana"). *See* "Mozartiana."
Swan Lake, The, Ballet, Op. 20 (1876), 172–3, 201, 241
Symphony, No. 1, G minor, "Winter Dreams," Op. 13 (1868), 76, 80, 89, 114, 447

Symphony, No. 2, C minor, "Little-Russian," Op. 17 (1873), 132, 134, 137
146, 148, 360, 397
Symphony, No. 3, D major Op. 29 (1875), 172, 174, 179, 289, 290
Symphony, No. 4, F minor, Op. 36 (1877), 202, 215, 222, 244, 255, 258, 265,
272, 275-7, 292-5, 326, 355, 367, 368
Symphony, No. 5, E minor, Op. 64 (1888), 561, 566, 574, 575, 580, 581, 719
Symphony, No. 6, in B minor (The Pathetic), Op. 74 (1893), 702, 703, 714-
16, 718-22

Trio, in A minor, for piano, violin, and 'cello, Op 50 (1882)
The Tempest, Fantasia for orchestra from Shakespeare's play, Op. 18 (1873),
92, 135-7, 140, 144-7, 159, 161-3, 211, 313, 318, 337-9, 340, 347, 465,
574, 626, 700

Undine, Opera (1869), 106, 113, 114, 116, 117, 132, 299, 316, 329, 359
Undine, Ballet (1886), 520

Vakoula the Smith.   See "Les Caprices d'Oxane" and "Cherevichek"
Valse-Scherzo, for violin and orchestra, Op. 34 (1877), 318
Variations on a Rococo Theme, for 'cello and orchestra, Op. 33 (1876), 194, 347
Vesper Service, The, Op. 52, 405, 408, 421, 437
Voyevode, The, Opera, Op. 3 (1868), 58, 82, 83, 94, 100, 102, 105, 329, 358
Voyevode, The, Symphonic Ballade on Poushkin's Poems, Op. 78, 662, 663,
667, 670-672, 719

Winter Dreams.   See "Symphony No. 1"

Year, The, "*1812.*"   *See* "Festival-Overture"

CPSIA information can be obtained
at www.ICGtesting.com
Printed in the USA
BVHW041327241220
596436BV00005B/203